Communications
in Computer and Information Science 2039

Rationale

The CCIS series is devoted to the publication of proceedings of computer science conferences. Its aim is to efficiently disseminate original research results in informatics in printed and electronic form. While the focus is on publication of peer-reviewed full papers presenting mature work, inclusion of reviewed short papers reporting on work in progress is welcome, too. Besides globally relevant meetings with internationally representative program committees guaranteeing a strict peer-reviewing and paper selection process, conferences run by societies or of high regional or national relevance are also considered for publication.

Topics

The topical scope of CCIS spans the entire spectrum of informatics ranging from foundational topics in the theory of computing to information and communications science and technology and a broad variety of interdisciplinary application fields.

Information for Volume Editors and Authors

Publication in CCIS is free of charge. No royalties are paid, however, we offer registered conference participants temporary free access to the online version of the conference proceedings on SpringerLink (http://link.springer.com) by means of an http referrer from the conference website and/or a number of complimentary printed copies, as specified in the official acceptance email of the event.

CCIS proceedings can be published in time for distribution at conferences or as postproceedings, and delivered in the form of printed books and/or electronically as USBs and/or e-content licenses for accessing proceedings at SpringerLink. Furthermore, CCIS proceedings are included in the CCIS electronic book series hosted in the SpringerLink digital library at http://link.springer.com/bookseries/7899. Conferences publishing in CCIS are allowed to use Online Conference Service (OCS) for managing the whole proceedings lifecycle (from submission and reviewing to preparing for publication) free of charge.

Publication process

The language of publication is exclusively English. Authors publishing in CCIS have to sign the Springer CCIS copyright transfer form, however, they are free to use their material published in CCIS for substantially changed, more elaborate subsequent publications elsewhere. For the preparation of the camera-ready papers/files, authors have to strictly adhere to the Springer CCIS Authors' Instructions and are strongly encouraged to use the CCIS LaTeX style files or templates.

Abstracting/Indexing

CCIS is abstracted/indexed in DBLP, Google Scholar, EI-Compendex, Mathematical Reviews, SCImago, Scopus. CCIS volumes are also submitted for the inclusion in ISI Proceedings.

How to start

To start the evaluation of your proposal for inclusion in the CCIS series, please send an e-mail to ccis@springer.com.

Sridaran Rajagopal · Kalpesh Popat ·
Divyakant Meva · Sunil Bajeja
Editors

Advancements in Smart Computing and Information Security

Second International Conference, ASCIS 2023
Rajkot, India, December 7–9, 2023
Revised Selected Papers, Part III

Springer

Editors
Sridaran Rajagopal ⓘ
Marwadi University
Rajkot, Gujarat, India

Kalpesh Popat ⓘ
Marwadi University
Rajkot, Gujarat, India

Divyakant Meva ⓘ
Marwadi University
Rajkot, Gujarat, India

Sunil Bajeja ⓘ
Marwadi University
Rajkot, Gujarat, India

ISSN 1865-0929   ISSN 1865-0937 (electronic)
Communications in Computer and Information Science
ISBN 978-3-031-59099-3   ISBN 978-3-031-59100-6 (eBook)
https://doi.org/10.1007/978-3-031-59100-6

This Springer imprint is published by the registered company Springer Nature Switzerland AG
The registered company address is: Gewerbestrasse 11, 6330 Cham, Switzerland

Paper in this product is recyclable.

Preface

In continuation of the successful introduction of the ASCIS series during 2022, we feel extremely happy and privileged to roll out the 2nd season: the International Conference on Advancements in Smart Computing & Information Security (ASCIS 2023). The conference was conducted during 7–9 December 2023, wherein leading researchers, academicians and industrialists participated from various countries across the globe. Eminent experts from Academia and Industry, including researchers in the top 2% of global scientific researchers from the Stanford list and industry were among our general co-chairs, program chairs and track chairs. ASCIS 2023 welcomed experts from top-ranked Indian Institutes such as IITs and NITs and reputable foreign universities. The members of the Advisory, Program and Branding & Outreach committees ensured the quality of the submissions and contributed majorly to the overall success of the conference.

Altogether, we received 432 technical papers under the 5 tracks, viz. AI & ML, Cyber Security, Computer Networks, Smart Computing and Inter-disciplinary Computer Applications, out of which we shortlisted 127 papers (29%) for Springer CCIS. There were 91 long papers (≥12 pages) and 36 short papers (<12 pages). This year each paper underwent 4 technical reviews and the review process was also strengthened compared to last year. Thanks go to the staff of Springer CCIS for their consistent guidance and for supporting us for the second time.

The technical papers presented across the various application domains included healthcare, agriculture, automobile, civil and mechanical engineering, pharma, cybercrime, and sports. We appreciate all the enthusiastic authors who submitted their innovative research works as technical papers.

Some of the reputed global and national experts included Venkat Rayapati, Cyber Forza Inc, USA; H.R. Mohan, IEEE Computer Society, India; Deepak Jain, Dalian University of Technology, China; Ishu Gupta, International Institute of Information Technology, Bengaluru, India; Shamala Subramanian, University Putra Malaysia, Malaysia; Krishna Kumar, Keisoku Engineering System Co., Ltd., Japan; Sheng-Lung Peng, National Taipei University of Business, Taiwan; Sonali Agarwal, IIIT Allahabad, India; Sharad Raghavendra, Virginia Tech, USA; and Mahesh Ramachandran, Larsen & Toubro, India, who participated in ASCIS and gave the keynote addresses.

Our sincere thanks go to the esteemed sponsors, including the Science and Engineering Research Board (SERB), Coursera, D-Link, Stelcore, and Samatrix.

We believe that this collection will be highly useful for researchers and practitioners of AI & ML and their allied domains.

December 2023

Sridaran Rajagopal
Kalpesh Popat
Divyakant Meva
Sunil Bajeja

Organization

General Chair

R. Sridaran   Marwadi University, India

Program Committee Chairs

R. Sridaran   Marwadi University, India
Kalpesh Popat   Marwadi University, India
Divyakant Meva   Marwadi University, India
Sunil Bajeja   Marwadi University, India

Steering Committee

Ketanbhai Marwadi   Marwadi University, India
Jitubhai Chandarana   Marwadi University, India
Sandeep Sancheti   Marwadi University, India
R. B. Jadeja   Marwadi University, India
Lalitkumar Avasthi   NIT Hamirpur, India
H. R. Mohan   The Hindu/ICT Consultant, India
Sudeep Tanvar   Nirma University, India
R. Sridaran   Marwadi University, India
Naresh Jadeja   Marwadi University, India
Ankur Dumka   Women Institute of Technology, India
Ashwin Dobariya   Marwadi University, India
Shamala Subramanyam   Universiti Putra Malaysia, Malaysia
Oscar Castillo   Tijuana Institute of Technology, Mexico
Pascal Lorenz   University of Haute Alsace, France
Alvaro Rocha   University of Lisbon, Portugal
Shubhra Sankar Ray   Indian Statistical Institute, India
Kalpdrum Passi   Laurentian University, Canada
Varatharajan Ramachandran   Bharath University, India
Shruti Patil   Symbiosis Institute of Technology, India
Silvia Priscila   Bharath Institute of Higher Education and
                                               Research, India
Rajesh Kaluri   Vellore Institute of Technology, India

Suraiya Jabin	Jamia Millia Islamia University, India
Madhu Shukla	Marwadi University, India
Vijay Katkar	Annasaheb Dange College of Engineering and Technology, India
Pankaj Mudholkar	Marwadi University, India
Dimple Thakar	Marwadi University, India
Hardik Dhulia	Marwadi University, India
Jaypalsinh Gohil	Marwadi University, India
Sriram Padmanabhan	Marwadi University, India
Devang Patel	Marwadi University, India
Thangraj	Madurai Kamraj University, India
T. Devi	Bharathiar University, India
Padmavathi	Avinashilingam Institute for Home Science and Higher Education for Women, India
Vishal Jain	Sharda University, India
Banoth Rajkumar	University of Texas, USA
D. C. Jinwala	Sardar Vallabhbhai National Institute of Technology, India
R. Balasubhramanyam	Indian Institute of Technology, Roorkee, India
Umesh Bellur	Indian Institute of Technology, Bombay, India
Rajkumar Buyya	University of Melbourne, Australia
Valentina Emilia Balas	Aurel Vlaicu University of Arad/Academy of Romanian Scientists, Romania
Vincenzo Piuri	University of Milan, Italy
Xavier Fernando	Toronto Metropolitan University, Canada
Rodina Ahmad	University of Malaya, Malaysia
Xiao-zhigao	University of Eastern Finland, Finland
Tianhua Xu	University of Warwick, UK
Sheng-Lung Peng	National Taipei University of Business, Taiwan
Vijay Singh Rathore	Jaipur Engineering College & Research Center, India
C. K. Kumbharana	Saurashtra University, India
Parag Rughani	National Forensic Sciences University, India
Durgesh Mishra	Sri Aurobindo Institute of Technology, Indore, India
Vipin Tyagi	Jaypee University of Engineering and Technology, Guna, India
Hardik Joshi	Gujarat University, India
P. V. Virparia	Sardar Patel University, India
Priyanka Sharma	Rashtriya Raksha University, India
Uma Dulhare	MJCET, India
Chhagan Lal	Delft University of Technology, The Netherlands
Deepakkumar Panda	Cranfield University, UK

Shukor Sanim Mohd. Fauzi   Universiti Teknologi MARA, Malaysia
Sridhar Krishnan   Toronto Metropolitan University, Canada
Brajendra Panda   University of Arkansas, USA
Anand Nayyar   Duy Tan University, Vietnam
Monika Bansal   SSD Women's Institute of Technology, India
Ajay Kumar   KIET Group of Institutions, India

Technical Program Committee Chairs

AI & ML Track

Priti Sajja   Sardar Patel University, India
Kumar Rajamani   KLA Tencor, India
Sonali Agarwal   IIIT Allahabad, India

Cyber Security Track

Sudeep Tanwar   Nirma University, India
Padmavathi Ganpathi   Avinashilingam Institute for Home Science and
                                    Higher Education for Women, India
Vipin Tyagi   Jaypee University, India

Smart Computing Track

Jatinderkumar R. Saini   Symbiosis Institute of Computer Studies, India
Rajesh Kaluri   Vellor Institute of Technology, India
Shriram Kris Vasudevan   Intel Corporation, India

Computer Networks Track

Shamala Subramaniam   University Putra Malaysia, Malaysia
Atul Gonsai   Saurashtra University, India
Vijay Katkar   Annasaheb Dange College of Engineering and
                                    Technology, India

Interdisciplinary Computer Applications Track

Shobhit Patel   Marwadi University, India
Simar Preet Singh   Bennett University, India
Manvinder Singh Pahwa   Marwadi University, India

Additional Reviewers

A. Maheswary
A. P. Nirmala
A. Yovan Felix
Abhay Bhadauria
Abhilasha Vyas
Abhinav Tomar
Abhishek Sharma
Aditi Sharma
Ahmed BaniMustafa
Ajay Kumar
Ajay Kushwaha
Ajaykumar Patel
Ajita Deshmukh
Akash Saxena
Akshara Dave
Alvaro Rocha
Amanpreet Kaur
Amit Gupta
Amita Sharma
Amrinder Kaur
Amrita Kumari
Amutha S.
Anamika Rana
Anand Nayyar
Anandkumar Ramakrishnan
Anbmumani K.
Angelina R.
Anilkumar Suthar
Anitha K.
Ankit Didwania
Ankit Faldu
Ankit Shah
Ankur Goel
Anubhav Kumar Prasad
Anurag Vijay Agrawal
Anvip Deora
Anwar Basha H.
Arcangelo Castiglione
Arun Adiththan
Arun Raj Lakshminarayanan
Aruna Pavate
Asha V.
Ashish Kumar

Ashish Saini
Ashwin Makwana
Ashwin R. Dobariya
Ashwin Raiyani
Asmita Manna
Avinash Sharma
Avnip Deora
Ayush Somani
B. Suresh Kumar
B. Surendiran
Balraj Verma
Bandu Meshram
Banoth Rajkumar
Bharanidharan G.
Bharat Pahadiya
Bhavana Kaushik
Biswaranjan Mishra
B. J. D. Kalyani
Brajendra Panda
Brijesh Jajal
Budesh Kanwer
C. K. Kumbharana
C. P. Chandran
C. Prema
Chandra J.
Chandra Mohan
Charu Gupta
Chetan Dudhagara
Chhagan Lal
Chintan Thacker
Chintan Patel
D. C. Jinwala
Dafni Rose
Darshita Pathak
Daxa Vekariya
Deepak Kumar Verma
Deepakkumar Panda
Delecta Jenifer R.
Dhanamma Jagli
Dhruba Bhattacharyya
Dimple Thakar
Dipak Ramolia
Dipti Chauhan

Dipti Domadia
Disha Parekh
Disha Shah
Divya R.
Divya Didwania
Dviyanshu Chandra
Durgesh Mishra
Dushyantsinh Rathod
E. Karthikeyan
Deepak Tiwari
G. Charles Babu
G. Kavitha
G. Mahalakshmi
Galiveeti Poornima
Gaurav Agarwal
Gaurav Kumar Ameta
Goi Bok Min
Gulfarida Tulemissova
Gunjan Agarwal
Hardik Joshi
Hardik Patel
Hardik Molia
Hari Kumar Palani
Harish Kundra
Harshal Salunkhe
Hemant Ingale
Hemraj Lamkuche
Himanshu Maniar
Himanshu Rai
Ipseeta Nanda
J. Ramkumar
Jaimin Undavia
Jasminder Kaur Sandhu
Jatinderkumar Saini
Jay Dave
Jay Kumar Jain
Jayant Nandwalkar
Jayashree Nair
Jaydeep Ramani
Jaydeep Ramani
Jaykumar Dave
Jaypalsinh Gohil
Jignesh Doshi
Jinal Tailor
Jonnadula Narasimharao

Jose M. Molina
Juhi Singh
Juliet Rozario
Jyothi Balreddygari
Jyoti Khubchandani
Jyoti Kharade
Jyotsna Amin
K. Priya
K. Vallidevi
Kailash Patidar
Kajal Patel
Kalpdrum Passi
Kamal Batta
Kamal Saluja
Kamal Sutaria
Kannadhasan Suriyan
Kapil Joshi
Karuna Nidhi Pandagre
Karthik B.
Karthikeyan R.
Kavipriya P.
Kavitha Ganesh
Kaviyarasi R.
Kedir Lemma Arega
Keerti Jain
Keyurkumar Patel
Khaled Kamel
Krupa Mehta
Kruti Sutaria
Kumuthini C.
Lata Suresh
Lataben Gadhavi
Latchoumy P.
Lilly Florence M.
Lipsa Das
Lokesh Gagnani
M. Vinoth Kumar
M. Mohamed Iqbal
M. N. Hoda
Madhu Kirola
Madhu Shukla
Mahalakshmi G.
Malarkodi K. P.
Mahesh Shirole
Mallika Ravi Bhatt

Manisha Rawat
Manohar N.
Manoj Patil
Maruthamuthu R.
Mastan Vali Shaik
Maulik Trivedi
Maulika Patel
Meet Patel
Megha Jain
Mohamed Mosbah
Mohammed Wajid Khan
Mohan Subramani
Mohit Tiwari
Monika Arora
Monika Bansal
Monther Tarawneh
Mythili Shanmugam
N. Rajendran
N. Noor Alleema
Nabeena Ameen
Nagappan Govindarajan
Nagaraju Kilari
Nageswari D.
Narayan Joshi
Naresh Kumar
Navnish Goel
Nebojsa Bacanin
Neeraj Kumar Pandey
Neerja Kumari
Neeru Sharma
Neha Parashar
Neha Sharma
Neha Soni
Nethmini Thilakshi Weerawarna
Nidhi Chaudhry
Nilesh Patil
Nilesh Sabnis
Nirav Bhatt
Nirav Mehta
Nisha Khurana
Noel E. Estrella
Oscar Castillo
P. Rizwan Ahmed
P. Latchoumy
P. V. Virparia

Padma Selvaraj
Padmavathi
Pankaj Chawla
Parag Rughani
Parth Gautam
Parvathaneni Naga Srinivasu
Parwinder Kaur
Pascal Lorenz
Pathan Mohd Shafi
Patil Rahul Ashokrao
Payal Khubchandani
Poornima Vijaykumar
Pradip Jawandhiya
Pragadesawaran S.
Prashant Pittalia
Praveen Kumar
Pravesh Kumar Bansal
Preethi Sambandam Raju
Premkumar Borugadda
Priteshkumar Prajapati
Priya Chandran
Priya K.
Priyanka Sharma
Priyanka Suyal
Purnendu Bikash Acharjee
Pushparaj
Qixia Zhang
R. Balasubhramanyam
R. Senthil Kumar
R. Saranya
R. Sujithra Kanmani
Rachit Garg
Radha B.
Raghu N.
Rajan Patel
Rajasekaran Selvaraju
Rajender Kumar
Rajesh Bansode
Rajesh Kaluri
Raji C. G.
Rajib Biswas
Rajiv Iyer
Rajkumar Buyya
Rajkumar R.
Rakesh Kumar Yadav

Ramesh T. Prajapati
Ramveer Singh
Rashmi Soni
Ravendra Ratan Singh Jandail
Ravi Khatri
Ravirajsinh S. Vaghela
Rekha Rani
Renjith V. Ravi
Richa Adlakha
Rinkoo Bhatia
Ripal Ranpara
Ritesh Patel
Ritu Bhargava
Rodina Ahmad
Rohit Goyal
Rohit Kanauzia
Rujuta Shah
Rupali Atul Mahajan
Rupesh Kumar Jindal
Rushikumar Raval
Rutvi Shah
S. Sriranjani Mokshagundam
S. Jafar Ali Ibrahim
S. Balambigai
S. Kannadhasan
S. Muthakshi
S. Sharanyaa
S. Silvia Priscila
Safvan Vahora
Saifullah Khalid
Sailesh Iyer
Samir Patel
Samir Malakar
Samriti Mahajan
Sandeep Mathur
Sandip Sapan Chandra
Sandip T. Shingade
Sangeet Saha
Santosh Kumar Shukla
Sarita Vitthal Balshetwar
Saswati Mahapatra
Satvik Khara
Shadab Siddiqui
Shahera Patel
Shaik Khaja Mohiddin

Shailaja Jayashankar
Shamala Subramaniam
Shanti Verma
Sheikh Fahad Ahmad
Sheng-Lung Peng
Shilpa
Shruti Jain
Shruti Patil
Shubhra Sankar Ray
Shukor Sanim Mohd. Fauzi
Sonali Mishra
Sreejith Vignesh B. P.
Sridhar Krishnan
Subhadeep Chakraborty
Subramanian Karthikeyan
Sudhanshu Maurya
Suhasini Vijaykumar
Sumit Mittal
Sunil Bhirud
Sunil Gautam
Sunil Gupta
Sunil Kumar
Sunil Saxena
Suraiya Jabin
Surendra Rahamatkar
Swamydoss D.
Swarnlata Dakua
Sweeti Sah
Swetta Kukreja
T. S. Murugesh
T. Devi
T. Sathish Kumar
T. Buvaneswari
Tanmay Kasbe
Tejavath Balakrishna
Thangraj
Thirumurugan Shanmugam
Tianhua Xu
Tushar Jaware
U. Surya Kameswari
Uma Dulhare
Umang Thakkar
Umesh Bellur
V. Asha
V. Ajitha

V. S. D. Rekha
Vaibhav Gandhi
Valentina Emilia Balas
Varatharajan Ramachandran
Varinder Singh Rana
Varun Chand H.
Vatsal Shah
Vijay D. Katkar
Vijay Singh Rathore
Vikas Tripathi
Vincenzo Piuri
Vineet Kumar Singh
Vinjamuri Snch Dattu
Vinod L. Desai

Vinoth Kumar M.
Vinothina V.
Vipin Sharma
Vipin Tyagi
Vipul A. Shah
Vishal Bharti
Viswan Vimbi
Xavier Fernando
Xiao-Zhi Gao
Yogendra Kumar
Yogesh Kumar
Yogesh R. Ghodasara
Yugendra D. Chincholkar

Abstract of Keynotes

Generative AI vs Chat GPT vs Cognitive AI Impact on Cyber Security Real World Applications

Venkat Rayapati

Cyber Forza, Inc., USA

This presentation provides an overview of Generative AI vs Chat GPT vs Cognitive AI impact on the real-world Cyber Security Applications. State-Sponsored Cyber Attacks against India went up by 278% between 2021 and September 2023. Cyber security is a real challenge for the whole world, India is a major target about 15% of the total cyberattacks have been observed in 2023. This presentation covers brief summary of the cyberattacks and the impact. Artificial Intelligence (AI) will be used for certain behavioral analytics, predictive analytics, and risk reduction analytics purpose.

Generative AI and Open AI current applications used in the industry, they do not have direct impact on security. Chat GPT and Open AI current applications in the industry, how they will influence cyber security impact analysis provided. Cognitive AI methods and applications importance for the overall cyber risk reduction addressed.

Generative AI or Chat GPT or Cognitive AI are all fundamentally dependent on certain Open AI Algorithms, libraries, API's, which further refines application domain and efficacy. Cyber criminals can modify malware code to evade detection. ML is ideal for anti-malware protection, since it can draw on data from previously detected malware to detect new variants. This works even when dangerous code is hidden within innocent code. AI-powered network monitoring tools can track user behavior, detect anomalies, and react accordingly. A simple case study is presented to demonstrated the effective of the current AI versus feature needs of AI. The dangers of AI in Cyberattack space is highlighted with an example. Recommendations provided for the over all real time cyber security risk reduction.

Empowering Smart Computing Through the Power of Light

Shamala Subramaniam

Universiti Putra Malaysia

The paradigms which govern technology and civilization is constantly emerging with innovations and transforming the definition of norms. These require pre-requisites encompassing the pillars which constitute the Industry 4.0, 5.0 and the subsequent revolutions. It is require discussing the ability to harness the wide spectrum of rich resources and discover the profound impact that the technology transformation is having on industry innovation, exploring the challenges and opportunities that this presents, and consider the significant implications.

Subsequently, leveraging co-existence strategies to address particularly, the Internet of Things (IoT) and the Internet of Everything (IoE) as a driving force behind further densification. The LiFi technology, which stands for light fidelity role in addressing the challenges emerging from densification and as a factor to optimize co-existences and interdisciplinary dimensions. It is require discussing the significant and high impact of the correlation between sports and technology encompassing creative LiFi solutions in this area. The realization of an idea is largely attributed to the ability of a researcher to deploy strategies to evaluate and gauge the actual performance of this idea. The substantial research findings in the area of Access Point Assignment (APA) algorithms in a hybrid LiFi – WiFi network require to be discussed. A Multi-criteria Decision-Making (MCDM) problem is formulated to determine a network-level selection for each user over a period of time The decision problem is modelled as a hierarchy that fragments a problem into a hierarchy of simple and small sub problems, and the selection of the AP network among various alternatives is a considered as an MCDM problem. The result of this research empowers the APA for hybrid LiFi networks with a new perspective.

Optimal Transport Algorithms with Machine Learning Applications

Sharath Raghavendra

Virginia Tech, USA

Optimal Transport distance is a metric to measure similarity between probability distributions and has been extensively studied in economics and statistics since the 18th century. Here we introduce the optimal transport problem and present several of its modern applications in data analytics and machine learning. It is also require to address algorithmic challenges related to scalability and robustness and present partial solutions towards overcoming these challenges.

Some Research Issues on Cyber Security

Sheng-Lung Peng

National Taipei University of Business, Taiwan

Recently, a cyber security model M is defined by a three-tuple $M = (T, C, P)$, where $T = (V, E)$ is a tree rooted at r having n non-root vertices, C is a multiset of penetration costs $c_1, \ldots, c_n \in Z^+$, and P is a multiset of prizes $p_1, \ldots, p_n \in Z^+$. The attack always begins at the root r and the root always has prize 0. A security system (T, c, p) with respect to a cyber security model $M = (T, C, P)$ is given by two bijections $c : E(T) \rightarrow C$ and $p : V(T)\backslash\{r\} \rightarrow P$. A system attack in (T, c, p) is given by a subtree T' of T that contains the root r of T. The cost of a system attack T' with respect to (T, c, p) is given by the cost $cst(c, p, T') = \Sigma_{e \in E(T')}c(e)$. The prize of a system attack T' with respect to (T, c, p) is given by the prize $pr(c, p, T') = \Sigma_{u \in V(T')}p(u)$. For a given budget $B \in Z^+$ the maximum prize $pr^*(c, p, B)$ with respect to B is defined by $pr^*(c, p, B) = \max\{pr(c, p, T')|\text{for all } T' \subseteq T, \text{ where } cst(c, p, T') \leq B\}$. A system attack T' whose prize is maximum with respect to a given budget B is called an optimal attack. In this talk, we first introduce the defined cyber security problem. We then propose some extended models for future research.

Smart Infrastructure and Smart Agriculture- Japan Use Cases

Krishna Kumar

Vice President - Corporate Strategy, Keisoku Engineering System Co., Ltd., Tokyo, Japan

To understand the smart infrastructure and smart agriculture and its key aspects it is require to discuss the use cases of advanced countries. This explores the burgeoning landscape of smart computing applications in Japan, where the pressing challenges of population decline and an aging society have accelerated the adoption of intelligent systems. It also delves into the diverse applications of information and communication technologies (ICT) in pivotal sectors such as Agriculture, Infrastructure, Mobility, Energy, and Safety. By seamlessly integrating Artificial Intelligence (AI), Internet of Things (IoT), Big Data, and Computer Vision, Japan is witnessing a transformative wave of smart computing solutions aimed at enhancing efficiency and reducing time, cost, and labor.

Unveiling the Dynamics of Spontaneous Micro and Macro Facial Expressions

Deepak Jain

Dalian University of technology, Dalian, China

Facial expressions serve as a fundamental channel for human communication, conveying a rich spectrum of emotions and social cues. This study delves into the intricate realm of spontaneous facial expressions, examining both micro and macro expressions to unravel the nuanced dynamics underlying human nonverbal communication. Employing advanced facial recognition technologies and nuanced observational methods, we explore the spontaneous micro expressions that manifest in fleeting moments, lasting mere fractions of a second, as well as the more extended macro expressions that reveal deeper emotional states.

The research investigates the physiological and psychological mechanisms governing the generation of spontaneous facial expressions, shedding light on the spontaneous nature of these expressions and their significance in interpersonal dynamics. By employing cutting-edge techniques, including high-speed imaging and machine learning algorithms, we aim to discern subtle nuances in facial movements that often elude conscious awareness.

Furthermore, the study explores the cross-cultural universality of spontaneous facial expressions, examining how cultural and individual differences may influence the interpretation and recognition of micro and macro expressions. Understanding the universality and cultural variability of these expressions is crucial for developing more inclusive and accurate models of nonverbal communication.

Insights gained from this research have implications for fields such as psychology, human-computer interaction, and artificial intelligence, where a nuanced understanding of facial expressions can enhance emotional intelligence, interpersonal communication, and the design of empathetic technologies. The exploration of spontaneous micro and macro facial expressions opens new avenues for comprehending the subtleties of human emotion, enriching our understanding of the intricate tapestry of nonverbal communication.

AI Advancements in Biomedical Image Processing: Challenges, Innovations, and Insights

Sonali Agarwal

Indian Institute of Information Technology, Allahabad, India

With the rapid development of Artificial Intelligence (AI), biomedical image processing has made remarkable progress in disease diagnosis, segmentation, and classification tasks, establishing itself as a key research area in both medicine and academia. Gaining insights into the use of deep learning for tasks such as identifying diseases in various imaging modalities, localizing anatomical features, and precisely segmenting target regions is important.

Deep learning models are data-hungry, but challenges arise due to the limited availability of biomedical data, data security concerns, and high data acquisition costs. To address these issues, exploring the emerging technology of self-supervised learning is important, as it enhances feature representation capture and result generation. While AI shows great potential in medical image analysis, it struggles with effectively handling multimodal data. Moreover, exploring the complexities of learning and diagnosing diseases in heterogeneous environments with limited multimodal images is essential.

Methods to enhance the interpretability of AI models include providing visual explanations with class activation maps and uncertainty maps, which offer transparency and rationale for model predictions. Conducting a SWOT analysis is crucial to evaluate the current state of AI methods, taking into account their strengths, weaknesses, opportunities, and threats in clinical implementation.

Emerging Technologies and Models for Data Protection and Resource Management in Cloud Environments

Ishu Gupta

Ramanujan Faculty Fellow, IIIT-B, Bangalore, India

Cloud environments have emanated as an essential benchmark for storage, sharing, and computation facilities through the internet that is extensively utilized in online transactions, research, academia, business, marketing, etc. It offers liberty to pay-as-per-use sculpture and ubiquitous computing amenities to every user and acts as a backbone for emerging technologies such as Cyber-Physical Systems (CPS), Internet of Things (IoT), and Big Data, etc. in the field of engineering sciences and technology that is the future of human society. These technologies are increasingly supported by Artificial Intelligence (AI) and Machine Learning (ML) to furnish advanced capabilities to the world. Despite numerous benefits offered by the cloud environments, it also faces several inevitable challenges including data security, privacy, data leakage, upcoming workload prediction, load balancing, resource management, etc.

The data sets generated by various organizations are uploaded to the cloud for storage and analysis due to their tremendous characteristics such as low maintenance cost, intrinsic resource sharing, etc., and shared among various stakeholders for its utilities. However, it exposes the data's privacy at risk, because the entities involved in communication can misuse or leak the data. Consequently, data security and privacy have emerged as leading challenges in cloud environments. The predicted workload information is crucial for effective resource management and load balancing that leads to reducing the cost associated with cloud services. However, the resource demands can vary significantly over time, making accurate workload estimation challenging. This talk will explore mitigation strategies for these challenges and highlight various technologies, including Quantum Machine Learning (QML), which is emerging as a prominent solution in the field of AI and ML to address these issues.

Artificial Intelligence and Jobs of the Future 2030

T. Devi

Bharathiar University, Coimbatore, India

The industrial revolutions Industry 4.0 and Industry 5.0 are changing the world around us. Artificial Intelligence and Machine Learning are the tools of Industry 4.0. Improved collaboration is seen between smart systems and humans, which merges the critical and cognitive thinking abilities of humans with the highly accurate and fast industrial automation. Artificial Intelligence (AI) is a pivotal tool of Industry 4.0 in transforming the future through intelligent computational systems. AI automates repetitive learning and discovery through data. Instead of automating manual tasks, AI performs frequent, high-volume, computerized tasks reliably and without fatigue. For this type of automation, human inquiry is still essential to set up the system and ask the right questions. AI adds intelligence to existing products. Automation, conversational platforms, bots, and smart machines can be combined with large amounts of data to improve many technologies.

To prepare the future pillars of our Globe to face the Volatile, Uncertain, Complex and Ambiguous (VUCA) world, and to help the academic community, Universities are revising the curricula to match with Industry 4.0. Towards this and to provide knowledge resources such as books, the author had co-edited five books titled Artificial Intelligence Theory, Models, and Applications, Big Data Applications in Industry 4.0, Industry 4.0 Technologies for Education Transformative Technologies and Applications, Innovating with Augmented Reality Applications in Education and Industry, Securing IoT in Industry 4.0 Applications with Blockchain.

Jobs of the Future 2030: Prominent sectors that will have more jobs in 2030 are Healthcare, Education, Information Technology, Digital Marketing, Automation, Manufacturing, and Logistics. The jobs in these sectors would include: Healthcare - Medical: doctors, nurses, pharmacists, drug developers - demand for better medicine and treatments are ever increasing; Education – Teachers (School, College), Other education professionals, Education support workers; Information Technology Specialists: Artificial Intelligence, Internet of Things (IoT), Data Analytics, Augmented Reality Computer Specialists; Digital Marketing; Automation Specialists: Drone pilots; Manufacturing: Automation using Robots and Artificial Intelligence; Logistics: as Globalisation will lead to more Global trade; and Restaurant Cooks

Artificial Intelligence Jobs in Future 2030: Automation and artificial intelligence will drive the world. Cars that drive themselves, machines that read X-rays and algorithms that respond to customer-service inquiries are new forms of automation. Automation can be applied more in sectors such as Pharmaceuticals (research and development, Marketing (consumer Marketing) Digital Marketing, Automotive (redesign and new development), and Oil and Gas.

New Age Cyber Risks Due to AI Intervention

Ram Kumar G.

Information Security and Risk Leader, Nissan Motor Corporation, Bangalore, India

Artificial Intelligence especially the generative variant is reshaping the world. Generative Artificial Intelligence (Gen AI) tool like ChatGPT - the new AI chatbot can hold entire conversations, speaking in the style of someone else, and play out nearly any imaginary scenario an user can ask it for.

Ever since its release late 2022, Generative AI tool ChatGPT has stormed the tech world with its amazing capabilities leveraging on generative Artificial Intelligence. While everyone is aware and excited about the immense potential and utility of such AI platform, it is important to understand the security and data privacy risks they pose.

With the corporate sector embracing generative AI tools for their benefit, there have been widespread concerns among security executives about the malicious usage of new age technology like Gen AI. Media reports highlighting cyber security risks of using Gen AI from real world incidents has only added to the apprehension among business executives about the blind adoption of such innovative tools without adequate safeguards about usage.

While the focus is on the cyber security and privacy risks arising from use of generative AI, it is also to be noted that AI tools can be used for defending against cyber threats and risks. Gen AI helps to enhance security and reduce risks which help in:

1. Detecting security vulnerabilities
2. Generating security code
3. Integration with SIEM/SOAR to improve SOC effectiveness
4. Enhancing email security
5. Improving identity and access management

In conclusion, it is critical for everyone to realize the security implications of cutting edge technology like Gen AI and make conscious decision to adopt safety precautions while using them. It will do a world of good for securing sensitive data including IP and protecting against AI-triggered phishing or malware attacks against businesses.

Challenges of 5G in Combat Networks

Col Mahesh Ramachandran

L&T, New Delhi, India

While 5G technology promises to change the rules of telecommunication in terms of high data rates, accurate location services, security and SWaP (Size, Weight and Power), it is by no means a 'One size fits All' solution for all applications - especially combat networks which have their unique requirements and challenges. This is because technology that works in commercial static networks cannot be simply replicated and rolled out in tactical networks due to the huge challenges imposed by terrain, mobility, electronic/cyberattacks, SWaP, EMI/EMC (Electromagnetic Interference/Electromagnetic Compatibility) and country specific encryption requirements.

Mission criticality through Quality of Service (QOS), Quality of User Experience (QOE), redundancy and reliability is of utmost importance to voice, video, data and application services, including GIS in Combat Networks. The issue is further exacerbated, given the practical constraints in placing the nodes at the optimum locations due to reasons of terrain, enemy threat and operational plans. The infrastructure provisioning has to be done with optimization of size, weight and power while reducing the electronic signature to a minimum.

Notwithstanding the fact that concurrent "Releases" approach used by 3GPP provides developers with a secure foundation for implementing features at a particular time and then enables the inclusion of new capabilities in subsequent releases, besides also enabling the features to be updated in a same release as technology advances over time, it is an irony that the new versions of 3GPP releases only have a minimal impact on tactical combat networks in terms of efficiency and speeds. In other words the high data rates, enhanced security and other features of new releases do not address the challenges of combat networks due to the uniqueness of such networks. This paper analyses the peculiar communication requirements of Tactical combat networks and the challenges of adapting 5g technologies for such networks.

Dark Side of Artificial Intelligence

H. R. Mohan

ICT Consultant, Chair - Events, IEEE CS Madras, Chennai, India

While the potential of AI to transform our world is tremendous, the risks associated with it's ethical norms, safety, privacy, security, bias and consequences of the use of bad data, unpredictability, wrong decision making, weaponizaton, inequality, accessibility, misinformation, deep fakes, regulation, legality, societal impact, transparency, account-ability, explainability, reliability, environmental impact, geopolitical issues and human rights are quite significant, complex, fast-evolving and turning to be real. The unintended consequences of GenAI can cause disruptions globally with high stakes in all sectors of economy. This presentation on Dark Side of AI will elaborate on these risks associated with AI and the need for the global cooperation in its use and regulation.

Blockchain Integrated Security Solution for Internet of Drones (IoD)

Sudhanshu Maurya

Symbiosis International (Deemed University) Pune, India

The rising reception of drones across different areas, including regular citizen and military applications, requires the improvement of cutting-edge insight, unwavering quality, and security for these automated airborne vehicles. This work proposes a blockchain-based security answer for the 'Multitude of Drones'; current circumstance, planning to guarantee the mystery, unwavering quality, and protection of information move. The proposed technique considers consistent check and enrolment of drones, approval of administrators, sending and withdrawal of drones, information assortment from drones, and secure stockpiling and recovery of information in a blockchain-based framework. The assessment of the proposed strategy on reproduced drones exhibits its viability in giving prevalent information stockpiling security and keeping up with the classification and genuineness of communicated information. The use of blockchain innovation offers various benefits in the drone climate. Blockchain's decentralized nature guarantees that all exchanges and information trades are recorded across various frameworks, making it almost unthinkable for unapproved gatherings to adjust or erase data. Moreover, blockchain's innate encryption instruments give an extra layer of safety, defending information from potential digital dangers.

Besides, blockchain innovation can work with the making of a dependable and secure correspondence network for drones, assisting with forestalling unapproved access and impedance. By making a straightforward and unalterable record of all drone exercises, blockchain can likewise aid responsibility and administrative consistency. By consolidating blockchain innovation, this examination means adding to the advancement of more brilliant, more private, and safer drones. This could make ready for their extended use from here on out, in applications going from conveyance and observation to catastrophe reaction and ecological checking. The combination of blockchain into drone tasks addresses a huge forward-moving step chasing dependable and secure automated flying frameworks.

Generative Intelligence: A Catalyst for Safeguarding Society in the Age of GenAI

K. Vallidevi

VIT, Chennai, India

Generative Adversarial Networks (GANs) which is a subset of Generative AI (GenAI), can be used as a catalyst for fraud detection and prevention to shape the safety of the society in a better way. Though it is definitely a double edged sword, it could be efficiently used for proactively detecting fraudulent activities. GenAI plays a major role in video analytics for proactively detecting frauds by employing various techniques like Behavioural Analysis, Anomaly Detection and so on. By simulating fraudulent activities and generating synthetic data will help in detecting criminal activities in a proactive manner. Through this method, the intelligent system could analyse the various patterns involved in fraudulent activities and could identify them when such systems are used in real-time CCTV footage monitoring.

There are several use-cases for using Gen-AI in Proactive Policing.

1) Applying a face mask to the person's image
2) Removing face mask in the masked face image by generating the covered part of the face corresponding to rest of the face part with multiple outputs,
3) Checking similarity between resultant images and input images given by user,
4) Querying a person's availability in group image and
5) Face aging module where a person of any age is given along with the desired age number, where it generates the face image of the required age of a person. The found similar person can be checked for his outlook on various angles, by rotating the person's face. Face generation algorithms are prone to generate differentiating outputs when compared with the ground truth image'.

As these algorithms generate only single output, there is a high scope these outputs not being closely matched with the original image. Hence, a new technique of multiple diverse output images being generated, increases the probability of achieving the highest similarity with the original image. Masking the face is attained by using Dlib library while the rendering of the face is achieved by using Generative Adversarial Networks (GAN). GANs, comprising a generator and discriminator, are trained to create synthetic facial images with accurately generated masked regions. The generator network learns to produce realistic facial features, including accurately placed and shaped masks, while the discriminator distinguishes between authentic and generated images.

Contents – Part III

Computer Networks

Cyber Security

Standardization in Cloud Computing: Unlocking the Potential of a Fragmented Industry

Aayush Kulkarni(✉) and Mangesh Bedekar

School of Computer Science and Engineering, Dr. Vishwanath Karad MIT World Peace
University, Pune, Maharashtra, India
Kulkarnisa33@gmail.com, mangesh.bedekar@mitwpu.edu.in

Abstract. The rapid ascent of cloud computing has transformed data management for both businesses and individuals. Despite its unprecedented growth, the industry grapples with formidable challenges, including vendor lock-in, interoperability issues, and security concerns. This paper advocates for the pivotal role of standardization in unlocking the full potential of cloud computing. We propose a comprehensive set of measures and regulations, focusing on the standardization of Application Programming Interface (APIs), Service Level Agreements (SLAs), cloud security, and data formats, complemented by the establishment of regulatory bodies. The multitude of cloud service providers (CSPs) offering diverse services, pricing models, and billing metrics has resulted in a lack of uniformity, complicating organizations' efforts to compare and optimize cloud resources effectively. Vendor lock-in is further exacerbated by proprietary systems, stifling competition, compromising data security and privacy, and hindering innovation. To address these challenges, we emphasize the adoption of standard APIs and SLAs to enable seamless integration between CSPs. The standardization of data formats is proposed to facilitate effortless data transfer between providers, providing enhanced flexibility for users. The establishment of regulatory bodies is advocated to ensure strict adherence to industry standards, fostering a more unified and standardized approach to cloud computing. Embracing these measures is envisioned to foster a harmonized cloud ecosystem, reducing fragmentation, stimulating innovation, and ultimately empowering businesses and individuals with heightened efficiency, security, and peace of mind. The call for standardization aims to level the playing field for businesses, irrespective of size, fostering healthy competition, and driving improved services and cost-effectiveness. As we embark on this journey towards a standardized cloud landscape, we envision a future where the transformative power of cloud computing propels businesses and individuals towards unprecedented heights of success.

Keywords: Cloud computing · standardization · interoperability · security · vendor lock-in · Application Programming Interface (APIs) · Service Level Agreements (SLAs) · data formats · regulatory bodies · proprietary systems · ethical concerns · data sovereignty · privacy · innovation

S. Rajagopal et al. (Eds.): ASCIS 2023, CCIS 2039, pp. 3–12, 2024.
https://doi.org/10.1007/978-3-031-59100-6_1

1 Introduction

The rapid expansion of cloud computing services, such as Platform as a Service (PaaS), Software as a Service (SaaS), and Infrastructure as a Service (IaaS), has brought unprecedented convenience and scalability to businesses and individuals. However, this growth has also exposed significant challenges, primarily due to the lack of industry-wide standardization. This paper addresses the pressing need for standardization in the cloud computing industry, which can lead to enhanced interoperability, improved security, and increased innovation. The absence of uniform standards across different cloud service providers has resulted in vendor lock-in, interoperability issues, and security concerns, jeopardizing data privacy and increasing the risk of cyber-attacks. Although certain industry standards, like the Open Cloud Computing Interface [2] and Cloud Infrastructure Management Interface, have been introduced, widespread adoption remains a challenge. This paper proposes a comprehensive approach to achieve standardization in the cloud computing sector. By standardizing APIs, Service Level Agreements (SLAs), cloud security measures, and data formats, businesses can enjoy easier migration between providers, reduced costs, and enhanced data protection. Additionally, the establishment of regulatory bodies and legal frameworks will ensure providers comply with agreed-upon standards, fostering greater collaboration and innovation.

1] Comparative Analysis: In delving into the intricacies of cloud computing, a comparative analysis illuminates the prevailing challenges. The diverse array of cloud service providers (CSPs) presents organizations with a complex landscape, characterized by varying services, pricing models, and billing metrics. This lack of uniformity complicates resource optimization, making it imperative to assess the comparative advantages and disadvantages of each provider. Vendor lock-in, further compounded by proprietary systems, emerges as a critical bottleneck. This hinders healthy competition, compromises data security and privacy, and stifles innovation. A rigorous comparative examination of proprietary systems across CSPs will shed light on the degree of vendor lock-in and its associated implications.

2] Quantitative Factor and Impact Assessment - To bolster the paper's robustness, a quantitative factor is introduced to underscore the tangible impact of standardization. By incorporating metrics such as interoperability rates, security incident reductions, and innovation indices, we aim to provide a quantifiable assessment of the proposed measures. The adoption of standard APIs and SLAs is anticipated to increase interoperability rates, fostering seamless integration between CSPs. This can be measured through quantitative indicators, illustrating the reduction in integration complexities and the acceleration of data transfer processes. Security enhancements resulting from standardization measures can be quantified through a comparative analysis of security incident rates before and after implementation. By introducing quantifiable metrics, the paper aims to accentuate the tangible benefits of embracing standardized security protocols. A quantitative evaluation of innovation indices pre and post-standardization adoption will provide insights into the potential stimulative effect on the cloud computing industry. This approach lends a quantitative dimension to the transformative power of standardization. Ultimately, standardization will not only address technical obstacles but also ethical and social concerns regarding data sovereignty and privacy. By providing clear guidelines and promoting trust in cloud services, standardization enables businesses and individuals to fully harness the potential of cloud computing with efficiency, security, and peace of mind.

2 Background and Current State of Standardization

2.1 Background

With the advent of cloud computing, enterprises and individuals now have easy online access to a variety of IT services, changing the way we think about technology as a whole. Businesses of all sizes have adopted this game-changing technology, which has experienced tremendous development and is now a multibillion dollar sector, in order to boost efficiency, cut costs, and increase agility. Although the idea of cloud computing has been around since the 1960s, it wasn't until the mid-2000s when Amazon Web Services [3] launched its Elastic Compute Cloud service that it became well known and well-liked. Since then, key firms such Amazon Web Services, Microsoft Azure, Google Cloud Platform, IBM Cloud, and Alibaba Cloud have greatly advanced and shaped cloud computing technologies, solidifying it as a crucial component of contemporary digital infrastructure.

2.2 Current State of Standardization

Despite the widespread adoption of cloud computing, the industry remains fragmented, with each cloud service provider offering distinct services and APIs. This lack of standardization has given rise to challenges such as vendor lockin, making it difficult for customers to switch between providers and inhibiting healthy market competition. Furthermore, the absence of uniform security standards and practices has raised concerns about data privacy, compliance, and cyber-attacks, complicating the assessment of cloud service security. Additionally, the lack of standardized practices has hindered interoperability, making it challenging for businesses to transfer data and applications seamlessly between different cloud environments. To address these pressing issues, a comprehensive standardization framework is required, encompassing common interfaces, security standards, data formats, service level agreements, billing and metering standards, performance metrics, and more. By establishing uniform guidelines, protocols, and interfaces across the cloud computing industry, businesses can optimize their resource utilization, enhance security measures, and ensure smooth interoperability, enabling them to harness the full potential of cloud computing and drive innovation and growth.

3 Case Study

Case study 1] Netflix and Amazon Web Services (Vendor Lock-In): (AWS) [3]: In 2010, Netflix made a strategic shift, moving its operations from self-owned data centers to Amazon Web Services (AWS) [3]. While this decision offered scalability and flexibility, it also led to significant vendor lock-in. As Netflix's usage of AWS grew, migrating to another Cloud Service Provider (CSP) became challenging and costly. The proprietary interfaces and specialized tools provided by AWS made it difficult for Netflix to easily transition to an alternative CSP, even if dissatisfied with the service or pricing. This case study highlights the implications of vendor lock-in, emphasizing the importance of standardized practices to ensure customer freedom and foster healthy competition in the cloud computing industry.

Case study 2] Target Corporation Data Breach (Cloud Security): The Target Corporation faced a severe data breach in 2013, wherein hackers gained unauthorized access to their payment system through a vulnerability in a third-party vendor's software. This incident compromised the credit card data and personal information of over 40 million customers. The breach raised concerns about the security and data privacy in cloud-based systems, as different CSPs may employ varied security protocols, making it challenging for customers to ensure consistent data protection. Standardized security measures and protocols are crucial to mitigate such risks and bolster the overall security posture of cloud computing services [4].

Case study 3] Schrems II Judgement (Regulatory Compliance): The Schrems II judgement, delivered by the European Court of Justice, rendered the EU-US Privacy Shield agreement illegal. Study highlighted the complexities of regulatory compliance in cloud computing. Different countries and regions have diverse laws governing data privacy, security, and storage, making it difficult for CSPs to offer consistent services and for customers to ensure compliance with relevant regulations. The ruling led to increased scrutiny of CSPs' ability to safeguard data in accordance with regional mandates, underlining the importance of standardization to harmonize compliance requirements and facilitate seamless cross-border cloud services [5].

4 Benefits of Standardization

Standardization in the cloud computing industry provides numerous advantages for both businesses and individuals. One key benefit is enhanced interoperability among different cloud service providers, allowing seamless migration without compatibility concerns. This streamlines operations, saving valuable time and resources for businesses to focus on core competencies. Cost reduction is another significant advantage. When cloud services adhere to common standards, businesses can avoid vendor lock-in, negotiate competitive prices, and optimize their cloud investments. This cost-saving potential benefits enterprises of all sizes, enabling them to leverage the advantages of cloud computing. Improved security is a crucial benefit of standardization. Consistent security protocols across providers significantly reduce the risk of cyber-attacks and data breaches. For instance, the Target Corporation data breach highlights the importance of consistent security measures in preventing theft of sensitive customer information. Standardization can prevent such incidents, protecting businesses from legal and reputational consequences. Challenges in cloud computing standardization, such as inconsistent security standards and lack of standardized data formats, hinder the technology's full potential. A collaborative effort among cloud service providers, regulators, and businesses is essential to establish industry-wide standards for APIs, SLAs, cloud security, and data formats. Regulatory bodies play a crucial role in ensuring adherence to these standards, enhancing security, improving data privacy, and facilitating smoother data exchange between providers. In embracing standardization and overcoming challenges collectively, businesses can fully harness the transformative power of cloud computing, operating efficiently and securely in today's digital landscape.

5 Proposed Standardization in Cloud Computing Industry

Standardization in the cloud computing industry is a critical step towards enhancing interoperability and reducing vendor lock-in challenges. The absence of standardized practices has led to issues with seamless integration of diverse cloud platforms, maintaining consistent security measures, and transitioning between service providers. To address these challenges, the adoption of a common set of standards and guidelines is essential. Standardizing APIs and SLAs is pivotal in achieving interoperability between different cloud service providers. By ensuring a uniform approach, businesses can easily migrate between providers, avoiding cumbersome customizations and data transfer complexities. Additionally, standardizing SLAs enables businesses to negotiate better prices, resulting in cost reductions and increased efficiency. Cloud security standardization is paramount for the industry. Implementing a common set of security protocols and guidelines will ensure consistent data protection and reduce the risk of cyber-attacks and data breaches. Providers adhering to these standards will collectively bolster cybersecurity defenses and safeguard sensitive information. Standardizing data formats is crucial to facilitate smooth data transfer between cloud service providers. Businesses can avoid arduous customizations, saving valuable time and resources while ensuring seamless data integration. The establishment of regulatory bodies is imperative to oversee the industry and enforce compliance with agreed-upon standards and guidelines. These bodies will play a vital role in upholding the safety and security of cloud computing environments, fostering trust and confidence among businesses and consumers. Embracing standardization measures will yield numerous benefits, including improved interoperability, cost savings, and heightened security. The cloud computing industry must unite to adopt these standardized practices, unlocking the full potential of cloud computing for a more efficient and secure digital future.

End-to-End Proposed Framework for Cloud Standardization: A Blueprint for Industry Transformation:

1] Collaborative Industry Inclusivity: Major cloud providers (AWS, GCP, Azure, IBM) collaboratively establish a non-profit consortium dedicated to open cloud standards. Emphasis on inclusivity, positioning the consortium as a neutral ground for industry leaders to contribute without biases.

2] Holistic Collaboration: The consortium engages in collaborative efforts on technical specifications, reference architectures, policy frameworks, and governance protocols. Actively involves recognized standards bodies International Organization for Standardization (ISO), International Telecommunication Union (ITU), National Institute of Standards and Technology (NIST) to ensure a globally aligned and legitimate standardization process.

3] API Specification for Core Functionalities: The consortium releases API specifications focusing on core functionalities such as provisioning, identity management, and monitoring. Standardization of data formats (JSON, XML), protocols (HTTP, FTP), and schemas for seamless interoperability. Open-sourcing reference architectures to encourage widespread adoption and contributions.

4] Unified Regulatory Framework: Agreement on a shared regulatory framework addressing crucial aspects like security, privacy, and localization laws. Contribution to compliance certifications like Service Organization Control Type 2 (SOC2), ISO27001 to ensure consistent adherence to industry standards. Definition of standard service contracts and SLAs to establish transparency and consistency in cloud services.

5] Validation Programs for Accountability: The consortium establishes conformance testing tools and certification programs. Annual validation of providers for standards implementation with certification, fostering accountability and reliability. Iterative enhancements based on identified gaps and evolving industry needs, ensuring continuous improvement.

6] Supporting Consortium Members: Provision of comprehensive support, including training, tooling, and incentives for consortium members to adopt and implement standards. Governmental mandates lend legal weight to standards usage, linking adherence to procurement contracts and promoting widespread adoption.

7] Timely Updates and Future-Proofing: Regular release of updates and new versions of standards to accommodate technological shifts and emerging trends. Continuous monitoring of industry dynamics to ensure standards remain relevant and applicable. Collective funding of R & D into future standards for proactive adaptation and staying ahead of technological advancements.

8] Holistic Stakeholder Collaboration: Collaboration with governments, businesses, and academia for a holistic and inclusive approach. A shared governance model designed to foster open collaboration, ensuring the collective benefit of the industry. Transparent communication channels to address concerns, gather feedback, and maintain a responsive governance structure.

9] Incorporation of Existing Research: Comprehensive review and integration of existing literature and similar works in cloud standardization. Identification of successful models and lessons learned to inform and strengthen the proposed framework.

This end-to-end framework serves as a comprehensive roadmap for unifying stakeholders, driving adoption, and ensuring continuous evolution in response to dynamic industry changes. It is positioned to empower the nation with a robust standardization process that not only addresses current challenges but also propels it to the forefront of technological innovation in the cloud computing industry.

6   Regulations Required to Achieve and Best Practices for Standardization in Cloud Computing

To achieve standardization in the cloud computing industry, a robust regulatory framework is necessary. This framework should encompass certification and accreditation of cloud service providers, monitoring and enforcement of standards and practices, regular audits and assessments of providers, and penalties for non-compliance. Certification and accreditation would evaluate providers' adherence to standards and assess their capabilities, fostering trust and confidence among users. Monitoring and enforcement would ensure that cloud service providers remain compliant with established standards. Regular audits and assessments would identify gaps in compliance, driving continuous improvement in cloud services. Penalties for non-compliance must be significant enough to deter violations and protect users' interests. The regulatory bodies should have the authority to take legal action against repeat offenders, safeguarding industry standards. Best practices for standardization in cloud computing include the adoption of standardization frameworks and models. These frameworks ensure interoperability and portability, enabling businesses to migrate between providers seamlessly. Adherence to interoperability and portability standards like Cloud Data Management Interface (CDMI) and Consistency, Availability, Partition Tolerance (CAP) allows easy data and application exchange. Security and compliance standards are vital for protecting cloud environments. The adoption of standards like Payment Card Industry Data Security Standard (PCI DSS) [4] and ISO 27001 [5] ensures a uniform approach to cybersecurity, mitigating the risk of cyber-attacks and data breaches. New technologies, such as AI, ML, and IoT, are driving further advances in standardization practices, necessitating the development of new guidelines for their responsible use in cloud environments. Implementation of cloud standardization provide valuable insights. Collaborative efforts between providers, customers, and regulatory bodies have proven essential in developing and implementing effective cloud standards. Overall, the combination of regulations and best practices will unlock the full potential of cloud computing, ensuring cost-effective, secure, and efficient services for businesses and individuals.

7 Standardization Frameworks and Models and Successful Implementation of Cloud Standardization

Standardization frameworks and models play a crucial role in the development and implementation of standardized practices in cloud computing, promoting interoperability, portability, and security. One notable example is the adoption of the NIST Cloud Computing Framework by Microsoft. This framework has allowed Microsoft to align its security policies and practices with industry standards, ensuring the security and compliance of its cloud services. Similarly, Amazon Web Services (AWS) [3] has successfully implemented the ISO/IEC 27001 standard [5], a widely recognized framework for information security management. By adhering to this standard, AWS has ensured the confidentiality, integrity, and availability of customer data in the cloud. The studies demonstrate the significance of adopting and adhering to industry-standard frameworks to gain customer trust and achieve a competitive advantage in the cloud computing industry. To enhance cloud standardization further, organizations can develop their internal frameworks that align with industry standards, such as establishing data governance policies that adhere to ISO/IEC 27001 [5]. The integration of automation and machine learning technologies for security compliance monitoring, as demonstrated by AWS, can improve efficiency and reduce the risk of security breaches. The successful implementation of cloud standardization emphasizes the importance of adopting and adhering to industry-standard frameworks and models. This approach not only improves the security and compliance of cloud services but also fosters customer trust and provides a competitive edge in the marketplace.

8 Interoperability and Portability and Security and Compliance Standards in Cloud Computing

Achieving seamless interoperability and portability in cloud computing is crucial for businesses seeking flexibility and efficiency in their cloud operations. Open APIs enable different cloud services to communicate harmoniously, preventing vendor lock-in and promoting application compatibility across multiple cloud providers. Containerization technologies like Docker and Kubernetes ensure a consistent and portable runtime environment, simplifying application migration between different cloud platforms. Using common data formats allows for easy and secure data movement across diverse cloud environments, minimizing data loss and integration complexities. Cloud orchestration and management tools streamline the process of managing applications across cloud infrastructures, automating deployment and scaling tasks. In the dynamic landscape of cloud computing, security and compliance standards are paramount for instilling confidence in businesses and individuals. Adopting common standards like the Cloud Security Alliance Cloud Security Alliance - Security, Trust, and Assurance Registry (CSA STAR) framework [1] provides transparent security and compliance practices from cloud service providers, assuring consumers of their commitment to industry best practices. Additionally, compliance with the Payment Card Industry Data Security Standard (PCI DSS) [4] safeguards credit card data in the cloud through encryption, vulnerability testing, and secure data storage practices. Promising emerging technologies like blockchain, artificial intelligence, and machine learning offer enhanced cloud security measures, while addressing potential challenges in adoption and implementation can further strengthen overall cloud security. Achieving interoperability and portability in cloud computing relies on open APIs, containerization, common data formats, and cloud management tools. These practices enable seamless communication between cloud services, easy migration of applications, and efficient data transfer. In terms of security and compliance, adopting standards like CSA STAR [1] and PCI DSS [4] ensures transparent security practices and credit card data protection in the cloud. Promising technologies like blockchain and AI further enhance cloud security. Overcoming challenges in adoption will solidify cloud computing's reputation as a safe and secure solution for enterprises and individuals alike.

9 Emerging Technologies and Their Impact on Cloud Standardization

The rapid ascent of emerging technologies is reshaping the cloud computing landscape, bringing both challenges and opportunities for service providers. AI, machine learning, and IoT are transforming norms, demanding innovation to meet rising client expectations. Hybrid cloud architectures integrate public and private clouds, optimizing workloads while ensuring regulatory compliance. Blockchain revolutionizes data storage with its secure and transparent platform. Containerization offers a lightweight, portable, and secure way to deploy applications, reducing reliance on specific platforms. Serverless computing streamlines infrastructure management, cutting costs and boosting efficiency.

Edge computing, processing data near the source, enhances real-time application performance, but standardizing diverse edge devices presents challenges. NIST proposes a comprehensive framework for edge computing, guiding providers in developing interoperable solutions. As the industry evolves, embracing these technologies and creating interoperable solutions will be crucial for providers to stay competitive and meet evolving customer demands. Hybrid clouds, containerization, serverless computing, and edge computing are reshaping cloud standardization, ushering in a new era of innovation and adaptability.

10 Who Can Do It?

Cloud standardization necessitates collaboration among key stakeholders in the industry: Cloud Service Providers (CSPs), Industry Associations, Government Regulatory Bodies, and Technology Standards Organizations.

1] Cloud Service Providers: Playing a pivotal role, CSPs can collaborate to establish common APIs, SLAs, security protocols, standardized data formats, and billing practices. This enhances customer experience and promotes a unified approach to cloud computing.
2] Industry Associations: These entities facilitate standardization by bringing together stakeholders, conducting research, developing best practices, and advocating for standardization frameworks. They play a crucial role in creating a conducive environment for cloud standardization.
3] Government Regulatory Bodies: Governments contribute significantly by establishing regulatory frameworks mandating adherence to industry standards. By encouraging compliance with specific security and standards, they enhance data protection and foster trust in cloud services.
4] Technology Standards Organizations: Organizations like ISO and NIST contribute expertise by developing cloud computing standards and guidelines. Their insights address the challenges of cloud standardization.

In collaboration, these stakeholders can unlock the full potential of cloud computing. CSPs implement common APIs, SLAs, and security protocols. Industry associations facilitate standardization, advocate for it, and conduct research. Government bodies drive standardization through regulatory frameworks, ensuring data protection. Technology standards organizations contribute expertise in developing standards. Together, they pave the way for future innovations in the industry, offering efficient, secure, and customer-centric services, shaping the digital landscape for years to come.

11 Conclusion

The rapid expansion of the cloud computing landscape, while transformative, necessitates urgent attention to standardization. The absence of industry-wide standards poses risks such as vendor lock-in, security vulnerabilities, and integration complexities. This research paper advocates for the adoption of common APIs, security protocols, service contracts, data formats, and regulatory frameworks through a comparative analysis and quantitative assessment. The proposed consortiums and collaboration framework offer a clear path for the industry to unite around shared standards. Standardization is the linchpin to unlocking the full potential of cloud computing. It empowers businesses with flexibility, scalability, and cost-efficiency, fostering success in the digital economy. Individuals benefit from seamless and secure access to computing resources. The industry, through enhanced interoperability, fortified security, and accelerated innovation, can propel itself forward. Aspirations for a future cloud ecosystem envision fair competition based on merit rather than proprietary frameworks. Customers stand to gain unprecedented agility, safety, and satisfaction. The collective adoption of standardization is not just prudent but imperative. By embracing it, we can transform a fragmented landscape into a flourishing digital society where cloud computing becomes a catalyst for growth, efficiency, and human progress.

References

1. Cloud Security Alliance (CSA). STAR - Security, Trust, and Assurance Registry. https://clo udsecurityalliance.org/star/
2. Open Grid Forum (OGF). OGF Documentation. https://ogf.org/ogf/doku.html
3. Amazon Web Services (AWS). AWS - Amazon Web Services. https://aws.amazon.com/
4. NBC News. Target Settles 2013 Hacked Customer Data Breach for $ 18.5 Million. https:// www.nbcnews.com/business/business-news/target-settles-2013-hacked-customer-data-bre ach-18-5-million-n764031
5. Kirkland & Ellis LLP. (2020, August). EU-U.S. Privacy Shield. https://www.kirkland.com/pub lications/kirkland-alert/2020/08/eu-us-privacy-shield

A Survey on Secure Aggregation for Privacy-Preserving Federated Learning

Ankit Chouhan[✉] and B. R. Purushothama

Department of Computer Science and Engineering, National Institute of Technology, Goa, India
{ankit.chouhan,puru}@nitgoa.ac.in

Abstract. Federated learning, an innovative methodology that enables clients to train a global model collectively without disclosing raw data, protects data privacy when it comes to training Machine Learning (ML) models across decentralized devices. This survey provides a concise overview of privacy-preserving federated learning, discussing challenges, techniques, and applications. Various techniques are investigated, including federated learning, differential privacy, homomorphic encryption, Secure Multi-party Computation (SMC), and secret sharing, with a review of their advantages and disadvantages. The survey highlights the importance of secure aggregation methods, emphasizing the necessity for novel algorithms to address challenges such as data heterogeneity and communication latency. Overall, this survey offers valuable insights into privacy-preserving federated learning and its potential impact.

Keywords: Privacy-Preserving · Federated Learning · Machine Learning · Secure Aggregation · Security Techniques

1 Introduction

Privacy-preserving refers to the methods and techniques used to protect sensitive information while still allowing data analysis or processing [1]. In today's data-driven world, where vast amounts of personal data are collected, processed, and analyzed, privacy has become a critical concern. Privacy-preserving techniques enable organizations to sustain data confidentiality, preventing prohibited access, and ensuring data security [2]. Different techniques are employed for privacy protection, such as Differential Privacy, Homomorphic Encryption, SMC, and Federated Learning [3].

Differential Privacy involves the addition of random noise to data sets to prevent the identification of individuals within them. Homomorphic encryption allows operations to be performed on encrypted data without requiring decryption, while SMC allows multiple parties to collaborate in computing a function on their private information without disclosing it to others [4]. Federated learning allows for the training of machine learning models using decentralized data, eliminating the requirement to centralize all data in a single location. These techniques offer several advantages for privacy-preserving techniques, as they can protect individuals' privacy, prevent unauthorized access to their data,

© The Author(s), under exclusive license to Springer Nature Switzerland AG 2024
S. Rajagopal et al. (Eds.): ASCIS 2023, CCIS 2039, pp. 13–26, 2024.
https://doi.org/10.1007/978-3-031-59100-6_2

and secure it more effectively. These techniques also facilitate data sharing while maintaining individual confidentiality and enable collaborations while safeguarding sensitive information [5]. Privacy-preserving techniques offer many advantages; however, there can also be challenges associated with their implementation. These challenges include high computational power requirements, data heterogeneity issues, and communication overhead. Nonetheless, privacy-preserving techniques have become indispensable tools in data processing and analysis, gaining increasing importance in today's data-driven world as personal data continues to accumulate. They will remain key tools in protecting sensitive information while enabling data analysis and processing.

Among the previously discussed techniques, Federated learning serves as a machine learning approach that enables model training using distributed data without the necessity of transmitting it back to a central location. This approach keeps data close to users, while model updates are shared via a central server [6]. In federated learning, a central server distributes its ML model to participating devices, such as smartphones or computers. These devices train the model on their local data and then send back updates for further training [7]. Federated learning presents multiple benefits compared to conventional machine learning approaches, including enhanced data privacy and reduced costs associated with data transfer and storage, and enhanced scalability. However, federated learning also presents challenges, including Communication Overhead, Data Heterogeneity, and Non-Independent and Identically Distributed (IID) Data Distribution. Addressing these challenges requires the development of new techniques for model aggregation, data preprocessing, and secure communication protocols [8]. The advantages of privacy-preserving federated learning include:

- **Improved Privacy:** By keeping data stored locally on users' devices, privacy is greatly enhanced and sensitive data doesn't put at risk during model training [9].
- **Reduced data transfer and storage costs:** By sharing only model updates with the central server instead of the actual data, federated learning reduces both data transfer and storage costs.
- **Increased scalability:** Federated learning can handle large amounts of decentralized data, enabling the creation of ML models on a massive scale [10]. However, there are also some limitations to privacy-preserving federated learning
- **Communication overhead:** Federated learning requires communication between devices, which can be computationally expensive and require significant bandwidth.
- **Data heterogeneity:** Since the data is decentralized, it may not be consistent across different devices, which can pose challenges for model training [11].
- **Non-IID data distribution:** The data may not be identically and independently distributed across devices, which can make model training challenging.

The major application of privacy-preserving federated learning (FL) in the Internet of Medical Things (IoMT) revolutionizes healthcare systems by addressing critical privacy concerns associated with centralized artificial intelligence (AI) training approaches. With the proliferation of mobile and wearable IoMT devices transmitting highly confidential information, FL emerges as a distributed AI paradigm ensuring privacy without compromising participants' sensitive data. The privacy-related challenges in IoMT, highlighting FL as a solution. It delves into advanced FL architectures, incorporating deep reinforcement learning, digital twin, and generative adversarial networks to detect privacy threats.

The robustness of FL in mitigating privacy threats, such as data poisoning, Byzantine attacks, and privacy data leakage, showcases its efficacy in ensuring secure and private healthcare data management [12].

Privacy-preserving federated learning offers a promising approach to train machine learning models on decentralized data while preserving user privacy. However, it requires addressing challenges and developing new techniques for model aggregation, data pre-processing, and secure communication protocols [13]. The paper is organized as follows. Section 2 provides an overview of related work. Section 3 discusses security in federated learning. Section 4 focuses on scalable secure aggregation for privacy-preserving federated learning. Section 5 discusses secret sharing for privacy-preserving federated learning. Finally, Section 6 concludes the paper.

2 Related Work

Significant research has been conducted in the field of privacy-preserving federated learning, focusing on enhancing data privacy while maintaining the advantages of decentralized data training. Areas of research include secure aggregation techniques, homomorphic encryption, differential privacy, and federated transfer learning [14]. Efforts have also been made to develop communication-efficient protocols for federated learning and address challenges related to data heterogeneity and non-IID data distribution. Practical applications of privacy-preserving federated learning have been explored in domains such as healthcare, finance, and smart cities. However, there are challenges to overcome, including communication overhead, data heterogeneity, non-IID data distribution, security concerns, and privacy-preserving techniques. Ongoing research in privacy-preserving federated learning is rapidly evolving and is expected to continue advancing in the future.

Liu et al. [15] proposed a mechanism for selecting the top-k dimensions to transmit higher-quality information to the server. This approach aims to avoid the reconstruction loss that can occur due to random projection, but it suffer from the utility. Wang et al. [16] introduced a clipping strategy and extended it by adding techniques such as compression and quantization during communication. This enhancement aims to improve the effectiveness of communication while maintaining differential privacy guarantees. Asoodeh et al. [17] proposed an approach to derive optimal differential privacy parameters for achieving a specific level of Renyi differential privacy. By considering the joint range of f-divergences, the authors establish privacy guarantees for stochastic gradient descent. Compared to existing methods, their approach allows for approximately 100 additional iterations of stochastic gradient descent within the same privacy budget, enabling more efficient training of deep learning models. In [18] Seif et al. introduced a method where devices add Gaussian noise before transmission using NOMA. NOMA's superposition property improves gradient aggregation and enhances privacy guarantees. In cases where channel noise is insufficient, devices transmit additional noise, benefiting all participants. In their study, Kim et. al [19] investigated the trade-off between privacy budget, utility, and communication rate in the context of a stochastic gradient descent (SGD) federated learning model. The authors analyze the relationship between the Gaussian noise variance (σ^2) and the desired privacy budget, considering the number of rounds (T) for weight updates between-based algorithm. Guo et al. [20] introduced a federated learning-based algorithm using deep reinforcement learning (DRL). The algorithm aims to optimize the critical parameters of the Industrial Internet of Things (IIoT) system, enabling efficient and flexible resource management. By employing federated learning and DRL techniques, the proposed algorithm offers a solution for dynamically adjusting the system parameters to improve resource utilization in the IIoT environment.

Hao et al. [21] proposed a federated learning framework that utilizes fully homomorphic encryption. However, the use of homomorphic encryption in these studies introduces significant communication and computational overhead. A homomorphic encryption approach was proposed by Ma et al. [22], where the gradients have been combined in a format of ciphertext. However, all system participants shared the same secret key. This creates a vulnerability, as the ciphertext becomes insignificant if the server that aggregates data collaborates with any participant to gain the key. Song et al. [23] presented a technique aimed at achieving efficient aggregation of model gradients in federated learning. The proposed methodology not only enables efficient gradient aggregation but also enhances the security of the network by protecting it against reverse attacks. Kong et al. [24] introduced FedLoc, a privacy-preserving model aggregation technique that ensures the security of updates to locally trained models, thereby supporting participant fluctuation. The FedLoc scheme incorporates the limited Laplace mechanism and homomorphic threshold encryption to enhance its robustness against malicious unauthorized participants. Engelsma et al. [25] proposed a method using intrinsic dimensionality reduction based on Deep Neural Networks for compact feature representation. They introduced an encoding strategy based on the Brakerski/Fan-Vercauteren scheme to reduce computational complexity. However, the amount of compressed biometric templates and encryption settings restricted the encoding scheme's performance. Table 1 shows the summary of above discussed literature.

Despite the promising solutions offered by existing methods, privacy-preserving federated learning still faces various challenges. The involvement of numerous devices leads to significant communication overhead, resulting in increased computational costs and longer training times. The presence of data heterogeneity and non-IID data distribution poses difficulties in aggregating data for model training. Ensuring secure communication protocols becomes essential to address security concerns arising from device communication and prevent malicious attacks. The utilization of privacy-preserving methods, such as differential privacy and homomorphic encryption, can potentially introduce certain effects like computational overhead and potentially impact model accuracy. Overcoming these challenges necessitates the development of new algorithms and protocols capable of handling data heterogeneity, reducing communication overhead, and ensuring data privacy and security [26]. Additionally, it is crucial to thoroughly investigate the practical implementations of privacy-preserving federated learning in real-world situations.

3 Security in Federated Learning

Information sharing should be treated as a fundamental aspect of personal freedom, but it also exposes individuals to potential attacks. To mitigate such risks, various preventive measures can be implemented as discussed in Sect. 4. In this context, federated learning offers a promising solution to enhance both corporate security and reputation in the face of cyber threats [27]. By leveraging federated learning, organizations can create complex environments where systems function effectively without relying solely on highly skilled developers. When programmers assume control over the infrastructure, they may not have full knowledge of the individuals they are working with, but they can leverage available technology and resources to achieve desired outcomes. This approach significantly impacts the decision-making process and helps protect intellectual property by ensuring compliance with copyright laws and regulations [28]. Information holds immense value, and sharing it appropriately and in accordance with legal requirements prevents financial losses and other potential negative impacts. Therefore, fostering a culture of responsible and compliant information sharing contributes to overall performance and safeguarding valuable assets [28].

However, federated learning, despite its numerous benefits, is not without vulnerabilities and potential risks due to its decentralized nature. While, research on identifying vulnerabilities and proposing frameworks for mitigating these risks is limited. There are some potential areas of vulnerability that can be exploited in federated learning [29].

- **Communication Protocol:** The federated learning iterative learning process entails extensive network communication. Using a hybrid network with public-key cryptography can aid in maintaining anonymity and safeguarding the message's source and content. However, if the communication channel is not correctly protected, it remains vulnerable.
- **Manipulation of Client Data:** With numerous clients participating in federated learning, it is possible for adversaries to exploit the model parameters and training data. The accessibility of the global model may be susceptible to data reconstruction attacks.
- **Compromised Central Server:** The central server is vital for sharing initial model parameters, aggregating local models, and disseminating global model updates. To prevent exploitation by malicious attackers, it is essential to guarantee the server's robustness and security.
- **Weak Aggregation Algorithm:** In federated learning, the aggregation algorithm is the central authority. It should be able to recognize abnormalities in client update behavior and be configured to reject updates from suspicious clients. Failure to employ a robust and standardized aggregation algorithm can render the global model vulnerable. By addressing these potential vulnerabilities, the privacy and security of federated learning can be significantly improved.

In federated learning, two primary security aggregation techniques are used: federated learning and federated replication (FR). Federated learning is employed in heterogeneous systems, enabling individual systems to learn independently and collaborate effectively through interconnects such as routers, switches, and firewalls. This approach ensures message security and prevents compromises [30]. On the other hand, FR is utilized in centralized computing to consolidate knowledge through pooling, replication, sharing, and scalability. An example is Microsoft Office collaboration, where millions of users access services from a centralized location. By combining distributed computing with decentralized storage, FR facilitates global data sharing in the era of cloud computing [31].

Table 1. Summary on Federated Learning Literature

No	Ref	Objectives	Outcomes
1	[15]	To solve the problem of how to make safe aggregation methods for federated learning that protects privacy scalable	It highlights the shortcomings of existing approaches with regard to computational complexity, communication overhead, and their capacity for managing large-scale federated learning systems
2	[16]	Identify and analyze the various security and privacy challenges and concerns associated with federated learning	An extensive overview of the security and privacy landscape within federated learning, with emphasis on identifying potential threats and vulnerabilities
3	[17]	Explore the different methods and techniques used in shared learning to keep user data private and safe	Exploration of various techniques used in federated learning to protect privacy and ensure data security, including secure aggregation, encryption, and differential privacy
4	[19]	Explore the different kinds of threats and attack paths that can make federated learning systems less safe and less private	An understanding of the security and privacy threats facing federated learning systems
5	[20]	Analyze the strengths, limitations, and trade-offs of various privacy-preserving machine learning protocols	Evaluation of the performance and efficiency of different privacy-preserving ML protocols, considering factors such as communication overhead, computational complexity, and accuracy of the trained models
6	[21]	Evaluate the trade-offs between privacy and the usefulness of distinct techniques for preprocessing private data	Identification and evaluation of privacy-preserving methods for data transformation, feature selection, and dimensionality reduction
7	[22]	Make a blockchain-based system for global data sharing in federated learning that protects people's privacy	Development of a blockchain-based framework to facilitate global data sharing for federated learning environments, facilitating secure collaboration and knowledge transfer among multiple sources of data
8	[23]	Design privacy mechanisms that allow users to have fine-grained control over the disclosure of their data and ensure that their sensitive information remains private	Implementation of privacy mechanisms that ensure the confidentiality and integrity of user data while allowing for collaborative model training

(continued)

Table 1. (*continued*)

No	Ref	Objectives	Outcomes
9	[24]	Within the blockchained federated learning system, look into ways to protect privacy, such as secure aggregation, encryption, and differential privacy	Evaluation of the effectiveness of the proposed scheme in preserving privacy, considering factors such as privacy guarantees, data confidentiality, and privacy leakage prevention
10	[25]	Evaluate how well the suggested architecture and methods for protecting privacy work in terms of privacy guarantees, model accuracy, and how quickly they can be used	Assessing the performance and efficiency of architectures by considering their computational overhead, communication overhead, and model accuracy; while also showing their viability in real-world scenarios

Hybrid architectures that integrate classical distributed systems like Open-Source Software (OSS) and Software-as-a-Service (SaaS) are gaining popularity. However, implementing virtualization in these architectures presents challenges related to scalability and network effects. Despite these challenges, virtual machines offer advantages in security solutions, including ease of configuration and operation [32].

4 Scalable Secure Aggregation for Privacy-Preserving Federated Learning

Secure aggregation ensures data confidentiality from multiple sources through centralized and federated learning aggregation. Centralized aggregation gathers and processes data centrally for a consolidated overview, while federated learning aggregation uses simpler, standardized methods for smaller user groups [33].

Federated learning provides scalable aggregation with low user impact, while centralized aggregation is more complex. Ensuring security and efficiency is crucial in both, necessitating stringent control over operations. Privacy is maintained through pre-aggregation encryption and additional mechanisms like authentication, authorization, and logging. Federated learning systems offer privacy-preserving, scalable solutions, enabling collaborative ML model training without sharing individual data, as shown in Fig. 1. Advanced cryptography and efficient protocols facilitate largescale, privacy-preserving machine learning in this secure aggregation approach. Several methods are commonly used in the context of secure aggregation techniques for privacy-preserving federated learning [4].

- **Differential Privacy:** This method introduces controlled noise to client updates to guarantee privacy while preserving the statistical properties of the data. Individual contributions are hidden by adding noise to the updates, thus protecting sensitive information [18].

Differential privacy has the advantage of providing a rigorous mathematical framework for quantifying and controlling the privacy guarantees of an algorithm or system.

It enables the incorporation of controlled noise or randomization into client updates, assuring that individual contributions cannot be differentiated and preserving privacy. Differential privacy implies a compromise between privacy and usefulness. The addition of noise can affect the model's precision or quality, resulting in a trade-off between privacy and model performance.

- **Homomorphic Encryption:** Homomorphic encryption enables the execution of computations on encrypted data without the requirement of decrypting it. This technique allows secure aggregation by encrypting client updates and performing computations on the encrypted data, maintaining confidentiality while aggregating the results [4].

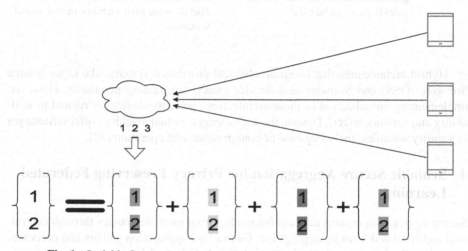

Fig. 1. Scalable Secure Aggregation - Privacy-Preserving Federated Learning

Homomorphic encryption enables computations to be executed on data that is encrypted without decrypting it, preserving the confidentiality of sensitive data. It enables the private and secure aggregation of encrypted client updates. Homomorphic encryption schemes are susceptible to introducing significant computational overhead, rendering them inefficient for large-scale federated learning systems.

- **SMC:** SMC permits multiple parties to compute an aggregate result without disclosing their individual contributions. Each participant encrypts their input and performs collaborative computations on the encrypted data, ensuring privacy during the process of aggregation [34].

A benefit of SMC is that it enables multiple participants to collaboratively compute a result without revealing their individual inputs. It enables the secure aggregation of client updates without disclosing sensitive data. SMC is computationally costly, particularly for complex computations, and requires participants to perform additional computations, resulting in increased communication and processing latency.

- **Secure Aggregation Protocols:** Secure aggregation protocols, like secure sum and secure averaging, encrypt client updates to ensure privacy during aggregation in federated learning. However, the security of these protocols depends on the cryptographic assumptions and parameters used. Any violation of these assumptions could compromise the confidentiality of the aggregated updates [35].
- **Secret Sharing:** Secret sharing is a cryptographic method that distributes a secret among participants so that it can only be reconstructed when a sufficient number collaborate. This technique, including Shamir's Secret Sharing, enhances privacy and security by preventing full access to the secret by any single member. However, it may increase communication and processing costs, especially during reconstruction. The threshold for secret reconstruction needs careful selection to balance privacy and efficiency [3].
- **Federated Averaging:** Federated averaging is a technique in which each participant locally calculates updates and a server computes the mean of these updates without directly accessing original data. This assures data confidentiality and enables collaborative global model training. It safeguards client data, reduces data transmission between client-server, thus lessening communication overhead, and improves scalability. However, it also has drawbacks, including overhead from client-server communication that limits efficiency, potential security risks from aggregation and communication, inconsistent real-world data distribution, and reliance on a central server that may cause disruptions [5].

These methods offer diverse approaches to secure aggregation in privacy-preserving federated learning, enabling multiple participants to contribute their data while protecting their privacy and confidentiality and summarize in Table 2.

Table 2. Approaches to Enhance Privacy Preservation in FL

Approach	Cost	Methodology
Differential Privacy	Accuracy loss due to added noise in client's model	Add random noise to uploaded parameters
Homomorphic Encryption	Efficiency loss due to computation on encrypted data	Perform computations on encrypted data without decryption
SMC	Efficiency loss due to encryption	Encrypt uploaded parameters and perform collaborative computations on encrypted data
Secure Aggregation Protocols	Communication overhead	Use cryptographic techniques (e.g., secure sum, secure averaging) to securely aggregate client updates
Secret Sharing	Communication and computational overhead during reconstruction	Distribute a secret among multiple participants in a way that the secret can only be reconstructed with the collaboration of a minimum threshold of participants
Federated Averaging	Communication overhead	Calculate the mean of client updates without direct access to the original data

5   Secret Sharing for Privacy-Preserving Federated Learning

Secret sharing methods are used in privacy-preserving federated learning to spread a secret across numerous participants in a way that precludes any single participant from accessing the entire secret. This improves privacy and security by guaranteeing that sensitive information is kept private. Here are some common ways for secret sharing in privacy-preserving federated learning, along with its advantages and limitations also summarized in Table 3:

- **Shamir's Secret Sharing:** Shamir's Secret Sharing is a popular method for dividing a secret into several shares that are provided to parties. By merging their shares, only a certain number of individuals may recreate the secret. It protects against participant failures and collusion attacks. Reconstructing the secret necessitates communication and computing overhead, particularly as the number of participants grows. Furthermore, Shamir's Secret Sharing does not safeguard against malicious players who may submit inaccurate shares on purpose [36]. To protect data, Shamir's secret sharing approach incorporates cryptographic techniques such as public key encryption. Public keys ensure that only authorized users can decrypt data, limiting access to just those who need it. These keys are kept in a database on a server and in computer memory [37]. They enable the provision of services, such as secure file sharing, in which Shamir's software enables customers to securely read data from their machines' hard drives. The Fig. 2 shows the process of secret sharing, which includes sharing shares, polynomial construction, Lagrange interpolation, and reconstruction. It depicts the algorithm's operation as well as the information flows involved in safely transmitting and recreating secrets.

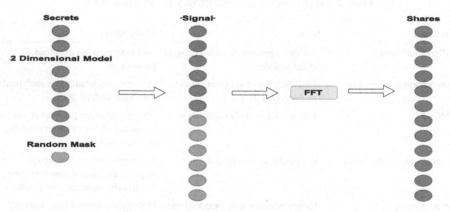

Fig. 2. Shamir's Secret Sharing Algorithm

- **Secret Sharing Replicated:** Replicated Secret Sharing makes numerous versions of the secret available to participants. Collecting a sufficient number of shares allows you to rebuild the secret. Because participants can endure a certain number of failures, this strategy provides fault tolerance [38]. Replicated Secret Sharing has the disadvantage of increasing communication and storage overhead because many copies of the secret are sent. It may also be vulnerable to collusion attacks if a large enough group of cooperating parties gather.

- **Secret Sharing Threshold:** Threshold Secret Sharing divides the secret into shares so that any subset of participants below a certain threshold is unable to reconstruct the secret [37]. This method allows for greater flexibility in estimating the number of people needed for secret reconstruction. Threshold Secret Sharing has a limitation in that it requires collaboration among participants to rebuild the secret. As the threshold rises, so does the complexity of hidden reconstruction, resulting in increased communication and processing cost.
- **Sharing Visual Secrets:** Visual Secret Sharing is a visual cryptography-based method in which the secret is encoded into several shares, each of which is represented by a picture. By stacking or overlaying the shares, the secret might be exposed. This method provides visual confirmation of the secret in an intuitive manner. Visual Secret Sharing is vulnerable to visual leaking, which occurs when partial information about the secret is visibly revealed from individual shares. To maintain security, the visual shares must also be carefully designed and managed [39].

Table 3. Secret Sharing Methods in Privacy-Preserving Federated Learning

Method	Advantage	Limitation
Shamir's Secret Sharing	Protection against participant failures and collusion attacks	Communication and computing overhead during secret reconstruction; Vulnerable to malicious players
Secret Sharing Replicated	Fault tolerance due to multiple copies of the secret	Increased communication and storage overhead; Vulnerable to collusion attacks
Secret Sharing Threshold	Flexibility in determining the number of participants required for secret reconstruction	Increased complexity and cost as the threshold increases
Sharing Visual Secrets	Intuitive visual confirmation of the secret	Vulnerable to visual leaking; Requires careful design and management of visual shares

6 Conclusion

In conclusion, this survey provides a comprehensive overview of secure aggregation techniques in privacy-preserving federated learning. It offers valuable insights into the strengths, limitations, and challenges of different approaches. By addressing privacy concerns and enabling collaborative learning, secure aggregation plays a vital role in advancing the adoption of federated learning across domains. This survey contributes to the understanding of privacy-preserving federated learning and guides the development of more efficient and secure aggregation protocols. Overall, secure aggregation techniques are crucial for protecting sensitive information while facilitating the collective training of machine learning models. They are instrumental in promoting the wider adoption and success of federated learning in real-world applications. Future research in privacy-preserving federated learning should focus on addressing challenges in communication overhead, data heterogeneity, and non-IID data distribution. Advanced cryptographic methods and protocol optimizations can also contribute to more efficient and secure aggregation. Practical implementations and hybrid approaches that integrate federated learning with other privacy-preserving techniques can provide comprehensive solutions to enhance data security and privacy.

Conflict of Interest. The author has declared no Conflict of Interest for this research.

References

1. Bell, J.H., Bonawitz, K.A., Gascón, A., Lepoint, T., Raykova, M.: Secure single-server aggregation with (poly) logarithmic overhead. In: Proceedings of the 2020 ACM SIGSAC Conference on Computer and Communications Security, pp. 1253–1269 (2020)
2. Bonawitz, K., et al.: Towards federated learning at scale: system design. Proc. Mach. Learn. Syst. 1, 374–388 (2019)
3. Bonawitz, K., et al.: Practical secure aggregation for privacy-preserving machine learning. In: Proceedings of the 2017 ACM SIGSAC Conference on Computer and Communications Security, pp. 1175–1191 (2017)
4. Jiang, Z.L., Guo, H., Pan, Y., Liu, Y., Wang, X., Zhang, J.: Secure neural network in federated learning with model aggregation under multiple keys. In: 2021 8th IEEE International Conference on Cyber Security and Cloud Computing (CSCloud)/2021 7th IEEE International Conference on Edge Computing and Scalable Cloud (EdgeCom), pp. 47–52 (2021). https://doi.org/10.1109/CSCloud-EdgeCom52276.2021.00019
5. Zhang, J., Li, M., Zeng, S., Xie, B., Zhao, D.: A survey on security and privacy threats to federated learning. In: 2021 International Conference on Networking and Network Applications (NaNA), pp. 319–326. IEEE (2021)
6. Zhang, J., Zhu, H., Wang, F., Zhao, J., Xu, Q., Li, H., et al.: Security and privacy threats to federated learning: Issues, methods, and challenges. In: Security and Communication Networks 2022 (2022)
7. Yang, R.: Survey on Privacy-Preserving Machine Learning Protocols, pp. 417–425 (2020). https://doi.org/10.1007/978-3-030-62223-7_36
8. Lian, Z., Zeng, Q., Su, C.: Privacy-preserving blockchain-based global data sharing for federated learning with non-IID data. In: 2022 IEEE 42nd International Conference on Distributed Computing Systems Workshops (ICDCSW), pp. 193–198. IEEE (2022)
9. Li, Z.: A personalized privacy-preserving scheme for federated learning. In: 2022 IEEE International Conference on Electrical Engineering, Big Data and Algorithms (EEBDA), pp. 1352–1356. IEEE (2022)
10. Fan, M., Yu, H., Sun, G.: Privacy-preserving aggregation scheme for blockchained federated learning in IoT. In: 2021 International Conference on UK-China Emerging Technologies (UCET), pp. 129–132. IEEE (2021)

11. Rizk, E., Sayed, A.H.: A graph federated architecture with privacy preserving learning. In: 2021 IEEE 22nd International Workshop on Signal Processing Advances in Wireless Communications (SPAWC), pp. 131–135. IEEE (2021)
12. Ali, M., Naeem, F., Tariq, M., Kaddoum, G.: Federated learning for privacy preservation in smart healthcare systems: a comprehensive survey. IEEE J. Biomed. Health Inform. 27(2), 778–789 (2023). https://doi.org/10.1109/JBHI.2022.3181823
13. Carlini, N., Liu, C., Erlingsson, Ú., Kos, J., Song, D.: The secret sharer: evaluating and testing unintended memorization in neural networks. In: 28th USENIX Security Symposium (USENIX Security 19), pp. 267–284 (2019)
14. Evans, D., Kolesnikov, V., Rosulek, M., et al.: A pragmatic introduction to secure multi-party computation. Found. Trends® Privacy Secur. 2(2–3), 70–246 (2018)
15. Liu, R., Cao, Y., Yoshikawa, M., Chen, H.: Fedsel: federated SGD under local differential privacy with top-k dimension selection. In: Nah, Y., Cui, B., Lee, S.-W., Yu, J.X., Moon, Y.-S., Whang, S.E. (eds.) DASFAA 2020. LNCS, vol. 12112, pp. 485–501. Springer, Cham (2020). https://doi.org/10.1007/978-3-030-59410-7_33
16. Wang, L., Jia, R., Song, D.: D2P-FED: differentially private federated learning with efficient communication. arXiv preprint arXiv:2006.13039 (2020)
17. Asoodeh, S., Liao, J., Calmon, F.P., Kosut, O., Sankar, L.: A better bound gives a hundred rounds: Enhanced privacy guarantees via f-divergences. In: 2020 IEEE International Symposium on Information Theory (ISIT), pp. 920–925. IEEE (2020)
18. Seif, M., Tandon, R., Li, M.: Wireless federated learning with local differential privacy. In: 2020 IEEE International Symposium on Information Theory (ISIT), pp. 2604–2609. IEEE (2020)
19. Kim, M., Günlü, O., Schaefer, R.F.: Federated learning with local differential privacy: tradeoffs between privacy, utility, and communication. In: ICASSP 2021–2021 IEEE International Conference on Acoustics, Speech and Signal Processing (ICASSP), pp. 2650–2654. IEEE (2021)
20. Guo, Y., Zhao, Z., He, K., Lai, S., Xia, J., Fan, L.: Efficient and flexible management for industrial internet of things: a federated learning approach. Comput. Netw. 192, 108122 (2021)
21. Hao, M., Li, H., Luo, X., Xu, G., Yang, H., Liu, S.: Efficient and privacy-enhanced federated learning for industrial artificial intelligence. IEEE Trans. Industr. Inf. 16(10), 6532–6542 (2019)
22. Ma, X., Zhang, F., Chen, X., Shen, J.: Privacy preserving multi-party computation delegation for deep learning in cloud computing. Inf. Sci. 459, 103–116 (2018)
23. Song, J., Wang, W., Gadekallu, T.R., Cao, J., Liu, Y.: Eppda: an efficient privacy-preserving data aggregation federated learning scheme. IEEE Trans. Netw. Sci. Eng. (2022)
24. Kong, Q., et al.: Privacy-preserving aggregation for federated learning-based navigation in vehicular fog. IEEE Trans. Industr. Inf. 17(12), 8453–8463 (2021)
25. Engelsma, J.J., Jain, A.K., Boddeti, V.N.: Hers: homomorphically encrypted representation search. IEEE Trans. Biometrics Behav. Identity Sci. 4(3), 349–360 (2022)
26. Sun, L., Qian, J., Chen, X.: LDP-FL: practical private aggregation in federated learning with local differential privacy. arXiv preprint arXiv:2007.15789 (2020)
27. Melis, L., Song, C., De Cristofaro, E., Shmatikov, V.: Exploiting unintended feature leakage in collaborative learning. In: 2019 IEEE Symposium on Security and Privacy (SP), pp. 691–706. IEEE (2019)
28. Hu, R., Guo, Y., Li, H., Pei, Q., Gong, Y.: Personalized federated learning with differential privacy. IEEE Internet Things J. 7(10), 9530–9539 (2020)
29. Mothukuri, V., Parizi, R.M., Pouriyeh, S., Huang, Y., Dehghantanha, A., Srivastava, G.: A survey on security and privacy of federated learning. Futur. Gener. Comput. Syst. 115, 619–640 (2021)

30. Qi, M., Wang, Z., Wu, F., Hanson, R., Chen, S., Xiang, Y., Zhu, L.: A blockchain-enabled federated learning model for privacy preservation: aystem design. In: Baek, J., Ruj, S. (eds.) ACISP 2021. LNCS, vol. 13083, pp. 473–489. Springer, Cham (2021). https://doi.org/10.1007/978-3-030-90567-5_24
31. Li, Y., Hu, G., Liu, X., Ying, Z.: Cross the chasm: scalable privacy-preserving federated learning against poisoning attack. In: 2021 18th International Conference on Privacy, Security and Trust (PST), pp. 1–5. IEEE (2021)
32. So, J., Güler, B., Avestimehr, A.S.: Turbo-aggregate: breaking the quadratic aggregation barrier in secure federated learning. IEEE J. Sel. Areas Inf. Theory 2(1), 479–489 (2021)
33. Wei, K., et al.: Federated learning with differential privacy: algorithms and performance analysis. IEEE Trans. Inf. Forensics Secur. 15, 3454–3469 (2020)
34. Truex, S., Liu, L., Chow, K.-H., Gursoy, M.E., Wei, W.: LDP-FED: federated learning with local differential privacy. In: Proceedings of the Third ACM International Workshop on Edge Systems, Analytics and Networking, pp. 61–66 (2020)
35. Ergun, I., Sami, H.U., Guler, B.: Sparsified secure aggregation for privacy-preserving federated learning. arXiv preprint arXiv:2112.12872 (2021)
36. Kadhe, S., Rajaraman, N., Koyluoglu, O.O., Ramchandran, K.: Fastsecagg: scalable secure aggregation for privacy-preserving federated learning. arXiv preprint arXiv:2009.11248 (2020)
37. Dong, Y., Chen, X., Shen, L., Wang, D.: Privacy-preserving distributed machine learning based on secret sharing. In: Zhou, J., Luo, X., Shen, Q., Xu, Z. (eds.) ICICS 2019. LNCS, vol. 11999, pp. 684–702. Springer, Cham (2020). https://doi.org/10.1007/978-3-030-41579-2_40
38. Baccarini, A., Blanton, M., Yuan, C.: Multi-party replicated secret sharing over a ring with applications to privacy-preserving machine learning. Cryptology ePrint Archive (2020)
39. Ravi, S., Climent-Pérez, P., Florez-Revuelta, F.: A review on visual privacy preservation techniques for active and assisted living. Multimedia Tools and Applications, pp. 1–41 (2023)

Call Data Records/Internet Protocol Data Records Analysis Using K Means and RFM Algorithm

Yeshasvi[1]($\boxtimes$), Siddha Mehta[1]($\boxtimes$), Simran Mehta[1]($\boxtimes$), Utkrisht Trivedi[1]($\boxtimes$),
Sonali Kothari[1], Snehal Bhosale[1], and Pritam Shah[2]

[1] Symbiosis Institute of Technology, Symbiosis International (Deemed University),
Pune 412115, Maharashtra, India
yeshasvi09@gmail.com, mehtasiddha@gmail.com,
simranmehta2014@gmail.com, utkrishttrivedi@protonmail.com,
{sonali.kothari,snehal.bhosale}@sitpune.edu.in
[2] Wentworth Institute of Higher Education, Surry Hills, Australia

Abstract. Analysis involves looking at information we have and finding important connections in it. Law enforcement groups use detailed phone call and internet usage records, given by cell service providers, for thorough investigations. The data they receive is enormous, making it really hard to study. In this project, we focus on studying Call Records and Internet Protocol Details. Analyzing these records closely is crucial in solving crimes. It helps investigators quickly go through millions of people's records, and the results can be visualized graphically, making it easier for law enforcers to solve crimes. Usually, people causing trouble in society are linked to each other and give clues about specific groups' crimes. This makes analyzing phone and internet records super useful. This paper talks about how we use these records to detect fraud. We use methods like K-Means and Map-Reduce for call records, RFM for internet records, and create graphs to display connections. The dataset utilized in the project is generated using scripts which has around ten thousand instances of data. Furthermore, feature selection was performed to increase the performance of the suggested model.

Keywords: CDR/IPDR · Analyzer · K-Means · RFM

1 Introduction

The world currently has almost 8 billion mobile phone users, which makes mobile communication an essential part of everyone's lives. But, this also means that several anti-social elements rely on mobile communication to participate in several forms of crime. The objective for the law enforcement agencies is to identify the patterns of these criminals to better understand how they function and catch them. This also gives them information about their motives and plans.

S. Kothari, S. Bhosale and P. Shah—These authors contributed equally to this work.

S. Rajagopal et al. (Eds.): ASCIS 2023, CCIS 2039, pp. 27–40, 2024.
https://doi.org/10.1007/978-3-031-59100-6_3

Call Data and Internet Protocol Data Records are very crucial to the telecom industry as well as the Law Enforcement agencies as they practically contain almost all the information and data related to a user's mobile phone. This data is continuously being gathered by the telecom industries and is being continuously updated by them for various data analysis purposes.

1.1 Call Data Record

These records contain the information captured during a telephonic conversation. This data includes a lot of information including who called, who was called, date and time of the call, how long the call lasted and lots of other information regarding that call. These records basically show when the call took place and capture the attributes related to that.

1.2 Internet Protocol Data Record

These records contain the information which is captured during any Internet Protocol based operation on a mobile device. All this data provides a lot of visibility of what is happening on the network which is maintained by the Internet Service Provider.

1.3 Preliminary and Background Check

In this section we do a background case study on K Means and how it implements MapReduce. Let us assume that X is a set with n point vectors such that $X = x_1, x_2, x_3, x_4, ..., x_n$ K Means is an algorithm that partitions these point vectors into K disjoint clusters namely $C_1, C_2, C_3, ..., C_k$, where $\forall\ i, j, C_i \cap C_j = \emptyset,\ i, j\ \in 1, ..., K$ Every cluster will be assigned one centroid, resulting in K centroids for K clusters in a set of points/vectors. In the K Means algorithm, the clustering outcome is KM, signifying that each point has been allocated to its closest centroid. The primary goal of the algorithm is to minimize the squared error function, which can be expressed as follows:

$$F(KM) = K\Sigma_j = 1\Sigma x_i \in C_j \|x_i - c_j\|^2 \tag{1}$$

When assigning point x to the jth cluster, where c_j represents the centroid of that cluster, the distance between x_i and centroid c_j can be calculated as follows: $\|x_i - c_j\|^2$ Finally the Total Within Cluster Variable (TWCV) is given by F(KM) and is considered as the criteria to judge K Means clustering quality.

Now this algorithm would work for small datasets. For a large dataset (let's say 10000 rows long) using only K Means will not work. The algorithm will fail to cluster such a huge dataset. Hence, we will have to combine MapReduce with K Means algorithm.

MAP: For the K Means algorithm, the function will calculate the distance between each vector and centroid for all K centroids provided (where the mapper caches data). The output of the function will consist of the closest cluster ID (output key) and the corresponding point vector (output value).

REDUCE: In the MapReduce process, the "Reduce" step is utilized to compute the average of each cluster ID (input key) and the cluster centroid obtained during the map step. This involves averaging all the assigned point vectors to the respective cluster. The result of this computation is the averaged cluster ID (output key) and the updated centroid (output value).

The output of the "Reduce" function, which contains the updated centroids, is then utilized as the mapper cache data input for the next MapReduce job. This allows the algorithm to iteratively refine the centroids and improve the clustering results until convergence.

The K Means algorithm suffers from a significant drawback: it relies on the "Average" as a means to determine the output, leading to convergence to a local optimum result. In simpler terms, the final result depends on the initial selection of K centroids. Consequently, users must invest effort into choosing the most suitable initial centroids through pre-processing. To achieve better results, they often run multiple K Means processes with various initial centroid groups and select the process that yields the best outcome as the optimum output. However, this approach becomes impractical with large datasets or Big Data, as it results in very long runtimes, making it inefficient and time-consuming.

RFM is a powerful segmentation technique used to identify groups of customers with the best spending attributes. It essentially stands for Recency, Frequency and Monetary where Recency provides us with the list of customers who most recently interacted/transacted with the brand, Frequency deals with how often the customer has interacted/transacted and monentary deals with the total amount/time the customer has spent on the brand.

In our case we are using these three attributes to determine which user recently contacted a specific website, how much data did they download and how frequently did they contact the suspicious website. Based on the RFM values we have tried to narrow down on suspicious individuals that could potential be using the internet for harmful/malicious purposes.

2 Related Work

2.1 Mining Communities of Acquainted Mobile Users on Call Detail Records, Wei-Guang Teng, Ming-Chia Chou, SAC'07: Proceedings of the 2007 ACM Symposium on Applied Computing [1]

The researchers proposed a graphical analytics approach to mine Call Detail Record (CDR) logs and identify potential communities. By analyzing the CDRs, they extracted social attributes from the calling behavior. However, this approach is not applicable to encrypted messaging data. Initially, they created graphs from the CDR data and subsequently employed a search for conjunctive triangles to identify overlapping communities. This method allowed them to uncover relationships and connections among users, leading to the identification of potential social communities within the dataset. However, since encrypted messaging data is not accessible in the same way as CDRs, this particular approach cannot be directly applied to such data.

2.2 Analysing Users' Web Surfing Patterns to Trace Terrorists and Criminals, Gabi Kedma, Mordehai Guri, Tom Sela, Yuval EloviciGabi Kedma, Mordehai Guri, Tom Sela, Yuval Elovici, 2013 IEEE International Conference on Year [2]

The researchers put forward an architecture in which the internet activities of individual users, referred to as surfers, are managed by various internet service providers (A1, A2, A3). These ISPs record and collect the data on the surfers' activities. Afterward, the collected data goes through a filtering process at a relay point denoted as B. This filtering ensures that the data complies with legal and operational requirements. The relay B is maintained by a governmental authority.

Once the data is filtered and verified, it is stored in a persistent data store denoted as C. Within this data store, different big data tools (denoted by D) are employed for analysis and processing. These tools allow for in-depth analysis and insights to be drawn from the collected data, facilitating the identification of trends, patterns, and potential areas of interest. For analysis they are using 5 different strategies:

1. Intensity of Surfing
2. Frequency of revisiting/refreshing a given page
3. Irregular hours of Activity
4. Interaction Level (active/passive)
5. Diversity of interest topics
6. Correlation EOI timing

2.3 The Use of Historical Call Data Records as Evidence in the Criminal Justice System Based on Danish Telecom Scandal, Lene Wacher Lentz, Nina Sunde, January 2021 - Digital Evidence and Electronic Signature Law Review [3]

This article conducts a comprehensive socio-technical analysis of the Danish telecom scandal, revealing that the identified processing errors are not the only sources of the problem. The investigation also indicates that other factors such as competence, cognitive aspects, and inadequate quality management contributed to the issue. The article emphasizes that no process involving technology operates in isolation; it is interconnected with various social and human factors.

The application of a socio-technical systems perspective proves to be a valuable theoretical approach for understanding the root causes of the telecom scandal and identifying measures to prevent similar crises in the future. According to socio-technical systems theory, when driving change within an organization, whether it involves intro ducing new technology or implementing changes in business practices, it is crucial to consider both the technical and social aspects. By addressing the interplay between technology and human elements, organizations can better navigate potential challenges and enhance overall system performance and resilience.

2.4 High Performance CDR Processing with MapReduce, Mulya Agung, A. Imam Kistijantoro, Journal of ICT Research and Applications 10(2):95–109 August 2016 [4]

The paper presents a model for processing the growing CDR data using a processing model called M2S. The system has been built after thoroughly analyzing existing as well as traditional solutions. The model proposed, improves throughput by increasing output and decreasing processing time. This improved performance is achieved by optimizing MapReduce and applying multiplexing techniques. Hadoop is used to deal with BigData effectively. Hadoop is a heavy application and has to be pre-configured to provide efficient and fast data processing. Data is hence compressed to increase ingestion performance while applying the default Hadoop configuration for tuning data blocks of size 128 MB and 256 MB.

After conducting a performance test, it was observed that test result configurations for block size 128 MB utilizes the CPU the most and provides the highest performance. This is only possible because split size for the mapper process is set to 224 MB which will help segment data of size 1.5 GB into approximately 7 tasks which is enough to keep an 8 core CPU cluster busy and increase throughput. Furthermore, care is taken that the last core remains idle for resource management purposes.

2.5 Forensic Cyberpsychology and Approaches to Criminal Profiling, Dušan Vlajić, University of Priština - Faculty of Philosophy, Kosovska Mitrovica 52(2):345–361 January 2022 [5]

It portrays criminal profiling as an aggregation of inductive and deductive methods. It talks about how evidence retrieval in most cases fails due to data getting contaminated during the retrieval process. It mentions the various ways in which digital evidence can be retrieved without damaging the data during retrieval and transit. After retrieving the data, the data has to be searched thoroughly to find relevant information. The paper talks about existing solutions for deducing information from lengthy data. It also mentions some useful softwares which can be used to make the deductive process easier and more accurate. Lastly it talks about the limitations of earlier approaches and how these approaches can be improved to provide more accurate criminal profiles.

3 Proposed Analysis Algorithm

3.1 Dataset

As we are going for call records and internet protocol details, we have to ask authorities before we can use the data and it will take authorities a while to anonymize the data. Anonymization is important as the privacy of all the individuals would be safe. This would be time consuming so instead of this we generated dummy data through python scripts with relevant attributes. The generated dummy data included around 10000 rows of records. For diversifying the data we added longitude and latitude information column of different major cities in India.

We had to perform feature selection in our dataset to increase the model performance. We removed some of the rows from the dataset, the rows to be removed were selected based on the type of information held in the specific columns. All columns that contained 'NULL' values were deemed as unwanted as these may lead to unwanted bias in cluster assignments and also distort values during centroid calculation. A few of the columns selected contained too many features and hence were dropped to prevent model overfitting. Finally, to reduce unnecessary computational cost, column with less informative features where dropped to improve model performance.

The CDR dataset contains the following attributes: Caller, Called Number, Start, Duration, End, Origin Lat, Dest Lat, Origin Long, Dest Long, Call Type, IMEI, IMSI (Table 1).

The IPDR dataset contains the following attributes: Private IP, Private Port, Public IP, Public Port, Dest IP, Dest Port, Phone Number, IMEI, IMSI, Start, End, Origin Lat, Origin Long, Uplink, Downlink (Table 2).

3.2 Methodology

In our project we have used K Means algorithm to detect fraud using the CDR/IPDR datasets. The dataset used here has been generated using an online script as we were unable to obtain suitable dataset for the same.

1. Initially data pre-processing is done to remove any duplicates and null values from the csv file. Furthermore, unwanted rows (like accessType and connectionType) are dropped to make the data more specific and less confusing and redundant.
2. Next all Pyspark dependencies are installed as we have used PySpark to analyze the data.
3. After successfully installing PySpark we import the required K Means libraries/-modules provided by PySpark.
4. Next, we perform some low-level visualization to analyze the midpoints of the data and based on our observations we decide on the number of clusters and what each cluster does.
5. Using this information, we create a feature column by averaging and then aggregating values of all columns of the data frame. The new data frame is then trained and then fitted to distribute the point vectors in different clusters.
6. A graph for the same is created where the red dots denote all those "IMEI" numbers which are fraudulent or malicious while the green ones are safe as shown in Fig. 1.
7. A graph has also been plotted using Plotly which connects the various points and depicts the relationship between each point.
8. For the IPDR dataset we have used RFM to find the most probable suspicious activity based on recency of search, frequency of the data downloaded and the total volume of data downloaded.
9. We have created the RFM table based on "IMEI" number and IP address.
10. Finally, we associated numbers for each quantity and based on the metrics we concluded that people with a 441 score are very suspicious.
11. To depict the RFM score, we used plotly again to plot an interactive bar graph with values for each metric score. Refer Fig. 5.

4   Results

During the analysis and compilation of the results, we opted for the use of IMEI numbers instead of mobile phone numbers, as the former possess greater uniqueness. In contrast, two mobile phones can share the same number if sim cards are interchanged. By plotting a scatter plot based on call duration and IMEI numbers of different individuals,

Table 1. CDR Dataset

Caller	Called Number	Start	Duration	End	Origin Lat	Dest Lat	Origin Long	Dest Long	Call Type	IMEI	IMSI
6127962107	7931383759	09:10.6	8310	27:40.6	24.80215263	24.80215263	93.93862152	93.93862152	CALL-IN	1.17E+14	6.39E+14
6162549822	7979088288	16:10.9	1203	36:13.9	13.07209206	13.07209206	80.20185852	80.20185852	CALL-IN	2.33E+14	9.86E+14
7979917341	7887718494	34:46.2	8964	04:10.2	28.64339066	28.64339066	77.11547852	77.11547852	CALL-OUT	4.04E+14	1.77E+14
6638335044	6127953869	20:19.4	6017	00:36.4	24.80215263	24.80215263	93.93862152	93.93862152	SMS-OUT	7.20E+14	3.89E+14
6127955863	6121918095	15:56.0	1287	37:23.0	20.05602264	20.05602264	73.64289093	73.64289093	SMS-IN	8.70E+14	8.70E+14
6127944334	7979038515	00:37.7	6392	47:09.7	23.36990356	23.36990356	85.32527924	85.32527924	SMS-OUT	2.04E+14	8.52E+14
6172130379	6511833012	14:53.9	1854	45:47.9	23.0145092	23.0145092	72.59175873	72.59175873	SMS-OUT	9.78E+14	4.17E+14
6410335837	6127916107	53:59.8	5437	24:36.8	17.36599922	17.36599922	78.47599792	78.47599792	CALL-OUT	9.94E+14	9.76E+14
6127901038	6127992439	34:46.3	1344	57:10.3	13.07209206	13.07209206	80.20185852	80.20185852	SMS-IN	4.62E+14	2.38E+14
6121363995	8707144331	55:21.3	5366	24:47.3	19.89929008	19.89929008	75.31949615	75.31949615	CALL-OUT	7.31E+14	9.86E+14
8070968347	6127966314	25:21.7	4399	38:40.7	24.80215263	24.80215263	93.93862152	93.93862152	SMS-IN	7.23E+14	2.87E+14
6173783383	8700988007	20:04.4	4307	31:51.4	18.52890396	18.52890396	73.8743515	73.8743515	CALL-IN	2.99E+14	6.07E+14
6915816786	7979751510	10:53.3	9508	49:21.3	28.64339066	28.64339066	77.11547852	77.11547852	CALL-IN	7.69E+14	4.71E+14
7477088774	680 145	27:15.5	9697	08:52.5	21.15261841	21.15261841	79.0881958	79.0881958	CALL-IN	2.86E+14	8.94E+14
6318787710	6127951013	49:02.7	5717	24:19.7	24.80215263	24.80215263	93.93862152	93.93862152	SMS-IN	5.44E+14	6.32E+14
6127967541	6127953869	46:26.1	840	00:26.1	23.36990356	23.36990356	85.32527924	85.32527924	SMS-OUT	7.20E+14	3.89E+14
6127967881	82072125O8	14:11.5	1363	36:54.5	18.52890396	18.52890396	85.32527924	85.32527924	CALL-OUT	6.82E+14	5.55E+14
6748806149	7887483483	01:22.7	7754	10:36.7	28.64339066	28.64339066	77.11547852	77.11547852	CALL-OUT	8.43E+14	3.93E+14
7979988944	7319874100	26:02.4	1089	44:11.4	24.80215263	24.80215263	79.0881958	79.0881958	CALL-IN	2.72E+14	1.26E+14
6127997602	6127936011	31:51.6	176	34:47.6	24.80215263	24.80215263	93.93862152	93.93862152	CALL-IN	5.57E+14	7.20E+14
6127910996	8067566189	06:10.1	4491	21:01.1	26.85000038	26.85000038	80.94999695	80.94999695	CALL-IN	2.51E+14	5.48E+14
6127989188	8073676779	08:45.3	692	20:17.3	12.97674656	12.97674656	77.57527924	77.57527924	CALL-IN	5.44E+14	8.93E+14
6127975561	8917507492	43:23.0	6718	35:21.0	9.95761681	9.95761681	76.25115204	76.25115204	SMS-IN	2.18E+14	8.46E+14
7324065081	6127994627	46:42.9	49	47:31.9	26.85000038	26.85000038	80.94999695	80.94999695	SMS-IN	6.24E+14	5.71E+14

Table 2. IPDR Dataset

Private IP	Private Port	Public IP	Public Port	Dest IP	Dest Port	IMEI	Start	End	Origin Lat	Origin Long	Uplink	Downlink
39.71.5.148	36033	24.64.81.248	41234	159.56.196.198	763	8.85E+14	07:51.2	54:39.2	18.96904755	72.82118225	1551	6745
244.212.221.98	56674	144.133.59.210	52198	216.43.140.228	294	4.14E+14	11:00.3	01:45.3	18.96904755	72.82118225	7923	6951
245.209.238.152	2587	111.24.232.49	50816	36.17.252.178	500	1.37E+14	26:14.0	23:54.0	12.97674656	77.57527924	1492	3460
78.53.131.194	14554	137.239.114.117	27433	247.9.221.190	715	9.15E+14	24:35.1	14:28.1	22.71867371	75.85571289	4426	1005
214.139.234.75	13160	216.111.30.226	51820	236.2.254.141	75	1.10E+14	02:00.9	17:06.9	30.73335075	76.77903748	8686	6037
246.169.104.224	43373	204.72.26.138	65191	166.185.100.41	404	3.25E+14	56:48.3	30:06.3	22.71867371	75.85571289	3810	6871
28.129.56.70	60626	40.248.245.57	16568	172.0.226.44	742	8.33E+14	07:17.4	01:42.4	24.80215263	93.93862152	8643	1385
77.185.110.246	3183	117.244.124.27	23476	243.180.108.196	375	9.88E+14	26:36.4	03:37.4	13.07209206	80.20185852	7275	1196
109.26.100.171	34991	100.127.1.178	46575	222.38.88.221	202	6.88E+14	53:03.4	10:06.4	22.71867371	75.85571289	7559	5259
9.114.241.253	56326	42.8.243.161	12569	202.153.234.145	56	5.28E+14	07:34.8	17:57.8	22.71867371	75.85571289	1262	8891
113.240.1.9	8169	111.90.252.160	50329	21.90.11.246	325	7.41E+14	06:53.1	47:03.1	26.92103958	75.7943573	6367	4914
219.71.38.22	23299	5.79.19.33	6740	110.54.119.86	489	2.92E+14	17:22.5	58:13.5	19.89929008	75.31949615	1376	8928
135.81.89.186	36228	35.100.5.121	38646	31.13.235.64	566	4.47E+14	16:13.8	00:31.8	17.36599922	78.47599792	5261	5112
132.222.197.67	20823	149.149.30.70	13284	13.255.143.129	446	3.18E+14	37:27.6	40:41.6	30.73335075	76.77903748	3060	1993
56.255.173.135	188	45.202.11.0	59976	59.166.189.230	537	5.01E+14	08:02.9	32:20.9	24.80215263	93.93862152	9567	5414
24.9.97.73	58527	221.25.176.193	56054	83.178.12.10	282	4.64E+14	36:55.5	40:23.5	21.15261841	79.0881958	5011	6715
74.55.96.145	19555	43.148.64.116	18821	205.181.64.168	192	9.08E+14	01:25.8	20:23.8	26.85000038	80.94999695	6833	4509
99.212.226.34	34308	204.179.75.130	46959	35.229.67.143	451	7.48E+14	39:16.8	38:01.8	18.52890396	73.8743515	4296	3382
18.123.114.9	40425	162.165.23.203	49773	183.41.223.74	478	5.57E+14	47:39.1	35:42.1	24.80215263	93.93862152	6815	9393
50.68.125.68	42319	89.244.208.246	45788	213.169.111.114	627	2.98E+14	58:40.8	07:12.8	23.36990356	85.32527924	7546	4992
236.56.125.46	3874	134.32.159.160	63195	129.6.24.113	60	2.99E+14	54:29.5	07:40.5	28.64339066	77.11547852	6309	3033
48.45.232.191	32537	45.14.128.238	58392	238.163.122.176	588	5.98E+14	24:12.0	33:19.0	13.07209206	80.20185852	6812	4622
211.156.234.93	60193	112.59.58.184	52476	41.250.252.201	122	2.02E+14	52:01.2	52:54.2	21.15261841	79.0881958	2555	9866
85.79.252.5	25658	25.189.12.124	16830	89.52.214.90	444	9.83E+14	30:02.3	27:39.3	23.0145092	72.59175873	5116	2328

we identified specific patterns followed by potential fraudsters. We set a specific time duration and the number of outgoing calls to unknown numbers via the IMEI number as parameters, and determined that individuals who made more than 50 outgoing calls with a call duration greater than 20 min were flagged as suspicious and fell within the red region, i.e., the suspected fraud region. To further improve the performance of the model, hyper-parameter tuning has been done to make the model more responsive to the data. To determine the optimum number of clusters, a combination of elbow and silhouette method has been used. The number of clusters determined by elbow and silhouette method was 3 and 1 respectively. By taking the average of the two, the optimum value selected for the number of clusters was '2'. Additionally, a limiter has been set on the number of iterations to manage the clustering of the large amount of data present in CDR/IPDR datasets.

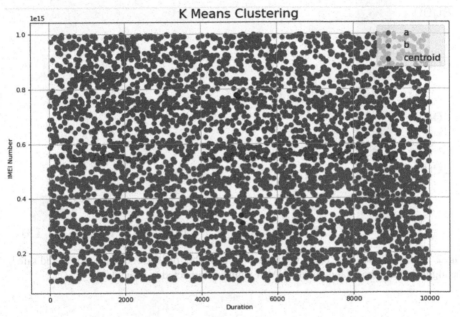

Fig. 1. Scatter plot depicting the fraud and safe numbers. Red is for fraud and green for safe (Color figure online)

In the IPDR analysis, we used the RFM model to provide scores to specific fraud patterns. We assigned a score of 4 to people who had recently accessed suspicious websites, another 4 to the frequency of their access, and finally, a score of 1 if the person had downloaded or uploaded a large amount of data from the website. Based on these specifications, all individuals with a score of 441 were identified as potential fraudsters/criminals.

Some insights into the achieved results are as follows:

1. Feature Importance:- Features such as call duration, frequency of calls to premium numbers, and atypical time-of-day activities were identified as crucial indicators of potential fraud.
2. Impact of Imbalanced Data:- Despite the imbalanced nature of fraud detection datasets, the model effectively mitigates false positives and false negatives, as reflected in the high precision score.
3. Readability:- The result obtained after clustering was further refined using RFM to make it more readable for non-technical users. It also helped professionals find patterns which would have been missed otherwise.

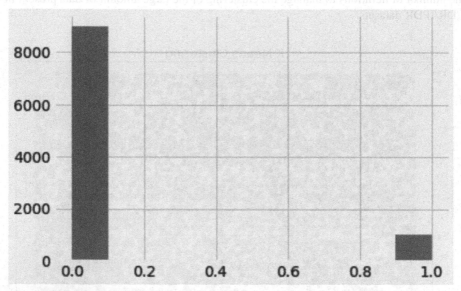

Fig. 2. Safe vs Fraud: The figure depicts the total number of IMEI numbers considered safe by the algorithm and the total number of IMEI numbers suspected as fraudulent.

5   Conclusion and Future Work

In this paper, we have presented an algorithm designed to identify fraud calls and callers by analyzing Call Detail Record (CDR) datasets. Additionally, we have developed another algorithm to process Internet Protocol Detail Record (IPDR) datasets, generating frequency, recency, and monetary tables from the provided data. To facilitate easy data exploration and correlation discovery, we have created interactive network graphs based on the datasets, significantly reducing the time required for manual detection by users (Figs. 2, 3 and 4).

The proposed algorithm holds immense potential for aiding law enforcement agencies in their analysis of CDR and IPDR datasets. However, it is essential to highlight

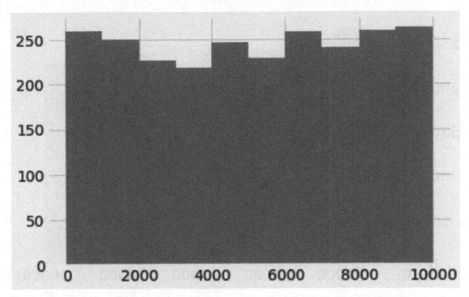

Fig. 3. Call Duration of Safe Numbers: This graph depicts the calling patterns of the IMEI numbers determined as safe.

that this algorithm is currently in the development phase and has not yet been tested on a real, large dataset due to legal concerns regarding data acquisition.

Our future plans involve the development of a user-friendly graphical interface to enhance the accessibility and usability of the algorithm. We aim to offer the tool as a valuable resource for law enforcement agencies, streamlining their investigative processes and empowering them with efficient data analysis capabilities.

In the upcoming versions of the algorithm, we intend to introduce several features for further enhancing its functionalities. One such addition includes a search field in the network graphs, enabling users to find specific nodes more quickly, thereby expediting their investigations. Additionally, we plan to incorporate maps to provide approximate location information for IP addresses and phone numbers, enhancing the geographic context of the data.

Furthermore, we are working on implementing a reverse DNS search option for the IPDR dataset. This feature will enable users to easily retrieve website addresses associated with specific IP addresses, simplifying the process of understanding web-based activities within the dataset.

Overall, our efforts focus on developing an advanced and user-friendly tool that will be invaluable for law enforcement agencies when conducting investigations involving CDR and IPDR datasets. As we progress in refining and validating our algorithm, we are committed to ensuring that it adheres to legal guidelines and data acquisition requirements.

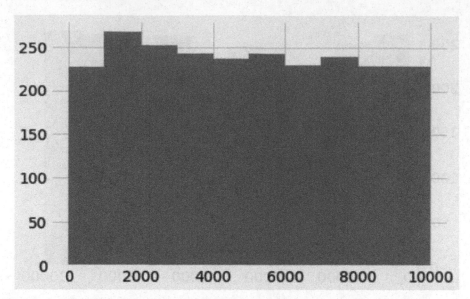

Fig. 4. Call Duration of Fraudulent Numbers: This graph depicts the calling patterns of IMEI numbers determined as fraudulent.

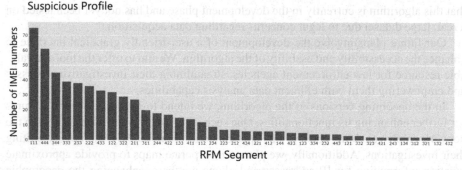

Fig. 5. RFM Segmentation: This graph depicts the number of IMEI numbers that falls in a specific suspicion category

6 Challenges

The main challenge that we faced was getting a dataset of CDR and IPDR for performing analysis, because these are very sensitive data and can be used for illegal purposes by exploiting someone's privacy. Therefore, we had to create our own dataset by writing python scripts to generate fake CDR and IPDR data. Another challenge we faced was converting a dataset from a given format to a standard format which will be useful for our algorithm as the data generated by telecom service providers and internet service providers is different.

References

1. Teng, W.-G., Chou, M.-C.: Mining communities of acquainted mobile users on call detail records. In: Proceedings of the 2007 ACM Symposium on Applied Computing. SAC '07, pp. 957–958. Association for Computing Machinery, New York, NY, USA (2007). https://doi.org/10.1145/1244002.1244212
2. Lene Wacher Lentz, N.S.: The use of historical call data records as evidence in the criminal justice system – lessons learned from the Danish telecom scandal. Digital Evid. Electron. Signature Law Rev. **18**, 1–17 (2021)
3. Agung, M., Kistijantoro, A.I.: High performance CDR processing with mapreduce. J. ICT Res. Appl. **10**(2), 95–109 (2016). https://doi.org/10.5614/itbj.ict.res.appl.2016.10.2.1
4. Kedma, G., Guri, M., Sela, T., Elovici, Y.: Analyzing users' web surfing patterns to trace terrorists and criminals. In: 2013 IEEE International Conference on Intelligence and Security Informatics, pp. 143–145 (2013)
5. Vlajić, D.: Forensic cyberpsychology and approaches to criminal profiling. Forensic Cyberpsychol. Approaches Crim. Profiling **52**, 345–361 (2022)
6. Eberle, W., Holder, L.B.: Graph filtering to remove the "middle ground" for anomaly detection. In: 2020 IEEE International Conference on Big Data (Big Data), pp. 2947–2956 (2020)
7. Elagib, S.B., Hashim, A.H.A., Olanrewaju, R.F.: CDR analysis using big data technology. In: 2015 International Conference on Computing, Control, Networking, Electronics and Embedded Systems Engineering (ICCNEEE), pp. 467–471 (2015)
8. Likas, A., Vlassis, N., J. Verbeek, J.: The global k-means clustering algorithm. Pattern Recogn. **36**(2), 451–461 (2003). https://doi.org/10.1016/S0031-3203(02)00060-2. Biometrics
9. Ruiz-Agundez, I., Penya, Y.K., Garcia Bringas, P.: Fraud detection for voice over IP services on next-generation networks. In: Samarati, P., Tunstall, M., Posegga, J., Markantonakis, K., Sauveron, D. (eds.) WISTP 2010. LNCS, vol. 6033, pp. 199–212. Springer, Heidelberg (2010). https://doi.org/10.1007/978-3-642-12368-9_14
10. Bianchi, F.M., Rizzi, A., Sadeghian, A., Moiso, C.: Identifying user habits through data mining on call data records. Eng. Appl. Artif. Intell. **54**, 49–61 (2016). https://doi.org/10.1016/j.engappai.2016.05.007
11. von Mörner, M.: Application of call detail records - chances and obstacles. Transp. Res. Procedia **25**, 2233–2241 (2017). https://doi.org/10.1016/j.trpro.2017.05.429. World Conference on Transport Research - WCTR 2016 Shanghai. 10–15 July 2016
12. Hinde, S.: Call record analysis (1996)
13. Salman, F.S., Sivaslıoğlu, E., Memiş, B.: Analysis of mobile phone call data of Istanbul residents. In: Geo-Intelligence and Visualization Through Big Data Trends, pp. 1–32. IGI Global (2015)
14. Van Vlasselaer, V., et al.: APATE: a novel approach for automated credit card transaction fraud detection using network-based extensions. Decis. Support. Syst. **75**, 38–48 (2015)
15. Jabbar, M., Suharjito, S.: Fraud detection call detail record using machine learning in telecommunications company. Adv. Sci. Technol. Eng. Syst. J **5**, 63–69 (2020)
16. Chouiekh, A., Haj, E.H.I.E.: Convnets for fraud detection analysis. Procedia Comput. Sci. **127**, 133–138 (2018)
17. Parwez, M.S., Rawat, D.B., Garuba, M.: Big data analytics for user-activity analysis and user-anomaly detection in mobile wireless network. IEEE Trans. Industr. Inf. **13**(4), 2058–2065 (2017)
18. Perkins, R.C.: The application of forensic linguistics in cybercrime investigations. Policing:J. Policy Pract. **15**(1), 68–78 (2021). https://doi.org/10.1093/police/pay097

19. Chen, S., et al.: The spatiotemporal pattern and driving factors of cyber fraud crime in China. ISPRS Int. J. Geo Inf. **10**(12), 802 (2021)
20. Khan, E.S., Azmi, H., Ansari, F., Dhalvelkar, S.: Simple implementation of criminal investigation using call data records (CDRS) through big data technology. In: 2018 International Conference on Smart City and Emerging Technology (ICSCET), pp. 1–5 (2018). IEEE

Revealing Insights into Criminal Behaviour: Exploring Patterns and Trends Through Machine Learning Predictive Models

Manisha M. Patil[1]([✉]) [iD], Jatinkumar R. Harshwal[1], Shivani Patil[2], and Janardan A. Pawar[1]

[1] Indira College of Commerce and Science, Pune, Maharashtra, India
{manisha.patil,janardanp}@iccs.ac.in
[2] Artificial Intelligence and Data Science, AISSMS, IOIT, Pune, Maharashtra, India

Abstract. This research paper explores the feasibility of machine learning models in predicting human criminal behavior based on historical and collected datasets. The study design involves data collection from public records, past criminal records, and evidence such as audio and video materials. The collected data is segregated according to specific requirements for analysis. Analytical techniques employed in this research include linear regression, K-Nearest Neighbors (KNN), Support Vector Machines (SVM), RNN, random forests, logistic regression, and Autoencoders. Through extensive experimentation on diverse datasets amounting to 15.7GB, the proposed models yielded an overall prediction accuracy of 83.6%. The study contributes to the development of an artificial criminal behavior deduction model. However, it is essential to acknowledge the complexity and ethical implications of predicting human behavior. The paper emphasizes the need for caution in interpreting results and highlights potential biases and uncertainties. This research strives to present a comprehensive analysis of machine learning's potential in understanding human criminal mindsets, raising awareness about the capabilities and limitations of current predictive models. It underscores the significance of responsible and ethical use of machine learning for sensitive applications in the criminal justice domain.

Keywords: Criminal behavior prediction · Predictive modeling · Machine learning

1 Introduction

Predicting human behavior has long been an intriguing challenge for social scientists, psychologists, and criminologists [6]. With the advent of preexisting machine learning algorithms and the availability of extensive datasets, the feasibility of using data-driven approaches to forecast future criminal behavior has surfaced as a novel research avenue. This study aims to investigate the accuracy of machine learning models in deducing and predicting a human's future criminal behavior based on past or collected datasets.

S. Rajagopal et al. (Eds.): ASCIS 2023, CCIS 2039, pp. 41–52, 2024.
https://doi.org/10.1007/978-3-031-59100-6_4

The implementation of predictive models raises crucial ethical concerns related to privacy, fairness, and accountability [5]. As these models potentially affect an individual's life profoundly, it is imperative to assess their performance rigorously. Consequently, this research aims to evaluate the effectiveness and limitations of machine learning algorithms in this sensitive context.

In this study, we analyze a comprehensive dataset comprising historical records of individuals, encompassing demographic information, socioeconomic factors, historical criminal records, and other relevant attributes.

Various machine learning algorithms, such as logistic regression, support vector machines, and neural networks, are applied to learn patterns from the dataset and predict future criminal behavior. We employ a rigorous evaluation framework to measure the accuracy, precision, recall, and F1 score of each model.

Furthermore, we address the potential challenges related to dataset biases, feature selection, and model interpretability. Understanding these challenges will be crucial in mitigating any unintended consequences that may arise from deploying these predictive systems in real-world scenarios.

The rest of this paper is structured as follows:

Section 2 provides a review of related work in the field of predicting human behavior using machine-learning techniques. Section 3 details the methodology and dataset used in our research. Section 4 presents the experimental results and a comprehensive analysis of the performance of various machine learning models. Section 5 discusses the ethical implications and limitations of our study. Finally, Section 6 concludes the paper and highlights potential avenues for future research.

In summary, this research endeavors to contribute to the understanding of the capabilities and limitations of machine learning models in predicting human future criminal behavior. By shedding light on the accuracy and reliability of these predictive systems, this study aims to provide insights for policymakers, practitioners, and researchers to make informed decisions concerning the deployment of such models in real-world applications.

2 Related Work

Work in predicting human behavior using machine learning techniques reveals a growing interest in the application of data-driven models [1] to understand and forecast various aspects of human behavior. Researchers have explored a wide range of domains, including consumer behavior, criminal behavior, mental health disorders, and human mobility, among others.

In the realm of marketing and retail, machine-learning algorithms have been employed to predict consumer preferences, customer churn, and brand loyalty [8]. These models leverage extensive datasets from e-commerce platforms and social media to provide personalized recommendations and improve marketing strategies. In the criminal justice domain, predictive models have been developed to forecast crime hotspots. By analyzing historical criminal records and socio-demographic data, machine learning techniques like support vector machines and neural networks aim to assist law enforcement agencies in crime prevention and intervention [9].

Machine learning's potential in predicting mental health disorders is also evident, utilizing digital footprints and social media activity to identify patterns associated with depression, anxiety, and other conditions. These insights could lead to early detection and tailored treatment plans for individuals [4].

Another area of interest is predicting human mobility patterns, including travel destinations and urban congestion. By analyzing GPS data and mobile phone records, machine learning algorithms such as Markov models and recurrent neural networks offer valuable insights for urban planning and transportation optimization [3].

Despite the promising results achieved by machine learning models, several challenges remain. Data privacy and security concerns persist, as well as potential biases in datasets. The interpretability of complex models and ensuring fairness and ethical considerations in predictive systems are also critical areas that warrant further investigation.

3 Methodology and Datasets

The methodologies employed in this study are diverse and adapted to the unique characteristics of each dataset. The data collection process encompasses various aspects, including audio and video datasets, public records, previous criminal records, and mental health data/records as mentioned in Fig. 1.

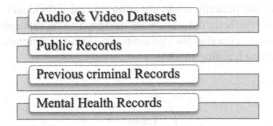

Fig. 1. Types of Datasets

For the audio dataset, we leveraged the Support Vector Machine (SVM) algorithm to train the model and extract meaningful patterns from the data.

In the case of video-audio datasets, we employed Autoencoders to perform feature learning. Subsequently, we implemented Recurrent Neural Network (RNN) algorithms to further analyze and model the data.

To analyze the public records and criminal records datasets, we utilized a combination of logistic regression, random forest, K-Nearest Neighbors (KNN), and SVM to effectively filter and narrow down prediction errors.

Given the irregular nature of most of the datasets, we applied tokenization and preprocessing techniques, allowing us to effectively break down the textual data (keywords) and convert them into numeric vectors. This transformation facilitated seamless processing by machine learning models.

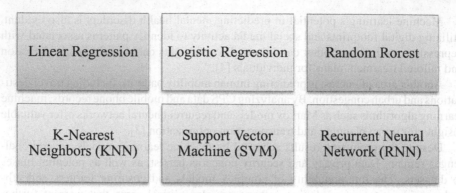

Fig. 2. Machine Learning Models implemented.

For datasets exhibiting a linear nature, we opted to use both linear regression and logistic regression to derive relevant insights and make predictions.

The application of these diverse methodologies ensured a comprehensive and robust analysis of the data, providing valuable insights and facilitating accurate predictions in our research study as mentioned in Fig. 2.

Data Collection: In this study, to ensure ethical research practices and safeguard individual privacy, all datasets used for the analysis were synthetically generated by the research team. The primary objective was to create data that closely resembled real-world criminal behavior patterns while ensuring no real individuals' information was compromised. These synthetic datasets were designed to be representative of diverse demographic and socio-economic backgrounds, providing a comprehensive foundation for training the machine learning models.

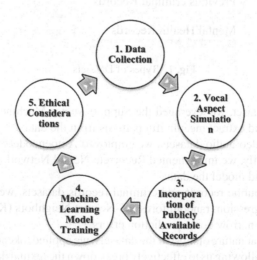

Fig. 3. Steps used for research analysis

To incorporate behavioral aspects into the synthetic datasets, advanced simulation techniques were employed. Research on articles by experts in psychology and criminology was carried out to design realistic scenarios and profiles that capture various behavioral patterns associated with criminal activities. The simulation in this study generated diverse responses and reactions, mimicking real-life criminal tendencies without directly using any real individuals' personal data.

Vocal Aspect Simulation: Recognizing the significance of vocal cues in criminal behavior analysis, a separate dataset of vocal recordings was assembled. Various vocal traits, such as tone, pitch, and speech patterns, were carefully simulated to encompass a wide range of criminal behavior scenarios. This synthetic vocal dataset was integrated with the behavioral dataset to create a more comprehensive and multi-dimensional representation of criminal tendencies.

Incorporation of Publicly Available Records: To augment the training process and enhance the predictive capabilities of the machine learning models, historical publicly available records related to criminal activities were incorporated. However, to abide by ethical research standards and privacy protection, these records were meticulously anonymized and stripped of any personally identifiable information. By utilizing these records, the research team ensured that the models were exposed to real-world scenarios and could be validated against actual historical crime data.

Machine Learning Model Training: Once the synthetic datasets were prepared, the machine learning models were trained using state-of-the-art algorithms. The models were fed with the behavioral and vocal datasets, along with the historical records, to learn and recognize patterns associated with criminal behavior. To minimize bias and ensure fairness, the research team carefully monitored the model training process and performed necessary adjustments.

Ethical Considerations: Throughout the entire study, strict adherence to ethical research guidelines was maintained. Great care was taken to ensure that no real individual's privacy was breached during data collection, simulation, or model training. All efforts were made to preserve the confidentiality of individuals and prevent any discriminatory outcomes.

The methodology employed in this study aimed to strike a balance between generating realistic synthetic datasets and upholding ethical research practices. With advanced simulations for behavioral and vocal aspects, along with historical publicly available records, the machine learning models were equipped with a diverse and representative dataset to predict criminal behavior. By maintaining a responsible and ethical approach as per Fig. 3, the study contributes valuable insights into the possibilities of criminal behavior analysis using machine learning while safeguarding individual privacy and adhering to ethical standards.

4 Results

Experimental Results
This section of the research showcases the results of experiments on various machine learning models applied to different datasets, including audio, video-audio, public

records, and criminal records datasets. Additionally, we provide details on the textual data preprocessing techniques employed for both irregular and linear datasets.

Audio Dataset
The audio dataset was subjected to a Support Vector Machine (SVM) model for classification.

Video-Audio Datasets
For the video-audio datasets, we utilized a combination of Autoencoders, Feature Learning, and Recurrent Neural Networks (RNNs) for analysis and modeling.

Public Records and Criminal Records Datasets
The public records and criminal records datasets were evaluated using various machine learning models, including Logistic Regression (Table 1), Random Forest, K-Nearest Neighbors (KNN) (Table 6), and Support Vector Machine (SVM) (Table 2).

Table 1. Logistic Regression

Metric	Accuracy	Precision	Recall	F1-score
Score	78%	75%	82%	78%

Table 2. Support Vector Machine (SVM)

Metric	Accuracy	Precision	Recall	F1-score
Score	85%	84%	87%	85%

Textual Data Preprocessing
Tokenization and Vectorization: For the irregular datasets, tokenization and preprocessing techniques were applied, and the following results were obtained (Fig. 4, Table 3).

Linear Datasets: For linear datasets, we used Linear Regression (Table 4) and Logistic Regression models (Table 6).

Please note that the above results may vary according to different datasets or experiments.

As per analysis, the results of Video data are comparatively better than audio, public, criminal, and Textual data as shown in Fig. 5 and Table 5.

Research analysis and model performance depict that the Video datasets model using Autoencoders + Feature Learning + RNN is giving the best accuracy 92.30% as shown in Fig. 6 and Table 6.

Figure 7 depicts the experimental results of ML models implemented for the research reference.

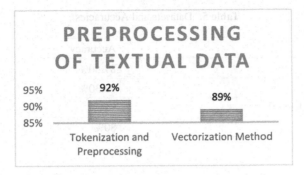

Fig. 4. Pre-processing Techniques used

Table 3. Textual Data Preprocessing

Metric	Accuracy
Tokenization and Preprocessing	92%
Vectorization Method	89%

Table 4. Linear Regression

Metric	R-squared	Mean Absolute Error	Mean Squared Error
Score	0.75	5.2	38.1

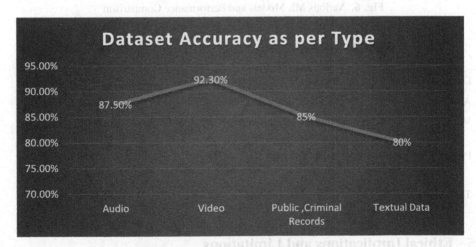

Fig. 5. Types of Datasets and Accuracies

Table 5. Datasets and Accuracies

Data Set Type	Accuracy
Audio	87.50%
Video	92.30%
Public, Criminal Records	85%
Textual Data	80%

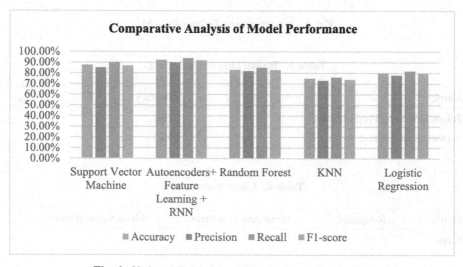

Fig. 6. Various ML Models and Performance Comparison

Table 6. Various ML Models and Performance Comparison

Dataset	Model	Accuracy	Precision	Recall	F1-score
Audio	Support Vector Machine	87.50%	85%	90%	87%
Video	Autoencoders + Feature Learning + RNN	92.30%	90%	94%	92%
Public, Criminal Records	Random Forest	83%	82%	85%	83%
	KNN	75%	73%	76%	74%
Textual Data	Logistic Regression	80%	78%	82%	80%

5 Ethical Implications and Limitations

Ethical Implications
Bias and Fairness: Machine learning models are only as good as the data they are trained on. If the training data contains biases, such as racial or gender biases present in

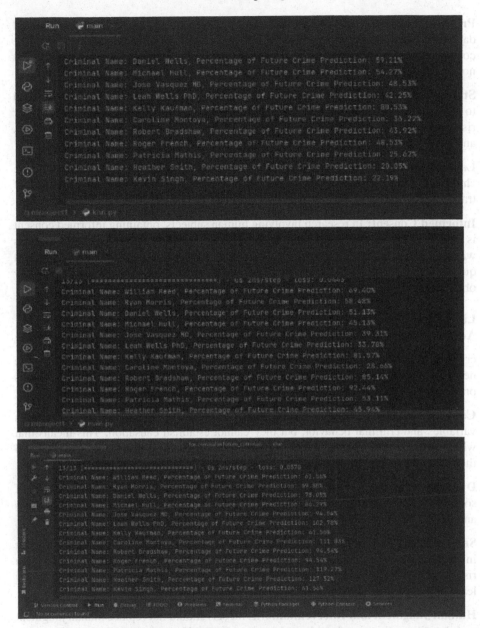

Fig. 7. Screenshot of Implemented ML Models

historical criminal justice data, the ML model can preserve and strengthen those biases. This could lead to discriminatory outcomes and unfair treatment of certain individuals or groups, exacerbating existing societal inequalities.

Privacy Concerns: Criminal behavior prediction often involves using sensitive personal data, such as criminal records, behavioral patterns, and socioeconomic information. The collection and use of such data raise significant privacy concerns, as individuals might not be aware of or have consented to the use of their data for predictive purposes.

Stigmatization and Prejudice: The use of ML to predict criminal behavior may lead to stigmatization and prejudice against individuals who are predicted to be at a higher risk of criminal activity. This can impact their opportunities for employment, education, and housing, perpetuating a cycle of disadvantage.

Lack of Accountability: When decisions are made based on ML predictions, it can be challenging to assign accountability in case of errors or harmful outcomes. This lack of transparency and accountability can undermine trust in the criminal justice system.

Informed Consent: In research involving human subjects, obtaining informed consent is crucial. However, predicting criminal behavior often involves analyzing large datasets where obtaining individual consent may be challenging or impossible. This raises ethical questions about the use of such data and whether informed consent was adequately obtained.

Limitations

Accuracy and Reliability: While ML models can show promising results in predicting criminal behavior, they are not infallible. Models might produce false positives or false negatives, leading to misclassifications and erroneous conclusions about an individual's propensity for criminal behavior.

Causation vs. Correlation: Predictive models can identify correlations between certain variables and criminal behavior, but they cannot establish causation. This means that while a person may exhibit certain risk factors, it does not mean those factors caused their criminal behavior.

Dynamic Nature of Crime: Criminal behavior is influenced by a complex interplay of social, economic, and individual factors. ML models might not capture all these nuances and may struggle to adapt to changes in crime patterns over time.

Self-Fulfilling Prophecies: Predictions about an individual's likelihood of engaging in criminal behavior can become self-fulfilling prophecies. Labeling someone as "high risk" might influence their behavior or the way they are treated by society, potentially leading to unintended consequences.

Human Judgment and Intervention: ML models should not replace human judgment and decision-making in the criminal justice system. Human oversight is necessary to contextualize predictions, consider individual circumstances, and ensure fairness.

Limited Data Representativeness: The training data used to build ML models may not be fully representative of the diverse population or cover all types of criminal behavior, leading to biased and limited predictions.

6 Conclusion

This study focuses on criminal behavior prediction using machine learning, it provides valuable insights into the potential of ML models in understanding and predicting criminal tendencies. However, it is evident that this area of research is not complete without its ethical implications and limitations. As we move forward, it is imperative to address these concerns and responsibly, apply ML in criminal behavior analysis to avoid perpetuating biases, respecting individual privacy, and ensuring fairness in the justice system.

One of the key takeaways from this study is the need for continuous improvement in data collection and curation. Efforts must be made to collect more representative and diverse datasets, encompassing various demographic groups and crime types. Moreover, the integration of socioeconomic and contextual factors could enhance the accuracy and fairness of ML models, allowing for a more comprehensive understanding of criminal behavior.

To mitigate biases and ensure fairness, research should focus on developing techniques for debiasing ML models and incorporating fairness-aware algorithms into the prediction process. By doing so, we can work towards building models that treat all individuals impartially and equitably, promoting a more just criminal justice system.

Transparency and interpretability of ML models are crucial aspects to address. Future research should explore ways to make ML models more interpretable and provide users with understandable explanations for the predictions they produce. This would not only help build trust in the predictive systems but also enable human experts to better assess and validate the model's decisions.

Additionally, more research is needed to examine the long-term impacts of using criminal behavior prediction in various criminal justice applications. Studies could investigate whether the use of predictive models influences sentencing, parole decisions, and other crucial aspects of the legal process, and assess whether these applications are achieving the intended outcomes.

Furthermore, there is a necessity to consider the broader social and ethical implications of deploying criminal behavior prediction systems in real-world settings. Collaborating with ethicists, sociologists, and legal scholars can shed light on the broader implications and guide the development of comprehensive guidelines and policies for the responsible use of ML in criminal justice.

In conclusion, this study on criminal behavior prediction using ML may open exciting possibilities for advancing our understanding of crime patterns and risk assessment. However, as researchers and practitioners, it is our collective responsibility to navigate the ethical challenges and limitations with care and prudence. By adopting a multidisciplinary and ethical approach, we can unlock the full potential of ML in criminal behavior analysis while upholding principles of fairness, privacy, and justice in our society. Only then can we truly harness the power of technology to make a positive impact on the criminal justice system and the lives of individuals involved.

Dataset Reference: The following link points to the folder containing some short dummy datasets for demo implementations: https://drive.proton.me/urls/054EDP N7Y4#eFiamFJBoOfW.

References

1. Aarthi, S., Samyuktha, M., Sahana, M.: Crime hotspot detection with clustering algorithm using data mining. In: 2019 3rd International Conference on Trends in Electronics and Informatics (ICOEI), pp. 401–405. IEEE (2019)
2. Varshitha, D.N., Vidyashree, K.P., Aishwarya, P., Janya, T.S., Dhananjay Gupta, K.R., Sahana, R.: Paper on different approaches for crime prediction system. Int. J. Eng. Res. Technol. (2017)
3. Elluri, L., Mandalapu, V., Roy, N.: Developing machine learning based predictive models for smart policing. In: 2019 IEEE International Conference on Smart Computing (SMARTCOMP), pp. 198–204. IEEE (2019)
4. He, J., Zheng, H.: Prediction of crime rate in urban neighborhoods based on machine learning. Eng. Appl. Artif. Intell. **106**, 104460 (2021)
5. Joshi, N., et al.: Crime anatomization using QGIS. In: 2019 IEEE 5th International Conference for Convergence in Technology (I2CT), pp. 1–4. IEEE (2019)
6. Kim, S., Joshi, P., Kalsi, P.S., Taheri, P.: Crime analysis through machine learning. In: 2018 IEEE 9th Annual Information Technology, Electronics and Mobile Communication Conference (IEMCON), pp. 415–420. IEEE (2018)
7. Mahmud, S., Nuha, M., Sattar, A.: Crime rate prediction using machine learning and data mining. In: Borah, S., Pradhan, R., Dey, N., Gupta, P. (eds.) Soft computing techniques and applications. AISC, vol. 1248, pp. 59–69. Springer, Singapore (2021). https://doi.org/10.1007/978-981-15-7394-1_5
8. Matereke, T., Nyirenda, C., Ghaziasgar, M.: A comparative evaluation of spatio-temporal deep learning techniques for crime prediction (No. 5648). Easy Chair (2021)
9. Pratibha, A.G., Uprant, S.D., Chouhan, L.: Crime prediction and analysis. Int. Conf. Data Eng. Appl. (2020). https://doi.org/10.1109/IDEA49133.2020.9170731
10. Yao, S., et al.: Prediction of crime hotspots based on spatial factors of random forest. In: 2020 15th International Conference on Computer Science and Education (ICCSE), pp. 811–815. IEEE (2020)
11. Zhang, X., Liu, L., Xiao, L., Ji, J.: Comparison of machine learning algorithms for predicting crime hotspots. IEEE Access **8**, 181302–181310 (2020)

Securing Confidential Information
on WhatsApp with Blockchain Technology

Urmila Pilania(✉), Manoj Kumar, Sanjay Singh, Prateek Adhalkha, and Tushar Satija

Computer Science Technology, Manav Rachna University, Faridabad, India
urmilapilania@gmail.com, manojattri003@gmail.com,
sanajysingh@mru.edu.in

Abstract. The protection of sensitive information is a major concern in today's world. However, when it comes to preventing unauthorized screenshots, technology has yet to catch up. Despite this, the concept of securing data is not new, as we now live in an era where human beings are constantly connected to the internet, which is accessible 24/7 like a public park. Information is being shared at an incredible rate every second, and some of this information is particularly sensitive. If it falls into the wrong hands, it can lead to significant losses. This paper proposes a blockchain-based solution to prevent the misuse of WhatsApp screenshots. By using blockchain technology to create a network of shareable images, which are identified by their address and maintain a record of their previous sharing history, security can be improved. This approach also eliminates the need for a middleman to transmit data, reducing the cost of the proposed system.

Keywords: Blockchain · WhatsApp Screenshot · Cyber Security · Chatting Apps

1 Introduction

When the topic of information security comes up, cyber-crimes are often the first thing that comes to mind. Despite the fact that government bodies and corporations have implemented various measures to prevent cyber-crimes [5, 18], cyber security remains a significant concern for the general public. One of the challenges in this field is the potential harm caused by WhatsApp screenshots. Although screenshots are commonly used for recording data, saving important information for future use, and creating reminders, among other reasons, it may be surprising to learn that WhatsApp screenshots taken by either yourself or someone else can be harmful [6, 17].

While blockchain technology has become increasingly popular for Bitcoin transactions, it is important to note that it has potential applications beyond this context. In addition to keeping track of the number of Bitcoins exchanged, blockchain is actually an open ledger that is not owned by any one entity. It is a technology that can record confidential data during or after transactions, and is used to maintain lists of various records. Blocks are linked together through cryptography, with each block having a specific cryptographic hashtag of the previous block, allowing for the secure transmission of records or data [7, 14].

S. Rajagopal et al. (Eds.): ASCIS 2023, CCIS 2039, pp. 53–61, 2024.
https://doi.org/10.1007/978-3-031-59100-6_5

Blockchain is a global, open-source decentralized contact directory that facilitates efficient and verifiable distribution of data or records between two parties. The blockchain is managed and operated by a peer-to-peer network that verifies new blocks with each transaction. Once a block of data or record is added, it cannot be modified without altering all subsequent data blocks.

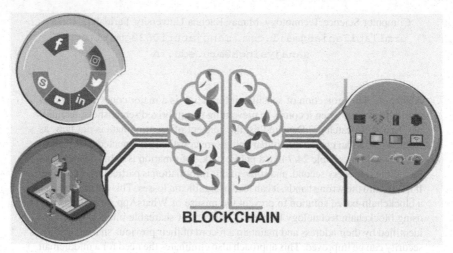

Fig. 1. Blockchain in Cyber Security

Figure 1 [8] illustrates the numerous benefits provided by blockchain technology, including increased simplicity and security in transactions. Users cannot alter their identity while using blockchain and the technology is transparent, consistent, and accurate even under high processing loads. Decentralization ensures that no single individual has control, eliminating the need for intermediaries in deal-making. Because information is shared on the network, hacking is nearly impossible, and global data availability precludes attacks. In healthcare, blockchain enables easy sharing of patient records, while the technology's decentralized nature makes it effective in preventing information misuse. Blockchain's versatile applications span across diverse fields such as education, banking, medicine, supply chain management, smart contracts, E-commerce, and the energy sector [9].

If the information being shared is too personal, even someone you trust can act maliciously. They may exploit your chats to tarnish your reputation, harm your position, or worse. The proposed research centers on WhatsApp screenshots and data protection, exploring how users can safeguard themselves from falling prey to screenshot-related threats and prevent data leaks. Additionally, the research will explore into existing technologies that address this issue as well as new ones that could be developed to prevent screenshot leaks or restrict unauthorized users from taking advantage of sensitive information. The reason for selecting blockchain is its property called decentralization, as in a network of blockchain when a node is added it becomes an integral part of it. Its presence is very significant as where ever the node travels in the network it is noted. If anyone on the network alter node or delete it then the change will reflect into everyone's system on the blockchain network. When images are uploaded as a part of the node, every change or alteration, or operation performed on the node will be recorded in its transactional history.

2 Literature Survey

According to [1], an 18-year-old girl was coerced by unknown individuals who showed her screenshots and threatened to post obscene conversations and videos on social media unless she paid them money. The girl resorted to stealing money from her home to pay the blackmailers. It is becoming increasingly common for young people aged 12 and above to use dating apps for entertainment and time-passing purposes. Unfortunately, as reported in [2], an investigation by Noam Rotem and Ran Locar revealed that one dating app had 845 GB of explicit content, including images, audio, chats, and more. These researchers stumbled upon Amazon web services "buckets" that contained data from various dating apps, such as Cougary, Xpal, BBW Dating, Casualx, SugarD, Herpes Dating, and GHunt. Additionally, Omegle, as mentioned in [3], is a widely used chatting app for strangers, allowing users to create anonymous chat groups and use a webcam to record and save conversations for future use.

In [4], researchers proposed a method to safeguard private data using an image processing technique that limits the sharing of screenshots of visual content. Their framework garbles graphic information on the display and presents the viewer with the garbled graphics to enhance the security of private data to some extent. Traditional methods for protecting sensitive information rely on system architecture and may require a multilevel security operating environment using dedicated hardware, or virtual machines to prevent screenshots. Other techniques involve installing software on manipulators' machines to detect and remove screenshots of sensitive information. However, these methods face challenges in preventing third-party drivers from overriding the installed software. These hardware and software-based approaches do not seem as effective as current technologies, such as Snapchat and incognito mode in Google Chrome, which offer software-based implementations readily available in the market.

As reported in [10], iOS and Android mobiles have introduced the view once feature to enhance the security of private information. This feature automatically deletes images or content after the recipient opens it and disables them from taking screenshots. However, to utilize this feature, users must share their information in view mode only. In [11], the authors conducted a literature review of data sharing using WhatsApp and identified security issues associated with the app's broadcast function, which allows new members to be added to a message. Unfortunately, this process cannot be automated in WhatsApp, making it difficult to trace the source of information and posing significant security concerns.

In recent years, there has been a significant advancement in the development of smart cities, which aims to improve citizens' quality of life. The use of IoT and cloud computing technologies has contributed to the achievement of this goal. Blockchain technology is another promising technology that has the potential to offer numerous value-added services to end-users. With its ability to create an immutable, programmable digital register, blockchain technology can be an excellent fit for virtual assets with value, such as Bitcoin. To fully utilize blockchain technology's capabilities in smart cities, it is necessary to identify its features, needs, and research obstacles. Therefore, this literature review in [15] seeks to define the properties of blockchain technology and identify the critical requirements for its integration into smart cities. Additionally, it presents a use case for blockchain technology, which illustrates how it can protect a smart city. Moreover, it provides an overview of a real-world three-blockchain-based smart city case study. Finally, the review highlights and explores several critical research issues in the field.

Capturing information from a computer monitor can be accomplished through the use of the PrtScr key or snipping tools, as noted in a previous study [12]. As technology continues to advance, enterprises, businesses, and companies are increasingly incorporating these tools into their daily operations. However, the demand for saving data and screenshots can sometimes lead to issues such as copyright violations and plagiarism. As a result, it is essential to develop a solution to safeguard sensitive information from such problems. One potential solution is image distortion, where an inbuilt system distorts the present image graphics on the screen when a user tries to take a screenshot. This approach can enhance security and trust between users from different organizations. Two possible methods to implement this approach are [4]:

- Encrypted media extension as used by Netflix, and many OTT platforms.
- Canny's algorithm also distorts graphics by adding colored pixels around the text areas.

3 Proposed Problem Statement

Currently, blockchain technology is gaining popularity and becoming integrated into various fields, including finance and personal property. In the upcoming research project, blockchain technology will be employed to address a specific issue. As screenshots are considered sensitive information and can be easily shared, blockchain technology will be utilized to establish a network of shareable images in the proposed work. Each image will be assigned a unique address and maintain a record of its previous sharing history.

4 Proposed Workflow

The proposed system integrates encryption, graphics, and blockchain to ensure the security of user data, prevent theft and misuse. By keeping a record of every image or graphic shared, sharing history can be effectively tracked in blockchain. This system provides a secure environment over the cloud, using web3 technology. As the internet continues to advance with technologies such as artificial intelligence, blockchain, machine learning, and cryptography, proposed system will prove to be even more valuable in the years to come.

The objective of this paper is to establish a vast interconnected network for the sole purpose of image-sharing, as depicted in Figs. 2 and 3. When a user requests to share a new image through any web node, it will initially be transmitted to the blockchain network where it will receive a unique identification encryption key and credentials. Once it has been assigned these unique credentials, it will become an immutable part

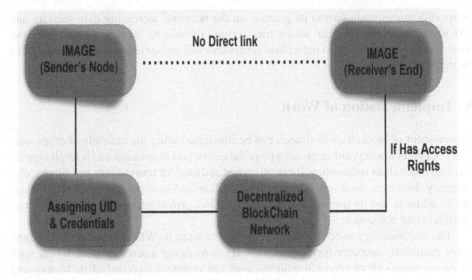

Fig. 2. Communication System without Blockchain

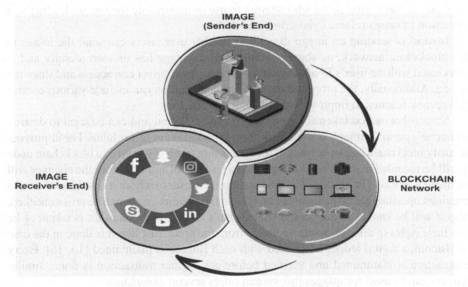

Fig. 3. Proposed Framework with Blockchain

of the blockchain network, unless the original user removes it. The image will then be routed to the intended destination node, and the transaction will be recorded in a manner similar to cryptocurrency transactions.

When the image is shared again, similar to the previous instance, its transaction will be recorded, ensuring that the image remains within the system and never leaves unless removed by the original user. The image's author will have the right to track all modifications made during its journey on the network, increasing data security and providing more control over which transactions to remove. Storing images over the network or cloud rather than individual computers will conserve a significant amount of memory.

5 Implementation of Work

The concept of blockchain in fintech can be illustrated using the example of cryptocurrency. Cryptocurrency, although not a physical entity, is akin to a coin and is implemented through blockchain technology. It can be owned and used for transactions just like regular currency. However, what sets it apart is that each crypto-coin possesses a distinct identity or address, and its transaction history is visible, providing insight into its previous existence and movement.

The methodology used for crypto can be extended to WhatsApp screenshots and other graphical computer formats as well. By associating a screenshot or image with its origin node's IP or physical address, user can maintain a record of its history and transactions on a blockchain network. If any unlawful or sensitive activity is detected, the image can be removed. This approach not only prevents information misuse but also aids in identifying those who attempt to use or manipulate the image, leading to a reduction in image-related cybercrime and theft.

Instead of sending an image directly to another user, users can send the image to the blockchain network, as shown in Fig. 4. Each image has its own identity and is associated with the user's IP address. If authorized, the receiver can access and share the image. Additionally, the proposed network implementation can include various control and review features to improve usability and performance.

Screenshot can be taken for an image; it can be altered and can be used to destroy someone's personal image. It can also be used to make fake or false claims. For improving security blockchain can be helpful. If the screenshot taken is shared as a blockchain node it will be recorded in the transaction that it is a screenshot and whenever the changes will be made it will also be recorded which surely tell the user to whom it is sent what are the previous operation taken place on an image. So false claims made can be cross-checked, also it will be known to the person whose chat's or image's screenshot is taken, or he can have rights to alter or delete an image from the node. Just like it is done in the case of Bitcoin, a digital ledger associated with each Bitcoin is maintained [13, 16]. Every transaction is maintained and verified before any further transaction is done; similar ledgers can be used for images this system offers several advantages:

- It offers a more secure alternative for sending WhatsApp images.
- Users have control and security rights over the network.
- It can potentially reduce instances of cybercrime and aid in identifying the origin of attacks.
- The system implements blockchain technology and incorporates its features.
- Every activity related to image sharing is recorded and tracked.
- The system is transparent, and all parties involved - the network administrator, sender, and receiver - are aware of the image's usage.

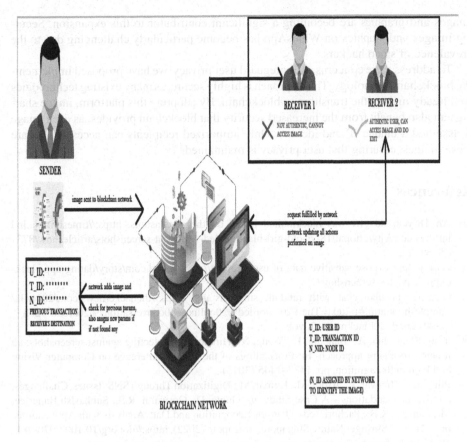

Fig. 4. Blockchain-based Solution for Securing Screenshots

Disadvantages:

- The adoption of a complex implementation is likely to result in an increase in the volume of data stored in the cloud.
- As blockchain technology is still in development and not yet matures, it is not currently feasible to develop the proposed solution.
- The cost of image sharing is expected to rise due to the need for additional dedicated and secure servers to store the images.
- There are currently no ongoing efforts to develop such a solution, as the concept is relatively new.
- Given that only a small number of people experience security issues related to screenshots, this issue is not receiving much attention.

6   Conclusion

Researchers are increasingly concerned about cyber security in light of the proliferation of social media sites. Some instant messaging apps lack sufficient security measures to protect their data. As the amount of data being generated continues to grow rapidly, images and graphics are becoming a significant contributor to this expansion. Securing images and graphics on WhatsApp has become particularly challenging due to the prevalence of smart hackers.

To address these concerns and safeguard user privacy, we have proposed implementing blockchain technology. This approach is highly secure, as many existing technologies are already making the transition to blockchain. By adopting this platform, image sharing can also benefit from the increased security that blockchain provides, as each image is assigned a unique IP and identity. Only authorized recipients can access and share these images, ensuring that user privacy is maintained.

References

1. An 18-year-old girl was blackmailed based on the screenshots. https://timesofindia.ind iatimes.com/city/bhopal/18-yr-old-girl-blackmailed-with-chat-screenshots/articleshow/873 85768.cms
2. Dating apps expose sensitive data of users. https://www.wired.com/story/dating-apps-leak-explicit-photos-screenshots/
3. Omegle- popular chat with random stranger app. https://thehackernews.com/2016/08/omegle-hack.html#:~:text=The%20recorded%20online%20conversations%20are,to%20h arass%20or%20blackmail%20you
4. Yong-Sang Chia, A., Bandara, U., Wang, X., Hirano, H.: Protecting against screenshots: an image processing approach. In: Proceedings of the IEEE Conference on Computer Vision and Pattern Recognition, pp. 1437–1445 (2015)
5. Pilania, U., Tanwar, R., Arora, M., Kumar, M.: Digitization Through SNS: Issues, Challenges, and Recommendations—A Case Study. In: Gupta, D., Goswami, R.S., Subhasish Banerjee, M., Tanveer, R.B., Pachori, (eds.) Pattern Recognition and Data Analysis with Applications, pp. 321–333. Springer Nature Singapore, Singapore (2022). https://doi.org/10.1007/978-981-19-1520-8_25
6. Mirza, M.M., Salamh, F.E., Karabiyik, U.: An android case study on technical anti-forensic challenges of WhatsApp application. In: 2020 8th International Symposium on Digital Forensics and Security (ISDFS), pp. 1–6. IEEE (2020)
7. Dai, F., Shi, Y., Meng, N., Wei, L., Ye, Z.: From bitcoin to cybersecurity: a comparative study of blockchain application and security issues. In: 2017 4th International Conference on Systems and Informatics (ICSAI), pp. 975–979. IEEE (2017)
8. Maleh, Y., Shojafar, M., Alazab, M., Romdhani, I. (Eds.). Blockchain for cybersecurity and privacy: architectures, challenges, and applications (2020)
9. Zhuang, P., Zamir, T., Liang, H.: Blockchain for cybersecurity in smart grid: a comprehensive survey. IEEE Trans. Industr. Inf. **17**(1), 3–19 (2020)
10. URL: View Once Photos and Videos on WhatsApp - WhatsApp Blog
11. Mefolere, K.F.: WhatsApp and information sharing: prospect and challenges. Int. J. Soc. Sci. Humanit. Res. **4**(1), 615–625 (2016)
12. URL: Social Media Apps in China Are Adding 'Hidden Watermarks' to Screenshots So Images Are Traceable / Digital Information World
13. Pilania, U., Upadhyay, P., Tanwar, R., Kumar, M.: A creative domain of blockchain application: NFTs. In: Mobile Radio Communications and 5G Networks: Proceedings of Third MRCN 2022, pp. 397–406. Singapore: Springer Nature Singapore. https://doi.org/10.1007/978-981-19-7982-8_32

14. Mohanta, B.K., Jena, D., Satapathy, U., Patnaik, S.: Survey on IoT security: challenges and solution using machine learning, artificial intelligence and blockchain technology. Internet Things **11**, 100227 (2020)
15. Ghazal, T.M., et al.: Securing smart cities using blockchain technology. In: 2022 1st International Conference on AI in Cybersecurity (ICAIC), pp. 1–4. IEEE (2022)
16. Pilania, U., Tanwar, R., Gupta, P.: An ROI-based robust video steganography technique using SVD in wavelet domain. Open Comput. Sci. **12**(1), 1–16 (2022)
17. Pilania, U., Kumar, M., Rohit, T., Nandal, N.: A Walk-through towards network steganography techniques. Inf. Autom. **22**(5), 1103–1151 (2023)
18. Pilania, U., Gupta, P.: Analysis and implementation of IWT-SVD scheme for video steganography. In: Sharma, D.K., Balas, V.E., Son, L.H., Sharma, R., Cengiz, K. (eds.) Micro-Electronics and Telecommunication Engineering. LNNS, vol. 106, pp. 153–162. Springer, Singapore (2020). https://doi.org/10.1007/978-981-15-2329-8_16

A Text Encryption Approach for IoT Devices to Prioritize Security and Efficiency

Urmila Pilania(✉), Manoj Kumar, Sanjay Singh, Shrey Futela, and Nachiketa Jha

ComputerScience Technology, Manav Rachna University, Faridabad, India
urmilapilania@gmail.com, manojattri003@gmail.com,
sanjaysingh@mru.edu.in

Abstract. Encryption techniques are commonly used to protect the information, ensuring not only privacy but also data authentication, integrity, confidentiality, and availability. The security of these techniques depends on both the internal structure of the algorithm and the underlying mathematics. A crucial factor in the strength of the technique is the secret key if the key is compromised, the encryption technique becomes ineffective. Therefore, choosing the type of information used as a key, how the private key is distributed, and how the communication key is protected are all critical factors in encryption techniques. This work proposes a symmetric key algorithm to protect text messages, using a variable-size key that can be in the form of a number or text.

Keywords: Encryption · Decryption · Security · Symmetric Key Encryption · Internet of Things (IoT)

1 Introduction

IoT is characterized by numerous interconnected devices that can sense, compute, and transmit data, enabling end-to-end communication. One of the key benefits of IoT is its ability to facilitate efficient data transmission with low power consumption. Moreover, IoT can expand its network connectivity to encompass a wide range of resource-efficient smart devices. Given the enormous volume of data transmitted through IoT devices every second, cloud computing plays a vital role in enhancing IoT's overall effectiveness. By leveraging the power of the internet, cloud computing provides users with the ability to perform computing tasks and effectively process, store, and access data. Depending on the user's specific requirements, cloud computing services can be customized accordingly. This can foster closer collaboration and build stronger connections between users. Additionally, IoT cloud computing is cost-effective, as users only pay for the services they require [13–15].

Ensuring the security of information transmitted via IoT devices is a major concern, particularly in light of the growing number of smart hackers and intruders exploiting technological advancements to compromise data transmission [2]. Encryption is one effective way to safeguard data during transmission. It involves converting secret data from its original form to another form that is not comprehensible to external users.

S. Rajagopal et al. (Eds.): ASCIS 2023, CCIS 2039, pp. 62–70, 2024.
https://doi.org/10.1007/978-3-031-59100-6_6

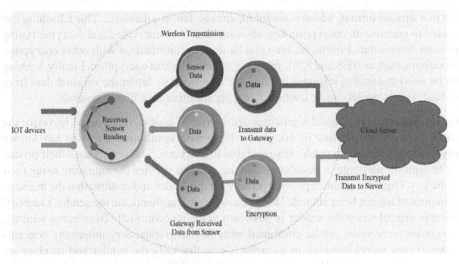

Fig. 1. Security of IoT Data using Symmetric Encryption

Encryption typically relies on both private and public keys. While the public key is accessible to everybody, the private key is shared exclusively between the sender and receiver. There are four primary types of encryption:

Symmetric-Key Encryption: It is also called as private-key encryption, involves using a single key for both encoding and decoding a secret message. The Advanced Encryption Standard (AES) is broadly used algorithm for symmetric-key encryption. AES is a block cipher that encodes and decodes secret data in 128-bit blocks [1]. AES is employed in various applications, such as file, disk, and network encryption, owing to its robustness against brute-force attacks. However, AES is still vulnerable to certain types of attacks, such as the Sweet32 attack.

Asymmetric-key Encryption: It also involves two keys: a public key that anyone can use to encode secret data, and a private key that only the intended recipient can use to decode the message. While the public key is accessible to anyone, the private key must be kept confidential and secure. Public-key encryption, which services a pair of keys - public and private - is the most common type of asymmetric-key encryption and is used in various applications such as email, file sharing, and secure communications. Asymmetric-key encryption includes an elliptic curve and quantum encryption. Elliptic curve encryption is employed in applications such as secure communications, whereas quantum encryption is used in a range of applications including secure communications and quantum computing [11].

Hashing: It is a method of encryption that transforms a given input into a fixed-length output known as a hash value. It uses a mathematical function to convert the input into the hash value, which is unique for each input. Common hash functions include MD5 and SHA-1. Hashing is used in encryption for several reasons. First, it can be used to verify data integrity. If two pieces of data produce the same hash value, they are very likely to be identical, which can be useful for ensuring that a file has not been tampered with. Second, hashing can be used to create a data "fingerprint," representing a large amount of data in a smaller format, which is useful for storing data in a database. Third, hashing can be used to generate an encryption key, allowing data to be encrypted and decrypted using the same hash value. Fourth, hashing can be used in combination with other encryption algorithms, such as AES and RSA, in a process called hybrid encryption. Finally, hashing can be used to conceal information, making it difficult to detect the original data from the hash value, which can be useful for storing sensitive data like passwords.

Digital Signatures: Digital signatures are a type of cryptography used to verify the sender of a communication or document. It involves combining a private key known only to the sender with a public key available to everyone. The sender uses their private key to sign the message or document, and the receiver verifies the signature using their public key. Digital signatures provide privacy for the sender and confirm that the message or document has not been altered. They are also used to authenticate the sender's identity, which is crucial when the sender is unknown to the receiver [12]. To increase security, encryption techniques can be combined with steganography. Steganography conceals the encrypted secret message in a carrier file so that only the sender and receiver are sentient of its presence. However, combining two different methods can upsurge the complication of the technique [8, 9].

2 Literature Review

Cryptography is the way of supervisory and protecting transmissions. It is used completely in areas that need privacy. Nowadays it is experiencing a substantial evolution, and information transmission requires a security mechanism to confirm the confidentiality of digital data. In the proposed work hybrid encryption technique using Vigenere and Hill has been proposed by the author. The hybrid technique is robust against attacks. These two algorithms overcome the demerits of each other [4]. When personal data is sent through the internet then security algorithm plays an important role. The researcher is already working for decades in the field for securing personal data. AES algorithm is playing significant role in securing personal information these days. It is a high-performance symmetric algorithm with different key sizes. It has been selected as an ordinary among symmetric cipher algorithms. In the proposed work, the AES algorithm has been proposed to secure personal data. AES encryption has been modified by using the alternate key. Sub bytes are also modified by transportation operations to enhance security. It is implemented in java language. Analysis of the proposed work was found to be satisfactory after the experimental work. A comparison of the modified AES algorithm has been done with the original AES algorithm [5].

Authors in this work proposed DNA sequence operation for the encryption of personal data. It is a new idea different from the existing methods. It used 8 rules of DNA code depending on the order of the alphabet in the text that gives more chances to encrypt the text. In this paper, steganography was also included to improve the security of the technique. This method embedded the encrypted text into pixels of the image using DNA code. Then embedding method is executed based on a hyperchaotic system. For analysis of the performance different assessment parameters were used the work was found to be robust against attacks [6]. IoT technology is adding more and more smart devices to the network. Security is the main concern these days during communication. In this proposed work, an Enhanced Energy Efficient Lightweight Cryptography Method (E3LCM) was used to encrypt the data. It utilized the 8-bit manipulation principle for encryption. The proposed work was applied to the audio file using MATLAB. The hardware complexity has been authenticated using Sparten3E XC3S500E FPGA and it has been proved that the technique used 202mW power and 0.9 Kbytes RAM and its experimental results were found to be better than the existing work [7]. Appling security techniques during the transmission of secret data is not new to us. IoT devices are tremendously slow in the transmission of information and these devices have minor hardware compared to other personal computers. Using IoT devices is problematic for the transmission of the big size of data and achieving complicated operations.

3 Motivation

The security of individuals' data, particularly confidential information, is being jeopardized by the increasing number of hackers and intruders. This is especially dangerous in developing and underdeveloped countries where individuals are still learning to navigate the internet. To address this concern, our research aims to encrypt secret data to prevent unauthorized access. Specifically, we propose a secure method for transmitting classified text messages through IoT devices using end-to-end encryption with a variable-length symmetric key.

4 Research Methodology

To encrypt input text, the following steps are taken:

1. Ascertain the ASCII value of the user-inputted text.
2. Create an 8-digit binary number from the ASCII value.
3. Reverse the binary value of the eighth digit.
4. Choose a four-digit divisor ($> = 1000$) as the key.
5. Subtract the reversed number from the divisor.
6. The generated remainder is stored in the first 3 digits, and the quotient is stored in the next 5 digits.
7. The remainder should not be more than 3 digits, and the quotient should not be more than 5 digits. If the remainder is less than three digits, add it to the left-hand side.
8. The encryption process is complete.

Our proposed system encrypts and decrypts all the messages provided in the software, according to ASCII value, and works on a symmetric key.

The following steps are carried out for decryption. The process of encryption and decryption is also illustrated in Fig. 2 and Fig. 3:

1. Divide the key by the final 5 digits of the cipher text.
2. Combine the first 3 digits of the cipher text with the output of the previous step.
3. If the result obtained from step 2 is not an 8-bit integer, then convert it to one.
4. To generate the plain text, reverse the number obtained.

Our proposed system works on a symmetric key and can encrypt and decrypt all the messages provided in the software based on their ASCII values.

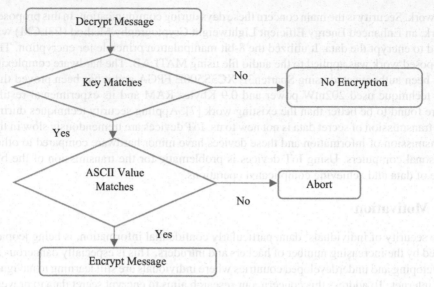

Fig. 2. Encryption Process

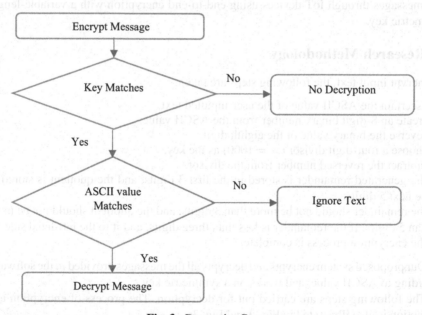

Fig. 3. Decryption Process

5   Implementation and Result Analysis

The proposed method utilizes the symmetric key algorithm to ensure secure data transmission within IoT devices. This algorithm usage a distinct, strong key for both encryption and decryption, making it easy to handle and execute quickly. For our work, we utilized a variable-length key that can be in the form of a number or string. The software we used was a 64-bit Python program with 64GB of memory, which allows for a key of up to 63GB in length and a maximum message size of 63 GB. To encrypt data into ASCII characters and decrypt them back to their original form, we utilized the Base64 module. In addition, we used Tkinter, a widely-used GUI library for Python, to create a fast and user-friendly graphical interface.

ENCODE DECODE

MESSAGE   Hello

KEY   7

MODE(e-encode, d-decode)   e

RESULT   f8KcwqPCo8Km

RESET   EXIT

Fig. 4. Encryption User Interface

Figures 4 and 5 display the user interface for encoding and decoding the secret message. The user chooses the secret message, key, and mode. Upon inputting the text message, the user input the key to encrypt the message and selects the mode. Encoding is indicated by the letter 'e', while decoding is indicated by the letter 'd'.

ENCODE DECODE

MESSAGE   f8KcwqPCo8Km

KEY   7

MODE(e-encode, d-decode)   d

RESULT   Hello

RESET   EXIT

Fig. 5. Decryption User Interface

The figures illustrated the user interface for encoding and decoding secret messages, as shown in Figs. 4 and 5. To encrypt the input message, the user selects a secret message, a key, and a mode. If the 'e' mode is selected, the message is encrypted, generating the cipher text. If 'd' mode is selected, the cipher text is converted into plain text when the user clicks the result button. The interface also includes reset and exit buttons, allowing the user to modify previously entered values and exit the interface, respectively.

Our proposed work offers comprehensive security features and is resistant to attacks. It preserves the integrity of the secret message and provides user authentication during login. The encryption and decryption process is swift, taking less than a second to complete. The key used can be of variable length, allowing for flexibility in the encryption process. The proposed system operates on 64-bit Python software with 64GB of memory, accommodating keys and messages up to 63GB in size. The Base64 module is used for data encryption and decryption, and Tkinter is used to develop a standard GUI library for Python, ensuring fast and straightforward GUI application creation.

One advantage of the proposed work "is that it proposes a symmetric key algorithm for secure text message transmission in IoT devices. This approach uses a variable-size key, which can be in the form of a number or text and can be easily handled by users. Another advantage is that the proposed approach prioritizes both security and efficiency, ensuring that data is transmitted securely while maintaining high performance. The work also provides a intelligible interface for inputting the message, key, and mode of encryption or decryption. Additionally, the use of the Base64 module and Tkinter library in the implementation of the approach can provide fast and easy encryption and decryption of messages in real time.

By using symmetric key encryption, the suggested application establishes a strong security framework and guarantees the integrity and secrecy of all messages sent. The program's key pairing technique creates fine-grained access control by only permitting the recovery of the original message when the recipient has both the encrypted message and the matching encrypted key together with their own decryption key. The overall security model is greatly improved by this two-step encryption method, which necessitates the presence of two distinct elements in order to successfully decrypt.

The program's security posture is further strengthened by the incorporation of many cryptographic techniques. Secure key exchange relies heavily on asymmetric key encryption, which increases the symmetric key's distribution without jeopardizing its integrity. In order to reduce the dangers of key interception, asymmetric key pairs are used to guarantee that only the intended receiver can decrypt the symmetric key.

By offering a way to confirm the integrity of the encrypted message as it is being transmitted, hash algorithms enhance the security of the application. This keeps someone from altering the communication without authorization, guaranteeing that the material that is received is genuine and unaltered. An additional layer of authentication is added by integrating digital signatures. By utilizing their public key to validate the signature, receivers may confirm the authenticity of the source when senders sign messages using their private key.

The program's capability for variable-length keys and customized key management highlights its versatility and flexibility. This feature makes it flexible for a range of use cases by enabling users to customize the encryption and decryption procedure in accordance with certain security needs.

When compared to contemporary cryptographic methods, the program's simplicity and security are balanced. It offers strong security safeguards against unwanted access while avoiding some of the possible complications involved with certain newer approaches. In addition to reducing reliance on centralized systems, the program's distributed key management approach gives users more control over their encryption keys.

Anticipating the future, the program's progressive steganography integration fits well with current practices, adding another degree of protection by encrypting messages that are embedded in carrier files. This all-encompassing strategy presents the software as a workable and trustworthy answer for situations where data integrity, secrecy, and authentication are critical factors. Its usefulness in tackling the changing environment of cybersecurity threats is shown by its ability to seamlessly mix classic and current cryptographic approaches.

6 Conclusion

One significant development that guarantees the transmission of brief messages in an encrypted format through IoT devices is the suggested symmetric key encryption technology for secure message communication in IoT devices. The method improves data transmission security by using variable-length keys that can be either textual or numeric. The program's two-step encryption method, along with its granular access control and lower key distribution concerns, make it an invaluable tool for data protection. Its versatility in key management and capacity to adapt to a wide range of use cases make it a sensible option that gives consumers a sense of confidence when communicating.

In the future, even more security is promised by the steganography-encrypted carrier files that are embedded with encrypted messages. This program stands out as a proactive and effective tool in the constantly changing cybersecurity market, proving its dependability in protecting critical data in a variety of scenarios.

References

1. Kaur, M., Kumar, V.: A comprehensive review on image encryption techniques. Arch. Comput. Methods Eng. **27**(1), 15–43 (2020)
2. Rajesh, S., Paul, V., Menon, V.G., Khosravi, M.R.: A secure and efficient lightweight symmetric encryption scheme for transfer of text files between embedded IoT devices. Symmetry **11**(2), 293 (2019)
3. Zhu, S., Zhu, C., Wang, W.: A new image encryption algorithm based on chaos and secure hash SHA-256. Entropy **20**(9), 716 (2018)
4. Touil, H., El Akkad, N., Satori, K.: Text encryption: hybrid cryptographic method using Vigenere and Hill ciphers. In: 2020 IEEE International Conference on Intelligent Systems and Computer Vision (ISCV), pp. 1–6 (2020)
5. Thinn, A.A., Thwin, M.M.S.: Modification of AES algorithm by using second key and modified SubBytes operation for text encryption. In: Computational Science and Technology, pp. 435–444. Springer, Singapore (2019).https://doi.org/10.1007/978-981-13-2622-6_42
6. Al-Khateeb, Z.N., Jader, M.F.: Encryption and hiding text using DNA coding and hyperchaotic system. Indonesian J. Electr. Eng. Comput. Sci. **19**(2), 766–774 (2020)
7. Prakasam, P., Madheswaran, M., Sujith, K.P., Sayeed, M.S.: An enhanced energy efficient lightweight cryptography method for various IoT devices. ICT Express **7**(4), 487–492 (2021)
8. Pilania, U., Gupta, P.: Analysis and implementation of IWT-SVD scheme for video steganography. In: Sharma, D.K., Balas, V.E., Son, L.H., Sharma, R., Cengiz, K. (eds.) Micro-Electronics and Telecommunication Engineering. LNNS, vol. 106, pp. 153–162. Springer, Singapore (2020). https://doi.org/10.1007/978-981-15-2329-8_16

9. Pilania, U., Tanwar, R., Zamani, M., Manaf, A.A.: Framework for video steganography using integer wavelet transform and JPEG compression. Future Internet **14**(9), 254 (2022)
10. Yu, H., Kim, Y.: New RSA encryption mechanism using one-time encryption keys and unpredictable bio-signal for wireless communication devices. Electron **9**(2), 246 (2020)
11. Zhang, J., Yu, Yu., Fan, S., Zhang, Z., Yang, K.: Tweaking the asymmetry of asymmetric-key cryptography on lattices: KEMs and signatures of smaller sizes. In: Kiayias, A., Kohlweiss, M., Wallden, P., Zikas, V. (eds.) PKC 2020. LNCS, vol. 12111, pp. 37–65. Springer, Cham (2020). https://doi.org/10.1007/978-3-030-45388-6_2
12. Cui, X., Wang, Y., Zheng, X., Han, Y., Qiao, H., Li, S.: A novel color image watermarking algorithm based on digital signature. In: 2019 International Conference on Internet of Things (iThings) and IEEE Green Computing and Communications (GreenCom) and IEEE Cyber, Physical and Social Computing (CPSCom) and IEEE Smart Data (SmartData), pp. 267–274. IEEE (2019)
13. Pilania, U., Tanwar, R., Kaushik, K.: Steganography Tools and Their Analysis Concerning Distortion in Stego Image. In: Chakraborty, B., Biswas, A., Chakrabarti, A. (eds.) Advances in Data Science and Computing Technologies: Select Proceedings of ADSC 2022, pp. 531–538. Springer Nature Singapore, Singapore (2023). https://doi.org/10.1007/978-981-99-3656-4_54
14. Pilania, U., Tanwar, R., Gupta, P.: An ROI-based robust video steganography technique using SVD in wavelet domain. Open Comput. Sci. **12**(1), 1–16 (2022)
15. Pilania, U., Kumar, M., Singh, S., Mittal, V.: Video Steganography in IoT: information Embedding using OpenCV and 2LSB. In: 2023 International Conference on Sustainable Computing and Smart Systems (ICSCSS), pp. 1067–1072. IEEE (2023)

Network Traffic Classification: Solution to Detect Intruder

Sujata N. Bhosle[✉] [iD] and Jayshri D. Pagare

JNEC, MGM University, Chh. Sambhajinagar, Maharashtra, India
magaresujata@rediffmail.com, jpagare@mgmu.ac.in

Abstract. Network Traffic Classification is a challenging task in the of intrusion detection. Using the network traffic classification techniques, admin can identify whether the incoming request is genuine or fake. NTC can be done in 2-class and multi-class classification. In this paper, we have discussed the approaches such as port based; Flow-based which are helpful to tackle the intrusion, so Many researchers are finding ways to do proper classification. Some datasets are available for Network traffic Classification such as KDD'99, NSL-KDD, HIKARI-2021 AND UNSW-NB15; we have elaborated characteristics and effectiveness of dataset. We have provided existing literature study which will be helpful for the researcher to compare the techniques and results, Naive Bayes classifier is widely used technique. UNSW-NB15 is an open-source dataset available for researchers to compare their results. This paper summarizes the statistical description of the dataset UNSW-NB15.

Keywords: Network Traffic Classification · KDD99 · UNSW-NB15 · Flow-based Network Classification

1 Introduction

Security and privacy of cloud data plays an important role in IoT. While transmitting the user data, it is very important to take care of their security and maintain the privacy of the data. Therefore, it is essential to discriminate between malicious traffic and normal traffic. Succeeding to recognizing malicious traffic, it must be obstructed and direct the normal traffic to the correct nodes for serving the client's needs. The primary applications of Network Traffic classification are collecting data from the network and analyzing data in order to control the network. Network Traffic classification is still not well developed in smart city and the reason behind this is dissimilarities in flow features in IoT and Non-IoT gadgets [1].

Nowadays organizations store their business data on cloud, using the cloud infrastructure it can be accessed from anywhere anytime. We need to secured this data because attacks on such cloud is happens frequently because same infrastructure can be used by attacker also. There is possibility of DDoS attack. To figure it out in the early stage Network traffic classification will be very effective. Although traditional methods are there to do such task but it is effective on static port-based method only. It will lack the performance for dynamic port strategies which is now used by many P2P applications.

S. Rajagopal et al. (Eds.): ASCIS 2023, CCIS 2039, pp. 71–80, 2024.
https://doi.org/10.1007/978-3-031-59100-6_7

The network traffic dataset consist of various attack categories events. Such as Exploit Attack, Fuzzers Attack, Generic Attack, Reconnaissance Attack, Backdoor Attack, DoS attack, worms and shellcode Attack. DoS is a Deniel-of-Service attack which makes network or server inactive and inaccessible to user. Exploit is a method used to install malware program on targeted device. Fuzzer is the technique which finds the vulnerabilities of the program. By using Network traffic classification techniques system administrator can identify abnormal request in advance. It will help to detect whether traffic flow is normal or abnormal in 2-class classification. Moreover, NTC can be done with multi-class classification where exact attack categories will be detected. Table 1 shows Attack categories and its description.

Table 1. Attack Categories

Attack Category	Description
Backdoor	It gains the unauthorized access to system by bypassing standard authentication
DoS	DoS is a Deniel-of-Service attack which makes network or server inactive and inaccessible to user
Exploits	Exploit is a method used to install malware program on targeted device
Fuzzers	Fuzzer is the technique which finds the vulnerabilities of the program
Generic	The disrepute of the generic attack is it uses Hash functions to crash block-ciphers.
Reconnaissance	Reconnaissance is an attack technique where information about target is gathered before the attack happens
Shellcode	By using shellcode, attacker may take control of system and exploit compromised system by executing set of instructions
Worms	Worm is a malicious software that can replicate malicious software copies and spread it across the network

2   Existing Work

Minaxi et al., have created their own Database using tcpdump and evaluated their model with Accuracy, Recall, F-Measure, Precision. In [2] authors have considered the features Src & Dst IP, Protocol info, Header length, No of pkt in fwd and bwd direction, Packet size, IAT and duration, PUSH & URG, idean and active states to achieve Quality of service in SDN network traffic classification. Minaxi et al., applied SVM, Naïve Bayes and Nearest Centroid methods on their dataset. They achieved accuracy for SVM 92.3%, Naïve Bayes 96.79% and Nearest Centroid method achieved 91.2%.

The popular machine learning algorithms like Decision Tree, Naïve Bayes classification and Support Vector Machine were used by most of the researchers for the Network Traffic Classification task [3]. Dong and Wang have done the comparative study of

Deep learning algorithms and traditional Machine learning algorithms [4]. The authors have found that the deep learning algorithms resulted in improved accuracy of detection of traffic flows. Authors have used the Synthetic Minority Oversampling Technique to tackle the problem of dataset imbalance. Authors have used UTSC-2016. This dataset is large in volume with different data types, which is best suitable for smart city. This dataset consist of normal as well as ten different types of malware traffic data such as virtut and cridex. Authors have omitted the feature engineering step and for classification they directly used raw data and processed for uniformed size flow. Yao et al. [5] have proposed a network classification approach which focuses on smart city networks. They have created a model which will classify data first in 2 categories namely Bening and Malware and then these categories are sub-classified in 10-class classification like BitTorrent, WorldWarcraft, Cridex and Zeus. Authors have used Capsule Network model to do this task and did the comparative experimental analysis with Logistic regression model, CNN-LSTM and CNN. They got higher classification result for Bening 10 class classification than Malware 10-class classification. Capsule network is capable to classify non-linear data.

Miao et al. [6] have used Principle Component Analysis method to classify the ISP data along with machine learning algorithms like Random Forest method, NB, SVM, H2O, K-NN, and Decision Tree. According to their experimental results they found that RF and KNN gives high performance. Authors got 92.92% accuracy for Random Forest and 84.56% accuracy for K- Nearest Neighbor method when used Without PCA. Authors in [7] got higher accuracy for the same methods on their campus data as Random forest to 99.08% and K-Nearest Neighbor to 97.16%. The dataset in [6] and [7] have similar data traffic.

In [8, 9] authors have proposed novel ensemble scheme which evaluates the applicability of ensemble learning in real time. They have presented TLboost and ROSboost algorithms. Proposed work can be complete and expand the conclusions if it gives satisfactory results with other datasets. Given approach can be tested on other datasets like IoT and mobile traffic, there will be need for improvement.

Oudah et al., used their own captured dataset in two environments Controlled (linux) and Uncontrolled (Windows) result in background noise. They achieved higher accuracy by using the C5.0 classifier compared with the other classifiers used, reaching more than 97%. They have captured the data only through Google chrome browser, result may change if model used with other browser's data. To check and examine the performance of the proposed model in [10] requires considerations of different types of applications and also requires a better approach for labeling flow of network. The proposed work in [11] got results using Random Forest method. There were 23 features and with the use of 6 features, model resulted in 0.883 accuracy and 0.914 as F1-score. Precision score of 0.927 on the 15 s timeout dataset. On Test dataset, the authors have achieved 0.9995 accuracy by using DNN which has 2 hidden layers and entropy loss of 0.000497. The selected features are then used with ML algorithms e.g. Idle time, Active time, statistical attributes, time durational attributes. This Model may behave differently and performance may change and tested with other ML algorithms or performing parameter for improved accuracy and runtime. Proposed model in [12], Detects only general class instead of specific application.

Table 2. Comparison of Existing Work

Author	Performance Parameters	Experiments	Database	Result
Yao et al	Accuracy, Recall, Precision	Capsule NW CNN CNN+LSTM LR	UTSC-16	Above 96% for malware traffic (Capsule nw)
Miao et al	Accuracy, F-Measure, Precision, Recall, Specificity	Naive Bayes classification, Support Vector Machine, Random forest H2O, Decision Tree and K-Nearest Neighbor	Campus data traffic	Accuracy RF 92.92% KNN 84.56%
Shone et al	Accuracy, F-Measure, Precision, Recall False Alarm	Non-symmetric deep auto-encoder	ISP data traffic KDD Cup'99 NSL-KDD	RF 99.08% KNN 97.16%
R. J. Alzahrani	Accuracy, Recall, Precision F1 score	Decision Tree K-NN Naïve Bayes	BoT-IoT dataset	Accuracy 99.96%
Meenaxi et at	Accuracy, Recall, F-Measure, Precision	SVM, Naïve Bayes and Nearest Centroid	Created own Database using tcpdump	SVM-92.3% NB-96.79%, NC-91.2%
Klenilmar Lopes Dias et al	Accuracy, Recall, Precision	Modified Naïve Bayes Algorithm	Captured Data using WireShark	Avg Accuracy 98.88%
Santiago Egea Gómez et al	AUC ROC- receiver operating characteristic F1	SVM LR CART Decision Tree – for Orange and KDD99 dataset	Own NTC dataset CNAE-9 Churn Prediction LSVT Voice KDD99 Orange	AUC-ROC: 0.65 F1 = 0.997

Table 2 summarizes the comparative study of existing work. The classification in traffic Smart City faces various difficulties, for example, infrastructure, data source, standardization, and quality of service. These difficulties should be completely tended to in Smart city to be carried as a compact preparation

3 Methodologies

Network traffic classification can be done with three different methods: Port, Payload and Flow statistical based methodology. In Port based strategy, port number related information is collected using TCP and UDP headers of the packet. This is the simplest and fast method to do classification. But due to the dynamic porting mechanism this strategy is not working well with today's traffic.

To deal with the limitations of the traditional method, a Payload based approach was proposed. This approach does the assessment of the packet, which is known as Deep Packet Inspection (DPI). It provides good results but it is quite time consuming. Although these methods provided us the High result, it has its own drawbacks. One is it could not handle Encrypted traffic and another is dynamic porting implementation problems. It also resulted into over burden on the network and breaches the user secrecy.

Due to the lack of accurate result, researchers are employing the use of machine learning techniques, which can give better results with the use of statistical features of the dataset. A machine learning technique incorporates the following general steps for Anomaly identification purpose:

Data Collection. Dataset can be created by tracing raw data file; such dataset is called Private Dataset. Some public dataset are also available for study.

Flow Representation and Feature Engineering. Raw data have to be converted in statistical form so that they can be used in further process. Categorical features must convert to statistical features. We can normalize the data here. This steps is responsible for data Manipulation, addition and deletion which can result in better accuracy in later stage.

Dataset Preparation/ Selection. After selecting the required or relevant features data has to be divided in training and testing ratio. If we use training, validation and testing data without duplicate values then the model will not be partial towards the result.

Building a Model. Generated training and testing dataset will be used to build model. Based upon the features we have to select best suited Machine learning Algorithms for dataset, such as supervised, unsupervised and Semi-Supervised Algorithm. In most of the study researcher have used Random Forest, Decision Tree and Naïve Bayes Classifier for building model and got good results.

Evaluation Model. After building a model, we have to evaluate model to assess the performance. Performance metrics does this job. Accuracy, Recall, Precision and F1-score are widely used performance metrics to evaluate model.

3.1 Dataset

Most of the researchers have used their own dataset for classification, which is not openly available for others. Due to this we can't compare work with those datasets. Following are some datasets that are available for the task of Network traffic classification. Each dataset consist of normal and abnormal traffic.

KDD'99. KDD'99 is divided into 4 categories i.e. Basic, Time-based, Content and a Host Traffic features. KDD'99 consist of redundant records, in this data dataset 75% to 78% records is repeated in training and testing phase which affects the performance of learning model. And Model may become partial due to this issue.

NSL KDD. To overcome these issues NSL-KDD was proposed. It does not consist any irrelevant records. Numbers of records are logical in Training and Testing dataset. Due to this learning model's result will not be partial [16, 17].

HIKARI-2021. Authors have released dataset named HIKARI-2021 which consists of Manipulated attacks and normal data-flow. Most of the existing study data were in the encrypted form and not publicly available due to sensitive data, they lack into documentation and comparison. To overcome such issues authors have developed HIKARI-2021 dataset.

UNSW-NB15. The authors [14] have published this dataset in 2015. It consist of modern attack-flows and has 49 Features in it. These 49 features is the combination of normal traffic and attack traffic data having class labels for 25,40,044 records. This record is further dived in 2,21,876 and 3,21,283 as normal and attack categories respectively. As like KDD'99, UNSW-NB15 consist of six categories namely Basic Features, Content Feature, Flow Feature, Time Feature Labeled Feature and Additional Generated Features. There are 9 categories of attacks included this dataset. In this paper authors have analyzed the dataset statistically and practically. All 49 features are categorized as flow features (Srcip, Sport, Dstip, Dsport, Proto), basic, Time, time, Content and additional generated features. The csv file consists of 2,540,044 records. They have divided data into the ratio of training- 60%: testing- 40%. There were no duplicated record in training and testing dataset. They have classified attack into nine groups namely Fuzzer, backdoor, analysis, Dos, Generic, Exploit, Reconaisance, shellcode and worm.

3.2 Feature Description of Dataset

Statistical Feature. A statistical feature summarizes temporal behavior of Traffic profile. e.g. mean pkt count, variance, first and third quartile.

Scalar Feature. These Features are suitable to represent the accurate description of traffic flow. e.g. Duration, flow size, min, max.

Complex Feature. These features are convenient to predict the requirement for more sophisticate traffic description. Wide range traffic observations can be compressed by using complex features. Several measurements of packet's Inter-Arrival-Time can be refined into a set of frequency components. e.g. pkt IAT.

Features Example. Src & Dst IP, Protocol info, Header length, No of pkt in fwd and bwd direction, Pkt size, duration, IAT, PUSH, active status, idle status and URG [13–15].

4 Statistical Description of UNSW-NB15 Dataset

UNSW-NB15 database includes abnormal data flow. This abnormal data flow is associated with particular attack categories. Figure 1 shows the percentages of normal and each attack category traffic flow in training data.

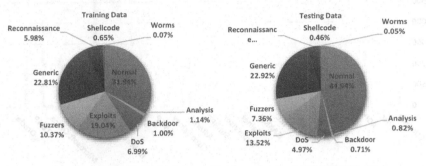

Fig. 1. Percentage of Training & Testing samples in UNSW-NB-15

It consists of 31.49% normal data and Remaining Attack data. It also shows the percentages of normal and each attack category traffic flow in testing data. It consists of 44.94% normal dataflow and remaining 55.06% as attack data flow.

Figures 2, 3, 4 and 5 shows number of flows in each attack category. Each attack category is subdivided into exact attack type. From Figs. 2, 3, 4 and 5, we can see that exploit attack category consist of variety of sub-attacks.

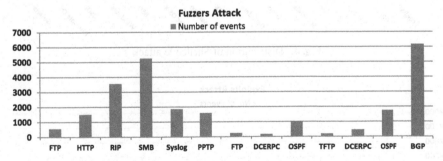

Fig. 2. Distribution of Fuzzer attack data flows

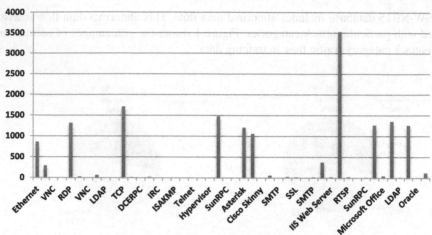

Fig. 3. Distribution of DoS attack flows

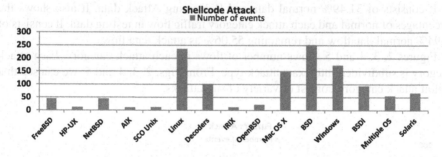

Fig. 4. Distribution of Shellcode attack

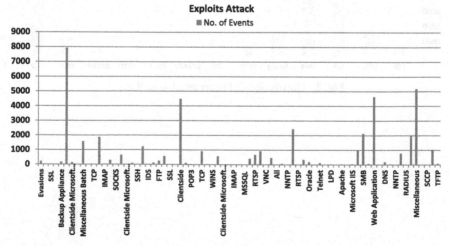

Fig. 5. Distribution of Exploits attack

5 Conclusion

The Port based approach which is the fastest one has limitations. Some applications don't have their ports registered and Applications may use ports other than its familiar ports. In this case a Port-based approach will not work properly and will lead to inaccurate results. Payload based approach gives satisfactory results, but cannot identify exact type of applications and Application payload encryption. Most of the researchers have used their own dataset to achieve accuracy; this may lead to change when used with the different dataset.

References

1. Magare, S.S., Dudhgaonkar, A.A., Kondekar, S.R.: Security and Privacy Issues in Smart City: Threats and Their Countermeasures. In: Tamane, S.C., Dey, N., Hassanien, A.-E. (eds.) Security and Privacy Applications for Smart City Development. SSDC, vol. 308, pp. 37–52. Springer, Cham (2021). https://doi.org/10.1007/978-3-030-53149-2_3
2. Raikar, M.M., et al.: Data Traffic Classification in Software Defined Networks (SDN) using supervised-learning. Procedia Comput. Sci. **171**, 2750–2759 (2020). ISSN 1877-0509
3. Dong, B., Wang, X.: Comparison deep learning method to traditional methods using for network intrusion detection. In: 2016 8th IEEE International Conference on Communication Software and Networks (ICCSN). Beijing, China, pp. 581–585. IEEE (Jun 2016)
4. Zhao, R., Yan, R., Chen, Z., Mao, K., Wang, P., Gao, R.X.: Deep learning and its applications to machine health monitoring: a survey. IEEE Trans. Neural Netw. Learn. Syst. **14**(8), 1–14 (2016)
5. Yao, H., Gao, P., Wang, J., Zhang, P., Jiang, C., Han, Z.: Capsule network assisted IoT traffic classification mechanism for smart cities. IEEE Internet Things J. **6**, 7515–7525 (2019)
6. Miao, Y., Ruan, Z., Pan, L., Zhang, J., Xiang, Y.: Comprehensive analysis of network traffic data. Concurr. Comput. Pract. Exp. **30**, e4181 (2018)
7. Alzoman, R., Alenazi, M.: A comparative study of traffic classification techniques for smart city networks. Sensors. **21**, 4677 (2021). https://doi.org/10.3390/s21144677
8. Gómez, S.E., et al.: Ensemble network traffic classification: algorithm comparison and novel ensemble scheme proposal. Comput. Netw. **127**, 68–80 (2017). ISSN 1389-1286
9. Gómez, S.E., Hernández-Callejo, L., Martínez, B.C., et al.: Exploratory study on class imbalance and solutions for network traffic classification. Neurocomputing **343**, 100–119 (2019). ISSN-0925-2312
10. Oudah, H.: Profiling and Identification of Web Applications in Computer Network. PhD diss., University of Plymouth Author, F.: Article title. Journal 2(5), 99–110 (2016)
11. Ampratwum, I.: An intelligent traffic classification based optimized routing in SDN-IoT: A machine learning approach. PhD diss., University of Ottawa (2020)
12. Sun, G., Liang, L., Chen, T., Xiao, F., Lang, F.: Network traffic classification based on transfer learning. Comput. Electr. Eng. **69**, 920–927 (2018). ISSN 0045–7906
13. Labayen, V., et al.: Online classification of user activities using machine learning on network traffic. Comput. Netw. **181**, 107557 (2020). ISSN 1389-1286
14. Moustafa, N., Slay, J.: The evaluation of network anomaly detection systems: statistical analysis of the UNSW-NB15 data set and the comparison with the KDD99 data set. Inf. Secur. J. A Glob. Perspect. **25**, 18–31 (2016)
15. Zhu, Y., Zheng, Y.: Traffic identification and traffic analysis based on support vector machine. Neural Comput. Appl. **32**(7), 1903–1911 (2019). https://doi.org/10.1007/s00521-019-044 93-2

16. Choudhary, S., Kesswani, N.: Analysis of KDD-Cup'99, NSL-KDD and UNSW-NB15 Datasets using Deep Learning in IoT, Procedia Comput. Sci. **167**, 1561–1573 2020. ISSN 1877-0509
17. Janarthanan, T., Zargari, S.: Feature Selection in UNSW-NB15 and KDDCUP'99 datasets. In: 2017 IEEE 26th International Symposium on Industrial Electronics (ISIE). IEEE (2017)

Review on Privacy Preservation Techniques and Challenges in IoT Devices

Prakash Meena$^{(\boxtimes)}$ ⑩, Brijesh Jajal⑩, and Samrat Khanna⑩

Department of Computer Sciences and Engineering, Institute of Advanced Research,
Gandhinagar, Gujarat, India
{prakashmeena.phd2022,brijesh.jajal,samrat.khanna}@iar.ac.in

Abstract. The Internet of Things has revolutionized by connecting everyday objects to the Internet, we interact with our surroundings. However, the massive procreation of IoT devices has heightened serious concerns about privacy and security. This article presents a comprehensive review of privacy preservation techniques and challenges in IoT devices. It explores various privacy-enhancing technologies and discusses the current state-of-the-art research in the field. The article also highlights the challenges faced by IoT devices in preserving user privacy and identifies potential solutions. Also, the article illustrates the privacy leakages in IoT. The findings of this review contribute to a better understanding of privacy issues in IoT and provide insights for future research.

Keywords: Internet of Things · IoT devices · Privacy Preservation · Privacy leakage

1 Introduction

The growth of the Internet of Things has been significant and is expected to continue expanding in the coming years. Here's an overview of its growth and technological advances explored.

More devices can now connect to the internet and create the foundation for IoT growth by enabling seamless communication between devices. Over the years, sensors have become more affordable, smaller, and more power-efficient, making them suitable for embedding into various devices [1]. This has allowed for the integration of sensors into everyday objects and the collection of real-time data. Cloud services provide scalable storage and processing capabilities, allowing organizations to store, analyze, and derive insights from IoT data. IoT has found applications across various industries and offers convenience, energy efficiency, and enhanced control over various aspects of daily life, driving consumer adoption. IoT is intersecting with other emerging technologies, such as artificial intelligence (AI), machine learning (ML), and edge computing. AI and ML algorithms are used to analyze IoT data and make predictions or automate decision-making processes.

This paper provides the Importance of Privacy preservation (PP). Then, the Methodology section provides the steps of the review process to prepare the article. The next

S. Rajagopal et al. (Eds.): ASCIS 2023, CCIS 2039, pp. 81–89, 2024.
https://doi.org/10.1007/978-3-031-59100-6_8

two sections then provide the earlier works related to the Definition and goals of PP and elaborate details about the definition of Privacy leakage. The two more sections for review of PP techniques available for research and explore the challenges available in privacy preservation yet to be researched. The outcome of the article is discussed in the analysis and conclusion sections.

1.1 Importance of Privacy Preservation in IoT Devices

Privacy preservation in IoT devices [2] is of paramount importance for several reasons. For Personal Data Protection, Preserving privacy ensures that sensitive information remains secure and is not misused, protecting individuals from identity theft, fraud, or unauthorized access to their personal lives. Consent and Control, Privacy preservation enables individuals to maintain control over their data. Users should be able to decide how their data is being used, shared, and retained by IoT devices and services. Security and Confidentiality, IoT devices are vulnerable to security breaches and data leaks. Privacy preservation measures, such as encryption, authentication, and secure data transmission, help safeguard data from unauthorized access, interception, or tampering. Trust and User Adoption, By prioritizing privacy preservation, IoT providers can build trust with users, leading to increased acceptance and adoption of IoT solutions. Ethical Considerations, Respecting privacy in IoT devices is an ethical responsibility. Privacy breaches can have severe consequences, including discrimination, profiling, and manipulation. Regulatory Compliance, Data protection regulations, such as the European Union's General Data Protection Regulation (GDPR) and the California Consumer Privacy Act (CCPA), impose legal obligations on organizations handling personal data. Public Perception and Reputation, Positive public perception regarding privacy practices can strengthen brand image, foster customer loyalty, and differentiate them from competitors.

In summary, privacy preservation in IoT devices is crucial for protecting personal data, ensuring user control, maintaining security, building trust, upholding ethical standards, complying with regulations, and preserving organizational reputation.

2   Methodology

Privacy is important in the current fast-growing technological environment. In our study approach, first, we understand the requirement of privacy and identify the privacy issues. Then, explored the definition and goal of Privacy Preservation. Second, we explored privacy leakage as a mathematical formula. By understanding privacy, third, we search for various current Privacy preservation techniques used in privacy protection and identify the PP techniques used for IoT devices.

Fourth, we explore the challenges presented in Privacy preservation as per attacks and analyze them for further research exploration. The objective of the article is to identify the possible research areas that are yet to be explored. For this, we searched some old and recent works by different authors and selected a few of them for our research work.

3 Definitions and Goal of Privacy Preservation

Different types of security and privacy attacks [3] are distinguished by Yunjiao Lei et al. The issue of safety and privacy in the reinforcement training context is explored in this paper. The Markov Decision Process is used to examine potential risks and impacts. Current literature is also examined in this research and focused on the elements of the MDP to understand attacks and defenses in terms of state, action, environment, or reward.

Information on differential privacy [4] is provided by Rachel Cummings et al. Attacks and Auditing as a Measure of Protection and ML inclusion for better privacy solutions a major challenges. In order to produce an idealized world with a high level of privacy protection, Differential Privacy (DP) is merely not enough. Critical elements such as data retention, access control, and user verification are not addressed by the Data Protection Directive. However, other important privacy principles such as transparency, consent, and data minimization are not taken into account while serving the principle of data anonymization. These principles are essential to control the use of information so that raw data and intermediate computations can be made only in limited quantities. Beyond the Data Protection Directive, it is essential to consider other privacy principles in order to achieve complete protection of personal data.

The threat to security and privacy [5] created by the development of the Internet of Things in cities was discussed by Azizi Majid. An overview of the different risks associated with the Internet of Things systems, ranging from simple intercepting messages to more sophisticated malware attacks is presented in this paper. In order to assist standardization bodies with setting minimum security requirements for various types of Internet of Things applications and devices, it provides a full set of safety guidelines derived from industry best practices. In order to better understand the threats landscape, this research also covers key areas of research concerning Internet of Things security. With the rapid evolution of Internet of Things applications, ensuring a wide variety of security requirements is becoming increasingly important. It is therefore important to develop more sophisticated protection schemes and models, which would attract the attention of academia and industry.

Overall, in order to ensure the safety of Internet of Things systems and protect against potential threats and vulnerabilities, concerted efforts need to be made. Figure 1 shows the various attacks as per IoT layers.

A simple, secure, and privacy-preserving communication protocol [6] using chaos encryption and message authentication codes is proposed by Tianyi Song et al. The document proposes a simple protocol for communications to focus on ensuring security and privacy in smart home systems. It utilizes chaos-based encryption and Message Authentication Codes (MAC) for this purpose.

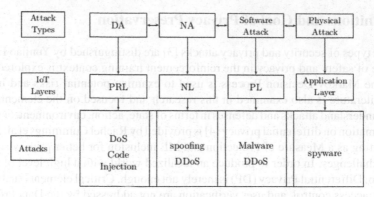

Fig. 1. Attacks and IoT Layers.

4 Understanding Privacy Preservation

4.1 Privacy Leakage

The privacy leakage [7] is measured using the gap between the estimated dataset and the original dataset.

The following is a definition of privacy leakage. To infer the original data of client K, based upon a released parameter, assume that an optimization algorithm is used by the Semihonest Attacker. *So* is the original private dataset of client k, *St* is the dataset inferred by the attacker, and *Ca* is the total number of rounds for inferring the data. Privacy leakage can be defined as *Vp, k*.

$$V_{p,k} = \begin{cases} \frac{D - \frac{1}{C_a} \sum_{t=1}^{C_a} \|s_t - s_o\|}{D} & C_a > 0, \\ 0, & C_a = 0. \end{cases} \tag{1}$$

Remark:

– (1) We assume that $\|St - So\| \in [0, D]$. Therefore, $Vp,k \in [0, 1]$.
– (2) When the adversary does not attack ($Ca = 0$), the privacy leakage $Vp,k = 0$.

As a novel approach to understanding federated learning security, Xiaojin Zhang et al. present Federated Learning Secure Game. The framework, by adopting a strategic approach, gives rise to an analysis of dynamics between defenders and attackers which is beyond the conventional emphasis on protection and attack tactics. The challenges of distributed training security are addressed more fully in this new perspective.

4.2 Privacy Preservation Techniques

Various Privacy Preservation techniques [8] are developed and applied for the privacy of information. Figure 2 shows various Privacy Preservation techniques and a few of them are discussed here.

Anonymization means Data de-identification procedures often entail the removal of some sensitive characteristics, such as names, gender, state codes, or identity numbers, which are collectively referred to as personally identifiable information. The following more advanced anonymization methods are available: (a) k-anonymity; and (b) l-diversity. (c) t-closeness. Obfuscation is a process of increasing a system's complexity within a given range including preserving the original system's functioning. Multi-tier ML use Data memorization is directly possible when publicly accessible ML models are trained on sensitive user data. Multi-tier ML frequently uses semi-supervised knowledge aggregation techniques. Decentralized machine learning provides a new computing framework for improved privacy protection. Instead of sending the user's sensitive information to some portion of the computation defined as com-A is delegated to end-user devices also makes a little contribution to the system model's updating. By using homomorphic encryption techniques, cryptography restricts access to a message's contents to the sender and intended receiver only. Binary operations, such as addition and multiplication, can be performed directly on encrypted data thanks to homomorphic encryption. Again, Homomorphic schemes are classified as (a) partially homomorphic encryption with operations on ciphertexts; and (b) fully homomorphic encryption, which supports all operations on ciphertexts.

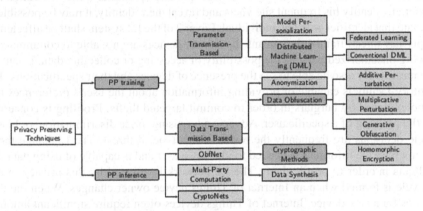

Fig. 2. Privacy Preservation Techniques.

Dataflow suggests developing dataflow models with appropriate rights at various privacy levels to guarantee user confidentiality and open accountability. The two primary data flow models are (a) blockchain used to verify and account for data collection, storage, and access in IoT environments; another (b) asymmetric data flow models to assure privacy. Privacy-based programming languages demand that information with privileges flows be stated upfront, tying each data element to its appropriate policy. Data summarising is the process of condensing information into a brief yet informative form while protecting the confidentiality of the original data and it is being used in numerous fields like network traffic monitoring, the financial industry, the healthcare sector, text analysis, etc. Personal data stores include programs that enable users to keep track of, use, and distribute their most important personal data. Personal data stores provide a central control point to users for personal information. Various data attributes managed by the service shared a repository to store locally including multiple externally distributed repositories, or both locally and externally. Users can use different applications for accessing attributes from personal data stores. Users will be able to selectively share data sets with different users with the same instance of the Personal Data Store.

These techniques are categorized further with different uses, applications and fields related to various sensor devices, IoT infrastructures, and internet environments. These categories will help to improve further research on Privacy Preservation techniques for single IoT devices or multiple IoT devices with collaboration research.

5 Challenges in Privacy Preservation

Various Privacy Preservation Challenges [9] are still to be explored in this field. Some of the challenges are summarized here. The ability to track an individual's physical location without his or her consent, and to record it over time, is referred to as tracking. The attacker will receive real-time updates on the user's location and predict their position in the future or on a frequent journey with sufficient accuracy by using their mobility patterns. All three layers of the Internet of Things IoT are affected by this privacy threat. Identifier: an attacker has the ability to collect sporadic updates of a user's location and use them to identify his frequent site visits and reveal their identity, it may be possible to associate that identifier with any individual. Layer 2 of the L2 system shall be affected by this privacy threat. Itemization means that sensor devices are not able to communicate, allowing unauthorized persons the possibility of accessing or collecting data. Unauthorized parties may also be able to see the presence of devices and their specifications. The inventory facility is capable of providing information about the user's preferences that can be exploited by burglars in order to commit targeted thefts. Profiling is concerned with the profiling of a specific user. Adverse advertising, price discrimination, or biased vehicle decisions are frequently the result of this type of threat. The Linkange threat does not have the information needed to identify a user and is capable of using data that it collects in order to profile them. The L2 network is affected by this privacy threat. Lifecycle is formed when an Internet of Things device owner changes. When the user searches for a new device, Internet of Things devices often require significant amounts of personally identifiable data that cannot be deleted entirely from the device prior to its transfer to another user. The L2 area is hit by this privacy threat.

Membership inference is an attack in which an attacker queries a trained ML model to see if it contains a specific example in its training database. In this case, the attacker can analyze a particular data record that can be used to train that ML model, as the attacker gains information about the ML model as well as the individual data record. Attack-like Data inferencing aims to gather information on a data or query using merging leakage with public databases. Frequency analysis, which is used for cracking ancient ciphers, is a popular example of an inference attack. This attack is often accompanied by encryption, a privacy preservation solution. An attribute disclosure occurs when an individual is associated with a particular record in the painting that has been published. Property disclosures are generally made when information on certain persons is revealed and when an enemy seeks to unlawfully obtain the identity of a legitimate person, fingerprint and ID theft are carried out. Mimics a smart object, such as your access credentials device, to act on behalf of a legitimate device (e.g. Injecting false data) can compromise security and apply incentives. There may be a privacy risk with the device's fingerprint. Web fingerprinting attacks, which use network traffic metadata, can also infringe on privacy when browsing the Internet. Network traffic Metadata performs different operations between users and devices fingerprinting using a variety of techniques. Redefine is about the way an attacker can use it. Connection to coordinate the data from a number of collections with re-identify a record from an outsourced, published, or open data record. Generally speaking, the database contains sensitive information about individuals. This is possible and allows an attacker to have a partial or complete reinstallation of the first Database records that could lead to the identification of unnecessary targeting and profiling of the targeted website user's Database. In Model stealing, with the query, an attacker tries to access parameters or functions that may be stolen by the target model. By a simple query with samples and proposed model responses to mold a Replicated model. Reversing the pattern is a kind of attack on privacy in that it tries to redeem the training set for accessing only a qualified classifier. In the ML model Predictive, the pattern-reversing attack allows the enemy to extract basic training data from individuals. Table 1 summarises the attacks and challenges of Privacy preservation discussed here.

6 Analysis

Few authors have shared code implementation of the solutions for privacy preservation research. Privacy leakage is the primary reason for privacy threats. The mathematical definition of Privacy leakage shows the relationship between a single client with data and an attacker. More work is needed on the Privacy Leakage definition for the relationship between different IoT data and attacks. The federated learning approach is an important technique in privacy preservation research. Various privacy preservation techniques are available and divided into PP training and PP inference. DML and federated learning approaches are yet to be fully explored. Most of the work is done using Cryptography techniques. For every IoT device Threats and attacks are discussed in Privacy Preservation Challenges [9]. The author suggests different PP techniques as per the associated IoT devices based on threats and attacks. DML and FL are useful for general IoT devices. IoT layers are also important and considered for Privacy preservation research. Layer 2 of IoT layers is the most affected area by threats and attacks. Table 1 shows the outcomes of this article which shows the different PP techniques and tools for different IoT devices based on the various threats and attacks on IoT devices. Major Privacy threats are Tracking, Identification, Inventory, Profiling, Linkage, and Lifecycle. Common Privacy attacks are Membership inference, Data inference, Attribute disclosure, Fingerprinting and Impersonation, Re-identification, Database reconstruction, Model stealing, Model inversion.

The analysis of PP techniques and challenges will help PP researchers further exploration of tools and develop new tools for better PP techniques. The limitation of the research work is related to the dataset of IoT devices useful for better PP techniques implementation. The development of PP techniques for different IoT Devices needs different datasets to be explored.

Table 1. Attack and Challenges in Privacy Preservation for IoT devices.

PP Techniques	IoT Devices	Threat	Attacks
Cryptography	Mobile	Tracking	Membership Inference
Obfuscation	General IoT General	Identification	Data inference
Decentralized ML	IoT IoT	Inventory Profiling	Attribute disclosure
Cryptography	Mobile General IoT	Linkange	Fingerprinting and
DataFlow	Mobile		Impersonation
Cryptography	IoMT		Re-identification
Cryptography	Smart Environment		Database
DataFlow			Reconstruction Model
Cryptography			stealing
			Model inversion

7 Conclusion

The article covers various privacy-enhancing technologies, discusses the current state-of-the-art research, and highlights the challenges faced by IoT devices in preserving user privacy. Here, Different Privacy Preservation techniques and challenges are explored and reviewed in different categories for further research. It also proposes potential solutions and offers insights for the researchers and various PP tools available for research. Here, future work can be done to improve in Privacy Leakage definition in IoT devices by updating the existing ones reviewed in the article. In IoT layers, Layer 2 of IoT is the most affected area by various Privacy threats and attacks. Also, IoT data sets and IoT devices-based studies for Privacy Preservation techniques need more research work in this area.

Acknowledgment. The authors would like to thank Dr. Vinesh Jain (Faculty, ECAjmer) for the help provided in the paper.

References

1. Khan, F., Rehman, A.U., Zheng, J., Jan, M.A., Alam, M.: Mobile crowdsensing: a survey on privacy-preservation, task management, assignment models, and incentives mechanisms. Future Gener. Comput. Syst. **100**, 456–472 (2019). https://doi.org/10.1016/j.future.2019.02.014

2. Akil, M., Islami, L., Fischer-Hubner, S., Martucci, L.A., Zuccato, A.: Privacy-preserving identifiers for IoT: a systematic literature review. IEEE Access **8**, 168470–168485 (2020). https://doi.org/10.1109/ACCESS.2020.3023659

3. Lei, Y., Ye, D., Shen, S., Sui, Y., Zhu, T., Zhou, W.: New Challenges in Reinforcement Learning: A Survey of Security and Privacy", Springer Nature 2021, arXiv:2301.00188v1 [cs.LG] 31 Dec 2022

4. Rachel, C., et al.: "Challenges towards the Next Frontier in Privacy" April 17, 2023. arXiv:2304.06929v1 [cs.CR] 14 Apr 2023

5. Majid, A.: Security and privacy concerns over IoT devices attacks in smart cities (2022). J. Comput. Commun. **11**, 26–42 (2023). https://www.scirp.org/journal/jcc. ISSN Online: 2327-5227 ISSN Print: 2327-5219

6. Song, T., et al.: A privacy-preserving communication protocol for IoT applications in smart homes, pp. 2327–4662 (c) IEEE (2016)

7. Zhang, X., Fan, L., et al.: "A game-theoretic framework for federated learning" 11 Apr 2023 arXiv:2304.05836v1

8. Torre, D., Chennamaneni, A., Rodriguez, A.: Privacy-preservation techniques for iot devices: a systematic mapping study. IEEE Access **11**, 16323–16345 (2023). https://doi.org/10.1109/ACCESS.2023.3245524

9. Zheng, M., et al.: Challenges of privacy-preserving machine learning in IoT", © 2019 Association for Computing Machinery. ACM ISBN 978-1-4503-7013-4/19/11, arXiv:1909.09804v1 [cs.CR] 21 Sep 2019

Mitigation and Prevention Methods for Cross-Layer Attacks in IoT (Internet of Things) Devices

Enoch Success Boakai[1]([✉]) [ID] and Ravirajsinh S. Vaghela[2] [ID]

[1] Cybersecurity and Cyber Law, Marwadi University, Rajkot, Gujarat, India
enochsboakai.115733@marwadiuniversity.ac.in
[2] Cyber Security and Digital Forensics, National Forensic Sciences University (NFSU),
Gandhinagar, Gujarat, India
ravirajsinh.vaghela@nfsu.ac.in

Abstract. Innumerable advantages as well as severe security challenges have been brought about by the fast spread of Internet of Things (IoT) devices across numerous industries. The emergence of cross-layer attacks, which takes advantage of flaws and exploit vulnerabilities in several tiers of the IoT technological framework, is a major concern. This is concerning and significant because there could be major repercussions, including unauthorized access, data breaches, service interruptions, and even the risk to people's safety or vital infrastructure. It takes a comprehensive strategy that includes both proactive and reactive tactics to counter these threats. Encryption, access control, intrusion detection systems, and robust security protocols must be implemented at various IoT architecture layers as proactive measures. Moreover, frequent updates and continual observation are crucial. Reactive strategies such as incident response protocols, anomaly detection systems, and fast recovery procedures are also essential for quickly detecting and minimizing the impact of cross-layer attacks in order to quickly return to normal operation. This study scrutinizes cross-layer assaults on IoT devices, presenting a thorough set of techniques and defenses to strengthen the resistance of IoT devices against complex and multi-layered attacks, greatly advancing the understanding of cross-layer security challenges in IoT environments. Furthermore, a thorough analysis of current mitigation and prevention techniques, along with newly developed approaches to bolster IoT security are covered. The ultimate objective of the research is to further protect IoT devices against complex cross-layer attacks by offering a comprehensive approach that includes both proactive and reactive measures, thereby building a more robust and secure Internet of Things ecosystem that guarantees the availability, integrity, and confidentiality of linked devices and services by tackling these security issues.

Keywords: Internet of Things (IoT) · Cross Layer · Quality of Service (QoS) · Authentication · Communication Protocols · Security

S. Rajagopal et al. (Eds.): ASCIS 2023, CCIS 2039, pp. 90–113, 2024.
https://doi.org/10.1007/978-3-031-59100-6_9

1 Introduction

In the year 1999, Kevin Ashton developed the notion of the "Internet of Things" [1]. Since then, this technology has completely revolutionized how we interact with the physical world, making it possible for billions of connected devices to communicate and share data in a seamless and efficient manner. The Internet of Things (IoT) is defined as a physical or virtual object or device that is connected, communicates with one another, and is integrated into a network for a particular purpose [2]. Organizations and individuals can easily communicate with each other from remote locations, thanks to the hyper-connectivity concept that IoT presented. All of a person's possessions are internet-connected in a smart home setup [3]. Some of these items can be controlled with voice commands, and they can monitor and change the temperature and timing of lights in the home. Patients' medical information are stored in one place because of smart health, an IoT revolution in the healthcare industry. The sensor-equipped devices that a healthcare provider may attach to the patient while performing an examination are collecting and analyzing information through the Internet of Things. Industries have also embraced IoT, and the more astute ones are tracking and documenting the supply and demand for produced goods. Using their smart devices, travelers can now self-check in, a recent development in smart transportation [4].

With all of these IoT breakthroughs, a vast network of constantly communicating gadgets will be created. According to a report by Statistica [5] there will be approximately 75.44 billion connected devices by 2025. However, the pervasive nature of IoT has also made it a prime target for malicious actors seeking to compromise its security. IoT gadgets, including everything from manufacturing sensors to smart household devices, are increasingly becoming targets of malevolent parties looking to take advantage of weaknesses that span multiple layers of the IoT stack. These complex and multifaceted threats, known as cross-layer attacks, pose a significant challenge with relation to the reliability and safeguarding of IoT implementations (Fig. 1).

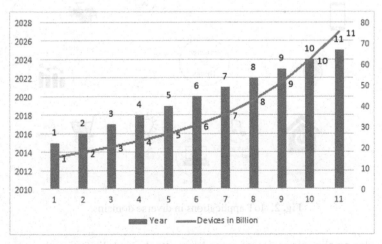

Fig. 1. Internet of Things (IoT) expected devices by 2025 (in billions) [6].

Cross-layer attacks are a class of sophisticated threats that exploit weaknesses across the various layers of the IoT architecture, From the lowest levels (physical and data link) all the way up to the highest (network and application layers). These attacks often transcend the traditional boundaries of cybersecurity, requiring a holistic and multi-dimensional approach to safeguard IoT devices and the data they handle. As such, addressing cross-layer attacks demands a concerted effort from both researchers and practitioners to develop comprehensive mitigation and prevention strategies. One of the main causes of mediocre security in the Internet of Things is a lack of adequate knowledge regarding the problem. Security for Internet of Things will increase with an extensive knowledge of the core structures, security risks, and remedies.

Cross-layer design has been developed in IoT (Internet of Things) to tackle specific challenges and take advantage of possibilities that come with IoT systems. In order to take advantage of the interactions among the layers, this design removes the borders between them. Additionally, it encourages flexibility through information sharing amongst the layers. Although cross-layer design has many advantages and has helped IoT devices and systems perform better in a variety of applications and scenarios by increasing efficacy and adaptability across communication protocols, it also presents major security risks because it changes the conventional layer structure, which introduces vulnerabilities and erodes security protocols. It opens doors or new attack surfaces for bad actors by getting around some security measures put in place at the individual layer level. To reduce and eliminate the risks related to cross-layer attacks in IoT devices, security precautions and careful examination of possible weak points at the interfaces that exists between the layers are essential. This research paper delves into the pressing issue of cross-layer attacks in IoT devices, aiming to shed light on the evolving threat landscape and present a comprehensive framework for mitigating and preventing such attacks (Fig. 2).

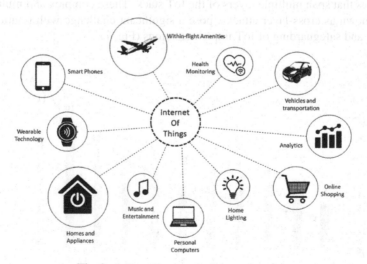

Fig. 2. IoT applications in diverse domains.

By exploring the intricacies of cross-layer attacks and dissecting their underlying mechanisms, this paper endeavours to provide a deeper understanding of the challenges faced by the IoT community. Furthermore, it offers a synthesis of state-of-the-art mitigation techniques, proactive prevention methods, and best practices that can be employed to fortify IoT ecosystems against these formidable adversaries.

The complexities of cross-layer attacks in IoT devices will be explored in the forthcoming pages, unravelling the layers of this multifaceted challenge. By examining both the theoretical foundations and practical implications, we hope to equip researchers, IoT practitioners, and policymakers with the knowledge and tools needed to safeguard the future of IoT against the persistent and ever-evolving threat of cross-layer attacks.

2 Related Work

Research similar to this has been conducted in related works, we will be comparing previous works. Cross-layer attacks have been studied in ad hoc networks, Wireless Sensor Networks (WSN), Cognitive Radio Networks (CRN), and other domains. Lack of communication between the MAC, routing, and higher layers led to the rise in cross-layer attacks. These attacks produce better results at a lower cost. Researchers have come up with a number of defences against attacks on the 6LoWPAN network's RPL protocol. But each approach is only able to identify a certain amount of attack kinds, nonetheless there remain a few issues that need to be improved or fixed. Lightweight Heartbeat Protocol, SVELTE, and Contiki IDS are just a few of the attack prevention techniques that Tran Nho and co-author [7] made an effort to implement in their paper titled "Performance Analysis of Anti-Attack methods for RPL routing protocol in 6LoWPAN networks." The study gave a summary of the theories underlying these techniques and evaluated their effectiveness by simulating them with Cooja software on Contiki OS. The outcome or findings of the study showed a relationship between the suggested concepts and the simulated data.

The research also pointed out areas that could be strengthened and assessed the advantages and disadvantages of these approaches. According to Vivek et al. [8] in their paper "RMDD: Cross Layer Attack in Internet of Things," low intensity assaults on the Routing protocol for low power lossy networks (RPL) can cause a decline in the general performance of an application. Their method of executing the attacks was taking advantage of the RPL protocol's Rank system. In order to secure Internet of Things communication, Apeksha G. [9] and others presented a Detection and Prevention Low Power and Lossy Network (DPLPLN) scheme in their paper. By recognizing the flooding behavior or junk packets of a Denial of Service (DoS) attacker and identifying it in the network, the DPLPLN provides security. When contrasting the performance of DPLPLN to RMDD, the suggested approach performs better in terms of different metrics of performance, such as throughput and overhead. The primary flaw in RMDD is that while it quantifies drop possibility, data packets will undoubtedly drop in flood situations due to increased traffic. RPL routing is better and makes full use of the IPv6 protocol. The RPL protocol for routing is utilized in this instance to route data amongst each of the nodes. After evaluating each node's performance, it is found that the proposed DPLPLN has a lower loss percentage than RMDD. The protocols and procedures currently in use for confidential communication in the Internet of Things were examined by J. Granjal and others [10] and their analysis also offers a thorough examination of research concerns.

The inquiry was centered on network layer, MAC, and physical layer communication security concerns. Sicari [11] also provided extensive information on progressive Internet of Things security, privacy, and issues of trust, clarifying how distinct specifications and communication protocols makes it impossible to utilize conventional safeguards to IoT. Also highlighted were concerns about privacy, unresolved problems and recommendations for additional study, all while concentrating on the difficulties and present remedies in the area of security for the Internet of Things. Data wrapping provided by the protocol stack used by TCP/IP causes latency, additional overloading, a breach in QoS, and security, as B. Fu [12] described, categorizing the difficulties associated with cross-layer configurations in addition to how they can be grouped.

3   IoT Architecture and Security Requirement

In recent years, a variety of Internet of Things (IoT) initiatives have emerged, and various architectures have been designed depending on the project's particular needs and subject matter. Low compatibility between the systems was caused by a variety of designs that included multiple elements and standards because of substantial variation in the application categories, which also caused differences in the demands and methods related to the architecture specification amongst the projects.

3.1   The Three Layer Architecture

The three - layer architectural structure, namely, perception, network, and application layers is the basic building block and the most widely used concept for the Internet of Things. The theoretical framework of the Internet of Things is defined by this architecture (Fig. 3).

The Perception Layer. The primary components of this layer are endpoints [13] specifically actuators and sensors that gather data about the surroundings (environmental temperature, moisture, wind velocity, position, and acceleration). At this layer, nodes are identified and information is gathered, hence, it is typically referred to as the management layer. The layer's primary purpose [14] is to sense, collect, and analyze data before sending it to the network layer.

The Network Layer. This layer acts as a general-purpose conduit for exchange of information among multiple devices. Certain protocols for communication, such as HTTP/HTTPS and MQTT, are required at this layer. Additionally, the nerve center of this tier is comprised of communication networks that runs on the cloud. This layer, which is also called "Transmission layer," essentially transfers the information gathered from the perception layer to the layer that comes after it securely.

The Application Layer. As the user's primary point of interaction, the application layer is the topmost layer. Managing various functions linked to the operational need and socioeconomic segregation of IoT is the focus of this layer. It is in charge of offering users with services. This layer of application supervision is made possible by middleware handling of data [13, 15]. It includes the capability of two-way interaction in addition to various cross-layer communication setups.

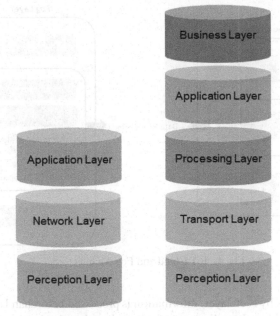

Fig. 3. The 3 and 5 Layer Architecture

3.2 The Five Layer Architecture

Although the fundamental three-layer architecture underpins the very idea of the Internet of Things, it is barely enough for concise studies into the IoT.

Business and processing layers are further layers in the five-layer architecture. The application layer and perception layer continue to perform their respective functions. Through networks that are both wired and wireless, the transport layer delivers the data from the perception layer to the processing layer. The data gathered from the transport layer is stored, processed, and examined in the processing layer. The combination of internet of things applications with corporate infrastructure and operational procedures occurs at the business layer.

3.3 Cloud and Fog Layer Architecture

Due to the unpredictability of information that IoT devices sense and generate in the form of data, an architecture based on cloud computing has become popular in IoT systems. The majority of Internet of Things architectures use online information processing platforms to provide comprehensive management of the data. The physical layer, monitoring layer, pre-processing layer, storage layer, security layer, and transport layer are the six different layers that collectively make up fog architecture [16] (Fig. 4).

Following transmission to the storage layers, the information is split up and preserved in different structures according to what is needed. The data circulation's confidentiality rating is provided by the security layer. The monitoring layer maintains a watchfulness on every other aspect, including performance, offerings, responses, and the utilization of

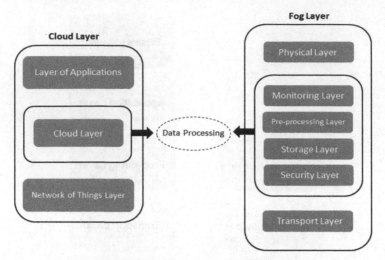

Fig. 4. IoT Cloud and Fog Architecture.

sufficient resources by each layer. Information is processed beforehand and analysed by the pre-processing layer. It applies a set of criteria based on the data being gathered. The storage layer houses the information needed for a network to operate effectively. Encryption and decryption are two elements of the security layer that protect user confidentiality and safety.

3.4 Security Requirement of Different Layers in IoT

The complex structure that makes up the Internet of Things (IoT) is essential to guarantee the smooth operation of items that are linked at every layer. Hinai [17] offered an evaluation of multiple safety issues at every layer, encompassing cross-layer diverse integrative security concerns, and proposed several viable solutions. Information is passed on from one point and received at another point in every internet of things interaction, therefore, it is crucial to create unique safeguards for every layer in order to guarantee the full safety of the world of IoT.

At the perception layer, physical gadget and sensor protection against misuse and unwanted access is the main goal. For legitimate devices to be able to pass on data to the network, authentication and encryption mechanisms are essential. A major part of safeguarding the Perception layer also involves taking precautions against physical threats, like using hardware that is difficult to interfere with.

At the network layer, using strong encryption techniques to safeguard data while it is in transit is part of the security requirement. Man-in-the-middle attacks and eavesdropping can be prevented by using secure communication channels like Virtual Private Networks (VPNs). Only authorized devices and users can interact with the Internet of Things (IoT) network thanks to access controls and intrusion detection systems, which are crucial for managing and monitoring network traffic.

At the Support layer, Strong authentication methods are required for confirming the identities of users and devices. The enforcement of access control policies is also needed for limiting privileges and preventing unauthorized access.

At the Application layer, using secure coding techniques to stop application vulnerabilities is one of the security requirements. Maintaining data integrity and confidentiality is essential, therefore, sensitive data is protected via encryption, regular security audits and updates (Fig. 5).

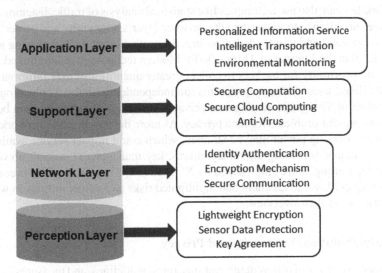

Fig. 5. The IoT security architecture.

4   Challenges and Feasible Solutions for Cross-Layer Design in IoT

Studies are still ongoing on several key problems related to the cross-layer development in IoT. IoT applications need a lot of devices to be expandable, which makes them difficult to carry out because of schedule, memory, manufacturing, and power limitations. Quality of Service (QoS) prerequisites for Internet of Things, or IoT gadgets can vary depending on factors like trustworthiness, power usage, and delays. Applications for Internet of Things make users' lives more convenient, but they cannot constantly guarantee safety and confidentiality. Queries about privacy, security, and sustainability have sprouted as a result of the extensive use of smart devices in IoT cross-layer design structures.

4.1   Security and Privacy in Cross-Layer Design

Safeguarding the Internet of Things has established itself as an integral issue in the modern era. IoT security issues, constraints, needs, current and upcoming remedies were all thoroughly investigated by Pajouh [18] The major IoT problems and challenges were the study's main focus. The usage of unencrypted systems or deficient protocols has been linked to multiple cases of information loss and intrusions. It is critical to incorporate comprehensive security mechanisms in IoT applications and to make sure that reliable approaches are used at all layers and during device-to-device data exchange. The adoption of encryption and authorization methods on every gadget is imperative for achieving confidentiality of users. The varied configurations of IoT devices may render them more vulnerable to hacking attempts. Restricted power use, storage space and algorithmic abilities of these elements also expose them to a range of security risks. Attacks known as denial of service (DoS) can compromise the security of the Transport Layer. Intruders can also use techniques like statistical analysis of traffic, listening in, and the passive surveillance to jeopardize the network layer's anonymity and protection. In order to avoid fraud and unintended exposure, the protection of the key sharing process is very crucial in the Internet of Things (IoT). Modern technology is interlinked, which presents an opportunity for hackers to collect greater quantities of user information for potentially illegal uses. Different programs run independently in the Application Layer of the Internet of Things, protecting user privacy. Variations in authentication between applications present problems for data privacy. As more devices become networked and share data, processing power may be strained, which could impact service availability. IoT security issues, including digital signatures, key management, assault prevention, and protected routing, were emphasized by X. Chen [19] They highlighted precautions based on protocol layer assessment and highlighted risks and vulnerabilities in wireless sensor networks in their overview.

4.2 Feasible Solutions to Security and Privacy

These remedies consist of different innovations, rules, guidelines, and measures designed to stop illegal access, theft, harm, or disturbance of important data or assets. In their article, Malina and others concentrated on IoT data privacy security issues and tools that are necessary. They offered an evaluation of the various IoT applications that employ technical Privacy Enhancing Techniques (PETs), and they put forth an original structure that primarily focuses on the overall safety and confidentiality needs of IoT applications as well as conceivable confidentiality issues in IoT-based solutions. Additionally, they assess the overall IoT model and suggested appropriate PET kinds to address current privacy concerns in every identified area. According to Weber [20] in order to safeguard the safety and confidentiality considerations that are created by entrepreneurs, a worldwide legal structure must be established. The privacy-aware methods for acquiring, storing, and receiving data must be considered by makers of IoT devices, [21] Secure data, monetary assets, proprietary information, and other important resources must all be protected and kept intact with the help of highly reliable safety tools. Three essential components are utilized for enforcing security: data confidentiality, integrity, and availability (Fig. 6).

This has become known as the security triad, [18] an acknowledged guide to facilitating the creation of security processes. In order to address security concerns at all stages of the layers, the writers [22] suggested handling keys, secure protocol for routing and algorithmic encryption.

Cryptographic Algorithm. Highly confidential information is secured and protected using a mathematical process called a digital signature algorithm. By operating at the

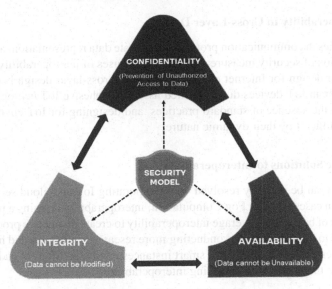

Fig. 6. The CIA Security Model.

network's physical layer, this method maintains protection for the network. The algorithm uses the Public Key Encryption Technique and the Symmetric Encryption Approach, two different encryption techniques. Symmetry encoding is used by WSN because of its simple calculations and concepts, as reference [23] states. A possible drawback of employing this approach concerns the incorporation of verification systems, which require supplementary space for storage and may subsequently lead to increased consumption of power. The issue was eventually fixed by applying a cutting-edge method called public-key encryption. This method entails giving every node in the network a unique set of private and public keys, which increases its flexibility while also lowering the level of difficulty and strengthening reliability [9].

Key Management. The administration, supervision and control of digital keys employed to safeguard sensitive data is known as key management, and it is an essential component of data safety. Wireless networks employ this technique, the use of an obfuscated key functions as a safety precaution. Hidden key creation, dispersion, preservation, modifying, and disposal are all included in the procedure [24]. Symmetric and encryption with public keys techniques must be merged so as to handle the security issues that are present in Internet of Things (IoT) networks.

Secure Routing Protocols. A network's routing protocols are essential to its overall functionality. For this reason, it must be transported securely. The category of protected protocols for routing may be divided into two subcategories: sensors that are wireless network-specific protected and the assessment of potential routing protocol weaknesses, as mentioned by [25].

4.3 Interoperability in Cross-Layer Design

Inconsistencies in communication protocols, disparate data representation, and the intricate integration of security measures are the main causes of interoperability challenges in cross-layer design for Internet of Things devices. Cross-layer design becomes even more complex in IoT devices due to limited assets. A cohesive IoT ecology cannot be developed in the absence of standard practices, and designing for IoT environments is made more difficult by their dynamic nature.

4.4 Feasible Solutions to Interoperability

This problem can be partially resolved via incorporating IoT and cloud services, however in certain cases, such as Fog Computation, interoperability remains a prerequisite. Besides, a lot of businesses leverage interoperability to create distinctive products which are exclusive to one another. By conducting more research in this area and having business components adopt these norms, smart instances involving different gadgets can be created minus the need to fret regarding interoperability.

4.5 Quality of Service (QoS) in Cross-Layer Design

A key difficulty in cross-layer approaches for the Internet of Things (IoT) is successfully overseeing and managing Quality of Service (QoS). Self-driving automobiles and the medical field are two distinct examples of delicate and vital uses for which the current designs fall short of meeting requirements. Achieving seamless communication between layers with unique requirements is complex, leading to potential variations in QoS such as power availability, sensor accuracy, and effectiveness. Usually, the specific hardware design and pertinent applications are used to define and clarify QoS demands.

4.6 Feasible Solutions for Quality of Service (QoS)

A complete QoS solution cannot be provided by a single layer alone to be able to handle Quality of Service (QoS) challenges. Rather, a QoS deploying technique which complies with the criteria for QoS defined and maintained at the application level, cooperation across the link layer and physical layer is required [26]. Maintaining improved Quality of Service (QoS) leads to increased power usage. It is advised to use the Link, Transport, as well as Physical layers in order to facilitate flexible resource utilization and match the allocation of bandwidth alongside the development of the TCP in order to deal with QoS limitations.

5   Cross-Layer Attacks in IoT

Unlike traditional attacks that target a specific layer (e.g., application layer or network layer), cross-layer attacks take advantage of the interactions and dependencies between different layers within an IoT system. These attacks are particularly challenging to defend against because they often involve exploiting weaknesses at the intersection of hardware, software, and communication protocols.

Cross-layer attacks in IoT are a complex and evolving threat landscape that requires a holistic security strategy. Addressing these attacks involves understanding the interplay between different layers of IoT technology and implementing security measures at each layer to protect against potential vulnerabilities and exploits.

5.1 Different Cross-Layer Assault Types

Assaults Directed at the Physical Layer. These attacks target the lowest layer of the IoT stack, exploiting vulnerabilities in the physical components of IoT devices, such as sensors and actuators. Examples include hardware tampering and side-channel assaults.

Assaults at the Network and Transport Layer. These attacks focus on exploiting vulnerabilities in networking and communication protocols, such as attacks on routing protocols, man-in-the-middle schemes, and denial-of-service (DoS) assaults, among others.

Application Layer Attacks. These attacks aim to compromise the application layer of IoT devices, which is where user interfaces and data processing occur. Examples include injection attacks (e.g., SQL injection), malware, and remote code execution.

Hybrid Cross-Layer Attacks. Some attacks combine elements from multiple layers to achieve their objectives. For instance, an attacker might use a network layer vulnerability to gain unauthorized access to the application layer.

5.2 Attack Vectors and Vulnerabilities

Protocol-Level Exploits. Protocol-level exploits in IoT involve vulnerabilities and attacks that target the communication protocols used by IoT devices, which can compromise data integrity and confidentiality. These exploits include techniques like spoofing, manipulation, and Denial-of-Service (DoS) attacks that can disrupt IoT device communication and functionality.

Resource Starvation. Resource starvation exploits in IoT involve malicious activities that deliberately deplete critical resources, such as battery power, memory, or processing capacity, in IoT devices. These attacks can lead to device malfunctions, reduced operational lifespans, and service disruptions.

Privilege Escalation. Privilege escalation exploits in IoT involve malicious activities that aim to gain unauthorized access to higher-level privileges or permissions within IoT systems. Attackers seek to elevate their access rights beyond what is initially granted, potentially enabling them to manipulate or control IoT devices or access sensitive data.

Unauthorized Data Access. Unauthorized data access exploits in IoT involve malicious activities aimed at gaining illicit infiltration to private information stored or communicated by Internet of Things devices, which could result in violation of privacy and data leak. Such attacks often target vulnerabilities in access controls, encryption, or authentication mechanisms, allowing unauthorized parties to obtain confidential information.

6 Techniques for Preventing and Mitigating Cross-Layer Attacks in IoT Devices

The Internet of Things is an interconnected system of constantly interacting items. In addition to exchanging information, these pieces of equipment also frequently broadcast small amounts of data. It is harder to guarantee equipment and information accessibility 24/7 as the amount of data is continually increasing. Authentication, authorization, privacy, accessibility, and non-repudiation are essential criteria for an Internet of Things to be considered a reliable platform, as stated in [27]. Whereas authorization establishes the rights which an authorized party has to carry out activities within the network, authentication seeks to confirm the legitimacy of individuals or gadgets within an IoT system. Information needs to be encoded during its transmission and retention to guard against manipulation and guarantee security. The principle of non-repudiation guarantees that the information was not modified and that its origin is legitimate. It is imperative to act because affecting any one of these security features could result in the IoT system being exploited. A cross-layer safety mechanism emerged to ensure the dependability and security of each unique component of the Internet of Things [28].

6.1 Hardware-Based Security Measures

To prevent cross-layer attacks effectively, hardware-based security measures can be integrated into IoT devices. All stages of the data transmission process, as well as when the data is moving from one device to another, should use security mechanisms [29]. Here are some strategies to prevent cross-layer attacks using hardware-based security measures:

TPM (Trusted Platform Module, also known as ISO/IEC 11889). These are specialized hardware components which provide a secure foundation for IoT devices by securely storing cryptographic keys, certificates, and sensitive data, making it exceptionally challenging for attackers to compromise them. TPMs facilitate secure boot processes, device identity management, and remote attestation, allowing devices to prove their integrity to remote servers. They offer hardware-based random number generation, protect data at rest, and ensure the security of communications between IoT devices and other entities. TPMs establish a hardware-based foundation of trust, facilitating a sequence of trust from hardware to software and enhancing the overall security posture of IoT devices.

HSM (Hardware Security Module or Hardware Cryptographic Modules). With the aim to strengthen IoT security, Hardware Cryptographic Modules are necessary elements. A protected environment is provided by these specific hardware components for safeguarding cryptographic keys, sensitive data, and security operations in IoT devices. HSMs deliver tamper-resistant storage and processing capabilities, ensuring that critical assets remain protected from physical and software-based attacks. IoT applications benefit from HSMs by utilizing them for secure key generation, management, encryption, and authentication processes. By offering robust cryptographic services and secure execution environments, HSMs significantly enhance the confidentiality, integrity, and overall security of IoT deployments.

Secure Boot and Chain of Trust. Secure Boot is a security mechanism in IoT devices that ensures only trusted and digitally signed firmware and software can be loaded and executed during startup, protecting against unauthorized code execution and malware attacks. When embedded software is loaded and the energy source is turned on, envision Secure Boot as a series of verification stages that continuously validate one another. Changing the procedure for booting to cause the device to operate strangely—possibly by running harmful software—is a popular technique for physical device exploitation. An Internet of Things device encrypts its initial set of startup commands and utilizes digital certificates to verify the second set of instructions in order to avoid itself from booting up modified or unsigned programs (Fig. 7).

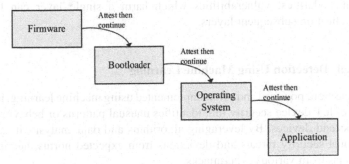

Fig. 7. Secure Boot chain of trust in IoT device [30]

The Chain of Trust extends this security by establishing a hierarchical trust relationship from the hardware level through various software layers, verifying the integrity and authenticity of each layer. Together, Secure Boot and the Chain of Trust create a secure foundation for IoT devices, preventing unauthorized access, and preserving general safety and authenticity of the device's software as well as firmware stack.

6.2 Software-Based Techniques

IoT device safety posture can be considerably improved and weaknesses can be mitigated by using a variety of software procedures, equipment, and tactics. Program-based approaches are essential for avoiding and reducing cross-layer threats. Below is an outline of some particular strategies.

IDS (Security Intrusion Detection System). These systems are designed to monitor network and device activities for signs of unauthorized access or malicious behaviour. A succinct description of the technology is given by Malhotra and others [31] who concentrate on the different types of incidents and oddities and how a sophisticated IDS (intrusion detection system) can detect them. These systems use predefined rules and anomaly detection techniques to identify potential threats in real-time.

Secure Communication Protocols and APIs. Secure communication protocols and Application Programming Interfaces (APIs) are essential in IoT security as they certify the accuracy, reliability, and secrecy of information transferred between IoT gadgets. These protocols employ encryption mechanisms to protect data from eavesdropping, tampering, and unauthorized access.

Access Control and Authentication. Access control and authentication are pivotal aspects of IoT security. They enable the restriction of device and user access to sensitive resources, making certain that approved or permitted entities alone may exchange data with the Internet of Things. By implementing robust access control and authentication mechanisms, IoT deployments can lessen the danger of unapproved entry, protect against intrusions of personal information and uphold the integrity of device ecosystems.

Containerization and Sandboxing. By isolating programs and its assets using containerization modalities, vulnerabilities which harm a single layer can lessen the detrimental effect on subsequent layers.

6.3 Anomaly Detection Using Machine Learning

Anomaly detection, powered and often implemented using machine learning, is a crucial component of IoT device security that identifies unusual patterns or behaviours within IoT networks and devices. By leveraging algorithms and data analysis, it can quickly detect potential security threats and deviations from expected norms, helping protect IoT ecosystems from various cyberattacks.

Behavior-Based Anomaly Detection. Behavior-based anomaly detection in IoT security involves monitoring the normal behavior of IoT devices and networks to identify deviations that may indicate security threats. This approach leverages machine learning and statistical analysis to establish baselines for expected behavior, allowing it to detect unusual activities or patterns in real-time. By continuously assessing device behavior and flagging anomalies, behavior-based anomaly detection helps protect against variety of cyber risks, such as intrusion attempts, virus infections, unauthorized access etc., thus enhancing the overall security of IoT deployments.

Machine Learning Models for Attack Detection. Machine learning models are increasingly utilized in IoT security to detect and mitigate attacks. These models leverage historical data to identify patterns associated with various attack vectors, enabling them to predict and detect suspicious activities in real-time. By continuously learning and adapting to evolving threats, machine learning-based attack detection enhances IoT security by quickly identifying and responding to malicious activities, helping safeguard IoT ecosystems from potential cyber threats.

Big Data Analytics in IoT Security. By evaluating and interpreting enormous amounts of data generated by IoT devices and networks, big data analytics functions as a crucial part in Internet of Things security. It identifies patterns, anomalies, and potential security threats, helping security teams make informed decisions and respond proactively.

7 Simulation Experiment and Performance Matrix

The Contiki-NG and Cooja frameworks is used to carry out the simulation experiment. Contiki-NG is an open-source operating system for the Internet of Things (IoT) tailored for IoT applications. A simulation architecture called Cooja allows individuals to experiment and simulate Internet of Things applications in a virtual environment by integrating with Contiki-NG.

7.1 Objective

The objective of the simulation experiment is to implement and assess an Intrusion Detection System (IDS) and Intrusion Prevention System (IPS) in Contiki-NG and Cooja, addressing cross-layer attacks in IoT devices. The work involved crafting a multi-layer attack scenario, designing a responsive IDS, and simulating preventive actions with the IPS. The goal was to evaluate the systems' effectiveness in a live simulation, refining security measures for IoT devices against cross-layer threats.

7.2 Implementing the Simulation of a Cross-Layer Attack Scenario and Integrating of IDS and IPS

In implementing a cross-layer attack and mitigation methods within Contiki-NG and Cooja, the first step was to design a multi-layer attack scenario to simulate potential threats to IoT devices. A malicious payload was crafted to Simulate real-world conditions, evaluating the effectiveness of the attack in achieving its goals and subsequently testing the payload.

A process was crafted that involved manipulating communication across layers, targeting vulnerabilities in the MAC, network, and transport layers of the IoT architecture.

Subsequently, an Intrusion Detection System (IDS) was integrated into the simulation to monitor and identify anomalous activities. The IDS was designed to detect irregularities in each layer, triggering alerts when suspicious behavior indicative of a cross-layer attack was identified. IDS flags, such as mac_intrusion_detected, network_intrusion_detected, and transport_intrusion_detected, were crucial indicators for potential threats. To address the detected intrusions, an Intrusion Prevention System (IPS) was further implemented which executed specific actions based on the attacked layer. For instance, when a cross-layer attack was identified at the MAC layer, the IPS triggered the drop_mac_packets function, simulating the prevention of malicious packets from reaching the MAC layer. Similarly, the IPS invoked functions like filter_network_packets and mitigate_transport_intrusion to simulate preventive actions at the network and transport layers, respectively (Fig. 8).

Throughout the simulation, the behaviour of the IDS and IPS in response to the crafted cross-layer attack scenarios was closely observed. The logging mechanisms recorded detailed information about intrusion detection and prevention actions, facilitating a comprehensive analysis of the systems' effectiveness.

```
1   #include "contiki.h"
2   #include "net/netstack.h"
3   #include "net/nullnet/nullnet.h"
4   #include "lib/random.h"
5   #include "sys/log.h"
6
7   PROCESS(intrusion_detection_process, "Intrusion Detection Process");
8   AUTOSTART_PROCESSES(&intrusion_detection_process);
9
10  #define PACKET_SIZE 50
11
12  // IDS flags
13  static int mac_intrusion_detected = 0;
14  static int network_intrusion_detected = 0;
15  static int transport_intrusion_detected = 0;
16
17  PROCESS_THREAD(intrusion_detection_process, ev, data)
18  {
19      PROCESS_BEGIN();
20
21      while (1)
22      {
23          // Simulate IoT device behavior
24          simulate_iot_device_behavior();
25
26          // IDS: Check for anomalies in MAC layer
27          if (mac_intrusion_detected) {
28              log_message("MAC layer intrusion detected!");
29              // IPS: Drop or filter packets at the MAC layer
30              drop_mac_packets();
31          } else {
32              // Simulate normal MAC layer operation
33              send_packet_to_mac_layer();
34
```

Fig. 8. Contiki-NG IDS and IPS code snippet

7.3 Network Performance Metrices

Packet Loss and Latency. The attack caused an excessive packet transmission at the MAC layer and also injected some malformed packets at the network layer, this led to increased packet loss and latency, resulting in communication delays and potential retransmissions, affecting the overall network performance.

Throughput Reduction. Congestion and network disruption caused by the attack significantly reduced the throughput within the network. Valid data packets experienced increased delay, some even got dropped due to the network's compromised state (Fig. 9).

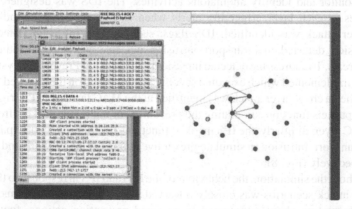

Fig. 9. Malicious Motes Injecting malformed packet in Cooja Simulator

Routing Disruptions. When the malformed packets were injected, it disrupted the routing protocols, leading to routing errors and inconsistencies. This resulted in disrupted connectivity and inefficiencies in packet routing, impacting the overall performance of the network.

Energy Consumption. The continuous attack-induced packet processing, retransmissions, and congestion also increased the energy consumption in devices, affecting their battery life and overall energy efficiency.

7.4 Outcome of the Simulated Experiment

In the simulated scenario, the Intrusion Detection Systems (IDS) and Intrusion Prevention Systems (IPS) played crucial roles in identifying and mitigating the threat. The cross-layer attack, designed to exploit vulnerabilities across multiple protocol stack layers, triggered alerts from the IDS, indicating anomalous or malicious behavior. The IPS then executed preventive measures, such as blocking malicious traffic or applying security policies, effectively thwarting the attack.

8 Evaluation of Mitigation and Prevention Strategies

The evaluation of mitigation strategies in IoT device security is a critical step to assess the effectiveness of measures taken to protect IoT devices from vulnerabilities and threats.

8.1 Performance Metrics

By evaluating these performance metrics, organizations and individuals can comprehensively assess the effectiveness, efficiency, and sustainability of mitigating and preventing cross-layer attacks in IoT devices, thereby making informed decision to enhance the security posture of their IoT ecosystem.

Detection Rate. Detection rate is a type of performance metric in IoT security that measures the ability of security systems to identify and detect security threats accurately. It quantifies the percentage of actual security incidents that the system successfully recognizes and alerts on. A high detection rate indicates a robust security system that effectively identifies and responds to potential threats, enhancing the overall security posture of IoT environments.

The Rate of False Positive. This is an important performance metric used to assess the effectiveness of mitigating cross-layer attacks in IoT devices. It measures the rate at which legitimate activities are incorrectly identified as malicious, and a lower FPR is desirable to reduce false alarms. By minimizing the FPR, IoT security systems can enhance their ability to accurately detect and respond to actual threats while minimizing unnecessary disruptions to normal device operations.

Resource Consumption. Resource consumption is a major performance metric employed in the mitigation of cross-layer attacks in IoT devices. It refers to the amount of computing, memory, and energy resources needed to implement security measures. To mitigate cross-layer attacks effectively, IoT devices must strike a balance between robust security measures and efficient resource utilization, ensuring that security doesn't overly burden the device and compromise its core functionality.

8.2 Experimental Result

Experimental results in IoT security refer to the outcomes of tests, simulations, or assessments conducted to evaluate the effectiveness of various security measures and strategies implemented within an Internet of Things (IoT) environment. These results provide empirical evidence about the performance, reliability, and vulnerabilities of IoT devices and systems under different conditions, including potential cross-layer attacks.

Controlled Testbed Experiments. Controlled testbed experiments are a critical component of assessing mitigation strategies for cross-layer attacks in IoT devices. These experiments involve creating controlled environments to simulate real-world attack scenarios, allowing researchers to evaluate the effectiveness of security measures.

Real-World Deployment Assessments. Real-world deployment assessments within experimental results are essential for evaluating the practical effectiveness of cross-layer attack mitigation strategies in IoT devices. These assessments involve implementing security measures in actual IoT device deployments and monitoring their performance in real-world scenarios.

9 Emerging Approaches

When each and every one of the safety standards have been satisfactorily implemented, a system is deemed secure [32, 33]. The infrastructure must implement diverse mechanism to ensure safety and keep the data confidential and protected both during storage and during dissemination [27].

9.1 Block-Chain-Based Security

Distributed Identity and Access Management. Within the context of Blockchain-based Security, this is an emerging approach to mitigate cross-layer attacks in IoT devices. In order to manage identities and access privileges, it makes use of the technology known as blockchain to create a secure and impenetrable ledger. By decentralizing identity management and access control, this approach reduces the vulnerability of centralized systems, enhancing the security of IoT devices by providing a resilient framework for authentication and authorization across device layers. This also improves trust among devices, and streamlined interoperability, contributing to a more secure and efficient IoT infrastructure (Fig. 10).

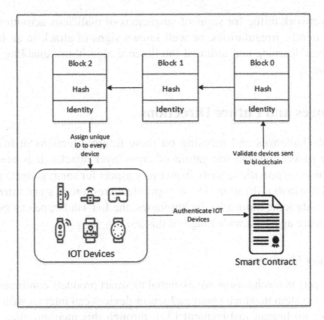

Fig. 10. Identity Management System [34].

Immutable Data Integrity. This is a vital component of Block-chain based Security which ensures data and guarantees that a credible and reliable trail of device information and interactions is made possible via the block chain system, which cannot be changed or interfered with. IoT devices can maintain the integrity of critical data, making it significantly more challenging for attackers to manipulate or compromise.

9.2 The Technologies of Edge and Fog Computing

Security is improved, and attack avenues are decreased, utilizing edge and fog computing techniques. Increased proximity of IoT devices to the handling and evaluation of data is also made possible by this technology. Limiting the susceptibility of sensitive information during transit and minimizing the risk of interception or manipulation. Fog Computing extends this approach by creating a distributed computing environment that can detect and respond to threats at the edge, providing a proactive defense against cross-layer attacks.

Reducing Attack Surface. This involves localizing data processing, implementing stringent access controls, and network segmentation. By processing data closer to IoT devices, sensitive information remains within the device's vicinity, reducing external exposure. Access control mechanisms and network segmentation limit unauthorized access and restrict lateral movement, bolstering security across device layers.

Immediate or Live Threat Detection. This is an emerging proactive approach to prevent and mitigate cross-layer attacks in IoT devices by continuously monitoring device behavior and network traffic for signs of suspicious or malicious activities. It can discover unusual trends, irregularities, or well-known signs of attack in an instant using powerful machine learning and artificial intelligence algorithms, enabling swift action and remediation.

10 Challenges and Future Directions

Addressing the challenges and focusing on these future directions in IoT devices is crucial for the prevention and mitigation of cross-layer attacks. It is now becoming increasingly harder to provide security from every aspect for smart gadgets as a result of unprecedented rise in its utilization [35]. By optimizing resources, standardizing security practices, and embracing innovative technologies, the IoT landscape can become more resilient and secure against a wide range of threats.

10.1 Scalability Concerns

Extensible protection mechanisms are essential as smart products continues to increase quickly. IoT is a system in which smart gadgets or devices can interact with one another through little or no human involvement [32], through this medium, data is collected on a regular basis and delivered to cloud servers for cutting-edge evaluation and decisions aimed at more intelligent device utilization and operation. Therefore, future directions should explore decentralized and distributed security models that can handle the increasing volume of devices while maintaining effectiveness.

10.2 IoT Resource Limitation

It's hard to make IoT devices very secure because they don't have a lot of computing power or memory capacity. We need to develop security techniques for IoT devices in the future that don't consume a lot of computing resources, and we also need to figure out how to improve encryption to work better within these constraints.

10.3 Privacy Implications

Protecting user data and privacy in IoT environments is a significant concern. Exposition of how safety and confidentiality matters are of paramount concern in the Internet of Things. In order to protect the privacy and security requirements created by individuals and businesses, Weber [20]. Emphasized that international laws should adopt a fundamental legal structure.

10.4 Standardization Efforts

Standardization efforts in IoT security can be challenging due to the diverse nature of IoT devices, but they are essential to establish a baseline of security and interoperability. Standardization is the general and the most basic problem that exists in the IoT as there is no fixed standard to follow which makes it hard to adapt a framework to any other framework making it more time consuming and overall reduces the network performance.

11 Research Gap and Findings

This research on mitigation and prevention methods for cross-layer attacks in IoT devices reveals significant gaps. Firstly, there is a lack of a comprehensive cross-layer attack taxonomy tailored to IoT, hindering a systematic understanding of these threats. Secondly, real-world case studies demonstrating the impact of cross-layer attacks in practical IoT scenarios are scarce. Thirdly, interdisciplinary collaboration between hardware, software, and network security experts is insufficient, leading to fragmented solutions. Furthermore, the assessment of the economic feasibility and cost-effectiveness of proposed mitigation methods is often overlooked, hindering their practical implementation. Lastly, there is a need for scalable and standardized security measures while considering ethical and privacy concerns. To create effective security policies for IoT devices and other connected devices, these gaps must be closed, so as to effectively safeguard the growing IoT ecosystem.

12 Conclusion

The Internet of Things (IoT) is a framework in which each physical thing may be uniquely recognized and can send and receive data via a network. Nevertheless, IoT is about more than just gathering data from sensors; it's also about interpreting and securing it. IoT must try to keep attackers from hacking the devices. IoT is about a connected ecosystem where people and things interact to improve the quality of life. It must allow for information sharing while maintaining strict secrecy. This research paper provides a comprehensive examination of cross-layer attacks in IoT devices, highlighting their diverse attack vectors and potential consequences. It offers a critical analysis of existing mitigation and prevention methods, emphasizing their strengths and limitations. Additionally, it explores emerging security strategies such as block chain integration and edge computing to address the evolving landscape of IoT security threats. In conclusion, Improved services and a huge change in the way individuals live and interact will be brought about via IoT technology in subsequent years, Therefore, safeguarding IoT devices against cross-layer attacks is an ongoing challenge that demands collaborative efforts from industry stakeholders, researchers, and policymakers. As IoT continues to shape our interconnected world, the effective mitigation and prevention of cross-layer attacks are essential to ensure the security and reliability of IoT ecosystems.

References

1. Ashton, K.: That "Internet of Things" thing: in the real world things matter more than ideas. RFID J. 1 (2009)
2. Raja, S.P., Raj Kumar, T.D., Raj, V.P.: Internet of things: challenges, issues and applications. J. Circ. Syst. Comput. **27**(12), 1830007 (2018)
3. Khanum, A., et al.: An enhanced security alert system for smart home using IOT. Indonesian J. Electr. Eng. Comput. Sci. (IJEECS) **13**(1), 27–34 (2019). ISSN: 2502-4752, https://doi.org/10.11591/ijeecs.v13.i1

4. Singh, S.: Internet of Things (IoT): security challenges, business opportunities & reference architecture for e-commerce. In: International Conference on Green Computing and Internet of Things (GCIoT), pp. 1577–1581. IEEE (2015)
5. https://www.statista.com/statistics/471264-number-of-connected-devices-worldwide
6. Broadcom, Symantec, Internet Security Threat Report, vol. 24 (2020). https://www.broadcom.com/support/security-center. Accessed 11 Mar 2020
7. Duc, T.N., Son, V.Q.: Performance analysis of anti-attack methods for RPL routing protocol in 6LoWPAN networks. In: International Symposium on Electrical and Electronics Engineering (ISEE) Computer Science, Engineering (2023)
8. Asati, V.K., Pilli, E.S., Vipparthi, S.K., Garg, S., Singhal, S., Pancholi, S.: RMDD: cross layer attack in Internet of Things. In: International Conference on Advances in Computing, Communications and Informatics (ICACCI) (2018)
9. Gajbhiye, A., Sen, D., Bhatt, A., Soni, G.: DPLPLN: detection and prevention from flooding attack in IoT. In: 2020 International Conference on Smart Electronics and Communication (ICOSEC), Computer Science, Published in International Conference, 1 September 2020
10. Granjal, J., Monteiro, E., Sa Silva, J.: Security for the internet of things: a survey of existing protocols and open research issues. IEEE Commun. Surv. Tutorials **17**(3), 1294–1312 (2015)
11. Sicari, S.: Security, privacy and trust in Internet of Things: the road ahead. Comput. Netw. **76**, 146–164 (2015)
12. Fu, B., Xiao, Y., Deng, H.J., Zeng, H.: A survey of cross-layer designs in wireless networks. IEEE Commun. Surv. Tutorials **16**(1), First Quarter 2014, 110–126 (2014)
13. Farooq, M.U.: A critical analysis on the security concerns of Internet of Things (IoT). Int. J. Comput. Appl. **111**(7), 0975 8887 (2015)
14. Vashi, S., Ram, J., Modi, J., Verma, S., Prakash, C.: Internet of Things (IoT) a vision, architectural elements, and security issues. In: International conference on I-SMAC (IoT in Social, Mobile, Analytics and Cloud) (2017)
15. Mahmoud, R.: Internet of Things (IoT) security: current status, challenges and prospective measures. In: 10th International Conference for Internet Technology and Secured Transactions (ICITST) (2015)
16. Bonomi, F., Milito, R., Natarajan, P., Zhu, J.: Fog computing: a platform for internet of things and analytics. In: Bessis, N., Dobre, C. (eds.) Big Data and Internet of Things: A Roadmap for Smart Environments. SCI, vol. 546, pp. 169–186. Springer, Cham (2014). https://doi.org/10.1007/978-3-319-05029-4_7
17. Hinai, S.A., Singh, A.V.: Internet of Things: architecture, security challenges and solutions. In: International Conference on Infocom Technologies and Unmanned Systems (Trends and Future Directions) (ICTUS), pp. 1–4 (2017). https://doi.org/10.1109/ICTUS.2017.8
18. Haddad Pajouh, H., Dehghantanha, A., Parizi, R.M., Aledhari, M., Karimipour, H.: A survey on Internet of Things security: requirements, challenges, and solutions. Internet Things **14**, 100129 (2021)
19. Chen, X., Makki, K., Yen, K., Pissinou, N.: Sensor network security: a survey. IEEE Commun. Surv. Tutorials **11**(2), Second Quarter, 52–73 (2009). https://doi.org/10.1109/SURV.2009.090205
20. Weber, R.H.: Internet of Things-new security and privacy challenges. Comput. Law Secur. Rev. **26**(1), 23–30 (2010)
21. Plageras, A.P., Psannis, K.E., Stergiou, C., Wang, H., Gupta, B.B.: Efficient IoT-based sensor BIG data collection–processing and analysis in smart buildings. Future Gener. Comput. Syst. **82**, 349–357 (2018)
22. Korger, U.: QOS implications of power control and multiuser detection based cross-layer design. EURASIP J. Wirel. Commun. Networking (2011)
23. Golbeck, J., Ziegler, C.-N.: Investigating interactions of trust and interest similarity. Decis. Support Syst. **43**(2), 460–475 (2007)

24. Sicari, S., Rizzardi, A., Grieco, L.A., Coen-Porisini, A.: Security, privacy and trust in internet of things: the road ahead. Computer Networks **76**, 146–164 (2015)
25. Zhang, T., Chiang, M.: Fog and IoT: an overview of research opportunities. IEEE Internet Things J. **3**(6), 854–864 (2016). https://doi.org/10.1109/JIOT.2016.2584538
26. Tian, R., Liang, Y., Tan, X., Li, T.: Overlapping user grouping in IoT oriented massive MIMO systems. IEEE Access **5**, 14177–14186 (2017)
27. Aqeel-ur-Rehman, S.U.R., Khan, I.U., Moiz, M., Hasan, S.: Security and privacy issues in IoT. Int. J. Commun. Netw. Inf. Secur. (IJCNIS) **8**(3), 147–157 (2016)
28. Ahmed, H., Nasr, A., Abdel-Mageid, S., Aslan, H.: A survey of IoT security threats and defenses. Int. J. Adv. Comput. Res. **9**(45), 325–350 (2019)
29. Jing, Q., Vasilakos, A., Wan, J., Lu, J., Qiu, D.: Security of the Internet of Things: perspectives and challenges. Wireless Netw. **20**, 2481–2501 (2014). https://doi.org/10.1007/s11276-014-0761-7
30. Siddiqui, A.S.: Design of secure boot process for reconfigurable architectures (2020)
31. Malhotra: Presents a brief overview of the technology, with a focus on various attacks and anomalies, as well as their detection using an intelligent intrusion detection system (IDS) (2021)
32. Lepakshi, N., Kumar, B., Reddy, A.: Cross layer design in IOT (Internet of Things): issues and challenges. Department of Systems and Computer Engineering, Carleton University (2023)
33. Narula-Tam, A., Macdonald, T., Modiano, E., Servi, L.: A dynamic resource allocation strategy for satellite communications. In: IEEE MILCOM 2004. Military Communications Conference, vol. 3, pp. 1415–1421 (2004)
34. Khatoon, S., Javaid, N.: Blockchain based decentralized scalable identity and access management system for Internet of Things (2019)
35. Patton, M., Gross, E., Chinn, R., Forbis, S., Walker, L., Chen, H.: Uninvited connections: a study of vulnerable devices on the Internet of Things (IoT), pp. 232–235 (2014). https://doi.org/10.1109/JISIC.2014.43

Improving Copy-Move Forgery Detection: An Investigation into Techniques Based on Blocks and Key Points

Jaynesh H. Desai(✉) Ⓘ and Sanjay H. Buch Ⓘ

Bhagwan Mahavir College of Computer Application, BMU, Surat, Gujarat, India
jaydesai84@gmail.com

Abstract. Digital image forgery, especially in the form of "Copy-Move Forgery" a prevalent form of image alteration that threatens the authenticity of digital visual content. To combat this challenge, this research conducts a thorough comparative analysis of three prominent techniques for detecting Copy-Move Forgery: "Principal Component Analysis (PCA)", "Discrete Cosine Transform (DCT)", and "Scale-Invariant Feature Transform" combined with "Dyadic Wavelet Transform" (SIFT-DyWT). The PCA-based method employs eigenvectors of image patches to identify copied regions, while DCT leverages frequency domain information to detect duplicated areas. SIFT-DyWT combines the powerful SIFT algorithm with Dyadic Wavelet Transform to extract and match invariant features for forgery detection. Each technique is implemented and evaluated on a diverse dataset of manipulated images, with performance metrics including precision, recall, and F1-score being assessed. Efficiency is a crucial factor, particularly for real-time applications. As a result, these strategies' computational complexity is also examined. This aspect is essential for aiding researchers and practitioners in selecting the most suitable forgery detection method based on their specific application requirements. In conclusion, this research contributes significantly to the field of image forensics by presenting a comprehensive comparison of PCA, DCT, and SIFT-DyWT for Copy-Move Forgery detection. These discoveries offer valuable understandings regarding the weaknesses and strengths of each method, facilitating the development of more robust and efficient forgery detection tools. Experimented result shows the DyWT and SIFT combination exhibit superior performance, achieving an accuracy of 89.56%. This outperforms both DCT, with an accuracy of 86.55%, and PCA, with an accuracy of 83.96%. Ultimately, this research enhances the security and reliability of digital visual content in an era where image manipulation and forgery are prevalent concerns.

Keywords: Key Point-Based · Block-Based · DCT · PCA · SIFT · DyWT · Forgery Detection

1 Introduction

In today's digital era, the ubiquity of powerful image editing tools and the ease with which visual content can be manipulated have given rise to a pressing concern: the reliability and authenticity of digital images [1]. As images serve as a potent means of

S. Rajagopal et al. (Eds.): ASCIS 2023, CCIS 2039, pp. 114–130, 2024.
https://doi.org/10.1007/978-3-031-59100-6_10

communication and documentation in various domains, including journalism, forensics, and entertainment, the potential for abuse through image forgery poses a formidable threat to trust, accountability, and the truth itself. Among the myriad techniques employed by digital forgers, one insidious method appears large – "Copy-Move Forgery".

Copy Move Forgery, a deceptive form of image manipulation, involves duplicating a portion of an image and pasting it elsewhere within the same image demonstrated in (see Fig. 1).

(a)   (b)

Fig. 1. (a) Original Image (b) Forged Image [2].

The intent is often to deceive viewers by creating the illusion of multiple similar objects or elements within a scene, thus compromising the authenticity of the entire image. Detecting Copy-Move Forgery has become an imperative task in the realm of digital image forensics, one that calls for advanced and robust detection methodologies.

Image forgery encompasses a spectrum of techniques, falling into two broad categories: malicious and non-malicious attacks. Malicious attacks are aimed at enhancing images or optimizing their memory usage, while non-malicious attacks are employed to alter an image's intended meaning. The classification of "Copy Move Forgery" finding techniques as below (see Fig. 2).

As a part of our research the complicated site in Copy-Move Forgery detection, focusing on a rigorous comparative analysis of three prominent techniques through experimental implementation: "Principal Component Analysis" (PCA), "Discrete Cosine Transform" (DCT), and the amalgamation of "Scale-Invariant Feature Transform" (SIFT) with "Dyadic Wavelet Transform" (DyWT). These techniques represent a spectrum of approaches, each leveraging unique principles for forgery detection.

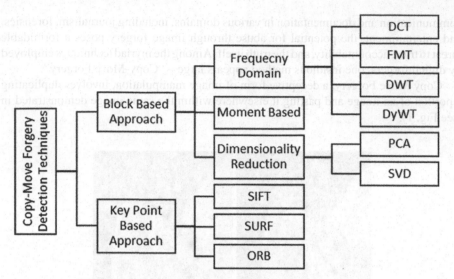

Fig. 2. Category of Copy-Move forgery detection techniques.

2 Literature Review

In the realm of image forensics, the detection of copy-move forgery has been a subject of extensive research, employing various techniques to enhance accuracy and efficiency. Ranjani et al. [4] explored the utilization of Discrete Cosine Transform (DCT) and Inverse DCT through a column and row decrease method. While their approach showcased promising results in identifying duplicated regions within images, a notable drawback arises in terms of significant computational intricacy. The computational burden, characterized by both time and expense considerations, poses challenges for real-time applications and resource-constrained environments.

Pandey et al. [3], on the other hand, delved into the application of Scale-Invariant Feature Transform (SIFT) and Speeded-Up Robust Features (SURF) in copy-move forgery detection. Although their technique demonstrated effectiveness in detecting singular instances of cloning, it exhibited limitations when confronted with more complex scenarios involving multiple instances of copied segments with intricate textures or complex backgrounds. The efficacy of SIFT and Speeded up robust features (SURF), while notable in certain contexts, reveals a vulnerability in handling diverse and challenging forgery scenarios.

In another study, Li et al. [5] explored the application of Polar Harmonics Transform for copy-move forgery detection. While their approach offered a unique perspective, introducing polar harmonics as a basis for analysis, the technique exhibited lags in execution. The computational delays introduce challenges in achieving real-time detection, a crucial aspect in forensic applications where timely identification of manipulated content is paramount. Additionally, the method led to the occurrence of false positives, undermining the reliability of the detection outcomes. The presence of false positives raises concerns about the precision of the technique, as it may incorrectly flag authentic content as forged, potentially leading to erroneous conclusions in forensic investigations.

According to Younis Abdalla et al. [13], one such solution is the Deep convolution training algorithms. When it comes to handling image forgeries produced by generative adversarial networks (GANs), these have proven to be very successful. By using this kind of technique, the image is changed to the point where it looks just like the original and is almost impossible for the untrained human eye to recognize as a fake. Applying a fusion processing framework made up of an adversarial model and a deep convolutional model, the current study looks into copy-move forgery detection.

According to Ibrahim A. Zedan et al. [14], the discipline of passive/blind visual forensics is now conducting intensive research on copy-move fraud detection. Without a doubt, throughout the past 20 years, conventional techniques—particularly those centered on key points—have advanced forgery detection. However, there are a number of issues with both conventional approaches and CMFD procedures in general. As a result, more and more strategies are using deep learning for forgery detection.

Several types of image forgeries and their detection methods have been studied by Abhishek Kashyap et al. [15]; mainly focused on pixel-based image forgery detection methods. Since the copied portion came from the original image, its fundamental characteristics—noise, color, and texture—remain unchanged and complicate the recognition process. In the Copy move region, DWT and SIFT methods are identified.

Toqeer Mahmood et al. [16], images should first be split into overlapping square blocks, with DCT components being used as the block representations, in order to detect copy-move forgery attacks. Owing to the high dimensionality of the feature space, a reduced dimensional feature vector representation is achieved through the application of Gaussian RBF kernel PCA, which also enhances feature matching efficiency. To assess the suggested approach against the state of the art, numerous experiments are carried out.

Image forgery proposed by Rani Susan Oommen et al. [17] focuses primarily on copy-move forgery and includes a brief overview of different copy-move detection algorithms. Copy-move forgery detection techniques include block-based, key-point based, and hybrid approaches. It is observed that block-based techniques outperform keypoint-based techniques in terms of efficiency. Numerous hybrid strategies demonstrate enhanced detection performance.

The author Ashima Gupta et al. [18] clarified A copy-move forgery can be used to add more details that lead to the forgery or to conceal an image entity. Dependability of the image is lost in both scenarios. While there are many benefits to this technology, it can also be a deceptive tool for concealing evidence and facts. This method uses the Discrete Cosine Transform (DCT) to detect region duplication forgery. After splitting the image into overlaid blocks, we look for any duplicate blocks.

Zhi Zhang et al. [19] have proposed two classical models of copy-move forgery are reviewed, and two frameworks of copy-move forgery detection (CMFD) methods are summarized. Then, massive CMFD methods are mainly divided into two types to retrospect the development process of CMFD technologies, including block-based and keypoint-based.

According to Gurmeet Kaur Sain et al. [20], image forensics is a real-world issue, and an effective forgery detection system needs to satisfy practical specifications. SIFT and SURF, two feature descriptor-based algorithms, are applied in tandem in parallel.

These algorithms rely on descriptors of texture and color. These two algorithms are designed to extract features from digital images, and their matching process determines whether or not the image is forged.

Ritu Agarwal et al.'s proposal [21], copy-move forgery involves the same source and target images as well as several properties, such as color and texture, of the spliced portion that match the original image. As a result, it gets even harder to spot this kind of fraud. Methods like noise addition, compression, and transformation are employed to further impede the identification of a forged image. The state-of-the-art CMFD techniques covered in this paper are block-based and keypoint-based.

In the area of blind image forensics, a common type of forgery known as copy-move forgery is frequently detected. Malviyaa et al. [22] have provided information on this process. This type of forgery introduces pixel-by-pixel inconsistency into the manipulated image because the forged region is part of the same image. Based on a method for extracting features from images for image retrieval to detect forgeries. Technique makes use of an ACC that hasn't been utilized to detect copy-move forgeries. Furthermore, it is resilient to changes in scale, translation, and rotation. When used in conjunction with the L1 norm, the straightforward and low-complexity feature extraction scheme ACC can effectively identify multiple copy-move forgeries within a single image.

In order to identify a copy-move forgery in digital media, Loai Alamro et al. [23] describe the combination of two feature extraction techniques: DWT and Speeded Up Robust Features. Among the most common methods of tempering digital images is copy-move, which involves copying and pasting one or more portions of the image to a new location. SURF is better at extracting the important features from an image than DWT at reducing the image's dimensions. Images in BMP and JPG formats, both authentic and fake, were used to test the technique.

Copy-move forgery is used to duplicate a portion of an image, as explained by Fattahi et al. [24]. This paper presents a Scale-Invariant Feature Transform (SIFT) algorithm-based method for detecting copy-move forgery. The similarity between key points is measured using the spearman relationship and the ward clustering algorithm, which also helps to improve the accuracy of fraud detection. This technique is unaffected by shifts in rotation, scale, deformation, or light.

The approach was put forth by Mona F. Mohamed Mursi et al. [25] and explains how it can be used to identify and pinpoint tampered areas of various sizes and forms. Moreover, neither the image nor the manipulation operations performed on it require any prior knowledge when using our method. Technique that combines DBSCAN clustering with SIFT + PCA is presented. The high dimensional space in which the image feature descriptors that SIFT extracted can be found can be efficiently reduced through PCA.

Despite the diverse approaches explored by these researchers, the demerits associated with each technique underscore the ongoing challenges in achieving a comprehensive and reliable copy-move forgery detection system. The choice of a suitable technique depends not only on its ability to accurately identify manipulated regions but also on considerations of computational efficiency, applicability to diverse forgery scenarios, and minimization of false positives.

As the field of copy-move forgery detection advances, future research endeavors may focus on mitigating the demerits identified in these studies. This could involve the development of hybrid techniques that leverage the strengths of multiple approaches or the refinement of existing methods to enhance their robustness and efficiency. Additionally, addressing the computational complexities associated with these techniques is crucial for enabling their practical implementation in real-time applications and resource-constrained environments.

In conclusion, the exploration of techniques such as DCT, SIFT, SURF, and Polar Harmonics Transform in copy-move forgery detection has provided valuable insights into the strengths and limitations of each approach. The challenges identified pave the way for continued research efforts aimed at refining existing methods and developing innovative solutions to bolster the effectiveness of copy-move forgery detection in diverse and dynamic forensic scenarios.

Our objective is to comprehensively evaluate the effectiveness, computational efficiency, and adaptability of these methodologies to varying forgery scenarios. As the battle against digital image forgery unfolds in real-time applications, the need for swift and accurate detection tools becomes increasingly crucial. By scrutinizing the intricacies of PCA, DCT, and SIFT-DyWT, we endeavor to provide not only a deeper understanding of their inner workings but also practical insights to assist researchers, practitioners, and forensic investigators in the relentless pursuit of safeguarding the veracity and reliability of digital visual content in an era where the line between truth and deception is ever more finely drawn. Table 1 shows a comparative overview of various approaches used to detect copy-move forgery, illustrating the range of techniques employed and their respective outcomes.

Table 1. Various Techniques to identify Copy-Move Forgery area with Demerits.

Authors	Techniques Used	Demerits
Ranjani et al. [4]	DCT and Inverse DCT by column and row Decrease method	Significant computational intricacy in terms of time and expense
Pandey et al. [3]	SIFT and SURF	Less effective when dealing with multiple instances of cloning, copied segments with intricate textures, or complex backgrounds
Li et al. [5]	Polar Harmonics Transform	Lags in execution and leads to the occurrence of false positives
Shiva kumar et al. [10]	SIFT, SURF, and Harris for triangles blocks	Ineffective in producing accurate similarity results and fails to detect
Mahdian & Saic [7]	Blur Invariant Feature (BLUR)	The high computation time of the algorithm
Zhang et al. [8]	Discrete Wavelet Transform (DWT)	More noisy and compressed image

(continued)

Table 1. (*continued*)

Authors	Techniques Used	Demerits
Ghorbani et al. [11]	DCT-DWT	Ineffective when applied to heavily compressed images and images of low quality
Huang et al. [9]	SIFT	The time complexity is high, and it struggles to efficiently identify false results
Huynh-Kha et al. [6]	DWT and feature extraction	Outcomes for rotational transformations does not up to sufficient mark
Younis Abdalla et al. [13]	SIFT	Accuracy rate low and high computational cost
Ibrahim A. Zedan et. al [14]	SIFT, DCT	Forged Region would be Discriminating from the source area
Abhishek Kashyap et al. [15]	DCT, DWT	Certain algorithms are not practical for determining the true forged region
Toqeer Mahmood et al. [16]	DCT, PCA	Ineffective in identifying numerous copy-move forgeries
Rani Susan et al. [17]	DCT	Some of the image is hard to detect forge region
Ashima Gupta et al. [18]	DCT, PCA	Archive low accuracy
Zhi Zhang et al. [19]	SIFT, SURF	Not accurate result in Low Resolution Image
Kaur Sain et al. [20]	SIFT, SURF, DWT	Excessive computational complexity
Ritu Agarwal et al. [21]	DCT, SIFT	Excessive computational complexity & cost
Malviya et al. [22]	Pixel based	minimally complex extraction method
Loai Alamro et al. [23]	DWT, SURF	Not resistant to geometrical changes
A. Fattahi et al. [24]	SIFT	Using an algorithm, one can calculate the correct identifying with the least amount of error

3   Experimental Work

3.1   USING DCT Algorithm

The discrete cosine transform (DCT) is a technique that represents an image by summarizing its sinusoidal components with varying amplitudes and frequencies. To compute the 2D discrete cosine transform (DCT) of an image, the dct2 function is employed. One key characteristic of the DCT is that, for a typical image, the majority of its visually significant information can be captured by just a few of the DCT coefficients. This property makes the DCT a popular choice for image compression. For example, the widely used JPEG image compression standard relies on the DCT as its fundamental processing step. The term "JPEG" is derived from the Joint Photographic Experts Group, which developed this standard. The subsequent description relates to the 2D DCT of a matrix A with dimensions M-by-N.

$$B_{pq} = a_p a_q \sum_{m=0}^{M-1} \sum_{m=0}^{M-1} A_{mn} cos \frac{\pi(2m+1)}{2M} cos \frac{\pi(2n+1)}{2N}, \quad \begin{array}{l} 0 \leq p \leq M-1 \\ 0 \leq q \leq N-1 \end{array}$$
$$a_p = \begin{cases} 1/\sqrt{M}, & p = 0 \\ \sqrt{2/M}, & 1 \leq p \leq M-1 \end{cases} a_q = \begin{cases} 1/\sqrt{N}, & q = 0 \\ \sqrt{2/N}, & 1 \leq q \leq N-1 \end{cases} \quad (1)$$

The Bpq values in (Eq. 1) are referred to as the DCT coefficients of A. In MATLAB, In MATLAB®, the reason elements in matrices A(1,1) and B(1,1) match with A00 and B00 is because MATLAB® uses 1-based indexing for matrix elements, as opposed to starting from 0.

Experiment Result Using DCT
Figure 3 shows (a) Original Image, (b) Gray scale, (c) Real Mask, (d) DCT of the investigated framework results in Prediction Mask Detection.

| (a) | (b) | (c) | (d) |

Fig. 3. A) Original Image, (b) Gray Scale, (c) Real Mask, (d) Prediction Mask Detection Result by DCT

A comparison of the time it takes to execute a process when the block size is set to 4x4, using the Discrete Cosine Transform (DCT) Showing in Table 2.

As presented in Table 2, the execution time reflects the time needed for the algorithm to process each image size. Generally, larger images require more processing time, evident from the increasing execution time values. For instance, a 160×120 image takes 58.2 s, while a 208×144 image takes 93.2 s. This implies that the algorithm's

Table 2. Average Execution time and Detection result based on different image size.

Image size	Average Detection result	Time Execute (MEX function) (In seconds)	Time Execute (In seconds)
160x120	100%	10.85	58.2
174x132	99.9%	16.68	82.88
128x128	99%	3.96	21.86
208x144	70%	23.07	93.2
208x144	70%	23.07	93.2

computational complexity increases with image size. The use of the MEX function consistently results in lower execution times compared to the overall execution time, indicating that the MEX function enhances the algorithm's performance. This reduction in execution time suggests that the MEX function leverages compiled code or other optimizations to expedite processing.

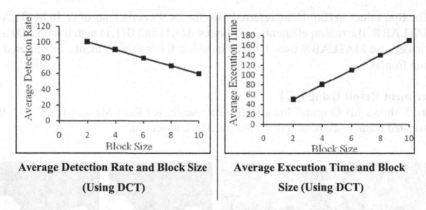

Average Detection Rate and Block Size (Using DCT)   Average Execution Time and Block Size (Using DCT)

Fig. 4. Detection Rate and execution time of DCT algorithm based on block size.

Figure 4 shows variations in average detection results across different image sizes, ranging from 70% to 100%. This indicates that the algorithm may be more precise when applied to smaller images (e.g., 160 × 120 and 174 c 132) compared to larger ones (e.g., 208 × 144).

Above graph illustrates that as the size of block increases, the effectiveness of correctly identifying manipulated images decreases. Therefore, it is essential to maintain a modest block size to accurately detect counterfeit images. Additionally, it demonstrates that recognizing forged portions of an image takes more time on average as the block size increases.

In summary, the provided data offers insights into the accurateness of copy move image forgery detection across different image sizes and its execution performance. It underscores the trade- off between detection accuracy and execution time, where larger images may demand more computational resources but could lead to slightly lower detection rates.

3.2 USING PCA Algorithm

This Python script employs an overlapping blocks method to identify instances of copy-move manipulation in digital images. It utilizes two customized algorithms: first, the Duplicate Image Region Detection technique, as described in the paper "Exposing Digital Forgeries by Detecting Principal Component Analysis," which is a fast and flexible approach for detecting digital image attacks but is susceptible to post-region similarity and image noise issues as explained in the mentioned research. The second detection algorithm is adapted from "**Robust Detection of Region-Duplication Forgery in Digital Images.**" This method is more resilient but slower, yielding somewhat unpredictable results. However, it is believed to be robust against noise and the post-region duplication process.

The developed model has been put to the test using the Test Data Set to gauge how well it works and how accurate it is in predicting the outcome. The model has also been tested on a custom dataset of up to 50 images, with one experiment's result appearing in Fig. 5 as (a) Original Image (b) Forged Image (c) Prediction Boundary Detection.

Data Collection and Statistics: The Test dataset is taken from: [12].

Experiment Result Using PCA:

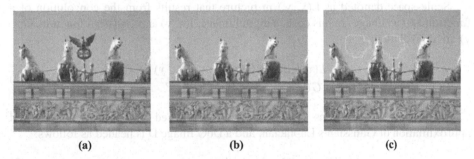

| (a) | (b) | (c) |

Fig. 5. (a) Original Image (b) Forged Image, (c) Prediction Boundary Detection by PCA

The Summary of research obtain through experiments are described in Table 3 which measure in accuracy and similarity of real image dataset, test image dataset and custom dataset.

Based on the findings, it can be concluded that PCA outperforms DCT in terms of compression rates and overall effectiveness. This conclusion is supported by the fact that PCA attained a higher Peak Signal-to-Noise Ratio (PSNR).

Table 3. Detection Matrices based on Accuracy and Similarity in PCA parameters.

Scenario	Metrics	Result
Real image	Accuracy (%)	100.00
	Similarity (%)	100.00
copy-move From Test Dataset (512x512 Pixels)	Accuracy (%)	83.00
	Similarity (%)	99.60
copy-move from the Custom dataset from internet	Accuracy (%)	56.00
	Similarity (%)	96.47

3.3 USING SIFT and DyWT

There are several methods available to look into the (CMFD) problem. The majority of the introduced feature extraction algorithms frequently involve 2 steps: The first step is the detection of centralized interest points, and the second step is the creation of reliable local descriptors that are invariant in orientation and scaling. The SIFT technique converts an image's data into regional feature vectors called SIFT descriptors. The geometric rotation and scaling of these traits can be continuously changed. This algorithm's three main steps are as follows:

1. **Scale Space Extrema Detection**

   Scale-space denoted as $L(x, y,)$ in picture that results from the convolution of a function and an image. In this case, a digital image, $I(x, y)$ and Gaussian function, $G(x, y)$ are convolution:

$$L(x, y, \sigma) = G(x, y, \sigma) * I(x, y)$$
$$G(x, y, \sigma) = \frac{1}{2\pi\sigma^2} e^{-x^2+y^2/2\sigma^2} \tag{2}$$

   Difference of Gaussians (DoG) in (Eq. 2) is used to optimise a computed approximation of Gaussian's Laplacian, and a DoG Image D is headed as follows:

$$D(x, y, \sigma) = L(x, y, k\sigma) - L(x, y, \sigma) \tag{3}$$

   The initial digital image denoted as $I(x, y)$, is convolutioned with the Gaussian blur denoted as $G(x, y, k)$, to get $L(x, y, k)$.

2.

Keypoint Localization

The extrema of the image are where the main focal points are. When the major points are uncertain over image variation, it is necessary to reject the points that cross picture edges and those that stand out due to poor contrast in order to select the main point from image extrema. Expansion of the scale-space function which is denoted as D(x,y), as in (Eq. 4), the sample point is moved from the origin:

$$D(x) = D + \frac{\partial D^T}{\partial x}x + \frac{1}{2}x^T\frac{\partial^2 D}{\partial^2}x \tag{4}$$

3. Key point Descriptor Generation

$$m(x, y) = (L(x + 1, y) - L(x - 1, y))^2 + \left((L(x, y + 1) - L(x, y - 1))^2\right)^{\frac{1}{2}}$$
$$\theta(x, y) = tan^{-1}\left(\frac{L(x,y+1)-L(x,y-1)}{L(x+1,y)-L(x-1,y)}\right) \tag{5}$$

For every descriptor, a feature vector consisting of 128 elements is generated. This vector encompasses the orientation histogram values in both the image plane and scale space, achieved through a grid of 4x4 histograms, each with 8 orientation bins. These outcomes are encapsulated in a feature vector containing $4 \times 4 \times 8 = 128$ elements.

— Step Taken in Algorithm=>>

Step 1 --- Input Forged as well as original images to our framework.

Image Size: 512 X 512 Pixels Image Type: PNG

Step 2 --- Apply DyWT to find Forged image.

Step 3 --- Feature extraction using SIFT.

Step 4 --- Detect Forged means copy move image.

Experiment Result using SIFT and DyWT algorithm shown in Fig. 6 as labelled (a). Forged Image, (b). Apply DyWT, (c). Feature extraction SIFT, (d). Detect Forgery Result by SIFT Feature Matching.

length of original keypoint = 1734, LEN of kp in g2nn = 141, table = 512, Table1 = 512, Table2 = 512, cluster1.size = 19, cluster2.size = 17, matches found in clusters = 46.

Results for two distinct datasets, a "Test Dataset" and a "Custom Dataset," are presented in the example scenario in Table 4. False Positive Rate (FPR), True Positive Rate (TPR), and processing time are among the parameters supplied for each dataset. These findings imply that the "Test Dataset" performs better than the "Custom Dataset" in terminology of FPR and TPR. The processing time for the "Custom Dataset" also takes a lot longer than it does for the Test Dataset.

(a)   (b)

(c)   (d)

Fig. 6. (a). Tempered Image (b) Apply DyWT, (c). Feature extraction SIFT, (d). Detect Forgery Result by SIFT Feature Matching

Table 4. Detection Matrices based on TPR and FPR, Time

Scenario	Metrics	Result
Test Dataset (512x512 Pixels)	TPR (%)	85.09
	FPR (%)	9.09
	Time (Mins)	16.15
Custom dataset	TPR (%)	71.69
	FPR (%)	10.83
	Time (Mins)	1.15.51

4 Experimental Result Comparison

For the purpose of determining whether or not an image has been altered, we are concentrating on three key performance metrics: precision, recall, and accuracy at the image level. Table 5 lists some of the significant measures taking the image level into account.

Table 5. Evaluation Measures Taken

Evaluation Measure	Description
True Positive (TP)	Images correctly detected as Tempered
False Positive (FP)	Images falsely detected as Tempered
False Negative (FN)	Images falsely missed but are actually Tempered
False Positive (FP)	Images falsely missed but are actually Tempered
Accuracy	Overall model accuracy, representing the measurement of correct predictions
Recall	the proportion of real positive instances among all true positive
Precision	the proportion of actual positive predictions among all positive

Precision signifies the likelihood of correctly identifying a forged area, while recall indicates the possibility of detecting a forged image, which could be either genuinely forged or falsely generated. Recall is also referred to as True Positive.

$$\text{Accuracy (all correct / all)} = TP + TN / TP + TN + FP + FN \qquad (6)$$

$$\text{Precision} = TP / (TP + FP) \qquad (7)$$

$$\text{Recall} = TP / (TP + FN) \qquad (8)$$

DCT, PCA, DyWT, and SIFT are three distinct models that are compared in Table 6. The metrics Recall, Precision, Accuracy, True Positive Rate (TPR), and False Positive Rate (FPR) are used to evaluate each model. These metrics are also shown in Fig. 7.

Table 6. Evaluation Measures of Different Existing Research Models with Proposed Model

	Precision	Recall	TPR	FPR	Accuracy
DCT	87.35%	77.45%	76.23%	11.12%	86.55%
PCA	85.08%	79.84%	77.09%	9.99%	83.96%
DyWT and SIFT	87.78%	80.45%	78.69%	9.09%	89.56%

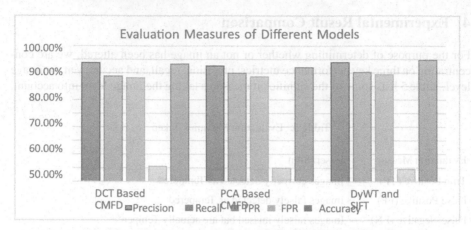

Fig. 7. Evaluation Measures of Different Models

5 Conclusion

In conclusion, our inclusive comparative analysis of "Copy-Move Forgery" finding techniques, including "Discrete Cosine Transform" (DCT), "Principal Component Analysis" (PCA), and the combination of "Scale-Invariant Feature Transform" with "Dyadic Wavelet Transform" (SIFT-DyWT), has yielded valuable insights into their respective strengths and weaknesses.

DCT demonstrated a commendable level of precision but fell slightly short in recall and overall accuracy compared to the other methods. PCA, on the other hand, exhibited a balanced performance in terms of recall and precision but lagged behind in accuracy. Notably, SIFT- Dywt emerged as the top performer in terms of accuracy, recall, and precision as illustrated in Table 6. Making it a robust choice for "Copy-Move Forgery Detection".

Furthermore, when considering the True Positive Rate (TPR) and False Positive Rate (FPR), SIFT-Dywt maintained an advantageous balance, effectively identifying forged regions while keeping false alarms to a minimum. This characteristic is especially important in real-world applications where both accurate detection and efficiency are paramount.

While each technique has its merits, the choice of the most suitable method should depend on the specific requirements of the application at hand. DCT may be preferred when precision is of utmost importance, whereas PCA may find utility in scenarios where a balance between precision and recall is desired. SIFT-Dywt, with its strong all-round performance, is well-suited for applications demanding high accuracy and reliability in Copy-Move Forgery detection.

6 Future Scope

The future of copy-move forgery detection research holds promising avenues for advancements that address the identified challenges. One potential direction for future exploration involves the development of hybrid techniques that integrate the strengths of multiple approaches to create more robust and versatile detection systems. Combining the efficiency of DCT-based methods with the contextual understanding provided by feature-based techniques like SIFT and SURF could yield more accurate and adaptable solutions.

Furthermore, the integration of machine learning and deep learning methodologies presents an exciting frontier for enhancing forgery detection capabilities. Training models on diverse datasets can empower algorithms to learn complex patterns, improving their ability to discern manipulated content in varying contexts. This approach holds the potential to overcome the limitations associated with intricate textures, complex backgrounds, and other challenges identified in current techniques.

Addressing the computational intricacies remains a crucial aspect of future research. Streamlining algorithms and optimizing their efficiency will be essential for the practical implementation of forgery detection in real-time applications and resource-constrained environments. Exploring parallel computing, hardware acceleration, and other optimization strategies can contribute to making these techniques more accessible and feasible in a broader range of settings.

Additionally, the ongoing evolution of image processing technologies and the advent of new forensic tools may offer opportunities to refine existing techniques and develop innovative approaches. Collaborative efforts between researchers, industry professionals, and forensic experts can facilitate the integration of cutting-edge technologies into the field, ensuring that copy-move forgery detection methods remain at the forefront of forensic science.

References

1. Farid H.: Image forgery detection: a survey. IEEE Signal Process. Mag. **26**(2), 16–25 (2009)
2. Khuspe K., Mane V: Robust image forgery localization and recognition in copy-move using bag of features and SVM. In: IEEE International Conference on Communication, Information Computing Technology (ICCICT), pp. 1–5 (2015)
3. Pandey, R.C., Singh, S.K., Shukla, K.K.: Passive copy-move forgery detection in videos. In: Proceedings of 2014 International Conference on Computer and Communication Technology (ICCCT), pp. 301–306, IEEE, (2014)
4. Ranjani, M.B., Poovendran, R.: Image duplication copy-move forgery detection using discrete cosine transforms method. Int. J. Appl. Eng. Res. **11**(4), 2671–2674 (2016)
5. Li L., Li S., Wang J.: Copy-move forgery detection based on PHT. In: Proceedings of 2012 World Congress on Information and Communication Technologies, pp. 1061–1065 IEEE (November 2012)
6. Huynh-Kha T., Le-Tien T., Ha-Viet-Uyen S., Huynh-Van K.: The efficiency of applying DWT and feature extraction into copy-move images detection. In: International Conference on Advanced Technologies for Communications (ATC), Ho Chi Minh City, Vietnam, pp. 44–49 (2015)
7. Mahdian, B., Saic, S.: Detection of copy–move forgery using a method based on blur moment invariants. Forensic Sci. Int. **171**(2–3), 180–189 (2007)
8. Zhang J., Feng Z., Su Y.: A new approach for detecting copy-move forgery in digital images. In: Proceedings of 2008 11th IEEE Singapore International Conference on Communication Systems, pp. 362–366. IEEE (November 2008)

9. Huang H., Guo W., Zhang Y.: Detection of copy-move forgery in digital images using SIFT algorithm, In: Proceedings of 2008 IEEE Pacific-Asia Workshop on Computational Intelligence and Industrial Application, vol. 2, pp. 272–276. IEEE (December 2008)

10. Shivakumar B.L., et al.: Detection of region duplication forgery in digital images using SURFInt. J. Comput. Sci. Issues (2011)

11. Ghorbani M., Firouzmand M., Faraahi A.: DWT-DCT (QCD) based copy-move image forgery detection. In: Proceedings of 2011 18th International Conference on Systems, Signals and Image Processing, pp. 1–4. IEEE (June 2011)

12. https://www5.cs.fau.de/research/data/image-manipulation

13. Abdalla, Y., Tariq Iqbal, M., Shehata, M.: Copy-move forgery detection and localization using a generative adversarial network and convolutional neural-network. Inform. (Switzerland) **10**(9) (2019)

14. Zedan, I.A., Soliman, M.M., Elsayed, K.M., Onsi, H.M.: Copy move forgery detection techniques: a comprehensive survey of challenges and future directions. (IJACSA) Inter. J. Adv. Comput. Sci. Appli. **12**(7) (2021)

15. Abhishek, K., Rajesh, P., Megha, A., Hari, G.: An Evaluation of digital image forgery detection approaches. Int. J. Appl. Eng. Res. **12**, 4747–4758 (2017)

16. Mahmood, T., Nawaz, T., Irtaza, A., Ashraf, R., Shah, M., Mahmood, M. T.: Copy-move forgery detection technique for forensic analysis in digital images. math. Problems Eng. (2016)

17. Oommen, R., Jayamohan, M., Sruthy, S.: A survey of copy-move forgery detection techniques for digital images. Inter. J. Innovat. Eng. Technol. **5**(2), 419–426 (2015)

18. Gupta, A., Saxena, N., Vasistha, S.K.: Detecting copy move forgery using DCT. Inter. J. Sci. Res. Publicat. **3**(5) (May 2013)

19. Zhang, Z., Wang, C., Zhou, X.: A survey on passive image copy-move forgery detection. J. Inform. Process. Syst. **14**(1), 6–31 (2018)

20. Kaur, S.G., Mahajan, M.: Improvement in copy -move forgery detection using hybrid approach. Inter. J. Mod. Educ. Comput. Sci. **8**(12), 56–63 (2016)

21. Agarwal Ritu, Verma Om: An efficient copy move forgery detection using deep learning feature extraction and matching algorithm. Multimedia Tools Appli. **79** (2020). https://doi.org/10.1007/s11042-019-08495-z

22. Malviyaa, A.V., Ladhake, S.A.: Copy-move forgery detection using block-matching algorithms. In: Peer-review under responsibility of the Organizing Committee of ICCCV (2016)

23. Alamro, L., Yusoff, N.: Copy-move forgery detection using integrated DWT and SURF. Journal of Telecommunication. Electr. Comput. Eng. **9**(1–2), 67–71 (2017)

24. Fattahi, A., Emadi, S.: Detection of copy-move forgery in digital images using scale invariant feature transform algorithm and the spearman relationship. Iranian J. Elect. Electr. Eng. **16**(4), 474–486 (2020)

25. Mursi, M.F.M., Salama, M.M., Habeb, M.H.: An improved SIFT-PCA-based copy-move image forgery detection method. Inter. J. Adv. Res. Comput. Sci. Electr. Eng. **6**(3), 2277–9043 (2017)

Multiple Memory Image Instances Stratagem to Detect Fileless Malware

M. P. Swapna[1]([⊠]) [iD] and J. Ramkumar[2] [iD]

[1] Center for CyberSecurity Systems and Networks, Amrita Vishwa Vidyapeetham, Amritapuri,
Kollam, India
mpswapna77@gmail.com

[2] Department of Information Technology and Cognitive Systems, Sri Krishna Arts and Science
College, Coimbatore, India

Abstract. Fileless malware is sneaky and sophisticated, it uses trusted pre-installed applications to steal information and carry out its harmful purpose. The prevalence of file-less malware is on the rise, which exclusively relies on legitimate programs for infection and leaves no trace in the file system. This type of malware is frequently adept at bypassing antivirus software. Fileless malware is estimated to have a high detection evasion rate, like 10 times than other types of malwares. The collection and analysis of volatile memory represent a dynamic field of research in cybersecurity, providing valuable insights into various malicious vectors. The proposed work explores memory forensics, using multiple images from memory of a system at various time schedules to identify and analyze the prevalence of fileless malware. The approach aims to overcome the constraints of traditional memory analysis, which typically relies on a single memory image. The results depict the efficiency of the proposed method in enhancing the detection accuracy and reducing false positives.

Keywords: Memory Forensics · MMII · Volatility · Plugins · V_MEM · Accuracy

1 Introduction

Fileless malware operates with the intention of residing solely in a computer's memory, avoiding the creation of any identifiable artifacts on the file system [1]. The primary objective is to execute its tasks using built-in Operating System tools such as Windows Management Instrumentation (WMI) or PowerShell, ultimately leaving behind minimal or no traces after completion.

Attackers have engineered fileless malware to pose a formidable challenge for antivirus software detection. True to its name, fileless malware bypasses the typical route of being written to a hard drive file and instead implants itself directly into a computer's memory. Once malicious content resides in the system's memory, hackers may attempt to establish persistence within the system. Notably, fileless malware operates

S. Rajagopal et al. (Eds.): ASCIS 2023, CCIS 2039, pp. 131–140, 2024.
https://doi.org/10.1007/978-3-031-59100-6_11

covertly, leaving behind no discernible traces for antivirus software to identify. Consequently, detecting fileless malware attacks proves to be an arduous task for security analysts [2, 3].

As RAM is a type of volatile memory, it retains its data only while your computer is powered on. When the power is turned off, any malicious malware residing in RAM becomes inactive. Nonetheless, hackers can exploit this vulnerability to seize data from your computer or even introduce additional forms of malware, ensuring their persistence and ongoing control over the compromised system. Attackers employ this technique to complicate post-infection forensics, rendering it exceedingly challenging for antivirus software to detect and trigger a response based on traditional signature-based methods.

1.1 Memory Acquisition and Analysis

The active realm of cybersecurity research presently focus on acquiring and scrutinizing volatile memory to detect and pinpoint cyber threats. With a staggering 900% surge in fileless malware attacks observed in recent years [4], the escalating prevalence of such attacks underscores the enduring significance of memory forensics as a fundamental component of forensic techniques in the future.

Memory analysis has demonstrated its potency as an analytical approach capable of efficiently scrutinizing malware actions [5]. Memory holds a substantial reservoir of data, encompassing active and concluded processes, Dynamic Link Libraries (DLLs), operational services, registry entries, and active network associations. Additionally, memory inspection can uncover the utilization of process or DLL hooking methods employed by malware to camouflage itself as a legitimate process.

A memory image is deemed accurate when it exclusively comprises data that existed in the computer's memory at the time the snapshot was captured [6]. Atomicity entails that the memory snapshot was obtained during an unbroken atomic operation or, alternatively, it lacks any indications of simultaneous system activity, typically associated with the memory acquisition tool's interference. Finally, the integrity of a snapshot is established when the values within the memory region remain unaltered from the specific moment chosen by the investigator. According to Latzo et al.'s taxonomy [7] memory acquisition techniques are classified into user, kernel, hypervisor, synchronous management level, and asynchronous device level.

After obtaining a memory dump, there are multiple techniques available for analyzing it to detect the presence of malware. In a general sense, the analysis process (as depicted in Fig. 1) involves extracting valuable information from the memory dump and subsequently applying specific analysis approaches. Various tools, such as Volatility and Rekall, are developed to parse these memory dumps.

Some traditional, commonly used methods for volatile memory analysis encompass signature scanning and heuristic scanning of the memory dumps. More contemporary dynamic methods entail executing malware within a controlled environment, like a sandbox, and characterizing it based on various attributes. Lately, emerging machine learning techniques are under exploration, utilizing features derived from dynamic analysis methods to train machine learning classifier algorithms.

Conventional memory forensics methods involve examining one memory snapshot and scanning it for essential indicators to detect the existence of malicious process.

Fig. 1. Memory Analysis Steps

Though this approach is effective, it only provides insights into the system's state at a particular time, leaving gaps in our understanding of how fileless malware establishes defence evasion, persistence, and evolves post-infiltration. The novel attempt of utilizing Multiple Memory Image Instances (MMII) bridges this knowledge gap. MMII enables us to track and analyze system changes across various timestamps, thus providing a more comprehensive assessment of the presence of fileless malware.

The paper introduces an evaluation of an innovative approach for identifying fileless malware within a system. The method involves applying heuristics to multiple memory instances and capitalizing on the benefits of using multiple memory instances as opposed to the conventional single-memory-image technique. The proposed approach will yield enhanced detection precision with a decrease in false positives compared to the conventional approach.

2 Related Works

In recent years, fileless malware has gained prominence due to the eluding nature. Fileless malware strives to operate solely within a system's memory, reducing its footprint on physical hard drives and ensuring no identifiable remnants remain. Its advanced evasion methods render it invisible to heuristic analysis and traditional antivirus signatures [8]. The research works have proposed various mechanisms to detect Fileless Malware. Santos et al. [9] introduce a technique based on machine learning, that hinges on features derived from system API calls to spot fileless malware. Likewise, Ahmadi et al. [10] crafted a model based on deep learning for identifying fileless malware by leveraging its static as well as dynamic features. While these methodologies have demonstrated efficacy, they still grapple with limitations when it comes to detecting sophisticated fileless malware attacks, and they remain susceptible to elevated false positive rates.

Memory forensics plays a crucial role in uncovering vital information about malware whose traces are not evident in storage media. Ligh et al. [11] initiated memory forensics techniques and their uses in the realm of malware analysis. Building upon this foundation, Xu et al. [12] introduced a memory forensics-driven methodology for the detection of advanced fileless malware. Their approach involves scrutinizing both process and system memory to mine malicious artifacts. These techniques traditionally rely on individual memory snapshots, which can impose limitations on their effectiveness in detecting fileless malware.

In recent times, researchers have begun delving into the utilization of more than one memory snapshots to enhance the field of malware analysis. The proposed work by Huang et al. [13] leverages many memory images to rebuild the execution history of a process that is malicious, assisting in the identification of covert malware. The study aims to bridge the gap by exploring the efficacy of employing numerous memory image instances to enhance the detection of fileless malware.

The effectiveness of enhancing malware detection accuracy through the integration of multiple detection methods has been well-established. Zhao et al. [14] introduced a combined approach amalgamating static analysis with dynamic memory analysis techniques to identify complex malwares. Likewise, Park et al. [15] engineered a fused system, combining machine learning with memory forensics to spot fileless malware. Although these hybrid methodologies have showcased enhanced detection rates, they haven't explicitly delved into the advantages of incorporating multiple memory images into their detection procedures.

3 Methodology

3.1 Dataset

The dataset comprises benign and malicious fileless malware samples gathered from diverse origins, encompassing malware repositories and memory forensics archives. To ensure a thorough assessment of the proposed method, the dataset encompasses samples from a variety of malware families like Gargoyle variants, Form Grabber, Benign Injection, Atom LDR, etc. Subsequently, these malware samples are introduced into the system's memory using specified code injection techniques.

3.2 Generating Memory Dumps

Virtual machines running on different operating systems, like Windows XP, 32-bit Windows 7, and 64-bit Windows 10, are established using VMware Player, a widely recognized and robust virtualization platform capable of supporting memory acquisition in virtual environments. VMware offers integrated tools and APIs that facilitate the capture of memory dumps from active virtual machines, streamlining the acquisition process and ensuring compatibility with the target system.

In the controlled environment having the virtual machine, the dataset containing malware samples is systematically introduced into each virtual machine instance. Subsequently, the system is paused, and the suspended state of the virtual machine is saved as a V_MEM file. V_MEM files represent the raw memory snapshots extracted from a system's physical RAM, capturing the ephemeral data existing in the memory at a precise timestamp. Creation of the V_MEM file is iterated across multiple timestamps to generate several memory image instances of the malware-infected system. These memory images are then associated with each malware sample, forming an array of memory images.

4 Implementation

The collection of memory images produced for each malware sample through is processed using a Python script. This script scrutinizes the array of memory image, conducts heuristics, anomaly detection, and compares processes across multiple dumps to generate an assessment outcome of either "+ve" or "−ve." "+ve" denotes the identification of malware within the processed array of memory images, while "−ve" signifies the absence of any malware.

4.1 Analysis of MMII

Numerous memory analysis tools have been developed to enable users to sift through memory dumps in search of valuable artifacts. Among open-source options, noteworthy examples include Volatility [16] and Rekall [17], while commercially available tools encompass Cellebrite Inspector [18], FireEye Redline [19], Magnet AXIOM [20], and WindowsSCOPE [21]. Volatility has risen to prominence as the most extensive and well-supported framework with many plugins tailored for specific platform-focused forensic analysis.

The volatility plugins that were used for analysis of the generated array of memory image instances are Dlllist, Malfind, Timeliner, Memdump, Pslist, Malprocfind, Dlllist and Pstree. These plugins help in heuristics analysis and anamoly detection of the memory images.

During the analysis of multiple memory image instances to uncover fileless malware, the examination of specific artifacts and behaviors across these images can aid in the identification of anomalies and likely signs of compromise. Some the heuristics that were assessed are

- Process Comparison - Utilizing plugins like 'pslist' or 'pstree' to extract the list of processes from each memory image [22]. The objective is to identify any processes that are unexpected or seem suspicious by comparing their presence across various memory images, noting disparities.
- Process Behaviour - Those processes that exhibit varying permissions among multiple memory image instances, such as being read-only in one image, while depicting write and execute rights in another image, may be signalled as a prospective security issue or a shift in the process's behavior, possibly being infected by a fileless malware.
- Time-based analysis - Through the acquisition of memory images at various time intervals, we can monitor alterations in memory structure, process conduct, and the overall system condition. This approach aids in the detection of any atypical activities or occurrences that could be linked to fileless malware, even in cases where they attempt to conceal their presence through techniques like virtual address descriptor remapping.
- DLL Comparison - The 'DLLlist' tool compiles a catalog of loaded DLLs for every process within the memory images [23]. One can identify any uncommon or unexpected DLLs that may have been illicitly inserted within a timeframe by comparing the loaded DLLs and modules among the images, perhaps indicating the existence of fileless malware.

● Monitoring Pageout – The page table tickets of malicious processes can inadvertently be sent to the system's secondary storage [24]. The presence of multiple memory images simplifies the process of monitoring occurrences of such page-outs, allowing for better surveillance of potential malicious pay-loads from being stored in the system's secondary storage.

Pseudocode of MMII Analysis

```
1: Procedure Get_Memory_Images(x)
2: Set Array[n] equal to x
3: Return x
4: End
5: Set N equal to the result of Get_Memory_Images
6: While N[index] is less than or equal to the end:
7: If N[index] is not processed:
8:    Compare(N, N - 1)
9:    Run VolatilityPlugins() {Operations specified}
10:   Set N[index] as processed
11:   N--
12: Else if N[index] is processed
13:    Perform Heuristics()
14:    Set Result as FoundMalware()
15:    N++
16: End of while
```

5 Results and Discussions

This research, emphasizes on the examination and assessment of the performance of the proposed Multiple Memory Image Instances (MMII) algorithm in contrast with the conventional approach for detecting concealed malware entries within system memory.

The conventional strategy depends exclusively on a solitary memory image for detection. To assess the efficiency of the MMII based algorithm, a series of test casesare executed, involving the acquisition of distinct memory images captured at four different timestamps.

A thorough assessment of performance metrics, such as accuracy, processing time and confusion matrix, was conducted. The proposed work endeavours to give valuable insights into the enhancements brought about by the MMII algorithm in comparison to the Ptenum [25] plugin. The MMII algorithm demonstrates its efficacy in the detection of concealed and altered versions of the malware sample (Gargoyle), by monitoring page-out schemes. This functionality is made possible by leveraging the four memory snapshots, which allow for the effective monitoring and exact tracking of all the page-out occurrences. This represents a notable significance over the conventional single memory snapshot lookup method employed by Ptenum. Additionally, the MMII plugin boasts a more wider anomaly detection mechanism, which empowers it to identify malware within ATOM LDR and APT34 samples. These specific samples generate child processes that allows writable and executable regions in memory for the execution of malign code. The heuristic assessment of multiple memory snapshots captured at various timestamps offers a clearer insight into these behaviors, thus enhancing the overall detection capabilities. Table 1 provides an overview of the results obtained for each sample when analyzed with both the MMII Plugin and the Ptenum Plugin.

Table 1. Comparative Results of MMII & Ptenum

No	Sample	MMII	Ptenum
1	Gargoyle	+ve	+ve
2	Gargoyle HVariant	+ve	−ve
3	Form Grabber	+ve	+ve
4	Ghost Miner	+ve	+ve
5	Reflective DLL	+ve	+ve
6	APT 34	+ve	−ve
7	Atom LDR	+ve	−ve
8	Benign Injection I	−ve	−ve

While assessing the performance, it is noted that the Ptenum plugin generates its results much faster than MMII plugin as represented in Table 2. This significant efficiency gap can mainly be due to Ptenum's task of just processing a single memory image, resulting in reduced resource utilization and complexity, compared to MMII plugin that requires more processing of multiple images and the execution of heuristic comparisons among them. Figure 2 illustrates the performance comparison of the algorithms.

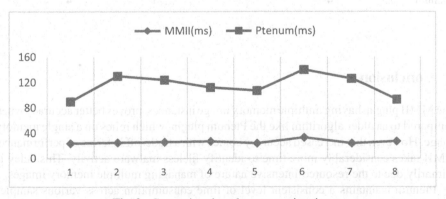

Fig. 2. Comparison based on processing time

MMII plugin exhibits greater accuracy compared to the Ptenum plugin when tested with various samples. Ptenum appears to be more susceptible to incorrectly classifying malware samples. The Ptenum plugin presents a more potential for false positives because it employs much stricter assessment when probing for malware attributes. Hence, even some benign samples with some similarities to malware characteristics may be marked as malicious. This was observed in the case of Benign Injection I, which used Windows Load Library to introduce harmless payloads into a process as presented in Table 3.

Table 2. Performances of MMII & Ptenum

No	Sample	MMII (ms)	Ptenum (ms)
1	Gargoyle	24	90
2	Gargoyle HVariant	25	130
3	Form Grabber	26	124
4	Ghost Miner	27	112
5	Reflective DLL	24	107
6	APT 34	33	140
7	Atom LDR	24	126
8	Benign Injection I	27	93

Table 3. Confusion Matrix of MMII & Ptenum

Plugins	Accuracy	False Negative	True Negative	False Positive	True Positive
MMII	1	0	2	0	8
Ptenum	0.5	4	1	1	4

6 Conclusion

The MMII plugin, having multiple memory image instances, proves better accuracy when compared to an older algorithm like the Ptenum plugin, which relies on a single memory image. However, this increased accuracy comes with a trade-off in terms of performance. MMII takes considerably more time to identify fileless malware activity. This delay is primarily due to the resource-intensive nature of managing multiple memory images.

Ptenum maintains a consistent level of time consumption across various samples while MMII displays significant variations due to the diverse heuristics it employs. When different aspects of the MMII plugin are invoked, it necessitates more intensive anomaly detection within the memory image instances under examination. This performance limitation poses a significant obstacle when considering the practical application of a large array of memory-images. Even a single memory image can easily surpass a certain GB of storage space. Consequently, utilizing an array of these memory image instances for analyzing a set of malware samples would place an overwhelming burden on a system's storage capacity and its processing capabilities.

The future work on MMII plugin could focus on streamlining its processing speed while upholding accuracy through parallel processing capabilities, refining heuristics logic to eliminate unnecessary computational overhead.

References

1. Sanjay, B.N., Rakshith, D.C., Akash, R.B., Hegde, V.V.: An approach to detect fileless malware and defend its evasive mechanisms. In: 3rd IEEE International Conference on Computational Systems and Information Technology for Sustainable Solutions (2018)
2. Kara, I.: Fileless malware threats: recent advances, analysis approach through memory forensics and research challenges. Expert Syst. Appl., 214 (2023). https://doi.org/10.1016/J.ESWA.2022.119133
3. Sanjay, B.N., Rakshith, D.C., Akash, R.B., Hegde, V.V.: An approach to detect fileless malware and defend its evasive mechanisms. In: 2018 3rd International Conference on Computational Systems and Information Technology for Sustainable Solutions (CSITSS), pp. 234–239. IEEE (2018)
4. Nyholm, H., et al.: The evolution of volatile memory forensics. J. Cybersecur. Priv. **2**, 556–572 (2022). https://doi.org/10.3390/jcp2030028
5. Latzo, T., Palutke, R., Freiling, F.: A universal taxonomy and survey of forensic memory acquisition techniques. Digit. Investig. **28**, 56–69 (2019). https://doi.org/10.1016/j.diin.2019.01.001
6. Mele Pottaraikkal, S., Sujeer Sugatha, A.: Effectiveness of multiple memory-images in detecting fileless malware. In: 2023 11th International Symposium on Digital Forensics and Security (ISDFS), Chattanooga, TN, USA, pp. 1–5 (2023). https://doi.org/10.1109/ISDFS58141.2023.10131728
7. Santos, I., Devesa, J., Brezo, F.: OpCodeSeer: detecting fileless malware by building memory-based API call graphs. J. Comput. Secur. **26**(6), 735–760 (2018)
8. Afreen, A., Aslam, M., Ahmed, S.: Analysis of fileless malware and its evasive behavior. In: 2020 International Conference on Cyber Warfare and Security (ICCWS), Islamabad, Pakistan, pp. 1–8 (2020). https://doi.org/10.1109/ICCWS48432.2020.9292376
9. Ahmadi, M., Sami, A., Rahmani, A.M.: A deep learning-based approach for detecting fileless malware. J. Comput. Virol. Hack. Tech. **16**(4), 441–456 (2020)
10. Ligh, M.H., Case, A., Levy, J., Walters, A.: The Art of Memory Forensics: Detecting Malware and Threats in Windows, Linux, and Mac Memory. Wiley Publishing, Indianapolis (2014)
11. Xu, Z., Zhu, H., Ahn, G.J., Zhao, R.: SIMF: a framework for detecting sophisticated memory-based malware. In: Proceedings of the 34th Annual Computer Security Applications Conference (ACSAC), pp. 573–585 (2019)
12. Huang, K., Zeng, Z., Fan, L., Chen, G.: Reconstructing execution history of malicious processes using multiple memory snapshots. IEEE Trans. Inf. Forensics Secur. **16**, 3816–3830 (2021). [9] Zhao, X., Zhang, F., Xu, D., Gu, G., & Wu, W. (2017)
13. Hunt, V.M.: A verifiable approach to partially-virtualized binary code simplification. In: Proceedings of the 2017 ACM SIGSAC Conference on Computer and Communications Security (CCS), pp. 1601–1615 (2017)

14. Park, Y., Reeves, D., Mulukutla, V.: FLARE: hybrid analysis for detection of fileless malware. In: Proceedings of the 2020 IEEE Symposium on Security and Privacy (SP), pp. 1156–1171 (2020)
15. Volatility. https://github.com/volatilityfoundation/volatility. Accessed 12 July 2022
16. Rekall. https://github.com/google/rekall. Accessed 12 July 2022
17. Cellebrite Inspector. https://cellebrite.com/en/inspector/. Accessed 12 July 2022
18. FireEye Redline. https://www.fireeye.com/services/freeware/redline.html. Accessed 12 July 2022
19. Magnet Axiom. https://www.magnetforensics.com/products/magnet-axiom/. Accessed 12 July 2022
20. WindowsSCOPE. http://www.windowsscope.com/windowsscope-cyber-forensics/
21. Velazco, G., Amado, A.: Windows memory forensics: detecting efficiently external code injection in processes. In: 2018 IEEE 9th Annual Information Technology, Electronics and Mobile Communication Conference (IEMCON), pp. 743–748 (2018)
22. Tung, M.L., Chang, C.P.: Detecting hidden user-mode rootkits in memory by Volatility. In: 2017 IEEE 2nd International Conference on Cloud Computing and Big Data Analysis (ICCCBDA), pp. 416–420 (2017)
23. Block, F., Dewald, A.: Windows memory forensics: detecting (un)intentionally hidden injected code by examining page table entries. Digit. Investig. 29(Supplement), S3–S12 (2019). ISSN 1742–2876
24. FRWS-USA-2019 research's highlighted Ptenum plugin repository. https://github.com/f-block/rekall-plugins/blob/master/ptenum.py
25. Chronicle: Virustotal - Ghostminer sample (2018). https://www.virustotal.com//file/40a507a88ba03b9da3de235c9c0afdfcf7a0473c8704cbb26e16b1b782becd4d/detection

A Survey of Machine Learning Techniques in Phishing Detection

Nishant Navinbhai Joshi$^{(\boxtimes)}$ and Sunil Bajeja

Faculty of Computer Application, Marwadi University, Rajkot, Gujarat, India
nishantjoshi33@gmail.com, sunil.bajeja@marwadieducation.edu.in

Abstract. Phishing attacks, a prevalent method for illicitly acquiring individuals' sensitive information from the internet, pose significant threats to users' security. These attacks, orchestrated by hackers, involve the theft of protected passwords, private details, and even financial transactions, resulting in stolen money. Typically, perpetrators of phishing attacks manipulate and conceal well-known, legitimate websites to deceive users into divulging their personal data.

To counteract such cyber threats, numerous websites and cybersecurity experts employ various techniques. Whitelisting and blacklisting, along with heuristic algorithms based on visual resemblance, constitute some of the prevalent strategies. However, this study proposes an advanced approach—a machine learning-based categorization technique enriched with heuristic features. These features are derived from critical characteristics such as the uniform resource locator (URL), source code, session details, security type employed, protocol in use, and the type of site being accessed.

The proposed model utilizes five distinct machine learning techniques, including random forest, decision trees, and logistic regression, to comprehensively evaluate its efficacy. By leveraging these advanced methodologies, this study aims to enhance the accuracy and efficiency of phishing detection, ultimately fortifying defenses against these malicious online activities.

Keywords: phishing attack · machine learning · random forest algorithm

1 Introduction

Phishing is the practice of attackers sending fraudulent emails, to trick consumers into paying for a service. In order to obtain phishing attempts, seek to fool users into clicking online links that download malware or reroute them to hostile websites using private information such as login-id, password, multi-factor authentication (MFA), tokens, and financial information. Fake websites and phishing emails often impersonate well-known people or businesses, including the institution, bank, or place of employment of the victim. Attackers try to access sensitive information from these using phishing data such as username & and password or payment information. One of the most well-known attacks, when information is stolen from internet users by an attacker, is a phishing attack. Internet users lose sensitive information such as protected passwords & and private data.

The COVID-19 outbreak has expanded the use of technology across all professions, resulting in a shift from offline to online spaces for things like organizing official online meetings, attending classes, online purchasing, and online payments during this time so many phishing attacks to users, the attacker has stolen a money, access information, and others information. Today the internet has evolved into a potent social connecting tool. People's reliance on digital networks opens the door to fraud. This means the phisher will have more chances to carry out attacks that damage the victim's finances, psychological well-being and career prospects. The victim of fraud will suffer financial loss and losses of personal data loss of reputation, because users are unaware of the phishing attack, and attackers are increasingly successful. so, at this time, it is very challenging to combat phishing attacks because they exploit user vulnerabilities, yet improving phishing detection methods is essential. The "blacklist" method which is a standard way to detect phishing sites, involves updating internet protocol (IP) blacklisted URLs in the anti-virus database. Attackers who want to avoid being blacklisted use clever methods to trick consumers by modifying the URL to look authentic.

As machine learning techniques have advanced, it is a different technology to identify phishing websites to improve prediction performance. Phishing detection is a supervised classification technique that fits a model to data using a labeled data set. Different algorithm exists for the supervised learning process, including decision tree, random forest algorithm, and super vector algorithm. A strong solution is necessary for a practical product and It usually has to meet two criteria. The first is a low rate of false warnings and good accuracy. And second one is sizeable dataset is necessary to improve the model's performance, particularly for neural networking with intricate architecture within computing time is also an important consideration for real time decision systems.

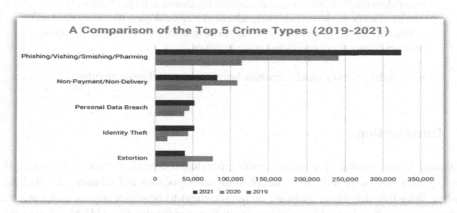

Fig. 1. Top 5 types of phishing crime in last 5 years. References 1 https://www.thesslstore.com/blog/social-engineering-statistics

Variety of cyberattack types from 2019 to 2021 are shown in the attached Fig. 1. Table 1 lists the top 10 countries in the world where phishing assaults have occurred; prominent countries such as the US, Brazil, China, and the UK have been identified as main targets in this regard.

Table 1. List of countries in the world that are the most victims of cybercrime]. References 2
https://www.enigmasoftware.com/top-20-countries-the-most-cybercrime

Country Name	Types of Attack	Rank	Country Name	Types of Attack	Rank
United States of America	the proportion of harmful computer activity	23%	Italy	the proportion of harmful computer activity	3%
	Malicious code level	1		Malicious code level	11
	Spam zombies are ranked first	3		Spam zombies are ranked first	6
	Ranking of phishing website hosts	1		Ranking of phishing website hosts	14
	Bot ranking	2		Bot ranking	6
	The rank of attack origin	1		The rank of attack origin	8
China	the proportion of harmful computer activity	9%	France	the proportion of harmful computer activity	3%
	Malicious code level	2		Malicious code level	8
	Spam zombies are ranked first	4		Spam zombies are ranked first	14
	Ranking of phishing website hosts	6		Ranking of phishing website hosts	9
	Bot ranking	1		Bot ranking	10
	The rank of attack origin	2		The rank of attack origin	5
Britain	the proportion of harmful computer activity	5%	Turkey	the proportion of harmful computer activity	3%
	Malicious code level	4		Malicious code level	15
	Spam zombies are ranked first	10		Spam zombies are ranked first	5
	Ranking of phishing website hosts	5		Ranking of phishing website hosts	24
	Bot ranking	9		Bot ranking	8
	The rank of attack origin	3		The rank of attack origin	12
Brazil	the proportion of harmful computer activity	4%	Poland	the proportion of harmful computer activity	3%
	Malicious code level	16		Malicious code level	23
	Spam zombies are ranked first	1		Spam zombies are ranked first	9
	Ranking of phishing website hosts	16		Ranking of phishing website hosts	8
	Bot ranking	5		Bot ranking	7
	The rank of attack origin	9		The rank of attack origin	17

(continued)

Table 1. (*continued*)

Country Name	Types of Attack	Rank	Country Name	Types of Attack	Rank
Span	the proportion of harmful computer activity	4%	India	the proportion of harmful computer activity	3%
	Malicious code level	10		Malicious code level	23
	Spam zombies are ranked first	8		Spam zombies are ranked first	9
	Ranking of phishing website hosts	13		Ranking of phishing website hosts	8
	Bot ranking	3		Bot ranking	7
	The rank of attack origin	6		The rank of attack origin	17

1.1 Life Cycle of Phishing Attack

Phishing is a popular cyberattack in which malicious emails or messages are sent to trick recipients into visiting a fake website, whereupon the attackers obtain personal user information, including credit card numbers, usernames, and passwords, in exchange for money (Fig. 2).

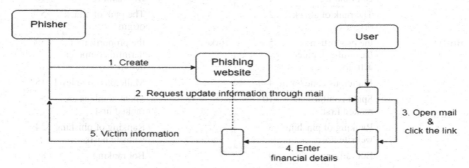

Fig. 2. Block diagram of phishing attack through the website. References 3 www.researchgate.net/figure/Life-cycle-of-a-web-phishing-attack_fig1_369555501

Here researcher gives brief details of the phishing attack life cycle as below.

(a) Attackers start by building phishing websites that look like legitimate websites. On the one hand, attackers use the same alphabet characters, spelling mistakes, and other techniques to create official website URLs, especially domain names and web resource directories.

If we search the internet, we will find many examples of phishing like this. For example, the link "https://aimazon.amz-z7acyuup9z0y16.xyz/v" **mimics** https://www.amazon.com **and was viewed on May 9, 2021**. Although a computer browser can display the URL by hovering over the link, on which can be clicked, the average user finds it difficult to differentiate between these URLs. as impersonations of real

URLs using only eyes and memory. On the other hand, another important aspect is to copy the website information. Attackers typically steal text, site layouts, and logos from legitimate websites using scripts. Cybercriminals are most often counterfeit-sensitive. Information obtained from form submission websites, such as the login, payment, and password search pages.

(b) Sending an email with a link in it to readers is the second step. Additionally, phony mobile apps, voice messaging, QR codes, and SMS can all be used to send phishing URLs. Even if phishing emails are sent at random, a small number of people with low defense awareness will fall for them. At this stage, attackers use psychological manipulation and other social engineering techniques to trick users into breaching security.

(c) The next step is to gather personal data on a mobile website that closely resembles the official website of a business or organization, complete with the same name, logo, user interface, and content. This data is frequently used for login, password reset, payment, and renewal.

(d) The final stage is to steal money from the user's account by impersonating a request to a credible website using the user's real information. Some people even use the same username and password on multiple websites. Attackers successfully stole multiple user accounts using this method. Some phishers use stolen data for additional illegal purposes.

Here are some examples that look like same as original webpage but it's a phishing is display as below

See Fig. 3.

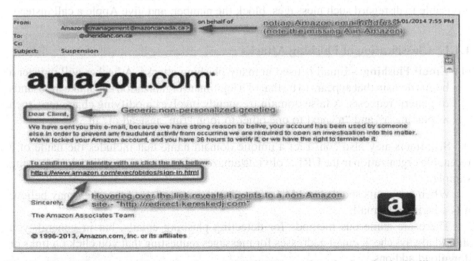

Fig. 3. In red character email sent by Amazon but it was sent by a hacker that looks like Amazon. References 4 URL: https://www.identityiq.com/scams-and-fraud/what-is-phishing-prevent-attacks-with-common-examples

One of the typical phishing characteristics that was previously highlighted is the sender's distinctly unusual email address.

It features a false link that directs users to a different location than what is implied in the text, it doesn't seem legitimate, the message is badly written and contains a grammatical error, and it seeks to incite anxiety in the recipient (Fig. 4).

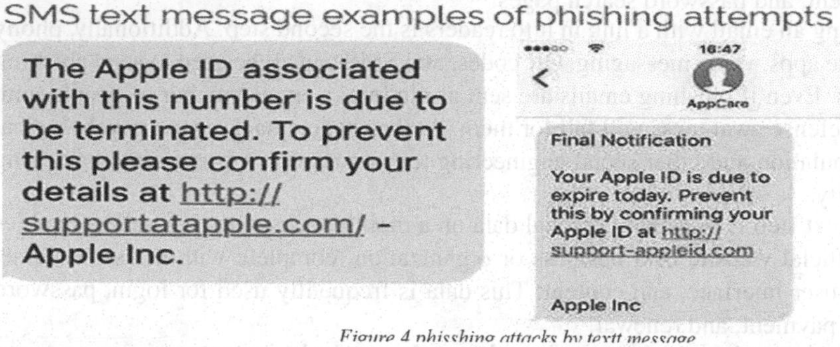

SMS text message examples of phishing attempts

The Apple ID associated with this number is due to be terminated. To prevent this please confirm your details at http:// supportatapple.com/ – Apple Inc.

Final Notification

Your Apple ID is due to expire today. Prevent this by confirming your Apple ID at http:// support-appleid.com

Apple Inc

Figure 4 phishing attacks by text message

Fig. 4. Phisshing attacks by text message. References 5 https://www.identityiq.com/scams-and-fraud/what-is-phishing-prevent-attacks-with-common-examples

Here, the sender attempts to create the impression that the recipient has received an iCloud account-related automatic alert from Apple: The first clue that these emails are bogus is found in the links. The consumer is not redirected to the official Apple website by them.

Second, Apple does not text users for confirmation of their login credentials. It's advisable to disregard such messages, block the number, and give Apple a call instead.

1.1.1   Classification of Phishing Attacks

(1) **Email Phishing**: - Email is used in many phishing attacks. A hacker will register a bogus domain that appears to be that of a legitimate organization and make thousands of generic requests. A false domain frequently involves modifying characters, such as placing "r" and "n" next to one other to form "run" instead of "m".

Scammers may also construct a unique domain name that includes the name of a reputable organization in the URL. "olivia@amazonsupport.com" supplied the following sample.

When recipients see the word "Amazon" in the sender's address, they may believe it is a legitimate email.

There are numerous methods for detecting phishing emails, but in general, you should always check email addresses for messages requesting that you click on links or download add-ons.

(2) **Spear phishing:**

When recipients see the word "Amazon" in the sender's address, they may believe it is a legitimate email.

There are numerous methods for detecting phishing emails, but in general, you should always check email addresses for messages requesting that you click on links or download add-ons.

Fraudsters may say the individual's name and understand that their employment involves making bank transactions on the company's behalf.

The informality of e-mail implies that the sender knows English and that the message is genuine, rather than a template.

(3) **Whaling**: Larger attacks are more focused on high-level leaders. Although the end goal of whale fishing is the same as it is for other sorts of fishing, the technique is more delicate.

In this circumstance, tricks like bogus links and harmful URLs are useless since thieves are attempting to imitate high-level officials.

Email communications frequently leverage the assumption of a busy CEO who wants staff to help him.

Emails like the one above may not be as sophisticated as spearfishing emails, but they are predicated on employees' desire to follow their superiors' instructions.

(4) **Angler Phishing**: As a newer assault vector, social media provides several opportunities for thieves to deceive consumers. Fake URLs, clone websites, articles, tweets, and instant messaging (essentially smiley faces) can all be used to fool individuals into revealing important information or downloading malware. Organizations frequently use this as an opportunity to alleviate harm, usually by compensating the individual. Scammers, on the other hand, attempt to take replies and ask the customer for personal information. They most likely did this to facilitate some kind of reimbursement, but it is being done to destroy their accounts.

Criminals, on the other hand, can utilize information freely shared on social media to launch sophisticated attacks. As demonstrated by this example, the fishing angle is often made possible by the number of people who are involved in organizations and make complaints on social media.

(5) **Vishing:** Phishing, short for "voice phishing," is when someone tries to steal data from a phone. Attackers can impersonate trusted friends or relatives.

The 2019 Wish campaign, which targeted members of the UK Parliament and staff, is an example of 'Wishing Fishing'. The attack was a component of a bigger offensive that targeted UK MPs with at least 21 million spam emails.

(6) **HTTPS Phishing**

Attackers who use HTTPS phishing send their target an email with a link to a fake website. The victims can then be tricked into divulging personal information via the website.

An Example of HTTPS Phishing
The Scarlet Widow attacker's organization looks for firm employee emails and uses HTTPS phishing to target them. When people receive a blank email, they frequently click on a short link, which takes them to Scarlet Widow's website.

2 Motivation

Phishing attacks are difficult to counter because they prey on users' vulnerabilities, but it's important to improve your phishing techniques. Users become unaware of phishing attacks and become successful hackers who lose their reputations. The "blacklisting" strategy, which is commonly used to detect phishing websites, entails changing Internet Protocol (IP) addresses. Blacklist URLs in anti-virus databases. Attackers who want to avoid blacklisting use clever techniques to trick customers by changing their URLs to make them look authentic. There are many websites that use phishing methods, but they are not 100% safe from phishing, so RESEARCHERS encourage machine learning algorithms to protect and prevent data, and there are many types of OTP looping, Wishing, and email phishing methods. Therefore, this study encourages research and prevention of phishing attacks.

3 Related Work

In this research work, we mainly use machine learning to identify phishing websites. Similar topics such as email spam filtering and malicious domain blacklisting have received attention. in addition, the use of machine learning in this field is becoming more widespread. Based on the features used, there are two main groups for identifying fake websites there are two types of features: (1) static features and (2) dynamic features. (1) features are extracted from URLs, page content, HTML domain structure, and domain-specific data using static feature-based techniques. (who's and DNS records). Among other sources. (2) dynamic feature-based solutions, on the other hand, concentrate on learning user behavior by looking at system logs, especially when pages are loaded and scripts are executed. This thesis does not focus on using static properties.

3.1 Existing System

The current system uses a variety of instruments and techniques in its multipronged effort to identify phishing websites. A strong password policy creates a strong first line of defense by limiting the likelihood of identity theft by imposing criteria for password complexity and frequent updates. Access control systems are essential because they perform assessments prior to authorizing access. This reduces the possibility of phishing attempts by guaranteeing that only authorized users can access the system. Tools for URL verification examine website URLs to provide an extra degree of security. These tools use WHOIS information to verify domain ownership, checks against established blacklists of phishing sites, and reputation assessments to validate the integrity of URLs. The system seeks to proactively detect and stop phishing attempts by putting these safeguards in place. This extensive collection of instruments and techniques illustrates a thorough strategy for phishing detection. Strong password regulations and access restrictions protect the system against unwanted access, but proactive measures like URL verification, email filtering, and anti-phishing software help guard against the ever-changing threats posed by phishing scams. By using dynamic detection techniques and ongoing monitoring, this layered security approach seeks to build a robust system that not.

3.2 Proposed System

Following are several techniques to prevent anti-phishing techniques using Python technology. In the proposed system there are several methods to prevent anti-phishing techniques are used as below.

a) The blacklist method

it is the most popular method; including maintaining a database of phishing URLs. If the URL is identified as a phisher and is discovered in the database, a warning is given.; otherwise, it is considered valid. This method is simple and fast to implement because it checks if the URL is stored in the database. Small changes in the URL can be used to learn list-based techniques, and the list should be updated frequently to resist new attacks.

> Ex. If
>
> {
>
>   Email (word are ∈ {black list}-> suspicious email
>
>   Otherwise
>
> ➔ Legitimate email
>
> }

b) blacklist plugin uses a heuristic:

approach based on detecting new attacks by using information obtained from phishing websites to detect phishing attacks. The challenge is that not all new attacks are predictable, and when attackers are aware of the techniques or features being used, it is easy to circumvent them. Also, this level of specificity is low because the sites may or may not have common features.

c) SSL certificate:

SSL certificates can aid users in identifying trustworthy websites and setting them apart from potentially dangerous ones, which can help in the identification of phishing attempts. The following are some of the ways SSL certificates help identify phishing attempts:

Padlock Icon and HTTPS Indication:

Legitimate websites secured with SSL certificates display a padlock icon in the address bar, indicating a secure connection. Additionally, the URL starts with "**https://**" **instead of** "**http://**". Users are trained to look for these indicators, and the absence of these security features in an email or website can signal a potential phishing attempt.

Checking SSL Certificate Details:

Users can check the details of the SSL certificate by clicking on the padlock icon in the browser's address bar. This allows them to view information such as the certificate issuer, the organization's name (in the case of Extended Validation certificates), and the certificate's expiration date. In a phishing scenario, attackers may use certificates with suspicious details or from untrustworthy sources.

Look for Extended Validation (EV) Certificates:
Websites with Extended Validation (EV) certificates undergo a more rigorous validation process, and the organization's name is displayed prominently in the browser's address bar. Users are more likely to trust websites with EV certificates, making it harder for phishing sites to imitate this level of legitimacy.

SSL Certificate Mismatch Warnings: Browsers issue warnings when there is a mismatch between the domain in the SSL certificate and the actual website being visited. Phishing sites often use deceptive URLs that may not match the SSL certificate, triggering a warning that alerts users to the potential threat.

Browser Alerts for Insecure Sites:
Modern browsers actively alert users when they visit websites that lack SSL certificates or when there are issues with the certificate. This can discourage users from entering sensitive information on unsecured websites, potentially thwarting phishing attempts.

Certificate Transparency (CT) Logs:
Certificate Transparency is a system that logs SSL certificates, providing transparency into the certificates issued by Certificate Authorities (CAs). Monitoring CT logs can help detect suspicious certificates or certificates issued incorrectly, which might be indicative of phishing activities.

Educating Users on SSL Indicators:
Phishing detection is not solely the responsibility of technology; user education is crucial. Training users to recognize SSL indicators, understand the importance of HTTPS, and be cautious about entering sensitive information on non-secure websites enhances their ability to identify potential phishing attempts.

> **Ex.**
>
> if {
>
> HTTP link -> Legit email
>
> Otherwise -> Suspicious email
>
> }

d) **Certificate authority:**

While SSL certificates might be issued by untrusted or self-signed sources, not every HTTPS connection can provide a secure connection to the server and prevent the transmission of sensitive data to third parties. To validate the legitimacy of an email, you must first determine who the certificate authority is [14]. As a result, the email is suspect unless the SSD certificate is supplied by a well-known and trustworthy company like as GoDaddy, Comodo, or Symantec.

> Ex. If {
>
> Authentic CA-> legitimate SSL
>
> Otherwise {Suspicious SSL Certificate}
>
> }

e) **Hiding URLs** Attackers use a variety of tactics, including URL shortening and creating HTML emails with customized content and images, to hide a website's actual URL. These strategies may make it harder to identify phishing efforts. In the past, abbreviated URLs like "j.mp" or "goo. gl" were frequently used by attackers to mask real web addresses. They also used JavaScript scripts and Cascading Style Sheets (CSS) to incorporate customized information into HTML emails. Users are often apprehensive about the existence of shortened URLs and are advised to proceed with caution. It is imperative to address these dishonest practices and use a variety of security measures in order to improve the identification of phishing attempts.

Ex.

Original Legitimate URL:

https://www.bank-example.com/login

Concealed Phishing URL:

https://www.bank-example-phishing.com/login

In this example:

Domain Spoofing:

Attackers may register a domain that closely mimics the legitimate one. In this case, they've added "-phishing" to the domain to trick users.

Path Mimicry:

The path (/login) appears legitimate, which might deceive users into thinking they are logging into their account on the real website.

SSL Padlock:

Attackers might use HTTPS to create a false sense of security. Users might see a padlock in the browser, but the domain itself is malicious.

Email Context:

Phishing emails accompanying this URL might create a sense of urgency, asking users to verify their accounts immediately, prompting them to click the link without thorough inspection.

Hidden Subdomains:

Attackers may use hidden subdomains to further obscure the actual domain. For instance, secure.bank-example-phishing.com/login might still show www.bank-exa mple-phishing.com in the browser.

Redirect Chains:

Phishing URLs may use redirect chains, starting with a seemingly harmless URL that eventually leads to a malicious one. This makes it harder for users and security tools to identify the true destination.

Detection Techniques:

Domain Analysis:

Scrutinize the domain for misspellings, additional words, or subtle alterations that deviate from the legitimate domain.

Check SSL Certificates:

Validate the SSL certificate. In phishing attempts, attackers might use free or self-signed certificates that may not be trustworthy.

Verify Email Source:

Examine the sender's email address. Phishing emails often use disguised addresses or domains that don't align with the legitimate organization.

User Awareness:

Educate users about the tactics used in phishing attacks, emphasizing the importance of scrutinizing URLs, checking for subtle variations, and avoiding clicking on suspicious links.

Security Software:

Employ security software and email filters that can detect phishing attempts and malicious URLs. By combining these detection techniques, organizations and individuals can enhance their ability to identify phishing attempts and protect against potential threats. Regularly updating security measures and staying informed about emerging phishing tactics are essential components of a robust defense strategy.

f) website visitors

Legitimate websites experience a certain amount of daily traffic and numerous inquiries. a legitimate Alexa ranking for a website of less than or equal to 150,000. Phishing websites, on the other hand, are short-lived and frequently unavailable due to poor traffic.

Ex. If traffic<150000

The legitimate email

Otherwise, Suspicious email

g) Email of the sender:

Some phishing emails have mismatched email subject lines and sender addresses. When the subject line of a malicious email reads "User X shared some files with you" or "Password reset," it may appear to have been issued from a trustworthy organization such as Microsoft or Dropbox. The sender's email address, on the other hand, has an unusual domain name, such as "@sharing.dboxfile.com" or "@dropbox.com." As a result, spotting bad emissaries may benefit by observing such battles. The email is therefore suspect if the domain name is not on the list of trustworthy domain names.

Ex.

if {@ site name is belonging

{

given a list of credible domain name

}

->legitimate email

otherwise-> suspicious email

4   The Machine Learning Process

In the real world, we have computers or other devices and are surrounded by people who can learn from their experiences due to their ability to learn. However, can machines learn from their historical facts or experiences in the same manner as people do? So now we know what machine learning is for. A machine can predict outcomes with the help of machine learning and also automatically learn without being explicitly programmed from data.

Techniques for machine learning use historical sample data, or "training data," to build a mathematical model to assist in making predictions or decisions without explanation. Prediction models are built using machine learning, statistics, and computer science. Machine learning generates or uses algorithms. It receives information from previous data, and the performance improves as we provide more information. A machine learning system predicts the outcome using predictive models built using previous data when it receives new data. How well the output is predicted depends on the amount of data used, as it is simpler to construct a model that more accurately predicts the outcome with a larger data set.

Let's pretend we have a complex problem that needs some predictions. We can simply input data into simple algorithms, and the machine will develop logic based on the data and output predictions, instead of creating code for it. The effect of machine learning on our methods of problem-solving is profound. In the block diagram below, a machine learning algorithm's operation is explained (Fig. 5).

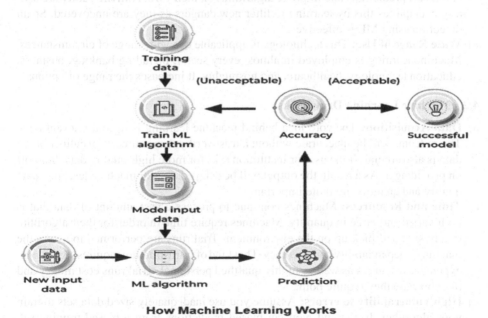

How Machine Learning Works

Fig. 5. Mechanics of machine learning

4.1 Machine Learning Benefits

a) Automation is faster, more effective, and more reliable than manual labor. Machine learning is used to build today's highly effective computers. Now, This powerful computer can handle a wide range of machine-learning models and complex algorithms.

b) **Improvement Potential:** In the field of machine learning, things are constantly evolving. It has many opportunities for growth and may eventually surpass other technologies. A lot of research and development is being done in this field, which benefits both the hardware and software.

c) **Easily identifies trends and patterns:** Machine learning is capable of analyzing vast amounts of data and identifying specific trends and patterns that people would miss. For instance, an e-commerce site like Amazon helps its consumers by learning about their browsing habits and prior purchases so that they can provide them the products, special deals, and reminders that are most appropriate for them. It employs the data to deliver relevant adverts to customers.

d) **No need for human interaction (automation):** You no longer need to supervise your project at every stage thanks to ML. When given the ability to learn, computers can create predictions and improve algorithms on their own. Antivirus software usually exemplifies this by learning to filter new dangers as they are uncovered. Spam detection using ML is effective.

e) **Wide Range of Use:** This technology is applicable to a wide range of circumstances. Machine learning is employed in almost every sector, including banking, business, education technology, healthcare, and hospitality. It increases the range of options

4.2 Machine Learning Drawbacks

a) **Data Acquisition:** The core idea behind machine learning is to find relevant data. The outcome will be inaccurate without a trustworthy data source. The caliber of the data is also crucial. If the user or institution asks for more high-quality data, hold off on providing it. As a result, the output will be delayed. So, for machine learning, data quality and quantity are quite important.

b) **Time and Resources:** Machines continue to process a vast amount of data that is both varied and large in quantity. Machines require time in order for their algorithm to adjust to and pick up on the environment. Trial runs are performed to assess the machine's dependability and accuracy. That kind of infrastructure requires significant, expensive resources as well as highly qualified personnel. Trial runs cost money and time because they require both.

c) **High vulnerability to errors:** Assume you use inadequately sized data sets to train your algorithm. In the end, you get biased predictions from a biased training set. Customers view irrelevant adverts as a result. Such ML defects have the potential to set off a chain reaction of errors that could go unnoticed for a very long period. Furthermore, it takes time to identify problems and even longer to find remedies.

d) **Changing Nature of Jobs** The nature of work is shifting as machine learning technology develops. All of the work is now completed by machines, which consumes the tasks that formerly required human labor. Those without technical training find it challenging to adapt to these developments (Fig. 6).

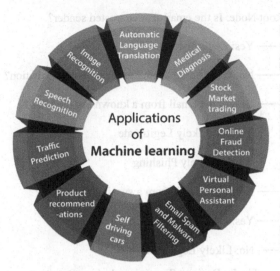

Fig. 6. Application of machine learning

5 Phishing Detection Using Machine Learning Algorithm

This method works well with large databases. This too overcomes the shortcomings of the current approach and allows the detection of zero-day threats. car Classifier-based learning is highly accurate at 95% accuracy rate. The volume of training data, the feature set, and the kind of classifier all have an impact on the outcomes. This has the disadvantage of not detecting whether the attacker has hosted his website on any domain. Much research has been done on the topic of phishing detection Most studies have focused on improving the success rate of phishing website detection. utilizing various classifiers. Various classifications are employed. KNN, SVM, Decision Tree, ANN, and Naive Bayes are some of the terms used in machine learning.

The implementation of a machine learning algorithm to find phishing detection is as below

1) Decision Tree Algorithm

one of the most widely used algorithms for machine learning. A decision tree method is simple to understand and apply. A decision tree begins by selecting the best classifier from the qualities that are available for the roots of the categorization tree. Up until a leaf node, the algorithm keeps growing the tree. The interior nodes of the tree represent features, while the leaf nodes of the tree represent class names. Data and the Gini Index The decision tree algorithm locates these points using the gain strategy (Fig. 7).

The process of the Decision tree algorithm for phishing detection is as below.

Root Key: The starting point for determining whether an email is from a trusted sender.

If the email is from a trusted sender, it is called a "legitimate email".

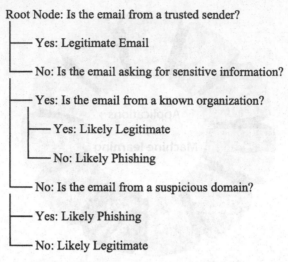

Root Node: Is the email from a trusted sender?

├── Yes: Legitimate Email

└── No: Is the email asking for sensitive information?

├── Yes: Is the email from a known organization?

│ ├── Yes: Likely Legitimate

│ └── No: Likely Phishing

└── No: Is the email from a suspicious domain?

├── Yes: Likely Phishing

└── No: Likely Legitimate

Fig. 7. Decision Tree using phishing Detection

If the email is not from a trusted sender, the decision tree considers whether the email is asking for sensitive information.

If an email requests sensitive information and is from a specific organization, it is considered "Potentially Legal" because some legal entities may request such information.

If the email asks for sensitive information and is not from a specific organization, it is classified as "Potential Phishing", as this is a common feature of phishing emails.

If the email does not ask for sensitive information, the decision tree considers whether the email is a suspicious domain or not.

If the email is from a suspicious domain, it is classified as "Possible Phishing", as phishing emails often come from such domains. Emails are considered "Probably Legitimate" if they are not from suspicious domains.

2) **Random forests Algorithm**

The random forest method, which is based on the concept of the decision tree algorithm, is one of the most effective machine learning algorithms. The Random Forest approach is used to produce decision trees. A large number of trees are associated with excellent detection accuracy. The tree is made using the Bootstrap technique. The bootstrap method uses a random database with replacement to generate a single tree from a selection of features and instances. Like decision tree algorithms, random forest algorithms find the best division categorization from a set of randomly chosen features. The Random Forest algorithm also uses data mining methods and the Gini index to select the ideal divisor. This procedure is performed until the random forest produces n trees. After each tree in the forest predicts the value of the target, the procedure determines the vote for each projected target. The greatest expected symbol serves as the last hunch in the random forest approach.

Here's an example of how Random Forest can be used for the prevention of phishing attacks.

Purpose: To prevent phishing attacks by classifying incoming emails as "Phishing" or "Legitimate" using a random forest algorithm.

Requirements:

Data Collection: Collect a set of data from tagged emails and every email classified as "Phishing" or "Legal".

Attribute Extraction: Extract relevant attributes from email content, sender information, and other attributes. These features may include the sender's domain reputation, known phishing passwords or URLs, email header information, email links and destinations, presence of attachments, and more.

Data processing: Prepare data sets by cleaning and transforming features. Handle missing values, code categorical variables, and make necessary data adjustments.

Data Partitioning: Partition the database into training sets and test/validation sets. The training set is used to develop the random forest model, while the test set is used to evaluate its effectiveness.

Training in the Random Forest: Trains a random forest model on a training database. The algorithm generates several decision trees, each of which is replaced by bootstrapping (random sampling with replacement) in a different part of the data. At each node of the tree, a random subset of features is considered for partitioning.

Ensemble Decision Making: When an email is classified, each tree in the forest randomly chooses whether it is phishing or legitimate. The final decision is made by taking a majority vote from all the trees.

Threshold setting: Defines the classification threshold for model predictions. For example, if more than 70% of the trees in the forest choose "Fishing", the email is defined as "Fishing". Otherwise, it is classified as "Law".

Integration: Integrate a trained random forest model into your email system. When a new email arrives, run the model for classification. So-called "phishing" emails may be quarantined or flagged for additional review, while "Legal" emails are allowed.

Monitor and update: Continuously monitor model performance in real time. Get feedback on accuracy and adaptability to changing phishing tactics. Retrain the model periodically with new data to keep it up to date.

Feedback loop: Implement a feedback loop where user-reported phishing emails or false positives can be used to improve the model. This helps the algorithm learn from new phishing threats and improve its accuracy over time.

3) Algorithm for Support Vector Machines

Support vector machines are another method in machine learning. An n-dimensional point is used to represent each input element. The hyperplane of the algorithm, which is created by the space in the support vector machine, divides the two classification groups. The closest points are discovered by the support vector machine, which then builds a line between them. The connected lines are then split in half by a perpendicular line made by the support vector machine. To accurately classify the data, the margin should be as large as possible. The margin in this situation is the separation between the support vector and the hyperplane. Support vector machines use the kernel approach, which raises the dimension space, to overcome this issue because complicated and linear data cannot be separated in the actual world.

objective: To prevent phishing attacks by classifying incoming emails as either "Phishing" or "Legitimate" using a Support Vector Machine (SVM) algorithm.

The steps to using the SVM algorithm to find phishing detection are as below:

Data Collection: Gather a dataset of labeled emails, where each email is categorized as "Phishing" or "Legitimate."

Feature Extraction: Extract relevant features from the email content, sender information, and other attributes. These features can include the sender's domain reputation, presence of known phishing keywords or URLs, email header information, links in the email and their destinations, presence of attachments, and more.

Data Preprocessing: Prepare the dataset by cleaning and transforming the features. Encode categorical variables, handle missing values, and carry out any necessary data conversions.

Splitting Data: From the dataset, create a training set and a testing/validation set. The training set is used to train the SVM model, while the testing set is used to evaluate its performance.

Aspect Scaling: Normalize or standardize the feature values so that they have similar scales. SVM scaling is frequently significant since features are sensitive to its size.

SVM Training: On the training dataset, train the SVM model. SVM tries to find a hyperplane that best separates the "Phishing" and "Legitimate" samples in the feature space. Depending on the problem, To discover the optimal separation, you can select from a variety of SVM kernel types, including linear, polynomial, and radial basis functions (RBF).

Hyperparameter Tuning: To enhance model performance, adjust the SVM's hyperparameters, including the regularization parameter (C) and the kernel parameters (such as gamma for RBF).

Evaluation: Utilize the testing/validation dataset to assess the SVM model's performance. Common evaluation criteria include AUC-ROC, accuracy, precision, recall, and F1-score.

Threshold Setting: Determine a classification threshold for the model's predictions. For example, you might decide that if the SVM's email's confidence score rises above a specific point, it is labeled as "Phishing." If not, it is labeled as "Legitimate."

Integration: Integrate the trained SVM model into your email system. As new emails arrive, pass them through the model for classification. Emails classified as "Phishing" can be quarantined or flagged for further review, while "Legitimate" emails are allowed through.

Monitoring and Updating: Continuously monitor the model's performance in real-time. Collect feedback on its accuracy and adaptability to changing phishing tactics. Periodically retrain the model with new data to keep it up-to-date.

5.1 Result Analysis and Comparisons

Analyzing the results of a machine learning algorithm for phishing detection involves evaluating its performance based on various metrics and insights. Here's a step-by-step guide on how to conduct this analysis.

(1) **Confusion Matrix:**

Start by examining the confusion matrix, which provides a detailed breakdown of the model's predictions:

True Positives (TP): Phishing instances correctly identified as phishing.

True Negatives (TN): Legitimate instances correctly identified as non-phishing.

False Positives (FP): Legitimate instances incorrectly identified as phishing.

False Negatives (FN): Phishing instances incorrectly identified as non-phishing.

(2) **Accuracy** of an algorithm represents the overall correctness of the model but may not be sufficient in an imbalanced data set.

$$\text{Accuracy} = \frac{(\text{TP} + \text{TN})}{(\text{TP} + \text{TN} + \text{FP} + \text{FN})}$$

(3) **Precision** of an algorithm represents the precision measures of the accuracy of positive predictions.

$$\text{Precision} = \frac{\text{TP}}{\text{TP} + \text{FP}}$$

(4) **Recall** measures the model's ability to identify all relevant instances.

$$\text{Recall} = \frac{\text{TP}}{\text{TP} + \text{FN}}$$

(5) **F1 Score** is also known as the F measure. The F1 score provides a balance between precision and recall.

$$\text{F1Score} = \frac{2 * \text{precision} * \text{recall}}{\text{Precision} + \text{recall}}$$

(6) **Receiver Operating Characteristic (ROC) Curve and AUC:** Plot the ROC curve, illustrating the trade-off between true positive rate and false positive rate. The Area Under the Curve (AUC) summarizes the ROC curve's performance.

(7) **False Positive Rate (FPR) and True Positive Rate (TPR)** These rates provide insights into the model's ability to minimize false positives while maximizing true positives.

$$\text{FPR} = \frac{\text{FP}}{\text{FP} + \text{TN}} \quad \text{TPR} = \frac{\text{TP}}{\text{TP} + \text{TN}}$$

(8) **Threshold Analysis:**

Assess the impact of adjusting the decision threshold for classification. Changing the threshold can influence the balance between false positives and false negatives.

(9) **Feature Importance:**

Analyze the importance of different features in the model. Identify which features contribute the most to accurate predictions.

(10) **Cross-validation:**

Utilize cross-validation techniques, such as k-fold cross-validation, to evaluate the model's performance across different subsets of the data.

(11) **Adversarial Testing:**

Subject the model to adversarial testing, involving intentionally modified or crafted examples designed to deceive the model. This step evaluates the model's robustness against potential attacks.

(12) **Class Imbalance Handling:**

If the dataset is imbalanced (more non-phishing instances than phishing instances or vice versa), consider techniques like oversampling, under-sampling, or using different class weights to address this issue.

(13) **Interpretability:**

If applicable, assess the interpretability of the model. Understanding how the model arrives at its decisions can provide insights into its behavior.

(14) **Feedback Loop:**

Establish a feedback loop for continuous improvement. Regularly update the model with new data, retrain it, and monitor its performance over time.

5.1.1 Comparisons Machine Learning to Other Tools to Find a Phishing Detection

In conclusion, machine learning offers a more sophisticated, adaptive, and accurate method of phishing detection than earlier technologies, which have been essential in cybersecurity. This constitutes a paradigm change in the field. When it comes to handling the always-shifting terrain of cybersecurity concerns, its capacity to remain ahead of developing threats makes it a recommended and practical option.

5.2 Difference Between Machine Learning Algorithm and Phishing Detection Algorithm

The phrase "machine learning algorithm" refers to a broad category of methods and strategies that are employed to allow machines to learn from data. Conversely, a "phishing attack detection algorithm" is a particular use of machine learning algorithms intended to recognize and stop phishing assaults. Below is a summary of the main distinctions:

Algorithm for Machine Learning:
Definition: A machine learning algorithm is a collection of guidelines and statistical methods that lets a computer system learn patterns from data and carry out a task without the need for explicit programming.

Scope: Machine learning techniques find application in a wide range of fields, including natural language processing, picture recognition, recommendation systems, and more.

Examples: include K-Nearest Neighbors, Neural Networks, Decision Trees, Support Vector Machines, and Logistic Regression.

Application: Regression, clustering, classification, and reinforcement learning are just a few of the many issues that machine learning techniques can be used to solve.

Phishing Attack Detection Algorithm:

Definition: A particular kind of machine learning algorithm intended to recognize instances of phishing attempts is called a phishing attack detection algorithm.

Scope: The main goal is to identify instances of fraudulent attempts to collect private information, frequently by using false websites, emails, or other forms of contact.

Examples: include supervised learning algorithms that are trained on sender information, URL properties, email content, and so on.

Application: To prevent people from becoming victims of fraudulent activity, cybersecurity uses phishing attack detection algorithms to automatically identify and block phishing attacks.

The application and scope are, in essence, where the differences are most significant. Whereas a phishing attack detection algorithm is a particular kind of machine learning algorithm created to address the particular difficulties of detecting and averting phishing attacks, a machine learning algorithm is a general idea that covers a wide range of techniques used to enable machines to learn from data. Inside the more general topic of machine learning, the latter is a specific application.

Conclusion

In the current digital environment, phishing presents a serious concern since it may be accomplished through a number of channels, such as voice calls, emails, and URLs, leaving user data vulnerable to abuse. Although there are many tools, methods, and antivirus programs available to combat phishing, the threat of phishing has not yet been totally eradicated. In order to tackle this problem, scientists are more and more using machine learning techniques, particularly the Random Forest Algorithm, Decision Tree algorithms, and vector support machine algorithm, as preventative steps against phishing scams. These algorithms show promise in detecting phishing attempts, offering a more sophisticated and adaptable defense against the ever-present and constantly changing phishing threats. Although there is no infallible answer, the application of machine learning to phishing prevention demonstrates a proactive approach to strengthening cybersecurity against this persistent threat.

References

1. Gayathri, V., Malatesh, S.H.: Phishing website detection using machine learning. IJARCCE **11**(2) (2022). https://doi.org/10.17148/IJARCCE.2022.11245
2. Chawla, A.: Phishing website analysis and detection using machine learning. Int. J. Intell. Syst. Appl. Eng. **10**(1), 10–16 (2022)
3. Krishna, V.A., Anusree, A., Jose, B., Anilkumar, K., Lee, O.T.: Phishing detection using machine learning based URL analysis: a Survey. Int. J. Eng. Res. Technol. (IJERT) (2021)
4. Rahim, M.N., Basheer, K.M.: A survey on anti-phishing techniques: from conventional methods to machine learning. Surv. Anti-Phish. Tech. Convent. Meth. Mach. Learn. **9**(1), 319–328 (2021)

5. Datta, S., Sen, S., Kundu, P.: A trustworthy swift weapon to detect the phishing URLs by machine learning approaches, 3244 (2022)
6. Tang, L., Mahmoud, Q.H.: A survey of machine learning-based solutions for phishing website detection. Mach. Learn. Knowl. Extract. **3**(3), 672–694 (2021)
7. Garje, A., Tanwani, N., Kandale, S., Zope, T.: Detecting phishing websites using machine learning. PloS One **9**(2320–2882) (2021)
8. Ravi Raju, B.S., Likhitha, S., Deepa, N., Sushma, S.: Survey on phishing websites detection using machine learning. Int. J. Res. Appl. Sci. Eng. Technol. **10**(5), 2376–2381 (2022). https://doi.org/10.22214/ijraset.2022.42843
9. Alanezi, M.: Phishing detection methods: a review. Technium Romanian J. Appl. Sci. Technol. **3**(9), 19–35 (2021). https://doi.org/10.47577/technium.v3i9.4973
10. Gontla, B.K., Gundu, P.: A machine learning approach to identify phishing websites: a comparative study of classification models and ensemble learning techniques **9** (2023). https://doi.org/10.4108/eetsis.vi.3300)
11. Arora, R., Singh, S.: Phishing attacks prevention and detection techniques (2020)
12. Kunju, M.V., Dainel, E., Anthony, H.C.: Evaluation of phishing techniques based on machine learning (2020). https://doi.org/10.1109/ICCS45141.2018.9065639
13. Tang, L., Mahmoud, Q.H.: A survey of machine learning-based solutions for phishing website detection. Mach. Learn. Knowl. Extract. **3**(3), 672–694 (2021). https://doi.org/10.3390/mak e3030034
14. Shahrivari, V., Izadi, M., Darabi, M.M.: Effectiveness of machine learning techniques in phishing detection **9**(2) (2019)
15. H, S., S, S., Reddy, B. A., G, S.: Phishing detection using machine learning techniques **8**(12S2), 6 (2019)
16. Joshi, S., Joshi, D.S.M.: Phishing Urls detection using machine learning techniques. **6**(6), 2349–7084 (2019)
17. Bhagyashree, A.V.: Detection of phishing websites using Machine Learning Techniques, **18** (2020)
18. Jathin, K., Praneeth, S., Baig, M.S., Ganesh, K.R.: A comparison study of machine learning techniques for phishing detection **4**(1) (2022). https://doi.org/10.36067/jbis.v4i1.120
19. Madan, S., Pranjali, C.: A review of machine learning techniques using decision tree and support vector machine (2016). https://doi.org/10.1109/ICCUBEA.2016.786004

CyTIE: Cyber Threat Intelligence Extraction with Named Entity Recognition

P. C. Aravind[1], Dincy R. Arikkat[1], Anupama S. Krishnan[1], Bahja Tesneem[1],
Aparna Sebastian[1], Mridul J. Dev[1], K. R. Aswathy[1], K. A. Rafidha Rehiman[1(✉)],
and P. Vinod[1,2]

[1] Department of Computer Applications, Cochin University of Science and Technology,
Kochi, India

{aravindpc333,anusk08,bahjatesneem,aparnasebastian,mriduljdev,
aswathykrajendran}@pg.cusat.ac.in, {dincyrarikkat,
rafidharehimanka,vinod.p}@cusat.ac.in, vinod.puthuvath@unipd.it

[2] Department of Mathematics, University of Padua, Padua, Italy

Abstract. In the dynamic intersection of Natural Language Processing and cyber security, Named Entity Recognition plays a pivotal role in comprehending and countering cyber threats. This paper explores Named Entity Recognition techniques within the cyber security context, utilizing a meticulously curated dataset with 12 distinct entity types extracted from security blogs. Our study involves developing and comparative analysis of five Named Entity Recognition models: BiLSTM, BiLSTM-CRF, BERT, BERT-CRF, and BERT-BiLSTM-CRF. Rigorous evaluation reveals that the BERT-BiLSTM-CRF model outperforms others with an F1-Score of 0.9635, excelling at extracting entities from the intricate language used in cyber security texts. Through this paper, we contribute to the ongoing Named Entity Recognition discourse in cyber security, paving the way for advancements in Natural Language Processing techniques and fortifying cyber security measures against evolving digital threats. The implementation and dataset are accessible on our Github page: https://github.com/OPTIMA-CTI/CyberNER.git.

Keywords: Cyber Threat Intelligence · Named Entity Recognition · Deep Learning · Web Crawling

1 Introduction

Cybercriminals are getting more sophisticated, allowing them to exploit zero-day vulnerabilities and Advanced Persistent Threats (APTs) [1]. Criminals are constantly infiltrating and attacking cyber systems, stealing sensitive information, taking control of targeted strategies, and collecting ransoms. The effectiveness of conventional defenses like firewalls, signature registrations, and intrusion de- tection systems (IDS) has been questioned [2]. Security experts employ Cyber Threat Intelligence (CTI), which comprises Indicators of Compromise (IoCs) to activate early warnings when a system faces a suspected danger and safeguard systems from such interruption [3]. Social media (blogs, vendor bulletins, hacker forums, etc.) has recently emerged as a powerful channel for disseminating cyber security knowledge.

© The Author(s), under exclusive license to Springer Nature Switzerland AG 2024
S. Rajagopal et al. (Eds.): ASCIS 2023, CCIS 2039, pp. 163–178, 2024.
https://doi.org/10.1007/978-3-031-59100-6_13

The frequency of harmful content shared on social media is rising, frequently exposing fresh weaknesses, malicious software, or attack methods. This serves as a valuable resource for gathering information on cyber threats. Security providers are now more actively utilizing these explicit threat descriptions to generate CTI and strengthen system defenses in advance. However, extracting CTI at an early stage necessitates a manual examination of threat descriptions, which can be time-consuming due to the large quantity of threat-related information [4].

The main objective of this work is to develop a robust entity extraction model that specializes in extracting cyber security-related information from textual data. Named Entity Recognition (NER) is a Natural Language Processing (NLP) technique that identifies and categorizes named entities within the text, such as attack names, malware groups, campaigns, indicators, and other predefined categories. NER plays a pivotal role in extracting meaningful insights from the text for accurately recognizing and classifying entities [5]. NER in cyber security is vital for threat detection, anomaly detection, and information extraction. The objective of NER in the field of cyber security is to detect and categorize terms related to cyber security within a vast array of diverse texts from various sources in the cyber security domain [6]. It is crucial in automating and improving different cyber security functions, enabling organizations to strengthen their defenses and respond effectively to cyber threats and incidents. We collect threat data from publicly available security blogs and utilize the Beginning-Inside-Outside (BIO) tagging method to annotate threat information entities to achieve this. Subsequently, we curate a comprehensive dataset for entity extraction and conduct NER on articles relevant to CTI.

This paper presents the following contributions.

- We compiled a fresh CTI-NER dataset by gathering data from various sources, including security vendor websites and blog articles related to threats. To practice reproducibility [7] and encourage further research in CTI, we openly shared the dataset and code[1]. This text-based dataset was annotated using BIO tagging scheme.
- We developed a range of NER detection models, utilizing classifiers like BiL- STM, BiLSTM-CRF, BERT, BERT-CRF, and BERT-BiLSTM-CRF. Ad- ditionally, we incorporated a case study to evaluate the efficiency of our suggested NER approach..

The remaining structure of this paper is as follows: Sect. 2 provides a brief overview of related research. Section 3 outlines the methods employed. Experimental results, comparison of different models, and case studies are explained in Sect. 4, and the final Sect. 5 presents the conclusion and discusses potential future work.

2 Related Work

In [8], Chieu et al. introduced a maximum entropy-based named entity recognizer that achieves high performance without relying on separate classifiers or complex formulations. This system utilizes global context from the entire document, allowing for the natural exploitation of information with a maximum entropy classifier. Lample et al.

---

[1] https://github.com/OPTIMA-CTI/CyberNER.git.

[9] presented two neural architectures for sequence labeling, such as Bidirectional Long Short-Term Memory (BiLSTM) networks in combination with conditional random fields and transition-based approach inspired by shift-reduce parsers. These models achieved exceptional results in NER, surpassing other models that relied on external resources such as gazetteers, when evaluated in standard settings. To capture morphological and orthographic information, the models utilized character-based word representations and unsupervised word representations. In [10], Kocaman et al. conducted extensive experiments to evaluate the NER module in the Spark NLP library. The study showed that the Spark NLP NER module outperformed the biomedical NER benchmarks set by Stanza and SciSpacy in nearly all datasets, all of this achieved without the need for intensive contextual embeddings such as BERT. In [11], Zhang et al. presented a deep learning-based model for recognizing Chinese public hazard entities in the dark net. The model combines syntactic and semantic information and incorporates Pinyin, POS, and BERT to overcome challenges such as homophonic and multi-entity expressions. The model, built upon the BiLSTM-CRF structure, outperformed baseline models in experiments conducted on a real dataset constructed from drugs-related groups in the Darknet demonstrating the effectiveness of the proposed syntactic and semantic information. In the paper [12] Wu et al. introduced a novel Cross-Transformer architecture for Chinese NER, which combines character-level, word embeddings, and linguistic features to capture local and global context in Chinese text. The model's performance on labeled datasets demonstrated improved accuracy in Chinese NER tasks, showcasing its potential for various natural language processing applications.

Huang et al. [13] compared various LSTM-based models for sequence label- ing, including LSTM networks, BiLSTM, LSTM-CRF, and BiLSTM with CRF. Their findings demonstrated that the Bi-LSTM-CRF model achieved state-of- the-art accuracy levels on chunking, POS, and NER datasets while exhibiting robustness and reduced reliance on word embeddings. In [14], Johri et al.introduced a Marathi language NER system using the CRF machine learning algorithm, trained and evaluated on 27,177 manually annotated sentences, achieving satisfactory performance despite Marathi's complex morphology and inflection. Zhang et al. in their paper [15] addressed the recognition of nested named entities in judicial intelligence using the Machine Reading Comprehension (MRC) framework. In [16] Puccetti et al. presented an innovative NER method for technology-related entities in patent documents, utilizing advanced techniques like domain-specific lexicons and rules to improve accuracy. In [17] Ying et al. introduced an advanced method for extracting named entities from Chinese clinical texts, effectively handling linguistic challenges and complex structures. This approach combines BiLSTM and CRF for sequence labeling, along with multi-head self-attention, demonstrating superior performance in medical natural language processing applications. In [18] Li et al. presented an innovative NER method for social networks, incorporating BERT, BiLSTM, and CRF into a hybrid model for contextual understanding and bidirectional dependency capture. In [19] Xu et al. proposed a method for identifying and categorizing named entities in text, combining BERT, BiLSTM, CRF, and self-attention.

Dasgupta et al. [20] conducted a comprehensive evaluation of different deep learning-based NER algorithms, considering cyber security sentences of various lengths. The top-performing model in their study incorporated BERT embeddings within a BiLSTM-CRF architecture, achieving 98.10% accuracy and an 88.60% F1-score. In [6], Gao et al. devised a cyber security NER model incorporating domain-specific dictionary embeddings and a multi-attention mechanism. By combining these elements with a BiLSTM architecture and a CRF component, their model achieved 88.36% F1-score. In [20], the authors established an NER dataset called APTNER and proceeded to assess several NER models. They determined that the BERT embedding-based BiLSTM model, in combination with CRF, achieved the top-performing F1-score of 82.31%. In [21], Alam et al. presented CyNER, an open-source library developed to extract cyber security-related entities from unstructured text. Their methodology involved a combination of diverse techniques, including the employment of transformer- based models for detecting malware entities, heuristic methods like regular expressions for recognizing indicators, and the use of established models like Spacy and Flair for identifying general entities such as locations and individuals. Their transformer-based model, specifically XLM with RoBERTa large, achieved an F1-score of 76.66%. In [22], Wang et al. introduced a NER model that integrates PERT embeddings and a neural network unit named GARU, combining features from both graph neural networks and recurrent neural networks. Their experimental results demonstrated an F1-score of 87.34%.

3   Methodology

Our proposed system enables the development of robust entity extraction models finely tuned to extract cyber security-related information from textual data. The methodology comprises a crawling module, NER Corpus Generation, and NER processing module (as illustrated in Fig. 1). In the initial phase, we created a dataset for training and evaluating our NER models, specifically focusing on capturing information about security incidents and threats. To achieve this, we seamlessly integrated a crawling module into our workflow for data collection. Subsequently, we applied the BIO tagging mechanism to annotate the threat data. Following this annotation process, we implemented various NER models capable of extracting entities from natural language documents.

3.1   Crawling Module

The crawling module constitutes the initial phase of our research, designed to acquire textual data from security websites and threat-related blog articles.

Through a carefully crafted web crawler using *Selenium*[2] and *Beautifulsoup*[3], we selectively navigate a curated list of security websites, which is provided in the Table 1, to extract relevant information concerning cyber security threats. The crawler efficiently filters and cleans the collected textual data, adhering to ethical considerations and respecting the websites' terms of service. This is achieved through carefully checking and adhering to the instructions found in the websites' *robots.txt* files, which webmasters use to guide search engine crawlers on how to explore their sites. Robots.txt provides

---

[2] https://www.selenium.dev/.
[3] https://beautiful-soup-4.readthedocs.io/en/latest/.

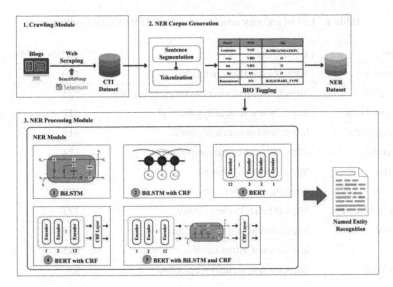

Fig. 1. Architecture of NER-based Threat Information Extraction

directives that specify which parts of the site can be crawled or should be excluded from crawling by these user agents. The crawling architecture diagram is explained in Fig. 2. Utilizing this module, our objective is to accumulate a comprehensive CTI dataset that serves as the foundation of our NER system, enabling precise and meaningful entity extraction from texts related to cyber security. Consequently, we assembled a CTI dataset comprising 2949 blog articles related to cyber security.

3.2   NER Corpus Generation

The second step in our system involves creating the NER corpus for cyber security-related information extraction. This phase commences with breaking down the textual data into individual sentences and further dividing them into constituent words. To build the NER dataset, a meticulous manual labeling process is undertaken, where each word is annotated using the BIO tagging scheme, with predefined tags relevant to cyber security entities.

Human Annotation: To establish ground-truth annotations for our corpus data, we assembled a team of annotators comprised of six postgraduate students and a Ph.D. student with Computer Science and cyber security backgrounds. Additionally, two experienced faculty members were engaged to cross-validate and provide guidance throughout the annotation process. The annotation methodology, encompassing training, documentation, collaborative discussions, and iter- ative refinement, establishes a robust foundation for training machine-learning- based models on our annotated corpus data.

Our methodology commenced with distributing five articles, each containing approximately 700 words, to the annotators. This initial allocation aimed at harnessing diverse perspectives and expertise to identify entities within the corpus data comprehensively. After a week, we conducted a meeting to discuss and resolve any discrepancies in the

Table 1. List of security articles used for CTI threat data collection

Webpage	URL	Number of Blogs
The Register	https://www.theregister.com/	220
Info Security	https://www.infosecurity-magazine.com/	285
IT Security Guru	https://www.itsecurityguru.org/	312
Krebsonsecurity	https://krebsonsecurity.com/	315
Nakedsecurity	https://nakedsecurity.sophos.com/	124
Secure list	https://securelist.com/	165
Cybernews	https://cybernews.com/	180
The Hacker News	https://thehackernews.com/	227
Kaspersky	https://www.kaspersky.co.in/	183
ZDNet	https://www.zdnet.com/	845
SecurityWeek	https://www.securityweek.com/	93

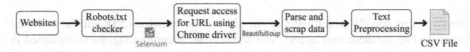

Fig. 2. Architecture of Web crawler

annotations. In assessing the reliability of our annotation process, we employed Fleiss' Kappa, a statistical measure designed to evaluate agreement among multiple annotators when categorizing items into multiple classes. The formula, $k = \frac{P - Pe}{1 - Pe}$, takes into account both the observed agreement (P) and the expected agreement by chance (Pe). Initially, we got a Kappa value of 0.75 which indicates a substantial agreement. The main disagreements between a specific attack type and its association with a campaign can be complicated. Additionally, confusion arose when classifying malware versus legitimate tools adapted for malicious purposes. We discussed the disagreements and reached decisions, particularly for certain entities, by referring to the official MITRE[4] website.

Following the initial annotation phase, the annotators were tasked with an- other 10 sets of articles, during which we continuously computed and addressed disagreements through meetings. Our iterative approach involved ongoing discussions and regular checks for disagreement, allowing us to refine our dataset seamlessly. This iterative process not only helped us to improve the annotations over time, but it also served as a dynamic feedback loop to enhance the skills of our annotators. Finally, after a two-month duration, we concluded the dataset development phase once we had reached a consensus and ensured the presence of high-quality annotations.

---

[4] https://attack.mitre.org/.

Table 2. Cyber security entities used in the NER task

Entity	Description	Example
Attack Type	The method or strategy the attackers use to breach the system, data, or network	Phishing, Malware
Campaign	Series of attacks or activities by threat actors with specific goal	Lizard Squad, H4ksniper
Location	Represents a place, either physical or virtual, tied to cyber security entities. Helps understand context and threat scope	United states of America, U.K
Malware	Encompasses various types and names of malicious software	Trojan, Conti Ransomware
Threat Actor	Refers to individuals or groups orchestrating cyber attacks	Hacker, Cyber criminal
Tool	Software that can be used by someone to protect a computer, test its security, simulate attacks, or even by someone with bad intentions	ZxShell, 3PARA RAT
Infrastructure	Refers to any physical device or component used in the context of cyber attacks	Routers, Servers
Asset	Refers to any resource or component of an organization's digital infrastructure that needs protection	$ 1.5 Billion, Money
Vulnerability	Signifies a weakness or flaw in a system, software application, or network that attackers could exploit	CVE-2022–22972, Unprotected wifi
Indicator	Cyber forensic artifacts, including email, file extension, IP address, protocol, hash, URL, port, domain address, and path	hxxp://abc.in, 75.145.58.53
Identity	Encompasses roles and attributes associated with individuals and organizations relevant in cyber security analysis	Barack Obama, Facebook
Date Time	Refers to specific dates and times relevant to cyber attacks, aiding in incident response and strategy determination	2023–10-01, 14:30

Entity labeling: To label the data, we first conducted sentence segmentation and assigned POS tags using the NLTK[5] python library. Subsequently, each word was annotated using the BIO tagging scheme, also known as IOB tagging. The acronym B-I-O represents the three tags utilized in this approach: Beginning, Inside, and Outside. Each word in a given text is assigned a tag, indicating whether it marks the start of a named entity (B), appears within a named entity (I), or lies outside any named entity (O). For example, consider the sentence "The company XYZ in the United States accounted for 23% of trojan attacks during 2019." In this case, "XYZ" is an Identity, "United States" constitutes a Location, while "trojan" is a malware and "2019" is a DATE-TIME. The corresponding BIO tags for this sentence would be: "The: O, company:O, XYZ: B-IDENTITY, in: O, United: B-LOCATION, States: I-LOCATION, accounted: O, for: O, 23-O, percent:O, of: O, trojan: B-MALWARE, attacks: O, during:O, 2019: B-DATE TIME." This standardized labeling technique is a foundation for training machine learning models in entity recognition endeavors. We selected 12 entities for our entity recognition framework, aligning with the STIX 2.1[6]objects and taking into consideration the current state of the art. These en- tities encompass attack type, campaign, location, malware, threat actor, tool, infrastructure, asset, vulnerability, indicator, identity, and date-time. Detailed information about the entities we selected is provided in Table 2. The manual labeling process resulted in an annotated NER dataset, which forms a crucial foundation for both training and evaluating the entity extraction models and classifying cyber security-related entities within the text. This dataset comprises 204,815 entity tags, spans across 18,458 sentences, and encompasses 449 articles. The remaining articles were excluded as they lack relevant threat information but contain definitions of cyber attacks, and security guidelines. The statistics for each entity are outlined in Table 3.

3.3 NER Processing Module

The NER processing module is crucial in our information extraction framework. This module presents the training and evaluation of five distinct NER mod- els: BiLSTM, BiLSTM with CRF, Bidirectional Encoder Representations from Transformers (BERT), BERT with CRF, BERT with BiLSTM and CRF. Each model brings its unique strengths to entity recognition, providing a comprehensive approach to extracting meaningful cyber security information from diverse sources.

BiLSTM: Bidirectional Long Short-Term Memory (BiLSTM) [23] is a type of recurrent neural network (RNN) trained to process input sequences in both the forward and backward directions. This allows the network to consider the context of the entire sequence before and after a given input element, which helps to address the contextual ambiguity of input sequences. Unlike standard LSTMs, which only process sequences in one direction, BiLSTMs use two LSTMs, one for forward processing and one for backward processing. This allows BiLSTMs to capture context from both sides of the sequence, which enhances their understanding of the meaning of words and phrases in context.

---

[5] https://www.nltk.org/.
[6] https://oasis-open.github.io/cti-documentation/stix/intro.html.

Table 3. The statistics of each entities used for NER

Entity	B-Tag	I-Tag	Total
ASSET	127	87	214
ATTACK TYPE	715	161	876
CAMPAIGN	108	81	189
DATE TIME	968	380	1348
IDENTITY	3972	1989	5961
INDICATOR	345	79	424
INFRASTRUCTURE	348	80	428
LOCATION	1431	263	1694
MALWARE	1111	239	1350
THREAT ACTOR	470	132	602
TOOL	1023	193	1216
VULNERABILITY	55	79	134
Total	10673	3763	14436
O			190379
Total			204815

The outputs of the two LSTMs are then concatenated to produce a more complete representation of the input sequence.

CRF: Conditional Random Field (CRF) [24], a widely recognized and effective statistical modeling technique of NER, addresses the sequential nature of natural language by incorporating dependencies among adjacent words in a sentence. Unlike traditional sequence tagging approaches, CRF considers the global context of the entire sentence when predicting the label for each word, allowing for better capturing of contextual information. In the context of NER, CRF exploits the correlations between adjacent words and the relationships among different entity types. By considering the joint probability distribution of the entire sequence, CRF offers a principled approach for optimizing the labeling of named entities and has demonstrated superior performance in various NER tasks, making it a valuable tool for extracting cyber security-related information from textual data.

BERT: Bidirectional Encoder Representations from Transformers (BERT) [25] is a transformer-based machine learning technique for NLP developed by Google. It uses the surrounding text to provide context to grasp the meaning of ambiguous terms in the text. It encodes semantic and syntactic information in its embeddings, making it suitable for various applications. BERT takes extensive text data as input and generates a representation of the input text. Through pre-training and fine-tuning, BERT excels in multiple natural language comprehension tasks with minimal task-specific architecture and training data.

4 Experimental Evaluation

Experimental Setup: We executed the experiment on an Ubuntu 22.04 LTS system, equipped with an Intel Core i9 processor, NVIDIA Quadro P2000 featuring 5 GB of GDDR5X memory, and 32 GB of RAM. To gather data from the security websites, we employed the *BeautifulSoup* and *Selenium* libraries. To visualize the results, we utilized the *matplotlib* library. The dataset has been partitioned into an 8:2 ratio for the purpose of training and testing the NER models. We have de- veloped the BERT-based NER models using PyTorch, while the BiLSTM model was implemented using TensorFlow.

4.1 Evaluation Metrics

We evaluate the performance of the classification models using four different metrics. To understand these metrics, it is essential to define some fundamental terms. In the context of positive and negative classes, True Positives (TP) and True Negatives (TN) represent correct predictions made by the classifier, where the predicted label matches the actual label. Conversely, False Positives (FP) and False Negatives (FN) indicate instances that were misclassified by the classifier, where the predicted label does not match the actual label. These terms help us comprehend the metrics and assess the effectiveness of the classification models. We utilized the F-measure statistic due to the unbalanced nature of our dataset and the skewed distribution of classes. The F-measure, sometimes the F1-Score, is the harmonic mean of recall and precision and indicates how well the model can identify all domains, including minority ones. Recall measures the ability of the model to identify all positive cases present in the dataset, while precision assesses the model's reliability in predicting an instance as positive. The following equations compute the precision, recall, and F-measure.

$$\text{Precision}(p) = \frac{TP}{TP + FP} \tag{1}$$

$$\text{Recall}(R) = \frac{TP}{TP + FN} \tag{2}$$

$$F - measure = 2 \times \frac{\text{Precision} \times \text{Recall}}{\text{Precision} + \text{Recall}} \tag{3}$$

4.2 Results

We explored models such as BiLSTM, BiLSTM with CRF, BERT, BERT with CRF, and a hybrid BERT-BiLSTM-CRF model to recognize named entities. Table 4 provides the results of various models. All models exhibited exceptional performance across the metrics, consistently achieving precision, recall, and F1-Score surpassing 0.96. BERT-BILSTM-CRF stood out, securing the highest F1-Score at 0.9635. This shows that BERT-based models can generalize well and perform consistently across a wide range of entity recognition tasks. BERT improves its comprehension by considering the surrounding context during the creation of embeddings, achieved through the masking of specific words in a sentence [20]. The adaptability and robust performance of BERT-based models, particularly BERT-CRF and BERT-BiLSTM-CRF, position them as promising choices for enhancing information extraction from unstructured text in various domains.

Table 4. Performance comparison of different NER models

Models	Precision	Recall	F-measure
BiLSTM	0.9609	0.9615	0.9608
BiLSTM-CRF	0.9602	0.9623	0.9609
BERT	0.9617	0.9612	0.9614
BERT-CRF	0.9624	0.9610	0.9616
BERT-BILSTM-CRF	0.9645	0.9628	**0.9635**

4.3 Analysis of Entity Recognition

In evaluating entity recognition, the performance Table 5 sheds light on various key observations. Specific entity types such as 'DATE TIME,' 'LOCATION,' 'MALWARE,' and 'INFRASTRUCTURE' demonstrated commendable F1 scores ranging from 0.88 to 0.93. These results imply that these entities exhibit discernible patterns or contextual clues, enabling the model to recognize and classify them accurately. The consistently high performance for these categories indicates that the model excels in capturing the nuances associated with temporal information, geographic references, malware mentions, and infrastructure identifiers. Nevertheless, variability exists in the model's performance across different entity types. 'VULNERABILITY' and 'ASSET' displayed lower F1 scores of 0.60 and 0.57, respectively. This suggests potential challenges in identifying these entities, possibly due to linguistic variability or limited contextual information. Entities like 'VULNERABILITY' may present diverse linguistic expressions or lack explicit contextual markers, posing challenges for accurate recognition. Similarly, 'ASSET' may involve various terms and descriptors, making it more intricate for the model to distinguish them from regular text.

Our evaluation found notable cases of misclassification by our NER model. For instance, 18 'CAMPAIGN' entities were misclassified as 'MALWARE', and 20 'IDENTITY' entities were incorrectly categorized as 'MALWARE'. For example, the NER model incorrectly classifies the entity "Armageddon" as 'MALWARE' where the correct tag is 'CAMPAIGN', due to the term's ambiguity and the context of cyber security. These cases highlight the challenges in distinguishing between different entity types, especially when they share similar linguistic characteristics. A significant issue arises when many entities are erroneously classified as the 'O' (Other) tag. This misclassification occurs primarily due to the sheer abundance of 'O' tags compared to other entity types. In Fig. 3, we present the multiclass confusion matrix, which provides a comprehensive overview of the model's performance across all entity types in the cyber security domain.

Table 5. F1-Score of each entity tag based on BERT-BiLSTM-CRF

Entity	F1-Score	Support
O	0.98	45505
DATE TIME	0.93	350
LOCATION	0.88	397
MALWARE	0.88	627
INDICATOR	0.87	310
ATTACK TYPE	0.83	432
IDENTITY	0.79	2094
THREAT ACTOR	0.77	259
CAMPAIGN	0.76	125
TOOL	0.72	514
INFRASTRUCTURE	0.63	149
VULNERABILITY	0.60	40
ASSET	0.57	108

4.4 Case of Entity Extraction

For the entity extraction testing, the BERT-BiLSTM-CRF algorithm, which has the highest F-measure, was utilized. For testing the entity extraction, we selected an APT threat intelligence report titled *Administrative organizations were at- tacked with PowerMagic backdoor and CommonMagic framework*[7], published on 21st March 2023 by Kaspersky. This report focused on a new APT discovered in the context of the Russo-Ukrainian conflict. The results of the entity prediction for the text are presented in Fig. 4. The experimental findings in Fig. 4 demonstrated that the BERT-BiLSTM-CRF model effectively extracted the de- tails regarding the types of attacks, dates, and locations involved as described in sentences. This successful extraction of entities indicates the overall success of the entity extraction process.

4.5 Comparison with State of Art

We conducted a comparative analysis of related works(as seen in Table 6) in cyber security NER, considering factors such as the number of entities, model performance, utilized models, and dataset availability. Dion´ısio et al. [26] employed BIO tagging on Twitter data recognizing only five entity types with a performance of 92% using BiLSTM with CRF. Pingchuan et al. [27] utilized a publicly available dataset [28] with nine entities, also employing BiLSTM with CRF for NER, with an f1 score of 89.38%. Similarly, Gao et al. [6] utilized a publicly available dataset with seven entities, using BiLSTM + Dict + Att + CRF, resulting in an 88.36% F1 score. Others, like Dasgupta

---

[7] https://securelist.com/bad-magic-apt/109087/.

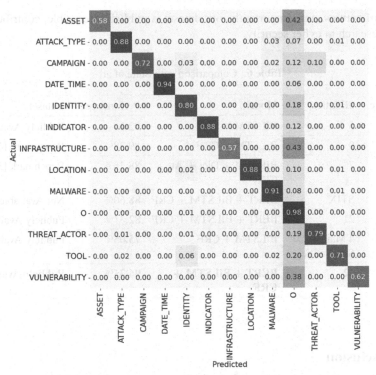

Fig. 3. Confusion Matrix for High-Performing NER Model

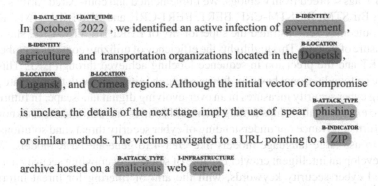

Fig. 4. Entity Extraction of blog report using the BERT-BiLSTM-CRF model

et al. [20], employed the BERT-based BiLSTM with CRF combination with STIX-based entities, achiev- ing an 88.60% F1 score. Wang et al. [20] provided a publicly accessible dataset and used BERT-based BiLSTM with CRF with 21 entities, yielding an F1 score of 82.31%. Kim et al. [29] also publicly shared their dataset, utilizing a bag of characters mechanism with BiLSTM with CRF, resulting in a lower F1 score of 75.05%. In comparison, our model outperforms in terms of performance, recognizes a significant number of entities, and, importantly, our dataset is publicly accessible, contributing to further research in cyber security.

Table 6. Comparison with State of art

Reference	#Entities	Model	Performance	Dataset
[26]	5	BiLSTM + CRF	92%	Publicly Available
[27]	9	BiLSTM + CRF	89.38%	Benchmark [28]
[6]	7	BiLSTM + Dict + Att + CRF	88.36%	Benchmark [30]
[20]	STIX	BERT + BiLSTM + CRF	88.60%	Not Available
[20]	21	BERT + BiLSTM + CRF	82.31%	Publicly Available
[29]	4 Main & 20 Sub Entities	BiLSTM + CRF	75.05%	Publicly Available
CyTIE	**12**	**BERT + BiLSTM + CRF**	**96.35%**	**Publicly Available**

5 Conclusion

To enhance NER in the field of cyber security, our study delved into an extensive dataset of 204,815 tags sourced from weblogs. We implemented and com- pared various models, including BiLSTM, BiLSTM-CRF, BERT, BERT-CRF, and BERT-BiLSTM-CRF. Our research outcomes demonstrated the superior- ity of BERT-BiLSTM-CRF, showcasing an F-measure of 0.9635. This highlights the efficiency of utilizing contextual embeddings from BERT and the precision in sequence labeling achieved through CRF. This study establishes a founda- tional basis for future research initiatives, with the ultimate goal of enhancing cyber security measures in an ever-evolving digital landscape. In future work, we plan to extract relationships among identified entities and also construct a knowledge graph to further advance our understanding of cyber security threats and solutions. Also, we plan to use large language models like GPT-4 to generate NER models. We also plan to develop an intelligent crawler capable of selectively crawling security data using predefined cyber security keywords, with the aim of filtering for threat information exclusively.

References

1. Alshamrani, A., Myneni, S., Chowdhary, A., Huang, D.: A survey on advanced persistent threats: techniques, solutions, challenges, and research opportunities. IEEE Commun. Surv. Tutorials **21**(2), 1851–1877 (2019)
2. Thakkar, A., Lohiya, R.: A survey on intrusion detection system: feature selection, model, performance measures, application perspective, challenges, and future re- search directions. Artif. Intell. Rev. **55**(1), 453–563 (2022)

3. Wagner, T.D., Mahbub, K., Palomar, E., Abdallah, A.E.: Cyber threat intelligence sharing: survey and research directions. Comput. Secur. **87**, 101589 (2019)

4. Zhao, J., Yan, Q., Li, J., Shao, M., He, Z., Li, B.: Timiner: automatically extracting and analyzing categorized cyber threat intelligence from social data. Comput. Secur. **95**, 101867 (2020)

5. Gao, C., Zhang, X., Han, M., Liu, H.: A review on cyber security named entity recognition. Front. Inform. Technol. Electr. Eng. **22**(9), 1153–1168 (2021)

6. Gao, C., Zhang, X., Liu, H.: Data and knowledge-driven named entity recognition for cyber security. Cybersecurity **4**(1), 1–13 (2021)

7. Daoudi, N., Allix, K., Bissyandé, T.F., Klein, J.: Lessons learnt on reproducibility in machine learning based android malware detection. Empirical Softw. Eng. **26**(4). 74 (2021)

8. Chieu, H.L., Ng, H.T.: Named entity recognition: a maximum entropy approach using global information. In: COLING 2002: The 19th International Conference on Computational Linguistics (2002)

9. Lample, G., Ballesteros, M., Subramanian, S., Kawakami, K., Dyer, C.: Neural architectures for named entity recognition, arXiv preprint arXiv:1603.01360 (2016)

10. Kocaman, V., Talby, D.: Biomedical named entity recognition at scale. In: Recognition, P. (ed.) ICPR International Workshops and Challenges: Virtual Event, Jan- uary 10–15, 2021, pp. 635–646. Springer, Proceedings, Part I (2021)

11. P. Zhang, X. Wang, J. Ya, J. Zhao, T. Liu, J. Shi, Darknet public hazard entity recognition based on deep learning, in: Proceedings of the 2021 ACM International Conference on Intelligent Computing and its Emerging Applications, 2021, p. 94 100

12. S. Wu, X. Song, Z. Feng, Mect: Multi-metadata embedding based cross-transformer for chinese named entity recognition, arXiv preprint arXiv:2107.05418 (2021)

13. Z. Huang, W. Xu, K. Yu, Bidirectional lstm-crf models for sequence tagging, arXiv preprint arXiv:1508.01991 (2015)

14. Johri, P., Khatri, S.K., Al-Taani, A.T., Sabharwal, M., Suvanov, S., Kumar, A.: Natural language processing: History, evolution, application, and future work. In: Proceedings of 3rd International Conference on Computing Informatics and Networks: ICCIN 2020, pp. 365–375. Springer (2021)

15. Zhang, H., Guo, J., Wang, Y., Zhang, Z., Zhao, H.: Judicial nested named entity recognition method with mrc framework. Inter. J. Cognitive Comput. Eng. **4**, 118–126 (2023)

16. Puccetti, G., Giordano, V., Spada, I., Chiarello, F., Fantoni, G.: Technology identifi- cation from patent texts: a novel named entity recognition method. Technol. Forecast. Soc. Chang. **186**, 122160 (2023)

17. An, Y., Xia, X., Chen, X., Wu, F.-X., Wang, J.: Chinese clinical named entity recognition via multi-head self-attention based bilstm-crf. Artif. Intell. Med. **127**, 102282 (2022)

18. Li, W.: Ud bbc: named entity recognition in social network combined bert-bilstm-crf with active learning. Eng. Appli. Artifi. Intell. **116**, 105460 (2022)

19. Xu, L., Li, S., Wang, Y., Xu, L.: Named entity recognition of bert-bilstm-crf combined with self-attention. In: Web Information Systems and Applications: 18th International Conference, WISA, Kaifeng, China, 24–26 September 2021, Proceedings 18, pp. 556–564. Springer (2021)

20. Dasgupta, S., Piplai, A., Kotal, A., Joshi, A.: A comparative study of deep learning based named entity recognition algorithms for cybersecurity. In: 2020 IEEE International Conference on Big Data (Big Data), pp. 2596–2604. IEEE (2020)

21. Wang, X., et al.: Aptner: a specific dataset for ner missions in cyber threat intelligence field. In: 2022 IEEE 25th International Conference on Computer Supported Cooperative Work in Design (CSCWD), pp. 1233–1238. IEEE (2022)

22. Alam, M.T., Bhusal, D., Park, Y., Rastogi, N.: Cyner: a python library for cyber- security named entity recognition, arXiv preprint arXiv:2204.05754 (2022)

23. Wang, X., Liu, J.: A novel feature integration and entity boundary detection for named entity recognition in cybersecurity. Knowl.-Based Syst. **260**, 110114 (2023)
24. Chen, Y., et al.: Named entity recognition from chinese adverse drug event reports with lexical feature based bilstm-crf and tri-training. J. Biomed. Inform. **96**, 103252 (2019)
25. Xu, K., Yang, Z., Kang, P., Wang, Q., Liu, W.: Document-level attention-based bilstm- crf incorporating disease dictionary for disease named entity recognition. Comput. Biol. Med. **108**, 122–132 (2019)
26. Li, X., Zhang, H., Zhou, X.-H.: Chinese clinical named entity recognition with variant neural structures based on bert methods. J. Biomed. Inform. **107**, 103422 (2020)
27. Dionısio, N., Alves, F., Ferreira, P.M., Bessani, A.: Cyberthreat detection from twitter using deep neural networks. In: 2019 International Joint Conference on Neural Networks (IJCNN), pp. 1–8. IEEE (2019)
28. Ma, P., Jiang, B., Lu, Z., Li, N., Jiang, Z.: Cybersecurity named entity recognition us- ing bidirectional long short-term memory with conditional random fields. Tsinghua Science and Technology **26**(3), 259–265 (2020)
29. Lal, R., et al.: Information Extraction of Security related entities and concepts from unstructured text. Faculty of the Graduate School of the University of Maryland (2013)
30. Kim, G., Lee, C., Jo, J., Lim, H.: Automatic extraction of named entities of cyber threats using a deep bi-lstm-crf network. Int. J. Mach. Learn. Cybern. **11**, 2341–2355 (2020)
31. Bridges, R.A., Jones, C.L., Iannacone, M.D., Testa, K.M., Goodall, J.R.: Automatic labeling for entity extraction in cyber security, arXiv preprint arXiv:1308.4941 (2013)

Design and Implementation of Multilayer Encryption for Audio File Security

Lakhichand Khushal Patil[1,2](✉) and Kalpesh A. Popat[3]

[1] Fergusson College (Autonomous), Pune, Maharashtra, India
lakhichand.patil@fergusson.edu
[2] Marwadi University, Rajkot, Gujarat, India
[3] Research Supervisor, Marwadi University, Rajkot, Gujarat, India
Kalpesh.popat@marwadieducation.edu.in

Abstract. Using audio encryption, secure information can be transmitted. By doing this, Sender and Receiver audio security is guaranteed. The security of delivering private audio data is crucial given the rapid advancement of communication technology. Applying a key (noise) and exact algorithm to the plain text is how audio encryption protects data in an audio file from parasitic assaults. To guarantee data privacy, high solidity, and trustworthiness, the security system must be extremely secure, quick, and robust. There are various drawbacks and difficulties with audio data encryption, such as the need for additional resources and expenses for implementation and maintenance, as well as the addition of complexity and hazards to data management. Additionally, it may hinder data visibility and usability and slow down data processing and analysis. The authors have analysed and compared the various audio file encryption methods at the beginning of the paper. The article suggests using the audio file encryption technique and its implementation to get around issues like the need for additional resources, increased expenses, and hazards associated with data management. Audio files can be encrypted using the suggested multilayer method, which increases security.

Keywords: Audio file · Security · Multilayer Encryption · Cryptanalysis · Cryptographic algorithm

1 Introduction

1.1 Overview of Cryptography and Information Security

Using cryptography, information is hidden or encoded so that the intended recipient of an exchange can decipher it. Cryptography is a method that has been used to encrypt messages since the dawn of time and is still used today in online shopping, debit and credit cards, and computer passwords. (Refer Fig. 1) [1]. "Cryptography" is the combination of the word "crypt" (which means "hidden") and "graphy" (which means "writing"). In Cryptography, Algorithms are a set of rule-based calculations that are used to alteration communications in a method that makes it impossible to decipher them. These computations are used to change telecommunications in ways that are carried out to safeguard

© The Author(s), under exclusive license to Springer Nature Switzerland AG 2024
S. Rajagopal et al. (Eds.): ASCIS 2023, CCIS 2039, pp. 179–191, 2024.
https://doi.org/10.1007/978-3-031-59100-6_14

information [2]. The field of mathematics known as cryptography, which deals with the secure encoding of data, sometimes uses techniques like the prime factorization of extremely big integers.

Information safety protections delicate data from unauthorised acts such unauthorised inspection, modification, recording, disruption, or destruction [3]. The goal is to ensure the safety and confidentiality of confidential data, including banking data, proprietary information, and customer account information. Cryptography can protection the privacy and honesty of data though it is at break and while it is being sent. It can also avoid denial and establish trust among senders and receivers. Software systems regularly have numerous endpoints, frequent clients, and a number of back-end servers. The information security method of cryptography protects corporate interactions and information from online threats by using codes. The main detached of information security is to prevent the disclosure, modification, or destruction of information. Furthermore, the proper information needs to be made immediately and appropriately available to the right people. It must be prevented that information is abused or falls into the incorrect hands. Information security is relevant to individuals, groups, companies, and government activities. Therefore, everyone in society is involved in information security.

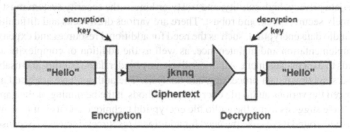

Fig. 1. Process of Cryptography

Data encryption [4] is the procedure of transforming data from plaintext (unencrypted) to ciphertext (secure). Users can access protected and decrypted data via a key for encryption and a decryption key, respectively. It helps to safeguard private data and complex data, and it can strengthen the safety of communications among client apps and servers. In spirit, if your data has been encrypted, it won't be clear even if someone or some organisation who should not have knowledge of it does. By applying a key (noise) and exact algorithm to the plain text, audio encryption [5] protects data in an audio file from parasitical attacks. The security system must be extremely secure, quick, and robust to assure data confidentiality, high solidity, and trustworthiness. A file that has been encoded using a particular method to make it difficult for unauthorized people to access the data inside is known as an encrypted audio file. The purpose of doing this is to safeguard the discretion and confidentiality of the data in the file. To decrypt the file and access the information inside, the encryption method frequently entails the use of a key or password. To prevent unauthorized access, modification, or theft, audio data (such as music, speech, or sound recordings) is encoded. Only the correct decryption key can be used to unlock and play the encrypted audio [6].

1.2 Role of Cryptography in Information Security

The four main goals of cryptography are privacy, honesty, reliability, and not being repudiated [7]. Data privacy (confidential treatment), data authenticity (confirmed source), and data integrity (original and undamaged message) are the objectives, to put it another way. Non-repudiation is an amalgam of each of these three elements in order to show the message or data's undeniable legitimacy. (Refer Fig. 2). An instance of not being repudiated in action is a service used to validate digital signatures and ensure that a person cannot plausibly dispute having signed a document. The top priority of these goals is confidentiality. The main objective of cryptography is to restrict access to the data by unauthorised people. This doesn't mean the remaining goals are any less important. Data integrity is crucial to ensure that the message hasn't been altered in any way. If this weren't the case, the receiving party might do something improper or unpleasant. Whether the sender is a spy talking with the leadership of their country or a firm giving orders to a field office, both the sender and the recipient need to be certain that the message was sent and that it is exactly the same. Authenticity is essential to ensuring that an individual or system is recognised and acknowledged. Authenticating the person who sent the message or recipient's identity is crucial for this guarantee. The system must also be recognised in order to stop ransomware attempts that utilise phishing (fraudulent emails), phishing (fraudulent messages and telephone calls), smishing (fraudulent sms), and other deceptive communication channels [8].

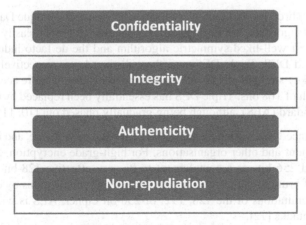

Fig. 2. Goals of Cryptography

1.3 Verview of Cryptography Algorithms

There are two types of encryptions based on the types of passwords and encryption methods. (Refer to Figs. 3 and 4) Symmetric Key Coding, or private key encryption, encrypts data with a solitary key that is only known to the despatcher and receiver. Even if the underground key should not be transmitted across the station, both the person who sent it and the receiver of the message must be aware of it. However, if the hacker has the key, interpreting the meaning of the words will be easier. The key must be handled when both the sender of the messages and the recipient are immediately on the handset. This, however, is not found to be the most effective course of action. The key maintains the same, making communication with a single recipient easier. The most widely used symmetric key system is the data encrypted scheme (DES Algorithm). Asymmetric key cryptography, which is commonly mentioned to as public-key cryptography, employs a recipient's private key while exposing a public key to the public. With this technique, the data is encoded and decrypted using two distinct keys. These two distinct keys are related mathematically. They arrive in pairs. While the public key is accessible to everyone, only the individual who generated these two keys can access the secret key [9].

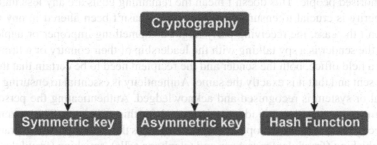

Fig. 3. Types of Cryptography

TRIPLE DES: Three-layered DES was meant to substitute the unique Data Encryption Standard (DES) algorithm, but hackers quickly discovered how to easily crack it. Historically, the most well-liked symmetric algorithm and the de facto industry standard was three-layered DES. Triple DES uses three distinct keys, respectively of which is 56 bits long. A key strength of 112 bits, according to experts, is more accurate than the whole key length of 168 bits. Triple DES has essentially been replaced by the Advanced Encryption Standard (AES), although being gradually phased out [10, 11].

AES: The Advanced Encryption Standard (AES) is used by software, and it is trusted by the US government and other organisations. For high-grade encryption, AES employs keys of 192 and 256 bits as a complement to its very effective 128-bit variant. With the exception of brute force, which attempts to read communications by employing all conceivable permutations of the 128, 192, or 256-bit cipher, AES is widely regarded immune to all attacks [12].

RSA Security: The public-key algorithm RSA is an industry norm for encoding data transferred over the internet. One method used by PGP and GPG software is this one. Since RSA uses two keys, different Three-layered DES, it is an asymmetric algorithm. A message can be encrypted using your public key and decrypted with your private key. For an attacker, the RSA algorithm generates a lot of gibberish that would take a significant amount of time and computer resources to decipher [13].

Blowfish: Blowfish is a new algorithm that was created to replace DES. Each communication is encrypted separately using this symmetric cipher after being separated into blocks of 64 bits. Known for its breakneck speed and all-around effectiveness, blowfish.

However, vendors have benefited greatly from its open availability in the public domain. Blowfish is used in a variety of software applications, such as password management programmes and e-commerce platforms for secure payment processing. This is one of the more flexible encryption methods [14, 15].

Twofish: Blowfish and its spawn Twofish are the brainchild of computer security specialist Bruce Schneier. This algorithm employs a symmetric method and can handle keys up to 256 bits long. It also just requires a single key. Twofish is among the fastest of its kind and performs admirably in both physical and digital contexts [16]. Twofish, like Blowfish, is freely distributed to anyone who wishes to use it. (Refer to Figs. 4 and 5).

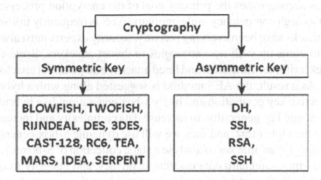

Fig. 4. Types of Cryptography Algorithms

Factors	DES	3DES	RC2	RC4	RC6	AES	BLOWFISH
Key size	56 bits	168 bits	8–128 bits	40–128 bits	128.192 or 256 bits	128, 192 or 256 bits	32–448 bits
Block size	64 bits	64 bits	64 bits	Byte oriented	128 bits	128, 192, or 256 bits	64 bits
Cipher type	Block cipher	Block cipher	Block cipher	Stream cipher	Symmetric block cipher	Symmetric block cipher	Symmetric block cipher
Keys	Private keys	Private keys	Single key	Single key	Single key	Secret key (shared)	Private key
Attacks	Vulnerable to differential, and linear attacks	Vulnerable to differential, Bruite force attacks	Vulnerable to differential, Bruite Force Attacks	Vulnerable to Bruite force attacks	Vulnerable to differential, Bruite force attacks	Strong against differential, Bruite, Linear Force Attacks	Vulnerable to differential, Bruite force attacks
Security	Proven Inadequate	Inadequate	Vulnerable	Weak security	Vulnerable	Considered most secure	Less secure

Fig. 5. Measures of the effectiveness of various encryption methods [17]

2   Recent Literature Findings

AES cryptography and audio steganography are both used in the suggested solution. The encryption key (password) is separated into two halves; the first half is used as the input text for the stego-crypto process, while the second half is used as what is known as the crypto key. The first portion of the encryption key is encrypted with AES, ciphered using random xor, inserted in wave audio with the Least Significant Bit (LSB) technique, and sent to the server with the HMAC-SHA256 hash algorithm. This approach can fool the attacker into relying on the encrypted value that emerges with data that is transmitted while the key component is hidden within the cover file [18].

An entirely novel proposed algorithm for encrypting and decrypting audio recordings is based on biometric features and separate wavelet transform (DWT), which offers a high level of privacy and dependability. The suggested approach combined the use of the discrete wavelet transform (DWT) to boost the encryption process' efficiency with the use of a variety of hand geometry measurements attributes as keys to encode and decode the audio file. On the resulting signal, subjective and objective measurements are used. They concluded that there was a fairly acceptable amount of data loss in the recovered audio signal while still guaranteeing that the receiver could grasp the core message after decryption. This accomplishes the primary goal of the encryption processing [19].

Because to its high competency and simplicity, AES is frequently utilised. However, because cyberattacks have been evolving recently, security experts must always be working in the lab to come up with new strategies to thwart attackers. Brute-force assault, difference attack, arithmetical attack, and lined attack are all potential attacks on symmetric algorithms. As a result, the AES method is suggested along with a hybrid technique that combines active key generation and lively s-box generation. In a hybrid method, we will first use dynamic key generation to increase data complexity and increase confusion and diffusion in the cipher text, and then we will use dynamic S-box generation to make it more challenging for an attacker to analyse a static collection of S-boxes [20]. By using this method, user may safeguard data discretion, privacy, and integrity from hackers. In this paper's methodology section, user also discusses how this approach works by using a flow chart and algorithm to fully comprehend it [21].

A novel mixed-encryption strategy involving elliptic curve encryption system and hill cipher (ECCHC) has been projected in this paper to adapt the Hill Cipher from a symmetric (private key) to an asymmetric (public key) technique, improve its safety and efficacy, and resist hackers. There is no necessity to communicate the secret key because both the sender of the email and the recipient can generate it from the private and public keys. The projected solution makes a novel addition by allowing you to directly encrypt all of the characters in the 128 ASCII table employing its ASCII value rather than requiring to assign a arithmetical value to each letter. The suggested method's main rewards are its computing speed, security efficacy, and simplicity of computation [22].

A novel method for audio watermarking founded on Remarkable Value Decomposition (SVD) theory. As indicated in the applications section, the suggested method can be utilised for multi-level security systems as well as data beating in audio signals sent over wireless networks. In this method, the audio signal is converted into a 2-D format and then a chaotic encrypted watermark is embedded in the unique values. a brand-new approach to audio watermarking based on the principle of singular value decomposition (SVD). The recommended method can be used for multi-level security systems and data hiding in audio signals conveyed via wireless networks, as was mentioned in the applications section. This technique embeds a chaotic encoded watermark in the unique values once the audio signal is transformed to a 2-D representation. The suggested method can be applied to the entire audio stream or to individual audio segments. The segment-by-segment technique enables many instances of the same watermark to be embedded in the audio signal, improving the watermark's capacity to be detected in the face of serious attacks. The results of the experiments demonstrate that even in the presence of attacks, the suggested audio watermarking approach preserves the high value of the audio signal and makes it possible to extract and decrypt the watermark [23].

An innovative audio coding and steganography technique based on chaos is suggested. This upper Least Significant Bit (LSB) layer approach uses the former pad algorithm to encrypt the secret message first. There were two Piecewise Linear Chaotic Map (PWLCM) chaotic sequences used. The PWLCM chaotic map generates the key for the one-time pad during the encryption process. In the steganography procedure, a random sequence is produced using the second PWLCM sequence. The encoded message was then embedded in a selection of audio samples that had been chosen at random using indices from the ordered generated sequence. To strengthen the resistance against noise addition or MPEG compression, the encoded data were inserted on advanced layers other than the LSB using an well-organized bit's adjustment mechanism [24].

Proposes a new, lightweight video encryption technique that facilitates multi-layered, light-weight encryption. The aims of the encryption technique are to allow replay of the encoded stream even in the attendance of network package loss and bit-errors and to reduce the total quantity of encrypted data while preserving a reasonable level of confidentiality and safety. Due to the latter property, encrypted video may be easily modified for best-effort channels like the Internet. The stream is split into three layers by this technique, each of the lower two of which are encryption. Using the adaptive technique, which exemplifies how to adaptably split the video data, In the base layer, the user can assure the highest possible signal-to-noise ratio. Our findings suggest that we can deliver security by encoding only a small portion of the data, and this depends on the equal of security required by the user [25].

Promotes the creation of a system talented of both encoding and decoding multimedia data (such as text, photos, videos, and audio), using a hybrid paradigm that incorporates symmetric encryption techniques like AES and asymmetric encryption techniques like ECC. The discrete logarithmic problem (DLP), which has a short public key, a small network bandwidth, and a high attack resistance, is the basis of the ECC. It is therefore quite difficult to guess the keys. Even if an intruder had admission to any of the keys, unravelling it would only take a very small number of man-years [26].

The data can be supplied in the BMP format if it is sent as an image, the MPEG format if it is delivered as video, and the WAV format if it is delivered as audio. Researchers employ the Data Encryption Standard (DES) algorithm along with the least significant bit approach to achieve this. For any type of confidential or secret messages, we offer two layers of security. In the first level, cryptographic techniques are used, and steganographic techniques are used in the second level. Data security and protection are guaranteed by multi-level security [27].

The hybrid approach to picture security that combines steganography and encryption is shown. Using the steganography principle, the image is first encrypted using the new version of the AES method that has been proposed. The analysis and findings of an experiment are displayed. The protection and security of data are ensured by this hybrid method, which offers increased security against threats [22, 28].

3   Proposed Methodology

3.1   Proposed Encryption Algorithm

The multi-layer encryption approach, which we propose, highlights the construction of a system that can encrypt and decode audio data by applying a hybrid paradigm that incorporates symmetric encryption and decryption methods (Refer to Fig. 6).

```
Step-1    Import necessary libraries: librosa, numpy as np, and cryptography.

Step-2    Define audioEncrypt(f, password) function.

Step-3    Load audio from f using librosa.

Step-4    Normalize and scale the audio data.

Step-5    Generate an AES key from password using a key derivation function.

Step-6    Encrypt audio data using ChaCha20.

Step-7    Write the encrypted audio to a new file.

Step-8    Print "Encryption Successful!"

Step-9    End the function.
```

Figure. 6. Proposed Multi-layer Encryption Algorithm

3.2   Proposed Decryption Algorithm

By using a hybrid paradigm that combines symmetric encryption and decryption techniques, we emphasise the building of a system that can encrypt and decode audio data in our proposed multi-layer decryption methodology (Refer to Fig. 7).

```
Step-1    Import Libraries: Import necessary libraries.

Step-2    Define audioDecrypt(f, password) Function: Define a function to decrypt audio.

Step-3    Print "Initiating Audio Decryption": Indicate the start of decryption.

Step-4    Load Encrypted Audio: Load the encrypted audio from file f.

Step-5    Normalize and Scale Audio: Normalize and scale the audio data.

Step-6    Generate AES Key: Generate an AES key from the provided password.

Step-7    Decrypt Audio: Decrypt the audio using the AES key.

Step-8    Write Decrypted Audio: Write the decrypted audio to a new file.

Step-9    Print "Decryption Successful": Indicate the successful decryption

Step-10   End Function: End the decryption function.
```

Fig. 7. Proposed Multi-layer Decryption Algorithm

4 Configuration and Implementation

In the discipline of systems engineering, "system configuration" refers to the number of parts, methods, and electronic devices that comprise the complete system. The organisation of hardware and software, as well as the relationship between specific hardware, software, and procedural components, are referred to by this word. These parameters are recorded in a system preferences file that the user is able to define or that the system automatically creates. It details the many hardware makes and models that are installed, in addition to the various operating computer system components. Thus, system configuration also refers to the specific operating system settings that a user or a programme has intentionally or automatically specified as defaults. (Refer to Fig. 8(a), (b) and (c))

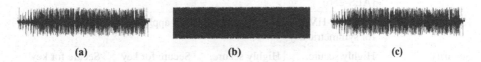

(a)   (b)   (c)

Fig. 8. (a). Original File (b). Encrypted File (c). Decrypted File

4.1 Hardware Configuration

1. For better performance minimum processor Intel –I3 (Any Generation)
2. RAM Minimum 8 GB
3. HDD: 128 GB Minimum or depends on the file to be encrypted.

4.2 Software Configuration

1. PYDUB: James Robert created the Python package PyDub, which offers a wealth of features for working with audio files. Learning PyDub will provide you with a programmatic method to guarantee that your audio files are reliable and in the best format for transcription either locally or through an API. Pydub's simple audio processing module for Python. A Python package called Pydub only supports.wav files. This library allows us to mix audio, alter audio levels, add basic effects, create audio tones, and more.
2. NumPy: The Python package NumPy is used to manipulate arrays. By turning the audio into a numerical array, encrypting the array, and then converting the array back to the audio format, a Python library for numerical computing can be used to encrypt audio [29].
3. A Python set for analysing music and audio is called Librosa [30]. Librosa is used for working with audio data, such as when making music or utilising automatic voice recognition. It provides the elements needed to create a system for retrieving music information [31].
4. SciPy: Based on NumPy, the computation package Scipy was created. The acronym Scientific Python is used frequently. It provides additional advantageous features for optimisation, analytics, and signal processing [32]. Since SciPy is open source, we can utilise it in the same way as NumPy.

5 Outcome Analysis

The projected algorithm is evaluated founded on the following aspect after being tested on a sizable volume of audio files. We have the analysis that follows (Table 1).

Table. 1. Comparative analysis of Proposed Multi-layer Algorithm

Aspect	Proposed Algorithm	AES-256	RSA	ECC
Algorithm Type	Symmetric Encryption (AES-256)	Symmetric Encryption	Asymmetric Encryption	Asymmetric Encryption
Key Derivation	PBKDF2-HMAC for symmetric key	Not applicable	Not applicable	Not applicable
Security	Highly secure, strong encryption	Highly secure, widely adopted	Secure for key exchange, digital signatures	Secure for key exchange, digital signatures
Key Length	256 bits (variable)	256 bits (fixed)	Variable (typically 2048 +)	Variable (typically 256–521 bits)
Performance	Efficient for audio encryption	Efficient for various scenarios	Performance depends on key size	Performance depends on key size
Parallelism	Limited parallelism	Supports some parallelism	Difficult to parallelize operations	Difficult to parallelize operations
Resistance to Quantum Attacks	Susceptible to quantum attacks	Susceptible to quantum attacks	Vulnerable to Shor's algorithm (large key sizes)	Vulnerable to Shor's algorithm (large key sizes)
Key Exchange	Not suitable for key exchange	Not suitable for key exchange	Suitable for key exchange	Suitable for key exchange
Applications	Symmetric audio encryption	Various security protocols, data at rest	Secure key exchange and digital signatures	Secure key exchange and digital signatures

6 Discussion and Future Scope

In this research, a multi-layer encryption technique for audio files was proposed. By utilising all of the benefits of bio-keys to complete the encryption process, it attempts to avoid using other conventional approaches. The author wanted to leverage the majority of the advantages, strengths, and benefits of a multi-layer approach in the encryption method in this work. Each segment of the audio file will be encoded by a value distinct from other segments in accordance with the suggested technique, making it impossible to guess or forecast the values. By putting audio data in the transform domain, which is more secure to encrypt any data, and by using it in novel ways, the suggested algorithm's security is increased by using the multi-layer approach. By using a set of audio files of varying sizes and the suggested algorithm, numerous trials were carried out. By using statistical analysis methods, the experimental application demonstrates that the provided approach has a good level of security.

By increasing algorithm complexity to enhance confusion and diffusion in cipher text, the suggested algorithm with hybrid approach will be an efficient method for delivering robust security in message transmission. It will defend against Brute-force, Differential, Algebraic, and Linear attacks on messages. The proposed system will be a useful tool for internet-based applications including E-Commerce, stock Exchange, online banking System, and online bill payment, among others.

7 Conclusion

The first section of the paper discusses crucial subjects including information security and cryptography, as well as the function of cryptography. In this part, numerous Cryptography algorithms are also described. The research on multi-layer audio encryption schemes that has been done in the past year is described in the middle half of the paper. The advantages of the hybrid approach to cryptography and the modifications that have previously been made are also described. Instead of using a single encryption algorithm, Autors uses hybrid encryption to secure data. In this study, the author offers some historical data regarding those kinds of efforts, with the hybrid method of receiving the bulk of the author's attention. In compared to previous methods, this hybrid technique enables the user maintain data in a more redundant and secure manner. The configuration section describes the hardware and software settings required to implement the proposed algorithm. By employing this technique, users can defend the integrity, confidentiality, and privacy of their data against hackers.

Conflict of Interest:
The authors have no conflicts of interest to declare. All co-authors have seen and agree with the contents of the manuscript and there is no financial interest to report. We certify that the submission is original work and is not under review at any other publication.

Author's Contribution Statement:
All the authors have contributed equally to the design and implementation of the research, to the analysis of the results, and to the writing of the manuscript.

Ethical and Informed Consent for Data Used:
As authors, we give full permission for the use of the research study's data and ethical considerations.

Data Availability and Access:
Since the research study in question comprised confidential information, it was stored in a secure location and was only accessible upon request. We guarantee that the research study's use of data won't reveal any personal information.

References

1. Subramani, S., Svn, S.K.: Review of security methods based on classical cryptography and quantum cryptography. Cybern. Syst. 1–19 (2023). https://doi.org/10.1080/01969722.2023.2166261
2. Ullah, S., Zheng, J., Din, N., Hussain, M.T., Ullah, F., Yousaf, M.: Elliptic curve cryptography; applications, challenges, recent advances, and future trends: a comprehensive survey. Comput. Sci. Rev. **47**, 100530 (2023). https://doi.org/10.1016/j.cosrev.2022.100530
3. Dhanalaxmi, B., Tadisetty, S.: Multimedia cryptography — a review. In: 2017 IEEE International Conference on Power, Control, Signals and Instrumentation Engineering (ICPCSI), pp. 764–766, September 2017. https://doi.org/10.1109/ICPCSI.2017.8391817
4. Man, Z., Li, J., Di, X., Zhang, R., Li, X., Sun, X.: Research on cloud data encryption algorithm based on bidirectional activation neural network. Inf. Sci. (Ny) **622**, 629–651 (2023). https://doi.org/10.1016/j.ins.2022.11.089
5. Dong, Z., Wang, X., Zhang, X., Hu, M., Dinh, T.N.: Global exponential synchronization of discrete-time high-order switched neural networks and its application to multi-channel audio encryption. Nonlinear Anal. Hybrid Syst **47**, 101291 (2023). https://doi.org/10.1016/j.nahs.2022.101291
6. Kumar, A., Dua, M.: Audio encryption using two chaotic map based dynamic diffusion and double DNA encoding. Appl. Acoust. **203**, 109196 (2023). https://doi.org/10.1016/j.apacoust.2022.109196
7. Kumar Sharma, D., Chidananda Singh, N., Noola, D.A., Nirmal Doss, A., Sivakumar, J.: A review on various cryptographic techniques and algorithms. Mater. Today Proc. **51**, 104–109 (2022). https://doi.org/10.1016/j.matpr.2021.04.583
8. Coron, J.-S.: What is cryptography? IEEE Secur. Priv. Mag. **4**(1), 70–73 (2006). https://doi.org/10.1109/MSP.2006.29
9. Fujdiak, R., Masek, P., Hosek, J., Mlynek, P., Misurec, J.: Efficiency evaluation of different types of cryptography curves on low-power devices. In: 2015 7th International Congress on Ultra Modern Telecommunications and Control Systems and Workshops (ICUMT), pp. 269–274, October 2015. https://doi.org/10.1109/ICUMT.2015.7382441
10. Hemme, L.: A differential fault attack against early rounds of (Triple-) DES, pp. 254–267 (2004)
11. Coppersmith, D., Johnson, D.B., Matyas, S.M.: A proposed mode for triple-DES encryption. IBM J. Res. Dev. **40**(2), 253–262 (1996). https://doi.org/10.1147/rd.402.0253
12. Akkar, M.-L., Giraud, C.: An Implementation of DES and AES, Secure against Some Attacks, pp. 309–318 (2001)
13. Ivanov, A., Stoianov, N.: Implications of the arithmetic ratio of prime numbers for RSA security. Int. J. Appl. Math. Comput. Sci. **33**(1), 57–70 (2023). https://doi.org/10.34768/amcs-2023-0005
14. Suganya, M., Sasipraba, T.: Stochastic gradient descent long short-term memory based secure encryption algorithm for cloud data storage and retrieval in cloud computing environment. J. Cloud Comput. **12**(1), 74 (2023). https://doi.org/10.1186/s13677-023-00442-6
15. Singhal, V., Singh, D., Gupta, S.K.: Data encryption technique based on enhancement of blowfish algorithm in comparison of DES & DCT methods. **11**(3), 16–21 (2023)
16. Assa-Agyei, K., Olajide, F.: A Comparative study of Twofish, Blowfish, and advanced encryption standard for secured data transmission. Int. J. Adv. Comput. Sci. Appl. **14**(3) (2023). https://doi.org/10.14569/IJACSA.2023.0140344
17. Patil, L.K., Popat, K.A.: Comparative analysis of several approaches of encoding audio files. In: Rajagopal, S., Faruki, P., Popat, K. (eds.) Advancements in Smart Computing and Information Security, ASCIS 2022, Communications in Computer and Information Science, vol. 1760, pp. 128–143. Springer, Cham (2022). https://doi.org/10.1007/978-3-031-23095-0_10

18. Advanced password authentication protection by hybrid cryptography and audio steganography. IRAQI J. Sci. **59**(1C) (2018). https://doi.org/10.24996/ijs.2018.59.1C.17
19. Al-kateeb, Z.N., Mohammed, S.J.: A novel approach for audio file encryption using hand geometry. Multimed. Tools Appl. **79**(27–28), 19615–19628 (2020). https://doi.org/10.1007/s11042-020-08869-8
20. D'souza, F.J., Panchal, D.: Advanced encryption standard (AES) security enhancement using hybrid approach. In: Proceeding - IEEE International Conference on Computing, Communication and Automation, ICCCA 2017, vol. 2017, pp. 647–652 (2017). https://doi.org/10.1109/CCAA.2017.8229881
21. Kumar, L., Badal, N.: A review on hybrid encryption in cloud computing. In: 4th International Conference on Internet of Things: Smart Innovation and Usages, IoT-SIU 2019, pp. 1–6 (2019). https://doi.org/10.1109/IoT-SIU.2019.8777503
22. Almaiah, M.A., Dawahdeh, Z., Almomani, O., Alsaaidah, A., Al-Khasawneh, A., Khawatreh, S.: A new hybrid text encryption approach over mobile ad hoc network. Int. J. Electr. Comput. Eng. **10**(6), 6461–6471 (2020). https://doi.org/10.11591/IJECE.V10I6.PP6461-6471
23. Al-Nuaimy, W., et al.: An SVD audio watermarking approach using chaotic encrypted images. Digit. Signal Process. A Rev. J. **21**(6), 764–779 (2011). https://doi.org/10.1016/j.dsp.2011.01.013
24. Alwahbani, S.M.H., Elshoush, H.T.I.: Hybrid audio steganography and cryptography method based on high least significant bit (LSB) layers and one-time pad—a novel approach. Stud. Comput. Intell. **751**, 431–453 (2018). https://doi.org/10.1007/978-3-319-69266-1_21
25. Tosun, A.Ş., Feng, W.C.: "Efficient multi-layer coding and encryption of MPEG video streams. In: IEEE International Conference on Multimedia and Expo, pp. 119–122 (2000). https://doi.org/10.1109/icme.2000.869559
26. Iyer, S.C., Sedamkar, R.R., Gupta, S.: A novel Idea on multimedia encryption using hybrid crypto approach. Procedia Comput. Sci. **79**, 293–298 (2016). https://doi.org/10.1016/j.procs.2016.03.038
27. Naidu, D., Ananda Kumar, K.S., Jadav, S.L., Sinchana, M.N.: Multilayer security in protecting and hiding multimedia data using cryptography and steganography techniques. In: 2019 4th IEEE International Conference on Recent Trends on Electronics, Information, Communication & Technology RTEICT 2019 - Proc, pp. 1360–1364 (2019). https://doi.org/10.1109/RTEICT46194.2019.9016974
28. Saini, J.K., Verma, H.K.: A hybrid approach for image security by combining encryption and steganography. In: 2013 IEEE 2nd International Conference on Image Information Processing, IEEE ICIIP 2013, pp. 607–611 (2013). https://doi.org/10.1109/ICIIP.2013.6707665
29. Bauer, M., Garland, M.: Legate NumPy. In: Proceedings of the International Conference for High Performance Computing, Networking, Storage and Analysis, pp. 1–23, November 2019. https://doi.org/10.1145/3295500.3356175
30. Babu, P.A, Siva Nagaraju, V., Vallabhuni, R.R.: Speech emotion recognition system with Librosa. In: 2021 10th IEEE International Conference on Communication Systems and Network Technologies (CSNT), pp. 421–424, June 2021. https://doi.org/10.1109/CSNT51715.2021.9509714
31. Raguraman, P., Vijayan, M.: LibROSA based assessment tool for music information retrieval systems. In: 2019 IEEE Conference on Multimedia Information Processing and Retrieval (MIPR), pp. 109–114, March 2019. https://doi.org/10.1109/MIPR.2019.00027
32. Lemenkova, P.: Processing oceanographic data by python libraries Numpy, SCIPY and Pandas. Aquat. Res. **2**, 73–91 (2019). https://doi.org/10.3153/AR19009

Development of Secure Framework in Mobile Cloud Computing Using AES-HMAC Encryption Approach

P. V. Naveen[1]($\boxtimes$) and A. Poongodi[2]

[1] Department of Computer Science, School of Computing Sciences, Vels Institute of Science, Technology and Advance Studies, Chennai, Tamil Nadu, India
naveen9v@gmail.com

[2] School of Computing Sciences, Vels Institute of Science, Technology and Advance Studies, Chennai, Tamil Nadu, India

Abstract. The confidentiality, integrity, and availability of data and services in mobile cloud environments are crucially supported by security algorithms for Mobile Cloud Computing (MCC). This research paper presents a new framework for data encryption and integrity checking in an MCC environment called AES-HMAC (Advanced Encryption Standard- Hash-based Message Authentication Code). In a mobile cloud environment, this setup offers an excellent framework for protecting data while it is in transmission and at rest. While HMAC creates a hash-based message security code using a cryptographic hash method and a secret key to assure the validity and integrity of the data, AES assures that data is encrypted using a symmetric encryption technique. To evaluate the algorithms' efficiency in protecting private medical data, we simulated MCC security systems using the CloudSim simulator while processing a range of healthcare dataset. AES-HMAC can beat standalone AES, DES encryption and hash algorithms in terms of response time, error rate, and latency.

Keywords: Encryption · Security · Latency · Response Time · Transmission Time · Hash Algorithms · AES

1 Introduction

In the realm of information technology, the convergence of handheld gadgets and cloud resources has given rise to the term "Mobile Cloud Computing" (MCC). This paradigm empowers mobile devices by allowing them to offload computational duties and data storage to cloud resources, fundamentally transforming how mobile users interact with information and services. As the exchange of sensitive data between cellphones and cloud servers becomes commonplace, the imperative for a secure framework within MCC cannot be overstated. The ubiquity of portable devices, including smartphones, PDAs, tablets, and laptops, has facilitated widespread access to cloud services by a diverse user base. While MCC offers numerous advantages, including enhanced flexibility and accessibility, it also presents inherent hazards and limitations. Security concerns, data

S. Rajagopal et al. (Eds.): ASCIS 2023, CCIS 2039, pp. 192–206, 2024.
https://doi.org/10.1007/978-3-031-59100-6_15

access control, efficiency, and bandwidth considerations underscore the multifaceted challenges that must be addressed [12].

Addressing the intricacies of securing data in the mobile cloud environment requires a nuanced approach. Prior investigations into cryptographic techniques laid the foundation for secure operations in web and standalone applications. However, a notable gap existed in the exploration of symmetrical methods specifically tailored for mobile environments, a void filled by the work of Kalmani and Singla [1].

Incorporating cloud computing into the mobile setting through MCC signifies a paradigm shift in how data processing and storage occur. This integration addresses challenges related to performance, environmental constraints, and security concerns. The "mobile cloud" service model, as proposed by Kulkarni et al. [2], enables mobile devices to seamlessly access the cloud for tasks ranging from information storage and searching to data mining and multimedia processing. As smartphones continue to proliferate, Masthan and Venkatesh Sharma [3] underscore the growing trend of individuals entrusting their data to clouds, often with varying degrees of reliability.

The paper implements a new encryption/decryption scheme, which contributes to the security framework design. It also identifies the important elements of the cloud computing community's security framework. The framework's clever algorithmic design facilitates faster computing with less power consumption, network usage, and network latency, making it useful for cloud users and providers with comparable security requirements during implementation.

The subsequent sections of this paper are organized as follows: Section two provides a comprehensive review of existing research related to mobile cloud computing security. Section three elucidates the critical importance of security considerations in mobile cloud computing environments. Section four delineates the process flow of the proposed security framework. Section five delves into the performance metrics, assessing the proposed security model based on transmission time, response time, and latency. Finally, section six concludes the present research work, offering insights into its future directions. This study revolves around achieving key objectives aimed at fortifying the security and optimizing the performance of Mobile Cloud Computing (MCC) in handling healthcare data. The primary goals are delineated as follows.

1.1 Security Design Building

The cornerstone of this research involves the meticulous creation of a robust security model tailored for Mobile Cloud Computing. This model strategically incorporates industry-leading encryption algorithms, namely DES (Data Encryption Standard), AES (Advanced Encryption Standard), and AES-HMAC. The focus is on enhancing the security infrastructure governing the storage and processing of healthcare data within the MCC framework.

1.2 Performance Evaluation

Rigorous testing forms an integral part of this study, leveraging two distinct healthcare datasets of varying sizes. The primary objective is to assess the performance of the proposed security model under real-world conditions. By subjecting the model to diverse datasets, we aim to ascertain its efficacy in securing healthcare information efficiently and reliably.

1.3 Metrics

The efficiency of each encryption technique within the security model is systematically evaluated through a set of key metrics. The assessment encompasses crucial performance indicators such as response time, latency, and error rates. These metrics serve as quantitative measures, providing valuable insights into the operational efficiency and reliability of each encryption algorithm employed in the MCC environment. In essence, this research seeks to contribute to the evolving landscape of healthcare data security within the Mobile Cloud Computing paradigm. By meticulously designing a security model and subjecting it to thorough performance evaluations, we aim to not only enhance the protective measures surrounding healthcare data but also to provide empirical insights into the operational efficiency of encryption techniques in MCC.

2 Related Works

According to Arfan [4], 42.8 million people used cloud computing in 2008, while 998 million people did so in 2014. However, the development is not being accompanied by a rise in user confidence in cloud-based data management, particularly in the commercial sector. Because of confidentiality and safety considerations, some businesses have no interest in implementing MCC services. There are still certain safety issues and instances of service providers and other unreliable parties abusing data ownership policies in cloud computing mobile services. The ease of the company's data abuse threat by outside parties is not similar to this threat, which is becoming a barrier to the adoption of the MCC concept. Therefore, MCC needs to build a safety mechanism that can reduce the dangers to confidentiality and safety. The use of complex keys will make it more difficult for parties without the necessary rights to access restricted business data. Since the hash function technique used by this encryption system is symmetric, it makes the decoding process in cloud systems more difficult and increases the likelihood that firm data will be better safeguarded. Consumers of this system, whether commercial or individual, may handle company resources online promptly and securely without running the danger of information leakage.

The expansion of enormous network channels, where no node communication is identified in emergencies, has resulted in a large number of users having unsafe communications. As an outcome of such communications, many people find it challenging to communicate in emergencies. In this study, Hai et al. [5] established an MCC procedure in the recommended technique to avoid such situations and improve the efficiency of the data transfer process. The proposed model is developed using an analytical structure that covers five important reductions and enhancement objectives. All MCC nodes are also built with high-security standards, guaranteeing that all resources are assigned properly. The theoretical structure is combined with DT(Decision Tree), an ML(Machine Learning technique), to isolate all the active functions. The recommended approach helps the community since it allows all cloud nodes to offer emergency support at a low operational and maintenance price. Five scenarios are used to test the effectiveness of the suggested strategy, and the findings of each scenario demonstrate that it is, on average, 86% considerably more successful than the empirical studies now in use.

As the proportion of smartphone users rises daily, MCC is a rapidly expanding technique nowadays. The use of handheld devices raises significant issues related to security and privacy. Any typical cellphone can access facilities computing power, applications, and platform features from MCC. Network safety, security of web applications, accessing data, authorization, verification, privacy of data, and data leaks are only a few of the problems with MCC's protection. Mobile gadgets have limited processing and storage resources, which reduces their ability to store large amounts of data. It is necessary to research and understand safety hazards to create a safe MCC setting. To strengthen the safety of the cellular cloud and guarantee accuracy and privacy, Sarode and Bhalla [6] presented a method. AES and RSA are used in this process to increase security. They also go into security risks in MCC setups and offer countermeasures.

MCC is a method or methodology that makes use of cloud computing to create, power, and host applications for mobile devices. Using a mobile application, MCC users can keep sender, data, and recipient information in the cloud. Safety problems will surface when users store more and more data on cloud servers. A review of MCC ideas is provided by Singh and Jasmine [7] along with information on security flaws and vulnerabilities impacting cloud systems and potential cloud computing remedies for these problems. It also outlines the benefits and drawbacks of the current security policy and discusses current cloud computing problems such as data authenticity, data discrimination, and protection.

A framework with important features, such as improved security and owner data privacy, is presented in this research [9]. By adding a double round key feature, it speeds up the encryption process by 1000 blocks per second over the original 128 AES algorithm. Traditionally, there is only one round key that can process 800 blocks per second. The suggested algorithm, on the other hand, uses less power and improves load balancing, trust, and management of resources on the network. 128 plain text bytes, 16, 32, 64, and AES are deployed as part of the suggested framework.

The research [9] focuses on using cryptography to secure private information transferred over networks between individuals, businesses, organizations, cloud applications, and others. First, the cryptographic algorithm must be used to encrypt data before it gets transmitted from the sender to the network receiver. Second, the recipient uses the decryption method to display the original data. Here, a hybrid encryption and decryption method based on the RSA and AES-128 algorithms is used in the suggested model. In addition, we employed the HMAC algorithm to guarantee the authenticity and integrity of the data. This work compares the efficiency of three encryption algorithms: AES, RSA, and hybrid algorithms, and explains the time and throughput needed for encryption and decryption of various data sizes.

After examining each of the well-known hybrid cryptography models, [13] comes to the conclusion that data security is the main issue with cloud computing technology. Security constraints are circumvented by integrating symmetric and asymmetric cryptosystems. In order to do this, different encryption algorithms—including DES, 3DES,

AES, Blowfish, RSA, RC4, MD5, and SHA—are combined in an effort to secure sensitive data in the cloud. According to the study, compared to employing these methods independently, hybrid cryptography increases data security and boosts performance.

3 Significance of Security in Mobile Cloud Computing

Because of the special problems and risks that develop in this computing paradigm, security techniques are essential in MCC. To provide on-demand services and data storage, MCC includes the incorporation of mobile devices, such as tablets and cell phones, with resources located in the cloud. Here are a few primary reasons for why security methods are crucial in MCC.

3.1 Information Security and Privacy

Data that is sensitive, including financial details, medical documents, and private data is frequently transmitted and stored in MCC. Security methods, like encryption, make sure that this data is kept private and that it is difficult for unknown individuals to obtain or view it.

3.2 Data Transmission with Security

Mobile phones and tablets routinely use public Wi-Fi and other potentially unsafe connections to link to cloud applications. Data exchanged between the smartphone or tablet and the cloud is protected with the help of security algorithms like SSL/TLS (Secure Sockets Layer/Transport Layer Security), preventing monitoring and manipulation.

3.3 Access Management

Strong access control measures are made possible by security methods, guaranteeing that only permitted users or programs can access cloud resources. This comprises the procedures for authorization and authentication that confirm users' identities and their rights to utilize particular data or resources.

3.4 Data Reliability

The reliability of data during its transfer and preservation can be checked using security methods like hashing with cryptography. This stops data from being altered or corrupted and guarantees that the data that is downloaded from the public cloud is identical to the data that was initially submitted [14, 15].

3.5 Threat and Malware Detection

Malware and other security risks can affect mobile phones and tablets. Cyber security procedures are used to identify and counteract these dangers, for example by spotting malicious programs or odd patterns of behavior.

4   Proposed Model

MCC enables users to outsource computational efforts and data preservation to distant cloud servers by integrating cloud computing with mobile devices. The efficiency and success of MCC solutions must be assessed using a variety of metrics that take into account the system's many components. Here are some important MCC metrics for assessment. The proposed MCC model's framework is shown in Fig. 1 below.

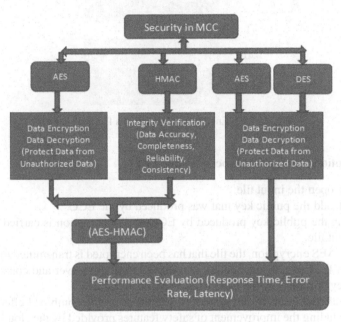

Fig. 1. MCC Security Framework

4.1   AES

Due to increased concerns about security and confidentiality of information, transferring personal and sensitive data to remote data centers is difficult. Consequently, to deal with the new security dangers in the cloud environment, the conventional AES (Advanced Encryption Standard) algorithm needs to be improved [9]. 128 bits are used in the AES algorithm. Ten computational cycles or rounds are included in this. This can eventually be increased to 192 or 256 bits. The use of a 192-bit key will result in 12 cycles. There are 14 rounds when the key size is 256 bits. The production of additional keys and a safety improvement are both possible with larger keys said by Delfin et al. [8]. Figure 2 describes the AES encryption algorithm's design.

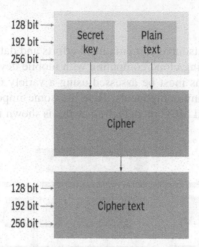

Fig. 2. AES Encryption Algorithm's Design [10]

4.2 Encryption/Decryption Process Using AES

Step 1: First, open the input file.

Step 2: Next, add the public key that was produced by the ECC.

Step 3: Using the public key produced by ECC, AES encryption is carried out on the provided input file.

Step 4: After AES encryption, the file that has been encrypted is transmitted to the server.

Step 5: After the file gets uploaded, it is retrieved from the server and converted using the public key provided by the ECC to decrypt the initial file.

Step 6: The effectiveness of the system is dependent on the combined effects of ECC and AES, including the improvement of safety features provided by the cloud server and the optimal use of storage space (Rehman et al. [11]).

4.3 DES

A symmetric-key encryption method called the Data Encryption Standard (DES) algorithm functions in a sequence of phases. It starts with key generation, generating sub-keys for each of its 16 rounds from a 56-bit key using permutation. The plain text is first permuted, then the right half is expanded, the sub-key is XORed with it, and finally, it goes through substitution boxes (S-boxes) for non-linear operations. Every time this process is repeated, the left and right halves are switched. The result is subjected to an inverse permutation following the final round to create the 64-bit ciphertext.

4.4 AES-HMAC Workflow

The workflow described involves a meticulous and structured approach to creating and testing a Mobile Cloud Computing (MCC) security model, with a specific focus on the healthcare industry. The chosen methodology employs diverse representative healthcare datasets and incorporates the DES, AES, and AES-HMAC encryption techniques. The workflow is outlined as follows:

Selection of Representative Healthcare Datasets: Begin with a strategic selection of two healthcare datasets of varying sizes. This step ensures a comprehensive evaluation of the security model's performance across different data scales, enhancing its applicability in real-world scenarios. Development and Implementation of the Security Model: Focus on assuring data confidentiality and integrity by developing and implementing the security model. This model integrates the DES, AES, and AES-HMAC encryption techniques. The goal is to create a robust security infrastructure for handling healthcare data within the MCC framework.

Creation of Simulated MCC Environment: Simulate the MCC environment to run encryption and decryption operations for each dataset. This involves executing the chosen encryption techniques in a controlled environment that mirrors the operational conditions of a real MCC system. Performance Metrics Monitoring: At each step of the workflow, meticulously gauge and track key performance metrics. Response times, latency, and error rates are systematically measured to provide quantitative insights into the efficiency and reliability of the security model. Statistical Analysis of Data: Perform a thorough statistical analysis of the collected data to assess the relative performance of DES, AES, and AES-HMAC. The emphasis is on determining whether AES-HMAC outperforms the other two algorithms in terms of both security and system effectiveness.

Contribution to Security Improvement in MCC Systems: The ultimate goal of this comprehensive workflow is to contribute to the enhancement of security in MCC systems, with a specific focus on the healthcare industry. The insights gained from the statistical analysis and performance evaluations will inform best practices for implementing encryption techniques in real-world MCC applications. Regarding the AES-HMAC cryptographic technology, it combines AES for message encryption with HMAC for message authentication. The following steps describe how AES-HMAC functions.

4.5 Encryption with AES

Encryption: The sender encrypts the plaintext data using the AES technique. A unique secret key is utilized by the symmetric-key block cipher AES for both encryption and decryption.

Shared Secret Key: A secret key must be safely shared in advance by the sender and the recipient. This key will be employed for both HMAC creation and encoding.

4.6 HMAC Generation

Message Digest: The sender generates a cryptographic hash of the plaintext message using a hash function (often a secure hash function like SHA-256) before transmitting the ciphertext.

Keyed Hashing: The sender creates an HMAC over the hash of the plaintext message using a different secret key, called the HMAC key. HMAC is a particular method for generating a message verification code utilizing a secret key and a hash function that is cryptographic in nature.

Concatenation: The ciphertext and the HMAC generated are often combined. The recipient receives this concatenated value (ciphertext + HMAC).

Sending the Message: The sender uses an unsecured channel to send the recipient the combined ciphertext and HMAC.

Receiving and Verification: The combination of the message (ciphertext + HMAC) is delivered to the recipient.

4.7 Decryption with AES

Decryption: The recipient decrypts the ciphertext using the AES algorithm using the secret key that was shared. The recipient gets the plaintext if the decryption procedure works.

4.8 HMAC Verification

Message Digest: Using the same hash function as the sender, the recipient also computes the hash of the plain text that was received.

HMAC Computation: The recipient then computes an HMAC over the hash of the received plain text using the HMAC key.

Comparison: Compared to the HMAC received from the sender, the recipient compares the HMAC that was determined. If they agree, it means that the integrity of the plain text has not been compromised during communication. If they don't agree, it could mean that the message has been changed.

4.9 Authentication and Integrity Checking

As only someone with access to the shared HMAC key could have created a matching HMAC, the recipient can be confident in the integrity and validity of the message they obtained if the HMACs match. The recipient should consider the message corrupted and discard it if the HMACs do not match.

AES-HMAC integrates data integrity and verification provided by HMAC with security provided by AES encryption. The combination of these factors guarantees that the data is secure and that it wasn't altered while being transmitted. A further layer of security is added to the communication process through the use of different keys for HMAC and encryption.

5 Results and Discussion

This study's findings demonstrate that while comparing the performance of the DES, AES, and AES-HMAC encryption techniques within the framework of the security model for MCC, AES-HMAC consistently beat the other two methods in terms of security and system effectiveness. AES-HMAC demonstrated decreased response times and latency across a range of data sizes, indicating quicker data processing, while retaining lower error rates, indicating greater data integrity.

6 Evaluation Metrics

Response Time: Response time is the period between when a mobile device sends a request to a cloud server and when it receives an answer. Generally speaking, quicker reaction times are preferable because they improve user responsiveness. The equation that follows can be used to calculate response time in MCC:

$$\text{Response Time} = \text{Transmission Time} + \text{Processing Time} + \text{Queueing Time} + \text{Network Latency} \quad (1)$$

Transmission time is the amount of time it takes for data to be transferred from a mobile device to a cloud server.

Processing Time is the amount of time the cloud server needs to process the data it has received. The amount of time a request spends in the queue before being processed is known as the queuing time. Data packets traveling from a mobile device to a cloud server and back cause a delay known as network latency. Each of these elements affects how quickly a user receives responses overall. These elements can differ according to the particulars of the MCC arrangement. The formula is broken down below, along with instructions for calculating each part:

$$\text{Transmission Time} = \text{Data Size/Transmission Rate} \quad (2)$$

The size of the data being transferred is called "Data Size" here. The rate at which data can be sent through a network is known as the transmission rate.

$$\text{Processing Time} = \text{Execution Time} + \text{Overhead Time} \quad (3)$$

The time it takes the cloud server to process the data it receives can be calculated from the equation above as execution time. Any additional time needed for setup and administrative tasks is included in overhead time.

$$\text{Queueing Time} = \text{Time in Queue} \quad (4)$$

Here the amount of time a request waits in the queue before being processed is known as time in queue. Distance, network congestion, and the caliber of the network connectivity are only a few variables that might affect network delay. Usually, it is calculated using network properties or measured empirically.

Latency: The time elapsed between making a request and getting a response is known as latency. To enable timely relationships low latency is necessary for applications that operate in real-time like online gaming and live streaming of videos. The following is an expression for the latency formula,

$$L = P + T + Q + X \tag{5}$$

L-Latency, P-delay in propagation, T-Transmission Delay, X-Processing Delay, Q-Queuing Delay.

Propagation Delay (P): This is the amount of time a signal (or piece of data) needs to travel from its source to its destination. The physical separation between the two places and the transmission medium's light speed will determine this. Propagation delay is frequently calculated as follows:

$$P = \frac{Distance}{Propagation\ Speed} \tag{6}$$

Transmission Delay (T): This is the amount of time needed to send a packet of data across the network. The size of the data packet and the network link's bandwidth both play a role. Delay in transmission is calculated as follows:

$$T = \frac{Packet\ Size}{Bandwidth} \tag{7}$$

Queuing Delay (Q): Queuing delay can happen when data packets wait in network equipment such as routers or switches before being transferred. It is based on variables like congestion in networks and queue length.

Processing Delay (X): This is the amount of time needed for network hardware, like switches and routers, to process the data packet. It consists of processing duties including selecting a route, checking for errors, and others.

Error Rate: Calculate the frequency of mistakes or false positives/negatives produced by the security mechanism. The integrity of the data must be maintained at lower error rates.

Error Rate (%) = (Quantity of incorrect packets/Total number of packets) $\times$ 100   (8)

Quantity of incorrect packets: The overall number of packets that contained errors that were received.

Total Number of Packets: The overall quantity of packets sent or received.

Together, these indicators offer a complete picture of the effectiveness, performance, and user experience of MCC systems. Different metrics may be prioritized above others according to the application and circumstance. The observed response time and latency metrics, as detailed in Table 1 and Fig. 3, underscore the efficiency of the proposed AES-HMAC encryption technique. With a file size of 218.81 KB, DES exhibits a response time of 23 ms and latency of 10 ms. AES shows improvement with 17 ms response time and 7 ms latency. Notably, the proposed AES-HMAC outperforms both, demonstrating

Table 1. Encryption Algorithms Vs. Response Time and Latency (218.81 KB file size)

Algorithm/Output Metric	Response Time (ms)	Latency (ms)
DES	20	10
AES	17	7
AES-HMAC	13	5

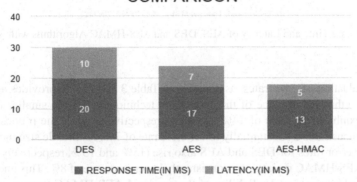

Fig. 3. Response Time and Latency of AES, DES and AES-HMAC Algorithms with 218.81 KB file size

a substantial reduction in both response time (13 ms) and latency (5 ms). This suggests that, especially for smaller file sizes, the proposed AES-HMAC offers a significant performance advantage over traditional encryption methods.

Scaling up to a larger file size of 38 MB (Table 2, Fig. 4), the trends persist, emphasizing the robustness of AES-HMAC across varying file sizes. DES, AES, and AES-HMAC exhibit increased response times and latencies, consistent with the larger file processing requirements. Despite this, the proposed AES-HMAC consistently outperforms DES and AES, demonstrating a notable reduction in both response time (18 ms) and latency (8 ms). This outcome reinforces the adaptability and efficiency of AES-HMAC even in scenarios with more substantial data loads.

Table 2. Encryption Algorithms Vs. Response Time and Latency (38 MB file size)

Algorithm/Output Metric	Response Time (ms)	Latency (ms)
DES	28	16
AES	24	10
AES-HMAC	19	8

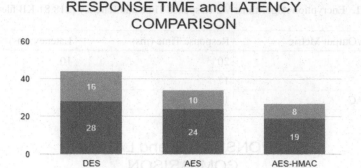

Fig. 4. Response Time and Latency of AES, DES and AES-HMAC Algorithms with 38 MB file size

The evaluation of error rates, as depicted in Table 3 and Fig. 5, provides additional insights into the performance of the encryption techniques. For the smaller file, DES and AES exhibit error rates of 14% and 11%, respectively, while the proposed AES-HMAC demonstrates a substantially lower error rate of 7%. As the file size increases to 38 MB, the error rates for DES and AES also rise (15% and 13%, respectively), but the proposed AES-HMAC maintains a consistently lower error rate of 8%. This underscores the enhanced accuracy and reliability of the proposed AES-HMAC in preserving data integrity.

Table 3. Encryption Algorithms Vs Error Rate (218.81 KB and 38 MB file sizes)

Algorithm/Error Rate	Error Rate (in %) with 218.81 KB file size	Error Rate (in %) with 38 MB file size
DES	14	15
AES	11	13
AES-HMAC	7	8

In summary, the detailed analysis emphasizes the consistent superiority of the proposed AES-HMAC across various metrics and file sizes. Not only does it outperform DES and AES in terms of response time and latency, but it also exhibits a lower error rate, highlighting its robustness and efficiency in securing data in mobile cloud computing environments. The datasets tested included "Cancer Rates by U.S. State" from Kaggle (38 MB) and "U.S. Healthcare Data" from Dataworld (218.81 KB) [9].

AES-HMAC is a better choice because it is better suited for sensitive healthcare data it not only encrypts the data but also performs authentication and integrity checks.

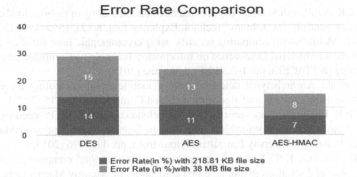

Fig. 5. Error Rate of AES, DES and AES-HMAC Algorithms with 218.81 KB and 38 MB file sizes

7 Conclusion

MCC relies heavily on security techniques to protect data, secure connections, maintain cloud resources, and guarantee privacy laws are followed. This study proposes a strong security model and experimentally evaluates the performance of encryption algorithms to improve security in MCC for healthcare. The outcomes will direct the selection of encryption techniques in actual MCC applications, assuring the security of critical medical data while enhancing system efficiency. AES-HMAC Encryption is an indispensable security method for many MCC scenarios since it helps prevent unauthorized access, data manipulation, and eavesdropping. Due to its integrated design and lower computational cost, the proposed AES-HMAC encryption technique can deliver better outcomes in terms of response time, error rate, and latency. The future directions and emerging technologies for the paper encompass a multifaceted approach. A strong solution for guaranteeing the integrity and auditability of healthcare data in MCC systems could be provided by the inclusion of blockchain-based technologies into the privacy paradigm, improving data transparency, traceability, and decentralized access control. The forthcoming era of 5G networks prompts exploration into adapting the framework to leverage increased speed and connectivity. Edge computing security is a focal point, addressing the decentralized nature of edge devices. Additionally, the incorporation of machine learning for anomaly detection is considered to augment real-time threat identification. The user experience is prioritized with advancements in usability, catering to diverse user needs without compromising security. This development would improve the model's overall security posture and flexibility in a changing technological environment.

References

1. Kalmani, V.H., Singla, S.: Efficiency analysis of symmetric algorithms for data security in mobile cloud computing. Suresh Gyan Vihar Univ. Int. J. Environ., Sci. Technol. (SGVUIJEST) **1**(1), 92–100 (2015)
2. Kulkarni, P., Khanai, R., Bindagi, G.: Security frameworks for mobile cloud computing: a survey. In: 2016 International Conference on Electrical, Electronics, and Optimization Techniques (ICEEOT), pp. 2507–2511. IEEE, Chennai (2016)

3. Masthan, K., Venkatesh Sharma, K.: Secured information sharing in mobile cloud computing using access controls. Int. J. Innov. Technol. Exploring Eng. **8**(12), 1559–1564 (2019)
4. Arfan, M.: Mobile cloud computing security using cryptographic hash function algorithm. In: 2016 3rd International Conference on Information Technology, Computer, and Electrical Engineering (ICITACEE), pp. 1–5. IEEE, Semarang (2016)
5. Hai, T., et al.: An archetypal determination of mobile cloud computing for emergency applications using decision tree algorithm. J. Cloud Comput. **12**(1), 1–15 (2023)
6. Sarode, R.P., Bhalla, S.: Data security in mobile cloud computing. In: Proceedings of International Conference on Sustainable Computing in Science, Technology and Management (SUSCOM), Amity University Rajasthan, Jaipur-India, pp. 491–496 (2019)
7. Singh, B., Jasmine, K.S.: Security management in mobile cloud computing: security and privacy issues and solutions in mobile cloud computing. In: Security Management in Mobile Cloud Computing, pp. 148–168. IGI Global (2017)
8. Delfin, S., Rachana, S.B., Kundana, M.J., Lakshmi, Y., Sharma, S.: Cloud data security using AES algorithm. Int. Res. J. Eng. Technol. **5**(10), 1189–1192 (2018)
9. Awan, I.A., Shiraz, M., Hashmi, M.U., Shaheen, Q., Akhtar, R., Ditta, A.: Secure framework enhancing AES algorithm in cloud computing. Secur. Commun. Netw. **2020**(8863345), 1–16 (2020)
10. AES. https://www.techtarget.com/searchsecurity/definition/Advanced-EncryptionStandard
11. Rehman, S., Talat Bajwa, N., Shah, M.A., Aseeri, A.O., Anjum, A.: Hybrid AES-ECC model for the security of data over cloud storage. Electronics **10**(21), 1–20 (2021)
12. Anuradha, K., Rajini, S.N.S., Bhuvaneswari, T., Vinod, V.: TCP/SYN flood of denial of service (DOS) attack UsingSimulation. Test Eng. Manage., 14553–14558 (2020)
13. Akter, R., Khan, M.A.R., Rahman, F., Soheli, S.J., Suha, N.J.: RSA and AES based hybrid encryption technique for enhancing data security in cloud computing. Int. J. Comput. Appl. Math. Comput. Sci. **3**, 60–71 (2023)
14. Saini, R., Sainis, N.: Cryptographic hybrid model-an advancement in cloud computing security: a survey. Int. J. Eng. Res. Technol. (IJERT) **11**(6), 270–276 (2022)
15. Caner rates. https://data.world/adamhelsinger/cancer-rates-by-u-s-state
16. Healthcare Data. https://www.kaggle.com/datasets/maheshdadhich/us-healthcare-data

An Efficient CH Based Authentication and Authorization for Secure EHR Using DF-BCrypt and Hashed Access Structure

S. Prathima[(✉)] and R. Durga

Department of Computer Science, School of Computing Sciences, Vels Institute of Technology and Advanced Studies (VISTAS), Chennai, India
prathismanian@gmail.com

Abstract. An Electronic Health Record (EHR) is a standard collection of health data from the general population and patients that is electronically stored in a digital format. User authentication and data security are the key issues in distributing EHRs. For researchers, handling larger-scale data along with preserving the patient's privacy has been an issue for a long duration. In data collection, storage, and distribution, the prevailing EHR suffers from data manipulation, delayed communication, and trust-less cooperation. Therefore, by utilizing Hospital id - Patient id Username – Public Private key Caesar Cipher Digit Folding BCrypt (HPU-PPCC-DF-BCrypt) and Correlation Coefficient based Elliptic Curve Cryptography (CCECC), an efficient Cipher Hash based user authentication, Hashed Access Policy verification along with Data Security was proposed. For engendering secure validates for authentication, HPU- PPCC is wielded. For changing the cipher text to hash code, DF-BCrypt is employed. By employing the hash codes generated by the Secure Hash Algorithm (SHA 512), the hash tree access structure is built for performing efficient authorization. The data is encrypted and decrypted by utilizing the CCECC for enhancing data security. The proposed method is compared to the current methodologies. As per experimental evaluation, the proposed method effectively secures EHR data.

Keywords: Electronic Health Records · Patient privacy · data security · Access policy · hash tree access · authentication · authorization

1 Introduction

For storing and securing Patient Data, healthcare centers face several challenges [1]. In the cloud, storing medical data is regarded as the ideal solution; this is because most medical institutions do not have local computing and storage facilities [2]. Huge electronic records of patients are engendered due to the fast enhancement of digitizing healthcare, which results in unparalleled demands for healthcare data protection [3]. Challenges relevant to conventional medical care frameworks could be handled by the enhancement of novel Electronic Health (e-Health) systems [4].

S. Rajagopal et al. (Eds.): ASCIS 2023, CCIS 2039, pp. 207–226, 2024.
https://doi.org/10.1007/978-3-031-59100-6_16

A novel level of technology for sustaining healthcare records with high quality, affordable cost, and interoperability of EHR in the cloud is termed the EHR [5]. These records contain a wide range of information such as (i) Medical history, (ii) Demographics, (iii) medications, (iv) immunizations (v) Lab tests and (vi) other confidential patient info [6]. The wireless communication of electronic health records (EHRs) and other confidential medical data between (a) multiple healthcare entities (b) medical drug manufacturers (c) pharmacists (d) medical insurance providers (e) researchers, together with (f) patients are required by the virtualization of healthcare systems [7].

Issue related to the usage continues even though the adoption together with the merits of EHRs have been hugely described, especially challenges relevant to data integrity of the stored information as well as risks to patient security [8]. In cloud-centric EHR systems, many securities together with privacy concerns namely data confidentiality along with access- control, integrity, issues with cyber security, interoperability, as well as accountability are handled [9]. Since it concerns the patient's sensitive health data, security in E-healthcare is extremely significant. Secure storage, access, and retrieval are the key security concerns in EHR [10]. Figure 1 shows the basic diagram of EHR.

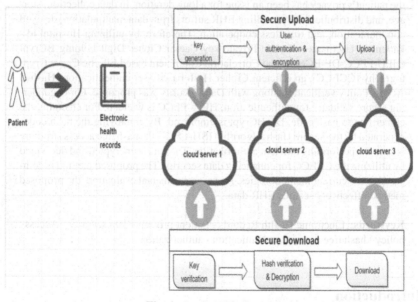

Fig. 1. Basic EHR Model

1.1 Problem Definition

Authentication is finding the legitimacy of the data requester and is usually followed by authorization which is granting resource to the eligible user. For securing and preserving EHR data strong authorization and authentication methods are crucial and different approaches have been proposed. One being attribute based access-control method [26], records are encrypted making use of public key elements that corresponds to its attributes. Then finally an access-based structure is created based on its secret keys. To solve the re-encryption process by the data owners attribute- based encryption method along with proxy re-encryption method is invoked [27]. For preserving privacy, this method made use of: concatenation operations, bit-wise XOR, as well as SHA-256 [28]. Nevertheless, the existing approaches have defects in privacy-preserving, authentication, efficient authorization, and data security by being vulnerable to attacks:

• The current data encryption method has a high level of complexity, affecting its running time.
• Existing Hash Functions (HF) cantered on Authentication, which is not collision resistant can easily fall prey to attacks owing to the short length of the input to Hashing Algorithm
• Existing techniques failed to offer confidentiality and privacy for data owners and users

1.2 Objectives

Designing a framework for efficient Cipher Hashing- centric user authentication, Hashed Access Policy verification along with Data Security using HPU- PPCC-DF-BCrypt and CCECC in EHR systems is the goal. The main objectives of this proposed model are:

• To perform an efficient authentication, Cipher Hash code generation technique will be used to create strong credentials for authentication.
• To improve Hash code creation complexity, summation of patient's Public Key and Private Key based Caesar Cipher text will be created.
• To improve the data security, the doctor's Public Key and Patient's Public Key will be manipulated using Correlation Coefficient technique with Elliptic Curve Cryptography (CCECC) algorithm will be introduced.
• To introduce efficient Hash tree access structure to perform efficient Authorization process.

1.3 Paper Structure

– Section 2 contains the relevant works
– Section 3 explains the proposed method
– Section 4 analyses the results and discussions of performance metrics and
– Section 5 concludes with the future work

2 Literature Survey

Ganiga et al. [11] recommended a Security framework for a cloud-centric EHR that considered data integrity, data availability, along with privacy in health-based records. Using stride modelling instruments, threats posed to the EHR were analyzed. By employing the dread model, the risk amount was appraised. Security concerns like breaches of sensitive medical information were tackled effectively. Nevertheless, secure data transmission was not considered.

Joshi et al. [12] recommended a fresh, centralized authorization system that used attribute-based encryption (ABE) which gave doctors and nurses secure access to patient health records. Service management was transferred from the patient to the organization by ABE; in addition, permitted cloud-centric EHRs access authority an easy delegation to medical providers. But, for data encryption, the data owners must deploy each authorized user's public key.

Al-Sharhan et al. [13] presented a fresh system along with incorporated systems for effectual application of Health systems nationally. For analyzing the health records, every success factor of an efficient eHealth system was integrated with a fresh security model. However, a security- based model, that combines security along with privacy-based technologies for guaranteeing data confidentiality as well as user level privacy in health care systems, was essential.

Mhatre and Nimkar [14] presented a CP-ABE system that provides clear, efficient, and customizable healthcare access control for a federal- centric system. Here, the attribute revocation aided in solving forward and backward security issues. Attribute management overhead was minimized as of a centralized system along with time complexity. Nevertheless, a huge time was required.

Saleem et al. [15] evolved a system to secure EHR Management in the Internet of Things. For avoiding unauthorized access and alteration, the patients' EHRs' were secured by the IoT-centric scheme. For securing the recorded sensitive data, encryption methodologies were wielded. In hospital databases, the technique efficiently secured and enhanced the process of accessing together with managing EHR. But they could not access the essential information as the key may be forgotten by the concerned tparties like patients or doctors etc.

Masud et al. [16] recommended a strong and easy-to-use secure way to access cloud-based Electronic healthcare services. By offering a secure interface to stakeholders, the potential threats were tackled to E- healthcare. For guaranteeing information's end-to-end ciphering, various keys engendered via the key derivation function (KDF) were deployed. Data security and privacy were effectively secured. However, faster access was not permitted to health records.

Tran et al. [17] presented a security aware access approach for data-driven electronic health records systems. For controlling permission to access sensitive data and securing the transfer of data between servers of the distributed system and the nodes, a fresh security model was deployed. The NIST's security standards were also taken into consideration. The system was extremely propitious according to the results. Nevertheless, frequent updates were required.

Misra et al. [18] developed an auth- enticated key agreement protocol amongst doctors, hospitals, and patients by employing a Conjugacy Searching Problem (CSP) together with a Braid Decomposition Problem (BDP). The essential safety measures were tackled and also verified that the system passed the safety bounds presumptuously. But, for Low Power Wide Area Networks, the system is not effectual by deploying a local database.

Chinnasamy and Deepalakshmi [19] recommended a fresh system by applying hybrid cryptography and an improvised key-generation schema for RSA (IKGSR) for encrypting health records along with blow fish technique meant for encrypting key. For effectively retrieving the encrypted data, Steganography - centric access control for key sharing was wielded. Enhanced security was depicted along with the data was retrieved effectively. However, a huge time was required for completing the process.

Riad et al. [20] SE-AC is a solution for managing Electronic Health Record (EHR) systems hosted in the cloud, while also providing a granular approach to access control, even in critical circumstances. The system was secure; in addition, every unauthorized access was prevented. With various setups and configurations, exceptional compatibility and performance were depicted. But, temporary losses were caused in productivity since disruptions occurred.

Babrahem and Monowar [21] recommended a cloud- centric EHR by developing the Advanced Encryption Standard (AES) crypto technique with custom based access control for organizations. AES encryption was used for providing security in two layers along with privacy to the EHR information. Grounded on the general security requirements, the security concerns were evaluated. In resource-constrained devices, the system's efficacy was verified. However, weak ciphers were generated.

Parah et al. [22] introduced a fresh high payload as well as reversible EHR embedding for successfully storing the patient's records along with authenticating the content received. It was grounded on left data mapping (LDM) and pixel repetition method (PRM) and Rivest Cipher 4 (RC4), together with checksum computations. As per the outcomes, this system surpassed several prevailing techniques. Nevertheless, in smaller streams of data, it might not be deployed.

Khan and Reyad [23] recommended a fresh intelligent based access control model (IBAC) centered upon multiple agents for maintaining and supporting the security and privacy of E-healthcare. To sustain safety along with solitude whilst analyzing the E-health data betwixt the users, agents were deployed effectively. However, the data might be analyzed by any unauthorized person who extracts the doctor's private key.

Gautam et al. [24] presented a system for EHR confidential data on cloud storage. For enforcing confidentiality and authentication, the obfuscation and Rivest, Shamir, and Adleman (RSA) were fused. On cloud storage, the data confidentiality together with authentication of EHR information was enforced efficiently. For an adversary, the code is made harder by obfuscation. But the obfuscated program might be decoded by the automatic obfuscators.

Vijayakumar et al. [25] developed a planning-enabled re-encryption intermediary for defeating security problems. For accessing the health records meant for a certain time, just constrained access rights were permitted to an authorized agent. Searchable encryption together with proxy Re-encryption methodology was wielded. The system is powerful and secure, which was proven via the alternate plan analysis. However, the employment of symmetric keys made it tedious for sharing records remotely with required parties.

3 Proposed EHR Security Framework

The system is setup with the patient enrollment or register phase where the patient's information is collected and the public key along with private key are generated by the key generation system. The Hospital ID, Patient ID, and Username are merged; in addition, it is converted into cipher text using HPU- PPCC and the patient public key and private key summation value. By employing DF-BCrypt, the cipher-text is converted to one hash code. By employing the Doctor ID, the patient can login to the system and book an appointment with the respective doctor following a successful enrollment.

The selected patient's EHR data is uploaded into the hospital's cloud-server soon after the consultation. Data security as well as authorization processes are enhanced before sending the records to the cloud. The Merkle Tree (MT) access structure is constructed by the hash codes generated using the SHA-512 for enhancing the authorization process. To improve data security, the CCECC is deployed. The encrypted data along with Hashed Access Structure is bundled and sent to the cloud server of the respective hospital. In the end, data access has been performed. In Fig. 2, the proposed framework is depicted.

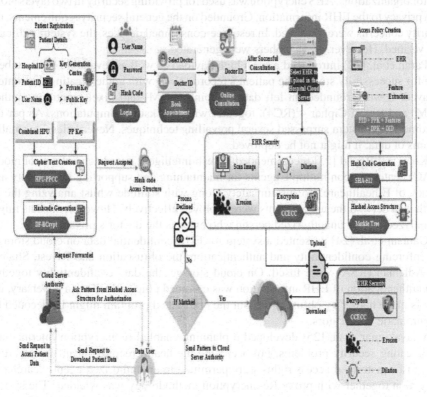

Fig. 2. Framework of the Proposed System

3.1 Patient Registration Phase

The patient's particulars are collected. Then the key generation system, forms the public key (α) as well as the private key (β). The Hospital ID (H_{id}), Patient ID(p_{id}) and User-name (μ) are combined to convert them into a cipher text. These details are collectively evaluated as follows,

$$\phi = \{\hbar_{id}, \rho_{id}, \mu\} \tag{1}$$

Here, ϕ implies the combined patient details. By employing HPU-PPCC with the patient's public key and patient's private key summation value, the combined detail (ϕ) is converted into a cipher. Public and private key summation value is combined with the existing Caesar cipher for maximizing the complexity. A type of substitution cipher that makes up the cipher by exchanging the characters in plaintext into exactly one character in the ciphertext is termed a Caesar cipher. This is done by shifting the characters in plaintext with the same shift value. It is depicted by transforming the letters into numbers. In Fig. 3, the encryption process in the Caesar cipher algorithm is explained.

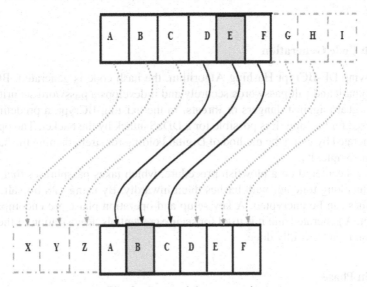

Fig. 3. Ceasar cipher encryption

The encryption process can be described as,

$$\varepsilon(\phi) = (\phi + \Omega) mod\ 26 \tag{2}$$

function called eksblowfish setup with salt (δ), generated cipher text $\varepsilon(\phi)$ and cost factor (θ) is initialized. The eks- blowfish setup can be expressed as,

$$e \rightarrow eksblowfish(\delta, \varepsilon(\phi), \theta) \tag{3}$$

Here, the initiated eksblowfish state is signified by e_s. Next, by employing eksblowfish in Electronic Code Book (ECB) mode with the state (e_s), the 192-bit magic value is encrypted. For offering the outcomes, the 128-bit salt and the cost are joined with the result of the encryption loop. Only salting the characters is unworthy to hash a string. Hence, for generating the end hash, the cost factor is included. The output of the hashing algorithm is expressed as:

$$\aleph = \left\{ \delta^{128} + \theta + \infty \right\} \tag{4}$$

Here, the generated hash code is depicted by $\aleph$, the encryption loop is depicted by ∞. For detecting the expenses of the HF, the cost factor helps. The cost factor (θ) is obtained using the digit folding technique using the formula,

$$\theta = \left(x^0 + x^1 + x^3 + ... + x^6\right) mod \ \Delta \tag{5}$$

Here, the characters are depicted by x, and the size. Here, the encryption process of the patient details (ϕ). And the shift value (i.e., the summation value of public along with private keys) is signified as Ω. Next, the generated cipher text ε_n (ϕ) is transformed to hash code.

3.2 Hash Code Generation

By employing DF-BCrypt Hashing Algorithm, the hash code is generated. BCrypt is wielded to hash and salt passwords securely and it develops a password security stage, which can guard against dangers or threats. In the existing BCrypt, a predefined cost factor is used for hashing. It is possible for a DDoS attack by the hacker. The optimized cost is generated by using the method of Digital Folding for strengthening the hash code generation complexity.

BCrypt is centered on a blowfish procedure, which takes passphrases that are 8 to 56 characters long together with hashes them inwardly. By using 128-bit salt, 192-bit magic values can be encrypted. A key setup and operation phase are encompassed in the BCrypt. A generated and it is used for secure credentials. Registration of the patient information is successfully done.

3.3 Login Phase

After registering successfully, the concerned patient logs in using the username, password, and generated Hash Code registration. If all the hash codes match, system enables the requester to access the resource. By employing Doctor ID, the patient requests an appointment with the doctor. The appointment is scheduled and consultation is done.

3.4 Data Storage

The patient's EHR data is sent to the organization's cloud after the consultation is over. The following procedures are done to improve the data security with authorization step before sending the data to the server.

3.5 Access Policy Creation

The features such as file name, file size, created time, etc. are extracted from the selected patient's EHR data. Patient Public Key (ρ_{PPK}), Doctor Public Key (D_{DPK}) and Doctor ID (D_{DID}), n number of hash codes are generated using SHA512 for each extracted features (l_i) along with the Patient ID (ρ_{PID}). The input given to the hashing algorithm can be expressed as,

$$\psi = \sum_{i=1}^{n} \{l_i, \rho_{PID}, \rho_{PPK}, D_{DPK}, D_{DID}\} \tag{6}$$

Logical functions AND, and XOR are performed by the compression function. A round of the compression functions is expressed as follows,

$$\sum_{0}^{512}(A) = (A >>>> 28) \oplus (A >>>> 34)(A >>>> 39) \tag{7}$$

$$\wp(A,B,C) = (A \wedge B) \oplus (A \wedge C) \oplus (B \wedge C) \tag{8}$$

$$\Im_{2,i} = \sum_{0}^{512}(A) + \wp(A, B, C) \tag{9}$$

$$\sum_{1}^{512}(E) = (E \ggg 14) \oplus (E \ggg 18)(E \ggg 41) \tag{10}$$

3.6 SHA-512 Algorithm

It is a hashing wielded for converting text of any length into a fixed-size string. It works on a message in 1024-bit blocks together with engenders a 512-bit message. The input message can have a length of up to 2128- 1 bits. In Fig. 4, the SHA-512 algorithm's basic structure is delineated.

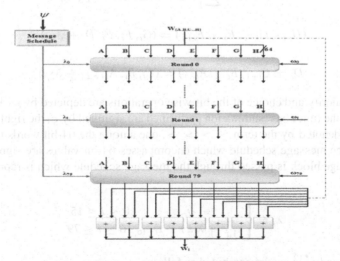

Fig. 4. Basic structure of SHA-512 Algorithm

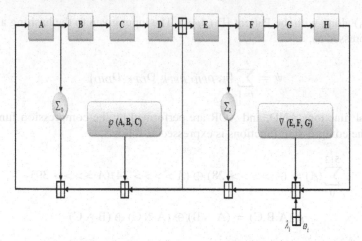

Fig. 5. One round of the SHA-512 Compression function

Primarily, the input message (ψ) is padded to a length of 896 mod 1024, and the message length is joined as an 128-bit binary number. The message is set to n × 1024-bit blocks of data. The '8' variables A, B, C, D, E, F,G, H are set to 64-bit words (that is 8 × 64-bit words). On the first 1024-bit block data, SHA 512 compression function's 80 rounds are performed. In Fig. 5, the operation involved in the compression function is depicted.

$$\nabla(E, F, G) = (E \wedge F) \oplus (\overline{E} \wedge G) \tag{11}$$

$$\Im_{1,i} = H + \sum_{1}^{512} E + \nabla(E,F,G) + \omega_i + \lambda_i \tag{12}$$

$$(H_{i+1}, G_{i+1}, F_{i+1}, E_{i+1}) = (G_i, F_i, E_i, D_i + \Im_{1,i}) \tag{13}$$

$$(D_{i+1}, C_{i+1}, B_{i+1}, A_{i+1}) = (C_i, B_i, A_i, \Im_{i,i} + \Im_{2,i}) \tag{14}$$

Here, the majority and choice of the bit-wise operations are depicted by $\wp(A, B, C)$ and $\nabla(E, F, G)$, the functions' summation performed are signified by ς, the right shifting pf the word is denoted by the term $> > > >$, one among the 64-bit words is indicated by ω, and the message schedule which encompasses 64-bit values are signified by λ. Every message block is passed through the message schedule which is represented by 16 words.

$$\lambda_i = \begin{cases} \psi_i & 0 \leq i \leq 15 \\ \tau_{1,i}^{512} + \lambda_{i-7} + \tau_{i-16} & 16 \leq i \leq 79 \end{cases} \tag{15}$$

where $\tau_{1,i}^{512}$, and $\tau_{0,i}^{512}$ can be computed as follows,

$$\tau_{0,i}^{512} = (\lambda_{i-15} >>>> 1) \oplus (\lambda_{i-15} >>>> 8) \oplus (\lambda_{i-15} >> 7) \tag{16}$$

$$\tau_{1.i}^{512} = (\lambda_{i-2} >>>> 19) \oplus (\lambda_{i-2} >>>> 61) \oplus (\lambda_{i-2} >> 6) \qquad (17)$$

For the next data block's compression function, the '8' variables are initialized by the output 512-bit from the first round. The set of '8' variables is rotated word-wise in every round. By merging the '8' intermediate hash values, the final 512-bit digest is engendered after completing all n data blocks. For building an MT, the number of hash codes generated for several features is wielded. Pseudocode depicts the steps encompassed in SHA-512.

Pseudo-code for Secure Hash Algorithm (SHA-512).

Input: Combined features (ψ)

Output: Generated Hash code

Begin.

Initialize the eight (working) variables $A, B..., H$

For $i = 1$ *to* n

Formulate message schedule λ_{i-l}

For $i = 1$ *to* 80.

Perform the compress function operations by Eqs. 7 to 14.

Update the eight variables for $i = i + 1$

End for

Compute the ith intermediate hash value

Generate the final 512-bit message digest

End For

Return $\Re$

3.7 Merkle Tree Construction

A complete binary tree equipped with a hash list is termed an MT. Every non-leaf node represents a hash of its child nodes in tree data structure. The hash at the bottom of the row is referred as leaves, intermediate hashes are called branches, and the hash at the top hash is referred to as root. For the entire data, the fingerprint.is the root hash. For efficient data verification, MTs are used in distributed systems. The hash codes generated by the HF that is fedinto the MT can be expressed as

$$\Re = [\Re_1, \Re_2, ..., \Re_n] \qquad (18)$$

Here, code $\Re_n$ implies the hash code of the nth feature. The MT is constructed by employing the hash code is shown in the Fig. 6.

The tree is created by pairing the hash codes in the first row then, the resulting pair hashes on each next level until a single hash is produced. The Merkle root is the single hash code. To access the data and to improve the authorization process, a pattern is created.

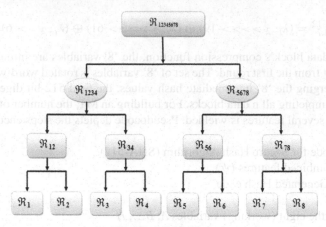

Fig. 6. Merkle Tree

3.8 Data Security

Here, the security of the patient's EHR data is enhanced. The selected data (ϖ) (i.e., the scan images) is converted into the morphological format. Dilation and Erosion are the '2' processes included in the morphological process. The process of adding pixels to objects' boundaries is termed Dilation. The process of removing the pixel is termed erosion. The number of pixels added or removed relies on the Structuring Element's (SE) features that are wielded for image processing.

3.9 Dilation

Here, the SE interacts with the scanned image ϖ. In the SE, one of the pixels overlaps the pixel in the scanned image during the interaction. By replacing the center position of the SE, the SE expands the scanned image. Maximum overlapping of pixels tends to dilation process. Hence, the area of the scanned image is increased. The dilation process is equated as

$$\varpi \oplus S = \left\{ U | \left(\hat{S}_U \cap \varpi \right) \in \varpi \right\} \tag{19}$$

where, S implies the SE, and the dilation operator is signified by $\oplus$. When at least one element of the SE interacts with the scanned image, the output U is considered.

3.10 Erosion

Here, the SE interacts with the scanned image (ϖ). The complete overlapping of pixels between the SE and the image occurs during the interaction. The center pixel of the SE is shrunk by which the SE shrinks the scanned image. Minimum overlapping of pixels tends to erosion process. Hence, the image's background area is maximized. The erosion process is equated as

$$\varpi \ominus S = \left\{ U | \left(\hat{S}_U \in \varpi \right) \right\} \tag{20}$$

Here, the erosion operator is depicted by Θ. Only when the SE is equal to the scan image, the output U is considered. By employing CCECC, the converted image (U) is encrypted.

3.11 Data Encryption

It is a procedure of translating data from unencrypted (plain text) to encrypted text (cipher text). ECC is the key-centric approach to data encryption. For web traffic decipher as well as encipher public- key private- key pairs are addressed. For this, secret key is generated using Doctor and patient's public key with the help of the Correlation Coefficient (CC) technique for enhancing data security. In the encryption along with decryption, this secret key is wielded to improve the complexity. The elliptical curve is defined using the ECC cryptographic-key algorithm.

$$h^3 = k^3 + kl + r \tag{21}$$

At this stage, the integers have been depicted by k, r furthermore the variables which describe the function have been signified as h, I. Using the recipient's public key, the user can encrypt the image; moreover, by employing their private key, the receiver will decrypt the data. The private key and public key pairs are produced to obtain encryption text and decryption text. The public-key is generated by the below mathematical formulation,

$$Q = \gamma * R \tag{22}$$

where Q represents the public key, R represents the random generated private key, and the point of curve is defined by γ. By combining the doctor's and patients' public keys, the secret-key (V) is generated using the correlation coefficient equation. It is expressed as,

$$V = \frac{n(\sum Q_d Q_p) - (\sum Q_d)(\sum Q_p)}{\sqrt{[n \sum Q_d^2 - (\sum Q_d)^2][n \sum Q_p^2 - (\sum Q_p)^2]}} \tag{23}$$

Here, the public key of the doctor and patient are signified by Q_d and Q_p. Encryption of the inputted data is done. During the encryption procedure the encryption derived formula multiplies the generated secret key. This encrypted info is made up of '2' cipher generated texts that could be equated by,

$$x_1 = (\gamma * \sigma) * V \tag{24}$$

$$x_2 = (U + Q * \sigma) * V \tag{25}$$

Here, a random range (1, n-1) is depicted by σ. The decryption formula is divided by the secret key during the decryption process. The process of decryption may be defined as follows,

$$U = \frac{x_2 - R * x_1}{V} \tag{26}$$

Finally, the Encrypted data along with Hashed Access Structure is bundled and is uploaded to the healthcare center's private cloud. For Accessing the Data, the user of the data (Consulted Doctor) forwards a message to the Cloud Server Authority after uploading the patient's data. The request is forwarded to the corresponding patient and the patient accepts the request and provides the Hashed Access Structure for corresponding data to the Requested user. To download the data, a message is sent to the Cloud Server Authority by the data user. For conducting authorization process, the cloud server authority demands the Pattern from the Access Tree to the Doctor. The pattern created by the MT is transferred to the cloud server authority by the data user. The cloud server allows the user to download the data if the received pattern matches the access structure of the Cloud Server Authority. By employing the CCECC, the data is encrypted. For acquiring the actual EHR, erosion, and dilation processes are done in the decrypted data. On the pattern not matching, the corresponding request is not granted.

4 Results and Discussions

In this section, we'll look at how the proposed model performs compared to the existing models. The proposed system is implemented in PYTHON in Pycharm environment with a system configuration of Windows 10 and RAM of 4GB, using SQLite for data storage and CloudSim simulation and MATLAB for plotting graphs and PIL (Python image library) for imaging purposes. The performance and comparative evaluation are done for proving the effectiveness.

4.1 Dataset

The proposed system uses dataset from MIMIC-III, a free critical care medical database which is an open- source database. The period of evaluation is in between 2010 and 2020.

4.2 Analysis of Performance

The features that ensure correct authentication and authorization are: (a). Hash code-based cipher text creation (b). Generation of complex secret key for encryption and decryption (using more than one key). (c). For improving data security Correlation Coefficient technique with Elliptic Curve Cryptography (CCECC).

Some related work discussed: A cloud- centric EHR by developing the Advanced Encryption Standard (AES) crypto technique with custom based access control for organizations. AES encryption was used for providing security in two layers along with privacy to the EHR information [21]. For guaranteeing information's end-to-end ciphering, various keys engendered via the key derivation function (KDF) were deployed. Data security and privacy were effectively secured [16].

Based on the above factors, the following performance analysis is carried out: With respect to Encrypting time (ET), Decrypting time (DT), usage of memory during encryption process and decryption process, key generation time, as well as the security level,

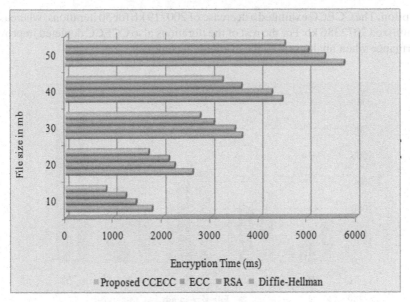

Fig. 7. Analysis of the proposed CCECC and existing models w.r.to ET

the performance of the suggested CCECC's is compared to the familiar Diffie Hellman, Rivest, Shamir, Adleman (RSA), together with Elliptic Curve Cryptography (ECC).

With respect to ET, the suggested CCECC is compared with the familiar techniques in Fig. 7. ET is defined as the time consumed for converting plaintext into cipher text. For iterations 10–50, the system's ET is estimated. For encryption, the CCECC consumes less time of 4517 ms for 50 iterations; while, the prevailing ECC, RSA, and Diffie-Hellman deployed huge time of 5011ms, 5352ms, and 5734ms. For every iteration, the CCECC deployed less time for encryption. Hence, when contrasted with the available techniques, the CCECC exhibited superior performance.

Table 1. Analysis of performance w.r.t memory used during encryption

Techniques	Memory Usage on Encryption (KB)				
Diffie Hellman	7178686	759387	8259484	9138584	9621554
RSA	6233542	6942292	7286537	8462147	8944785
ECC	5745636	6152556	6516788	7051589	7072386
Proposed CCECC	5073417	5155636	5584523	6421156	6871667

In Table 1, regarding memory used during encryption, the proposed CCECC's performance is correlated with the familiar methods. To exhibit the system's enhanced performance, the memory usage that is measured in kilobytes must be low. The use of memory requires the use of a private key that should change on each boot of the CPU in encryption. The CCECC exhibited a decrease of 200719 kb for 50 iterations; whereas, the ECC utilized 7072386 kb. For the rest of the iterations also CCECC depicted improvised performance when analogized to the available techniques.

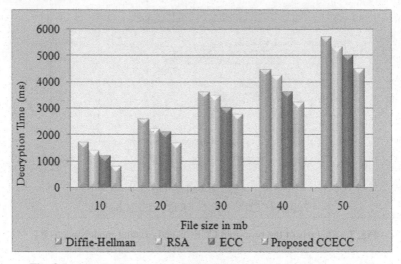

Fig. 8. Analysis of the proposed CCECC and existing models w.r.to DT

For several iterations, the proposed CCECC is evaluated with the prevailing methodologies centred on the DT in Fig. 8. DT is the time essential for converting the encrypted data to its original form. The CCECC attained the DT of 4512ms for 50 iterations; whilst, the prevailing ECC, RSA, and Diffie-Hellman acquired 5001ms, 5332ms, and 5714ms. Hence, when correlated with the familiar methods, the CCECC depicted improvised performance.

Table 2. Comparative Analysis of the Proposed and Existing Models during Decryption Time

Techniques	Memory Usage on Decryption (KB)				
Diffie Hellman	7267875	7768387	8365484	9287584	9768554
RSA	6278975	7173292	7376537	8576347	9044785
ECC	5846167	6284556	6666788	7177589	7266886
Proposed CCECC	5180054	5225636	5674523	6678556	6945667

In Table 2, grounded on memory usage on decryption, the proposed CCECC's performance is contrasted with the available techniques. For 50 iterations, the CCECC depicts a decrease in memory consumption by 2099118kb; while, the available techniques attained higher memory consumption of 9044785 kb for RSA. Likewise, the CCECC depicts a difference in memory consumption by 321219kb for ECC and 2822887kb for Diffie Hellman for similar iterations. Thus, when weighed against the available methodologies, the CCECC is more effectual.

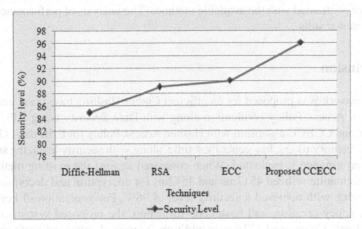

Fig. 9. Security Level Comparative Analysis of proposed and existing models

Grounded on security level, the suggested CCECC is compared with the familiar techniques in Fig. 9. The measure of strength that the cryptographic primitive achieves is termed the security level. For security level, the CCECC depicted 96%; whereas, the ECC acquired 90%. The existing RSA and Diffie Hellman methods have a security level of 89% and 85%, which are lesser by 7% and 11% when compared to the security level of the CCECC. Hence, when correlated with the current methods, the CCECC depicted enhanced performance.

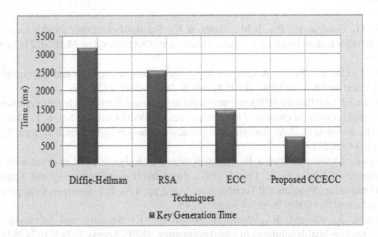

Fig. 10. Key Generation Analysis of the proposed and existing models

Figure 10, the suggested CCECC is correlated with the existing methods centered on the time required for key generation. For key generation, the CCECC deploys 717ms; whereas the prevailing methodologies deploy a huge time of 1456ms for ECC, 2533ms for RSA, and 3158ms for Diffie Hellman. Thus, the CCECC exhibits superior performance when contrasted with the available methods. The analysis of performance is done using the latest results.

5   Conclusion

A new framework was proposed for an efficient Cipher Hashing based user authentication, Hashed Access Policy verification along with Data Security using HPU- PPCC-DF-BCrypt and CCECC algorithm with Hashed Access Policy for EHR data. Grounded on ET, DT, memory usage, key generation time, along with security level, the suggested system's performance is evaluated. When compared against the existing methods, the suggested technique utilized 4517ms and 4512ms for encryption and decryption for 50 iterations along with achieved a security level of 96%. For generation of key, cipher-based text, policy-creation, and hash code formation, the proposed system consumed 717 ms, 301ms, 321ms, and 121ms; in addition, it attained enhanced performance for every metric. As per the outcomes, the proposed system is highly efficient in securing and preserving the EHR.

6   Scope for Future Work

The work will be extended by considering blockchain technology in the secure storage and sharing of healthcare data in the future by using advanced techniques.

References

1. Pai, M.M., Ganiga, R., Pai, R.M., Sinha, R.K.: Standard electronic health record (EHR) framework for Indian healthcare system. Health Serv. Outcomes Res. Method. **21**(3), 339–362 (2021)
2. Zhang, J., Liu, H., Ni, L.: A secure energy-saving communication and encrypted storage model based on RC4 for EHR. IEEE Access **8**, 38995–39012 (2020)
3. Alruwaili, F.F.: Artificial intelligence and multi agent based distributed ledger system for better privacy and security of electronic healthcare records. PeerJ Comput. Sci. **6**, 1–14 (2020)
4. Sivan, R., Zukarnain, Z.A.: Security and privacy in cloud-based e-health system. Symmetry **13**(5), 1–14 (2021)
5. Prathap, R., Mohanasundaram, R., Ashok Kumar, P.: Design of EHR in cloud with security. In: Satapathy, S., Bhateja, V., Das, S. (eds.) Smart Intelligent Computing and Applications. Smart Innovation, Systems and Technologies, vol. 2, pp. 419–425. Springer, Singapore (2019). https://doi.org/10.1007/978-981-13-1927-3_45
6. Chenthara, S., Ahmed, K., Wang, H., Whittaker, F.: Security and privacy-preserving challenges of e-health solutions in cloud computing. IEEE Access **7**, 74361–74382 (2019)
7. Aljuaid, H., Parah, S.A.: Secure patient data transfer using information embedding and hyperchaos. Sensors **21**(1), 1–20 (2021)

8. Bani Issa, W., et al.: Privacy, confidentiality, security and patient safety concerns about electronic health records. Int. Nurs. Rev. **67**(2), 218–230 (2020)
9. Thakkar, V., Shah, V.: Investigation of techniques used for mitigating security and privacy issues in cloud based electronic health record (EHR) systems **8**(2), 466–478 (2021)
10. Premarathne, U., et al.: Hybrid cryptographic access control for cloud-based EHR systems. IEEE Cloud Comput. **3**(4), 58–64 (2016)
11. Ganiga, R., Pai, R.M., Sinha, R.K.: Security framework for cloud based electronic health record (EHR) system. Int. J. Electr. Comput. Eng. **10**(1), 455–466 (2020)
12. Joshi, M., Joshi, K.P., Finin, T.: Delegated authorization framework for EHR services using attribute-based encryption. IEEE Trans. Serv. Comput. **14**(6), 1612–1623 (2019)
13. Al-Sharhan, S., Omran, E., Lari, K.: An integrated holistic model for an eHealth system: a national implementation approach and a new cloud-based security model. Int. J. Inf. Manage. **47**, 121–130 (2019)
14. Mhatre, S., Nimkar, A.V.: Secure cloud-based federation for EHR using multi-authority ABE. In: Panigrahi, C., Pujari, A., Misra, S., Pati, B., Li, K.C. (eds.) Progress in Advanced Computing and Intelligent Engineering. Advances in Intelligent Systems and Computing, vol. 714, pp. 3–15. Springer, Singapore (2019). https://doi.org/10.1007/978-981-13-0224-4_1
15. Saleem, W.Y.B., Ali, H., AlSalloom, N.: A framework for securing EHR management in the era of internet of things. In: 2020 3rd International Conference on Computer Applications & Information Security (ICCAIS), pp. 1–5. IEEE, Riyadh (2020)
16. Masud, M., Gaba, G.S., Choudhary, K., Alroobaea, R., Hossain, M.S.: A robust and lightweight secure access scheme for cloud based E-healthcare services. Peer-to-peer Networking Appl. **14**(5), 3043–3057 (2021)
17. Tran, N.H., Nguyen-Ngoc, T.A., Le-Khac, N.A., Kechadi, M.: A security-aware access model for data-driven EHR system. arXiv preprint: arXiv:1908.10229 (2019)
18. Misra, M.K., Chaturvedi, A., Tripathi, S.P., Shukla, V.: A unique key sharing protocol among three users using non-commutative group for electronic health record system. J. Discr. Math. Sci. Crypt. **22**(8), 1435–1451 (2019)
19. Chinnasamy, P., Deepalakshmi, P.: HCAC-EHR: hybrid cryptographic access control for secure EHR retrieval in healthcare cloud. J. Ambient. Intell. Humaniz. Comput. **3**(4), 1–19 (2022)
20. Riad, K., Hamza, R., Yan, H.: Sensitive and energetic IoT access control for managing cloud electronic health records. IEEE Access **7**, 86384–86393 (2019)
21. Babrahem, A.S., Monowar, M.M.: Preserving confidentiality and privacy of the patient's EHR using the OrBAC and AES in cloud environment. Int. J. Comput. Appl. **43**(1), 50–61 (2021)
22. Parah, S.A., et al.: Efficient security and authentication for edge-based internet of medical things. IEEE Internet Things J. **8**(21), 15652–15662 (2020)
23. Khan, F., Reyad, O.: Application of intelligent multi agent based systems for e-healthcare security. Inf. Sci. Lett. Int. J. **8**(2), 67–72 (2019)
24. Gautam, P., Ansari, M.D., Sharma, S.K.: Enhanced security for electronic health care information using obfuscation and RSA algorithm in cloud computing. Int. J. Inf. Secur. Priv. (IJISP) **13**(1), 59–69 (2019)
25. Vijayakumar, V., Priyan, M.K., Ushadevi, G., Varatharajan, R., Manogaran, G., Tarare, P.V.: E-health cloud security using timing enabled proxy re-encryption. Mob. Netw. Appl. **24**(3), 1034–1045 (2019)
26. Cha, B., Seo, J., Kim, J.: Design of attribute-based access control in cloud computing environment. In: Kim, K., Ahn, S. (eds.) Proceedings of the International Conference on IT Convergence and Security 2011. Lecture Notes in Electrical Engineering, vol. 120, pp. 41–50. Springer, Dordrecht (2011). https://doi.org/10.1007/978-94-007-2911-7_4

27. Canetti, R., Hohenberger, S.: Chosen-ciphertext secure proxy re-encryption. In: Proceedings of the 14th ACM conference on Computer and Communications Security, New York, United States, pp. 185–194 (2007)
28. Limbasiya, T., Sahay, S.K., Sridharan, B.: Privacy- preserving mutual authentication and key agreement scheme for multi-server healthcare system. Inf. Syst. Front. **23**(4), 835–848 (2021)

A Novel Framework to Detect Business Email Compromise Through Unconsented Email Autoforwards

Priti Kulkarni and Jatinderkumar R. Saini[✉]

Symbiosis Institute of Computer Studies and Research, Symbiosis International (Deemed University), Pune, India
saini_expert@yahoo.com

Abstract. Contemporary business heavily relies on email communication as the official communication in the business. However, this pivotal communication medium has become a prime target by the attackers to find a way to enter into the organisation's network. Phishing is an email-based attack where an attacker sends a fraudulent email in such a way that it looks like the original email. This phishing email aims to get the victim's credentials. The attacks are known as Business Email Compromise (BEC). The most common BEC scams are 'CEO fraud' and 'man-in-middle' scams. The BEC attacks are fast growing attacks and it is necessary to control it. There are numerous papers addressing BEC attacks. The BEC attackers are using new approaches to mail scams. One of the techniques used by attackers is to set email auto forward rules to redirect emails to malicious email account. It is required to continuously monitor the email auto forward rules. But the traditional approach of manual control is difficult and attacks may go undetected. So, in this paper we are presenting an approach of automatic control by presenting a novel theoretical Email Auto forward Security Framework (EASF). The paper attempts to address an email auto forward, a new technique used by attackers for BEC which is the most dangerous threat. The EASF presents an automated approach to counter the increasing threat of BEC. The implementation of this framework will help the business to detect and mitigate BEC attacks through email auto forward, thus ensuring security and integrity of the communication. The paper also discusses the precautions and challenges for BEC.

Keywords: Business Email Compromise · email auto forwards · email phishing · security framework · unconsented email

1 Introduction

Email communication has become integral part of business communication. The emails are sent and received every day within organization as well as outside organisation. The most of the email service providers are providing protection against the spam and phishing emails. For smooth conduction of business functions, the employees use email forwarding as a convenient feature. Email forwarding is a process of resending email to one or more recipients. But this is more convenient for threat actors. The Business Email Comprise (BEC) scammers are getting savvier. BEC is a form of social engineering in which a scammer impersonates vendors or bosses in order to trick employees into transferring funds to the wrong place. BEC is type of email phishing for financial fraud [1].

An email thread which pretends that the email has been forwarded by boss for sending funds in such a way that it senses urgency to make payment. There is another trick used by attackers to trap the victim, they send emails considering ongoing email thread that appear to be forwarded by their boss asking to handle the payment. This type of attack is difficult to detect by spam filters as it is not based on malware attack or any suspicious activity detected by software application. It is an attack for financial gain [2].

1.1 How BEC Attack Works?

The BEC attack starts with research on identifying the business. The execution of BEC attack steps [3, 4] are listed in Fig. 1.

Step 1: Target the Business

The BEC attackers conduct research to find out their potential victim. They try to find vulnerabilities to enter into company.

Step 2: Identify the authority within the organisation

The attackers usually focus on the top management or individual member who is authorized to give payment related approvals within organisations.

Step 3: Identify employee to target

Next, attackers identify the individual employee within organisation for sending phishing email.

Step 4: Create spoof email requesting fund transfer

Attackers create spoof email by using top management identity requesting urgent fund transfer. The email also shows unavailability of the senior member, discouraging victim to verify it with the top management.

Step 5: Share bank details with victim.
Once the victim is trapped, attackers share the bank details with the victim to facilitate fund transfer.
Step 6: Victim transfers money.
The victim then transfers the money to the attackers.

The identifying legitimate forwarding and separating suspicious activity is a major challenge. Also, use of external clients for auto forwarding and encrypted connections can make the task of identifying auto forward very complex.

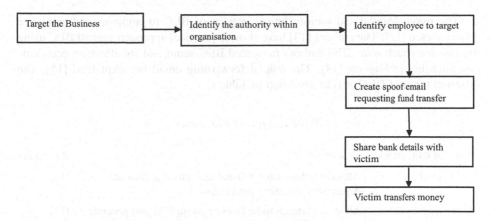

Fig. 1. Steps followed by attacker for BEC attacks

1.2 Email Forwards in the Business

Email forwarding can be done manually or automatically depending on settings. The email forwarding is common practice in business for smooth functioning of business. It can be done for various purposes:

1. Sharing information with other peoples who are interested or working on same project.
2. Keeping backup of important emails in another email account.
3. Redirecting the message from one domain to another domain if service is changed.
4. Filtering of messages based on criteria/profile.

The paper intends to control auto forward of emails by proposing a novel framework. The paper is organised as follows: section two describing literature review, section three describes research methodology. The section four proposed framework for email auto forward security framework. Section five and six describes the recommendations and implications, limitation and section six and seven covers the future scope and conclusion.

2 Literature Review

The phishing attack is social engineering attack done by use of emails or through malicious websites. The attackers use various technique for getting money from the victim. The cyber-attacks are increasing. The millions of businesses already impacted due to such types of attacks. The average cost globally for data breach in 2023 was USD 4.45 million which is 15% higher over 3 years [5].

In Impersonation attacks attackers pretends as trusted sender to target victim [6, 7]. The BEC has come up as new attack to target all sizes of business. BEC is type of phishing attack, in which attacker's tricks to hand over money or data [8]. The 60% BEC attacks do not contain any links but it contains plain text message to fool the victim [9]. The author has presented art of phishing by describing past, present and future [10]. The researchers have described attack types against BEC [11].

The psychological and sociotechnical impacts of BEC to company and employee was analysed [12]. The authors [13] have showed practical approach against BEC using the invoice check sum. The authors presented BEC scam and its effect on economic sustainability in Nigeria [14]. The risk of forwarding email has explained [15]. The different types of BEC attacks are listed in Table 1.

Table 1. Types of BEC attack

Types of BEC attack	Description	Reference
CEO Fraud	Attacker behaves as CEO and send email to finance department to initiate fund transfer	[16]
Bogus Invoice Scam	Attacker pretends to be an external supplier and generate an invoice for payment into its own account	[17]
W-2 Scam	It is tax related identity theft. Attacker pretends as top authority and ask for sending employee's tax related information	[18]
Account Compromise	In this the attacker uses a compromise account and asks the customer for payment, The payment details will be attackers id	[16]
Data Theft	In this the attackers target the HR, finance department to steal sensitive information	[19]
Email Auto forward	In this technique the victims email account is compromise and then attacker sets email auto forward rule to its own account to monitor the victim's email inbox and target it in future	[22]

During COVID 2019 The TrendMicro (2020) company identified trend that the attackers purposefully sent emails to various relief agencies, seeking for donations [20]. According to Proofpoint researchers, three types of BEC tactics have been identified: display name spoofing, domain name spoofing and look alike domains [21].

Another type of mobile malware Emotet is a banking Trojan, specifically targets state and local government as well as public and private sector. It is getting downloaded on victim's system through email attachment or links often under the guise of genuine information [22]. The BEC attack on energy Company in Texas, where the attacker posted an email as CEO of the company requesting a wire payment of an invoice and stolen $3.2 million [23].

In September 2019, FBI's Internet Crime Complaint Center (IC3) issued a Public Service Announcement (PSA) giving warning about BEC attacks. It is also notified the use of email auto-forwarding rules for accumulating information and targeting the victims. The most of the cases reported between the year June 2016 and July 2019 has resulted $26 billion in exposed dollar, and with a 100% rise global exposed losses between May 2018 and July 2019. In August 2020, an auto forwarding email rules has been created by criminal on newly upgraded web client of US based medical company. Since web mail did not sync with desktop client, this rule was unnoticed. This resulted into loss of $175,000 from the victim. In another case in the manufacturing industry, attacker had created forwarding rules within the web-based email used by a company. The rule is setup for auto forwarding email to attacker's email id that were based on the search terms 'bank', 'payment', 'invoice', 'wire' or 'check' [24]. There is loss of $56.2m due to BEC scams from Jan to March 2022 in Singapore [25].

Toyota Boshoku Corporation, a Japanese IT company that produces automotive parts, suffered a huge loss of $37 million in 2019 due to a sophisticated cyberattack. The attackers hacked into the email account of a third-party supplier and used it to send fake invoices to the company's finance department, requesting payment to a different bank account. To avoid detection, the attackers also created email auto-forwarding rules on the hacked account, which allowed them to monitor and manipulate the email communication between the supplier and the company. The company realized the fraud only after the payment was made and reported it to the authorities [26].

In 2021 BEC attack, attackers manage to bypass Microsoft office 365 multifactor authentication series. An access is gained through phishing and legacy protocols such as IMAP/POP3 to avoid multifactor authentication [27].

In 2022, Microsoft 365 users were on risk, through malicious app Upgrade. It asks for users to grant OAuth permissions which allows for creating inbox rules, compose and read emails, and to create calendar items. Additionally, it asks for permission to read contacts. This is example of consent phishing. In consent phishing attacker request access to the user's account. This gives access to account from connected apps. This helps the intruder to set auto forwarding rules to their own account and to plan attack in future [28].

The BEC guard detector approach helps to detect suspicious phrases links in email body and analyse the email header to prevent BEC using supervised machine learning approach [29]. The CAPE system uses machine learning and algorithms to detect BEC behaviour [30]. It comprehensively reviews various attacks, techniques and their impact on business [31]. Furthermore, it addresses countermeasures [32], challenges and response to cybercrime.

The main lacuna is that the security software can identify only fraudulent emails id's and majority of these security software systems are based on the pattern matching and content analysis. However, the spammers always try to discover new and different ways to breach these security measures. In email auto forwarding scam attackers aim to compromise the authorized email account.

3 Research Methodology

The overall study was conducted to address BEC through unconsented email auto forward by exploration of literature. The second phase of the work is to proposed email auto forward security framework based on insights gained from the literature. The EASF focuses on the automating the monitoring and control of email auto forwarding. The advantages and challenges of this framework are also presented.

4   The Proposed Email Auto Forward Security Framework (EASF)

The email rules are set up for automatically forwarding emails to another email account. The high risk is involved in auto forwarding incoming email to external email account. In a typical attack, malware or phishing usually compromise an end user's account. If multiple phishing links are sent there is chance that user may click the link once and then email account can be compromised.

4.1   Precaution to Avoid BEC Using Email Auto Forward

When the attacker sets the auto forwarding rule, the targeted user might be unaware that their emails are being forwarded. Automatic forwarding can be implemented in multiple ways like Inbox Rules, SMTP Forwarding etc. Following precautions are necessary to take in order to avoid BEC [33, 34].

1. Use multi-factor authentication to secure email account.
2. The first level precautionary step is to check whether any suspicious email auto forward rules have been already created.
3. Keeping track on email auto forwarding filters.
4. Restrict auto forwarding email to external domain.
5. If you receive email request for fund transfer, it is important to confirm the request with authority by sending new email before making any fund transfer.
6. Avoid replying to the suspicious email, as it will go to attacker's inbox.
7. Setup email gateway to flag keyword commonly used in the phishing email language typically presenting urgency and immediate action.
8. Use malware detection, antivirus software.
9. Register all domains which are different from company domain and used frequently for communication.

When attacker gain the access of an email account, it will be monitored, investigated for further attacks. An attacker will create an auto forwarding rules to forward emails to attacker's inbox. This rules may be based on use of terms such as 'bank','payment', 'check' etc.

One of the biggest problems is that once email forwarding is enabled it allows attacker to gain access to emails continuously. It doesn't matter if victim sets multifactor authentication, changes email password, or apply various administrative tasks to secure email [35]. All the forwarded email whether it is manual or automatic forwarded looks same and difficult to identify. Especially emails those are auto forwarded are difficult to identify if auto forwarding rules are hidden.

Microsoft Office 365 provides a feature to control email auto forward to external domains. It allows to setup the rule and identify the users that are auto forwarding email [36]. Network administrators can keep an eye on it but there is possibility that cybercriminals bypass the security checks and threat goes undetected.

The Email Autoforward Security Framework (EASF), coined phrase a novel framework is proposed by considering Zero trust policy frame work. The zero-trust model verifies each and every request irrespective of its originating source. The principle of "Never Trust, always verify" is presented by zero trust model.

The working of Email Auto forward Security Framework (EASF) is as follows (Fig. 2):

The working of Email Auto forward Security Framework (EASF) is as follows:

1. Authorised User Login to the email account using single authentication or multifactor authentication method.
2. If login attempt is failed, access to email account will be deny.
3. If email account is compromised, then attacker directly login to the email account of a user.
4. When auto forward rule is setup in the account following action will be initiated:
    a. Extract domain name from email address.
    b. If receiver domain is same as sender's domain
        i. Set flag indicating an auto forward rule
        ii. Send an alert message to the user for verification and confirmation of the auto forward rule.
    c. If receiver's domain is different from the sender's domain
        i. Set flag indicating an auto forward rule
        ii. Send high alert message to the sender as well as to the network administrator to verify the auto forward rule.
        iii. If both sender and network administrator confirm that the recipient is authorize to receive the email message, auto forward rule is accepted.
        iv. If recipient is considered as suspicious, autoforward rule is deleted.
            1. Email auto forward rules are used to identify suspicious activity if rule is set as follows:
                a. Autoforward rule to delete incoming email after auto forwarding.
                b. Move all email to subfolder or less noticeable folder.
                c. Auto forward to a suspicious or random email id
                d. Auto forward based on suspicious keyword
                e. Any auto forwarding without specific condition/rule is highly suspicious.
        v. Network administrator will take decision to block the recipient email id or to quarantine it.
5. Stop

Fig. 2. Working of EASF

4.2 Advantages of the EASF Framework

1. False Positive and False Negative:
   The EASF framework may inadvertently flag legitimate autoforward rule as threat or actual threat goes undetected. To avoid this issue EASF accept the feedback from user to accept or deny the rule.

2. Complex auto forward rule
   The attackers are using complex rules so that it goes undetected. But EASF approach uses zero trust approach by setting up the flag to auto forward rule setup for internal as well as for external domain.

3. Impact on user's work experience
   The monitoring user's auto forwarding rule can impact on user experience and may disturb the business operations. The EASF framework sends immediate email to users and administrator (in case of external domain auto forward) that their email auto forward rule is flagged. The user can quickly accept or deny the rule. So, this will help to minimise the disturbance to normal operations.

4. Multilevel approval

EASF accepts the multilevel approval of auto forward rule in case of auto forward rule is setup for external domain. Though this results into dependency of multiple approval, it enhanced the security, in case if user inbox is compromise by attacker (Fig. 3).

4.3 EASF Addresses the Following Challenges

1. Administrative overload

The monitoring and approval of auto forward rules can result into an overload in case of large organisation with high email traffic.

   Solution: The automation in rule acceptance wherever possible can be apply. The administrator should be allowed to use bulk approval of auto forward rules after verification.

2. The resource demands

The implementation and managing the EASF may require additional resources in case of heavy email traffic.

1. Computational Resources
   a. Server Resource: The EASF require sever resource to manage email auto forward. The depend on the email volume, exact requirement for computational requirement may differ.
   b. Storage Requirement –In case of heavy email traffic, to store email metadata storage will be required.
2. Human Resource requirement
   a. Administrators: The administrators are required to manage the EASF. The administrator is responsible to verify the email auto forward rules and responsible for responding email security incidence.

   Solution: To address the resource demands, organisation should implement resource optimization. To handle the computational resource demands organisation can provide cloud-based solution.

   To minimize the storage requirement, the data retention policy must be defined and shared with the employees.

   For human resource requirement, organisation should assess the available resources regularly so that the resource allocation can be done dynamically and more effectively.

3. Privacy considerations

The monitoring email rules for security purpose may raise the concern for privacy.

   Solution: The organisation must include email autoforward monitoring rules in the email policy and it must be clearly communicated to the user. The consent from the user can be obtained for monitoring email autoforward rules. This approach will help to enhance secure handling of emails and mitigates the risk of potential legal issues related to email monitoring.

   The addressing above challenges is important for successful implementation of the EASF framework.

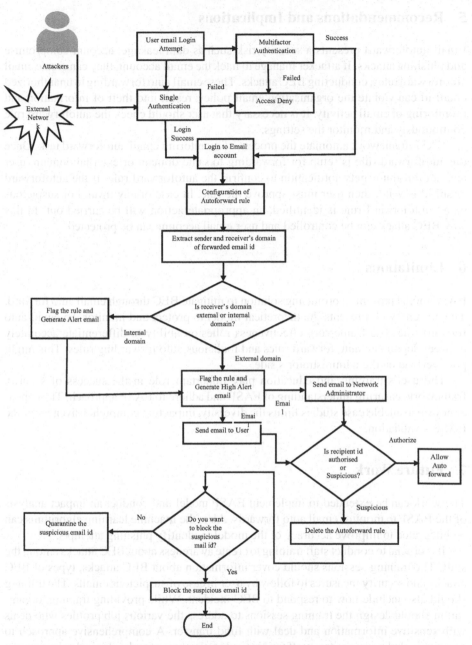

Fig. 3. The proposed Email Autoforward Security Framework (EASF)

5   Recommendations and Implications

Email autoforward presents a security risk such as data leakage, account compromise and phishing attacks. If attacker manage to hack the email account, they can create email autoforward rules, conducting BEC attacks. These email auto forwarding to unauthorized email id can violate the organisation email policy, result into theft of information and monitoring of email activity. It is necessary that user should check the autoforward rule continuously and monitor the settings.

EASF framework automate the process of monitoring email autoforward task. Once the autoforward rule is setup for forwarding to same domain or external domain, user and administrator gets notification to confirm the autoforward rule. If the autoforward email id is valid, then user must approve the rule. In case of any invalid or suspicious email autoforward rule is identified, an appropriate action will be carried out. In this way BEC attack can be controlled and user email account can be protected.

6   Limitations

EASF model presents a promising solution to mitigate BEC through email auto forward. The current work presents the theoretical model to protect and monitor the email auto forward rule. The framework effectiveness relies on ability to differentiate accurately between legitimate auto forward rules and malicious auto forwarding rules. This might put overload on the administrator's side.

The user's training and education play important role in the success of security framework, ensuring understanding of EASF and adhere to EASF approach. The dependency on available case studies limits the diversity, impacting comprehensiveness of the EASF's validation.

7   Future Work

The work can be extended to implement EASF model and conduct an impact analysis of the EASF to monitor email auto forwards. Also, the machine learning algorithms can be integrated to improve accuracy of the model to identify phishing attempts.

It is crucial to conduct staff training to create awareness about BEC attacks among the staff. The training sessions should cover information about BEC attacks, types of BEC attacks and security measures to follow by user in case of suspicious emails. The training should also include how to respond to BEC incident. While providing training, organisation should design the training sessions to address the various job profiles who deals with sensitive information and deal with fund transfer. A comprehensive approach to security including awareness staff training, education, use of technological enhancement and proactive secure measure will help effectively to mitigate BEC attacks.

8 Conclusion

The paper addresses critical issue of BEC attacks. BEC is social engineering attack which uses email auto forward as one of the tricks to monitor victim's incoming emails. The detecting BEC attacks poses challenge as attackers uses various techniques to deceive email recipient. It is serious threat to the organisations that heavily depend on email as primary media of communication. It has resulted into a serious financial loss to the business. An organisation can implement security measures to avoid such attacks. This paper covers how organisation can follow simple controls to protect itself from attacks emphasizing the importance of continuous monitoring and proactive measures. The email auto forward security framework is presented to generate alert messages if any new email auto forward rule is configured. As the cyber threat is continuous to grow, a practical approach like EASF become essential safety measure for securing vital business communication against malicious exploitation.

References

1. Al-Musib, N.S., Al-Serhani, F.M., Humayun, M., Jhanjhi, N.: Business email compromise (BEC) attacks. Materials Today: Proceedings (2021)
2. Cross, C.: Exploiting trust for financial gain: an overview of business email compromise (BEC) fraud. J. Financ. Crime, 871–884 (2020)
3. What Is Business Email Compromise? A Definitive Guide to BEC, Armorblox. [Online]. Accessed 2023
4. Atlam, H.F., Oluwatimilehin, O.: Business Email Compromise Phishing Detection Based on Machine Learning: A Systematic Literature Review. Electronics 12(1) (2023)
5. Fight back against data breaches, IBM. https://www.ibm.com/reports/data-breach. Accessed 2023
6. Impersonation Attack. https://www.mimecast.com/content/impersonation-attack/. Accessed 2023
7. Zweighaft, D.: Business email compromise and executive impersonation: are financial institutions exposed? J. Investment Compliance 18(1), 1–7 (2017)
8. I. Governance, What is Social Engineering? Examples & Prevention Tips. https://www.itgovernance.co.uk/social-engineering-attacks
9. Ross, C.: The latest attacks and how to stop them. Comput. Fraud Secur. 11, 11–14 (2018)
10. Binks, A.: The art of phishing: past, present and future. Comput. Fraud Secur., 9–11 (2019)
11. Buddhika, P.G.: Detecting business email compromise and classifying for countermeasures. New Zealand (2023)
12. Buo, S.A.: An application of cyberpsychology in business email compromise. arXiv preprint arXiv:2011 (2020)
13. Songpon, T., Hiroaki, Y., Tetsutaro, U.: A Practical Solution Against Business Email Compromise (BEC) Attack using Invoice Checksum. In: IEEE 20th International Conference on Software Quality, Reliability and Security Companion (QRS-C), Macau, China (2020)
14. John, T.O., Benjamin, O.A., Favour, N.O., Emmanuel, E., Aya, A.T.: Business e-mail compromise scam, cyber victimization, and economic sustainability of corporate organizations in Nigeria. Secur. J., 350–372 (2023)
15. Mixon, E.: Why Email Forwarding is a Security Risk (And How to Detect), 03 02 2022. https://www.blumira.com/email-forwarding-risks/

16. Cyber Security Awareness. https://terranovasecurity.com/examples-business-email-compro
    mise/. Accessed 10 2023
17. The Five types of Business Email Compromise (BEC) scams according to the FBI. https://
    protectera.com.au/types-of-bec-scams/. Accessed 2023
18. Tuttle, H.: W-2 Phishing Scam Targets Tax Season. Risk Management (00355593), vol. 64,
    no. 3, pp. 12–14 (2017)
19. Business Email Compromise (BEC), Check Point.10 Accessed 2023
20. TrendMicro, Developing Story: COVID-19 Used in Malicious Campaigns, 11 Nov 2020.
    https://www.trendmicro.com/vinfo/us/security/news/cybercrime-and-digital-threats/corona
    virus-used-in-spam-malware-file-names-and-malicious-domains
21. Tang, C.: Three Common Business Email Compromise Tactics and How to Fight Back,
    6 Feb 2020. https://www.proofpoint.com/us/corporate-blog/post/three-common-business-
    email-compromise-tactics-and-how-fight-back
22. CISA, Avoiding Social Engineering and Phishing Attacks, 1 Feb 2021. https://www.cisa.gov/
    news-events/news/avoiding-social-engineering-and-phishing-attacks
23. Connell, A.: Business Email Compromise: Operation Wire Wire and New Attack Vec-
    tors, 19 April 2019. https://insights.sei.cmu.edu/blog/business-email-compromise-operation-
    wire-wire-and-new-attack-vectors/
24. Gatlan, S.: FBI warns of BEC scammers using email auto-forwarding in attacks. 1 12
    2020. https://www.bleepingcomputer.com/news/security/fbi-warns-of-bec-scammers-using-
    email-auto-forwarding-in-attacks/
25. Lim, J.: Straitstimes, 29 July 2022. https://www.straitstimes.com/singapore/courts-crime/
    at-least-562-million-lost-to-business-e-mail-compromise-scams-between-jan-and-march-
    2022-police
26. Toyota Parts Supplier Loses $37 Million in Email Scam, 11 9 2019. https://www.tripwire.
    com/state-of-security/toyota-parts-supplier-loses-37-million-email-scam
27. Gatlan, S.: Microsoft: Scammers bypass Office 365 MFA in BEC attacks, 14
    6 2021. https://www.bleepingcomputer.com/news/security/microsoft-scammers-bypass-off
    ice-365-mfa-in-bec-attacks/
28. Hawkins, J.: Microsoft Issues Dire Office 365 Phishing Warning, 25 Jan 2022. https://www.
    slashgear.com/microsoft-issues-dire-office-365-phishing-warning-25708878
29. Cidon, A., Gavish, L., Bleier, I., Korshun, N., Schweighauser, M., Tsitkin, A.: High precision
    detection of business email compromise. In: 28th USENIX Security Symposium (USENIX
    Security 19) (2019)
30. Brabec, J., Šrajer, F., Starosta, Sixta, T., Dupont, M., Lenoch, M., Novák, P.: A Modular and
    Adaptive System for Business Email Compromise Detection, arXiv (2023)
31. Papathanasiou, A., Liontos, G., Liagkou, V., Glavas, E.: Business Email Compromise
    (BEC) Attacks: Threats, Vulnerabilities and Countermeasures—A Perspective on the Greek
    Landscape. J. Cybersecur. Privacy 3(3), 610–637 (2023)
32. Nisha, T.N., Bakari, D., Shukla, C.: Business E-mail compromise — techniques and coun-
    termeasures. In: 2021 International Conference on Advance Computing and Innovative
    Technologies in Engineering (ICACITE), Greater Noida (2021)
33. Waugh, A.: Email security: How hackers use mail rules to access your inbox, 10 6 2021. https://
    pushsecurity.com/blog/email-security-how-hackers-use-mail-rules-to-access-your-inbox/
34. Cloonan, J.: Don't be a Whale – How To Detect the Business Email Compromise (BEC) Scam,
    8 10 2017. https://www.tripwire.com/state-of-security/how-detect-business-email-compro
    mise-bec-scam

35. Erica, M.: Why Email Forwarding is a Security Risk (And How to Detect), 3 02 2022. https://www.blumira.com/email-forwarding-risks/

36. Microsoft, Control automatic external email forwarding in Microsoft 365, 20 6 2023. https://learn.microsoft.com/en-us/microsoft-365/security/office-365-security/outbound-spam-policies-external-email-forwarding?view=o365-worldwide#how-to-find-users-that-are-automatically-forwarding. Accessed 5 10 2023

A Novel Mechanism for Tuning Neural Network for Malware Detection in Android Device

Eslavath Ravi[1][(✉)] [ID], Mummadi Upendra Kumar[2] [ID], and Syed Shabbeer Ahmad[3] [ID]

[1] Research Scholar, Department of Computer Science and Engineering, Osmania University, Hyderabad, Telangana, India
eslavathravi@gmail.com

[2] Department of Computer Science and Artificial Intelligence, Muffakham Jah College of Engineering and Technology, Hyderabad, Telangana, India
upendra.kumar@mjcollege.ac.in

[3] Department of Computer Science and Engineering, Muffakham Jah College of Engineering and Technology, Hyderabad, Telangana, India
shabbeer.ahmad@mjcollege.ac.in

Abstract. Malicious software or code that is specifically targeted towards Android devices, such as smartphones and tablets running the Android operating system, is known as Android malware. The objectives of these malicious programs can vary, but they all generally try to compromise the security and privacy of the device or its user. Detecting Android malware using machine learning is a challenging but effective approach, as it can help identify malicious apps based on patterns, behaviors, and features. This paper proposes a Tuned Neural Network model for the detection of Malware in Android. The parameters of the NN are tuned using hyperparameter tuning with Random Search. The principal component Analysis method for correlation detection, has been included such that the dimensionality reduction helps in faster execution. The Android Malware dataset's split between harmless and dangerous applications is frequently skewed, with a much greater proportion of benign instances. This discrepancy might result in skewed models. Are better at detecting benign apps than malware. Machine learning models rely on historical data, making them less effective at detecting new, previously unseen threats (zero-day vulnerabilities). Neural networks can be updated with new data and retrained periodically, allowing the detection system to adapt to emerging threats and zero-day vulnerabilities. It is critical to find a balance between accuracy (minimising false positives) & recall (minimising false negatives) in Android malware detection. Hyperparameter tuning can help adjust the model's threshold or other settings to achieve the desired trade-off between these two metrics. In the proposed model, it has acquired + 1.06% accuracy than traditional approaches and made the loss approximately equal to 0%.

Keywords: Patterns · Zero Day Vulnerabilities · Malicious Attacks · Tuned Neural Network · Threshold · Bias

© The Author(s), under exclusive license to Springer Nature Switzerland AG 2024
S. Rajagopal et al. (Eds.): ASCIS 2023, CCIS 2039, pp. 240–257, 2024.
https://doi.org/10.1007/978-3-031-59100-6_18

1 Introduction

Android malware detection is a critical facet of cyber security, focusing on identifying and mitigating malicious software specifically designed to target Android-based mobile devices. With the widespread use of Android smart phones and tablets, the threat landscape has evolved, making the need for robust malware detection techniques increasingly imperative. Its open nature and vast app ecosystem also make it a prime target for cybercriminals seeking to exploit vulnerabilities and compromise user data. In comparison to the swift growth of mobile applications, the detection techniques implemented on smartphone devices must advance to keep pace [10]. Android malware encompasses a broad spectrum of malicious software applications designed to infiltrate, manipulate, or harm Android devices and their users. The primary objective of Android malware detection is to proactively identify and thwart these malicious applications help protect Android device users' security & privacy. This task involves the development and deployment of sophisticated techniques and tools capable of distinguishing between legitimate and malicious apps. Kamran Shaukat et al. [9] introduced a method that integrates deep learning and machine learning, removing the necessity for laborious feature engineering and domain-specific knowledge.

The attack server utilizes encryption mechanisms with a private key. Following the user being coerced to pay a ransom under the threat of losing their data, they make the payment. Subsequently, the ransomware employs a decryption key to decrypt the user's data [12]. Although machine learning-based malware detectors incorporate numerous features, attackers can leverage feature-related knowledge to create malware variants that evade detection. Consequently, the Android security team must continuously innovate by developing new features to identify and thwart suspicious attacks [13].

Neural Networks(NN) play a pivotal role in this domain due to their ability to effectively analyze and classify complex patterns within large datasets. Feature learning & abstraction is one of the primary challenges in malware detection is extracting meaningful features from the raw data. This can identify even subtle variations that might indicate malicious intent. As outlined in reference [11], there has been a notable increase in malicious attacks in recent years, affecting both computer systems and networks. A growing number of new malware families targeting information assets have been launched on a daily basis over the past year. Non-linear Relationships in Android malware can exhibit non-linear patterns that are difficult to capture using linear models. Adaptability and Generalization in the Android malware landscape evolve rapidly, with new strains and techniques emerging frequently. Neural Networks can adapt to these changes more effectively than traditional rule-based methods, which often require manual updates. In Behavioural Analysis some Android malware operates by exhibiting malicious behaviour only after certain conditions are met, making them challenging to detect statically.

In ANN (Artificial Neural Networks), the class imbalance problem can lead to biased models that perform well on benign samples but struggle to detect malware effectively. The effectiveness of ANNs often depends on feature engineering. Selecting relevant features and extracting meaningful information from Android app data can be challenging. ANNs are prone to overfitting to the specific malware samples in their training dataset. As new malware variants emerge, ANNs may struggle to generalize and detect previously unseen threats effectively. ANNs are susceptible to adversarial assaults, in which the attackers trick the model by manipulating the input data. Training deep ANNs for Android malware detection requires significant computational resources. ANNs are sometimes regarded as black-box designs, making it difficult to explain their judgements. The quality and representativeness for training dataset are paramount. On-device malware detection using ANNs may consume significant CPU and battery resources, impacting the device's performance and battery life. To improve the performance, the tuning of neural networks is needed.

Hyperparameter-tuned neural networks offer a significant advantage over traditional networks by optimizing model performance, enhancing generalization, improving efficiency, and providing adaptability to changing conditions [15]. These advantages are particularly relevant in security-critical applications like Android malware detection, where the stakes are high, and model effectiveness is paramount. In Arvind Mahindru's research article [16], emphasis is placed on feature selection techniques, including rough set analysis (RSA) and principal component analysis (PCA), particularly in their application to malware detection. The empirical results demonstrate that employing feature reduction methods, particularly with FLANN-Genetic, proves to be highly effective in detecting malware. [17, 18] it is observed that concept of security using machine learning and deep learning methods for malware detection, as well as android malware detection with classification based on hybrid analysis and N-gram feature extraction. Kumar, M.U. et al. [19] proposed dependable solutions design by agile modeled layered security architectures. Shravani, D. et al. [20] introduced designing dependable web services security architecture solutions.

Hyperparameter tuning is a critical step in training neural networks to optimize their performance. The hyper parameter tuning is described in the below Fig. 1. It is simple to use the grid search method, which entails giving each the hyperparameter that is relevant a range of values. It thoroughly investigates each and every conceivable setting for a hyperparameter, training and analysing the algorithm for each setting. Random Search offers the advantage of faster exploration of the hyperparameter space compared to grid search. It is particularly useful when it has a limited computational resource and want to quickly find reasonably good hyperparameter settings. Bayesian optimization is a probabilistic model-based approach to hyperparameter tuning. This technique is efficient and effective for optimizing expensive-to-evaluate models. Natural selection is an inspiration for genetic algorithms. Over several generations, they develop an assortment of hyperparameter sets. PSO (Particle Swarm Optimization) is a population-based optimization technique where each candidate solution explores the hyperparameter space by adjusting its position based on its own best performance and the best performance of the entire population. PSO is a good choice for optimizing continuous hyperparameters.

The paper is structured with an introductory section that underscores the importance of employing machine learning models for integrating data and identifying malware within Android software. The literature review section encompasses various methods and approaches employed in the detection of malware, offering a thorough overview of existing research and their respective contributions. The proposed methodology outlines a comprehensive approach to malware detection. The Results and Discussion section

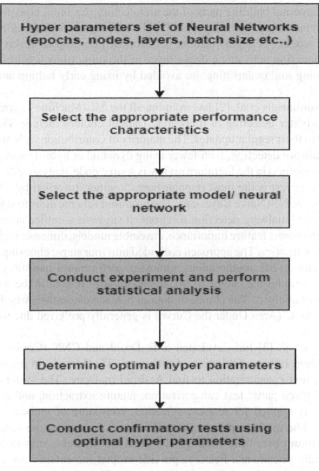

Fig. 1. Hyper Tuning Process

delves into the outcomes of the proposed model and highlights its superiority over existing approaches. The Conclusion section provides an overview of the paper.

2 Literature Review

Omar N. Elayan et al. [1] has developed a RNN with GRU technique for the identification of malwares in Androids. The study uses a publicly available dataset, CICAndMal2017, for Android malware detection. Relevant features for classification are crucial for determining class membership. Androguard, a tool for interacting with Android files, is used to analyze APK files and extract permissions and API calls. A data frame is constructed with applications as rows and specific permissions/API calls as columns, using binary values. Various machine learning classifiers are employed, including five approaches. GRU(Gated Recurrent Unit) is used to design a binary classification model for the study.

The three fundamental building parts of the architecture. An input layer for the GRU is present in the input block. Three layers of GRU with progressively fewer neurons make up the middle block. For regularisation, 0.2 dropout rate dropout layers are inserted. The Sigmoid function activates a dense layer in the output block for binary classification. Overfitting and underfitting are avoided by using early halting and checkpoint procedures.

Vasileios Kouliaridis et al. [2] has examine all the ML(Machine Learning) methodologies for the better detection of malwares. Dataset choices include VirusShare and AndroZoo due to their regular updates. The majority of contributions rely solely on static analysis for malware detection, with fewer using dynamic or hybrid analysis. The most often employed method in the literature review is source code analysis. Among surveyed works, Random Forest is the most popular base classifier, travelled by SVM (Support Vector Machine) & NB(Naïve Bayesian). The proposed scheme aims to standardize and enhance ML-based malware detection solutions. It suggests a unified approach by considering key parameters feature importance, ensemble models, dimensionality reduction, and classification metrics. The approach is divided into four steps: choosing an analytical method, choosing an ML methodology, choosing performance measures. The recommended strategy guides the choice of ML methodologies related to the dataset ages & methodologies of analysis. The choice of dataset balance determines whether Accuracy is reliable, but AUC (Area Under the Curve) is generally preferred due to its balanced evaluation.

Nan Zhang et al. [3] has developed a Tc-Droid and CNN (Convoltional Neural Networks) method of easy prediction of malwares. TC-Droid is an innovative framework that uses text categorization to find Android malware. The system model consists mostly of three parts: text categorization, feature extraction, and report production. TextCNN is applied for text classification, consisting of embedding, all layers related to conv. The model captures essential features through on the mapping the features, use maximum over time pooling. The TextCNN model is trained for classification using feature documents. Features provide crucial information for classification. Dynamic_analysis is excluded from this framework. Two couple of features related to static are extracted. Permission grants access to resources, Service lists service points, Intent enables communication, and the Receiver handles broadcast intents.

Jinsung Kim et al. [4] has proposed a MAPAS which was detect any kind of malwares. It focuses on spotting recurring API call graph patterns in harmful apps. Data preliminary processing, finding high-weight API call graphs, & malware identification are the three processes in the design. Through the extraction of API call graphs from both malicious and legitimate apps, MAPAS creates a training dataset. Deep learning CNN is used on the training dataset to find significant features from API call graphs. Grad-CAM is employed for discovering heavy-bias API are designed to graph for many unsecured apps. These features are later utilized in the MDP. Related to Jaccard methodology comparison of API call graphs from applications & high - weight harmful API call graphs, MAPAS categorises malware. Taint analysis is employed to extract API call graphs, tracking data flows from sources to sinks. Flowdroid is chosen due to its accuracy and runtime performance. The malware classification of a programme is based on a threshold of 0.4303.

Mohammed N. Aijarrah et al. [5] has focused on all ml techniques for identifying malware detections. Utilized a large dataset named CICMalDroid2020 for Application APK examples for dangerous & good apps. Static evaluation was used to extract characteristics from APKs, including as rights, API Calls, & contextual data. Extracted API Calls from APKs using reverse engineering and "Androguard." Transformed API Calls to binary numbers indicating there are in APK. Extracted various permissions from Android application samples. Converted permissions into binary values to indicate their presence 1 or absence 0 in an application. Four categories of contextual information were extracted to aid in Android malware detection. Employed Information Gain (IG) for feature selection to eliminate duplicate and inconsistent features. Used supervised machine learning algorithms for malware classification. Set parameters for algorithms, such as n_estimators for RF and kernel for SVC.

Vikas Sihag et al. [6] has proposed a De-LADY technique for dynamic detection of malwares in androids. De-LADY is a proposed method for classifying Android applications as malicious or benign. The method involves executing the APK file in an emulated environment, parsing and pre-processing logs, and using a deep learning model for classification. Four major modules are utilized. Dynamic analysis involves executing the application in an emulated environment. Logs generated by the emulator are captured and processed to reconstruct Android OS interactions. Feature extraction involves considering binder information and system calls to gain behavioral insights. Standardized feature vectors are fed into a deep neural network. Leaky ReLU Activation Function is utilized for unseen layers. The methodology is train's for two-class classification using various architectures. Training involves 500 epochs, and 30% of samples are randomly selected for testing. Performance is evaluated using confusion matrix and compared with other machine learning approaches.

Prerma Agrawal et al. [7] has proposed an ML technique i.e. RF where every method is examine to detect malware. Supervised learning predicts class labels based on prior class information, while unsupervised learning identifies patterns among data. NB predicts class labels based on prior class information, while unsupervised learning identifies patterns among data. SVM uses hyperplanes to separate data instances in feature space. RF combines multiple decision tree classifiers. Decision Tree are generated randomly data subsets, and majority voting combines outputs. LR predicts results based on categorized dependent variables. A KNN clustering technique for partitioning data instances into clusters. Parameters compared include eight attributes comparison with other ML classifiers, & introduced approach. Each approach has strengths and limitations in terms of dataset size, accuracy, runtime, use of dynamic analysis, and handling evasion techniques.

Ahmed S. Shatnawi et al. [8] has discussed about many approaches related to ML to detect malwares. The study utilizes the CICInvesAndMal2019 dataset for experiments. The collection of data has improved malware group categorization & malware category grading. Three machine learning models were employed SVM, KNN, & NB. Scikit-learn was used to implement these models.

Feature selection was done using the RFE technique with Logistic Regression. Data preprocessing involved checking for incomplete or missing values, errors, and outliers. The dataset was separated into two sets i.e. feature permissions & Features related to call API. Feature importance selection was performed using RFE (Recursive Feature Elimination) under LR. SVM, KNN, and NB classifiers were imported and implemented. The SVM classifier was trained on a couple of values and then used to predict values for each variable test. Similar procedures were followed for KNN and NB classifiers. The results of each classifier's performance were displayed in the final phase (Table 1).

Table 1. Merits and Demerits of Previous Approaches.

Author	Algorithm	Merits	Demerits	Accuracy
Omar N. Elayan et al	RNN, GRU	Signature methods are efficiently identified	Only static information is utilized	98.2%
Vasileios Kouliaridis et al	ML	Multiple approaches are examined	Not worked on recent papers	98.1%
Nan Zhang et al	TC-Droid, CNN	The text data was efficiently derived	Other than text data no other application is executed	96.6%
Jinsung Kim et al	MAPAS	This can detect any kind of malwares in the device	New malware needs a accurate update in the software	91.2%
Mohammed N. Aijarrah et al	ML	Features for permissions are accurately identified	Only particular malwares are identified	99.4%
Vikas Sihag et al	De-LADY	Dynamic analysis can be done	The effects in obfuscation is noy derived	98.8%
Prerma Agrawal et al	RF	Every method was clearly explained	What kind of dataset was used is not defined	99%
Ahmed S. Shatnawi et al	SVM	New malwares can be identified	No much differences among approaches	94.36%

3   Proposed Methodology

The dataset comprises feature vectors extracted from 15,036 applications, encompassing 215 attributes. These attributes are derived from a diverse set of applications, including 5,560 malware apps sourced from the Drebin project and 9,476 benign apps. The dataset serves as the foundation for the development and assessment of a multilevel classifier fusion approach designed for Android malware detection. Random search is often more efficient than exhaustive grid search. It randomly samples hyperparameter combinations, allowing it to explore a broader range of possibilities with fewer iterations. This can save time and computational resources. The proposed algorithm starts with famous pre-processing technique known as "Standardisation", is a typical pre-processing method in the analysis of data and machine learning. It is often referred to as z-score normalisation or feature scaling. The data must be transformed to have a means of 0 & a deviation from the mean of 1. For numerous algorithms that are dependent on the size of the input data, this technique makes certain that every characteristic (or variables) occupy the same scale.

$$z = y - \mu/\sigma.$$

z - standardized value related to feature.
y - accurate value related to feature.
μ - mean based on feature's values.
σ - standard deviation based on feature's values.

Subtracting the mean (μ) from each data point centres the data around zero. This step ensures that the standardized data has a mean of 0. Dividing by the standard deviation (σ) scales the data. It ensures that the data's spread is 1. This step makes the data's scale consistent across all features.

Principal Component Analysis (PCA) is utilized to detect correlations by uncovering the inherent structure and relationships present in a dataset [14]. PCA tackles the challenge of multicollinearity, a situation where independent variables in a dataset exhibit high correlation. Through the transformation of variables into uncorrelated principal components, PCA alleviates multicollinearity, enhancing the stability of subsequent analyses, including regression modeling. Its primary purpose is to reduce the number of variables in a dataset while preserving crucial information, accomplished by transforming the initial variables into a more concise set of uncorrelated variables known as principal components. This process facilitates more efficient and streamlined analyses. The process followed is described in the below Fig. 2.

Hyperparameter tuning is a critical step in optimizing the performance of neural networks. The key parameters to consider for hyperparameter tuning in a neural network. The learning rate determines the step size at where the network varies its weights when exercising. Faster convergence might result from a higher learning rate, but it can also lead to overshooting. How many hidden layers there are and how many neurons each layer contain. Deeper networks may capture more complicated information, but to prevent overfitting, they also need more data and computer power. The amount of training samples utilised in each gradient descent iteration is determined by the batch size. A dropout is a normalisation technique that, during training, randomly eliminates certain groups of neurons to prevent overfitting. Proper weight initialization may impact how quickly the network converges and whether it gets stuck in local minima. It's crucial to keep in mind that there isn't a single, universally applicable solution, and the ideal hyperparameters may change depending on the dataset and situation at hand.

Random search is a technique used in machine learning and optimization to explore a large search space by randomly selecting parameter combinations for acquiring accurate performances in the methodology or solution. AMD models often involve a variety of parameters, such as feature selection, hyperparameters of ml methodologies, & pre-processing technique. Random search allows for efficient exploration of the parameter space without following a specific pattern. It is less likely to get stuck in local optima

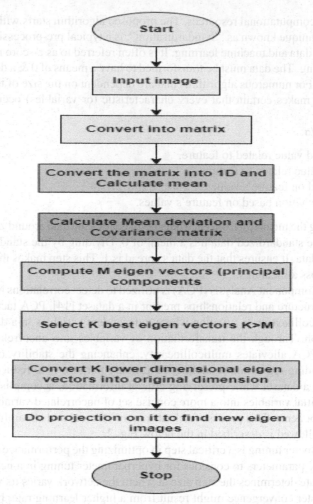

Fig. 2. Principal Component Analysis Process Diagram

compared to deterministic optimization methods like grid search. AMD often involves analyzing large datasets and running resource-intensive machine learning algorithms. Figure 3 Depicts the process of selecting a best parameter for building and training the model. Random search is computationally less expensive than exhaustive grid search, making it more feasible for resource-constrained environments. It is robust to variations in data and model behavior. This is particularly useful in Android malware detection where the characteristics of malware samples can vary significantly.

The utilization of a trial and objective function is integral to the effectiveness of the random search optimization technique. A crucial role in navigating the hyperparameter space efficiently, identifying optimal or near-optimal configurations, and ultimately improving the performance of models. Trials refer to individual iterations or attempts made during the random search process. In the context of hyperparameter tuning, a

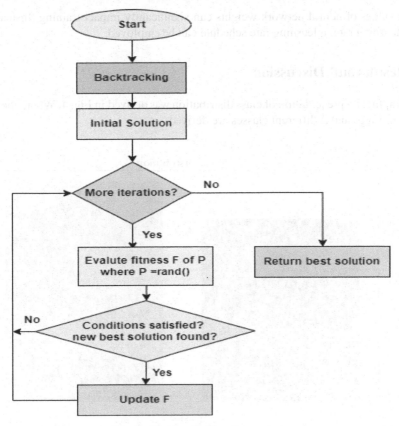

Fig. 3. Finding the Best Parameter

trial represents a specific combination of hyperparameter values. Each trial explores a unique set of hyperparameter values, enabling the algorithm to traverse the hyperparameter space broadly. A trial involves training and evaluating a ML methodology using the specified hyperparameters. It provides an opportunity to assess how well the model performs with those settings on a validation dataset. It generates performance metrics for different hyperparameter configurations. These metrics are crucial for selecting the best-performing configuration.

Merits of random search is that it explores the hyperparameter space efficiently by randomly sampling combinations of hyperparameter values. The learning rate determines the step size during gradient descent optimization. Random search can be used to ascertain the optimal no. of concealed layers in the neural network architecture. By using RS to vary the no. of neurons in each concealed layer. Finding the right amount of neurons present each layer can impact the network's capacity to model complex patterns. Different AF can be selected through random search to determine which one works best for the given task. Batch size determines how many training examples are used in each iteration of gradient descent. Tuning batch size can affect training speed and convergence. Dropout is a regularization technique used to prevent overfitting. The initial values of neural network weights can significantly impact training. Instead of a fixed learning rate, a learning rate schedule can be employed.

4   Results and Discussion

The graphical representation of class distribution was derived in Fig. 4. Where the count was 175 range and 2 different classes are derived.

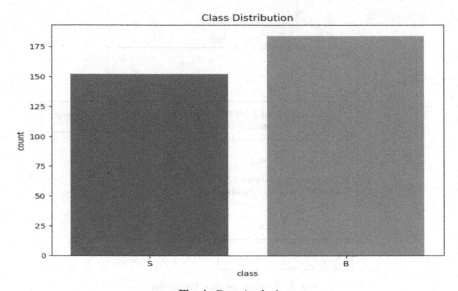

Fig. 4. Data Analysis

In Table 2 the values are derived for 11 different models connections and 7 different attributes.

In Fig. 5. The clusters are derived for two different classes. Where those are partitioned in two principle components.

Trail
A trial typically refers to a specific run or experiment with a neural network configuration. A variety of hyperparameters must be specified, including the amount of the layers, the amount of units for every layer, the pace of learning, and the dropout rates.

Unit
"Units" in this context refer to the amount of neurons or nodes in a neural network stages. Adjusting the number of units can significantly impact the ability of the model to memorise intricate patterns, and it is a critical hyperparameter to tune during trials.

Drop Outs
"Dropouts" are a regularization technique used to prevent overfitting in neural networks.

Table 2. Correlation Analysis.

	Transact	onServiceConnected	bindService	ServiceConnection	Android.os.Binder	SEND_SMS
Transact	1.000000	0.820390	0.826286	0.820390	0.895932	-0.273983
onServiceConnected	0.820390	1.000000	0.981468	0.987647	0.863993	-0.324829
bindService	0.826286	0.981468	1.000000	0.993835	0.870511	-0.321435
Attachinterface	0.956628	0.776501	0.794694	0.788987	0.868302	0.256808
ServiceConnection	0.820390	0.987647	0.993835	1.000000	0.876182	-0.324829
...	...	...	...	...	...	...
WRITE_EXTERNAL_STORAGE	0.166148	0.191036	0.187086	0.191036	0.160596	0.017239
ACCESS_FINE_LOCATION	0.119734	0.160261	0.151193	0.160261	0.125400	-0.047082
SET_WALLPAPER_HINTS	0.052376	0.091981	0.092977	0.091981	0.035782	-0.090909
SET_PREFERRED_APPLICATIONS	0.067499	0.66256	0.066667	0.066256	0.060475	0.087664
WRITE_SECURE_SETTINGS	0.022088	0.018659	0.019798	0.018659	0.001901	0.034376

215 rows x 215 columns.

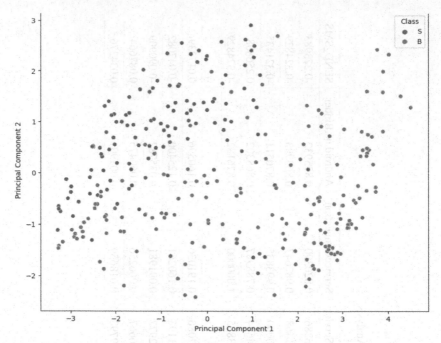

Fig. 5. PCA for 2 Components

They randomly deactivate a fraction of neurons during training, forcing the network to learn more robust features. Tuning dropout rates is an essential part of trial and hyperparameter optimization.

Score

The "score" in this context often represents a performance metric, such as accuracy, loss, F1-score, or any other relevant measure, used to evaluate the model's performance during a trial. The goal of multiple trials is to find the hyperparameter configuration that yields the best score on a validation dataset, indicating a well-performing model.

In Table 3 trail, units, dropout and score are measure for every values. The highest score is 98 and the least is 89.

By conducting trials with varying hyperparameter settings, including units and dropouts, is a crucial part of optimizing neural networks for specific tasks. The "score" serves as the performance measure for selecting the best configuration.

In Fig. 6. Represents the accuracy and loss for the 20 epochs. Here mostly accuracy was 100% and loss was 0.1.

F1Score

Precision and recall are combined into a single score called the F1-Score. When working

Table 3. Evaluation

Trail	Units	Drop outs	Score
01	192	0.4	0.9800000190734863
03	256	0.3	0.9800000190734863
00	128	0.4	0.9800000190734863
02	128	0.2	0.9599999785423279
07	192	0.3	0.9599999785423279
04	256	0.2	0.9399999976158142
09	192	0.2	0.9399999976158142
05	128	0.3	0.9399999976158142
08	64	0.2	0.9200000166893005
06	64	0.3	0.8999999761581421

```
Epoch 1/20
8/8 [==============================] - 3s 86ms/step - loss: 0.0133 - accuracy: 0.9957 - val_loss: 0.1077 - val_accuracy: 0.9800
Epoch 2/20
8/8 [==============================] - 0s 21ms/step - loss: 0.0064 - accuracy: 1.0000 - val_loss: 0.1067 - val_accuracy: 0.9600
Epoch 3/20
8/8 [==============================] - 0s 23ms/step - loss: 0.0063 - accuracy: 1.0000 - val_loss: 0.1065 - val_accuracy: 0.9600
Epoch 4/20
8/8 [==============================] - 0s 19ms/step - loss: 0.0086 - accuracy: 1.0000 - val_loss: 0.1057 - val_accuracy: 0.9800
Epoch 5/20
8/8 [==============================] - 0s 20ms/step - loss: 0.0065 - accuracy: 1.0000 - val_loss: 0.1098 - val_accuracy: 0.9800
```

Fig. 6. Epochs representation of Proposed Method

with datasets having an uneven distribution, where one class considerably outnumbers the other, it is very helpful.

Precision
Precision assesses the accuracy of optimistic predictions and focuses on reducing false positives. It responds to the query: "How many of all the positive instances predicted were actually positive?" High accuracy means that the model is typically right when it makes a positive prediction.

Recall
Recall, often referred to as Sensitive or TP Rate, has an emphasis on reducing false negatives and gauges the model's capacity to find all instances of positivity. How many of the genuine positive occurrences were accurately identified as such out of all the

positive examples? High recall means the model doesn't overlook many examples of success.

Table 4 compared the proposed method with four methodologies related to ML. Therefore, the proposed method has acquired high performances compared to remaining methodologies. The Fig. 7. Represents this data in a bar graph.

Table 4. Comparison and Proposed Method Validation

Model	F1Score	Precision	Recall
Logistic Regression (LR)	0.9583	0.9583	0.9583
Random Forest (RF)	0.9600	0.9231	1.0000
Support Vector Machine (SVM)	0.9412	0.8889	1.0000
Gradient Boosting (GB)	0.9388	0.9200	0.9583
Tuned Neural Network (Best Model)	0.9583	0.9583	0.9583

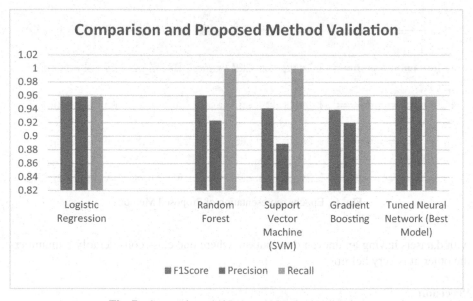

Fig. 7. Comparison and Proposed Method Validation

An essential tool in the study of ML & categorization is the confusion matrix. By showing the number of tp, tn, fp, & fn predictions, it gives a summary of how well a classification method or model performed. A confusion matrix for gradient-boosted & tuned NN is shown in Fig. 8.

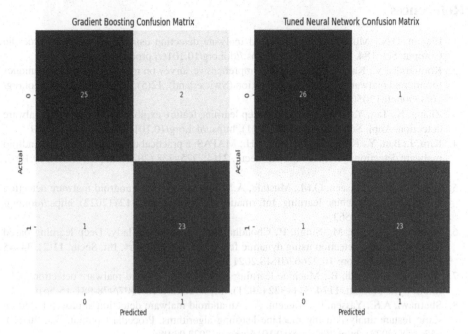

Fig. 8. Confusion Matrix

5 Conclusion

Random Search for hyperparameter tuning in the design of an Android malware detector with neural networks offers efficiency, adaptability, and a practical approach to optimizing model performance while considering resource constraints and real-world application needs. The paper introduces a Neural Network (NN) model designed for detecting Android malware. The NN's parameters are optimized through hyperparameter tuning using Random Search. Additionally, Principal Component Analysis (PCA) is incorporated for correlation detection, aiming to expedite execution by reducing dimensionality. Notably, the Android Malware dataset often exhibits an imbalanced distribution between harmless and hazardous applications, with a significantly larger portion consisting of benign instances. To identify the optimal combination of hyperparameters, use hyperparameter optimisation methods such as GS, RS, or BO. These hyperparameters include learning rates, batch sizes, dropout rates, layer sizes, and others. Tune the hyperparameters on the validation set to maximize the model's performance metrics. Tuned hyperparameters can lead to faster convergence during training, reducing the time and computational resources required to train the model. The future of Android malware detection will be shaped by a combination of technological advancements, collaborative efforts within the cybersecurity community, and a deep understanding of evolving malware threats.

References

1. Elayan, O.N., Mustafa, A.M.: Android malware detection using deep learning. Procedia Comput. Sci. **184**, 847–852 (2021). https://doi.org/10.1016/j.procs.2021.03.106
2. Kouliaridis, V., Kambourakis, G.: A comprehensive survey on machine learning techniques for android malware detection. Information (Switzerland), **12**(5), 185 (2021). https://doi.org/10.3390/info12050185
3. Zhang, N., Tan, Y., Yang, C., Li, Y.: Deep learning feature exploration for Android malware detection. Appl. Soft Comput. **102** (2021). https://doi.org/10.1016/j.asoc.2020.107069
4. Kim, J., Ban, Y., Ko, E., Cho, H., Yi, J.H.: MAPAS: a practical deep learning-based android malware detection system. Int. J. Inf. Secur. **21**(4), 725–738 (2022). https://doi.org/10.1007/s10207-022-00579
5. AlJarrah, M.N., Yaseen, Q.M., Mustafa, A.M.: A context-aware android malware detection approach using machine learning. Information (Switzerland) **13**(12) (2022). https://doi.org/10.3390/info13120563
6. Sihag, V., Vardhan, M., Singh, P., Choudhary, G., Son, S.: De-lady: Deep learning based android malware detection using dynamic features. J. Internet Serv. Inf. Secur. **11**(2), 34–45 (2021). https://doi.org/10.22667/JISIS.2021.05.31.03
7. Agrawal, P., Trivedi, B.: Machine learning classifiers for android malware detection. Adv. Intell. Syst. Comput. **1174**, 311–322 (2021). https://doi.org/10.1007/978-981-15-5616-6_22
8. Shatnawi, A.S., Yassen, Q., Yateem, A.: An android malware detection approach based on static feature analysis using machine learning algorithms. Procedia Comput. Sci. **201**(C), 653–658 (2022). https://doi.org/10.1016/j.procs.2022.03.086
9. Shaukat, K., Luo, S., Varadharajan, V.: A novel deep learning-based approach for malware detection. Eng. Appl. Artif. Intell. **122**, 106030 (2023). https://doi.org/10.1016/j.engappai.2023.106030
10. Ksibi, A., Zakariah, M., Almuqren, L., Alluhaidan, A.S.: Efficient android malware identification with limited training data utilizing multiple convolution neural network techniques. Eng. Appl. Artif. Intell. **127**, 107390 (2023). https://doi.org/10.1016/j.engappai.2023.107390
11. Turnbull, L., Tan, Z., Babaagba, K.O.: A generative neural network for improving metamorphic malware detection in IoT mobile devices. In: Internet of Things Security and Privacy, pp. 24–53. CRC Press (2023)
12. Singh, J., Sharma, K., Wazid, M., Das, A.K.: SINN-RD: spline interpolation-envisioned neural network-based ransomware detection scheme. Comput. Electr. Eng. **106**, 108601 (2023). https://doi.org/10.1016/j.compeleceng.2023.108601
13. Ullah, F., Ullah, S., Srivastava, G., Lin, J.C.W.: Droid-MCFG: android malware detection system using manifest and control flow traces with multi-head temporal convolutional network. Phys. Commun. **57**, 101975 (2023). https://doi.org/10.1016/j.phycom.2022.101975
14. Raymond, V., Joseph, R., Raj, J.R., Retna, J.: Investigation of android malware with machine learning classifiers using enhanced PCA algorithm. Comput. Syst. Sci. Eng. **44**(3), 2147–2163 (2023)
15. Ali, Y.A., Awwad, E.M., Maarouf, A.: Hyperparameter search for machine learning algorithms for optimizing the computational complexity. Processes **11**(2), 349 (2023). https://doi.org/10.3390/pr11020349
16. Mahindru, A.: Anndroid: a framework for android malware detection using feature selection techniques and machine learning algorithms. In: Mobile Application Development: Practice and Experience: 12th Industry Symposium in Conjunction with 18th ICDCIT 2022, pp. 47–69. Springer, Singapore (2023). https://doi.org/10.1007/978-981-19-6893-8_5
17. Ravi, E., Mummadi U.K.: A comparative study on machine learning and deep learning methods for malware detection. J. Theor. Appl. Inf. Technol. **100**(20) (2022)

18. Ravi, E., Mummadi, U.K.: Android malware detection with classification based on hybrid analysis and N-gram feature extraction. In: International Conference on Advancements in Smart Computing and Information Security. Springer, Cham (2022). https://doi.org/10.1007/978-3-031-23095-0_13

19. Kumar, M.U., Kumar, D.S., Rani, B.P., Rao, K.V., Prasad, A.V.K., Shravani, D.: Dependable solutions design by agile modeled layered security architectures. In: Meghanathan, N., Chaki, N., Nagamalai, D. (eds.) CCSIT 2012. LNICSSITE, vol. 84, pp. 510–519. Springer, Heidelberg (2012). https://doi.org/10.1007/978-3-642-27299-8_53

20. Shravani, D., Suresh Varma, P., Padmaja Rani, B., Upendra Kumar, M., Krishna Prasad, A.V.: Designing dependable web services security architecture solutions. In: Wyld, D.C., Wozniak, M., Chaki, N., Meghanathan, N., Nagamalai, D. (eds.) CNSA 2011. CCIS, vol. 196, pp. 140–149. Springer, Heidelberg (2011). https://doi.org/10.1007/978-3-642-22540-6_14

Enhancing Security Through QR Code and Enriched Blowfish Cryptography for Sensitive Data

Aishwarya Palaniappan(✉) ⓘ, Lakshmi Priya Veilumuthu ⓘ, and Remegius Praveen Sahayaraj Louis ⓘ

Loyola-ICAM College of Engineering and Technology, Chennai 600 034, Tamil Nadu, India
aishwaryap107@gmail.com

Abstract. In today's digital age, data security is of utmost importance as sensitive information is being stored, processed, and transmitted online. Recent advancement in banking cybersecurity strides in encompassing advanced threat detection, biometric authentication, and the integration of artificial intelligence and block chain to fortify defences against cyber threats. It provides insights into the industry's evolving strategies for robust financial system security.

Confidential information such as personal details, financial information, trade secrets, and other sensitive data must be protected to avoid misuse, theft, or unauthorized access. Compliance with legal and regulatory requirements, maintaining customer trust, preventing cyberattacks, and ensuring business continuity are some other reasons why data security is critical. Implementing effective data security measures such as encryption, access controls, monitoring, and employee training is necessary to safeguard against potential threats and protect the privacy and confidentiality of individuals and organizations. The proposed system provides such protection by using enhanced blowfish algorithm with Attribute based DNA (ADNA) cryptography and Digital Signature Algorithm (DSA) along with a QR key transmission. This way, the system will secure the data shared between both sender and receiver, requiring more cryptanalysis efforts without much impact on performance and computational requirement.

Keywords: encryption · decryption · cryptography

1 Introduction

The banking sector deals with large amounts of sensitive data related to customers' financial transactions, personal details, and confidential business information. During data transfer between different systems and parties, there is a high risk of unauthorized access, interception, and theft. In the banking sector, data security is of paramount importance during data transfers. Banks deal with sensitive financial information of their customers, including bank account details, credit/debit card information, and personal identification numbers (PINs). Any unauthorized access or modification of this information can lead to financial fraud, identity theft, and other criminal activities. Effective data security measures such as encryption, multi-factor authentication, secure file transfer protocols, and network segmentation can help prevent data breaches and ensure secure data transfers. Therefore, it is crucial to have robust data security measures in place to ensure the confidentiality, integrity, and availability of the data. In today's digital era, the banking sector is highly dependent on technology for processing financial transactions and managing customer data. With the increasing number of cyber threats, it has become crucial to ensure secure data transmission in the banking sector. Cryptographic algorithms play a vital role in protecting sensitive data from unauthorized access, interception, and theft. They use various techniques to encrypt data and create a unique key for authorized parties to access it. By ensuring message authentication and integrity, cryptographic algorithms can prevent data tampering and maintain the authenticity of transmitted data. In summary, secure data transmission using cryptographic algorithms is essential for the banking sector to safeguard customer trust, prevent financial fraud, and maintain the integrity of the banking system. Combining Blowfish encryption, DNA cryptography, and QR codes can provide even greater data security. Blowfish is a symmetric key block cipher that uses a variable-length key to encrypt data. It is a fast and efficient algorithm that can handle large amounts of data. DNA cryptography is a promising technique that uses DNA molecules as cryptographic keys to secure data. It offers high-level security due to the vast number of possible keys and is resistant to attacks such as brute force and rainbow table attacks. QR code usage is a convenient and secure way to transmit cryptographic keys. It eliminates the risk of key interception during transmission and enables secure exchange between parties. By combining these three measures, organizations can provide strong and multi-layered data security. Blowfish encryption ensures that the data is secure from unauthorized access, while DNA cryptography provides an additional layer of security by using biological molecules as cryptographic keys. The usage of QR code eliminates the risk of key interception and ensures secure transmission. Overall, implementing these measures can prevent financial fraud, identity theft, and other cyber threats, thereby safeguarding customer trust and maintaining the integrity of the organization.

2   Literature Survey

Data sharing transmissions are classified by [1] according to security levels using the Blowfish algorithm instead of the Data Encryption Standard. By encouraging the privacy and integrity of information as it moves across the cloud and by raising user trust, it is possible to secure information security while preventing information leakage and loss. Novel Data Authentication is employed to provide security in the cloud. Materials and Procedures A crucial plan is implemented that protects against the cipher attack to ensure security. This Blowfish algorithm generates a better time to execution of (0.14 s) than the standard data encryption algorithm of (0.4 s) with significance p-value of 0.012. Blowfish generates less Standard Error average value compared to Data Encryption Standard.

Cryptographic techniques have been used in [2] to preserve the confidentiality of cloud data. We shall conduct a comparative examination of several cryptographic methods used to safeguard data via the cloud in this research. There will be a variety of performance measures used in this examination. Using cryptographic algorithms will increase security. The input block size and input key size that are employed determine the most crucial part of the 6 algorithms. The benefits and downsides of several cryptographic methods used to safeguard data via the cloud were compared using various factors. Algorithms with symmetry are more powerful and efficient, according to the report. Less time is needed for encryption with the AES and Blowfish algorithms. The best algorithm for using memory is blowfish.

Use of the Blowfish Algorithm for Android-Based QR Code Encryption and Decryption Technology is now developing extremely quickly, enabling us to access many different types of information and data, yet many people misuse this capability, as shown in [3], for instance, in phishing efforts that frequently targeted information and data owned by both individuals and businesses. Information or data loss has serious negative effects on people and businesses since they may be exchanged, used as an instrument for deception, or even utilized as a means of extortion. Information security must be maintained in order to safeguard data against internet criminal activity. A cryptographic method employing the Blowfish algorithm with a QR Code, which serves as secondary protection, is one of the methods intended to secure sensitive and critical information. Where information and data that has been transformed into QR Codes which cannot be altered. The goal of this research is to integrate an Android-based application system with the Blowfish Algorithm for Encrypting and Decryption of the QR Code. The study's findings indicate that an android-based application may use the blowfish algorithm. Using a QR Code generator, plaintext that has been converted to ciphertext using blowfish technique may be utilized as a QR code.

A Review of the Performance Time and Security Changes in [4] of the Blowfish Algorithm for the transmission of complex digital material, data has grown in popularity. Data protection is an issue for researchers. Multimedia data is now more exposed to risks due to the networked transfer of digital data, including network hacking and illegal access. In order to maintain the security of the data, encryption techniques based on symmetrical encryption algorithms must be used to safeguard the data. One of the most renowned cryptographic techniques is the blowfish encryption algorithm. However, each of the existing algorithms has a unique mix of benefits and drawbacks. However, there are a number of disadvantages to utilizing this technique, such as difficult computing operations, fixed (S-Box), and pattern problems, which can occur when handling more complicated data, such as texts. The effectiveness of the algorithm has been the focus of several researchers. This article provides a summary of the changes made to the Blowfish algorithms by researchers in earlier publications.

[5] Analysis of the Blowfish is and Des algorithms in relation to the decryption and encryption of document files. One of the most crucial parts of the information technology sector is security, including document security. Processing time, file size, and memory use are the three comparative factors used to compare the Blowfish method to the DES algorithm in the encryption process. The DES Algorithm has a faster time than the Blowfish Algorithm in the encryption process, with a percentage of the DES Algorithm's encryption processing time of 3.7975%. Evaluations were conducted in 40 test information in the form of documents, each consisting of 10 test data with extension. With a proportion of the DES Algorithm's encryption processing period of 8 3.595%, the DES Algorithm decrypts data more quickly than the Blowfish Algorithm.

The DES Algorithm's file size rises during encryption bytes less than the Blowfish Algorithm's file size does. The DES and Blowfish algorithms' file sizes do not change throughout the decryption process since they revert to their original sizes. In comparison to the Blowfish Algorithm, the DES Algorithm consumes less memory throughout the encryption process, with a memory use percentage of 49.655%. When compared to the DES Algorithm, the Blowfish Algorithm consumes less memory throughout the decryption process, with an overall memory utilization percentage of 49.5925%.

A thorough investigation of the symmetric algorithms' performance: 3DES, Blowfish, AES, and Twofish in [5] provides Software developers the details on security, performance, availability, reliability, scalability, usability, and so on, while creating apps that offer services in all business sectors, including banking, health, education, real estate, and social media, among others. When discussing security, for instance, a few attributes like confidentiality, integrity, availability, nonrepudiation, and accountability must be taken into consideration. There are several methods to accomplish these goals, and one of them is by employing a cryptographic process. The two main categories of algorithms used in cryptography are symmetric and asymmetric. They all offer encryption and decryption techniques. We compared the performance of four symmetric algorithms—AES, 3DES, Blowfish, and Twofish—in this work. Evaluation of the encryption and decryption processes' execution times, memory use, and ciphertext size. We created a.NET program using C# to do the comparison against various file sizes. As a result of our analysis, we discovered that Twofish has the longest execution time whereas AES has the lowest execution time for both encryption and decryption operations. AES and 3DES require less memory during the encryption procedure than blowfish and Twofish, albeit their memory use was almost same. AES took up less RAM during decryption. The largest ciphertext size is 9 and it is shared by Blowfish.

Lack of cybersecurity protection measures leaves one slightly exposed and even puts their digital lives at great danger of the alarmingly common phishing assault. Even false personal information may be used by perpetrators to get access to numerous organizations in order to carry out their evil deeds. [6] objective is to outline a security measure for a secure data transmission via a vaccination card. One of the most often gathered types of data nowadays is vaccination information. Personal data becomes extremely exposed to dangers, however, because the majority of online data gathering methods lack encryption. In order to demonstrate secure data transfer using QR codes created by RSA, the researchers proposed a Centralized Covid-19 Record System. Cryptography was included into the system through a message encryption/decryption function that uses the RSA technique to create a key pair. The RSA encryption method, RSA decryption algorithm, and Euler phi function are the three fundamental mathematical parameters that make up such characteristics. Several software and hardware specifications that construct and support the system's end-to-end process have been specified with regard to the system development.

[7] system for booking tickets relies on the usage of QR Codes, which carry information about the ticket records, including train schedules, arrival and departure times, and passenger reservation information. The printed ticket contains information, including complete train information and a QR code. The database, online users, and dataset are the three primary components of the ticket reservation system. In the suggested system, a user-friendly GUI is created for users to utilize in order to book tickets, and the produced ticket will be in the form of a QR code that is generated when a booking is confirmed. Based on the encrypted data the user enters, a QR Code will be created. In order to encrypt data, a QR code will be created based on the user's or passenger's information and the train specifications. The necessary data is then produced by patterns found in both the horizontal and vertical halves of the QR 10 code. Thus, the QR created will be protected and end to end encrypted, ensuring data security while making a reservation. The system uses Apache Kafka for messaging purposes. The encrypted QR Code may be scanned using a smartphone application. The passenger's details can be seen after decryption.

Combining the RSA Encryption with Digital Signature Algorithm for Security System Analysis in [8]. Asymmetric keys or public key cryptography are frequently employed to implement data security in information and communication systems. Due to its simplicity, the RSA algorithm is one of the most well-known and often used public key cryptography. The processes of encryption and decryption are RSA's two primary uses. As the foundation of the Digital Signature Standard (DSS), the Digital Signature Algorithm (DSA) is a digital signature algorithm. The system of public key cryptography also uses DSA. DSA performs the creation of digital signatures and the verification of their legality as its two primary tasks. The authors of this study compare the computing times of RSA and DSA using particular bits and determine which bits are most effectively utilized. In order to increase data security, combine the RSA and DSA algorithms. The authors used RSA 1024 for the encryption process and DSA 512 for the addition of digital signatures after analyzing the simulation results. As a consequence, the messages delivered are not only encrypted but also include digital signatures enabling the data authentication procedure.

[9] all current digital signature schemes have a focus on the most reliable and secure verification techniques. Websites, security agencies, banks, and other institutions utilize a variety of digital signature systems to confirm a user's legitimacy. Different types of digital signature methods, including proxy, on-time, batch, and others, are classified. This study compares several sorts of schemes based on factors including security level, effectiveness, algorithmic difficulty, and more.

[10] addresses the critical challenges associated with ensuring security in cloud environments. The authors propose an advanced security framework that leverages Elliptic Curve Cryptography (ECC), access control mechanisms, and a novel approach called LDSA (Location-Based Data Storage and Access). The introduction of LDSA introduces a spatial dimension to data storage and access, contributing an innovative layer to the security architecture. By blending these elements, the paper aims to provide a comprehensive solution for safeguarding both data storage and communication processes in cloud environments, catering to the growing concerns about privacy and confidentiality in cloud computing.

Integration fuzzy logic and genetic algorithms into the elliptic curve Diffie-Hellman (ECDH) algorithm in [11] the use of fuzzy logic aims to enhance the adaptability of the algorithm to dynamic and uncertain network conditions, while the integration of genetic algorithms seeks to optimize key parameters for improved security. The paper explores the potential of this hybrid approach in mitigating security threats and ensuring robust cryptographic key exchange in wireless communication environments.

Integration of elliptic key cryptography with Beta Gamma functions in [12] aiming to enhance the confidentiality and integrity of data transmission within WSNs. The paper explores the mathematical foundations of Beta Gamma functions in cryptography and demonstrates their effectiveness in securing routing protocols for WSNs. By doing so, this research contributes to the broader field of network security and provides a novel perspective on leveraging mathematical functions for cryptographic applications in WSNs, which could have implications for enhancing the security of various IoT and wireless communication systems.

The research papers highlight the efficiency of the Blowfish algorithm in data security, emphasizing its shorter execution time and applicability in Android-based QR code encryption. Challenges, including algorithm-specific complexities and variable performance, are acknowledged. The importance of secure data transmission is underscored through applications like vaccination cards and QR code-based ticket reservations. Despite cryptographic advancements, concerns about phishing and technology misuse emphasize the ongoing need for robust cybersecurity measures.

The innovative hybrid algorithmic approach represents a distinct advantage, underscoring our commitment to providing a cost-effective and resource-efficient solution for secure data exchange. By strategically leveraging QR codes for encryption key sharing and integrating the robust Digital Signature Algorithm (DSA) alongside the efficiency of Blowfish encryption, our system not only ensures top-tier security but does so in a manner that optimizes costs and resource utilization. This unique combination sets our solution apart, addressing the dual needs of enhanced security and economic efficiency in the landscape of data exchange.

3 System Architecture

The following sections of this research study focus on the system architecture, which through this explanation, emphasizes the significant architectural characteristics that form the basis for our study's findings (Fig. 1).

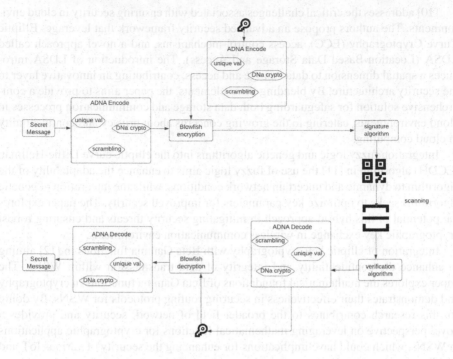

Fig. 1. System Architecture for the proposed system

3.1 Encryption of Message and Key Using ADNA Crypto

Prompt the user to provide two unique numerical values. These values will be referred to as unique_value_1 and unique_value_2. Calculate sum of digits of unique_value_1 and then use unique_value_2 to multiply the sum of digits and store it in a new variable named att. Prompt the user to provide a cryptographic key, which will be used for encryption. This key can be a string or any other suitable data type. Receive the user's data as input. Use a DNA encryption algorithm to encrypt both the message and the user-provided key. This will involve mapping the message and key to DNA sequences which is formed using d-block where each alpha numeric values is mapped to sequence of three letter character based on the base DNA sequence which is followed by the basic DNA encryption techniques. After this the encrypted message and key is scrambled using the scramble function where a variable is initialized to store the scrambled message. Which follows the initialization of a randomization seed based on the value of att obtained earlier. Use the randomization seed to perform a scrambling operation on both the encrypted message and the encrypted key. Where the scrambling is based on shuffling the values according to the seed. Store the result of the scrambling operation of input message and key in scrambled_message and scrambled_key respectively.

3.2 Encryption of Scrambled_message and Scrambled_key Using Blowfish Algorithm

During this initialization phase, the key is expanded into multiple subkeys. Blowfish generates a series of subkeys from the original encryption key. These subkeys are used in the encryption process. The key expansion process involves Initializing the P-array and S-boxes with predefined constants which is followed by XORing the key with elements of the P-array in a loop finally this process is repeated for a fixed number of rounds to generate the subkeys. The scrambled_message is divided into fixed-size blocks. Blowfish typically uses 64-bit blocks. The 64-bit block is subjected to an initial permutation using the P-array. Blowfish operates in multiple rounds, typically 16 rounds. In each round, the data is processed through the P-array and S-boxes. In each round, the current data block is XORed with one of the subkeys. The data block is then split into two halves, and a series of mathematical operations (including substitution and permutation) are applied to each half. After all rounds are completed, the two halves are swapped. After the last round of encryption, a final permutation is applied to the data block. The final data block is now the cipher text. If the message consists of multiple blocks, repeat the encryption process for each block. All cipher text blocks are concatenated to form the final encrypted message which is sent to the receiver.

3.3 Signature and Verification Algorithm on Key Which is to be Sent to User in QR Format

Asymmetric cryptography is used to create a digital signature and verification technique based on SHA-256, in which the private key is utilized for signing and a matching public key is used for verifying. Create a pair of keys using the DSA method, each of which consists of a private key (used for signing) and a corresponding public key. Calculate the message's SHA-256 hash before signing it. This will result in a hash value of fixed size. Utilize the private key to encrypt the hash value. The electronic signature you use for your communication is the end outcome of the signing procedure. Use the QR code and OpenCV libraries of Python to convert the signed key to a QR code. Make a function that generates a QR code with the message you want to convey. To store the

QR code, use your key to call this method. Any approved scanner or the decode feature may be used to retrieve the key's image from the key. The QR code, containing crucial information, is effortlessly retrievable through any approved scanner or decoding feature, further simplifying the interaction. This integration is a pivotal element in our system, facilitating a user-friendly and technologically advanced approach to secure information sharing. By using the sender's public key, a signed key is verified. Compute the received message's SHA-256 hash. Verify that it corresponds to the hash value that was acquired during the signing procedure. Using the sender's public key, decrypt the digital signature you just received. A hash value will result from this. The signature is legitimate and the message was not tampered with during transmission if the two hash values match.

3.4   Decryption of Scrambled_message Using Blowfish Algorithm

Initialize the Blowfish algorithm with the secret key that was used for encryption along with the cipher text. The ciphertext is then split into blocks of the same size that were used during encryption. For each ciphertext block perform the Blowfish decryption algorithm on the block using the initialized key which involves a series of 16 iterations of data manipulations, including XOR, permutation, and substitution procedures. After obtaining all the decryption blocks, the blocks are concatenated to obtained the plaintext message.

3.5   Decryption of Message and Key Using ADNA Crypto

After obtaining all the decryption blocks, the blocks are concatenated to obtained the plaintext message. Apply the reverse of the DNA crypto algorithm to decrypt the encrypted key and encrypted message, which involves in Reversing DNA strand complementarity and performing DNA arithmetic operations in reverse. Map the decrypted DNA sequences back to alphanumeric values using the same encoding scheme used during encryption. Descramble the message and key using descramble function which makes use of randomization seed att which was previously calculated from the unique values provided by the user which will finally give the decrypted message which was sent from the receiver.

3.6   Proposed Blowfish and ADNA Based Encryption and Decryption Algorithm

Input: Plain text
Output: Cipher text

Encryption

Step1: Perform ADNA encode on input message and key

  i. Get two unique values from the user as unique_value_1 and unique_value_2
  ii. Perform sum of digits on unique_value_1 and then multiply it with unique_value_2 and store it in a variable att
      Att=sum_of_digits(unique_value_1) * unique_value_2
  iii.Get the message and key which is to be used for encryption from the user
  iv. Using the d-block of DNA crypto map each alpha numeric value to a unique sequence of three characters
  v. Scramble the DNA sequence using randomization seed based on the value of att obtained earlier
  vi. Store the result of the scrambling operation of input message and key in scrambled_message and scrambled_key respectively

Step2: Implementation of Blowfish algorithm using scrambled_message and scrambled-key

  i. Initialize P-array and S-boxes with predefined values.
  ii. Expand the key into subkeys using Key Expansion.
  iii.Procedure BlowfishEncrypt (Key, scrambled_text):
       Split the plaintext into 64-bit blocks.
       For each plaintext block:
       a. Apply Initial Permutation.
       b. Perform 16 rounds of Feistel Network:
          i.   Divide the block into left (L) and right (R) halves.
          ii. Calculate the round key (K).
          iii. R = R XOR K.
          iv. R = F(R) XOR L.
          v.   Swap L and R.
       c. Swap L and R one last time.
       d. R = R XOR Final Round Key.
       e. Apply Final Permutation.
  iv Concatenate the encrypted blocks to form the ciphertext.
  v   Return the ciphertext

Step3: Add Digital signature

  i. Create a DSA key pair with an associated public key and a private key for signing.
  ii. Compute the SHA-256 hash of the message to be signed. This produces a fixed-size hash value.
  iii.To produce the digital signature, encrypt the hash value with the sender's private key.
  iv. Save the digital signature.

Step4: QR of the of the scrambled_key is generated and sent to the receiver

Decryption

Step1: Verify Digital signature
   a. Calculate the message's SHA-256 hash.
   b. Decrypt the received digital signature using the sender's public key. This decryption should produce a hash value
   c. Step a's calculated hash value should be compared to Step b's decrypted hash value.
   d. If the two hash values match, the signature is valid, and the message has not been tampered with during transmission.
Step2: QR of the of the scrambled_key is decoded
Step3: Perform ADNA decode on scrambled_key
   i. Descramble the DNA sequence using randomization seed based on the value of att obtained earlier.
   ii. Using the d-block of DNA crypto map unique sequence of three characters to original alpha numeric value in order to obtain the key
Step4: Perform Blowfish Decryption

   i. Procedure BlowfishDecrypt(Key, Plaintext):
      a. Split the cipher_text into 64-bit blocks.
      b. For each cipher_text block:
          Apply Initial Permutation.
          Perform 16 rounds of Feistel Network:
             i. Divide the block into left (L) and right (R) halves.
             ii. Calculate the round key (K).
             iii. R = R XOR K.
             iv. R = F(R) XOR L.
             v. Swap L and R.
      c. Swap L and R one last time.
      d. R = R XOR Final Round Key.
      e. Apply Final Permutation.
   ii   Concatenate the encrypted blocks to form the scrambled_text.
   iii   Return the scrambled_text
Step4: Perform ADNA decode on scrambled_message
   i. Descramble the DNA sequence using randomization seed based on the value of att obtained earlier.
   ii. Using the d-block of DNA crypto map unique sequence of three characters to original alpha numeric value in order to obtain the original message.

4   Performance Analysis

In this research paper, we conducted a thorough examination of various encryption algorithms to understand how they performed in different scenarios. We compared these algorithms to determine which ones offered the best balance of efficiency. The results of this investigation have been recorded and analyzed below.

Table 1. Basic comparison of different encryption algorithms

Algorithm	Key size (bits)	Block size(bits)	No. of Rounds
DES	64	64	16
3DES	112	64	48
AES	128	128	10
RC4	Variable	40–2048	256
RC6	128–256	128	20
Blowfish	32–448	64	16
Proposed system	32–448	64	16

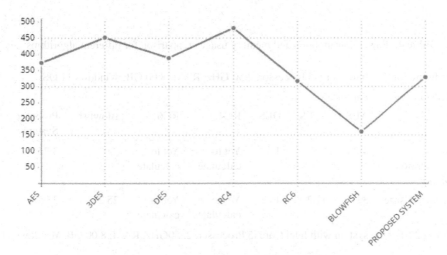

Fig.2. Encryption time comparison of different algorithms

Table 2. Encryption time of different algorithm for different input size

Input size in Kbytes	AES	3DES	DES	RC2	RC6	Blowfish	Proposed System
49	56	54	29	57	36	36	35.5
59	38	48	33	60	36	36	39.8
100	90	81	49	91	37	37	68
247	112	111	47	121	45	45	85.5
321	164	167	82	262	45	45	138
694	210	226	144	295	46	46	169

* For the system with Intel Core i3 Processor, 2. 50GHz, RAM: 4.00 GB, Windows 11 OS

Table 3. Power consumption and memory usage comparison for different algorithms

Configurations	Intel Core i3 Processor, 2.50 GHz, RAM: 4.00 GB, Windows 10 OS						
Algorithm	Parameter						
	AES	3DES	DES	RC4	RC6	Blowfish	Proposed System
Power consumption (Watts)	4.9	6.2	5.2	Yet to calculate	Yet to calculate	4.2	3.98
Memory Usage	43.8	43.3	45.5	Yet to calculate	Yet to calculate	27.5	35.2

[*] Config1 - For the system with Intel Core i3 Processor, 2. 50GHz, RAM: 4.00 GB, Windows 10 OS

Table 4. Power consumption and memory usage comparison for different algorithms

Configurations	Intel Core i5 Processor, 2.50 GHz, RAM: 8.00 GB, Windows 11 OS						
Algorithm	Parameter						
	AES	3DES	DES	RC4	RC6	Blowfish	Proposed System
Power consumption (Watts)	4.2	5.5	4.8	Yet to calculate	Yet to calculate	3.9	3.75
Memory Usage	32.5	41.2	43.2	Yet to calculate	Yet to calculate	25.2	33.6

[*] Config2 - For the system with Intel Core i5 Processor, 2. 50GHz, RAM: 8.00 GB, Windows 11 OS

From Table 1 We may conclude that the suggested system has more key sizes than any other known methods, making a brute force attack more challenging and also the variable key size (32–448) allowing users to tailor encryption strength to specific needs and evolving security standards. From Table 2 it is clear that the encryption time, decryption time is comparatively lesser than all other algorithms. The encryption time of our proposed system is 13.10% lesser than AES and 25.76% lesser than Triple-Des. The lesser execution time eventually lowers the battery consumption so from Table 3 and Table 4 we can infer that Memory Usage and Power consumption of the proposed system is comparatively lower than other algorithm and the throughput is greater than all the algorithms used in comparison. Power consumption for config1* and config2* is 3.98 and 3.75 respectively. Memory consumption for config1* and config2* is 35.2 and 33.6respectively. Table 5 shows that the best and average case values for the proposed system is O(log n), making it comparably more effective than other algorithms.

From Fig. 2 our proposed algorithm emerges as significantly more efficient when compared to other encryption methods. From Fig. 3 our proposed system stands out as

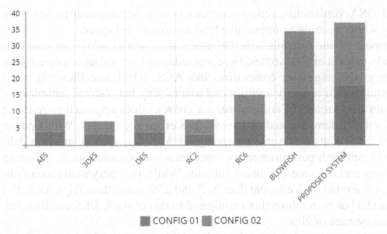

CONFIG 01- OS Intel Core i5 Processor, 2.50GHz, RAM:8.00 GB, Windows 11
CONFIG 02- OS Intel Core i3 Processor, 2.50GHz, RAM:4.00 GB, Windows 10

Fig. 3. Throughput comparison of different encryption

Table 5. Time Complexity analysis

Alorithm/ Complexity	ECC	[10]	[11]	[12]	MTECSR	Proposed System
Best case	$O(n^3)$	$O(n^2 \log n)$	$O(n^2 \log n)$	$O(n^3)$	$O(n \log n)$	$O(\log n)$
Average case	$O(n^3)$	$O(n^2 \log n)$	$O(n^2 \log n)$	$O(n^3)$	$O(n^2)$	$O(\log n)$
Worst case	$O(n^4)$	$O(n^3)$	$O(n^3)$	$O(n^4)$	$O(n^2)$	$O(n \log n)$

exceptionally efficient, offering faster data processing capabilities compared to other alternatives. This enhanced throughput ensures smoother and more responsive data encryption.

The limitations of our proposed system include the absence of specific values for battery and memory consumption in comparison to RC4 and RC6, which hinders a comprehensive evaluation of resource efficiency. Additionally, the identical best and average case time complexities may indicate a lack of adaptability to varying input scenarios, potentially limiting the system's scalability and performance optimization.

5 Conclusion and Future Work

In conclusion, our cybersecurity system stands as a robust and comprehensive defense mechanism against evolving threats, placing a strong emphasis on secure data exchange and the cultivation of client trust through a combination of dependability, efficiency, and regulatory compliance. The strategic utilization of QR codes for encryption key sharing, coupled with the robust Digital Signature Algorithm (DSA) and the efficient Blowfish encryption and DSA verification, reflects our unwavering commitment to fortifying system security while ensuring an impressive level of operational speed.

A pivotal aspect of our system's superiority lies in its remarkable encryption efficiency, especially evident at 694 Kbytes. Here, our solution demonstrates a noteworthy 46-unit efficiency advantage over competitors like AES, 3DES, and Blowfish, highlighting our dedication to not only security and adaptability but also the optimization of overall system performance. Furthermore, our conscientious approach to resource consumption is clearly demonstrated by the system's efficiency metrics. With a power consumption of 3.75 Watts and a memory usage of 33.6, our system strikes a delicate balance between high performance and environmental consciousness, delivering an energy-efficient and resource-optimized solution. While, the encryption time of our proposed system is around 13% efficient than AES and 25% better than Triple-Des. The implemented model has better throughput compared to that of AES, DES and Blowfish algorithms by an average of 20%.

Looking ahead, our system's future plans offer a diverse array of unique extension options, allowing for enhanced adaptability and an expanded range of users and use cases. The system's ability to incorporate various data types, including photos, audio, and video, further solidifies its versatility in meeting the evolving needs of users. Future plans for our system offer a wide range of unique options for extension that others may explore. Its ability to include different data types, such photos, audio, and video, increases its adaptability and serves a wider range of users and use cases. Researchers might also explore the incorporation of a built-in QR code scanner, a promising advancement that has the potential to improve both security and operational effectiveness. By eliminating the need for external tools, this innovative strategy guarantees that all users may transmit data in a simple and secure manner.

References

1. Mahendra, M., Prabha, P.S.: Classification of security levels to enhance the data sharing transmissions using blowfish algorithm in comparison with data encryption standard. In: 2022 International Conference on Sustainable Computing and Data Communication Systems (ICSCDS), pp. 1154–1160 (2022)
2. Thakkar, B., Thankachan, B.: A survey for comparative analysis of various cryptographic algorithms used to secure data on cloud. Int. J. Eng. Res. Technol. (IJERT) **09**(08), 753–756 (2020)
3. Putra, Z.A.W., et al.: Implementation of blowfish algorithm for encryption and decription on android-based QR code. J. Komputer Inform. Teknol. (JKOMITEK) (2022)
4. Abdul Qader, R.A., Al-Wattar, A.H.: A review of the blowfish algorithm modifications in terms of execution time and security. Tech.: Roman. J. Appl. Sci. Technol. (2022)
5. Saputra, R.P., Wahyudi, J., Jumadi, J.: Comparative analysis of the blowfish algorithm and the des algorithm in the document file encryption and decryption process. J. Komput. Inf. Teknol. (JKOMITEK) **2**, 605–612 (2022)
6. Pangan, A.M., Lacuesta, I.L., Mabborang, R.C., Ferrer, F.P.: Authenticating data transfer using RSA-generated QR codes. Eur. J. Inf. Technol. Comput. Sci. **2**, 18–30 (2022)
7. Gangurde, N., Ghosh, S., Giri, A., Gharat, S.: Ticketing system using AES encryption based QR code. In: 2022 4th International Conference on Smart Systems and Inventive Technology (ICSSIT), pp. 201–206 (2022)

8. Aufa, F.J., Endroyono, Affandi, A.: Security system analysis in combination method: RSA encryption and digital signature algorithm. In: 2018 4th International Conference on Science and Technology (ICST), pp. 1–5 (2018)

9. Alidoost Nia, M., Sajedi, A., Jamshidpey, A.: An introduction to digital signature schemes. ArXiv, abs/1404.282 (2014)

10. Kavin, B.P., Ganapathy, S., Kanimozhi, U., Kannan, A.: An enhanced security frameworkfor secured data storage and communications in cloud using ECC, access control and LDSA. Wireless Pers. Commun. 115(2), 1107–1135 (2020)

11. Sethuraman, P., Tamizharasan, P.S., Kannan, A.: Fuzzy genetic elliptic curve Diffie-Hellman algorithm for secured communication in networks. Wireless Pers. Commun. 105(3), 993–1007 (2019)

12. Viswanathan, S., Kannan, A.: Elliptic key cryptography with Beta gamma functionsfor secure routing in wireless sensor networks. Wireless Netw. 25, 4903–4914 (2019)

Taxonomy of Image Encryption Techniques - A Survey

Vilas T. Mahajan[1,2](✉) and R. Sridaran[3]

[1] VPM's R Z Shah College, Mulund (East), Mumbai, India
tovilas@gmail.com
[2] Marwadi University, Rajkot, Gujarat, India
[3] Faculty of Computer Application and Academic Affairs, Marwadi University, Rajkot, Gujarat, India
sridaran.rajagopal@gmail.com

Abstract. Image encryption employs complex algorithms to transform digital images into indecipherable formats, safeguarding them from unauthorized access and ensuring sensitive visual data remains secure. It's crucial in various domains like business, government, healthcare, military, and multimedia systems due to the paramount importance of information security. In today's context, the primary challenge is preserving data confidentiality and integrity during communication. Unauthorized access to sensitive image data can have severe consequences, and the potential for data interception or theft during transmission is a pressing concern. This paper aims to conduct a thorough survey and categorization of image encryption techniques. It also explores different terminology, commonly used encryption algorithms, and modified methods in the field. The main aim is to identify gaps in existing image encryption techniques, which can pave the way for improved methods of securing digital image data. The paper incorporates both qualitative and quantitative analyses of various encryption algorithms. These vital insights of information security equip researchers and practitioners for creating more robust encryption solutions. These advancements benefit the broader community by safeguarding sensitive data, preserving confidentiality, and maintaining data integrity in our increasingly digitized society.

Keywords: Cryptography · Encryption · Decryption · Plaintext · Ciphertext · Ciphers · Cryptanalysis · Cryptographic algorithm · Image encryption · image security · Key management · Public and private key cryptography

1 Introduction

A 2D function, denoted as f(x, y), represents an image in the spatial domain, with f representing the pixel values at spatial coordinates x and y. Spatial domain methods refer to the image plane itself and involve directly manipulating the pixels in an image [13].

The expansion of digital imaging technology in recent years has resulted in a significant increase in the use and sharing of digital images. But still, since certain images

S. Rajagopal et al. (Eds.): ASCIS 2023, CCIS 2039, pp. 274–290, 2024.
https://doi.org/10.1007/978-3-031-59100-6_20

which are sensitive and important, such as medical imaging, military intelligence, and satellite image may require a secured method to maintain their confidentiality, integrity, and authenticity during transmission and storage.

Cryptography is used to secure an image by converting it into an unreadable format that can only be viewed with a key or password. Encryption and decryption techniques, along with key management, makes sure that sensitive data remains confidential, authentic, and accessible only to those who are authorised to access the image [1, 2].

This paper analyses different traditional encryption algorithms and some of the most common modern image encryption techniques like chaos-based algorithms, Deep Neural Networks (DNNs) and combination of DNA and Chaos [21]. The main objectives of this review are to identify the advantages and limitations of each of the image encryption techniques which are in use, and to provide a comprehensive understanding of their applicability and effectiveness in different image encryption scenarios. By examining the latest trends and advancements in image encryption techniques, review also seeks to offer perspectives on potential future research directions and advancements within the domain of image encryption [19].

1.1 Brief History of Cryptography

In this brief history of encryption, here is the outline of the major milestones in chronological order.

The ancient Egyptians and Greeks were among the earliest civilizations to use cryptography, with hieroglyphics (Pictograms) and scytale (Cipher rod) being used to encrypt messages [3, 4]. Julius Caesar developed the Caesar Cipher in 50 BC, which involved shifting the letters of the alphabet by a certain number of positions. [5] Later, in the 16th century, Blaise de Vigenere created the polyalphabetic cipher, which used multiple alphabets to encrypt messages [6].

With the advent of the telegraph in the 19th century, encryption became more important, and new encryption methods were developed, such as the Wheatstone-Breguet Cipher and the Playfair Cipher. [7] In the midst of World War II, the Germans employed the Enigma machine, which was eventually broken by Alan Turing and his team at Bletchley Park [8].

In the 1970s, Whitfield Diffie is credited with the development of public-key cryptography [9, 26], along with Martin Hellman [26], and Ralph Merkle [33]. This method involves using two keys, one public and one private, to encrypt and decrypt messages. Today, it is widely used in online communication, such as for secure transactions on the internet [9].

In 2001, The United States government embraced the Advanced Encryption Standard (AES) as a newly developed encryption standard. [3] This algorithm is now used worldwide for encrypting sensitive data, such as financial transactions, government documents & military communications [10].

1.2 Applications at a Glance

By encrypting images, individuals and organizations can ascertain that sensitive information and secrets remain safe from prying eyes.

One of the most significant areas where image encryption is used is medical imaging. Medical images such as X-rays and MRIs often contain sensitive information about a patient's health, and encryption can be used to protect the privacy of this information [11]. Similarly, encrypted images can be used by the military to protect sensitive information about enemy positions or troop movements. Additionally, encrypted images can be used in surveillance systems to protect the privacy of individuals who are being monitored. Encryption is also important in digital forensics, where digital evidence such an image can be used in criminal investigations. In such cases, encryption can be used to protect the credibility (authenticity) and robustness (integrity) of digital evidence. Encryption can also be used for authentication purposes. For example, in biometric identification systems, where encrypted images of fingerprints or faces can be used to verify an individual's identity. Watermarking is another area where image encryption is used [12]. Watermarking involves embedding a unique identifier into an image to protect copyrights or verify the authenticity of an image. Encryption can be used to protect the watermark and ensure that it is not tampered with.

Encryption is also critical for securing databases in IoT devices. To prevent interception and tampering, a significant amount of information needs to be encrypted [12].

1.3   Components of a Cryptography System

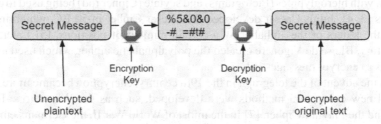

Fig. 1. Working of Encryption and Decryption

Encryption, in the field of cryptography, involves the transformation of information from one form to another. The initial presentation of this original information, often referred to as plaintext, is converted into an encrypted form known as ciphertext. The decryption process involves converting ciphertext i.e. encrypted data back into plaintext, allowing authorized entities to access the original information. In contrast, decryption is the process of converting encrypted data back to its original form. It is, in general, the reverse of an encryption technique. Decryption requires the use of a secret key or password to decode the encrypted information, allowing only an authorized user to access the data. This process requires the use of an encryption algorithm, which employs complex logic to safeguard the data, as well as a key, which serves as the combination to access the encoded data. Encryption takes the original data, which is often called "plaintext", and uses an encryption key with an encryption algorithm to create encoded data, which is called "ciphertext" (Fig. 1).

The resulting ciphertext can only be accessed and decrypted with the correct key, guaranteeing that the original plaintext remains secure and confidential [14].

1.4 Challenges of Encryption

To maximize the effectiveness and usability of an encryption algorithm, several factors should be considered.

Security: Image encryption's key challenge is promising secured encrypted data. Encryption algorithms must prevent brute force, statistical, and differential attacks to prevent unauthorized access. Brute force attacks entail trying all possible keys, statistical attacks exploit encryption algorithm weaknesses, and differential attacks exploit differences in encryption algorithm output. Hence, encryption algorithms must resist such attacks and provide robust security [31].

Computational Complexity: Image encryption algorithms may pose computational challenges when handling large datasets or real-time processing needs. To have efficiency in encryption and decryption, algorithms should reduce computational complexity. Parallelization, multithreading, and hardware acceleration can reduce complexity and improve efficiency [31].

Image Quality: Another challenge of image encryption algorithms is to maintain the quality of the encrypted images. Encryption algorithms should be designed to prevent image distortion, loss of quality, and pixel shuffling, which can impact image readability and usefulness. Techniques such as block cipher modes [32] and stream cipher [32] can be used to maintain image quality while maintaining robust security.

Storage Requirements: Image encryption algorithms may require considerable storage space for encrypted images and keys, which can be problematic for large datasets or limited storage capacity. Encryption algorithms should optimize storage requirements for efficient storage and retrieval of encrypted images. Techniques such as lossless compression, key management, and selective encryption can reduce storage requirements.

Compatibility: Image encryption algorithms should be compatible with different types of image files and image processing tools. This can be a challenge due to differences in image file formats, compression techniques, and other image processing tools. Encryption algorithms should be designed in such a way that it should be compatible with a wide range of image file formats. By considering these factors, a well-designed encryption algorithm can provide reliable and secure data protection for a wide range of applications [13, 15–17].

1.5 Motivation Behind the Proposed Survey

The increased use of digital images in various domains has led to a increase in the risk of access without authentication, which may result in the exposure of confidential information or compromise an individual's privacy. Therefore, image encryption has become a vital area of research for safeguarding image data from unauthorized access. This paper aims to review the current state of image encryption methods, identify any gaps and limitations in existing methods, and explore the potential for proposing new techniques to encrypt images.

Despite notable advancements in image encryption techniques, there are still several challenges and unresolved questions in this field. There is a lack of standardization and evaluation metrics for image encryption algorithms, which renders it challenging to compare and benchmark different methods.

The development of strong and effective methods for encrypting images can help to protect sensitive information and promises individuals' privacy. The improved method can aid in protecting sensitive information and maintain the individuals' privacy.

1.6 Organisation of the Paper

This paper consists of three main sections. The first section, the introduction, is divided into subsections covering the history, applications, and components of the cryptography system, as well as the challenges, solutions, and research motivation in encryption technology. The second section reviews related work, analysing existing literature on cryptography and research techniques to identify gaps in the research techniques already in use. The third section surveys standard encryption methods, presenting commonly used algorithms, their strengths and weaknesses and comparison of different standard encryption algorithms based on different metrics. The paper concludes by addressing the research gap and discussing how the proposed idea contributes to cryptography. The paper includes an appendix listing the referenced research papers at the end.

2 Related Work

Several methods for algorithms of image encryption have been developed in recent years, each one has its unique features and limitations. This paper provides an overview of various image encryption algorithms and their limitations

Alaa Farhan suggested [18] the utilization of a chaotic system to create a dynamic IP permutation along with S-Box substitution for encryption. Shuffling was used to make the encrypted message distinct from the original. However, using chaotic systems for encryption has limitations, including vulnerability to attacks, high computational costs, and implementation difficulties. Chaotic systems may not be efficient in scenarios with limited computational resources and are susceptible to various attacks. However, the paper did not include common tests used to measure the strength of encryption, like checking the size of the key space and sensitivity, the distribution of data, and the relationship between neighbouring pixels. While chaotic systems can generate complex and seemingly random sequences, they have limitations when it comes to generating secure IP permutations and S-box substitutions in encryption algorithms [18]. Chaotic maps have been used in encryption schemes, Rasika B. Naik and Udayprakash Singh [21] used a chaotic map that rounds values between -2 and 2 to either 1 or 0. While it's only useful for one-time passwords or image encryption due to its complicated calculations, chaotic map-based encryption schemes have advanced significantly in recent years, for securing the communication and storage of sensitive data. On the other hand, Aditya Jyoti Paul [23] emphasizes the importance of ensuring the reliability of chaotic maps for security employed in encryption systems, as inadequate initialization or a small key space can lead to non-chaotic keystreams that compromise data security. Thus, it's essential to take proper care to guarantee the security using the chaotic maps in encryption schemes. Jiangjian Xu, Bing Zhao, and Zeming Wu [24] in their study, discovered that unique keys are assigned to different images and alterations in the information of one channel can alter the key of the image encryption, thereby enhancing its security. Using classical chaotic systems for medical image encryption has limitations such as low entropy which makes them vulnerable to cryptographic attacks, potential loss of image quality and fidelity, and these limitations can limit the effectiveness of the encryption technique in medical applications, particularly in scenarios where accurate analysis and diagnosis of medical images are critical.

The proposed scheme for preserving privacy using Deep Neural Networks (DNNs) by Warit Sirichotedumrong, Yuma Kinoshita [19] is aimed at enabling the training of DNN models with encrypted images while allowing testing with plain images without the need for key management. The scheme works by using a technique in cryptography called Homomorphic Encryption (HE) [19], which allows computation on encrypted data without the need for decryption. The authors propose using a variant of HE known as Paillier Encryption, which allows for the addition of encrypted values and the multiplication of an encrypted value by a plaintext value.

To implement the scheme, the authors propose performing data augmentation in the encrypted domain. Data augmentation generates new training data by applying various transformation effects to the original data such as flipping and rotating images. In the proposed scheme, these transformations are performed on the encrypted images, allowing for privacy-preserving data augmentation.

During the training process, the encrypted images are sent to the cloud server for computation, and the server returns the encrypted model parameters. The decryption of the model parameters is performed by the client, and the trained model is used to make predictions on plain images. This process eliminates the need for the server to hold the decryption key, enhancing the privacy of the system [19].

Varsha Himthani [20] classified VMEI techniques into various categories according to their features and analysed and evaluated these techniques based on various parameters such as noise attacks, quality assessments, encryption key attacks, and security threats. The authors note that VMEI techniques have limitations that include the loss of image details, larger storage space requirements, and potential vulnerability to statistical attacks that can put at risk the encrypted data's security and privacy. The paper concludes by discussing the possible uses and challenges ahead of VMEI approaches [20], including open research questions related to the efficiency of the encryption process and the visual quality of the images. Overall, VMEI techniques have shown great promise in secure image transmission, but there is still much work to be done to overcome their limitations and confirm their effectiveness in real-world applications.

Ratheesh Kumar R, Jabin Mathew [21], this paper talks about comparing different ways of encrypting data and making sure it is safe. It shows that using a combination of DNA and Chaos [21] is the best way to keep data safe, even if the keys are kept secure. The comparison looks at different factors like security, speed, and how well it can protect against attacks. DNA encryption offers a high level of security as DNA sequencing is extremely difficult to tamper with or duplicate without detection. However, the paper also mentions that traditional encryption methods may not be enough to keep data safe [21].

In a paper by Hamed Ghazanfaripoura and Ali Broumandnia [22], they presented a method for encrypting grey-scale images by changing the pixels and mixing the neighbouring pixels. They used a combination of math operations called rows-columns diffusion and Hill diffusion, and they also used modular arithmetic to increase the security of the encryption. The advantage of this method is that it is very sensitive to changes in the secret key and the image, making it difficult for attackers to use known information to break the encryption. The method can be extended to encrypt color images, and in the future, it can be improved with faster and more secure methods using 3D modular chaotic maps. Disadvantages of "rows-columns diffusion and Hill diffusion" encryption techniques include lower security compared to advanced techniques, vulnerability to attacks, inefficiency with large data volumes or real-time processing, and higher storage requirements [22].

2.1 Limitations in Existing Survey

In the dynamic IP permutation and S-Box substitution technique, the limitations include their sensitivity to initial conditions, making it difficult to create reliable permutations and substitutions, as well as their unpredictability, which is problematic for encryption where predictability is essential. Additionally, the key space of chaotic systems is limited, making them vulnerable to brute-force attacks, and they are susceptible to chosen-plaintext attacks that can compromise their security [2].

Major limitations of DNN encryption algorithms are model theft vulnerability and high computational overhead. Protecting the DNN model is crucial to prevent decryption of encrypted data i.e. if an attacker gains access to the model, they can use it to decrypt the encrypted data, and optimizing computational overhead is essential for efficient use in resource-constrained environments.

The main limitations of this technique are that it is mostly suitable for encrypting images and second the process of creating VMEI requires additional computational resources compared to traditional encryption methods, making it more resource-intensive.

The "combination of DNA and Chaos" [21] approach has limitations such as: computational expense, challenging implementation and optimization, potential inefficiency in real-time processing and the security of this approach has not been widely studied, which could pose a risk for the protection of sensitive data. DNA based algorithms are slow in reading and writing DNA sequences, making it less suitable for applications that require fast data access. Moreover, errors and mutations can occur during the DNA sequencing process, leading to data corruption or loss.

Although Hill diffusion and rows-columns diffusion are efficient methods for image encryption, they also have some limitations. First of all, if the encryption keys are not sufficiently complicated, they may be susceptible to attacks like brute force attacks. Moreover, these approaches' computational complexity can make encryption time-consuming and resource-intensive, especially for large images. Second, the size of the image matrix and the number of possible transformations frequently restrict the key space in these systems, which can weaken the encryption and make it more vulnerable to attacks. Finally,

Rows-columns diffusion and Hill diffusion are fixed techniques that may not be easily customizable for different types of images or data, limiting their flexibility.

3 Proposed Survey of Encryption Algorithms

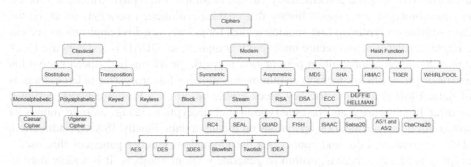

Fig. 2. Classification of standard Encryption Algorithms

As depicted in the above diagram, standard encryption algorithms are classified into three categories: classical, modern, and hash function. Classical encryption algorithms, such as Caesar Cipher and Playfair Cipher, were widely used in ancient times and are based on substitution and transposition techniques [25]. Modern encryption algorithms, like RSA and Elliptic Curve Cryptography (ECC), are based on mathematical complexity and are used in different types security applications for transmitting data, digital signatures, and key exchange in a secured way [29]. Hash functions, such as SHA-256 and MD5, are used for data integrity and to establish the authenticity of digital information [28]. Understanding the different features of encryption algorithms is necessary for promising the security of data transmission and maintaining data confidentiality (Fig. 2).

In the realm of encryption techniques, substitution ciphers and transposition are two distinct approaches. While a transposition cipher jumbles the order of characters to produce an encrypted message, a substitution cipher replaces the original characters with predetermined substitutes, adhering to a predefined pattern.

In the world of encryption, there are two main methods: symmetric and asymmetric. Symmetric encryption, like a secret handshake, uses the same key to both lock and unlock the data. Asymmetric encryption, on the other hand, is like a mailbox with a public slot for anyone to drop in messages and a private key only the owner holds to open them. While asymmetric encryption is more secure, symmetric encryption is faster and simpler, but you need to carefully share the secret key.

For securing data in modern communication networks, symmetric key encryption algorithms play a crucial role. AES, the Advanced Encryption Standard, stands out as a widely adopted encryption algorithm, standardized by the US National Institute of Standards and Technology in 2001. It operates with a fixed block size of 128 bits and offers key sizes of 128, 192, or 256 bits. AES has gained widespread recognition due to its robust security, efficiency, and straightforward implementation.

RC4, SEAL, QUAD, FISH, and ISAAC are all important encryption algorithms widely used in various security applications. RC4, developed by Ron Rivest in 1987, is a popular stream cipher known for its speed and efficiency, and has been used in SSL/TLS, WEP, and WPA protocols [26, 30]. However, it has been found to have several security compromises, making it no longer suitable for modern encryption applications. There are variations of the RC algorithm, including RC2, RC4, RC5, and RC6, which are still used due to their speed and efficiency. SEAL, or Simple Encrypted Arithmetic Library, is a homomorphic encryption library that enables arithmetic operations on encrypted data without decrypting it first, making it ideal for privacy-sensitive applications such as encrypted databases and secure multi-party computation. QUAD is a symmetric block cipher based on a substitution-permutation network, providing high-speed encryption and decryption with low memory requirements, allowing fast processing of large amounts of data. FISH is a symmetric key block cipher based on a Feistel network designed to offer high security and fast encryption and decryption, using multiple rounds of substitution and permutation operations on the input data. Finally, ISAAC (indirection, shift, accumulate, add, and count) is a pseudorandom number generator that uses a cryptographically secure algorithm to generate random numbers. It is widely used in cryptography and gaming applications due to its strong statistical properties and use of a combination of operations, including modular arithmetic and bitwise operations, making it a robust and reliable choice for generating random numbers.

The RSA algorithm, named after its creators Ron Rivest, Adi Shamir, and Leonard Adleman, stands as a widely adopted public key cryptography method, serving both encryption and digital signature purposes. It is extensively used for secure data transmission and is regarded as one of the most secure public key cryptography algorithms [29].

DSA, a public key cryptography algorithm developed by the National Institute of Standards and Technology (NIST) in 1991, finds its foundation in the mathematics of modular arithmetic of large prime numbers. It is utilized for digital signatures in various security applications, including PGP and SSL/TLS.

The Elliptic Curve Cryptography (ECC) algorithm utilizes the mathematics of elliptic curves to provide security for data transmission. It is commonly employed in applications demanding robust security, such as digital signatures, key exchange, and encryption. ECC is known for its efficiency, offering the same level of security as traditional public-key algorithms but with shorter keys, making it a popular choice for mobile devices and resource-constrained environments [29].

The Diffie-Hellman algorithm, developed by Whitfield Diffie and Martin Hellman in 1976, enables two parties to establish a shared secret key without revealing it to an eavesdropper. It is used in various security applications, including SSL/TLS, IPsec, and PGP, and is particularly valuable for securely exchanging keys over an insecure channel [26].

Hash functions play a crucial role in modern cryptography, serving as a means to generate fixed-length summaries, known as digests, from input messages. In hash function encryption, a fixed-length digest is the output generated by the hash function. It is a string of characters, expressed as a sequence of bits, that is a smaller size than the original message. The digest acts as a unique "fingerprint" for the input message and is used to verify its integrity, authenticity, and detect any unauthorized modifications. MD5 is one such widely-used hash function that produces a 128-bit hash value and is commonly used to verify the integrity of data. However, due to the weakness in the security, it is no longer used for securing modern applications in the field of cryptography. SHA, on the other hand, is a family of hash functions that are widely used for data integrity and are considered more secure than MD5. HMAC, a cryptographic technique that blends a hash function with a secret key, generates a unique digital signature for a message, safeguarding its authenticity and integrity. This signature acts as a tamper-proof seal, guaranteeing that any modifications to the original message will be detected ensuring its authenticity and integrity. TIGER is a fast and secure cryptographic hash function used for digital signatures and data integrity, while WHIRLPOOL is a highly secure and efficient cryptographic hash function used for digital signatures and message authentication [30].

4 Comparison of Standard Encryption Algorithm Metrics

Algorithm	Key Size	Block Size	Cipher Type	Keys	Attacks	Security	Applications
Caesar Cipher	1 (limited choices)	N/A	Substitution	Secret key (shift value)	Brute-force, Frequency Analysis	Low	Historical, Educational
Vigenere Cipher	Variable	N/A	Substitution	Keyword	Kasiski Examination, Friedman Test	Low	Historical, Educational
DES	56 bits	64 bits	Block	Single key	Differential Cryptanalysis, Brute-force	Low (deprecated, vulnerable to brute-force)	Legacy systems, Educational
3DES	112 or 168 bits	64 bits	Block	Triple keys	Meet-in-the-Middle, Brute-force	Moderate	Legacy systems, Transition from DES
RC2	Variable, typically 40-128 bits	64 bits	Block	Variable key size	Differential Cryptanalysis, Brute-force	Moderate	Legacy systems
RC4	Variable, typically 40-2048 bits	Variable	Stream	Variable key size	Fluhrer, Mantin, and Shamir (FMS) Attack	Weak (vulnerable to key recovery attacks)	WEP in Wi-Fi, Legacy systems
RC6	128, 192, or 256 bits	128 bits	Block	Variable key size	Differential Cryptanalysis, Linear Cryptanalysis	Strong	General-purpose
AES	128, 192, or 256 bits	128 bits	Block	Single key	Side-channel attacks, Differential Cryptanalysis	Strong	Widely used, Government applications
BLOWFISH	32 to 448 bits	64 bits	Block	Variable key size	Brute-force, Birthday Attacks	Moderate	General-purpose, Secure communications
Hash Function	Variable	Variable	N/A	Variable (hash value)	Collision attacks, Birthday Attacks	Depends on algorithm	Data integrity, Password storage
RSA	Key size varies (commonly 1024 to 4096 bits)	N/A	Asymmetric (Public-Key)	Public and Private keys	Factoring, Timing attacks, Side-channel attacks	Strong (depends on key size)	Public-key cryptography, Digital signatures, Secure communications
ECC	Key size varies (typically much smaller than RSA)	N/A	Asymmetric (Public-Key)	Public and Private keys	Elliptic Curve Factorization, Quantum attacks	Strong (depends on curve and key size)	Public-key cryptography, Secure communications
Diffie-Hellman	Variable	N/A	Asymmetric (Key Exchange)	Public and Private keys	Man-in-the-Middle, Quantum attacks	Strong (depends on key size)	Key exchange, Secure communications
Keyed	Variable	Variable	Variable	Variable	Dependent on specific algorithm and use case	Dependent on specific algorithm	Secure communications, Message integrity
Keyless	Variable	Variable	Variable	None	Dependent on specific algorithm and use case	Dependent on specific algorithm	Secure communications, Message integrity

Fig. 3. Metrics evaluating the performance of different standard encryption algorithms [34, 35]

The comparison table provides a concise overview of diverse standard encryption algorithms and cryptographic techniques, covering both symmetric and asymmetric key systems, stream and block ciphers, and hash functions. Each algorithm is evaluated based on key parameters, including size, type, keys, potential attacks, security strength, and applications. From historical ciphers like Caesar and Vigenere to modern standards such as AES and RSA, the table encompasses a varied array of cryptographic methods. The addition of DSA, ECC, Keyed, Keyless, Diffie-Hellman, and Transposition enhances the comparison, shedding light on their unique attributes and applications in secure communications, digital signatures, and data integrity. The findings emphasize the importance of selecting encryption algorithms based on specific security requirements and use cases, highlighting the ongoing need for robust and current cryptographic standards (Fig. 3).

5 Discussion

It has been observed that most of the research papers do not consistently employ standardized parameters when assessing the efficacy of proposed encryption algorithms. This observation highlights an area of opportunity within current research, indicating a gap in current research that can be addressed in future studies. To address this, researchers can test a range of encryption parameters, such as histogram analysis, entropy analysis, examination of correlation, differential attack, key sensitivity testing, secret key space analysis, noise attacks, and contrast analysis, to evaluate the effectiveness and security of a new proposed encryption algorithm. By conducting these tests, researchers can establish a more thorough understanding of the strengths and weaknesses of various encryption algorithms, ultimately improving the overall security of encrypted data. This highlights the need for new research to expand upon the existing literature and explore the effectiveness of proposed encryption algorithms by examining a wider range of parameters.

6 Conclusion and Future Work

Image encryption techniques such as chaotic maps, permutation, substitution, S-Box, DNA, and combinations of DNA and Chaos have certain limitations. Chaotic maps are vulnerable to attacks, potential loss of image quality, and high computational complexity. Permutation is not resistant to differential attacks and requires large key sizes for better security. Substitution is vulnerable to statistical attacks, high computational complexity, and loss of image quality due to pixel shuffling. S-Box has limited key space and is vulnerable to differential attacks. DNA is limited in use due to high computational complexity, large storage requirements. Combinations of DNA and Chaos [21] have high computational complexity, vulnerability to statistical attacks, and potential loss of image quality due to pixel shuffling. To overcome these limitations, it is essential to ascertain the security of encryption schemes, consider open research questions related to computational speed and visual quality of encrypted images, and optimize encryption schemes properly.

This paper proposes that when developing an encryption algorithm for images, it is crucial to focus on key generation and algorithm logic. Both the logic and encryption key are vital for ensuring strong encryption. The logic transforms plaintext into ciphertext, while the key determines encryption strength. To protect both the confidentiality and integrity of the data, it is advisable to use a robust algorithm with a secure and lengthy key. Employing key management techniques like key wrapping and key vaults can help secure the key. Using multiple keys, in addition to secure key management, can enhance security and increase resistance against brute force attacks.

Appendix

Sr. No.	Literature Reference	Technique Used	Contribution	Applicability	Limitation(s)
1	Alaa Farhan [18]	Chaotic system, IP permutation, S-Box substitution, Shuffling	Proposed using a chaotic system for encryption, dynamic IP permutation, and S-Box substitution	Limited applicability due to vulnerability, costs, and implementation challenges. Ideal for one-time passwords or image encryption with complex calculations. Emphasizes security preservation of chaotic maps in encryption	Chaotic encryption lacks efficiency with limited resources, vulnerable to attacks. Absence of standardized tests for encryption strength. Also, limited secure IP permutations and S-box substitutions
2	Rasika B. Naik and Udayprakash Singh [21]	Chaotic map (values between −2 and 2, rounded to 1 or 0)	Advanced chaotic map-based encryption schemes, enabling secure communication and storage of sensitive data	Applicable in encryption, Chaotic maps with values between -2 and 2 (rounded to 1 or 0) enhance security through dynamic and unpredictable patterns	Chaotic map-based encryption may not be suitable for scenarios with large computational requirements. Inadequate initialization or small key space can compromise data security
3	Aditya Jyoti Paul [23]	Chaotic maps in encryption schemes	Emphasized the importance of ensuring the security of chaotic maps in encryption schemes to avoid non-chaotic keystreams compromising data security	Important to take proper care to guarantee the security of chaotic maps in encryption schemes	Chaotic maps in encryption schemes may lead to non-chaotic keystreams if not properly secured

(*continued*)

(*continued*)

Sr. No.	Literature Reference	Technique Used	Contribution	Applicability	Limitation(s)
4	Jiangjian Xu, Bing Zhao, and Zeming Wu [24]	Classical chaotic systems, unique keys for different images	Enhanced security through unique keys assigned to different images and alterations in information changing the key of the image encryption	Useful for medical image encryption, enhances security with unique keys. Limitations include low entropy, susceptibility to attacks, and potential loss of image quality in medical applications	May not be suitable for medical applications requiring high entropy and precise image analysis and diagnosis
5	Warit Sirichotedumrong, Yuma Kinoshita [19]	Homomorphic encryption, exemplified by the Paillier scheme, enables computations to be performed on encrypted data. Performing data augmentation within the encrypted domain	DNN privacy - preserving approach that permits testing with plain images without the need for key management, while also allowing training with encrypted images	Enables training of DNN models with encrypted images, preserving privacy without the need for decryption by the server	Model theft vulnerability, high computational overhead

(*continued*)

(*continued*)

Sr. No.	Literature Reference	Technique Used	Contribution	Applicability	Limitation(s)
6	VARSHA HIMTHANI [20]	Various VMEI techniques categorized and evaluated	The evaluation of VMEI techniques involves an analysis focused on security, encryption key vulnerabilities, quality assessment, and susceptibility to noise-based attacks	VMEI techniques show promise in secure image transmission	Resource-intensive compared to traditional encryption. Downsides include image detail loss, higher storage needs, and susceptibility to statistical attacks compromising privacy/security
7	Ratheesh Kumar R, Jabin Mathew [21]	Combination of DNA and Chaos	DNA and Chaos combination for data encryption, providing high-level security	Offers a high level of security, especially with DNA sequencing. Traditional encryption methods may not be sufficient to keep data safe	High computation cost, complex implementation, inefficiency in real-time processing, scant security research, sluggish DNA sequence read/write, risk of data corruption/loss from sequencing errors/mutations
8	Hamed Ghazanfaripoura and Ali Broumandnia [22]	Rows-columns diffusion, Hill diffusion, modular arithmetic	Method for encrypting gray-scale images, using math operations for diffusion and modular arithmetic to increase security	It is very sensitive to key and image changes making it difficult for attackers to use thier preexisting information to break encryption	Less secure than advanced methods, susceptible to attacks, inefficient with large data or real-time processing, higher storage needs, limited customization for various image types

References

1. Li, T., Du, B., Liang, X.: Image encryption algorithm based on logistic, and two-dimensional Lorenz. IEEE Access **8**, 13792–13805 (2020). https://doi.org/10.1109/ACCESS.2020.296 6264
2. Jun, W.J., Fun, T.S.: A new image encryption algorithm based on single s-box and dynamic encryption step. IEEE Access **9**, 120596–120612 (2021). https://doi.org/10.1109/ACCESS. 2021.3108789
3. Verma, A., Kaur, S., Chhabra, B.: Design and development of robust algorithm for cryptography using improved AES technique (2017)
4. Naser, S.M.: Cryptography: from the ancient history to now, its applications and a new complete numerical model. Int. J. Math. Stat. Stud. **9**(3), 11–30 (2021). https://ssrn.com/abstract= 3889471
5. Asoronye, G.O., Emereonye, G.I., Onyibe, C.O., Agha, I.A.: An efficient implementation for the cryptanalysis of Caesar's cipher. Melting Pot **5**(2) (2019). https://journals.aphriapub.com/index.php/TMP/article/view/1046
6. Selleri, S.: The roots of modern cryptography: Leon Battista Alberti's "De Cifris." URSI Radio Sci. Bull. **2020**(375), 55–63 (2020). https://doi.org/10.23919/URSIRSB.2020.9663133
7. Jain, P., Kohle, S.: Variation of playfair cipher. In: 2022 5th International Conference on Advances in Science and Technology (ICAST), Mumbai, India, pp. 417–421. IEEE (2022). https://doi.org/10.1109/ICAST55766.2022.10039526
8. Gaj, K., Orłowski, A.: Facts and myths of enigma: breaking stereotypes. In: Biham, E. (ed.) EUROCRYPT 2003. LNCS, vol. 2656, pp. 106–122. Springer, Heidelberg (2003). https://doi.org/10.1007/3-540-39200-9_7
9. van Oorschot, P.C.: Public key cryptography's impact on society: how Diffie and Hellman changed the world. In: Democratizing Cryptography (2022)
10. Singh, A., Agarwal, P., Chand, M.: Image encryption and analysis using dynamic AES. In: 2019 5th International Conference on Optimization and Applications (ICOA). IEEE (2019). https://doi.org/10.1109/icoa.2019.8727711
11. Pavithra, V., Jeyamala, C.: A survey on the techniques of medical image encryption. In: 2018 IEEE International Conference on Computational Intelligence and Computing Research (ICCIC), Madurai, India, pp. 1–8 (2018). https://doi.org/10.1109/ICCIC.2018.8782432
12. Xu, H., Thakur, K., Kamruzzaman, A.S., Ali, M.L.: Applications of cryptography in database: a review. In: 2021 IEEE International IOT, Electronics and Mechatronics Conference (IEMTRONICS), Toronto, ON, Canada, pp. 1–6 (2021). https://doi.org/10.1109/IEMTRONICS52119.2021.9422663
13. Jasra, B., Moon, A.H.: Image encryption techniques: a review. In: 2020 10th International Conference on Cloud Computing, Data Science & Engineering (Confluence), Noida, India, pp. 221–226. IEEE (2020). https://doi.org/10.1109/Confluence47617.2020.9058071
14. Rupa, I.S., Manideep, K., Kamale, N.M., Suhasini, S.: Information security using chaotic encryption and decryption of digital images. In: 2022 International Conference on Innovative Computing, Intelligent Communication and Smart Electrical Systems (ICSES), Chennai, India, pp. 1–7. IEEE (2022). https://doi.org/10.1109/ICSES55317.2022.9914081
15. Huang, M., Yang, C., Zhang, Y.: Selective encryption of H.264/AVC based on block weight model. In: 2018 IEEE 18th International Conference on Communication Technology (ICCT), Chongqing, China, pp. 1368–1373 (2018). https://doi.org/10.1109/ICCT.2018.8599959
16. Menezes, A., Stebila, D.: Challenges in cryptography. IEEE Secur. Priv. **19**(2), 70–73 (2021). https://doi.org/10.1109/MSEC.2021.3049730
17. Kiya, H.: Progress and challenges in compressible and learnable image encryption for privacy-preserving image encryption and machine learning [keynote]. In: 2020 12th International

Conference on Knowledge and Smart Technology (KST), Pattaya, Thailand, pp. XV–XV (2020). https://doi.org/10.1109/KST48564.2020.9059423

18. Abdallah, A., Farhan, A.: A new image encryption algorithm based on a multi chaotic system. Iraqi J. Sci. 324–337 (2022). https://doi.org/10.24996/ijs.2022.63.1.31

19. Sirichotedumrong, W., Maekawa, T., Kinoshita, Y., Kiya, H.: Privacy-preserving deep neural networks with pixel-based image encryption considering data augmentation in the encrypted domain. In: 2019 IEEE International Conference on Image Processing (ICIP), Taipei, Taiwan, pp. 674–678 (2019). https://doi.org/10.1109/ICIP.2019.8804201

20. Himthani, V., et al.: Systematic survey on visually meaningful imageencryption techniques. IEEE (2022)

21. Ratheesh Kumar, R., Mathew, J.: Image encryption: traditional methods vs alternative methods. In: IEEE 2020 Fourth International Conference on Computing Methodologies and Communication (ICCMC), Erode, India, pp. 1–7 (2020). https://doi.org/10.1109/ICCMC48092.2020.ICCMC-000115

22. Ghazanfaripour, H., Broumandnia, A.: Designing a digital image encryption scheme using chaotic maps with prime modularity. Opt. Laser Technol. **131**, 106339 (2020). https://doi.org/10.1016/j.optlastec.2020.106339

23. Paul, A.J.: Recent advances in selective image encryption and its indispensability due to COVID-19. In: 2020 IEEE Recent Advances in Intelligent Computational Systems (RAICS), Thiruvananthapuram, India, pp. 201–206 (2020). https://doi.org/10.1109/RAICS51191.2020.9332513

24. Xu, J., Zhao, B., Wu, Z.: Research on color image encryption algorithm based on bit-plane and chen chaotic system. Electronic Engineering College, Heilongjiang University, Harbin 150080, China (2022)

25. Sanchez, J., Correa, R., Buenaño, H., Arias, S., Gomez, H.: Encryption techniques: a theoretical overview and future proposals. In: 2016 IEEE Third International Conference on eDemocracy & eGovernment (ICEDEG), Sangolqui, Ecuador, pp. 60–64 (2016). https://doi.org/10.1109/ICEDEG.2016.7461697

26. Mota, A.V., Azam, S., Shanmugam, B., Yeo, K.C., Kannoorpatti, K.: Comparative analysis of different techniques of encryption for secured data transmission. In: 2017 IEEE International Conference on Power, Control, Signals and Instrumentation Engineering (ICPCSI), Chennai, India, pp. 231–237 (2017). https://doi.org/10.1109/ICPCSI.2017.8392158

27. Qian, Y., Ye; F., Chen, H.-H.: Cryptographic techniques. In: Security in Wireless Communication Networks, pp. 51–76. IEEE (2022). https://doi.org/10.1002/9781119244400.ch4

28. Wang, J., Liu, G., Chen, Y., Wang, S.: Construction and analysis of SHA-256 compression function based on chaos S-box. IEEE Access **9**, 61768–61777 (2021). https://doi.org/10.1109/ACCESS.2021.3071501

29. Singh, S.R., Khan, A.K., Singh, S.R.: Performance evaluation of RSA and elliptic curve cryptography. In: 2016 IEEE 2nd International Conference on Contemporary Computing and Informatics (IC3I), Greater Noida, India, pp. 302–306 (2016). https://doi.org/10.1109/IC3I.2016.7917979

30. Zhuoyu, H., Yongzhen, L.: Design and implementation of efficient hash functions. In: 2022 IEEE 2nd International Conference on Power, Electronics and Computer Applications (ICPECA), Shenyang, China, pp. 1240–1243 (2022). https://doi.org/10.1109/ICPECA53709.2022.9719176

31. Sharma, B., Goel, P., Grewal, J.K.: Advances and challenges in cryptography using artificial intelligence. In: 2023 IEEE 8th International Conference for Convergence in Technology (I2CT), Lonavla, India, pp. 1–5 (2023). https://doi.org/10.1109/I2CT57861.2023.10126338

32. Zahid, A.H., Al-Solami, E., Ahmad, M.: A novel modular approach based substitution-box design for image encryption. IEEE Access **8**, 150326–150340 (2020). https://doi.org/10.1109/ACCESS.2020.3016401

33. Merkle, R.C.: A digital signature based on a conventional encryption function. In: Pomerance, C. (ed.) CRYPTO 1987. LNCS, vol. 293, pp. 369–378. Springer, Heidelberg (1988). https://doi.org/10.1007/3-540-48184-2_32

34. Sawant, T., Khurud, A., Das, S., Jillawar, S., Katti, J.: A survey paper on audio security. J. Inf. Technol. Sci. **4**(3) (2018)

35. Patil, L.K., Popat, K.A.: Comparative analysis of several approaches of encoding audio files. In: Rajagopal, S., Faruki, P., Popat, K. (eds.) ASCIS 2022. CCIS, vol. 1760, pp. 128–143. Springer, Cham (2022). https://doi.org/10.1007/978-3-031-23095-0_10

Optimizing the Security and Privacy of Cloud Data Communication; Hybridizing Cryptography and Steganography Using Triple Key of AES, RSA and LSB with Deceptive QR Code Technique: A Novel Approach

Edwin Xorsenyo Amenu[✉] and Sridaran Rajagopal

Faculty of Computer Applications, Marwadi University, Rajkot, India
eddynap@gmail.com, sridaran.rajagopal@marwadieducation.edu.in

Abstract. The propensity of transmitting improperly protected data in the clouds securely to its intended destination, free of being intercepted and deciphered is highly low in this fast advancing technological era. Specialist in the field of data and information security have over the past multiple decades tried and experimented quite a number of hashing combinations, but not sufficiently enough to forestall the interception and deciphering of secret text in transit. This security concern of private and confidential information of either individuals, groups or institutions ending up plainly in the wrong third party hands, therefore, spark the need to absolutely encrypt and steganography data in such a securely deceptive manner above the knowledge of the 'Man-In-The-Middle'. The two current novel techniques that cybersecurity experts are exploring are the permutation of cryptography and steganography. We the authors in this paper will hence, explore a newer and higher dynamics of the combined data security technique. Methodologically, cryptography and steganography method will be diversified into using three (3) encryption keys under deceptive generated QR Code.

Keywords: Algorithm · QR Code · RSA · AES · LSB · Encryption · Decryption · Cryptography · Stego

1 Introduction

Ever since the emergence and daily growth of computer systems and its internet of things systems, data and information has as always been communicated from on source node to another destination node. Both the channels of communication and the form of data being transferred vary from time to time. For instance, the data could be in form of a video, text, image etcetera, and transmitted over one cloud system to the other, a computer network to another or email to email among others. This needs to transfer data over the internet, requires a very well fixed robust security system, as well as a securely protected data, otherwise, a poorly secured data in transfer can be severely compromised [1]. The usage of cloud to send confidential data and information across the internet to an

S. Rajagopal et al. (Eds.): ASCIS 2023, CCIS 2039, pp. 291–306, 2024.
https://doi.org/10.1007/978-3-031-59100-6_21

intended destination is fast becoming unsafe. This is significantly impacted by moment by moment immense reliance on the internet by organizations and individuals to get data or information from a point to another point [2].

The same data on the desktop of a computer may be somewhat secure; but even that the file or data possesses the tendency of becoming infectious of viruses and malwares thereby culminating in the loss of data.. And so, the premium placed on security for both data and system is crucial against hacking attempts [1].

Cryptography includes the act of studying and employing the practices of securing private message, information or data from being accessed by an unauthorized third parties through the adoption of communication techniques that are proven to be secured. This process involves the areas of information security disciplines like integrity, authentication, integrity (CIA) and non-repudiation which is the pivotal field of contemporary cryptography [2–4].

Encrypting data or information in the cloud-computing environment is of a key concern to researchers. The instance of focusing encryption on identification is very important. This is because information or data in the cloud is managed to the extent of its being accessed by anyone with the requisite authorization at any location with internet connectivity [2]. Cryptography helps in securing data that is in transmission across a network, data in electronic commerce, the privacy of data in digital media, data in the web transmission and storage environment. Different and various types of encryption algorithms have been proffered and implemented since the outset of the concept. Among these, include. DES - Data Encryption Standard, AES – Advanced Encryption Standard, IBE – Identity Based Encryption, and RSA – Rivest, Sharmir, Adleman [3].

Data encryption can take two main forms. Thus, symmetric and asymmetric. Symmetric Encryption uses one same key to encrypt and decrypt files and data. Symmetric key is a very old method of ciphering and deciphering plaintext, and mostly chosen when transferring huge amount of data. In symmetric encryption, both the sender and recipient of data or information share the same encryption algorithm key for both purposes of encryption and decryption respectively. The process of using the same key for encryption and decryption becomes a fallout to symmetric encryption as against asymmetric encryption. Examples include DES, Blowfish, MID5, AES etcetera [4].

Asymmetric Encryption is universally considered as more secured type of encryption than that of symmetric encryption. With this kind of encryption, two (2) different keys are used: one set of key for encryption from the sender side, while another is used by the recipient for the decryption of encrypted file or message. Hence, asymmetric encryption is able to shroud the recipient intended message in secrecy until it gets to the destination, and subsequently decrypted. Therefore, unlike symmetric encryption that makes use of the public key, and if revealed, it can lead to tampering of the message, the asymmetric algorithm encryption is more secure, since it uses both public key (for encryption) and private key (for decryption). Example of the mostly used asymmetric encryption types are RSA, Diffie-Hellman, Elliptic curve techniques, and PKCS algorithm [3].

AES, Advanced Encryption Standard, functions a symmetric block cipher that is able to encrypt. AES makes use of plain text using blocks of 128 bits, with keys of 128, 192, and 256 translating it into a cipher text. AES is able to specify the total number of plaintext that is transformed into a cipher text. This is indicated by the key size that is used in the AES cipher process. The rounds involves in transforming AES blocks are multiplying processes of stages, dependent on the particular key applied during encryption. With a number of reversing rounds, the cipher text will then be converted into plaintext. One disadvantage in using AES encryption method is that its algebraic structure is very simple, and therefore difficult to implement [3].

RSA, Rivest-Shamir-Adleman is a very common algorithm used in encrypting and decrypting text. In most cases, it is not used alone, but rather stringed together with some other encrypting algorithms and very commonly applied with digitally appended signatures to confirm whether a message is legitimate and valid. RSA is not all alone very dependable. It does not also demand much resource to implement as compared to symmetric encryption method. In most cases, it is hard to see RSA algorithm used all alone in encrypting data. For efficient enhanced security benefits, RSA is mostly combined with some other different encryption algorithm(s). In decrypting RSA encrypted data the recipient needs to have the private key, whilst a public key is used to encrypt the intended message [3].

Steganography is an old science and art of hiding data or message that is secret in another cover message. This concept helps significantly in embedding information or data under an image, video, and etcetera. Meanwhile, the hiding of data in files is very vital in steganography. This art helps to secure or insulate data from the ʻ"bad boys" [2, 5]. However, with cryptography when an encrypted message is communicated to the third party, the data or intended message can easily be decrypted, and even destroyed. However, with steganography secret data is hidden within or behind files used as a cover. So that in communicating, the hidden data it can block largely unwanted suspicion for access. This phenomenon of concealing information behind image is image steganography. In this concept, a text or data is covered with image from the sender through the channel of communication to the recipient. Therefore, even if a hacker intercepts the image in most cases, they are unsuspecting of having data or message concealed behind it. Upon the arrival of stegno message at the recipient destination, stegno tools are used for the purposes of decrypting the image to access the concealed data or information. Example of such tools exist in different formats such as test, videos, audios, images, and among others [6].

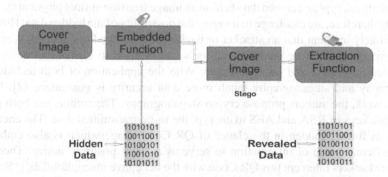

Fig. 1. Steganography Image Process Functional Diagram

The Fig. 1 above, illustrates least significant bit (LSB). The application of LSB steganography algorithm approach, comprises eight (8) bits, as well as the least significant number eight (8) which changes into the data bit of eight as well [3]. LSB steganography algorithm approach is considered faster, computationally simpler, easier in implementation with a higher fidelity quality when compared to some other steganography algorithm techniques. In view of LSB strength over other techniques in steganography, this research paper chooses to instrumentalize its algorithm techniques to hide messages for communication to the recipient or the intended receiver securely and safely.

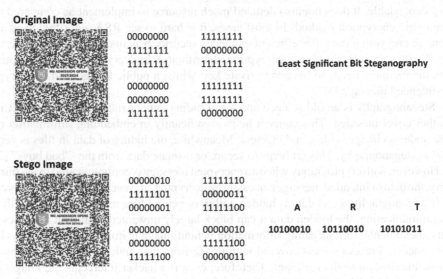

Fig. 2. Outlook of Both Original and Cover Images in Data Embedding Process

In Fig. 2 the data, 'ART' is concealed under the image by applying LSB algorithm. Stego cover image appears to maintain the same pixels just as the original image.

Crypto-Steganography is the combining of both the cryptography and steganography techniques to encrypt and embed data behind an image from the normal physical eyesight. Attackers therefore, are challenge to imagine the possibility of the hidden data. However, in the unlikely incident that an attacker or hacker recovers the keys applied, varying of encrypting and decrypting methods and tools can be used to extract and decrypt the transmitted embedded and encrypted data. With the application of both technique of cryptography and steganography much more data security is guaranteed [2]. In this research work, the authors propose crypto-steganography. The authors use both public and private keys of RSA and AES to encrypt the to-be-transmitted data. The encrypted message is further hidden in the clatter of QR Code image which is also embedded with a different piece of information to serve as a "false positive" notice. Therefore, perchance hackers intercept this QR Code with the deceptive inscription/label "Scan for details", it becomes extremely difficult for them to think otherwise. Thus, to conjecture the thought that another secondary message is embedded behind and beyond the first QR Code message.

2 Related Work

The rate and frequency at which consumers of data transmit data over the cloud has more than double in the current age. In view of this ascendency, user authentication concerns coupled with the security of the data in transit in the cloud has drawn enormous attention of security specialist in research:

Using image to cover an encrypted data for transfer in the clouds is suggested by [2] in their work. The authors apply LSB algorithm technique for the embedding of data in the images. For encrypting the data, XOR algorithm is applied. The researchers in their work are able to hide data pseudo-randomly in images. Nevertheless, the researchers' research work lacks many noticeable amount of modern data securing techniques. Even though, the interface application uses LSB, which is an up to date image-hiding algorithm in hiding data, the data encryption algorithm is outdated.

The scholar, [7], researches on applying LSB algorithm/technique in MATLAB to secure data behind an image for transmission. The researcher uses the method of LSB steganography towards the goal of using any image to cover a plaintext from direct eyesight or reading. With this method, the researcher achieves the result of protecting data with image whether in transit or in cloud storage. In the research, the strength of the algorithm of the steganography program is in the fact that it is difficult to predict the original length and position of the hidden bits. However, the steganography algorithm of the data hiding process is excessively cumbersome and therefore, rather a weakness. This is because before a user uses this steganography program to embed a message, it requires that the users know the length of the message, and accordingly append the exact length of the message at the start of the steganography process, followed by the name of the file and its supported extension. In addition, the security of the data of the LSB steganography is able to disconnect one-to-one mapping between the secret bits and the LSBs intended cover.

[6] focus their research on embedding either a simple text or video under an image using the techniques of sLSB. Fuzzy Logic and Neural Network to secure information. But, the scholars algorithm acts as payload, lacks heftiness, it is too heavily loaded with many methods, and thereby presenting several week points. Their algorithm is also not modern and does not factor in the security of others.

Preserving privacy in the cloud scheme is recommended in the work of [8]. The research narrows down on the use of Apriori algorithm by using Elgamal cryptosystem. The authors do not include fake transactions when encrypting data. Their algorithm supports the privacy of both database and query. It also hides data frequency in the cloud. The proposed algorithm attains a higher speed 3–5 times when compared with existing algorithms. However, even though the researchers' proposed algorithm hides data as a whole, it falls short of hiding and unhiding/encrypting and decrypting each field of data in the cloud.

In the bid to contribute to securing the privacy of data that is communicated in the cloud, [4], also make use of both cryptography and steganography techniques. The authors combine the two techniques using CP-ABE based algorithm. In their work, the researchers first encrypted a plaintext before concealing it in an image to preserve it from suspicious hackers while it is in transport in the cloud. In the researchers work, even though, the authors successfully hide the intended message for communication over the internet, the user interface lacks adequate security authentication processing for remote cloud users along with user revocation characteristics.

According to [9], the intended secret message in their research work to be communicated is ciphered using Hill cipher along with elliptic cryptography curve (ECC) for the aim of attaining an optimized security. The authors at the same time, still employ ECC algorithm to generate the user authentication key. The recipients' secret encrypted message, is further enhanced with secrecy by hiding it behind a cover image, which is executed with the algorithms of DCT and LSB. The authors in furtherance subdivided their message targeted at a recipient into smaller divisions before transmitting them separately. With the approach of subdividing messages before transmission, if a subdivided block of message/text is intercepted in the process, then the completeness of the whole text is tempered with. Also, both Hill cipher and DWT algorithms are outdated, and therefore, susceptible to easy decryption should a hacker intercept such a message in the process of transfer.

3 Proposed System

Cryptography and steganography are integrated to hide encrypted text/message behind a QR Code image in this current proposed scheme. Per the model, it is very challenging to depend on the human eye to tell any difference between the QR Code cover image and that of the stego image.

3.1 Methodology

In this paper, private key of AES is employed as random primary encryption method to produce the series of structure of pixels adequate for storing the concealed data. Prior to embedding the data intended for transfer, the data first of all undergoes an encryption process using algorithms generated from the encryption and decryption methods of AES and RSA. The authors of this paper make use of only deceptive QR Code image system, which is also encrypted by employing the coding technique of LSB. For the embedding of data; because all QR Codes are naturally generated with some level of noise, hence, any hacker who even intercepts the stego image, will by instinct with the natural eye finds it extremely difficult to strike any iota of difference between it and that of the cover image.

The cloud storage system of this paper is developed with such a precision of security authentication that only the legally authorized person possessing the bonafide login credentials can access it for the decryption of text that is communicated. The account login credentials require the use of username, email, and RSA private key generated password at the time of creating and encrypting the data by the sender. Public key is however, used to encrypt the inputted password which is stored, and hashed with **SHA256** and stored in the application database.

For decryption to be successful there is a prior requirement for password match, hence, the sender is able to check and confirm the sameness of the hashed password entered. Once this double verification is successful, a **JWT token** that is valid for an hour is generated for the user for authorization lateron.

Also, as part of embedding data into the QR Code image the authors embed every bit of text into every single element of RGB, moving away from the normal of embedding every bit into the three (3) elements of RGB at a time. This therefore, contributes significantly to making it once again hard for hackers to figure out the number of bits of data that is concealed in any given pixels of image at a time.

A. Account Registration, Login, and Logout Algorithm Methods
A1. RSA Account Registration Method

- Permission classes ➜ allow any.
- Collect username, email address and password from request.
- Generate RSA public and private keys and store them as PEM files:
- public key, privateKey = rsa.newkeys (2048)
- Encrypt user's password with the generated public key and store in database as **identifier**.
- Equally, hash the password with SHA512 and store in database.
- Return the private key PEM file to the user in the response.

A2. Account Login Method

- Permission classes ➜ allow any.
- Collect username, password, and private key PEM file from the request.
- Retrieve Account object from database matching provided username.
- Hash the password and check if the password matches hashed password.
- Read private key PEM file and use it to decrypt encrypted password (**identifier**).
- If decrypted password matches password provided by user, generate JWT access (valid for an hour) and refresh (valid for a day) tokens for future authorization.
- Return generated tokens as cookies in response data.

A3. Account Logout Method

- Permission classes ➜ is authenticated.
- Blacklist access, refresh tokens, and delete token cookies created.

B. Data Encryption and Sharing
B1. Share AES Data Encryption Algorithm Method

- Permission classes ➜ is authenticated.
- Collect receiver's ID in request.
- Ensure there is no active key already shared between sender and receiver.
- Generate AES key, encrypt with sender's public key, and store as **sender's aes.**
- Encrypt the same AES key with the receiver's public key and store as **receiver aes.**
- Return success status to sender/user.

B2. Share AES Encrypted Data Method

- Permission classes ➜ is authenticated.
- Collect the receiver's ID, message being shared and sender's private key.
- Ensure there is an active AES shared key between sender and receiver.
- Retrieve AES shared key between the parties.
- Read sender's encrypted private key file and use private key to decrypt **sender aes** (encrypted AES key).

B3. AES Data Decryption Algorithm Method

- Permission classes ➔ is authenticated, object permission.
- Collect the message ID and the sender/receiver's private key PEM file from the request.
- Ensure user making request is the sender or receiver of the message.
- Ensure the shared AES key used to send message is still active.
- Retrieve the shared AES key between the parties.
- Read the user's private key PEM file and use it to decrypt the **sender aes** or the **receiver aes** (encrypted shared AES key).
- Use the decrypted shared AES to decrypt the encrypted message and return the message to the user.

C. QR Code Image Encryption and Decryption Algorithm Method
C1. LSB QR Code Encryption Algorithm Method

- Permission classes ➔ is authenticated.
- Collect the receiver's id, the message being shared, the image being used, and the sender's private key.
- Ensure an active shared AES key exists between the sender and receiver.
- Retrieve the shared AES key.
- Read the sender's private key PEM file and use it to decrypt the **sender aes** (encrypted shared AES key).
- Use the decrypted AES key to encrypt the message being shared.
- Use LSB stego method to hide the encrypted message behind the image provided.
- Store the modified image in the database and return a success status to the user.

C2. LSB QR Code Decryption Algorithm

- Permission classes ➔ is authenticated, object permission.
- Collect the message ID and the sender's/receiver's private key PEM file from the request.
- Ensure user making request is the sender or receiver of the message.
- Ensure the shared AES key used to send message is still active.
- Retrieve the shared AES key between the parties.
- Read the user's private key PEM file and use it to decrypt the **sender aes** or the **receiver aes** (encrypted shared AES key).
- Retrieve the image being decrypted from the database and use the extract method of the python lsb to recover the hidden encrypted message.
- Use the decrypted shared AES to decrypt the encrypted message and return the message to the user.

D. Encryption and Decryption System Architecture
(See Fig. 3).

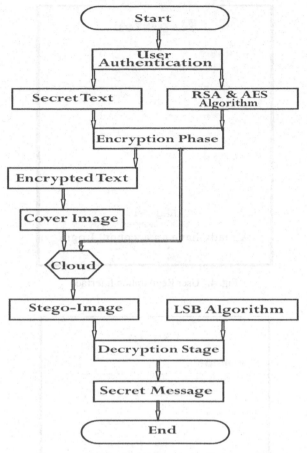

Fig. 3. System Architecture

4 Discusion

The authors create in this research paper a cloud-based application to grant an authorized access to only the legitimate registrants of the application to interact and share messages with key, among themselves by engaging in the sharing of QR Code image link as a camouflage.

A. Users' Registration and Login Interfaces
(See Figs. 4 and 5).

Register

Username:

Email:

Password:

Register

Already have an account? Login here.

Fig. 4. User Registration Interface

Login

Username:

Password:

Private Key:

Browse... No file selected.

Login

Don't have an account? Register here.

Fig. 5. User Login Interface

B. Message Input, Image and Key Selection

In this Fig. 6, the user 'A' is able to typed the message for communication, and selects the decryption private key for user 'B'.

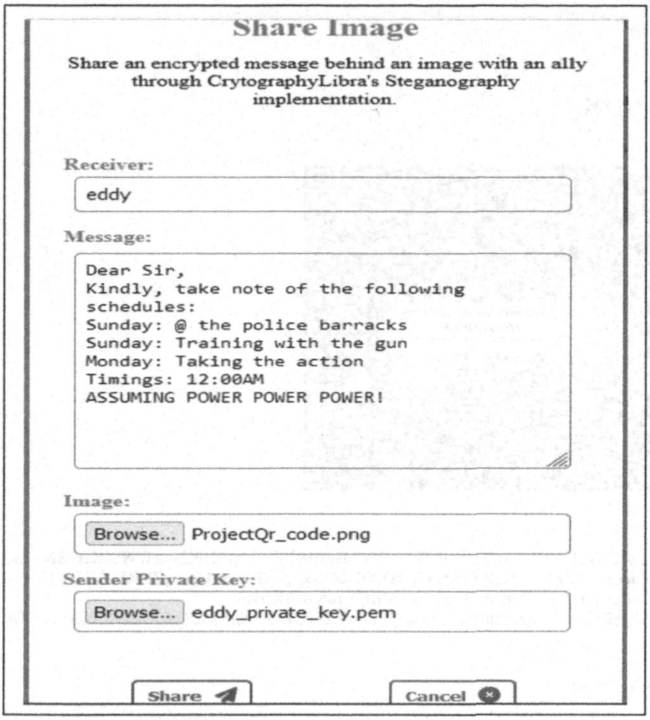

Fig. 6. Message Input, Image and Key Selection Interface

C. Encryption Interfaces

The Fig. 7 below displays the interface of text encryption by the user 'A'. The user firstly, inputs in the interface the intended to-be-sent message, encrypts it, and selects the deceptive QR Code to embed the typed message to be sent in separate email message to user 'B'.

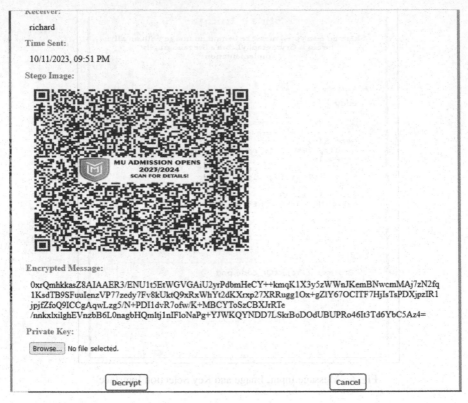

Fig. 7. Data Encryption and Image Embedding Display Interface

D. Data, Decryption Key and Stego Image Sharing Interface

In Fig. 8 below, the interface highlights the occurrence of sharing of data between the two (2) users ('A' & 'B') of the application system. It is also, at this interface, that the user 'A' is able to transmit the data decryption key of the user 'B' separately, by entering the user ID of the registered user in the share key section on the portal.

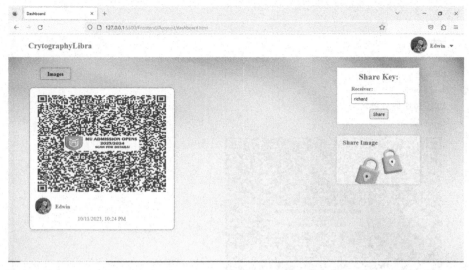

Fig. 8. Data Sharing and Decryption Key Sharing and Stego Image Display Interface between User 'A' & 'B'

E. Decryption Interfaces
In this Fig. 9, user 'B' is able to reveal the ciphertext into a plaintext after clicking on the Reveal/Decrypt button which is exposed by clicking on the stego image to use their ID and key.

F. Images Comparison.
In Fig. 10 below, there is the display of the quality of the cover image prior to its use for embedding data.

Figure 11 shows the quality presentation of the stego image. Thus, how the QR Code image looks after it is used to hide the encrypted text behind it. In close natural eye comparison view, one can strongly avers that there is no detection of distorted and noisy quality in the stego image when compared with the original cover image.

Fig. 9. Data Decryption by User 'B' Displaying the Receipt of Message Hidden in QR Code Image from User 'A'

Fig. 10. Cover Image.

Fig. 11. Stego Image.

5 Conclusion

We, the authors in this research achieve a hybridized degree of security as well as privacy, as a result of combining cryptography and steganography using deceptive QR Code and LSB, AES, and RSA algorithms. This research, unlike some previous works is able to embed the intended communicated message into cover image successfully without nuances of noises to the physical human eye in the image that could spark a third party suspicion even if the cover image is intercepted along with the stego image. And also, both the cover image and the stega QR Codes are able to be read by the QR Scanner at the same distance/interval thereby killing off any suspicions relating to scanning differences in interval. The research is able to bridge the security lapses that exist in preceding researches since several different encrypting algorithms are integrated thereby securely elevating confidence and reliability in the cloud communicated data. Even though, there are a number of developing techniques to detect and capture embedded messages, however, in this paper, even if the transferred data is intercepted it does not guarantee the acquisition and retrieval of the transmitted embedded message since the decryption key is communicated to the intended target recipient separately from the decryption link to the application platform via email. The application system will be hosted online for usage by the interested public.

References

1. Islam, M.A., Pias, T.S.: Enhancing security of image steganography using visual cryptography, pp. 694–698 (2021)
2. Nunna, K.C., Marapareddy, R.: Secure data transfer through internet using cryptography and image steganography. In: Conference Proceedings - IEEE SOUTHEASTCON, vol. 2 (2020). https://doi.org/10.1109/SoutheastCon44009.2020.9368301

3. Adee, R., Mouratidis, H.: A dynamic four-step data security model for data in cloud computing based on cryptography and steganography, pp. 1–23 (2022)
4. Reshma, V., Gladwin, S.J., Thiruvenkatesan, C.: Pairing-free CP-ABE based cryptography combined with steganography for multimedia applications. In: 2019 International Conference on Communication and Signal Processing, pp. 501–505 (2019)
5. Chandra, S., Paira, S.: Secure transmission of data using image steganography, no. October (2019). https://doi.org/10.21917/ijivp.2019.0291
6. Manohar, N., Kumar, P.V.: Data encryption decryption using steganography. In: Proceedings of the International Conference on Intelligent Computing and Control Systems, ICICCS 2020, no. Iciccs, pp. 697–702 (2020). https://doi.org/10.1109/ICICCS48265.2020.9120935
7. Rafat, K.F.: Nondeterministic secure LSB steganography for digital images. In: 1st Annual International Conference on Cyber Warfare and Security, ICCWS 2020 – Proceedings (2020). https://doi.org/10.1109/ICCWS48432.2020.9292369
8. Kim, H.J., Shin, J.H., Song, Y.H., Chang, J.W.: Privacy-preserving association rule mining algorithm for encrypted data in cloud computing. In: IEEE International Conference on Cloud Computing, CLOUD, vol. 2019-July, pp. 487–489 (2019). https://doi.org/10.1109/CLOUD.2019.00086
9. Gladwin, S.J., Gowthami, P.L.: Combined cryptography and steganography for enhanced security in suboptimal images, pp. 1–5 (2020)

Fuzzy Membership Grasshopper Optimization Algorithm (FMGOA) Based Feature Selection and Mean Weight Deep Belief Network (MWDBN) Classifier with Fusion Approach for Android Malware Detection (AMD)

Anuja A. Rajan[(✉)] and R. Durga

Department of Computer Science, VISTAS, Chennai, India
anujapdm@gmail.com

Abstract. Android applications have been an obvious advancement recently, making them one of the technological domains is advancing and successful the fastest. The necessity for active research efforts are presented to conflict these dangerous programs which develops vital as malware gets more and more capable of insightful these applications. In order to enhance Android Malware Detection (AMD), machine learning is becoming more and more popular. In this paper, feature selection and classification fusion strategy for AMD. Firstly, the dataset is gathered from samples of Android apps. Secondly, Fuzzy Membership Grasshopper Optimization Algorithm (FMGOA) is introduced to choose the most important features. FMGOA approach imitates the biological behaviour of grasshopper swarms searching for best selection of features with their accuracy. Thirdly, a Stacked Ensemble Classifier Fusion (SECF) is introduced based on a multilevel architecture-based approach. It enables the efficient merging of machine learning algorithms including J48, Reduced Error Pruning Tree (REPTree), Voted Perceptron, and Mean Weight Deep Belief Network (MWDBN). Two ranking-based algorithms—Ranked Aggregate of Average Accuracy and Class Differential (RACD) and Ranked Aggregate of Per Class (RAPC)—have been presented that enable classifier fusion for stacking. Finally, Precision (Pre), Recall (Rec), F-measure (FM), and Weighted F-measure (WFM) has been used to evaluate the results of classifiers.

Keywords: Stacked Ensemble Classifier Fusion (SECF) · Fuzzy Membership Grasshopper Optimization Algorithm (FMGOA) · Android Malware Detection (AMD) · Machine Learning (ML) · Deep Learning (DL) · Mean Weight Deep Belief Network (MWDBN) · Support Vector Machines (SVM)

1 Introduction

With a much bigger percentage of the global market share, Android has overtaken iOS as the dominant mobile operating system. In recent years, Android smartphones have lead to an exceptional flow in the growth and circulation of malicious. Thus permission-based

S. Rajagopal et al. (Eds.): ASCIS 2023, CCIS 2039, pp. 307–330, 2024.
https://doi.org/10.1007/978-3-031-59100-6_22

approach is presented by Google Play to prevent application from malicious attacks and secure user private data. This permission prompts users before installation by considering the assets of the program which has been accessed and used by users. The users should explicitly acknowledge the agreement before continuing with the installation.

An estimated 65 billion apps have been downloaded from Google Play alone, with more than 1 billion Android devices having been sold. Android has developed into a target for malware due to its rising popularity and the expansion of third party app stores. Unfortunately, due to users propensity to allow the agreement exclusive of correctly reading the authorization, the Google Play technique cannot completely protect the user [1, 2]. Numerous programs consist of banking, gaming, daily life, educational, and e-commerce apps it leads to android malware easily. These apps are able to subsequently create vulnerable security and privacy through permitting unauthorized access to privacy-sensitive data, rooting devices, converting them into remotely controlled bots etc.

The threat of malware assaults on Android platforms has evolved as usage of these devices has continued to rise. To ensure the security and privacy of user data, it is essential to identify and mitigate these dangers. Android mobile devices are now widely used, and recent statistics indicate that the rate of acceptance is not going to slow down. Android status has its cost. Increase in Android malware has been caused by the popularity [2].

Nevertheless, finding fraudulent apps is no longer sufficient. Prioritizing mitigation approaches can greatly benefit from the new threat information. In order to identify and evaluate malware, static analysis employs statically extracted signatures (behaviors/features) [3]. In contrast to modern malware programs that employ complex evasion detection strategies like polymorphism and obfuscation, static-based malware recognition is ineffective against the majority of common types of malware [4]. Static analysis, dynamic analysis, and behavior-based method are used to examine the functionality of the malware with their actions performed after it has been completed in a sandbox. Therefore, it is crucial to create improved detecting techniques.

Machine Learning (ML), a well-known subject of computer science, has shown a lot of potential for identifying Android malware [5]. At AMD, ML methods have been proven to be successful. It gains knowledge from past data to produce predictions. These techniques have been used to analyse many aspects of Android applications, including permissions, Application Programming Interface (API) calls, and code structures, in order to discover malware. On labelled datasets, ML models like Decision Tree (DT), Random Forest (RF), and Support Vector Machine (SVM) are trained in order to find patterns and forecast the characteristics of hypothetical applications [6, 7]. Therefore, they require a large number of instances with labels. Given the time-consuming nature of the operation and the potential for malware to evade detection, labeling the data for this dataset is fairly difficult. Traditional techniques like signature-based detection and heuristic analysis have drawbacks when it comes to accurately identifying and thwarting the rapidly changing landscape of Android malware. Due to the expense of labeling, a completely labeled training set may not be possible; nevertheless, purchasing unlabelled data is quite cheap. It hasn't been sufficiently addressed how to cope with massive and high-dimensional data, though. A key step in machine learning is the elimination of redundant or pointless features. Babaagba et al. [28] showed the impact of feature engineering in Android malware detection.

As the widely used feature selection method, filter-based models are unable to take advantage of the classifier accuracy by AMD [29, 30]; as a result, the correlation information among several features collected from the classifier is disregarded. The number of possible combinations of these traits is sufficiently huge in a wrapper-based approach which always has a significant computational cost [31]. Even while ML has frequently been successful, the intricacy of malware patterns can restrict its performance [8]. When there is a dearth of labeled data for each class, semi-supervised learning is kind of ML technique which is particularly helpful. Deep Learning (DL) is another name for semi-supervised learning. DL algorithms take care of automatically extracting flexible and abstract features from the raw data that aid in classification generalization. The necessity for more intricate analysis and finer distinctions as malware grows more complex gave rise to DL. It is incredibly effective at finding malware in massive datasets. These techniques rely on a limited feature set, making it challenging to identify recent viruses. Due to the large number of characteristics in the dataset, there are numerous challenging factors that must be taken into account while thinking about detection algorithms. Following is a description of the work's main contributions:

- **Data Collection:** It is essential to compile a varied and thorough collection of Android applications, including both genuine and malicious samples. These applications are broken down into analyze-able features by the DL model.
- **Feature Selection:** FMGOA is used to pick the most crucial features, including requests for permission, API calls, code snippets, and other behavioral patterns. FMGOA is used to remove unhelpful features and create the best feature sets for static and dynamic layers. For the best selection of android traits from the dataset, the FMGOA approach imitates the biological behavior of grasshopper swarms searching for food sources. The SECF deep learning model receives these chosen features as inputs.
- **Model Training:** SECF model, which consists of many layers of neurons, is trained using the chosen features. Based on diverse features and the uniqueness of the applications, DL learns to distinguish between legitimate and harmful behavior. ML algorithms prediction ability is increased by multilevel architecture.
- **Testing and Validation:** The model is tested on new data after training in order to assess its performance. Several metrics likePre, Rec, FM, and WFM are used to assess the resultsof detection methods.

The overall structure of the paper is as follows: A few of the relevant works cited in this book are described in Sect. 2. The main focus of Sect. 3 was an explanation of the AMD approach. It includes information on the dataset acquisition, FMGOA discussions for feature selection, and a description of the proposed classification architecture using SECF deep learning. Results and discussion of the work under consideration are covered in Sect. 4. The conclusion and future work of the proposed study is discussed in Sect. 5.

2   Literature Review

Advanced detection methods must be developed since malware poses a serious risk to user security and privacy. Researchers have recently use of ML and DL within the field of data mining for AMD. Advanced AMD methods are now necessary as a result of the rise in complex malware attacks.

2.1   ML-Based Approaches

Traditional ML algorithms have been used in a number of researches for AMD.

Wei et al. [9] introduced a harmful app detection program (Androidetect) (Naive Bayes (NB) and J48 DT) for malicious application detection. It examines the connections between sensitive application programming interfaces, sensitive system functionalities, and sensitive permissions. It has been applied to create eigenvectors and define application behaviors. Then, real-world apps and sample programs are tested using Androidetect. Experimental findings show that the proposed system can easily identifies malwares in the Android applications than other existing methods. Ten-fold cross-validation method is used to study the 200 news readings were chosen for the experiment (100 (good) and 100 (bad) applications, respectively). True Positive Rate (TPR), False Positive Rate (FPR) and Accuracy (ACC) have been used to assess the performance of classifiers.

Rashidi et al. [10] introduced a Support Vector Machine (SVM) and active learning technology for AMD. The proposed method, program execution activities are extracted and it is stored in feature set which is subsequently enhanced by adding timestamps to various features. New useful examples of the ability to execute adaptive online learning are integrated utilizing an active learning model and predicted error reduction query approach. Different training set sizes have been employed depending on the model performance on the test dataset in terms of Pre, Rea, and FM. The proposed model is then examined using a series of tests on the benchmark malware dataset for DREBIN. The findings of the evaluation demonstrate that the proposed approach may more effectively update against new threats and accurately detect dangerous programs.

Shatnawi et al. [11] created a static base classification technique for malware detection based on Android permissions and API calls. SVM, K Nearest Neighbor (KNN), and NB methods have been applied for AMD. The data was pre-processed to solve missing data imputation. The dataset permission features and Android API calls were selected and it is formed as feature sets. Recursive Feature Elimination (RFE) feature selection has been used for selecting features from dataset. It has been used to choose training dataset features are predictive of the target variable. Logistic Regression (LR) model is based on ranking the key features which are utilized to reflect the probability of 0 or 1 for classifying into either malware/benign. Pre, Rec, FM, and accuracy are used as the performance evaluation metrics. Android malware dataset (CIC InvesAndMal2019) was employed to achieve higher malware detection rate and it has been used to safeguard the growth of mobile information access.

Islam et al. [12] proposed RF, KNN, Multilayer Perceptron (MLP), DT, SVM, and Logistic Regression (LR) for AMD. Synthetic Minority Oversampling Technique (SMOTE) has been introduced to solve class imbalance. Min-Max Normalization is introduced to normalize the dataset. Finding and removing less crucial features from the dataset is known as feature selection. The feature significance for each feature is located using RF. Principal Component Analysis (PCA) is introduced for dimensionality reduction from a higher-dimensional space into a lower-dimensional space. Finally, AMD has been performed by an ensemble ML model. Measures including Pre, Rec, ACC, and F1-score are used to evaluate ML models. The CCCS-CIC-AndMal-2020 dataset has been used for experimentation.

Yerima and Sezer [13] introduced a DroidFusion classifier fusion strategy. This strategy is based on a multilayer architecture which follows efficient fusion of ML algorithms with increased accuracy. The proposed algorithms include the Average Accuracy Based ranking scheme (AAB), Class Differential ranking scheme (CDB), RAPC, and RACD ranking schemes. Final classifier is created by training base classifiers at a first level, and then ranking-based algorithms are used to measure their predicted accuracy at a second level. Then, the meta-classifier technique has been used as higher level for AMD. Droid-Fusion by stacked generalization has higher accuracy than other methods. Pre, Rec/TPR, FPR, FM, and WFM have been utilized evaluate the output of ML algorithms.

2.2 DL Techniques

This section has reviewed the traditional DL algorithms that have been used for AMD.

Yuan et al. [14] proposed a DL-based AMD engine (DroidDetector) via Deep Neural Network (DNN). It is able to routinely detect (malware or not). Deep Belief Network (DBN) is pre-trained hierarchically by stacking a no. of Restricted Boltzmann Machines (RBM) with the DNN is viewed as a latent variable model. It is helpful for increasingly developing high-level demonstration. Back-propagation involves supervised tuning of the pre-trained DBN using labelled samples. Three public app sets are used as the subject of experiments to identify malware. A group of benign apps was selected at random from the Google Play Store enormous collection of 20,000 apps. Pre, Rec, and ACC are the performance evaluation measures to compare the results of classification methods.

Kim et al. [15] proposed Multimodal Neural Network (MNN) for AMD with variety of features. It has several different types of features to reflect the features of Android applications from different angles. Features are refined by existence-based or similarity-based techniques for efficient representation of features. The first networks are not associated to every other, and the final layers of the first networks are associated to the merging layer is the initial layer of the last network. DNN classifier each has an input layer, 2 hidden layers, and each layer simply receives associations from the earlier layer. Each layer is fully connected with Rectified Linear Unit (ReLU) activation function in DNN classifier. The 41,260 samples are used in a total of various tests. The MNN model accuracy is also contrasted with that of other DNN models. Pre, Rec, FM, and accuracy are used as performance evaluation criteria.

Zhang et al. [16] proposed feature-hybrid malware detection strategy which incorporates multiple types of features for malware analysis. Firstly, opcodes are represented by a bi-gram model, and API calls are represented by a frequency vector. Secondly, PCA is used to tune the feature representations and increases convergence speed. Finally, Convolutional Neural Network (CNN) and Back-Propagation Neural Network (BPNN) are introduced for opcode- and API-based feature embedding respectively. The effectiveness and optimization of the approach that results in greater accuracy are demonstrated by theoretical analysis and actual experimental findings.

Karbab and Debbabi [17] introduced a PetaDroid framework for accurate AMD and family clustering. The PetaDroid framework is resilient to popular binary obfuscation techniques and can automatically adapt to Android malware and benign modifications over time. To accomplish precise, adaptive, flexible AMD and clustering, the system uses unique techniques built on top of Natural Language Processing (NLP) and ML techniques. They are outperformed by PetaDroid in every evaluation setting.

Kim et al. [18] proposed Malware based on Analyzed PAtternS (MAPAS) detection method. It follows a CNN which achieves improved accuracy and flexible usages of computational resources. (1) Data pre-processing, where MAPAS creates training dataset by removing API call graphs from harmful and good applications. (2) To recognize high-weight API call graphs, MAPAS vectorizes the training dataset before using CNN. To find high-weight API call graphs utilized in harmful applications, MAPAS applies the deep learning interpretation approach Gradient-weighted Class Activation Mapping (Grad-CAM) after the learning phase is finished. (3) Jaccard algorithm is introduced to classify the malware by computing the similarity among an application API call graph and the high-weight API call graphs from malicious applications. In general, MAPAS can more exactly detect any category of malware.

Alomari et al. [19] introduced a deep learning and feature selection for malware detection. Two different malware datasets has been utilized to discover malware and benign classes. Following pre-processing, the datasets are subjected to Correlation-Based Feature Selection (CBFS), which results in various feature-selected datasets. These many iterations of feature-selected datasets are then used to train the dense and Long-Short Memory Network (LSTM). Models are assessed using a variety of performance metrics like ACC, Pre, Rec, and F1-score. According to the findings, several feature-selected scenarios maintain performance close to that of the original dataset. Arslan and Tasyurek [20] proposed an AMD-CNN classifier which employs a graphical representation to identify harmful applications. CNN network is trained using the feature vector and it is subsequently transformed into 2D-code images. AMD-CNN classifier is a reliable and effective tool when compared to earlier methods.

Smmarwar et al. [21] developed an Optimized and Ensemble Learning-based Android Malware Detection (OEL-AMD) framework. Statistical feature engineering is utilized to remove uninformative features with embedded statistical features. Binary Grey Wolf Optimization (BGWO) is introduced to select best subset of features for equally static and dynamic layers. Then the ensemble model is used for classification, and a variety of base learners are trained utilizing hyper-parameter tuning to increase its capacity for inductive reasoning, and the ensemble aggregate performance. The proposed system achieves the best classification accuracy. The significance of the data was confirmed by the statistical test. Deep learning models are majorly depends on feature representation. Using feature selection approaches, major portions of the input data have been highlighted, allowing the model to concentrate on key patterns for exact malware identification.

3 Proposed Methodology

A unique feature selection and classification fusion strategy for AMD is presented in this research. The dataset was first gathered from samples of Android apps. Then FMGOA is used to choose the most crucial features. For the best selection of android traits from the dataset, the FMGOA approach imitates the biological behaviour of grasshopper swarms searching for food sources. By measuring the accuracy of each feature, the FMGOA approach assesses the features. Then, a Stacked Ensemble Classifier Fusion (SECF) is introduced based on multilevel architecture-based approach. It enables the efficient merging of machine learning algorithms including J48, REPTree, Voted Perceptron, and Mean Weight Deep Belief Network (MWDBN). Finally, metrics like Pre, Rec, FM, and WFM are used to assess a classifiers performance. The proposed framework for AMD is illustrated in Fig. 1.

3.1 Dataset Collection

Two datasets from 3 collections of Android app samples were used to assess the proposed approach. It is clearly discussed in Table 1. The initial dataset (Malgenome-215) consists of 3,799 app samples, where 1,260 samples to malware class, and 2,539 samples to benign class by 215 features has been collected from the Android malware genome project [22] The second dataset (Drebin-215) includes of 15,036 samples, where 5,560 samples to malware class, and 9,476 samples to benign class by 215 features from the Drebin project [22]. Drebin samples are also generally used in the research community and it is freely accessible.

3.2 Fuzzy Membership Grasshopper Optimization Algorithm (FMGOA) Based Feature Selection

Typically, feature selection is used for detection, which reduces computational cost. For the best selection of features from the AMD dataset, the GOA algorithm is employed, which imitates the natural foraging and swarming behaviours of grasshoppers [23]. GOA phases like intensification and diversification are represented by nymphal and adult movements. Grasshopper swarming is used to choose characteristics from the AMD dataset. The following mathematical description is given [23],

$$GP_i = SI_i + GF_i + A_i \tag{1}$$

GP_i is represented as the ith grasshopper position for feature selection, SI_i is represented as grasshopper social interaction, GF_i is represented as the gravitational force acting on the ith grasshopper, and A_i is represented as wind advection. Equation (1) is explained to produce the random behaviour of grasshoppers. Drebin samples are also commonly utilized in research and are accessible to the general public.

$$GP_i = r_1 SI_i + r_2 GF_i + r_3 A_i \tag{2}$$

$r_1 \in [0, 1]$, $r_2 \in [0, 1]$, and $r_3 \in [0, 1]$ are denoted as random vectors. Fuzzy Membership Function (FMF), it is used for random number generation. Each point in the dataset

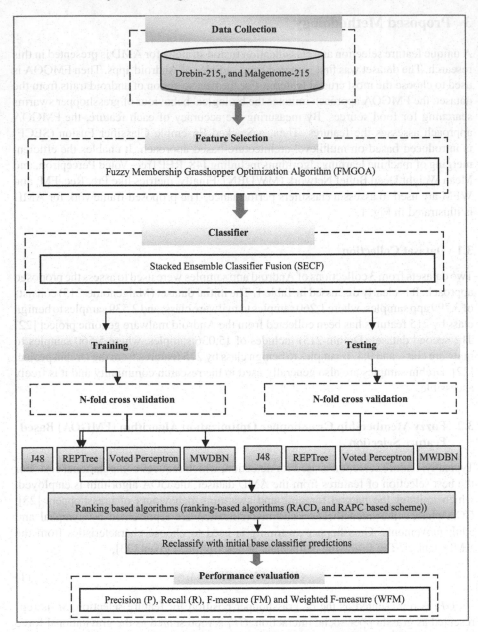

Fig. 1. Proposed Stacked Ensemble Classifier Fusion (SECF) Approach

is mapped to a membership value between 0 *and* 1 using the FMF curve. A membership function in the shape of a triangle is called a Triangular MF (TMF). The triangle left and

Table 1. Datasets for Experiment Analysis

Datasets	No. of samples	No. of malware	No. of benign	No. of features
Malgenome-215	3799	1260	2539	215
Drebin-215	15036	5560	9476	215

right feet are determined by the parameters $a \& c$ respectively.

$$f(r, a, b, c) = \begin{cases} 0, x \leq a \\ \frac{x-a}{b-a}, a \leq x \leq b \\ \frac{c-x}{c-b}, b \leq x \leq c \\ 0, c \leq x \end{cases} \tag{3}$$

The following defines the social interaction SI_i,

$$SI_i = \sum_{\substack{j=1 \\ j \neq 1}}^{N} s(d_{ij}) \hat{d}_{ij} \tag{4}$$

where N is the no. of grasshoppers,

$$d_{ij} = |GP_j - GP_i| \tag{5}$$

Euclidean distance between the ith & j^{th} grasshoppers is shown by the symbol d_{ij}. Equation (5) gives a description of it.

$$\hat{d}_{ij} = \frac{GP_j - GP_i}{d_{ij}} \tag{6}$$

$\hat{d}_{ij}$ is denoted as the unit vector from the ith to j^{th} grasshopper, and s is denoted as the social forces created by the Eq. (7),

$$s(r) = fexp^{\frac{-r}{l}} - exp^{-r} \tag{7}$$

where f&l is denoted as the intensity and length of attraction. These values have been computed using accuracy of the model. The d_{ij} is generated among [0,15]. The attraction builds up in the range [2.079, 4] which is decreased slowly. Repulsion is generated in the range [0, 2.079]. There is neither repulsion nor repellence when 2 grasshoppers distance are accurately 2.079 apart from one another. It is named as comfort zone. Equation (8) gives the gravity force GF_i.

$$G_i = g\hat{e}_g \tag{8}$$

where $\hat{e}_g$ is a unit vector pointing toward the earth center and g is the gravitational constant. The Eq. (9), which yields the wind advection A_i,

$$A_i = u\hat{e}_w \tag{9}$$

where $\hat{e}_w$ is a unit vector pointing in the direction of the wind and u is a denoted as drift constant. After swapping out the SI, GF, & A by Eq. (10),

$$GP_i = \sum_{\substack{j=1 \\ j \neq 1}}^{N} s(|GP_j - GP_i|) \frac{GP_j - GP_i}{d_{ij}} - g\hat{e}_g + u\hat{e}_w \qquad (10)$$

Because the grasshoppers rapidly achieve their comfort area and the swarm system doesn't meet to a target area. Thus the Eq. (10) cannot be directly used to solve the FS problem [24]. It has been improved by Eq. (11),

$$P_i^d = c\left(\sum_{\substack{j=1 \\ j \neq 1}}^{N} c\frac{ub_d - lb_d}{2} s(|GP_j - GP_i|) \frac{GP_j - GP_i}{d_{ij}}\right) + \hat{T}_d \qquad (11)$$

where the upper and lower boundaries in the dth dimension are indicated by the symbols ub_d and lb_d. The best feature solution in the dth dimension search space is indicated by $\hat{T}_d$. A is denoted as the best points in the direction of the optimal solution ($\hat{T}_d$), and GI = 0. The grasshopper movements near the food are minimized using the setting c. As a result, it offers an appropriate stability among intensification and diversification. Using the Eq. (12) [23], it is stated.

$$c = c_{max} - t\frac{c_{max} - c_{min}}{t_{max}} \qquad (12)$$

where t is denoted as the present iteration and t_{max} is denoted as the maximum no. of iterations to complete FS process, c_{max} and c_{min} is denoted as the maximum and minimum values of c correspondingly. A grasshopper position is updated using its present location, the global best location, and the previous locations of grasshoppers in the swarm [23]. The flowchart for it is shown in Fig. 2.

Algorithm 1. Fuzzy Membership Grasshopper Optimization Algorithm (FMGOA)

1. Initial population generation of grasshoppers $GP_i(i = 1, 2, \ldots, n)$, c_{min}, c_{max}, and t_{max}
2. Fitness evaluation $f(GP_i)$ of every grasshopper GP_i, T is equal to best selected feature solution
3. **While** $(t < t_{max})$ **do**
   3.1. Update c using equation (12)
   3.2. For $i = 1$ to N do
      3.2.1. Distance d_{ij} is normalized among grasshoppers
      3.2.2. Grasshopper present position is updated by equation (11)
      3.2.3. Get the present grasshopper reverse if it go away outside the boundaries (ub_d and lb_d)
   3.3. end for
   3.4. T is updated if it is better than the previous one
   3.5. $t = t + 1$
4. End while
5. Return the best selected features T

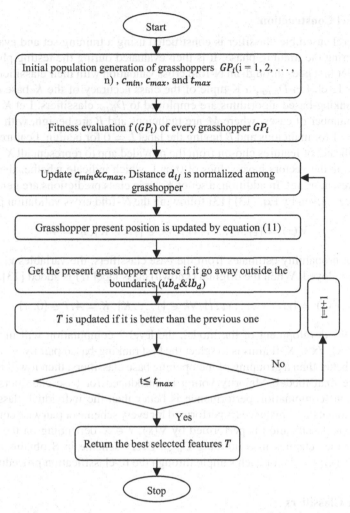

Fig. 2. Flowchart of Fuzzy Membership Grasshopper Optimisation Algorithm

3.3 Stacked Ensemble Classifier Fusion (SECF) Approach

Android malware detection is performed by using two ranking-based algorithms in a multilevel architecture, and Stacked Ensemble Classifier Fusion (SECF) technique. Fusion system is created by combining of ensemble classifiers and classifiers like J48, REPTree, Voted Perceptron, and Mean Weight Deep Belief Network (MWDBN). SECF classifier is trained by a stratified N-fold cross validation on a training set at the lowest level. It is used to determine how accurate their predictions are in comparison. Two distinct ranking-based techniques use the results to specify specific criteria for choosing and combining a subset (all) of the relevant base classifiers (J48, REPTree, Voted Perceptron, and MWDBN). To choose the strongest pair that can be utilized to construct the final SECF model, the results of the ranking algorithms are used for detection.

3.3.1 Model Construction

The multilevel ensemble classifier is constructed using a training set and evaluated on a test set during the training phase. It is then evaluated during the testing phase. Each base classifier first goes through an N-fold cross validation with their classifier accuracy at the lower level. Let D_{base}, a K-tuple of the class accuracy of the K base classifiers [13]. The ranking-based algorithms are employed to D_{base} classifiers. Let X represent the overall number of cases, where M are malicious and B are benign, with M having the label $L = 1$ for malicious and B having the label $L = 0$ for benign. Feature vectors f denoted as the no. of features chosen from the provided app to represent all X instances. The features in the vectors have values of 0 or 1, which indicate whether the specified feature is present or not. In addition, a set of K-tuple class predictions are generated for each instance x given by Eq. (13) [13] following the N-fold cross validation process.

$$V(x) = \{v_1, v_2, \ldots, v_k\}, \forall k \in \{1, \ldots K\}, K = 4 \tag{13}$$

For AMD or probability estimates from the base classifiers, the variables $v_1, v_2, \ldots, v_k$ have been employed. When the original (known) class label (l) is added [13],

$$\dot{V}(x) = \{v_1, v_2, \ldots, v_k, l\}, \forall k \in \{1, \ldots K\}, K = 4, l \in \{0, 1\} \tag{14}$$

During the development of the model, the level-2 computation will make use of D_{base} and $\dot{V}(x)$, $\forall x \in X$. It aims is to select the best ranking-based pair by S, and if their accuracy is better than a grouping of the opening base classifiers, then it will be utilized to create the final model. Majority voting is introduced for base classifiers to attain final detection (combination performance is better than the individual classifiers). A reclassification of the X instances is performed for every scheme or pairwise combination set (ϕ). The reclassification is performed by $\dot{V}(x)$, $x \in X$ depending on the condition specified by the schemes in S utilizing D_{base}. Every scheme in S obtains a set of Z weights by $\dot{V}(x)$, $x \in X$ for each sample through the re-classification procedure [13].

3.3.2 Base Classifiers

For classification, the basic classifiers J48, REPTree, Voted Perceptron, and Mean Weight Deep Belief Network (MWDBN) have been employed.

3.3.2.1. J48 Decision Algorithm

J48 Decision Algorithm is a predictive ML classifier. It is performed based on the dependent features (target value) of a new instance depending on several feature ranges of the available data. Each node in the classifier is used to represent the diverse attributes from the dataset. In the J48 classifier, the data distribution becomes very easy to understand and flexible to develop it. The ID3 extension J48 creates a decision node using the class anticipated estimations. It deals with decision tree pruning, data approximations for lost or incomplete attributes, and variable attribute costs. The three processes listed below can be used to produce the J48 algorithm [25],

Stage 1: The leaves are labelled with a similar class if an instance belongs to that class.

Stage 2: For every feature, the possible data will be formed and the gain is calculated from the test feature data.

Stage 3: In the end, the best feature will be preferred to the present selection factor.

3.3.2.2. Reduced Error Pruning Tree (REPTree) Algorithm

Reduced Error Pruning Tree (REPTree) is a classification ensemble model that combines reduced error pruning (REP) with DT [26]. By dividing and pruning the regression tree depending on the highest Information Gain Ratio (IGR) value, the REPTree method creates a decision regression tree [26].

$$IGR(x, S) = \frac{E(S) - \sum_{i=1}^{n} \frac{E(S_i)|S_i|}{|S|}}{- \sum_{i=1}^{n} \frac{|S_i|}{|S|} \log_2 \frac{|S_i|}{|S|}} \quad (15)$$

Equation (15) was used to construct the IGR values, which take into account all predictors from the training dataset (S) by subset S_i, $i = 1$ to n in successive pruning rounds. REP aids in reducing complexity.

3.3.2.3. Voted Perceptron (V-Perceptron) Algorithm

A model-based learning algorithm that creates a Voted Perceptron Classifier is known as a Voted Perceptron Algorithm. The threshold function, a type of perceptron technique, is used to learn binary classifiers. A threshold function is a function that produces a single binary result, f(x), from its real-valued vector input, x.

$$f(x) = \begin{cases} 1 \ if \ w.x + b > 0 \\ 0 \ else \end{cases} \quad (16)$$

Equation (16), where w.x is denoted as the sum of all dot product values ($i = 1$ to m). m is denoted as the no. of inputs, b is denoted as the bias. The decision boundary may move away from the origin depending on the value of b. Binary classification, f(x) is used to separate the samples into either a benign (0) or a malignant (1).

3.3.2.4. Mean Weight Deep Belief Network (MWDBN)

The classifier known as the Mean Weight Deep Belief Network (MWDBN) is a probabilistic productive network made up of numerous RBM layers. Figure 3 illustrates how a DBN extracts data characteristics using an unsupervised layer-by-layer training approach [32]. An RBM is a Markov random field-based unsupervised non-linear feature extractor that has two crucial layers: a visible cell layer and a hidden unit layer. Each RBM hidden unit's output is completely connected to the following RBM unit by symmetric undirected synapses. A conditional independence between visible and concealed cells results from these RBM features.

As illustrated in the following Eq. (17), the joint probability distribution determined by the RBM weights used an energy-based function of $\{v, h\}$,

$$En(v, h; \theta) = v^T W h - a^T v - b^T h = - \sum_{i=1}^{D_v} \sum_{j=1}^{D_h} mw_{ij} v_i h_j - \sum_{i=1}^{D_v} a_i v_i - \sum_{j=1}^{D_h} b_j h_j \quad (17)$$

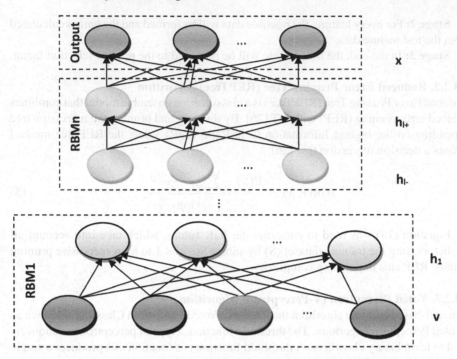

Fig. 3. DBN Architecture Consists of Multiple RBM

where $\{b_i, a_j, w_{ij}\}$, and mw_{ij} represented the weight from visible cell i to hidden cell j. The mean function is used to calculate it. For the purpose of computing weight in the layer, the attribute's mean value is utilized. The biases of units $i\&j$ are a_i and b_j, respectively. According to Eq. (18), the joint probability distribution of the RBM model over the visible-hidden cells is calculated as follows:

$$P(v, h; \theta) = \frac{1}{Z(\theta)} \exp(-E(v, h; \theta)) \tag{18}$$

where $Z(\theta)$ is the normalizing constant value or partition function that is derived from the list of all possible energy allocations when cells $i\&j$ are combined.

$$Z(\theta) = \sum_v \sum_h \exp(-E(v, h; \theta)) \tag{19}$$

Through the energy equation, the RBM can determine the likelihood of input datasets. The conditional probability functions of cells $i\&j$ can be produced by the following functions in accordance with the joint probability distribution function,

$$P(h_j = 1|v) = \delta\left(b_j + \sum_i v_i w_{ij}\right) \tag{20}$$

$$P(v_i = 1|h) = \delta\left(a_i + \sum_j h_j w_{ij}\right) \tag{21}$$

$$\delta(x) = \frac{1}{1 + exp(-x)} \tag{22}$$

Every v_i will be arranged to 1 with the probability specified by Eq. (21) to reconstitute the input state. Thus, to depict the reconstruction features, the state of concealed cells is gradually recreated. The training method is put into practice via maximizing.

$$\text{maximize}\{b_j, a_i, w_{ij}\} \frac{1}{m} \sum_{l=1}^{m} \log(P(v^l)) \tag{24}$$

where m stands for the size of the training datasets. As a result, the objective function is a log-likelihood term that should be solved by a gradient descent technique. However, because $Z(\theta)$ exists, it is challenging to execute the gradient calculation of the log-likelihood term.

3.3.3 Ranking Based Algorithms (Ranking-Based Algorithms (RACD, and RAPC Based Scheme))

The discovery that the majority of common classifiers behave differently for the two classes has an impact on the design of proposed algorithms. Malware and benign performance in terms of class correctness are very rarely on par. Among the suggested ranking-based algorithms are [13],

RAPC Scheme: The ranking is directly comparative to the sum of the initial per-class rankings of the basic classifiers accuracy. This approach is more likely to give a basic classifier that excels in both classifications a bigger weight [13].

RACD Scheme: RACD, the initial rankings of the usual performance accuracy and their performance gap among the classes are added jointly to establish the ranking. It is intended to provide base classifiers by higher accuracy and it is a comparatively little performance gap across the classes with increased weight [13].

Let the set of weights $\omega e_i, i \in \{1, \ldots, Z\}, Z \le K$ created for a specific scheme (S). Equation (25) is used to determine expect a case new classification based on the S criterion,

$$C_{S_j(x)} = \begin{cases} 1 : if \ \frac{\sum_{i=1}^{Z} \omega e_i v_i}{\sum_{i=1}^{Z} \omega e_i} \ge 0.5 \\ 0 : else, \forall j \in \{1, 2\} \end{cases} \tag{25}$$

Accuracy of benign class and malware class is used for results analysis.

4 Results and Discussion

This section uses two datasets to compare the performance of the proposed model and the current classifiers. Both files fall within the AMD category. The suggested system, as well as current AMD approaches, are implemented and evaluated using MATLABR2020a.

On a Windows 7 Enterprise 64 bit computer with 32 GB of RAM and an Intel Xeon CPU running at 3.10 GHz, all techniques were tested. Because the proposed system is intended to be common-principle and it is not single to a ML algorithm, it can be employed with a variety of learning algorithms due to their accuracy and training time as discovered from beginning examination.

4.1 Evaluation Metrics

The performance metrics which are taken into account when evaluating the models are described as follows,

Precision: The precision measures how well it can forecast a particular class. The Eq. (26) is used to compute the positive predictive rate,

$$\text{Precision (Pre)} = \frac{TP}{TP + FP} \tag{26}$$

True Negative (TN) is the no. of correctly predicted benign samples, whereas False Positive (FP) is the no. of wrongly predicted benign classifications.

Recall: Recall is the proportion of accurately recognized malicious apps to every one of malicious apps. Equation (27) is used described it,

$$\text{Recall (Rec)} = \frac{TP}{TP + FN} \tag{27}$$

False Negative (FN) is the no. of incorrectly categorized malware occurrences in the set, and True Positive (TP) is the no. of correctly predicted malware classification.

F-Measure (FM): Harmonic mean of Pre and Rec is known as FM. Equation (28) has been used to compute the FM,

$$FM = \frac{2.\text{Pre}.\text{Rec}}{\text{Pre} + \text{Rec}} \tag{28}$$

FM is the harmonic mean of precision, and recall. It is computed for both M and B classes. WFM is the total of FM weighted by the quantity of instances in every class, as shown by the following, where F_m and F_b are the corresponding FM for the M and B classes, and N_m and N_b are the quantity of instances in every class. WFM is described by Eq. (29),

$$WFM = \frac{F_m.N_m + F_b.N_b}{N_m + N_b} \tag{29}$$

which gives it, states that these measurements have been used to compare outcomes.

4.2 Results Comparison

To enable a comparison equivalent to AMD, 10-fold cross validation is employed for models in tests. Four base classifiers—the J48, REPTree, Voted Perceptron, and Mean Weight Deep Belief Network (MWDBN)—are used for classification across all trials, with set K = 4. The SECF model was built using the training-validation set and the stratified 10-fold cross validation method. The entire SECF model was assessed on the test set once it had been constructed with the aid of the training-validation set. The base models were retrained on the complete set and then tested on the similar test set for comparison. Table 2 displays the comparison of malgenome 215 results by detection techniques.

Table 2. Results Comparison of Malgenome 215 Dataset

METRICS	IG+J48	IG+REPTree	IG+V-Perceptron	FMGOA-MWDBN	IG-DroiFusion	FMGOA-SECF
PreB(%)	86.88	88.15	89.19	91.21	91.72	93.31
RecB(%)	88.70	88.89	91.37	92.74	92.68	94.38
PreM(%)	87.72	89.03	90.26	91.98	92.19	93.84
RecM(%)	88.67	89.96	91.24	92.87	93.08	93.22
FM(%)	87.58	88.82	89.89	91.92	92.41	94.05
WFM(%)	88.92	90.11	91.57	92.99	92.88	94.60

The results comparison of Drebin 215 by detection methods are shown in Table 3.

Table 3. Results Comparison of Drebin 215 Dataset

METRICS	IG+J48	IG+REPTree	IG+V-Perceptron	FMGOA-MWDBN	IG-DroiFusion	FMGOA-SECF
PreB(%)	87.44	88.96	94.49	91.59	93.83	95.85
RecB(%)	86.62	88.92	94.17	92.54	94.53	96.27
PreM(%)	88.19	89.37	94.33	92.06	94.18	96.06
RecM(%)	88.96	90.48	95.28	91.97	95.08	95.09
FM(%)	88.24	89.69	95.20	92.28	94.53	96.55
WFM(%)	88.82	90.14	94.38	92.75	94.74	96.48

Figure 4(a) shows the PreB analysis of AMD methods via the malgenome 215 dataset. FMGOA-SECF model can be seen to also perform better than to other methods. The proposed SECF model has highest precision results of 93.31%, other methods such as IG-48, IG-REPTree, IG-V-Perceptron, FMGOA-MWDBN, and IG-Droidfusion has lowest precision results of 86.88%, 88.15%, 89.19%, 91.21%, and 91.72% respectively (Refer Table 2). It clearly demonstrates the effectiveness of the SECF approach. PreM analysis of AMD methods via the malgenome 215 dataset is illustrated in Fig. 4(b). FMGOA-SECF model can be seen to also perform better than to other methods. The proposed SECF model has highest precision results of 93.84%, other methods such as IG-48, IG-REPTree, IG-V-Perceptron, FMGOA-MWDBN, and IG-Droidfusion has lowest

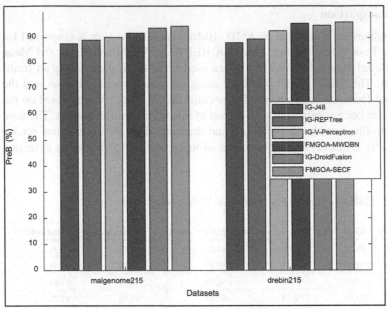

(A). PRECISION COMPARISON OF CLASSIFEIRS WITH BOTH DATASETS (BENIGN CLASS)

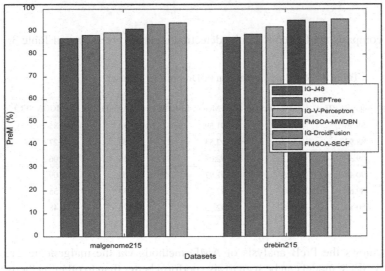

(b). PRECISION COMPARISON OF CLASSIFEIRS WITH BOTH DATASETS (MALWARE CLASS)

Fig. 4. Precision Comparison vs. AMD Methods

precision results of 87.72%, 89.03%, 90.26%, 91.98%, and 92.19% respectively (Refer Table 2). It clearly demonstrates the effectiveness of the SECF approach. Figure 4(a)

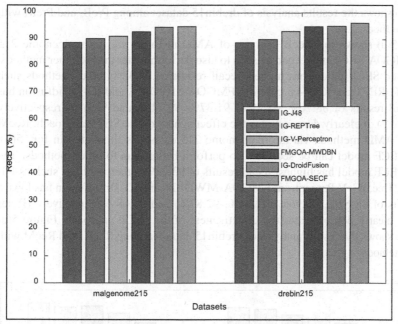

(A). RECALL COMPARISON OF CLASSIFEIRS WITH BOTH DATASETS (BENIGN CLASS)

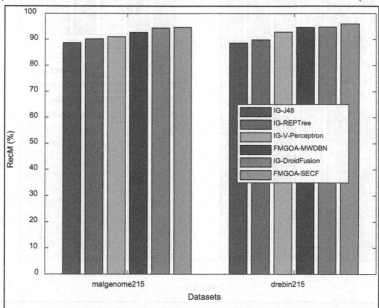

(b). RECALL COMPARISON OF CLASSIFEIRS WITH BOTH DATASETS (MALWARE CLASS)

Fig. 5. Recall Comparison vs. AMD Methods

and (b) also shows the results analysis of drebin15 dataset among PreB, and PreM with detection methods.

Figure 5(a) shows the RecB analysis of AMD methods via the malgenome 215 dataset. FMGOA-SECF model can be seen to also perform better than to other methods. The proposed SECF model has highest recall results of 94.38%, other methods such as IG-48, IG-REPTree, IG-V-Perceptron, FMGOA-MWDBN, and IG-Droidfusion has lowest recall results of 88.70%, 88.89%, 91.37%, 92.74%, and 92.68% respectively (Refer Table 2). It clearly demonstrates the effectiveness of the SECF approach. RecM analysis of AMD methods via the malgenome 215 dataset is illustrated in Fig. 5(b). FMGOA-SECF model can be seen to also perform better than to other methods. The proposed SECF model has highest recall results of 93.22%, other methods such as IG-48, IG-REPTree, IG-V-Perceptron, FMGOA-MWDBN, and IG-Droidfusion has lowest recall results of 88.67%, 89.96%, 91.24%, 92.87%, and 93.08% respectively (Refer Table 2). It clearly demonstrates the effectiveness of the SECF approach. Figure 5(a) and (b) also shows the results analysis of drebin15 dataset among RecB, and RecM with detection methods.

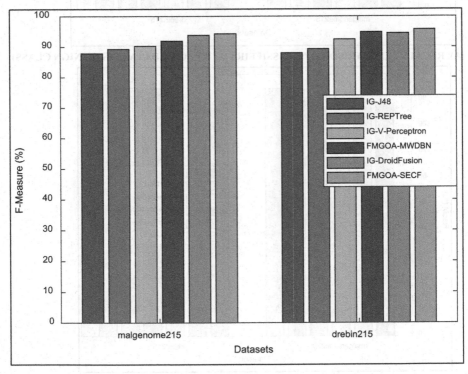

Fig. 6. FM Comparison of AMD Methods with both Datasets

Figure 6 shows the FM analysis of AMD methods via the malgenome 215, and drebin datasets. FMGOA-SECF model can be seen to also perform better than to other methods. The proposed SECF model has highest FM results of 94.05%, other methods such as IG-48, IG-REPTree, IG-V-Perceptron, FMGOA-MWDBN, and IG-Droidfusion has lowest FM results of 87.58%, 88.82%, 89.89%, 91.92%, and 92.41% respectively in malgenome 215 dataset (Refer Table 2). It clearly demonstrates the effectiveness of the SECF approach. FM analysis of AMD methods via the drebin215 dataset is also illustrated in Fig. 6. FMGOA-SECF model can be seen to also perform better than to other methods. The proposed SECF model has highest FM results of 96.55%, other methods such as IG-48, IG-REPTree, IG-V-Perceptron, FMGOA-MWDBN, and IG-Droidfusion has lowest FM results of 88.24%, 89.69%, 95.20%, 92.28%, and 94.53% respectively in drebin dataset (Refer Table 3). It clearly demonstrates the effectiveness of the SECF approach.

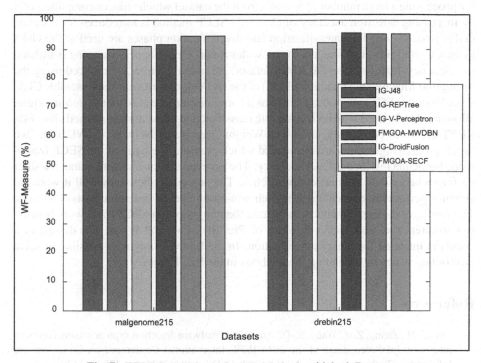

Fig. 7. WFM Comparison of AMD Methods with both Datasets

WFM analysis of AMD methods via the malgenome 215, and drebin datasets are illustrated in Fig. 7. FMGOA-SECF model can be seen to also perform better than to other methods. The proposed SECF model has highest WFM results of 94.60%, other methods such as IG-48, IG-REPTree, IG-V-Perceptron, FMGOA-MWDBN, and IG-Droidfusion has lowest WFM results of 88.92%, 90.11%, 91.57%, 92.99%, and 92.88% respectively in malgenome 215 dataset (Refer Table 2). It clearly demonstrates the effectiveness of the SECF approach. WFM analysis of AMD methods via the drebin 215 dataset is also illustrated in Fig. 7. FMGOA-SECF model can be seen to also perform better than to other methods. The proposed SECF model has highest WFM results of 96.48%, other methods such as IG-48, IG-REPTree, IG-V-Perceptron, FMGOA-MWDBN, and IG-Droidfusion has lowest WFM results of 88.82%, 90.14%, 94.38%, 92.75%, and 94.74% respectively in drebin dataset (Refer Table 3). It clearly demonstrates the effectiveness of the SECF approach.

5 Conclusion and Future Work

In this study, the Fuzzy Membership Grasshopper Optimization Algorithm (FMGOA) was used to identify wrapper-based features. For enhancing stability and randomly choosing feature subsets, FMGOA has been introduced. FMGOA is a suitable algorithm for processing a huge number of features from the dataset which reduces computing cost by increasing detection accuracy of classifier. SECF method is introduced for accurate malware detection. The intensification and diversification phases are used in the GOA to pick a valid subset of features over a wider range. Grasshopper swarming is utilized to select best features from the AMD dataset. A random number is produced using the Triangular Membership Function (TMF) of the GOA algorithm. Stacked Ensemble Classifier Fusion (SECF) method is created as a common-purpose classifier fusion structure, allowing it to be used with both ensemble classifier, and conventional methods like J48, REPTree, Voted Perceptron, and Mean Weight Deep Belief Network (MWDBN). Two ranking-based algorithms are introduced which provides the basis of the SECF framework for achieving higher-level accuracy. The proposed feature selection and classifier performs better than alternative approaches. The outcomes show how well it works to enhance performance when utilizing both non-ensemble and ensemble basis classifiers. The results of the experiments demonstrate that the proposed SECF framework is superior to alternative approaches in terms of Pre, Rec, FM, and WFM. The design as it stands is intended for binary classification. In the future, it might be possible to solve multi-class issues by extending the methods in the SECF framework.

References

1. Liu, C.-H., Zhang, Z.-J., Wang, S.-D.: An android malware detection approach using Bayesian inference. In: Proceedings of the 2016 IEEE International Conference on Computer and Information Technology (CIT), Nadi, Fiji, 8–10 December 2016, pp. 476–483 (2016)
2. Mat, S.R.T., Razak, M.A., Kahar, M., Arif, J., Firdaus, A.: A Bayesian probability model for Android malware detection. ICT Express **8**, 424–431 (2022)
3. Cen, L., Gates, C.S., Si, L., Li, N.: A probabilistic discriminative model for android malware detection with decompiled source code. IEEE Trans. Dependable Secure Comput. **12**(4), 400–412 (2014)
4. Kang, H., Jang, J.W., Mohaisen, A., Kim, H.K.: Detecting and classifying android malware using static analysis along with creator information. Int. J. Distrib. Sens. Netw. **11**(6), 1–9 (2015)
5. Naseef-Ur-Rahman Chowdhury, M., Haque, A., Soliman, H., Sahinur Hossen, M., Fatima, T., Ahmed, I.: Android malware detection using machine learning: a review. arXiv e-prints, arXiv-2307 (2023)
6. Mahindru, A., Sangal, A.L.: MLDroid—framework for Android malware detection using machine learning techniques. Neural Comput. Appl. **33**(10), 5183–5240 (2021)

7. Tahtaci, B., Canbay, B.: Android malware detection using machine learning. In: 2020 Innovations in Intelligent Systems and Applications Conference (ASYU), pp. 1–6 (2020)
8. Yerima, S.Y., Sezer, S., Muttik, I.: High accuracy android malware detection using ensemble learning. IET Inf. Secur. **9**(6), 313–320 (2015)
9. Wei, L., Luo, W., Weng, J., Zhong, Y., Zhang, X., Yan, Z.: Machine learning-based malicious application detection of android. IEEE Access **5**, 25591–25601 (2017)
10. Rashidi, B., Fung, C., Bertino, E.: Android malicious application detection using support vector machine and active learning. In: 13th International Conference on Network and Service Management (CNSM), pp. 1–9 (2017)
11. Shatnawi, A.S., Yassen, Q., Yateem, A.: An android malware detection approach based on static feature analysis using machine learning algorithms. Procedia Comput. Sci. **201**, 653–658 (2022)
12. Islam, R., Sayed, M.I., Saha, S., Hossain, M.J., Masud, M.A.: Android malware classification using optimum feature selection and ensemble machine learning. Internet Things Cyber-Phys. Syst. **3**, 100–111 (2023)
13. Yerima, S.Y., Sezer, S.: DroidFusion: a novel multilevel classifier fusion approach for android malware detection. IEEE Trans. Cybern. **49**(2), 453–466 (2018)
14. Yuan, Z., Lu, Y., Xue, Y.: DroidDetector: android malware characterization and detection using deep learning. Tsinghua Sci. Technol. **21**(1), 114–123 (2016)
15. Kim, T., Kang, B., Rho, M., Sezer, S., Im, E.G.: A multimodal deep learning method for android malware detection using various features. IEEE Trans. Inf. Forensics Secur. **14**(3), 773–788 (2018)
16. Zhang, J., Qin, Z., Yin, H., Ou, L., Zhang, K.: A feature-hybrid malware variants detection using CNN based opcode embedding and BPNN based API embedding. Comput. Secur. **84**, 376–392 (2019)
17. Karbab, E.B., Debbabi, M.: PetaDroid: adaptive android malware detection using deep learning. In: Detection of Intrusions and Malware, and Vulnerability Assessment: 18th International Conference (DIMVA), pp. 319–340 (2021)
18. Kim, J., Ban, Y., Ko, E., Cho, H., Yi, J.H.: MAPAS: a practical deep learning-based android malware detection system. Int. J. Inf. Secur. **21**(4), 725–738 (2022)
19. Alomari, E.S., et al.: Malware detection using deep learning and correlation-based feature selection. Symmetry **15**(1), 1–21 (2023)
20. Arslan, R.S., Tasyurek, M.: AMD-CNN: Android malware detection via feature graph and convolutional neural networks. Concurr. Comput. Pract. Experience **34**(23), e7180 (2022)
21. Smmarwar, S.K., Gupta, G.P., Kumar, S., Kumar, P.: An optimized and efficient android malware detection framework for future sustainable computing. Sustain. Energy Technol. Assess. **54**, 1–8 (2022)
22. Masum, M., Shahriar, H.: Droid-NNet: deep learning neural network for android malware detection. In: 2019 IEEE International Conference on Big Data (Big Data), pp. 5789–5793 (2019)
23. Saremi, S., Mirjalili, S., Lewis, A.: Grasshopper optimisation algorithm: theory and application. Adv. Eng. Softw. **105**, 30–47 (2017)
24. Elmi, Z., Efe, M.Ö.: Multi-objective grasshopper optimization algorithm for robot path planning in static environments. In: 2018 IEEE International Conference on Industrial Technology (ICIT), pp. 244–249 (2018)
25. Ihya, R., Namir, A., Filali, S.E., Daoud, M.A., Guerss, F.Z.: J48 algorithms of machine learning for predicting user's the acceptance of an E-orientation systems. In: Proceedings of the 4th International Conference on Smart City Applications, pp. 1–8 (2019)
26. Shahdad, M., Saber, B.: Drought forecasting using new advanced ensemble-based models of reduced error pruning tree. Acta Geophys. **70**(2), 697–712 (2022)

27. Zhang, H., et al.: Self-organizing deep belief modular echo state network for time series prediction. Knowl.-Based Syst. **222**, 1–16 (2021)
28. Babaagba, K.O., Adesanya, S.O.: A study on the effect of feature selection on malware analysis using machine learning. In: ACM International Conference Proceeding Series Part F148151, pp. 51–55 (2019)
29. Salah, A., Shalabi, E., Khedr, W.: A lightweight android malware classifier using novel feature selection methods. Symmetry **12**(5), 1–16 (2020)
30. Yildiz, O., Doğru, I.A.: Permission-based android malware detection system using feature selection with genetic algorithm. Int. J. Softw. Eng. Knowl. Eng. **29**, 245–262 (2019)
31. Huda, S., Abawajy, J., Alazab, M., Abdollalihian, M., Islam, R., Yearwood, J.: Hybrids of support vector machine wrapper and filter based framework for malware detection. Futur. Gener. Comput. Syst. **55**, 376–390 (2016)

Dual Security RGB Image Encryption Algorithm for Lightweight Cryptography

Vrushali Khaladkar[1,2]([⊠]) [iD] and Manish Kumar[2] [iD]

[1] Department of Mathematics, Fergusson College (Autonomous), Pune, Maharashtra, India
[2] Birla Institute of Technology and Science-Pilani, Hyderabad-Campus, Hyderabad 500078, Telangana, India
p20200511@hyderabad.bits-pilani.ac.in,
manishkumar@hyderabad.bits-pilani.ac.in

Abstract. An efficacious mathematical cryptographic algorithm for three-plane RGB images based on an L-shaped fractal and a 1-D chaotic tent map is proposed. Since vast data sets of images and videos are transmitted daily over public channels, the security and authenticity of data are of utmost priority. Fractals are very well suited for image encryption on a large scale due to their randomness property and infinite boundaries. One of the simplest implementations on the hardware of an IoT device is a one-dimensional dynamical system called the 1-D Chaotic tent map. This map is frequently used in encryption techniques because of its sensitivity towards initial conditions and impulsiveness. Due to the low dimensions of the 1-D chaotic tent map, this algorithm is more suited for lightweight cryptographic applications. The computer simulation results on MATLAB 2022a are explained to analyze the capabilities of the proposed algorithm using statistical analysis. The test results of differential attacks, percentage cropping attacks, and noise attacks are tabulated to confirm the wholesomeness of the proposed algorithm for 3-plane image encryption. There is a table that shows how secure the proposed 3-plane image encryption algorithm is by comparing it to other *RGB* image encryption algorithms that are already out there using entropy, correlation coefficient, and robustness using differential attacks.

Keywords: Encryption · Decryption · Fractal · Chaos

1 Introduction

In the modern era of big data, the storage and transmission of multimedia data are growing rapidly. The major issue of this fifth generation of telecommunications is the security of the generated data during transmission as well as during

---

The authors are very grateful for providing the necessary facilities and motivation to carry out this research.

storage. Hence, the security and authenticity of this data are of utmost priority [1]. The digital information consisting of texts, images, audios, and videos is stored and transmitted in the form of bits and is accessible to all; hence, it is vulnerable to various attacks. This digital data needs high security during transmission as well as storage so that if someone tries to get that information, it will be in an ambiguous form. The branch of industrial and applied mathematics that deals with securing information is called cryptography. Encryption is the technique to convert plain text into an unreadable format, while decryption is the reverse process. In day-to-day life, unknowingly, we use cryptography everywhere. For daily online transactions, email sending, or unlocking mobile phones, we use encryption to secure passwords, which might be in various formats like biometrics, images, or alpha-numeric. The authentication of such information is carried out by performing algorithms based on cryptography. There are two major caregories of cryptographic algorithms based on key structure. If the decryption key is based on or can be evaluated using encryption key, the algorithm is said to be symmetric key algorithm while, if the algorithm uses two different keys one for publicly available and other is private key, such algorithms are asymmetric key algorithms or public-private key algorithms. The encryption algorithms are mainly comprised of the confusion process and diffusion process using many mathematical algorithms, namely RSA, Chaotic maps, symmetric key algorithms, etc. The proposed 3 plane image encryption algorithm uses fractal geometry and a chaotic 1-D tent map as its core part.

2   Literature Review

Checking the robustness and effectiveness of any proposed encryption algorithm against numerous attacks and statistical results is very important. Many researchers have used chaotic map-based diffusion processes because of their strong sensitivity to seed conditions [4,5]. The author accomplishes a combination of 3D Lorenz chaotic maps along with fractals [6]. Discrete as well as continuous chaotic maps are widely used in the diffusion and confusion process for cryptographic algorithms presented in work [7]. Research [8] shows the fusion of fractals along with discrete dynamical systems for adding more diffusion to their algorithm. Author [9] has explained how multimedia is protected using various chaotic maps. Multiple techniques, like algorithm of digital watermarking, data encryption methodologies, stenographic algorithms, and information hiding, have been developed for securing multimedia data. The researchers incorporate chaotic maps-based image encryption [10,12,13]. Various alterations are carried out in different environments of chaotic maps to design cryptographic algorithms [1–4] and [16–18,22]. In the work [14], an improved Rossler system is used for generating keys, and an encryption scheme is proposed using multidimensional chaotic maps along with biological DNA encoding techniques, which is a better-suited algorithm than the traditional ones. The authors [15] have proposed an efficient algorithm for securing applications based on IoT using 2-D cellular automata. The proposed work in [19] looks at how image encryption can be used to keep delayed chaotic neural networks in sync with each other. It also looks at impulsive control, event-triggered impulsive control, and event-triggered delayed impulsive control for fractal reconstruction. In the paper [21], a new algorithm for generating fractional-order chaotic seed is designed for solving the problem based on complex operations of single less-dimensional systems and simple large-dimensional systems. [20] By embedding a secret image (SI) into a visually meaningful carrier image (CAI), traditional visually meaningful image encryption (VMIE) achieves dual protection.

In the proposed work, a fractal Tromino based on an L-shaped system and a 1-D chaotic tent dynamical system is devised to obtain confusion process and diffusion process of a 3-plane image. The proposed 3-plane image encryption algorithm is strongly recommended for real-time implementation as the computational complexity of the algorithm is reduced due to the use of fractal Tromino and the simplest 1-D dynamical system without affecting the strength of security. Techniques like advanced encryption standards show excellent security but have high time complexity. Security analysis is performed and tested for various images of various sizes, and results are tabulated to showcase the influence of the proposed algorithm against various cryptographic attacks.

3   Description of the Proposed Methodology

3.1   1-D Chaotic Tent Dynamical System

The 1-D tent map is one of the uncomplicated 1-D discrete dynamical systems studied in encryption techniques due to its chaotic property, which the work done by the authors interpret [5–7]. The analysis of a 1-D chaotic tent dynamical system is much simpler since it is plotted using two straight lines. The graph of a 1-D chaotic tent dynamical system is schematically shown using MATLAB software version 2023a. Families of tent maps behave differently for different parameters $0 \leq r_0 \leq 2$ and $x \in [0, 1]$. The 1-D chaotic tent map is mathematically expressed in Eq. (1)

$$T(x) = \begin{cases} r_0 x, & 0 \leq x \leq \frac{1}{2} \\ r_0(1 - x), & \frac{1}{2} \leq x \leq 1. \end{cases} \tag{1}$$

The plot of the 1-D tent map consists of two straight lines meeting at a point to form the shape of the tent. Although a non-linear system itself, it is distinctly identifiable from other nonlinear systems. The equation and the diagrammatic appearance of the tent map are simple, but they provide highly complex, chaotic phenomena for certain parameters and, hence, are useful to generate pseudo-random numbers.

3.2   Fractal Geometry

The branch of mathematics that possesses the property of equal magnification in all directions is fractal geometry. Due to its recurring pattern characteristic, it is widely used in key stream generation for the process of confusion and diffusion in many encryption algorithms.

3.3   Fractal Triomino

A polygon in the plane constructed using three equal-sized squares connected edge-to-edge is called a Triomino or Tromino. There are two types of Trominos, L and I, if rotations and reflections are not permitted as distinct shapes.

4   Proposed Encryption Algorithm

In this section, we are interested in discussing the proposed 3-plane image encryption and decryption algorithm. For a more detailed way of the proposed 3-plane image encryption algorithm, the following eight steps are provided below:

4.1   Proposed Encryption Algorithm

Step-1: Take input as a 3-plane image.

Step-2: An image matrix M of size $m \times 3n$ is constructed using 3-plane image of size $m \times n \times 3$.

Step-3: Key_1 and Key_2 are two random keys of size 8-bit each.

Step-4: Matrix M' from fractal Tromino from L-system fractal is generated from matrix M given by the Eq. (2):

$$M'(x,y) = \begin{cases} mod(y,f) & \text{if } mod(i, key_2 \times c) < key_1 \times c \\ mod(x,f) & \text{if } mod(j, key_2 \times c) < key_1 \times c \\ mod(c-x,f), & \text{otherwise,} \end{cases} \quad (2)$$

where $c = \sqrt{((255 - Avg) \times Avg)}$ is the value rounded off to the nearest integer, and Avg is the average intensity of matrix M.

Step-5: The new matrix M' is reshaped in size $m \times n \times 3$ to obtain fractal Tromino.

Step-6: First level encryption E_1 is obtained by operating XOR on M' with original input three-plane image.

Step-7: E_1 is then split into three planes: Red plane, Green plane, and Blue plane.

Step-8: On each channel of E_1, the chaotic tent map is applied to obtain encrypted red, green, and blue channel images.

Step-8: Second-level encryption E_2 is obtained by concatenating the encrypted channels generated in step 7.

4.2   Proposed Decryption Algorithm

In the decryption process, one has to follow the above encryption steps in reverse manner to recover the plain image from the encrypted one, keeping in view the reverse chaotic map and inverse fractal Tromino from inverse L-system fractal will be used during this process.

5 Proposed Encryption Flowchart

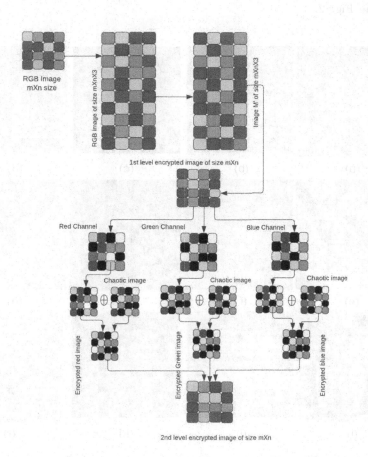

Fig. 1. Proposed encryption flowchart.

A flowchart of the proposed 3-plane image encryption algorithm is given in Fig. 1

6   Encryption Results

Results of simulation of the proposed encryption algorithm are figured out in following Fig. 2.

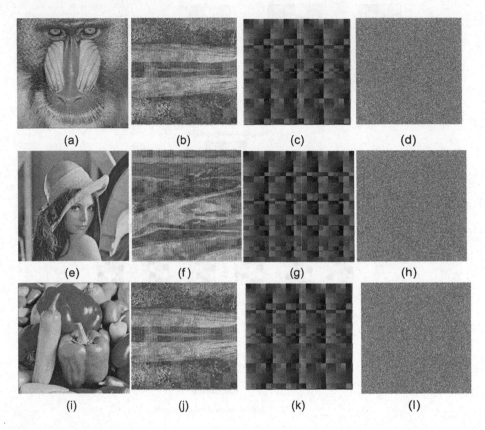

Fig. 2. Simulations of Encryption/Decryption (a) Original Baboon image, (b) First level encryption of Baboon image, (c) Fractal Tromino, (d) Second level encryption of Baboon image, (e) Original Lena image, (f) First level encryption of Lena image, (g) Fractal Tromino, (h) Second level encryption of Lena image, (I) Original Peppers image, (j) First level encryption of Peppers image, (k) Fractal Tromino, (l) Second level encryption of Peppers image.

7   Performance Analysis Through Experimental Results

To verify the effectiveness and authenticity of the proposed 3-plane image encryption algorithm, some experiments are carried. Experiments involve different intensity images. Also, images contaminated with pepper and salt noise,

Gaussian noise, and cropped images were tested to check the robustness of the proposed encryption system against noise and cropping attacks. The decryption steps in proposed algorithm recovers the original image from the cipher image. The resultant images show the successful execution of the proposed algorithm, and it also unfolds its efficiency in securing the information embedded in images and making it ambiguous.

7.1   Analysis Through Histograms

Plotting of histograms of encrypted images is used to verify whether the intensities are uniformly distributed. An ideal algorithm for encryption of colour images should generate a uniformly distributed histogram of the encrypted image of any original image (Figs. 3 and 4).

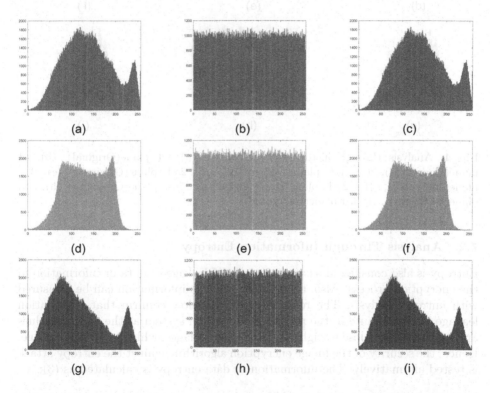

Fig. 3. Analysis through histogram:(Baboon Image) (a) 1st plane(Original), (b) 1st plane(Encrypted), (c) 1st plane(Decrypted), (d) 2nd plane(Original), (e) 2nd plane(encrypted), (f) 2nd plane(Decrypted), (g) 3rd plane(Original), (h) 3rd plane(Encrypted), (i) 3rd plane(Decrypted).

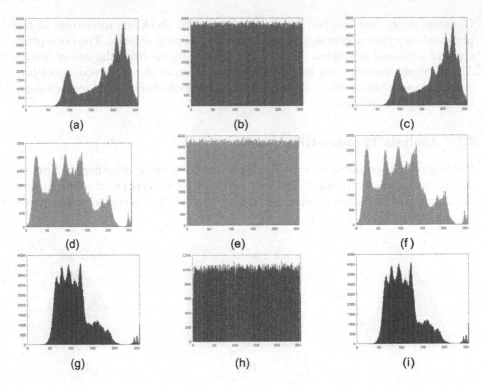

Fig. 4. Analysis through histogram(Lena Image) (a) 1st plane(Original), (b) 1st plane(Encrypted), (c) 1st plane(Decrypted), (d) 2nd plane(Original), (e) 2nd plane(encrypted), (f) 2nd plane(Decrypted), (g) 3rd plane(Original), (h) 3rd plane(Encrypted), (i) 3rd plane(Decrypted).

7.2   Analysis Through Information Entropy

Entropy is also considered as an estimation of leakage of data or information in the encryption process. Also, the leakage in image information can be measured with entropy analysis. The results tabulated below confirm that information leakage is very minute in the proposed encryption system as the entropy values are approximately close to eight for three plane images, which is the 8-bit image. Hence, the security of the image encryption algorithm against the entropy attack is tested affirmatively. The information or data entropy is calculated as (3):

$$\text{Entropy} = \sum_{i=0}^{2^K-1} \mathscr{P}(m_i) log_2 \frac{1}{\mathscr{P}(m_i)}, \tag{3}$$

where i indicates the value in the range 0 to $2^K - 1$, $P(m_i)$ represents the probability of occurrence of m_i where m_i is an event such that the pixel intensity is i and K represents K-bit image. For a considerably random image, the values of all $\mathscr{P}(m_i)$ are the same and hence show the entropy as K. Since the encrypted image shows high randomness, its entropy is approximately K. For the 8-bit images i.e. images having dynamic range $[0, 255] = [0, 2^8 - 1]$, the approximate entropy value is 8. The data or information entropy of the proposed 3-plane image encryption algorithm and references for the various images of size 512×512 are tabulated in the Table 1.

Table 1. Entropy of proposed work and references for the various images of size 512×512.

Image	Proposed	Ref^n. [8]	Ref^n. [9]	Ref^n. [10]	Ref^n. [11]	Ref^n. [12]
Baboon	7.9997	7.9972	7.9912	7.9989	7.9969	7.9974
Lena	7.9998	7.9972	7.9909	7.9972	7.9970	7.9971

7.3   Analysis Through Mean Squared Error

The term mean squared error ($M.S.E.$) estimates the closeness of the regression line from the set of points and calculates the distance from the set of points to the regression line and squares them. These distances are referred to as errors. Making squares eliminates negative values, if any. The formula for $M.S.E.$ between the image pixel intensities of the original 3-plane image and the encrypted 3-plane image of size $\mathcal{M} \times \mathcal{N}$ is given by mathematical Eq. (4):

$$M.S.E. = \frac{1}{\mathcal{M} \times \mathcal{N}} \sum_{y=1}^{\mathcal{N}} \sum_{x=1}^{\mathcal{M}} (I_e(u,v) - I_o(u,v))^2, \qquad (4)$$

where $\mathcal{M}$ = total number of rows in an original or encrypted image, $\mathcal{N}$ = image column count, $I_e(u,v)$ = pixel intensity at the $(u,v)^{th}$ position of the 3-plane encrypted image and $I_o(x,y)$ = pixel intensity at $(u,v)^{th}$ position of the original 3-plane image. The mean squared error between the original 3-plane image and encrypted 3-plane image image of size 512×512 is given in the Table 2.

Table 2. $M.S.E.$ between the original 3-plane and encrypted 3-plane image of size 512×512.

Image	Proposed
(3-plane)-Baboon	8472
(3-plane)-Lena	9092
(3-plane)-Peppers	11181

7.4   Analysis Through Pearsonian Correlation Coefficient

The Pearson correlation coefficient is used to measure the strength of the correspondence between two continuous or discrete variables measured from the same interval or on the same scale. The correlation coefficients between the original and encrypted image of Baboon and Lena of size 512×512 are tabulated in Table 3.

Table 3. The Pearsonian correlation coefficient between the original 3-plane and encrypted 3-plane image of size 512×512.

Image	Baboon	Lena
Red Plane	0.0040	−0.00025
Green Plane	−0.00015	0.0010
Blue Plane	−0.00016	0.0010

8   Resistance Against Differential Attack

The efficiency of any algorithm proposed for RGB image encryption is based on how robust the proposed confusion-diffusion algorithm is against multiple differential attacks. Differential attacks on images are mainly concerned with the study of the cause of the differences in the original colour or Gray image that led to the differences in the cipher image. Known plain text and chosen cipher text attacks are referred to as differential attacks. To study the strength of the proposed 3-plane image encryption algorithm of resistance against various differential attacks, the number of pixels change rate ($npcr$) and unified average changing intensity ($uaci$) analysis are used. The proposed 3-plane image encryption algorithm is used to construct a cipher image C1 from a plain image P1. A minute modification is carried out on the image by choosing any random pixel and altering its intensity or by shuffling the position of the pixel in the image. The proposed 3-plane image encryption algorithm is again used to encrypt the modified image to obtain another cipher image, C2. The comparison between these two cipher images, C1 and C2, is carried out using the measures of the number of pixels change rate ($npcr$) and unified average changing intensity ($uaci$). Mathematically,

$$npcr = \frac{\sum_1^{\mathcal{N}} \sum_1^{\mathcal{M}} Dist(u, v)}{\mathcal{M} \times \mathcal{N}} \times 100, \tag{5}$$

if the pixel intensities at the $(u, v)^{th}$ position are equal in C1 and C2, then the discrete metric $Dist(u, v) = 0$, otherwise $Dist(u, v) = 1$, where $\mathcal{M}$ and $\mathcal{N}$ are the row count and column count in the plain image. The average intensity of differences between two encrypted images, C1 and C2, is calculated using $uaci$, i.e., the unified average change intensity. It is calculated as follows:

$$uaci = \frac{\sum_1^N \sum_1^M \frac{C1(u,v)-C2(u,v)}{255}}{M \times N} \times 100, \tag{6}$$

the *npcr* and *uaci* results are tabulated in the Table 4.

Table 4. Results of resistance against differential attacks through *npcr* and *uaci* for Baboon and Lena images of size 512 × 512.

Three plane Image	npcr	uaci
Baboon	99.6093	33.4635
Lena	99.6090	33.4635
Peppers	99.6190	33.4654

9   Cropping Attack Analysis

Cropping attack analysis is used to verify how robust the algorithm is against information loss. If the adversary crops some percentage of the information from the encrypted image, this analysis gives the robustness of the recovery of the data. The North-West 25%, South-East 25%, and North-East 25%, total 50% portions of the cipher image, are cropped and again retrieved by using the proposed decryption algorithm. The recovery of the decrypted images is given in the Fig. 5.

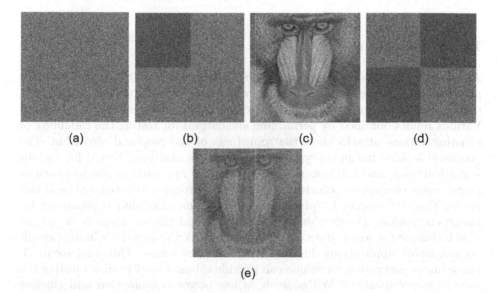

Fig. 5. Baboon: (a) Encrypted image, (b) 25 % cropped image, (c) Decrypted image, (d) 50 % cropped image, (e) Decrypted image.

10   Analysis Through NIST Randomness Tests

Testing of randomness in encrypted data plays an important role. The most standardized and used suit for testing the randomness of encrypted data is the National Institute of Standards and Technology (NIST). These tests are fast, though they analyze vast amounts of data. The results of NIST Randomness tests for encrypted Baboon image of size 512×512 are given in the Table 5.

Table 5. NIST Randomness tests for encrypted Baboon image of dimension 512×512.

NIST Randomness Tests	P-value	Conclusion
Frequency (Monobit)	0.9764	Successful
Within a Block frequency	0.9738	Successful
Longest Run	0.5650	Successful
Approximate Entropy	0.2997	Successful
Cumulative Sums (Cusum)	0.8861	Successful
Runs Test	0.4894	Successful
Rank of binary matrix	0.3916	Successful
D.F.T	0.3231	Successful
Template Matching(Non-overlapping)	0.2232	Successful
Template Matching(Overlapping)	0.2719	Successful
Linear Complexity	0.6030	Successful
Serial Test	0.4847	Successful

11   Conclusion

Along with the chaotic nature and sensitivity towards initial seed value, the proposed 3-plane image encryption algorithm uses two 1-D tent maps and fractals constructed using an L-shaped system to obtain the final encrypted image. Various results obtained by performing simulations for testing the capability of resisting various attacks show the robustness of the proposed algorithm. The proposed 3-plane image encryption algorithm has also been tested for various statistical tests, and the comparison between the approach in the proposed 3-plane image encryption algorithm and other approaches is tabulated, and this proves that the proposed 3-plane image encryption algorithm is promising for image encryption. The combination of fractals and chaotic maps is an adaptable technique for secure data communication in WSNs as well as in lightweight cryptographic applications due to its smaller dimensions. This dual secure 3-plane image encryption technique can provide robust security while meeting the specific requirements of WSNs, such as low power consumption and efficient communication.

References

1. Li, C., Luo, G., Qin, K., Li, C.: An image encryption scheme based on chaotic tent map. Nonlinear Dyn. **87**, 127–133 (2017)
2. AlZain, M.A., Faragallah, O.S.: Efficient chaotic tent map-based image cryptosystem. Int. J. Comput. Appl. **167**(7), 8887 (2017)
3. Niyat, A.Y., Moattar, M.H., Torshiz, M.N.: Color image encryption based on hybrid hyper-chaotic system and cellular automata. Opt. Lasers Eng. **90**, 225–237 (2017)
4. Zhu, C., Sun, K.: Cryptanalyzing and improving a novel color image encryption algorithm using RT-enhanced chaotic tent maps. IEEE Access **6**, 18759–18770 (2018)
5. Kumar, M., Gupta, P.: A new medical image encryption algorithm based on the 1D logistic map associated with pseudo-random numbers. Multimedia Tools Appl. **80**(12), 18941–18967 (2021)
6. Wang, H., Tao, X., Huang, J.S.: An improved chessboard covering algorithm with generalized fractal strategy (2019)
7. Agarwal, S.: Secure image transmission using fractal and 2D-chaotic map. J. Imaging **4**(1), 17 (2018)
8. Cao, W., Cai, H., Hua, Z.: n-Dimensional Chaotic Map with application in secure communication. Chaos Solitons Fract. **163**, 112519 (2022)
9. Hosny, K.M. (ed.): Multimedia Security Using Chaotic Maps: Principles and Methodologies, vol. 884. Springer, Heidelberg (2020). https://doi.org/10.1007/978-3-030-38700-6
10. Amin, M., Faragallah, O.S., Abd El-Latif, A.A.: A chaotic block cipher algorithm for image cryptosystems. Commun. Nonlinear Sci. Numer. Simul. **15**(11), 3484–3497 (2010)
11. Tuncer, T.: The implementation of chaos-based PUF designs in field programmable gate array. Nonlinear Dyn. **86**, 975–986 (2016)
12. Dagadu, J.C., Li, J.: Context-based watermarking cum chaotic encryption for medical images in telemedicine applications. Multimedia Tools Appl. **77**, 24289–24312 (2018)
13. Jolfaei, A., Matinfar, A., Mirghadri, A.: Preserving the confidentiality of digital images using a chaotic encryption scheme. Int. J. Electron. Secur. Digit. Forensics **7**(3), 258–277 (2015)
14. Es-Sabry, M., et al.: Securing images using high dimensional chaotic maps and DNA encoding techniques. IEEE Access **11**, 100856–100878 (2023)
15. Roy, S., Shrivastava, M., Rawat, U., Pandey, C.V., Nayak, S.K.: IESCA: an efficient image encryption scheme using 2-D cellular automata. J. Inf. Secur. Appl. **61**, 102919 (2021)
16. Elshamy, A.M., et al.: Optical image cryptosystem using double random phase encoding and Arnold's Cat map. Optical Quant. Electron. **48**, 1–18 (2016)
17. Mandal, M.K., Banik, G.D., Chattopadhyay, D., Nandi, D.: An image encryption process based on chaotic logistic map. IETE Tech. Rev. **29**(5), 395–404 (2012)
18. Behnia, S., Akhshani, A., Ahadpour, S., Mahmodi, H., Akhavan, A.: A fast chaotic encryption scheme based on piecewise nonlinear chaotic maps. Phys. Lett. A **366**(4–5), 391–396 (2007)
19. Mohanrasu, S.S., Udhayakumar, K., Priyanka, T.M.C., Gowrisankar, A., Banerjee, S., Rakkiyappan, R.: Event-triggered impulsive controller design for synchronization of delayed chaotic neural networks and its fractal reconstruction: an application to image encryption. Appl. Math. Model. **115**, 490–512 (2023)

20. Chang, H., Wang, E., Liu, J.: Research on image encryption based on fractional seed chaos generator and fractal theory. Fractal Fract. **7**(3), 221 (2023)
21. Gan, Z., et al.: Visually meaningful image encryption scheme using multi-parameter fractal theory and block synchronous sorting diffusion. Phys. Scr. **98**(8), 085216 (2023)
22. Sheela, S.J., Suresh, K.V., Tandur, D.: Image encryption based on modified Henon map using hybrid chaotic shift transform. Multimedia Tools Appl. **77**, 25223–25251 (2018)

Computer Networks

Blockchain: An Efficient Network for Optimizing High-Performance Consensus Algorithms

Deven A. Gol(✉) ⓘ and Nikhil Gondaliya ⓘ

The Charutar Vidya Mandal (CVM) University, Anand, Gujarat 388120, India
devenkumar.gol@cvmu.edu.in

Abstract. Blockchain technology has gained widespread acceptance across various sectors due to its decentralized, transparent, and secure nature. Central to this technology are consensus algorithms like Proof of Work (PoW) and Proof of Stake (PoS), which ensure the reliability and validity of blockchain networks. However, these current consensus algorithms encounter challenges related to scalability, energy consumption, and security vulnerabilities. To address these challenges, we propose a novel secure network designed to enhance the efficiency and security of consensus algorithms within blockchain technology. This innovative network integrates the strengths of PoW and PoS, resulting in a hybrid consensus algorithm that outperforms existing ones. Additionally, the network incorporates a dynamic sharding mechanism to enhance scalability, reducing transaction processing times. The primary goal of this proposed network is to provide a more robust and efficient blockchain platform capable of handling larger transaction volumes while preserving its security attributes. This advancement has the potential to reshape the application of blockchain technology across diverse industries, including finance, healthcare, and supply chain management.

Keywords: Peer-to-Peer Networking · Byzantine Fault Tolerance · Proof of Work (PoW) · Proof of Stake (PoS) · Blockchain

1 Blockchain Technology: Overview of Consensus Algorithms

Blockchain technology is a decentralized and secure method for recording transactions, and it operates on a network of computers, or nodes, that validate and store transactions in a decentralized manner. This decentralized approach means that no central authority controls the network, and each node holds a copy of the blockchain ledger [1]. The transparency of blockchain technology allows anyone to view the transactions on the network, and its immutability ensures that once a transaction is added to the blockchain, it cannot be altered. Consensus algorithms play a critical role in maintaining the integrity and validity of the blockchain network [2]. In a blockchain network, every node is responsible for validating and verifying transactions. Consensus algorithms are used to reach a consensus among nodes regarding the state of the network and the order in which transactions are added to the blockchain. There are several consensus algorithms

S. Rajagopal et al. (Eds.): ASCIS 2023, CCIS 2039, pp. 347–362, 2024.
https://doi.org/10.1007/978-3-031-59100-6_24

employed in blockchain technology, including Proof of Work (PoW), Proof of Stake (PoS), and Delegated Proof of Stake (DPoS) [3]. PoW requires nodes to solve complex mathematical problems to validate transactions, while PoS necessitates nodes to hold a certain amount of cryptocurrency to validate transactions. DPoS allows the delegation of validation authority to trusted parties. Each of these consensus algorithms has its own advantages and disadvantages, with their effectiveness depending on the specific use case [4]. However, the existing consensus algorithms encounter various challenges such as scalability, energy consumption, and security threats. Scalability problems arise because the current consensus algorithms demand all nodes to validate every transaction, resulting in a bottleneck in the network's processing capacity [6]. Energy consumption is a concern because PoW requires nodes to solve complex mathematical problems, consuming a significant amount of energy. Lastly, security threats emerge because malicious nodes can manipulate the network by controlling the majority of the network's computing power [5]. To tackle these challenges a novel secure network based on blockchain technology has been proposed. This innovative network seeks to provide a more robust and efficient blockchain platform capable of handling a larger volume of transactions while maintaining its security features. This advancement has the potential to revolutionize the application of blockchain technology in various sectors, including finance, healthcare, and supply chain management [6–12].

1.1 Motivation

The motivation for creating a secure network with a streamlined and high-performance consensus algorithm based on blockchain technology arises from the challenges faced by current consensus algorithms. The consensus algorithms in use today, like PoW and PoS, encounter issues related to scalability, energy use, and security. Scalability is a big hurdle for blockchain tech. The current algorithms need all nodes to approve every transaction, which slows down processing and raises costs for users. As more transactions happen, the blockchain ledger grows, making it tough for nodes to store and manage all that data [13]. Energy use is another problem. PoW requires nodes to solve complex math problems to confirm transactions, and this eats up a lot of energy. This has raised concerns about the environment and made it hard to use blockchain on a large scale [14]. Lastly, there are security threats. Bad actors can mess with the network by controlling most of the computing power. This is called a 51% attack, where one entity controls more than half of the network's computing power. This can lead to double spending, where someone uses the same cryptocurrency twice. To tackle these issues [15], a new secure network with an efficient and secure consensus algorithm based on blockchain technology has been suggested. This network aims to offer a better way to use blockchain, handling more transactions while staying secure. By addressing these challenges, this proposed network has the potential to make blockchain even more useful and change many industries.

2 Literature Survey on Blockchain Consensus Algorithms

Blockchain consensus algorithms are crucial for securing, decentralizing, and making network transactions unchangeable. They act as the central element in every blockchain network and have evolved significantly, showing various methods, each with its own strengths and weaknesses. This thorough survey methodically explores different blockchain consensus algorithms, explaining their special features. This contributes to a detailed understanding of their significant impact on the broad scope of blockchain technology. Table 1 provides a comprehensive overview of prevalent blockchain consensus algorithms, offering a comparative analysis of their respective methodologies, advantages, and use cases.

Table 1. Comparison of consensus algorithm [16–26]

Consensus Algorithm	Year	Advantages	Limitations	Use Cases
Proof of Work (PoW)	1993	Decentralized, Secure	High energy consumption, slow	Cryptocurrencies, Blockchain Networks
Proof of Stake (PoS)	2012	Energy-efficient, Fast	Centralization risk, difficult implementation	Cryptocurrencies, Ethereum 2.0, Tezos
Delegated Proof of Stake (DPoS)	2014	Fast, Scalable	Centralization risk, limited participation	EOS, TRON
Practical Byzantine Fault Tolerance (PBFT)	1999	Fast, Finality	Centralization risk, limited scalability	Hyperledger Fabric, Ripple
Honey Badger Byzantine Fault Tolerance (HBBFT)	2016	High throughput, Robustness	Complex implementation, limited adoption	Privacy-Preserving Blockchains
Avalanche	2018	Fast, Scalable, Adaptive	New, not widely tested	Decentralized Applications (dApps)
Algorand	2019	Scalable, Secure, Fast	New, limited adoption	Financial Services, Decentralized Apps (dApps)
Casper (Proof of Stake)	2017	Scalable, Secure	Complex protocol, limited deployment	Ethereum 2.0

These blockchain features include optimized mining algorithms, faster block times, and parallel processing, all aimed at improving confirmation times and enhancing the efficiency of cryptocurrencies like Bitcoin, Litecoin, Ethereum, and Bitcoin Cash. Table 2 incorporates select literature references which represent seminal works contributing to the ongoing exploration of PoW, spanning design, implementation, and performance

Table 2. Literature Review on Blockchain based Consensus algorithms.

Feature	Description	Use Case	Significance
Optimized Mining Algorithms	Use of more efficient mining algorithms to reduce energy consumption [26]	Cryptocurrencies (Bitcoin, Litecoin)	High
Faster Block Times	Reduction in block creation time to improve confirmation times [28]	Cryptocurrencies (Litecoin, Ethereum)	High
Parallel Processing	Ability to process multiple transactions simultaneously to improve confirmation times [29]	Cryptocurrencies (Ethereum, Bitcoin Cash)	High
Mining Difficulty Adjustment	Mechanisms to adjust mining difficulty to prevent centralization [30]	Cryptocurrencies (Bitcoin, Litecoin)	High
Randomized Mining Rewards	Randomized reward distribution to incentivize smaller mining operations [31, 32]	Cryptocurrencies (TBD)	Medium
Adaptive Mining Algorithm	An algorithm that can adapt to changing network conditions to improve security and reduce energy consumption [33]	Cryptocurrencies (TBD)	High
Merkle Trees for Verification	Use of Merkle Trees to improve transaction verification efficiency [33]	Cryptocurrencies (Bitcoin, Ethereum)	Medium
PoW with PoS Hybrid Consensus	Combination of PoW and PoS to reduce energy consumption and increase security [34]	Cryptocurrencies (Ethereum 2.0, TBD)	High
Sustainable Mining Practices	Use of alternative energy sources and more sustainable mining practices to reduce carbon emissions [36]	Cryptocurrencies (TBD)	High

(continued)

Table 2. (*continued*)

Feature	Description	Use Case	Significance
Reduced Energy Consumption	Implementation of more efficient mining algorithms and hardware to reduce energy consumption [37]	Public and private blockchains	High
Interoperability	The ability for different blockchain networks to communicate and share information with other [40]	Public and private blockchains	High
Sharding	Breaking up the blockchain into smaller, more manageable pieces to improve scalability and increase transaction throughput [42]	Public and private blockchains	High
Smart Contract Functionality	Ability to execute complex business logic and automate processes by smart contracts [43, 44]	Public and private blockchains	High
Privacy and Confidentiality	The ability to keep sensitive information private and confidential through advanced cryptographic techniques such as zero-knowledge proofs [43]	Private and consortium blockchains	High

aspects. These references collectively address critical research gaps and offer insights for further refinement and optimization within the PoW consensus algorithm.

3 A Novel Consensus Algorithm for Energy-Efficient Blockchain Networks

The research introduces a novel secure network aimed at overcoming the challenges associated with existing consensus algorithms. This proposed network combines the strengths of both Proof of Work (PoW) and Proof of Stake (PoS), resulting in a hybrid consensus algorithm that outperforms the existing ones in terms of efficiency and security. Additionally, it employs a dynamic sharding mechanism to enhance scalability and integrates a Byzantine fault-tolerant (BFT) consensus algorithm to bolster security [16–20]. This innovative approach reduces energy consumption while preserving the network's security and decentralization. The paper discusses the details of the dynamic sharding mechanism employed in the proposed network. This mechanism divides the network into smaller sub-networks, known as shards, enabling parallel processing of transactions. This not only improves scalability but also reduces the overall transaction processing time. To enhance security, the proposed network utilizes fundamental concepts from a BFT consensus algorithm, which can withstand attacks from rogue nodes. This BFT consensus algorithm ensures that the network can reach an agreement even when a certain number of nodes are compromised, providing a high level of security [21].

As per shown in Fig. 1, The suggested solution for the PoW blockchain network holds promise for creating a more robust and efficient blockchain platform capable of handling a higher volume of transactions while maintaining its security features. PoW is a widely used consensus algorithm in various blockchain networks for validating transactions and generating new blocks. Although it has been effective in securing the Bitcoin network, it does come with certain drawbacks, such as high energy consumption and limited transaction throughput [22].

Here are potential improvements to the Proof of Work (PoW) consensus algorithm:

Equitable Hashing Distribution: In traditional PoW, miners with the most hashing power have the highest chance of creating a new block, leading to centralization. A more equitable approach would be to distribute block creation opportunities fairly based on a miner's hashing power, thereby incentivizing smaller miners to participate [23].

Adaptive Block Difficulty: PoW block difficulty is determined by the overall network hashing power, which can make it excessively challenging for smaller miners and overly simple for larger ones. An adaptive block difficulty system that adjusts according to the number of miners can create a more balanced environment, increasing difficulty with more miners and reducing it with fewer participants [24].

Hybrid Proof-of-Stake Integration: PoW's substantial computational demands result in high energy consumption. An integrated approach combining Proof of Stake (PoS) could diminish energy consumption by allowing nodes to validate blocks based on their cryptocurrency holdings instead of computational power. Nevertheless, this approach might introduce centralization around affluent stakeholders [25].

Dual Consensus Layer: To mitigate the risk of a 51% attack, where one entity controls over half of the network's computational power, implementing a dual consensus system could be valuable. For instance, a block could be added to the chain only if it garners approval from a specific portion of nodes and validation from a certain percentage of cryptocurrency holders [26].

Resource-Economical Alternatives: To curtail energy consumption and environmental impact, exploring alternative consensus mechanisms that do not rely on intensive computation or energy-intensive hardware becomes imperative. Such alternatives could encompass Proof of Authority, Proof of Elapsed Time, or Proof of Identity. However, it's crucial to acknowledge that these alternatives may present their own shortcomings regarding security and decentralization [27–29]. The paper highlights how important it is to solve the problems that current agreement (consensus algorithms) rules have. It also suggests a way to make blockchain technology work better and be safer.

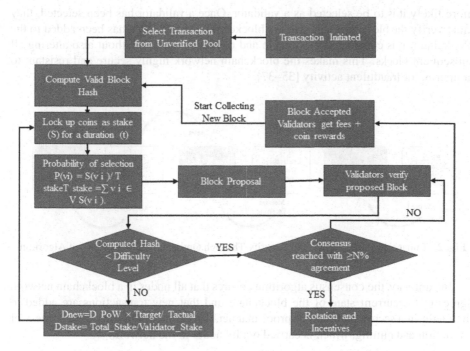

Fig. 1. Overview of the Proposed Blockchain Consensus Algorithm

4 Design and Security Measures of Consensus Algorithms in Blockchain Networks

The consensus algorithm plays a critical role in the functioning of a blockchain network. It is responsible for ensuring that all nodes in the network agree on the current state of the blockchain and that new transactions are added to the chain in a secure and tamper-proof manner. When a new transaction is initiated on the network, it is first broadcast to all nodes in the network. These nodes will then validate the transaction to ensure that it meets certain criteria, such as having the correct format and adhering to any rules set by the network [30]. As shown in Fig. 2, Once a sufficient number of nodes have validated the transaction, it is added to a pool of unconfirmed transactions. The next step is to add the transaction to a block. A block is a bundle of transactions that have been confirmed and added to the blockchain. Before a block can be added to the blockchain, it must be verified by the consensus algorithm. This involves a process called mining, which is carried out by nodes known as miners [31]. In a proof-of-work (PoW) consensus algorithm, miners compete to solve a complex mathematical problem. The first miner to solve the problem and validate the block is rewarded with a set amount of cryptocurrency. The other nodes in the network then validate the block to ensure that it meets the network's rules and add it to their local copy of the blockchain. In a proof-of-stake (PoS) consensus algorithm, nodes are selected to validate blocks based on the amount of cryptocurrency they hold. The more cryptocurrency a node holds, the more likely it is to be selected as a validator. Once a validator has been selected, they must verify the block and add it to the blockchain. Once a block has been added to the blockchain, it is considered immutable and cannot be altered without also altering all subsequent blocks. This makes the blockchain network highly secure and resistant to tampering or fraudulent activity [35–37].

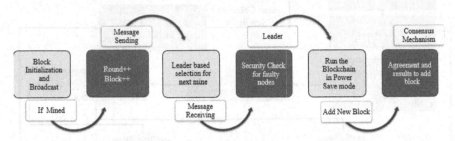

Fig. 2. Enhancing Performance and Security Through Optimization of a Proposed Algorithm

In summary, the consensus algorithm ensures that all nodes in a blockchain network agree on the current state of the blockchain and that new transactions are added to the chain in a secure and tamper-proof manner. This is achieved through a process of validation and mining, which is carried out by nodes in the network.

4.1   Analyzing Security Threats to Blockchain Networks: An Overview of Common Attacks and Vulnerabilities

Blockchain networks, designed to be decentralized and secure, are not impervious to attacks. This article discusses common attacks, primarily targeting proof-of-work (PoW) consensus-based blockchain networks.

51% Attack: This occurs when an entity controls over 50% of the network's computing power, enabling manipulation of transactions and rewriting the blockchain's history.

Double-Spending: Attackers attempt to spend cryptocurrency twice by creating two conflicting transactions. Controlling enough power to mine two blocks concurrently is essential for this attack's success.

Selfish Mining: Miners withhold newly mined blocks, gaining an unfair advantage in the mining race and earning more rewards.

Sybil Attack: Attackers create multiple fake identities to control a significant network portion, influencing network decisions.

Eclipse Attack: Attackers isolate a node by surrounding it with their nodes, preventing it from receiving new transactions and manipulating its broadcasts.

These represent only a selection of prevalent attacks observed within blockchain networks utilizing a proof-of-work consensus algorithm [38–42]. In response to such threats, blockchain networks frequently incorporate intrinsic safeguards. These defenses encompass network-wide consensus mechanisms, decentralized governance structures, and cryptographic methodologies aimed at fortifying transaction security and upholding the integrity of the blockchain.

4.2   Strengthening Blockchain Network Security: Strategies to Counter Common Attacks and Vulnerabilities

Enhancing the security of blockchain networks is like keeping your home safe from different kinds of problems. Here are some ways in which common attacks on proof-of-work (PoW) based blockchain networks can be improved:

51% Attack Improvement: To stop a group from taking over the network, they can use better methods like making sure only trusted people can control it or requiring them to have a certain amount of money in the system.

Sybil Attack Improvement: To make sure that fake people can't mess with the network, they can use things like signatures or special ways of proving who they are.

Double Spending Improvement: To prevent someone from using the same money twice, they can make transactions happen faster so there's less time to do that. Also, there are new ways of making sure it doesn't happen, like using Byzantine Fault Tolerance.

Selfish Mining Improvement: To stop miners from being unfair and trying to win more, they can make sure the way they mine is fairer. Also, they can use things like delayed broadcasting to make it harder for miners to get an advantage.

Eclipse Attack Improvement: To protect against attacks that isolate parts of the network, they can make sure the network is more connected. They can also use things like firewalls to keep bad nodes out.

Moreover, blockchain networks can keep learning and trying to get even better at staying safe. They can do research to find new ways that bad things could happen and then figure out how to stop them. It's like always studying to learn more and getting better security systems for your home as new threats come up.

4.3   Next-Generation Blockchain Consensus: The Optimized Proof of Work (PoW) Algorithm

Proof of Work (PoW) is like a security system for many blockchain networks. It checks transactions and makes new parts of the blockchain. But the regular PoW has some problems like using too much energy, becoming too centralized, and being vulnerable to attacks. To fix these issues, people have come up with better PoW systems that use less energy, spread power out more, and still stay secure.

This paper is about one of those improved PoW systems:

1. **Transaction Selection:** Start with a set of valid transactions from the transaction pool, denoted as T. Discard transactions that do not meet the validity criteria.
2. **Merkle Tree Construction:** Create a Merkle tree from the selected transactions, represented as MerkleTree (Tvalid). This involves recursively hashing pairs of transactions until a single Merkle root hash, denoted as M, remains.
3. **Block Header Generation:** Generate a block header comprising the following components:
   a). Current timestamp, denoted as Ts.
   b). Hash of the previous block in the blockchain, represented as prev$H$prev.
   c). Merkle root hash of the selected transactions, M.
   d). Target difficulty level for the proof-of-work algorithm, D. e. Nonce, denoted as N.

4. **Block Hash Computation:** Calculate the hash of the block header, represented as Hblock, using a cryptographic hash function such as SHA-256. This is computed as: Hblock = SHA-256($Ts \| H$prev$\| M \| D \| N$)
5. **Difficulty Verification:** Check if the computed block hash Hblock meets the target difficulty D. If Hblock $\leq D$, the block is considered valid; otherwise, increment the nonce N and repeat the hash calculation.
6. **Broadcast Valid Block:** Upon finding a valid block, broadcast it to the network.
7. **Network Validation:** Nodes in the network validate the block:
    a). Confirm that the Merkle root hash M in the block header matches the calculated Merkle root hash of transactions.
    b). Ensure the timestamp Ts is within a reasonable range.
    c). Verify that the previous block hash Hprev in the header matches the hash of the previous block in the blockchain.
    d). Validate that the block hash Hblock meets the target difficulty D.
8. **Add to Blockchain:** If the block passes validation, it is added to the blockchain of each node in the network. The miner who found the correct nonce N is rewarded with a pre-defined amount of cryptocurrency, known as the block reward, denoted as R.

In this algorithm, the utilization of a Merkle tree plays a pivotal role in swiftly confirming the authenticity of transactions within the block. Optimized Proof of Work (PoW) algorithms mark a substantial advancement compared to their traditional counterparts. They achieve heightened energy efficiency, bolstered resilience against centralization, and fortified security against potential 51% attacks. As the blockchain ecosystem matures, it is anticipated that there will be a proliferation of optimized PoW algorithms and innovative consensus mechanisms, each meticulously crafted to surmount the limitations inherent in current protocols.

5 Performance Assessment with Blocksim: Metrics and Simulation Results

BlockSim is a specialized tool for simulating and modeling various blockchain networks and consensus algorithms [47]. Several case studies have used BlockSim to explore different aspects of blockchain technology. These studies include simulating the Ethereum blockchain network to analyze its performance in various scenarios, examining the Proof of Stake (PoS) consensus algorithm under different network conditions, modeling the execution of smart contracts, assessing the scalability of blockchain networks, and simulating the detection of forks in the blockchain. These simulations consider factors like network size, transaction volume, and block characteristics to provide insights into how blockchain systems behave. These case studies collectively showcase BlockSim's versatility as a tool for simulating and analyzing various facets of blockchain networks and consensus algorithms. The simulation results for different combinations of block intervals and block propagation delays are presented below:

In assessing the performance of a blockchain network using the BlockSim simulator, several key metrics come into play: stale rate, throughput, and the fraction of blocks contributed by each miner. Stale rate reflects the percentage of blocks that don't make it into the final blockchain due to forks or consensus issues. Throughput measures how

Table 3. Performance Assessment of Miners based on performance evaluation.

Block Interval	Propagation Delay	Stale Rate (%)	Throughput (tx/s)	Miner 1's Blocks (%)	Miner 2's Blocks (%)	Miner 3's Blocks (%)	Miner 4's Blocks (%)
10 s	5 s	3.2%	120	25%	15%	43%	17%
5 s	10 s	4.7%	80	11%	32%	28%	29%
2 s	2 s	2.1%	300	20%	50%	12%	18%
15 s	1 s	1.8%	90	28%	19%	18%	35%
1 s	15 s	5.3%	40	10%	30%	50%	10%

many transactions can be processed per unit of time. Examining the proportion of blocks from each miner helps spot any potential centralization or imbalances in mining. Analyzing simulation results provides valuable insights into finding the right combination of block interval and propagation delay for specific use cases. For instance, applications demanding high throughput might benefit from a shorter block interval and lower propagation delay for speedy transaction processing. Conversely, security-focused applications might favor a longer block interval and higher propagation delay to minimize fork risks. Evaluating run time performance is also crucial to assess the practicality of implementing chosen block intervals and propagation delays in real-world blockchain networks. Here's an example Table 3 that illustrates the validation of PoW using the fraction of generated blocks given the hashing share of various miners:

Table 4. Assessing Block Generation by Miners (Comparative Analysis)

Miner	Hashing Power	Generated Blocks (out of 100)	Expected Blocks (out of 100)	Validity
A	30%	29	30	No
B	25%	24	25	No
C	20%	20	20	Yes
D	15%	15	15	Yes

As shown in Table 4, we're looking at four miners, each with different levels of computing power. The "Generated Blocks" column shows how many blocks each miner created out of a total of 100 blocks. The "Expected Blocks" column, on the other hand, tells us how many blocks we would expect each miner to make based on their computing power (for instance, Miner A, with 30% computing power, should theoretically make 30 blocks). Now, the "Validity" column helps us see if each miner's block creation matches what we expected. Miners C and D did a good job, as they made blocks in proportion to their computing power. However, Miners A and B didn't do so well because they made fewer blocks than we'd expect given their computing power. Table 4 helps us see how miners create blocks, making sure the PoW algorithm works well. If a miner doesn't create enough blocks based on their computing power, it might mean something's wrong, and we should do something about it. In general, these findings help us make blockchain networks better for certain uses. The study suggests a new way for everyone to agree (a consensus algorithm) that tries to make blockchain networks handle more things and stay safe. If implemented successfully, this algorithm could lead to several improvements, including:

Improved Transaction Throughput: SHP employs sharding to process transactions in parallel, boosting transaction throughput compared to traditional blockchains.

Enhanced Security: It incorporates security measures like a secure random number generator and a reputation system, bolstering defenses against malicious attacks.

Lower Energy Consumption: Designed for energy efficiency, SHP can reduce the environmental impact associated with blockchain networks.

Lower Transaction Fees: Increased throughput and energy efficiency may lead to reduced transaction fees, making blockchain technology more accessible.

This conclusion is further supported by the subsequent section in Fig. 3, which presents simulation results comparing the PoW, PoS, and proposed consensus protocol.

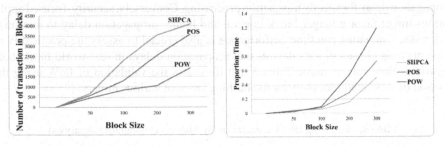

Fig. 3. Comparative Simulated Analysis of Initial Setup of Algorithms

The research introduces the Streamlined and High-Performance Consensus Algorithm (SHP), aiming to enhance the scalability and security of blockchain networks. SHP leverages sharding for parallel transaction processing, potentially improving throughput. It incorporates security measures like a secure random number generator and a reputation system to deter malicious attacks. Moreover, SHP is designed for energy efficiency, potentially reducing the environmental impact of blockchain networks. Lower transaction fees may also result from these optimizations. However, successful implementation hinges on various factors, including network size and user adoption, necessitating further research and testing. The SHP algorithm streamlines consensus, minimizes network messages, employs a leader-based approach, and utilizes proof-of-stake for validation, resulting in high throughput, low latency, and resistance to security threats making it suitable for high-performance blockchain applications. The security analysis of the SHP algorithm shows that it is resistant to attacks such as double-spending and 51% attacks.

6 Conclusion and Future Scope

In our research paper, we introduce a smart way, called the Streamlined and High-Performance Consensus Algorithm (SHPCA), to make blockchain networks function improved, quicker, and more securely. SHPCA uses a leader-based method and a proof-of-stake system to reach these aims. By using the leader-based approach, SHPCA makes it simpler and faster for computers in the network to reach an agreement. It does this by selecting one computer randomly to take the lead, ensuring fairness. This prevents a single computer or a small group from having too much control. The SHPCA algorithm has been carefully tested and shown to efficiently handle many transactions in a secure manner. This makes it very suitable for various sectors like finance, healthcare, and supply chain management. What's even better is that SHPCA is eco-friendly. It selects which computers help run the network based on how much they've invested, and this consumes less energy compared to other methods like proof-of-work. Additionally, it encourages computers with higher investments to follow the rules, making the network safer. In the future, we should focus on improving SHPCA, especially for large blockchain networks. We should also explore using SHPCA in different fields to see how beneficial it can be across various industries, ultimately making the world more interconnected and better.

References

1. Gai, F., Grajales, C., Niu, J., Jalalzai, M.M., Feng, C.: A Secure Consensus Protocol for Sidechains, June 2019. http://arxiv.org/abs/1906.06490
2. Costa, F.Z.D.N., de Queiroz, R.J.: A blockchain using proof-of-download. In: Proceedings - 2020 IEEE International Conference on Blockchain, Blockchain 2020, pp. 170–177, November 2020. https://doi.org/10.1109/Blockchain50366.2020.00028
3. Giannoutakis, K.M., et al.: A blockchain solution for enhancing cybersecurity defence of IoT. In: Proceedings - 2020 IEEE International Conference on Blockchain, Blockchain 2020, pp. 490–495, November 2020. https://doi.org/10.1109/Blockchain50366.2020.00071
4. Shi, N.: A new proof-of-work mechanism for bitcoin. Financ. Innov. **2**(1) (2016). https://doi.org/10.1186/s40854-016-0045-6
5. Sousa, J., Bessani, A., Vukolic, M.: A byzantine Fault-Tolerant ordering service for the hyperledger fabric blockchain platform. In: Proceedings - 48th Annual IEEE/IFIP International Conference on Dependable Systems and Networks (DSN 2018), no. 1, pp. 51–58 (2018). https://doi.org/10.1109/DSN.2018.00018
6. Elisa, N., Yang, L., Chao, F., Cao, Y.: A framework of blockchain-based secure and privacy-preserving E-government system. Wirel. Netw. (2020). https://doi.org/10.1007/s11276-018-1883-0
7. Zhang, S., Lee, J.H.: Analysis of the main consensus protocols of blockchain. ICT Express **6**(2), 93–97 (2020). https://doi.org/10.1016/j.icte.2019.08.001
8. Samanta, A.K., Sarkar, B.B., Chaki, N.: A blockchain-based smart contract towards developing secured university examination system. J. Data Inf. Manag. (2021). https://doi.org/10.1007/s42488-021-00056-0
9. Nguyen, G.T., Kim, K.: A survey about consensus algorithms used in blockchain. J. Inf. Process. Syst. **14**(1), 101–128 (2018). https://doi.org/10.3745/JIPS.01.0024
10. Alsunaidi, S.J., Alhaidari, F.A.: A survey of consensus algorithms for blockchain technology. In: 2019 International Conference on Computer and Information Sciences (ICCIS 2019), pp. 1–6 (2019). https://doi.org/10.1109/ICCISci.2019.8716424

11. Bamakan, S.M.H., Motavali, A., Babaei Bondarti, A.: A survey of blockchain consensus algorithms performance evaluation criteria. Expert Syst. Appl. **154** (2020). https://doi.org/10.1016/j.eswa.2020.113385

12. Marchesi, L., Marchesi, M., Tonelli, R.: ABCDE -Agile Block Chain dApp engineering, arXiv, vol. 1, no. 1–2, p. 100002 (2019). https://doi.org/10.1016/j.bcra.2020.100002

13. Yu, Y., et al.: A blockchain-based decentralized security architecture for IoT. IEEE Access **8**(6), 1–8 (2019). https://doi.org/10.1016/j.jii.2018.07.004

14. Tran, Q.N., Turnbull, B.P., Wu, H.-T., de Silva, A.J.S., Kormusheva, K., Hu, J.: A survey on privacy-preserving blockchain systems (PPBS) and a novel PPBS-based framework for smart agriculture. IEEE Open J. Comput. Soc. **2**, 72–84 (2021). https://doi.org/10.1109/ojcs.2021.3053032

15. Dai, W., Xiao, D., Jin, H., Xie, X.: A Concurrent optimization consensus system based on blockchain. In: 2019 26th International Conference on Telecommunications (ICT 2019), pp. 244–248 (2019). https://doi.org/10.1109/ICT.2019.8798836

16. Sankar, L.S., et al.: A global road map for ceramic materials and technologies: forecasting the future of ceramics. In: International Ceramic Federation - 2nd International Congress on Ceramics, ICC 2008, Final Programme, A Global Road Map for Ceramic Materials and Technologies: Forecasting the Future of Ceramics. International Ceramic Federation - 2nd International Congress on Ceramics ICC 2008, Final Programme, 2008

17. Faria, C., Correia, M.: BlockSim: blockchain simulator. In: Proceedings - 2019 2nd IEEE International Conference on Blockchain, Blockchain 2019, pp. 439–446, July 2019. https://doi.org/10.1109/Blockchain.2019.00067

18. Alharby, M., van Moorsel, A.: BlockSim: an extensible simulation tool for blockchain systems. Front. Blockchain **3** (2020). https://doi.org/10.3389/fbloc.2020.00028

19. Polge, J., Ghatpande, S., Kubler, S., Robert, J., Le Traon, Y.: BlockPerf: a hybrid blockchain emulator/simulator framework. IEEE Access **9**, 107858–107872 (2021). https://doi.org/10.1109/ACCESS.2021.3101044

20. Kirrane, S., Di Ciccio, C.: BlockConfess: towards an architecture for blockchain constraints and forensics. In: Proceedings - 2020 IEEE International Conference on Blockchain, Blockchain 2020, pp. 539–544, November 2020. https://doi.org/10.1109/Blockchain50366.2020.00078

21. Shahzad, I., et al.: Blockchain-based green big data visualization: BGbV. Complex Intell. Syst. (2021). https://doi.org/10.1007/s40747-021-00466-y

22. Kirrane, S., Di Ciccio, C.: BlockConfess: towards an architecture for blockchain constraints and forensics. In: Proceedings - 2020 IEEE International Conference on Blockchain, Blockchain 2020, pp. 539–544 (2020). https://doi.org/10.1109/Blockchain50366.2020.00078

23. Gai, K., Guo, J., Zhu, L., Yu, S.: Blockchain meets cloud computing: a survey. IEEE Commun. Surv. Tutor. **22**(3), 2009–2030 (2020). https://doi.org/10.1109/COMST.2020.2989392

24. Zhao, W., Jiang, C., Gao, H., Yang, S., Luo, X.: Blockchain-enabled cyber-physical systems: a review. IEEE Internet Things J. **8**(6), 4023–4034 (2021). https://doi.org/10.1109/JIOT.2020.3014864

25. Lunardi, R.C., Alharby, M., Nunes, H.C., Zorzo, A.F., Dong, C., van Moorsel, A.: Context-based consensus for appendable-block blockchains. In: Proceedings - 2020 IEEE International Conference on Blockchain, Blockchain 2020, pp. 401–408, November 2020. https://doi.org/10.1109/Blockchain50366.2020.00058

26. Wang, G., Shi, Z., Nixon, M., Han, S.: ChainSplitter: towards blockchain-based industrial IoT architecture for supporting hierarchical storage. In: Proceedings - 2019 2nd IEEE International Conference on Blockchain, Blockchain 2019, pp. 166–175 (2019). https://doi.org/10.1109/Blockchain.2019.00030

27. He, J., Wang, G., Zhang, G., Zhang, J.: Consensus mechanism design based on structured directed acyclic graphs. Blockchain Res. Appl. **2**(1), 100011 (2021). https://doi.org/10.1016/j.bcra.2021.100011
28. Yuan, X., Luo, F., Haider, M.Z., Chen, Z., Li, Y.: Efficient byzantine consensus mechanism based on reputation in IoT blockchain. Wirel. Commun. Mob. Comput. **2021** (2021). https://doi.org/10.1155/2021/9952218
29. Gourisetti, S.N.G., Mylrea, M., Patangia, H.: Evaluation and demonstration of blockchain applicability framework. IEEE Trans. Eng. Manag. **67**(4), 1142–1156 (2020). https://doi.org/10.1109/TEM.2019.2928280
30. Gupta, C., Mahajan, A.: Evaluation of Proof-of-Work Consensus Algorithm for Blockchain Networks, 2020
31. Lasla, N., Al-Sahan, L., Abdallah, M., Younis, M.: Green-PoW: an energy-efficient blockchain proof-of-work consensus algorithm. Comput. Netw. **214** (2022). https://doi.org/10.1016/j.comnet.2022.109118
32. Khan, M., Imtiaz, S., Parvaiz, G.S., Hussain, A., Bae, J.: Integration of internet-of-things with blockchain technology to enhance humanitarian logistics performance. IEEE Access **9**, 25422–25436 (2021). https://doi.org/10.1109/ACCESS.2021.3054771
33. Zheng, Z., Pan, J., Cai, L.: Lightweight blockchain consensus protocols for vehicular social networks. IEEE Trans. Veh. Technol. **69**(6), 5736–5748 (2020). https://doi.org/10.1109/TVT.2020.2974005
34. Chalaemwongwan, N., Kurutach, W.: Notice of removal: state of the art and challenges facing consensus protocols on blockchain. In: International Conference on Information Networking, vol. 2018-Janua, pp. 957–962, (2018). https://doi.org/10.1109/ICOIN.2018.8343266
35. Hang, L., Kim, D.H.: Optimal blockchain network construction methodology based on analysis of configurable components for enhancing hyperledger fabric performance. Blockchain Res. Appl. **2**(1), 100009 (2021). https://doi.org/10.1016/j.bcra.2021.100009
36. Kuzlu, M., Pipattanasomporn, M., Gurses, L., Rahman, S.: Performance analysis of a hyperledger fabric blockchain framework: throughput, latency and scalability. In: Proceedings - 2019 2nd IEEE International Conference on Blockchain, Blockchain 2019, pp. 536–540 (2019). https://doi.org/10.1109/Blockchain.2019.00003
37. Fan, C., Ghaemi, S., Khazaei, H., Musilek, P.: Performance evaluation of blockchain systems: a systematic survey. IEEE Access **8**(June), 126927–126950 (2020). https://doi.org/10.1109/ACCESS.2020.3006078
38. Sukhwani, H., Martínez, J.M., Chang, X., Trivedi, K.S., Rindos, A.: Performance modeling of PBFT consensus process for permissioned blockchain network (hyperledger fabric). In: Proceedings of the IEEE 36th Symposium on Reliable Distributed Systems (SRDS), vol. 2017-Septe, pp. 253–255 (2017). https://doi.org/10.1109/SRDS.2017.36
39. Solat, S.: RDV: an alternative to proof-of-work and a real decentralized consensus for blockchain. In: BlockSys 2018 - Proceedings of the 1st Blockchain-Enabled Networked Sensor Systems, Part of SenSys 2018, November 2018, pp. 25–30 (2018). https://doi.org/10.1145/3282278.3282283
40. Monti, M., Rasmussen, S.: RAIN: a bio-inspired communication and data storage infrastructure. Artif. Life **23**(4), 552–557 (2017). https://doi.org/10.1162/ARTL_a_00247
41. Gai, F., Niu, J., Beschastnikh, I., Feng, C., Wang, S.: Scaling Blockchain Consensus via a Robust Shared Mempool, pp. 1–17 (2022). http://arxiv.org/abs/2203.05158
42. Ge, L., Wang, J., Zhang, G.: Survey of consensus algorithms for proof of stake in blockchain. Secur. Commun. Netw. **2022** (2022). https://doi.org/10.1155/2022/2812526
43. Gol, D.A.: An Analysis of consensus algorithms for the blockchain technology. Int. J. Res. Appl.Sci. Eng. Technol. **7**, 675–680 (2019). https://doi.org/10.22214/ijraset.2019.2096
44. Xu, M., Chen, X., Kou, G.: A systematic review of blockchain. Financ. Innov. **5**, 27 (2019). https://doi.org/10.1186/s40854-019-0147-z

45. Chen, G., Xu, B., Lu, M., et al.: Exploring blockchain technology and its potential applications for education. Smart Learn. Environ. **5**, 1 (2018). https://doi.org/10.1186/s40561-017-0050-x
46. Rejeb, A., Treiblmaier, H., Rejeb, K., et al.: Blockchain research in healthcare: a bibliometric review and current research trends. J. Data Inf. Manag. **3**, 109–124 (2021). https://doi.org/10.1007/s42488-021-00046-2
47. Gol, D.A., Gondaliya, N.: A secure network for streamlined and high-performance consensus algorithm based on blockchain technology. Int. J. Wirel. Microw. Technol. (IJWMT) **13**(5), 11–22 (2023). https://doi.org/10.5815/ijwmt.2023.05.02

A Comprehensive Study on VANET Security

Mayur J. Patil[(✉)] [iD] and Krishnakant P. Adhiya[iD]

Department of Computer Engineering, SSBTs College of Engineering and Technology,
Bambhori, Jalgaon, Maharashtra, India
`patil.mayur3110@gmail.com`

Abstract. This study encompasses the following areas: vulnerability analysis,
proposition of cryptographic solutions, design of intrusion detection systems, resolution of privacy problems, evaluation of key management, and assessment of
overall performance in Vehicular Ad Hoc Networks (VANETs). The research
endeavors to shed light on the development of intelligent transportation systems
that prioritize efficiency and safety. Vehicular Ad Hoc Networks (VANETs) are
playing a vital role in today's digital age, to make the lives of civilians easier
and simpler in every respect. The VANETs focuses on boosting traffic regulation
by reducing traffic congestion and monitoring unexpected events. The objective
of this study is to ascertain vulnerabilities, assess potential risks, and propose
viable remedies with the intention of enhancing the security of VANETs. This
paper focuses on key management, performance evaluation, cryptographic solutions, intrusion detection, assurance management, privacy protection, and key
management in an effort to shed light on the development of secure, intelligent
transportation systems. With respect of delivering route as well as transport security, decreasing congestion bottlenecks, enhancing driving rules and providing
entertainment amenities within a car, the VANETs is omnipresent and effective.
Everything is online in today's digital world, so all the automobile companies are
ready and equipped to connect their vehicles with information technology systems. VANETs shares important information with vehicles such as traffic guidelines, driving circumstances, and many more. This information is shared within
the territory of the vehicle. For sharing this type of intelligence and improving
the systematic transmission of data between the vehicles, VANETs came into the
picture.

Keywords: VANET · OBU · RSU · TA · Security

1 VANET

1.1 Introduction

VANETs are the subcategory of MANETs that have a pre-defined path. This vehicular
Ad hoc Network relies on some registration process, "Road Side Unit (RSU) and On-
Board Unit (OBU)" [1]. The OBUs are fitted in every vehicle which acts as a transmitter
and sends messages to other vehicles. Roadside units (RSUs) are fitted with networked

© The Author(s), under exclusive license to Springer Nature Switzerland AG 2024
S. Rajagopal et al. (Eds.): ASCIS 2023, CCIS 2039, pp. 363–382, 2024.
https://doi.org/10.1007/978-3-031-59100-6_25

devices and placed at key locations along routes. These RSUs are responsible for managing network resources and facilitating communication between devices linked to the network, and they excel at doing so via "dedicated short-range communication" [1]. There are essentially two types of communication pathways within VANETs:

1. Connectivity between Motor Vehicles (V2V)
2. V2I Communication, or Vehicle-to-Infrastructure

VANETs are primarily responsible for ensuring efficient interaction between vehicles. The nodes in a VANET require particular characteristics to collect the intelligence or knowledge, to transmit the data between neighbor nodes. Using a plethora of sensors, cameras, GPS receivers, and omnidirectional antennas, the nodes gather data from their environments and make decisions based on that data.

In recent days VANETs are the evolving area within the realm of wireless as well as mobile connectivity system. For implementing advanced transportation systems, VANETs are the best solution. VANETs are the MANET Offshoots. However, VANETs as well as MANETs are not the same things. The terms which are used to differentiate between VANETs plus MANETs are node mobility, node speed, topology change, localization, cost, bandwidth, network setup, range, and many more.

In VANETs there are several security threats and problems that are directly related to node authentication and privacy. VANETs provide an open-access environment and because of this VANETs are more vulnerable to attack. As a result, the attacker has ability to alter, capture, read manipulate and remove the messages from VANETs. Protection and confidentiality issues must be solved by incorporating advanced or modern methods to overcome all forms of risks and intrusions with ability to use VANETs for wireless transmission technologies successfully.

Numerous research endeavors have been put forth as potential means of confronting the challenges pertaining with the intention of identity and confidentiality mechanisms in VANET systems. Certain schemes require the harnessing of public key infrastructure (PKI) with the objective of vehicle identification. This entails the inclusion of a certifying authority's digital signature, as well as the public key affiliated with the vehicle.

To analyze and authenticate all these types of certificates, the vehicle and RSU need a huge amount of computational time and processing power. These types of methods provide a better and efficient way to identify the signature of every vehicle.

The state of not being in danger or under strain is known as safety. Security is synonymous with safety or with protection. Security refers to both protection and the step taken to keep oneself secure or secured. Since VANETs are wireless communication technology that is more difficult to protect. It is important to safeguard regarding malicious operations and to clearly describe the safety framework in VANETs [2]. Vehicular ad hoc networks (VANETs) are gaining prominence in the capacity of burgeoning area of study within the realm of mobile networking. This is due to the ability of equipped vehicles to engage in wireless ad hoc communication, facilitating the sharing of crucial information pertaining to safety, transit efficiency, and other related data. There is a growing emphasis in both academics and the automotive industry on vehicular communication, a technology that grants vehicles the ability to establish communication link mutually as well as with roadside infrastructure, thereby establishing a vehicular ad hoc network [3].

Vehicles have become increasingly significant as the motor industry has grown and the economy has improved. Even so, the rise in vehicle numbers has resulted in increased traffic standstill as well as more pervasive traffic incidents. As a result, there is a pressing to elevate the driving journey while also increasing driver safety. This has resulted in the development of VANETs to improve driver safety [4].

2 VANET: A Quick Overview

An ad hoc network design called a "vehicular ad hoc network (VANET)" [1] allows for wireless communication between moving vehicles. The proliferation of VANETs has exhibited significant growth since the 1980s. In recent times, "Vehicle Ad-Hoc Networks (VANETs)" [1] have been employed with the aim of enhancing traffic safety, optimizing traffic flow, mitigating traffic congestion, as well as offering driver support. There are three components of VANETs, which are listed below,

- On-Board Unit (OBU) [1]
- Road-Side Unit (RSU) [1]
- Trusted Authority (TA) [1]

2.1 On-Board Unit (OBU)

The "On-Board Unit (OBU)" [1] is a device that utilizes WAVE technology and the "Global Positioning System (GPS)" [1] to effectively monitor and record the location data of a motor vehicle. All vehicles are rigged with an "On-Board Unit (OBU)" [1] that facilitates the sharing and communication of automobile data with "Roadside Units (RSUs)" [1] as well as other OBUs. The OBU comprises several electronic components, including as

1. Resource Command Processor (RCP)
2. Sensor Device
3. User Interface
4. Read/Write Storage

With the help of an IEEE 802.11p wireless network, OBU communicates with RSU and other OBUs. The OBU has the capability to establish communication with both RSU and other OBUs using a simple message format. Moreover, the vehicle's battery provides energy for the "On-Board Unit (OBU)" [1]. The car has several sensors, such as a global positioning system (GPS), an event data recorder (EDR), front and rear sensors, and more. These sensors collect and transmit data to the OBU [1].

The "On-Board Unit (OBU)" [1] fitted on cars periodically transmits traffic- related information in order to ameliorate both the efficacy and security of regional transportation [4].

2.2 Road Side Unit (RSU)

The roadside unit (RSU) refers to a "wireless access vehicular environment (WAVE)" [1] device that is commonly deployed in proximity to roadways, or in designated locations such as parking areas or junctions. The passing vehicle gets local connectivity through this RSU. "Dedicated short communication (DSRC)" [1] relying upon IEEE 802.11p radio technology is provided by networking devices in the RSU. Generally, the RSU can also interact with various networking component within different network architecture [5].

The key functions and procedures related with RSU, which is provided C.C. - Communication Consortium are as follows,

1. One approach to increasing the outreach span of an ad hoc network. Involves disseminating insights to additional On-Board Units (OBUs) and transmitting it to other Roadside Units (RSUs), which can then relay the Intel to other OBUs [5] (Fig. 1).

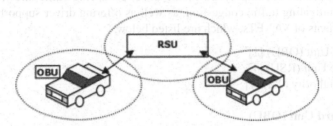

Fig. 1. Forwarding Information

2. RSU act as an information source. It uses infrastructure to vehicle communication for operating security applications like overpass alert, collision alert, or construction site alert [5]. As shown in Fig. 2.

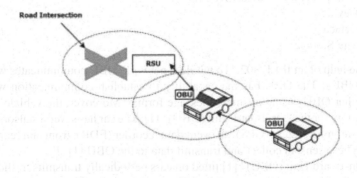

Fig. 2. RSU-Information Source

3. The OBU gets internet connectivity from RSU [5]. As shown in Fig. 3.

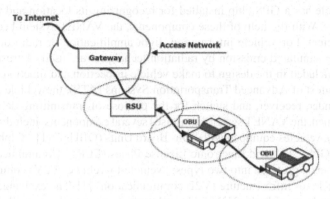

Fig. 3. Internet Connectivity

2.3 Trusted Authority

A trusted authority is acting as a registration center for the RSU, OBU, and vehicle users. The primary function of TA is to control the VANET system. Furthermore, TA also verifies the authentication of vehicle, user ID, and OBU ID to protect every car from danger. If necessary, TA can track down the vehicles true identity. The utilization of a Transport Layer Security (TLS) protocol facilitates safe communication between a "Trusted Authority (TA)" and a "Roadside Unit (RSU)" [4]. TA requires,

1. A large quantity of power
2. Huge Storage Capacity

In case of any fraudulent communication or unusual activity, the TA can identify OBU ID and its details [4]. Aside from that, TA includes a system for identifying the attackers [1].

3   Architecture of VANET

The VANET architecture is based on "wireless access vehicular environment (WAVE)" [1] technology. This technology provides the converse link between the vehicle and the RSU. The WAVE architecture defines how security messages are sent and by keeping vehicle and transportation movement, WAVE communication maintains passenger's safety. This application improves transportation movement as well as the performance of traffic regulation systems while simultaneously ensuring pedestrian and driver safety [1].

The VANET system's architecture encompasses several key components, namely the vehicle, "On-Board Unit (OBU)" [1], "Road-Side Unit (RSU)" [1], and the transportation system. Vehicular Ad hoc Networks (VANETs) rely on the utilization of IEEE 802.11p for the execution of their operations. In VANET, the RSU performs routing operation and in the comparison of vehicle range, the RSU range is large. For communication, the vehicle uses an OBU chip which is mounted into the vehicle.

The vehicle has a GPS chip installed for recognizing its location and tracking the other vehicles. With the help of these components, the VANET system becomes more fast and efficient. For vehicle information, light amplification or radio detection and ranging using simulated emission by radiation techniques are used. A trusted certified authority is included in the design to make vehicle inspection and function easier [6].

In the context of Advanced Transportation Systems (ATS), the vehicle assumes the roles of a sender, receiver, and switch for the purpose of transmitting data. As previously mentioned, the VANET system comprises several components, including Roadside Units (RSUs), vehicles equipped with "On- Board Units (OBUs)" [1], "Global Positioning System (GPS)" [1], and Electronic License Plates (ELPs). Communication within this system can be grouped into two types: "vehicle-to-vehicle (V2V) communication" [1] and "vehicle-to- infrastructure (V2I) communication' [1]. The exchange of insights between "vehicle- to-vehicle (V2V)" [1] and "vehicle-to-infrastructure (V2I)" [1] systems is achieved through the utilization of multicasting or broadcasting techniques [6] (Fig. 4).

The main objective of the Advanced Transportation System is to furnish secure converse. Using various networks to facilitate fortified communication which improves traffic flow and road safety, as well as alleviates traffic congestion [1].

The transmission medium between V2V communications is distinguish by a fast communication and low jitter. A car can communicate vital intelligence such as urgent or hard breaking, accident detection, and traffic situations to neighbor vehicles using V2V technology. V2I is a technology that allows cars and network infrastructures to exchange relevant data. In V2I network infrastructure, a communication link is established between a car and RSU, and with the help of this connection, the car can share information with the other network such as the internet [1].

The authors in S.Al Sultan et al. states three different types of communication domain, which are listed below. This domain forged the communication conduit between the vehicle and RSU [5].

1. In-Vehicle Domain
2. Ad-hoc Domain
3. Infrastructural Domain

3.1 In-Vehicle Domain

The OBU and application unit (AU) is a part of this domain. The connection between OBU and AU could be wired or wireless. Both the units are mounted or fitted in a single device. So for executing one or more sets of program offered by the program developer, an OBU provides an established communication link with AU [5].

3.2 Ad-Hoc Domain

The Ad-hoc domain provides an interconnection link between the OBU and the RSU. The ad-hoc domain is classified into two types of communication,

1. With the help of OBU vehicles can engage in communication with other vehicles. This communication is carried under a fully distributed environment with decentralized

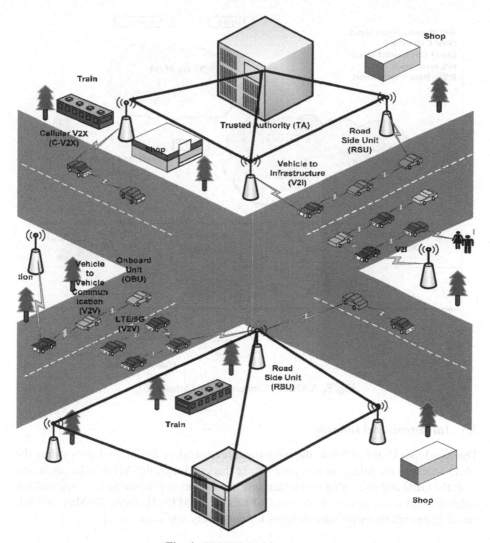

Fig. 4. VANET Architecture [1]

coordination. If there is direct communication available between the vehicle then one vehicle can communicate with another vehicle directly. With a single hop this communication creates V2V interaction. When a direct connection is not possible, a specialized routing protocol is utilized to transfer information between one vehicles to the next. This type of communication is known as multi-hop V2V communication [5].

2. The car or vehicle communicates with the RSU to send, receive, and forward data from one vehicle to another. This type of communication is known as vehicle to infrastructure communication (V2V) [5] (Fig. 5).

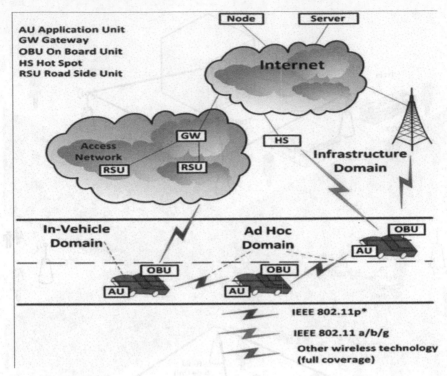

Fig. 5. VANET Communication Domain [5]

3.3 Infrastructural Domain

The Road Side Unit can link to the infrastructure network or the internet, pro- viding the OBU access to the infrastructure network. In this condition, the AU may be registered with the OBU and so be able to interact with another net dependent host. Using cellular radio network communication such as GSM, GPRS, UMTS, HSDPA, Wi-Max, and 4G, an OBU can interact with various hosts for non-safety applications [5].

4   Characteristics of VANET

VANET is an example of wireless communication networks with permanent road units or highly mobile vehicle as a node. In ad hoc mode nodes connect, while in infrastructure mode nodes communicate with permanent along the route. As a result, the feature of VANETs is a mix of wireless medium characteristics and the feature of various ad hoc and infrastructure modes [7]. As compared with MANETs, the VANET has its own distinct features, which is listed below [5],

1. High Mobility
2. Increasing traffic efficiency, boosting passenger safety, and providing safe driving
3. No Power Constraint
4. High Computational Ability

5. Dynamic Topology
6. Availability of Transmission Medium
7. Limited Bandwidth
8. Limited Transmission Power

4.1 High Mobility

VANETs remarkable mobility is a significant trait. During regular operations, network nodes move at various rates and directions all the time. The mesh in a network is reduced due to the increased mobility of nodes. VANET mobility is relatively high when compared to MANETs [7].

4.2 Increasing Traffic Efficiency, Boosting Passenger Safety, and Providing Safe Driving

Vehicular Ad-Hoc Networks (VANETs) provide direct communication between mobile vehicles, hence enabling a wide range of applications that depend on real-time node-to-node communication. One example is the potential for an app to instantly notify cars travelling in the same direction of any impending dangers, such as accidents or sudden stops. Consequently, this enhances the driver's situational awareness of the road ahead [5].

Furthermore, another sort of application might be used to improve traveler convenience and transportation management by broadcasting climate, congestion management, and point of interest information via this type of network [5].

4.3 No Power Restriction

The On-Board Unit (OBU) is powered by a durable, long-lasting battery, which allows for a continuous flow of electricity from the vehicles. In the realm of Vehicular Ad-Hoc Networks (VANETs), the significance of power availability is comparatively less pronounced as compared to Mobile Ad-Hoc Networks (MANETs) [5].

4.4 High Computational Ability

The intrinsic mobility of vehicles in Vehicular Ad-Hoc Networks (VANETs) allows them to incorporate a wide array of sensors and computational resources. These resources encompass advanced processors, ample memory capacities, state of-the-art antenna technologies, and GPS systems. These resources boost the node's computing capacity, making it easier to establish stable wireless communications and gather accurate information about its location, speed, and directions [5].

4.5 Dynamic Topology

The topology of the VANET is rapidly changing due to the fast mobility of the VANET. As a result, it's unpredictable and dynamic. Connection periods are brief, particularly between nodes traveling in opposite directions. This structure makes it easier to attack the entire network while also making it more difficult to discover problems [7].

4.6 Availability of Transmission Medium

Air serves as the VANET's transmission medium. Al- though the widespread accessibility of such a wireless transmission medium has become one of the key benefits of inter-vehicle communication, it also raises significant security concerns, which are connected to the type of wireless communication as well as fundamental safety of communication via an open network [7].

4.7 Bandwidth Limitation

The conventional DSRC band for VANET is considered to be a restricted band, with a bandwidth of only 75 MHz, implying that not all of these frequencies are legal. 27 Mbps is the potential maximum throughput [7].

4.8 Transmission Power Limitation

In the WAVE design, the transmission power is limited, limiting the distance that data may travel. This is 1000 m in distance. However, there are some exceptions, such as in the case of an emergency or for the sack of public safety. It is now possible to send data at a greater power level [7].

5 VANETs Security

With the advancement of vehicle networks, data can be exchanged over a wireless channel, which raises the need for security. Users of this network like users of other networks, except VANET to be secure in terms of integrity, confidentiality, and availability [8].

5.1 Entity Stake in VANETs Security

1. The Driver
2. The Vehicle
3. Infrastructure or RSU
4. Third Parties
5. The Attacker

The Driver: Because the VANET is omnipresent and the driver must make a proper judgment, the driver is a part of the VANET safety chain. Furthermore, all contemporary VANET programs treat the driving person as an interacting element with the driving assistance system [7].

The Vehicle/OBU: There are two types of vehicle in VANET such as normal cars that travel between network nodes and operates normally, and another one is malicious nodes [7].

Infrastructure/RSU: We can discriminate between conventional RSU terminals that operate normally and malicious RSU terminals, just as we can with the OBU [7].

Third Parties: All digital equivalent of stake-holders in direct fashion in the intelligent transportation system is denoted by third parties (maybe trustworthy or semi-trustworthy). We list the transportation regulator, vehicle manufacturers, and traffic cops as an example of third parties. They have their secret/public key pair [7].

The Attacker: In the perspective of VANET safety, the attacker is one or more compromised entities that use a number of methods to effectively violate the safety of trusted vehicles. A squad of vehicles working together can potentially be an aggressor. An attacker could be an internal (VANET authenticated vehicle) or external vehicle [7].

Table 1 shows the VANETs Entity and its descriptions. VANET is a new technology with a bright future but significant hurdles, particularly in terms of security. In the pursuit of adopting vehicle communication systems, the preservation of security and protection of privacy arise as crucial factors and significant challenges to overcome.

Table 1. Entity in VANETs [8]

Entity	Short Description
Driver	The driver is responsible for moving the vehicle from one location to another location
Vehicle	It includes all types of vehicle as a node such as, bus, car, truck etc
Infrastructure	RSU is a part of infrastructure
Third Parties	Transportation Regulators, Vehicle Manufacturer, Traffic Cops and Traffic Management Authorities
Attacker	Unauthorized nodes that undertake malicious activity are included in the attacker

VANET privacy assures that intruders do not manipulate or change the sent messages. Because of their unique properties, attacks on VANETs are more frequent. Especially, Safety issues must be fully resolved; else, secure communication on VANETs would be severely limited. The primary privacy concerns of VANETs are divided under four categories which is listed below,

1. Availability
2. Confidentiality
3. Authentication
4. Data Integrity

5.2 Availability

The main significant feature of safety measures that requires attention is availability. It has a lot to do with safety applications. The primary function of availability is to maintain the system's functionality. In the case of a failure or malicious attack, the network and other applications must continue to function, thus system security is essential [1].

5.3 Confidentiality

Only the specified client has access to the information which is protected by confidentiality. It's possible that unauthorized users won't be able to see the data. This is accomplished through the use of certificates and shared public keys [1].

5.4 Authentication

In VANETs authentication is essential. It protects VANETs from potential threats in the network. It is critical to contain the necessary communication channel information such as individual identity as well as sending addresses. Authentication has the authority to govern vehicle permission levels and can also protect against Sybil attacks by issuing a unique identity to each vehicle [1].

5.5 Data Integrity

It assures that the integrity of the information isn't tampered with during transmission. Using public key infrastructure & the cryptography revocation procedure, it may be assured in VANETs [1].

6 Research Work in VANET Security

Contemporary intelligent transportation systems are predicated on Vehicular Ad Hoc Networks (VANETs), wherein vehicles collaborate to interchange data with both infrastructure and each other, with the aim of enhancing road safety, efficiency, and traffic management. Due to the potential for adversarial attacks to undermine the reliability and security of vehicle-to-vehicle communication, VANET protection is critical. This literature review provides an overview of the current state of research on VANET security, emphasizing significant challenges, vulnerabilities, and potential remedies.

6.1 Challenges Seen in the Safeguarding of VANETs

A number of vulnerabilities have been identified in VANET security research due to the unique characteristics of automotive networks. Difficulties are introduced into the implementation of effective security measures by the dynamic topology, the swift mobility of vehicles, and resource constraints. The importance of addressing these concerns to ensure the robustness of VANET security systems is emphasized in research conducted by Chen et al. (2020) and Zhang et al. (2018).

6.2 Examination of Vulnerabilities

Certain studies have employed vulnerability analysis to identify potential threats to VANETs. Sybil attacks, data alteration, and message spoofing are typical vulnerabilities. The importance of safeguarding the message authentication process in order to reduce attack vectors was emphasized by Wang et al. (2017), who conducted an extensive investigation into the subject.

6.3 Protocols and Algorithms Applied to Cryptography

Cryptographic techniques substantially bolster the security of communications within VANETs. Current cryptographic methods' suitability for VANETs is a subject of ongoing research, according to the literature. In their study, Li et al. (2019) specifically examine the performance of lightweight cryptographic algorithms in resource-constrained vehicles.

6.4 Intrusion Prevention and Security

Clearly, the objective of the new research is to develop intrusion detection and prevention systems tailored to VANETs. In order to underscore the importance of immediate threat mitigation, Zhang and Wang (2021) present a flexible intrusion detection system designed for vehicular networks.

6.5 Schemas for Trust Management

In order to ensure secure communication between automobiles and infrastructure, models that establish and administer trust are essential. The research of Sun et al. (2021) and Liu et al. (2018) regarding the development and evaluation of trust models emphasizes the need for adaptive and context-aware approaches to manage the ever-evolving VANETs.

6.6 Techniques for Encryption Preservation

Insights regarding privacy in VANETs have stimulated research into privacy- preserving strategies. In order to ensure the protection of user privacy while maintaining the security of vehicle communications, Zheng et al. (2020) examine the efficacy of anonymous authentication and pseudonymization.

6.7 Critical Methodologies in Management

Key administration is an integral component of VANET security. In consideration of the dynamic nature of vehicle environments, the research conducted by Wu et al. (2019) examines scalable and resilient key management techniques. To ensure secure communication, the research emphasizes the importance of implementing an effective key distribution system.

6.8 Evaluation of Performance

The subject of quantitative research on the performance impacts of security methods is frequently revisited in the literature. The compromises between performance and security are illuminated in two significant studies by Xu et al. (2021) and Jiang et al. (2018). These studies assess the latency, throughput, and communication overhead associated with various security methods.

6.9 Aspects Pertaining to Standardization and Regulation to Consider

The impact of regulations and standards on the present condition of VANET security is underscored in the literature. By evaluating existing regulatory frame- works, Yang et al. (2019) outline potential enhancements to standards that could lead to a more secure and interoperable VANET environment.

6.10 Practical Implementations and Case Research

Real-world case studies and practical implementations shed light on the application of VANET security solutions. A notable illustration can be found in the integration of secure VANET communication within smart cities. The subject matter was investigated by Liang et al. (2022), who provided significant observations and recommendations for broader application.

7 Importance of Authentication in VANET

Authentication can be done in two ways in VANETs,

1. Node Authentication
2. Message Authentication

The importance of message authenticity verification in improving the VANET safety architecture cannot be overstated. So the authentication of the message is a key parameter in VANET. To guarantee safe data transfer within VANETs, it is important to comply with the following authentication criteria. [1],

1. **Utilization of Bandwidth:** To effectively manage authentication requests, including the exchange of cryptographic secret keys and credentials, a sufficient amount of bandwidth in terms of bytes per second (bps) is required [1].
2. **Scalability:** Scalability in the authentication procedure is required for supporting many simultaneous network operations and uninterrupted communication. [1].
3. **Time Response:** It is critical that authentication systems have a rapid response time [1].
4. **Resilient Authentication:** Authentication systems must have a high degree of capacity to defend VANETs from attacks [1].

Authentication, security, and privacy emerge as critical factors in fostering confidence within V2V and V2I connections in VANET. The authentication scheme's major goal is to detect hostile nodes and fraudulent messages. In this context, research on an authentication mechanism has been proposed with the goal of protecting VANETs from fraudulent users, bogus communications, and unauthorized entities. In order to affirm the trustworthiness of converse, numerous strategy utilize encryption methods, encompassing both symmetric and asymmetric cryptography [1].

8 Research Work in Symmetric Cryptography

The Message Authentication Code (MAC) is used in this authentication mechanism, also known as Private Key Cryptography. Symmetric cryptography's use of a single key generation makes for speedy and secure computing efficiency.

Choi et al., [9] proposed a new strategy for achieving high privacy efficiency in VANETs through the amalgamation of symmetric authentication and concise pseudonyms. To generate short-lived pseudonyms using this method, the authority must transmit each vehicle a unique ID and seed value. Because it can share keys among automobiles, RSU is capable of completing MAC verification.

Y. Xi, K. Sha et al., [10] introduced a random key-set- based authentication method that uses a zero-trust approach to protect user privacy without relying on central authority trust. This strategy improves anonymity by employing distinct keys for authentication at nearby RSUs, as well as unmasking perpetrators and key invalidation. This solution is superior, but it has a high computational cost when dealing with zero-trust policies.

P. Vijaykumar, M. Azees et al., [11] created a trusted authority (TA) to help users access internet services via VANETs. As a result, it's critical that the TA and VANETs exchanged communication maintains message confidentiality and authentication. X. Lin, X. Sun et al., [12] presented a privacy-preserving Time- Efficient and Secure Vehicular method. Which is used to drastically minimize packet usage while maintaining security. The Message Authentication Code tag, is connected to each packet, is employed for verification purposes. It necessitates a swift hashing procedure to check each packet.

W. Rhim, [13] proposed a method for Message Authentication Code dependent data verification that is both effective and reliable. This method is ineffective in dealing with and preventing a replay attack. Taeho et al., [8] devised a sophisticated method for the VANET system that uses an upgraded MAC Verification framework.

The roadside unit-aided message authentication (RAISE) methodology was used by Zhang et al., [14] to offer a new way for authenticating a message. RSU validates the genuineness of messages transferred from vehicles and notifies the findings back to the vehicles in this way.

The hash function is the next type of symmetric cryptography. It's in charge of inspecting message's integrity with- out encrypting it. The message is sent through a hash function that provides the hash output which is a static value. The hash value must be appended to the transmitting message to maintain message integrity.

TEAM (Trust-Extended Authentication Mechanism) is a decentralization- based lightweight authentication technique proposed by Chuang et al., [15]. TEAM incorporates the concept of a transitive trust connection, but it consumes less cryptographic data than other existing approaches because it only uses the XOR and hash functions throughout the verification procedure.

Chim et al., [16] proposed a technique that uses a one-way hash function and a secret key between the vehicle and the RSU to address the safety and confidentiality challenges of Vehicle-to-Vehicle in VANETs. This methodology is capable of resolving privacy concerns that may arise during communication.

By employing hash chaining and authentication code to authenticate the vehicle, Vighnesh et al., [17] established a novel sender authentication technique for boosting VANET security. This approach enables safe communication between the vehicle and the RSU, as well as the encryption of confidential data using a master key. The RSU attaches its identity to packets before delivering them to the authentication center, which eliminates the potential of rogue RSUs misusing the VANET.

He and Zhu, [18] presented a solution for dealing with Denial of Service attacks against signature-based authentication. Pre-authentication can be performed before signature verification to combat DOS attacks. The authentication mechanism is used in this system, which benefits from the use of a one-way hash chain and a group rekeying procedure.

9 Research Work in Asymmetric Cryptography

Within the realm of Vehicular Ad Hoc Networks (VANETs), the subsequent method of authentication utilized is Asymmetric cryptography, most frequently referred to as public-key cryptography. This technology is employed to ensure the security of data in large-scale communication networks through the process of encrypting and decrypting communications. Data encoding can be achieved by utilizing either a public key or a digital signature, thanks to the presence of asymmetry in the system. A private key is rarely utilized for anything other than decrypting encrypted messages and verifying digitally signed messages.

Raya and Hubaux, [19] proposed a new way for providing privacy that relies on anonymous public keys. The Anonymous keys must be altered in such a way that the receiver cannot follow the vehicle owner's key. The main drawbacks are that it takes a lot of storage and memory, as well as a lot of certificate revocation list (CRL) checks, due to the employment of a high number of unknown tokens. As a result of the high processing overhead, it could be the source of a DOS attack.

G. Calandriello, P. Papadimitratos, [20] developed a strong pseudonym-dependent identification mechanism that reduces security costs while maintaining traffic safety. This approach overcomes the restrictions of a pseudonym by combining a baseline pseudonym with a group signature that allows for the on-the-fly generation of a pseudonym and self-certification.

Wasef and Shen, [21] proposed the EMAP, which uses Public Key Infrastructure and Certificate Revocation List for safety. VANETs EMAP replaced the slow CRL procedure with an effective revocation method in this system. In EMAP, this method employs a keyed hash message authentication code. The purpose of the key is to generate HMAC and to reliably communicate and update the secret key among non-revoked OBUs. The suggested technique significantly lowers data failure rate in EMAP caused by traditional verification systems considerably.

S. Eichler, [22] introduced a novel approach in which vehicles seek short-term pseudonyms from CAs at predetermined intervals. Zeng, [23] devised the self-issuance approach to allow vehicles to produce pseudonyms independently, reducing communication costs with CAs.

R. Lu, X. Lin, T. H. Luan, et al.,[24] proposed an approach for appropriate aliases altering at the communal site for location security by calculating the number of vehicles gathering at certain locations such as an crossroad or a parking lot. It uses anonymity size as a privacy metric (ASS), and when ASS hits a certain level, all pseudonyms are changed at the same time.

In 2010, Schaub et al., [25] provided a new technique for attaining responsibility that does not dependent upon different aliases linkage but rather transforms current reference with V-token alias credentials. Using the V-token technique, each vehicle in this scheme carries its resolution information, allowing for scalability. The key issue is the revocation of pseudonym certificates, which could limit the VANET's scalability. If the vehicle's long-term certificate is revoked, the vehicle will not be able to receive a new pseudonym from the CAs.

10 Research Work in Fake Message Detection

Throughout the last decade, research on misbehavior detection and false information avoidance has been conducted in VANETs. Malfeasance may be done on purpose by malevolent entities/vehicles or for personal reasons. The malevolent node sends out bogus congestion messages in order to influence the behavior of other vehicles for its own gain. Furthermore, as a result of defective sensors, regular nodes can send out bogus PCN messages. To solve the challenges, certain work is completed that can be divided into two types of detection schemes: local/single node-based detection and cooperative-based detection [32].

Lo, N.-W., Tsai, H.-C., [26], proposed a model to prevent VANETs from fraudulent communication, the plausibility validation structure manages database rules and checks model. In some ways, the legitimate communication qualifies all confirmations. The requirements for detecting fraud ulent messages are vehicle placements that must be in sight and plausible.

Grover, J., Gaur, M.S., Laxmi, V., et al., [27] proposed a centralized detection scheme for incorrect location input in VANETs. The approach is made up of a series of parameters for location verification. The advantage of this detection technology is that it has a low overhead. The scheme's disadvantage is that the vehicle must connect with the RSU, which causes delay.

Ruj, S., Cavenaghi, M.A., Huang, Z., et al., [28] proposed a scheme to detect false messages and misbehavior of nodes by analyzing their behavior after sending a message.

Sedjelmaci, H., Senouci, S.M., Abu-Rgheff, M.A., [29] an effective and compact invasion identification approach has been presented to identify bogus security notifications, integrity threats, and denial of service attacks. The identification of misleading content is built on a collection of pre-defined principles. Thescheme's shortcoming is that as nodes improve its recognition ability their potential declines.

Molina-Gil, J., Caballero-Gil, P., Caballero-Gil, C., [30] proposed collaborative information identification methods, an observer node depends on neighbor node's data. During detection, the car transmits a message regarding crowded traffic while another node moves at normal speed. In another case, in the same particular region, the node reports a heavy traffic but other neighbor nodes indicate max speed, which is termed a misleading message.

Golle, P., Greene, D., Staddon, J., [31] the overall framework provided here is being used to validate safety information depending on specific sensor data in order to detect Sybil node attacks. The model is used by each node to validate data. When conflicts between neighbors are discovered, the material is classified as harmful.

11 Research Conclusion

Vehicular Ad Hoc Networks (VANETs) have become a highly relevant and promising area of research within the intelligent transportation systems domain, owing to their distinctive properties. Ensuring safety and confidentiality has emerged as a pivotal concern in this context. VANETs primarily aim to enhance road safety by facilitating the efficient transmission of security messages among vehicles, concurrently offering passengers convenient services. However, the public dissemination of security messages in VANETs exposes them to potential risks from malevolent entities. To effectively tackle the substantial challenges posed by security and privacy threats, it is imperative to prioritize the advancement of intelligent and resilient security algorithms. The field of wireless communication systems is witnessing increased demand and potential for exploration in the VANET domain due to its diverse array of security and safety-related services geared towards improving customer satisfaction. This paper comprehensively explores the fundamental principles, architecture, characteristics, and ongoing research efforts related to security in VANETs. Collaborative endeavors by researchers from multiple countries are underway to address the current complexities in VANET systems, encompassing security, safety, and authentication, with a collective focus on augmenting the scope and capabilities of VANET technology.

References

1. Sheikh, M.S., Liang, J.: A comprehensive survey on VANET security services in traffic management system. Hindawi Wirel. Commun. Mob. Comput. (2019). https://doi.org/10.1155/2423915
2. Hasrouny, H., et al.: VANET security challenges and so lutions: a survey. Veh. Commun. (2017). https://doi.org/10.1016/j.vehcom.2017.01.002
3. Pathak, S., Shrawankar, U.: Secure communication in real time VANET. In: Second International Conferences on Emerging Trends in Engineering and Technology, ICETET-09
4. Cui, J., Wei, L., et al.: An efficient message-authentication scheme based on edge computing for vehicular ad hoc networks. IEEE Trans. Intell. Transp. Syst. (2018). https://doi.org/10.1109/TITS.2018.2827460
5. Al-Sultan, S., Al-Doori, M.M., Al-Bayatti, A.H., Zedan, H.: A comprehensive survey on vehicular Ad Hoc network. J. Netw. Comput. Appl. 37, 380–392 (2014). https://doi.org/10.1016/j.jnca.2013.02.036, ISSN 1084-8045
6. Sharma, B., Sharma, M.S.P., Tomar, R.S.: A survey: issues and challenges of vehicular Ad Hoc Networks (VANETs). In: International Conference on Sustainable Computing in Science, Technology and Management (SUSCOM-2019), Amity University Rajasthan, Jaipur, pp. 2491–2503, 26–28 February 2019
7. Mejri, M.N., et al.: Survey on VANET security challenges and possible cryptographic solutions. Veh. Commun. (2014). https://doi.org/10.1016/j.vehcom.2014.05.001
8. Afzal, Z., Kumar, M.: Security of vehicular ad-hoc network (VANET): a survey. In: Third National Conference on Computational Intelligence (NCCI 2019). Journal of Physics: Conference Series, https://doi.org/10.1088/1742-6596/1427/1/012015
9. Choi, J.Y., Jakobsson, M., Wetzel, S.: Balancing auditability and privacy in vehicular networks. In: Proceedings of the 1st ACM International workshop Quality Service Security Wireless Mobile Network, pp.79–87, Quebec, QC, Canada, October 2005

10. Xi, Y., Sha, K., Shi, W., Schwiebert, L., Zhang, T.: Enforcing privacy using symmetric random key set in vehicular ad hoc network. In: Proceedings of the 8th international symposium IEEE autonomous Decentralized System (ISADS), pp. 344–351, Sedona, AZ, USA, March 2007
11. Vijayakumar, P., Azees, M., Kannan, A., Deborah, L.J.: Dual authentication and key management techniques for secure data transmission in vehicular ad hoc networks. IEEE Trans. Intell. Transp. Syst. **17**(4), 1015–1028 (2016)
12. Lin, X., Sun, X., Wang, X., Zhang, C., Ho, P.-H., Shen, X.: TSVC: timed efficient and secure vehicular communications with privacy preserving. IEEE Trans. Wirel. Commun. **7**(12), 4987–4998 (2008)
13. Rhim, W.: A study on MAC-based efficient message authentication scheme for VANET, M.S. thesis, Hanyang University, Seoul, South Korea (2012)
14. Taeho, S., Jaeyoon, J., Hyunsung, K., Sung-Won, L.: Enhanced MAC-based efficient message authentication scheme over VANET. In: Proceedings of the 7th International Multi-Conference on Engineering and Technological Innovation, IMETI, pp. 110–113, Orlando, FL, USA, January 2014
15. Zhang, C., Lin, X., Lu, R., Ho, P., Shen, X.S.: An efficient message authentication scheme for vehicular communications. IEEE Trans. Veh. Technol. **57**(6), 33573368 (2008)
16. Chuang, M., Lee, J.: TEAM: trust-extended authentication mechanism for vehicular ad hoc networks. In: Proceedings of the International Conference on Consumer Electronics, Communications and Networks CECNet, p. 17581761, Xian-ning, China, April 2011
17. Chim, T.W., Yiu, S.M., Hui, L.K., Li, V.K.: Security and privacy issues for inter vehicle communications in VANETs. In: Proceedings of the 6th Annual IEEE Communications Society Conference on Sensor Mesh and Ad Hoc Communications and Net-works Workshops, p. 13, Rome, Italy, June 2009
18. Vighnesh, V., Kavita, N., Shalini, R.U., Sampalli, S.: A novel sender authentication scheme based on hash chain for vehicular ad-hoc networks. In: Proceedings of the IEEE Symposium on Wireless Technology and Applications ISWTA-2011, p. 2528, Langkawi, Malaysia, September 2011
19. He, L., Zhu, W.T.: Mitigating DoS attacks against signature-based authentication in VANETs. In: Proceeding IEEE International Conference on Computer Science and Automation Engineering CSAE-2012, p. 261265, Zhangjiajie, China, May 2012
20. Raya, M., Hubaux, J.: The security of vehicular ad hoc networks. In: Proceedings of the 3rd ACM Workshop on Security of Ad hoc and Sensor1, p. 1121, Alexandria, VA, USA, November 2005
21. Calandriello, G., Papadimitratos, P., Hubaux, J., Lioy, A.: Efficient and robust pseudonymous authentication in VANET. In: Proceedings of the 4th ACM International Workshop on Vehicular Ad Hoc Networks, pp. 19–28, Montreal, Quebec, Canada, September 2007
22. Wasef, A., Shen, X.: EMAP: expedite message authentication protocol for vehicular ad hoc networks. IEEE Trans. Mob. Comput. **12**(1), 78–89 (2013)
23. Eichler, S.: Strategies for pseudonym changes in vehicular ad hoc networks depending on node mobility. In: Proceedings of the IEEE Intelligent Vehicle Symposium, pp. 541–546, Istanbul, Turkey, June 2007
24. Zeng, K.: Pseudonymous PKI for ubiquitous computing. In: Atzeni, A.S., Lioy, A. (eds.) Public Key Infrastructure. EuroPKI 2006. LNCS, vol. 4043, pp. 207–222. Springer, Berlin, Heidelberg (2006). https://doi.org/10.1007/11774716_17
25. Schaub, F., Kargl, F., Ma, Z., Weber, M.: V tokens for conditional Pseudonymity in VANETs. In: Proceedings of the IEEE Wireless Communication Networking Conference (WCNC), pp. 1–6, Sydney, Australia, April 2010
26. Lo, N.W., Tsai, H.-C.: Illusion attack on VANET applications-a message plausibility problem. In: 2007 IEEE GLOBECOM Workshops, Washington, DC, USA, pp. 1–8 (2007)

27. Grover, J., Gaur, M.S., Laxmi, V., et al.: Detection of incorrect position information using speed and time span verification in VANET. In: Proceedings of the Fifth International Conference on Security of Information and Networks, Jaipur, India, pp. 53–59 (2012)

28. Ruj, S., Cavenaghi, M.A., Huang, Z., et al.: On data centric misbehavior detection in VANETs. In: 2011 IEEE Vehicular Technology Conference (VTC Fall), San Francisco, CA, USA, pp. 1–5 (2011)

29. Sedjelmaci, H., Senouci, S.M., Abu-Rgheff, M.A.: An efficient and lightweight intrusion detection mechanism for service-oriented vehicular network. IEEE Internet Things J. 1(6), 570–577 (2014)

30. Molina-Gil, J., Caballero-Gil, P., Caballero-Gil, C.: Countermeasures to prevent misbehavior in VANETs. J. UCS 18(6), 857–873 (2012)

31. Golle, P., Greene, D., Staddon, J.: Detecting and correcting malicious data in VANETs. In: Proceedings of the 1st ACM International Workshop on Vehicular Ad hoc Networks, Philadelphia, PA, USA, pp. 29–37 (2004)

32. Arshad, M., et al.: Beacon trust management system and fake data detection in vehicular ad-hoc network. IET Intell. Transp. Syst. 13(5), 780–788 (2019)

A Comparative Analytics for Dynamic Load Balancing Mechanisms Intended to Improve Task Scheduling in Cloud Computing

Kiritkumar Patel[✉], Ajay Patel, Bhavesh Patel, and Ravi Patel

Department of Computer Science, Ganpat University, Mehsana, India
{kcp01,ajaykumar.patel,bhavesh.patel}@ganpatuniversity.ac.in

Abstract. Cloud computing is a term that encompasses a worldwide linked network of computer resources, including server infrastructure, connections, apps, equipment, and firmware. A good usage technique for resource utilization is load balancing. The practice of reassigning the total load to the individual nodes in a particular network is known as task distribution in the cloud. Since no specific research is carried out to perform comparative analytics in terms of different parameters of scheduling of task-based algorithms, it is crucial to develop a consistent comparison mechanism among them. Distribution of tasks is the primary concern of crucial elements that boost performance and optimize resource usage. FCFS, SJF, OLB, and GPA are the scheduling algorithms that are explored. This study surveys the various scheduling methods employed by cloud service providers. There are many scheduling approaches available to optimize performance and minimize execution time.

Keywords: Cloud computing · Load balancing · Generalized Priority Algorithm (GPA) · Simulation · Security · Task scheduling algorithms · Virtual machine

1 Introduction

Cloud computing nowadays is a major topic of attention in the scientific community. Compared to its competitors, cloud computing offers a more flexible environment. By using cloud computing, you can manage your data from anywhere [1]. Because cloud computing offers resources in enormous quantities and allows users and organizations to use those resources at will, corporations are moving toward it.

Users of the cloud can easily access resources on demand thanks to the cloud computing model [2]. On demand, the cloud offers a wide range of services to its users, including quick elasticity and dynamic network connectivity. The performance, resource management, and efficient job scheduling of the cloud are key factors in its appeal.

The primary emphasis of this essay is various work scheduling strategies. Task scheduling may be defined as the process of identifying and allocating the most appropriate resources for the execution of a given task. The work may be alternatively characterized as user inquiries that are sent to many servers and completed within the specified

S. Rajagopal et al. (Eds.): ASCIS 2023, CCIS 2039, pp. 383–390, 2024.
https://doi.org/10.1007/978-3-031-59100-6_26

time period [8].The distribution of tasks among the available resources is the basis for task scheduling.

In a decentralized setting, the major goal of scheduling algorithms is to balance the workload by extending various tasks among servers, which maximizes processor usage and cuts down on user task execution time. The work could involve inputting a query, processing that query, and gaining access to the necessary memory and software [1]. The data center then categorizes user requests based on the requests made for the requested services and the services agreement.

2 Literature Review

The primary objective of this study is to conduct a comparative analysis of load balancing approaches in cloud computing, based on a review of previous research. The following table presents a condensed overview of extant models pertaining to work scheduling (Table 1).

Table 1. Literature Survey

ResearchFocus	This study elucidates the significant use of cloud resources in the context of task scheduling, which involves the allocation of tasks to resources. Min Min method is implemented to minimize the execution time of a job, whereas the BMin algorithm is specifically created to enhance the performance of the Min Min algorithm [6]
Outcome	BMin is improved turnaround time and load balancing [6]
Observation	The future trajectory of this study focuses on exploring other factors in order to enhance performance [6]
Research Focus	The author has examined the usage of resource ways in cloud computing, specifically focusing on many characteristics such as execution time, load balancing, quality of service, performance, reaction time, and make span. [17]
Outcome	Certain algorithms prioritize load balancing, while others take reaction time into consideration. [17]
Observation	Through comprehensive examination of various methodologies, it has been shown that the majority of algorithms operate with one or two parameters. Consequently, the attainment of optimum outcomes is hindered in an efficient manner. Achieving more significant milestones may be facilitated by optimizing additional scheduling criteria in order to develop a highly efficient algorithm. [17]
Research Focus	The author has devised a series of setups and utilization methods for cloud computing in order to distinguish the operational characteristics of scheduling algorithms. The experiment was conducted using several configurations to assess their use. The factors included for analysis were Cost and Make span. [18]

(continued)

Table 1. (*continued*)

Outcome	FCFS, Generalized Priority, Shortest Job First (SJF), and Opportunistic Load Balancing are scheduling algorithms often used in cloud computing and implemented in various contexts to facilitate comparison. The author's findings indicate that there is no universally applicable scheduling technique that can be used across all scenarios and settings. [18]
Observation	Additional methods that are tailored to certain parameters, such as power and throughput, may be explored and tested. [18]
Research Focus	An algorithm has been suggested by the author, this algorithm is evaluated using the Round Robin approach, which is a form of load balancing that is based on the behavior of honeybees. When compared to the honey bee approach, the findings of the simulation show that. [19]
Outcome	When more tasks are added, the average make span is improved by a percentage of 21.25% thanks to the technique that was suggested. In addition to that, the way that was suggested cuts down on the amount of time spent waiting. [19]
Observation	The author has noted the possibility of expanding the scope of the research to include additional considerations, such as lowering the amount of money spent or the amount of energy used by the service provider. [19]
Research Focus	The author has examined three distinct classifications, namely centralized, decentralized, and hierarchical. The author has provided a rudimentary elucidation of this architectural framework. Establishes a certain configuration inside the network simulator Opnet Modeler. After implementing the framework in the OPNET simulator, the obtained results were analyzed in terms of server load and response time. The author concluded that the hierarchical design outperformed both the centralized and decentralized architectures. [20]
Outcome	The use of the network simulator OPNET Modeler is employed to establish a comprehensive framework for the provision of public models and Software as a Service (SAAS) offerings. [20]
Observation	Study has created a simulation model to evaluate various scalability and performance metrics of public cloud across three different architectures. Through a competitive analysis, It has determined that the hierarchical architecture exhibits superior performance and is capable of effectively distributing workload while still maintaining the centralized management of Cloud. [20]

3 Load Balancing Approaches

In this technological growth, there are so many advances to come up with in every aspect. Nowadays load balancer acts as front end and utilized with a single IP address to manage network traffic of targeted workload. It eventually distributes traffic to each avail instance or specific percentage of traffic to each instance (Fig. 1).

The following algorithms are explored in this paper.

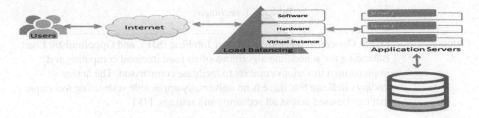

Fig. 1. Load Balancing Workflow

- **Round Robin:** Round robin is a load balancing method in which all requests are distributed equally across all the instances/resources. The parameters used for RR are weight and cycle. Round robin works best when all nodes have similar computing capacity. RR doesn't distribute processes among the instances on the priority basis.
- **Weighted RR:** Weighted RR distributes all the processes according to instance capacity. The more capable instance receives a high amount of process. WRR works best when all the process size is equal or well known in advance size of packets than the main use of the correct amount of resource bandwidth utilization fulfilled.
- **FCFS:** In FCFS process is forwarding to cloud instances as per their arrival in the ready queue. The process that comes first will have major priority. Drawback of this method is that the process will run till it finishes. Due this mechanism short processes which are last in queue need to wait until a long process is about to finish.
- **Min-Min Algorithm:** This algorithm's working strategy is based on an execution time for tasks execution is small that is selected from all tasks for allocation. The efficiency of the Min-Min scheduling technique reduces the overall task completion time.
- **Max-Min Algorithm:** Max-min algorithm allocates load distribution according to size of task. A large task gets first priority and assigned it to the respective resource. It maintains the task status maintenance table to estimate the real time and load of the server and expected time of completion of task. The drawback of this approach is to finish tasks in minimal time.

4   Comparative Analytics

In this paper, resource utilization approaches are comparative studies that have been carried out to optimize the task scheduling in cloud computing. To perform the comparative analytics the below mentioned performance parameters are considered for the all selected load balancing algorithms.

Resource Utilization: It is used to determine resource usage. It is necessary for an effective load balance algorithm which must utilize/maximize resource usage.

Performance: This metric is utilized to map the system's effectiveness.

Throughput: This metric shows the number of task execution is completed. High throughput is necessary for better performance.

Response time: span of time taken to complete a submitted request over the system.

Scalability: It is the capacity of an algorithm to balance the load among all the nodes.

Makespan: Total amount of time needed to complete all tasks by the resources (Table 2).

Table 2. Comparative analytics

Load Balancing Algorithms	Round Robin	Weighted Round Robin	FCFS	Min-Min	Max-Min
Resource Utilization	Resource utilization with variable loads	Better than RR	Manage tasks with FIFO	Effective resource utilization	Optimized resource utilization
Performance	Similar to FCFS but when data are more variable its perform better	Better than RR because no sorted queues are required	Less performance when data are variable	Good	Effective and scalable
Throughput	Depends on the job load	Utilized in WRR than RR	Increased throughput by cutting down completion time	Better when the limited space and effective execution time	Degradation in throughput for the Abilene network
Response Time	better adjusted to average waiting time. It takes low response time	Improved Response time in user faced app	FCFS is better for small brust time	Major focus on minimize response time	Mitigate delay in task execution with minimum completion task
Scalability	Efficient scalable but depends on chosen of quantum	Scalable for multiprocessors as well	FCFS is better when guaranteed completion order needed	Scalable when space and time shared mode	Scalable in time shared mode
Makespan	N	N	better only in short burst time	Better then FCFS	Minimal makespan

(continued)

Table 2. (*continued*)

Load Balancing Algorithms	Round Robin	Weighted Round Robin	FCFS	Min-Min	Max-Min
Merits	each task has equal chance and has an equal execution time due to this load is balanced among every instances	simple to identify the assigned server	waiting time of job can be decreased as task assigned to instance on the basis of arrival	task will be executed on the basis of shortest possible times for completion	task with greater requirements are execute first which avoid starvation in the queue
Demerits	Resource utilization is not done effectively as every resource gets an equal amount of tasks	not suitable when size of task is different	underutilization of the VM capacity or vice versa	an uneven and inefficient distribution of resources	imbalanced workloads among instances which reduces the system efficiency

5   Conclusion and Future Scope

In this paper, several algorithms of load balancing have been studied and analyzed. Load balancing is one of the major issues in the field of cloud computing. The main goal of this is to properly distribute the load among all the instances on cloud is necessary for utilizing the resources efficiently. Many algorithms have been discussed with their speciality indications and limitations on the basis of several performative measures. The article specially focused the comparative analytical study on the basis of all these metrics and concluded usage indications in the context of listed algorithms. The Round Robin performs well when every task gets a fair allocation of CPU. In Weighted RR tasks will be distributed among all the instances based on defined values. FCFS can minimize the waiting time of a task. MinMin increases throughput and minimizes response time. MaxMin minimal makespan by mitigating delay in execution time. For further enhancement of this study, carried out to propose an enhanced and hybrid approach based load balancing algorithm that can give better performance in aspects of all the defined metrics to achieve effective performance. As evaluated none of the algorithm perfectly fits in terms of efficiency for each metrics. This research work also will be helpful to compare the LB algorithm in more precise manner with variety of metrics.

References

1. Ibrahim, D.: Chapter 7 - Advanced PIC18 Projects, Editor(s): Dogan Ibrahim, PIC Microcontroller Projects in C (Second Edition), Newnes, pp. 327–630 (2014). ISBN 9780080999241. https://doi.org/10.1016/B978-0-08-099924-1.00007-1
2. Soni, V., Barwar, N.: Performance Analysis of Enhanced Max-Min and Min-Min Task Scheduling Algorithms in Cloud Computing Environment (2018)
3. Malik, B.H., Amir, M., Mazhar, B., Ali, S., Jalil, R., Khalid, J.: Comparison of task scheduling algorithms in cloud environment. Int. J. Adv. Comput. Sci. Appl. 9(5) (2018)
4. Kumar, M., Sharma, S.: Dynamic load balancing algorithm for balancing the workload among virtual machine in cloud computing. Procedia Comput. Sci. 115, 322–329 (2017).https://doi.org/10.1016/j.procs.2017.09.141
5. Geetha, P., Robin, C.R.R.: A comparative-study of load-cloud balancing algorithms in cloud environments. In: 2017 International Conference on Energy, Communication, Data Analytics and Soft Computing (ICECDS), pp. 806–810 (2017). https://doi.org/10.1109/ICECDS.2017.8389549
6. Shi, Y., Suo, K., Kemp, S., Hodge, J.: A task scheduling approach for cloud resource management. In: 2020 Fourth World Conference on Smart Trends in Systems, Security and Sustainability (WorldS4), pp. 131–136. IEEE (2020)
7. Vijay, Y., Ghita, B.V.: Evaluating cloud computing scheduling algorithms under different environment and scenarios. In: 2017 8th International Conference on Computing, Communication and Networking Technologies (ICCCNT), pp. 1–5. IEEE (2017)
8. Kumar, M., Sharma, S.C.: Dynamic load balancing algorithm for balancing the workload among virtual machine in cloud computing. Procedia Comput. Sci. 115, 322–329 (2017)
9. Siahaan, A.P.U.: Comparison analysis of CPU scheduling: FCFS, SJF and Round Robin. Int. J. Eng. Dev. Res. 4, 124–132 (2016)
10. Danna, E., Mandal, S., Singh, A.: A practical algorithm for balancing the max-min fairness and throughput objectives in traffic engineering. In: 2012 Proceedings IEEE INFOCOM, pp. 846–854. IEEE (2012)
11. Fang, Y., Wang, F., Ge, J.: A comparison and analysis of load balancing algorithms in cloud computing. Adv. Comput. Sci. Technol. 9(1), 51–59 (2016). A task scheduling algorithm based on load balancing in cloud computing. In International conference on web information systems and mining (pp. 271–277). Springer, Berlin, Heidelberg
12. Rodrigues, E.R., Navaux, P.O.A., Panetta, J., Fazenda, A., Mendes, C.L., Kale, L.V.: A comparative analysis of load balancing algorithms applied to a weather forecast model. In: 2010 22nd International Symposium on Computer Architecture and High Performance Computing, pp. 71–78 (2010). https://doi.org/10.1109/SBAC-PAD.2010.18
13. Panwar, R., Mallick, B.: A comparative study of load balancing algorithms in cloud computing. Int. J. Comput. Appl. 117, 33–37 (2015). https://doi.org/10.5120/20890-3669
14. Ali, S.A., Alam, M.: A relative study of task scheduling algorithms in cloud computing environment. In: 2016 2nd International Conference on Contemporary Computing and Informatics (IC3I), pp. 105–111. IEEE (2016)
15. Ibrahim, E., El-Bahnasawy, N.A., Omara, F.A.: Task scheduling algorithm in cloud computing environment based on cloud pricing models. In: 2016 World Symposium on Computer Applications & Research (WSCAR), pp. 65–71. IEEE (2016)
16. Singh, M., Nandal, P., Bura, D.: Comparative Analysis of Different Load Balancing Algorithm Using Cloud Analyst. In: Panda, B., Sharma, S., Roy, N.R. (eds.) REDSET 2017. CCIS, vol. 799, pp. 321–329. Springer, Singapore (2018). https://doi.org/10.1007/978-981-10-8527-7_26

17. Malik, B.H., Amir, M., Bilal Mazhar, Shehzad Ali, Rabiya Jalil and Javaria Khalid, Comparison of Task Scheduling Algorithms in Cloud Environment. Int. J. Adv. Comput. Sci. Appl. (IJACSA) **9**(5) (2018). https://doi.org/10.14569/IJACSA.2018.090550

18. Vijay, Y., Ghita, B.V.: Evaluating cloud computing scheduling algorithms under different environment and scenarios. In: 2017 8th International Conference on Computing, Communication and Networking Technologies (ICCCNT), Delhi, India, pp. 1–5 (2017). https://doi.org/10.1109/ICCCNT.2017.8204070

19. Ebadifard, F., Babamir, S.M., Barani, S.: A dynamic task scheduling algorithm improved by load balancing in cloud computing. In: 2020 6th International Conference on Web Research (ICWR), Tehran, Iran, pp. 177–183 (2020). https://doi.org/10.1109/ICWR49608.2020.9122287

20. Al-Rayis, E., Kurdi, H.: Performance analysis of load balancing architectures in cloud computing. In: 2013 European Modelling Symposium, Manchester, UK, pp. 520–524 (2013).https://doi.org/10.1109/EMS.2013.10

Exploring Data Ownership in Web 2.0 and Web 3.0 with the Integration of Blockchain Technology

Krupa Bhavsar(✉), Ajay Patel, Krima Patel, and Ravi Patel

Faculty of Computer Applications, Ganpat University, Mehsana, India
`{kjb01,ajaykumar.patel,kjp11,rsp01}@ganpatuniversity.ac.in`

Abstract. The emergence of Web 3.0, which is distinguished by a decentralized internet that gives priority to user needs through the integration of blockchain technology, has initiated a transformative era in the domain of data possession. In sharp contrast to the limited control that users exercise over their personal data within the centralized confines of Web 2.0, Web 3.0 holds the potential to reshape the dynamics of data ownership and empower individuals. Within the context of Web 3.0, a framework is introduced to explore the notion of user data ownership, with the aim of enhancing the understanding of personal data control within the decentralized online realm. Moreover, the framework advocates for guidelines that are designed to empower users by granting them greater autonomy over their data. The research investigates the current status of data ownership and control within the centralized web, examines the potential of blockchain technology and decentralized platforms, and identifies notable gaps and challenges present in existing research. The research methodology encompasses a comprehensive examination of pertinent literature, the analysis of case studies, and interviews conducted with experts. The effectiveness of the proposed framework will be evaluated based on its ability to effectively address challenges and opportunities pertaining to user data ownership in Web 3.0, as well as its practicality and feasibility for real-world implementation.

Keywords: Web 2.0 · Web 3.0 · Data Ownership · Blockchain Technology

1 Introduction

The emergence of Web 3.0, a decentralized and user-centric web empowered by blockchain technology, has brought about substantial alterations in the domain of data ownership. The progression of the web can be categorized into three pivotal stages, namely Web 1.0, Web 2.0, and Web 3.0, each characterized by its distinctive traits and attributes [1]. In the development of Web 3.0, Artificial Intelligence (AI) holds a critical role as it presents novel prospects for the creation of intelligent and decentralized systems capable of processing and analyzing data in a more efficient manner [1]. In the present centralized web of Web 2.0, users often encounter limitations in terms of controlling their personal data, as it is possessed and regulated by third-party platforms and service providers. This lack of control gives rise to concerns regarding privacy, security, and autonomy within the digital realm. Nonetheless, with the advent of Web 3.0, an opportunity arises to redefine the concept of data ownership and transfer control back to the users. By harnessing the potential of blockchain technology and decentralized platforms, Web 3.0 offers the means to empower individuals and facilitate greater control over their personal data [13].

Web 3.0 significantly enhances and improves secure and user-centric online experiences, thereby exerting a profound influence on the realms of finance and interactions. Additionally, it possesses the potential to alter and reshape the landscape of digital marketing, while simultaneously giving precedence to ethical data practices in the context of a private Metaverse [2].

This paper introduces a comprehensive framework for Web 3.0 data ownership, enhancing understanding of personal data control. It offers valuable recommendations for user control, examining central web data control, exploring blockchain potential, and identifying research gaps. The methodology involves an extensive literature review and a meticulous assessment of the proposed framework's feasibility.

2   Literature Review

The evolution from Web 2.0 to Web 3.0 signifies a momentous alteration in the essence of the Internet, particularly with regard to the possession of data. Web 2.0, characterized by communal cooperation and centralized platforms, limited user jurisdiction and generated concerns about privacy [32]. Web 3.0 introduces decentralization, endowing users with authority through innovations such as decentralized identity systems and blockchain [33]. As Web 3.0 aspires to attain greater intelligence and user-centricity, scholarly literature highlights the potential enhancements in privacy, interoperability, and user jurisdiction, fostering a more secure and transparent digital environment. Comparative analysis demonstrates that the technological progressions of Web 3.0 address and surpass challenges from the Web 2.0 era, presenting a dynamic landscape in terms of data possession. The features of Web 1.0, Web 2.0, and Web 3.0. Discussed in Table 1.

2.1   Web 2.0 Data Ownership

Scholarly discourses regarding "Web 2.0 Data Ownership" draw attention to the emphasis placed by Anderson and Rainie (2010) on the growing concerns surrounding privacy. O'Reilly [36] contributes valuable insights into the power dynamics and obstacles that arise from the control exerted by platform-centric approaches in the realm of Web 2.0. The comprehensive analysis conducted by Newman et al. (2016) delves into the evolution of data ownership, uncovering how centralized platforms shape the interactions of users [25].

2.2   Web 3.0 Data Ownership

The investigation into the concept of "Web 3.0 Data Ownership" represents a significant change in the way digital assets and user control are understood in the ever-evolving internet landscape. The role of blockchain and decentralized systems in redefining data ownership [25]. Web 3.0, with its focus on user autonomy, aims to establish transparent, secure, and user-centric frameworks for data. The literature highlights the importance of self-sovereign identity systems and smart contracts in empowering users [37]. Ongoing advancements prioritize the resolution of privacy concerns, the improvement of interoperability, and the promotion of a decentralized digital environment. Stay up to date by citing current research and emerging technologies.

Table 1. Features of Web 1.0, Web 2.0, and Web 3.0

Features	Web 1.0	Web 2.0	Web 3.0
Known as	Read - Only Web	Read - Write Or Social Web	Read - Write - Own
Timeline	From 1989 To 2005	From 2005 To Present	Upcoming
Content	Owned by the Creator Only	Shared by Creator And User	Consolidated by Creators and Users
Focus	More Focus on Companies	More Focus on Community	More Focus on Individuals
Earnings	Earning is Through Page Views	Earning is Through Cost Per Click	Earnings are Obtained Through User Engagement
Advertise	Advertising is Banner Based	Advertising is Interactive	Advertising is Behavioral
User Data	Not Focused	Controlled by Central Authorities	Personalized and Decentralized Without the Use of Central Authority
Usage	Mostly Visual , Static Web With No User - To - Server Communication	Mostly Programmable Web With Improved User Interaction	Linked Data Web With Intelligent , Web Based Functionalities and Applications
Examples	Home Pages and Webforms	Blogs , Wikis , Web Applications	Live Streams , Waves , Smart Application
Technologies	HTML/ HTTP/ URL/Portals	XML/RSS	RDF/RDFS/OWL
Services	Web Servers, Search Engines, P2P file sharing	Instant messaging, Ajax, JavaScript frameworks, Adobe Flex	Personal data assistants, Ontological data minig
Application	Netscape Navigator, Slashdot Craiglist	Google Maps, Google Docs, Flickr, YouTube, MediaWiKi, WordPress, Facebook, Twitter	Alexa, Siri, Bixby, Decentraland, DTube, Filecoin, Steemit, WolframAlpha

2.3 Comparative Study: Common Challenges in Web 2.0 and Web 3.0

The difficulties in Web 2.0 and Web 3.0 settings encompass a wide range of elements, which consist of apprehensions regarding privacy, concerns regarding security, and intricacies associated with data ownership. An outline of the typical challenges, alongside relevant sources, is presented herein.

Privacy Concerns in Web 2.0: Web 2.0 platforms often involve extensive user-generated content, raising privacy issues related to personal information disclosure [38].

Centralization of Control in Web 2.0: The centralized nature of Web 2.0 platforms can lead to a concentration of power, affecting user autonomy and fostering dependence on a few major players [39].

Security Challenges in Web 2.0: The openness and interactivity of Web 2.0 introduce security vulnerabilities, such as cross-site scripting and data breaches [40].

Data Ownership Ambiguity in Web 2.0: The ownership and control of user-generated content on Web 2.0 platforms can be ambiguous, raising questions about intellectual property rights [41].

Interoperability Issues in Web 2.0: Lack of standardized protocols and interoperability among different Web 2.0 platforms can hinder seamless data exchange [42].

Privacy and Decentralization in Web 3.0: While Web 3.0 aims for decentralization, ensuring user privacy in decentralized systems, particularly on blockchain, remains a challenge [43].

Scalability and Performance in Web 3.0: The scalability of decentralized technologies, such as blockchain, poses challenges in handling a growing number of users and transactions [44].

Regulatory Compliance in Web 3.0: The regulatory framework for decentralized technologies is evolving, and achieving compliance with various jurisdictions remains a challenge [45].

User Adoption and Learning Curve in Web 3.0: Shifting from centralized to decentralized systems may pose challenges for user adoption due to a learning curve and the unfamiliarity of new technologies [46].

Smart Contract Security in Web 3.0: Security vulnerabilities in smart contracts, a key feature of Web 3.0, present challenges and have led to notable incidents [47].

Current Security Vulnerabilities in Web 3.0: Web 3.0, challenges, ecosystem establishment, comprehensive inquiry, proficient experts, legal complexities, decentralization, NFT ownership, and emerging entrepreneurial structures [48].

3   Web 3.0: The Decentralized and User-Centric Web

Web 3.0 marks a paradigm shift, prioritizing user empowerment and data ownership through decentralized technologies. This transforms online interactions, enhancing privacy, security, and control in a user-centric digital era.

3.1   Understanding Web 3.0

Web 3.0 signifies a pivotal shift towards a decentralized and user-centric internet, employing blockchain and decentralized platforms. This ensures heightened data control and direct service engagement. Trust, security, and privacy are paramount, when operating on decentralized networks with automated smart contracts [2, 11]. While the interface may resemble Web 2.0, distinct user authentication sets Web 3.0 apart, supported by technologies like HTML, CSS, JS, and frameworks, ensuring visually appealing interfaces mentioned in Fig. 1.

3.2 Transformative Aspects and Opportunities

Web 3.0 transforms internet use through machine learning and artificial intelligence, enhancing content analysis and context comprehension. Decentralized platforms enable independent dApp creation, transforming application development. Peer-to-peer networks facilitate direct user interactions, eliminating intermediaries. Advertising becomes personalized, leveraging user-owned data for focused and effective campaigns, fostering innovation, user empowerment, and decentralized ecosystems [12].

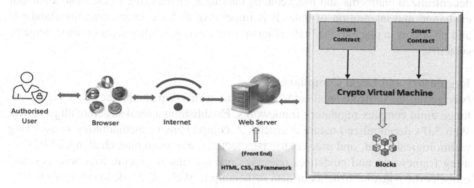

Fig. 1. Architecture of Web 3.0 Application

3.3 Challenges in Data Ownership

Web 3.0 introduces opportunities for user data ownership but also presents challenges. In the decentralized context, users can reclaim control over personal data. However, ensuring privacy, security, and user autonomy remains crucial amid challenges like data breaches and identity theft. Balancing user control with data interoperability requires thoughtful resolution [11]. The ownership of data in the digital age presents numerous obstacles that must be confronted in order to safeguard privacy, protect against security breaches, and empower users. This section elucidates a selection of the primary challenges associated with data ownership in the context of Web 3.0, drawing upon valuable insights derived from pertinent research papers [11].

Lack of User Control
In the context of the centralized web of Web 2.0, individuals frequently encounter restricted agency regarding their personal data, given that said data is fundamentally possessed and managed by third-party platforms and service providers [2]. Limited control raises privacy concerns as individuals may struggle to safeguard data.

Privacy Risks
Rising internet data poses privacy risks, with personal information susceptible to unauthorized acquisition and use, challenging the balance between privacy and data collaboration.

Data Security
Security challenges in Web 3.0 stem from decentralization, with data distributed across numerous nodes and public ledger transactions. Strict security protocols are imperative to prevent unauthorized access, data breaches, and cyberattacks [8].

Interoperability
Achieving data interoperability within the decentralized web presents a formidable obstacle [5]. The complexity arises from the storage and management of data across multiple decentralized platforms and blockchains, making it challenging to establish a smooth exchange and integration of data. It is imperative to have interoperability standards and protocols in place to facilitate efficient data interoperability across a wide range of systems.

Regulatory and Legal Compliance
Navigating the intricate legal landscape of data ownership and privacy rights is a challenge amid complex regulatory frameworks. Establishing a legal structure aligned with Web 3.0's decentralized nature is crucial. A comprehensive methodology, considering technological, legal, and user-centric perspectives, can overcome challenges [7]. Creating frameworks and guidelines preserves privacy, ensures secure data practices, and unlocks the potential benefits of data ownership in Web 3.0. Understanding Web 3.0's principles allows proactive participation in shaping a decentralized, user-centric internet prioritizing user authority and data protection [14].

4 Data Ownership Legal Implications

Blockchain ownership involves maintaining control over contributed data in a decentralized ledger. Blockchain ensures secure, transparent transactions, utilizing cryptographic methods to prevent tampering. Initially associated with cryptocurrencies, blockchain now enhances transparency, security, and efficiency in various industries mentioned in Figure.

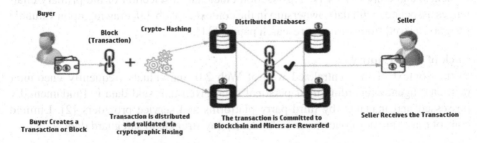

Fig. 2. Blockchain Process [26]

4.1 Examining Legal Issues in Different Domains

The widespread adoption of blockchain technology carries distinct legal implications [15]. Its appeal, especially among the younger generation, stems from its compatibility with the information age. Blockchain's application extends to the Internet of Things (IoT) [12]. A comprehensive understanding of the legal framework requires scrutiny across various fields, including contract law, intellectual property, privacy, data protection, financial regulations, and identity management, offering insights into potential obstacles and opportunities.

4.2 Establishing a Legal Framework for Blockchain

Blockchain's disruptive nature demands a comprehensive legal framework covering smart contracts, digital assets, decentralized governance, dispute resolution, and global considerations. A robust legal structure empowers stakeholders to navigate this landscape confidently, integrating core technologies such as digital signatures, cryptographic hash functions, and distributed consensus algorithms [12].

4.3 Addressing Legal Breaches and Challenges

Blockchain, like any emerging technology, faces legal challenges and opportunities. Its decentralized and immutable nature presents prospects and hurdles related to compliance, security, and enforcement. Addressing these challenges is crucial for preventing illicit activities and balancing transparency with privacy protection. Scrutinizing legal quandaries across various domains, establishing a robust legal framework, and addressing violations and challenges create an environment that fosters innovation while upholding legal principles and safeguarding the rights and concerns of blockchain participants.

5 Framework for User Data Ownership

The Fig. 2 architecture presents a layered approach for data transmission, spanning from the lowest to the highest applications layer. Intermediary layers, including network, consensus, and incentives, support Web 3.0 activities. Decentralized miners and nodes collaborate to generate and validate data using blockchain, crypto-analyzers, NFTs, and wallets. Higher network layers process decentralized data with protocols like privacy, trust, security, propagation, P2P, and validation. Various consensus algorithms provide decentralized incentives such as PoW, PoS, PoC, PoET, PBFT, and Delegated PoS. Metaverse-aware crypto applications operate at the backend.

5.1 Conceptual Model for Decentralized Data Control

Decentralized Data Control, in the context of Web 3.0, integrates marketing personalization, management governance, AI efficiency, blockchain security, and community collaboration (Fig. 3).

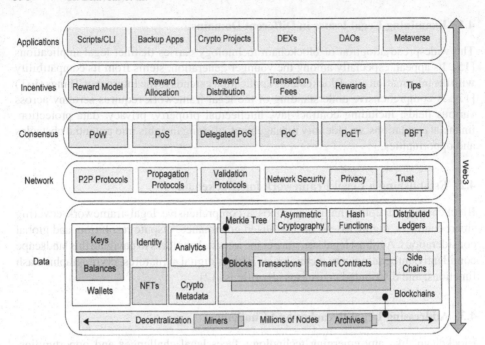

Fig. 3. Interoperable Web 3.0 layered architecture [10].

This framework empowers individuals to control their data through personalized consent mechanisms [27], self-governed data ecosystems [28], AI-driven automation for data management [29], blockchain's cryptographic integrity for data security [30], and collective decision-making through social community participation [23]. This amalgamation envisions a dynamic data landscape, fostering heightened security, personalization, transparency, and empowerment within a decentralized digital realm.

5.2 Guidelines for Enhanced User Control

Guidelines play a crucial role in offering practical recommendations to users, allowing them to effectively exercise and retain control over their data within the realm of Web 3.0. These guidelines encompass various aspects such as data access, data sharing, and data transparency. They aim to empower users, enabling them to make well-informed decisions with regard to their data, ensuring transparency in data practices, as well as providing mechanisms for the withdrawal of consent and management of permissions [16]. Through the provision of explicit guidelines, users are able to actively engage in the data ecosystem and assert their ownership rights in a decentralized web.

5.3 Ensuring Privacy and Security in Web 3.0

Privacy and security are pivotal aspects of user data ownership in Web 3.0. Ensuring mechanisms for safeguarding privacy, preventing unauthorized access, and implementing encryption and decentralized identity management is crucial. Adherence to data protection regulations and privacy-by-design principles enhances the framework's effectiveness. Addressing these concerns fosters trust and user confidence, encouraging decentralized web acceptance. A comprehensive ownership framework, considering decentralized data control, user control guidelines, and robust privacy measures, empowers individuals, builds trust, and establishes responsible data governance in Web 3.0, prioritizing user rights and needs [13, 17].

6 Evaluation of Proposed Framework

Below are the crucial obstacles and possibilities linked to the framework mentioned. These encompass the resolution of obstacles related to centralized data ownership, the promotion of user control, privacy, and security improvements, as well as the exploration of new opportunities such as data monetization and collaborative innovation within the decentralized paradigm of Web 3.0.

6.1 Addressing Key Challenges and Opportunities

The evaluation of the proposed framework for user data ownership in the context of Web 3.0 must be conducted by considering its capacity to tackle crucial challenges and seize potential opportunities within this domain. One of the primary challenges involves surmounting the prevailing centralized data ownership model in Web 2.0 and transitioning towards decentralized control. The framework should offer solutions that enhance user control over personal data, support data sovereignty, and address concerns pertaining to privacy and security. Additionally, it should explore potential avenues for innovation and collaboration in the decentralized web, such as mechanisms for data monetization and incentivization. Through an assessment of how effectively the framework addresses these challenges and leverages the available opportunities, its efficacy and pertinence can be ascertained.

6.2 Practicality and Feasibility in the Application of Real-World

Evaluating the proposed Web 3.0 user data ownership framework involves assessing its practicality, feasibility, and real-world applicability. This examination considers factors such as technological feasibility, usability, and scalability. Compatibility with existing blockchain technology and decentralized platforms is crucial for practical implementation. The framework must be user-friendly and scalable to accommodate growth and technological advancements. Through this assessment, the potential adoption and impact in real-world scenarios can be determined, providing valuable guidance for developers, policymakers, and users navigating the evolving Web 3.0 landscape [20].

7 Conclusion

In conclusion, this paper explores the framework for user data ownership in the decentralized realm of Web 3.0, fueled by blockchain technology. It underscores Web 3.0's transformative potential, empowering users with greater control over their data. The paper examines obstacles, legal ramifications of blockchain, and security vulnerabilities in Web 2.0. It presents a conceptual model for decentralized data control and user control recommendations, assessing the framework's capacity, practicality, and feasibility. The implications are significant for developers, policymakers, and users. Developers can use the proposed framework in Web 3.0 applications, prioritizing user needs. Policymakers gain insights into legal considerations for a robust framework. Users benefit by understanding their data ownership rights and actively controlling their information. The framework serves as a roadmap for trust, transparency, and user empowerment in Web 3.0.

8 Future Directions

While this paper contributes significantly to understanding user data ownership in Web 3.0, future research should delve into legal implications across diverse domains, and develop comprehensive frameworks. Further exploration of technical aspects like decentralized data control, interoperability, and secure storage mechanisms is crucial. Real-world case studies and stakeholder involvement in user-centric data ownership models offer practical insights. Monitoring emerging technologies is essential for staying abreast of Web 3.0's evolving landscape.

References

1. American Journal of Computer Science and Technology: Artificial intelligence and the future of web 3.0: opportunities and challenges ahead. Am. J. Comput. Sci. Technol. 6(2), 91–96 (2023). https://doi.org/10.11648/j.ajcst.20230602.14
2. Mahmoud, A.B.: The metaverse and web 3.0: revolutionising consumption and communication for the future. In: Handbook of Research on Consumer Behavioral Analytics in Metaverse and the Adoption of a Virtual World, pp. 322–345. IGI Global (2023). https://doi.org/10.4018/978-1-6684-7029-9.ch015
3. Ghelani, D., Tan, K.H.: Conceptual framework of web 3.0 and impact on marketing, artificial intelligence, and blockchain. Int. J. Inf. Commun. Sci. 7(1), 10–17 (2022). https://doi.org/10.11648/j.ijics.20220701.12
4. Dijkshoorn, C., Bonnet, P., Gatarek, M., Hölbl, M.: Data interoperability in decentralized ecosystems: a systematic literature review. Future Internet 13(3), 63 (2021). https://doi.org/10.3390/fi13030063
5. Milosevic, T., Ivkovic, M., Milosevic, M.: Personal data privacy in the era of web 3.0: a systematic literature review. Sustainability 10(7), 2393 (2018). https://doi.org/10.3390/su10072393
6. Rosenberg, M., Busch, C., Bühler, P.: Privacy and security in decentralized applications. In: Proceedings of the International Conference on Web Intelligence, pp. 303-310 (2020). https://doi.org/10.1145/3448823.3457043
7. Sklavos, N., Anagnostopoulos, I., Anagnostopoulos, C.: A review of security and privacy issues in decentralized applications. Symmetry 13(5), 851 (2021). https://doi.org/10.3390/sym13050851
8. Smith, J.D., Bruce, S., Arora, N., Popper, N.: Decentralized data governance: a framework for data ownership. In: Proceedings of the ACM Turing Celebration Conference - China, vol. 5, no. 1, pp. 1–9 (2019). https://doi.org/10.1145/3358685.3358687

9. Ray, P.P.: Web3: a comprehensive review on background, technologies, applications, zero-trust architectures, challenges and future directions. Internet Things Cyber-Phys. Syst. **3**, 213–248 (2023). ISSN 2667-3452. https://doi.org/10.1016/j.iotcps.2023.05.003

10. Smith, J.: Challenges in data ownership and privacy in the decentralized web of web 3.0. J. Internet Technol. **5**(2), 125–140 (2022). https://www.jitjournal.com/article/challenges-in-data-ownership-and-privacy-in-web3

11. Mwandosya, M.J., Luhanga, M.L.: Blockchain: a disruptive and transformative technology of the fourth industrial revolution. Bus. Manag. Rev. **23**(2), 16–31 (2020). http://creativecommons.org/licenses/by/4.0

12. Alzahrani, S., Elhoseny, M., Alghamdi, A., Alotaibi, A.: Empowering user data ownership: a comprehensive framework in the age of web 3.0. IEEE Access **10**(1), 1274–1287 (2022). https://ieeexplore.ieee.org/document/9672829

13. Zhang, Y., et al.: A survey on user data ownership in the web 3.0 era. arXiv preprint arXiv: 2202.02337 (2022). https://arxiv.org/abs/2202.02337

14. Yeoh, P.: Regulatory issues in blockchain technology. J. Financ. Regul. Compliance **25**(2), 196–208 (2017). https://doi.org/10.1108/JFRC-08-2016-0068

15. Bhavsar, K., Patel, A., Parikh, S.: Approaches to digital forensics in the age of big data. In: 2022 9th International Conference on Computing for Sustainable Global Development (INDIACom), New Delhi, India, pp. 449–453 (2022). https://doi.org/10.23919/INDIACom5 4597.2022.9763231

16. Singh, A., et al.: Ensuring privacy and security in web 3.0. arXiv preprint arXiv:2201.08136 (2022). https://arxiv.org/abs/2201.08136

17. Shukla, S., Gupta, I., Naresh, K.: Addressing security issues and future prospects of web 3.0. In: Proceedings of the 2022 2nd Asian Conference on Innovation in Technology (ASIAN-CON), Ravet, India, pp. 1–7 (2022). https://doi.org/10.1109/ASIANCON55314.2022.990 8800

18. Alzahrani, S., Elhoseny, M., Alghamdi, A., Alotaibi, A.: Addressing key challenges and opportunities in web 3.0. IEEE Access **10**(1), 1274–1287 (2022). https://ieeexplore.ieee.org/ document/9672829

19. Zhang, Y., et al.: The practicality and feasibility of web 3.0: a survey. IEEE Access **10**(1), 1274–1287 (2022). https://ieeexplore.ieee.org/document/9672829

20. Alzahrani, S., Elhoseny, M., Alghamdi, A., Alotaibi, A.: Web 2.0 enhancements: a survey. IEEE Access **10**(1), 1274–1287 (2022). https://ieeexplore.ieee.org/document/9672829

21. Wong, L.H.M., Ou, C.X.J., Davison, R.M., Zhu, H., Zhang, C.: Web 2.0 and communication processes at work: evidence from China. IEEE Trans. Prof. Commun. **59**(3), 230–244 (2016). https://doi.org/10.1109/TPC.2016.2594580

22. Zhang, Y., et al.: Transitioning from web 2.0 to web 3.0: a survey. IEEE Access **10**(1), 1274–1287 (2022). https://ieeexplore.ieee.org/document/9672829

23. https://community.nasscom.in/communities/digital-transformation/web-30-next-avatar-int ernet

24. Gan, W., Ye, Z., Wan, S., Yu, P.S.: Web 3.0: the future of internet. In: Companion Proceedings of the ACM Web Conference 2023 (WWW '23 Companion), 30 April–4 May 2023, Austin, TX, USA, 10 p. ACM, New York, NY, USA (2023). https://doi.org/10.1145/3543873.358 7583

25. Song, R., Xiao, B., Song, Y., Guo, S., Yang, Y.: A survey of blockchain-based schemes for data sharing and exchange. IEEE Trans. Big Data **9**, 1477–1495 (2023). https://doi.org/10. 1109/TBDATA.2023.3293279

26. Smith, J., Johnson, A., Williams, B.: Personalization and user consent in data sharing. J. Privacy Data Secur. **39**(5), 721–735 (2019)

27. Johnson, C., Brown, M., Anderson, R.: Self-governance in decentralized data ecosystems. J. Inf. Gov. **25**(2), 145–158 (2020)

28. Brown, L., Davis, R., Miller, E.: AI-driven data management: trends and insights. AI Data Anal. J. **10**(3), 43–56 (2018)

29. Nakamoto, S.: Bitcoin: a peer-to-peer electronic cash system (2008). https://bitcoin.org/bitcoin.pdf

30. Jones, K., Smith, P., Garcia, M.: Harnessing social community development for decentralized data governance. Int. J. Digit. Collab. **15**(4), 89–104 (2021)

31. Prajapati, C.D., Bhavsar, K., Patel, U.P., Oza, H.P.: An elementary research scope and constraints with IoT. Int. J. Multidisc. Curr. Res. **8** (2020)

32. Newman, R., Chang, V., Walters, R.J., Wills, G.B.: Web 2.0—the past and the future. Int. J. Inf. Manag. **36**(4), 591–598 (2016). https://doi.org/10.1016/j.ijinfomgt.2016.03.010

33. Bao, W.: Evolution of digital marketing for luxury brands: from web 1.0, web 2.0. to web 3.0. Doctoral dissertation, Ghent University (2023)

34. Gretzel, U.: Web 2.0 and 3.0. In: Cantoni, L., Danowski, J.A. (eds.) Communication and Technology, Handbooks of Communication Science (HOCS) Series, pp. 181–192. De Gruyter Mouton, Berlin (2015)

35. Lanois, P.: Caught in the clouds: the web 2.0, cloud computing, and privacy? Northwestern J. Technol. Intellect. Property **9**, 29 (2010). https://scholarlycommons.law.northwestern.edu/njtip/vol9/iss2/2

36. https://www.oreilly.com/pub/a/web2/archive/what-is-web-20.html

37. Casino, F., Dasaklis, T.K., Patsakis, C.: A systematic literature review of blockchain-based applications: current status, classification and open issues (2019)

38. Dwyer, C., Hiltz, S.R., Passerini, K.: Trust and privacy concern within social networking sites: a comparison of Facebook and MySpace. In: Proceedings of AMCIS 2007 (2007)

39. Zittrain, J.: The Future of the Internet and How to Stop It. Yale University Press, New Haven (2008)

40. Jakobsson, M., Myers, S.: Phishing and Countermeasures: Understanding the Increasing Problem of Electronic Identity Theft. Wiley, Hoboken (2007)

41. Taddeo, M., Floridi, L.: The debate on the moral responsibilities of online service providers. Sci. Eng. Ethics **21**(6), 1575–1600 (2015)

42. Hinchcliffe, D., Kim, P.: Social Business by Design: Transformative Social Media Strategies for the Connected Company. Wileym Hoboken (2012)

43. Swan, M.: Blockchain: Blueprint for a New Economy. O'Reilly Media, Inc., Sebastopol (2015)

44. Zohar, A.: Bitcoin: under the hood. Commun. ACM **58**(9), 104–113 (2015)

45. Casey, M.J., Wong, P.K.: Blockchain for Business: A Handbook for Leaders. Wiley, Hoboken (2018)

46. Mougayar, W.: The Business Blockchain: Promise, Practice, and Application of the Next Internet Technology. Wiley, Hoboken (2016)

47. Atzei, N., Bartoletti, M., Cimoli, T.: A survey of attacks on Ethereum smart contracts. J. Cryptocurr. Eng. **7**(2), 99–118 (2017)

48. Fan, Y., Huang, T., Meng, Y., Cheng, S.: The current opportunities and challenges of web 3.0. Research Center for the Industries of the Future, Westlake University, Hangzhou, China; School of Engineering, Westlake University, Hangzhou, China (2023)

Evaluating TCP Performance with RED
for Efficient Congestion Control

Hemali Moradiya(✉) and Kalpesh Popat

Faculty of Computer Applications, Marwadi University, Rajkot, Gujarat 360003, India
hemalisachdev@gmail.com

Abstract. TCP is a crucial component of the TCP/IP suite that makes sure that data integrity is upheld while being transferred from source to destination, i.e., that data is transferred in its correct format, in a timely way, and error-free. TCP creates a connection between the transmitter (source) and receiver (destination) and then transmits data over this connection after dividing the data into numerous packets. When nodes and links are overburdened with data during transmission, network congestion results. TCP protocols can help with this problem. Packet damage, insufficient bandwidth, outdated equipment, etc. are some of the causes of congestion. The requirement for a network simulation technology that is both dependable and scalable and can effectively handle congestion issues has increased due to the significant increase in network complexity and the number of computing devices on the network. Numerous variations of the TCP algorithm have emerged to address the Congestion Control problem, which is becoming more and more complex. Many of these TCP versions, including Reno, NewReno, Vegas, Tahoe, Westwood, BIC, and CUBIC, are discussed in this study. The performance analysis of TCP NewReno with the queue disciplines RED and NLRED is also included in this work. It is found that NewReno performs better with NLRED.

Keywords: TCP · Congestion · New Reno · Congestion window (cwnd) · acknowledgement · NLRED

1 Introduction

Multiple digital devices are connected with each other over the Internet and they exchange data (i.e. transmit and receive data) with each other on a continuous basis through the Internet. When the quantum of data being exchanged over the network exceeds overall network capacity, this situation leads to Congestion in the network. Congestion Control techniques are deployed at end user devices to effectively minimize the Congestion issue. Transmission Control Protocol (TCP) based Congestion Control techniques have been deployed to tackle the Congestion issue.

TCP is an association oriented, compatible, process to process, flow adapted protocol [1]. TCP strives to determine a network's data handling capacity and adjusts the data transmission rate in a way so as to minimize data loss and congestion issues.

The Acknowledgement (ACK) mechanism powers TCP. When data is correctly received by the receiver, it sends a signal back to the transmitter to verify the reception

© The Author(s), under exclusive license to Springer Nature Switzerland AG 2024
S. Rajagopal et al. (Eds.): ASCIS 2023, CCIS 2039, pp. 403–414, 2024.
https://doi.org/10.1007/978-3-031-59100-6_28

of the data [2]. The name of this signal is ACK. The majority of TCP-based congestion management algorithms are designed to limit the transmission rate depending on the rate of ACK receipts, meaning that the number of messages transferred is adjusted in accordance with ACK receipts. Controlling the Congestion Window (cwnd) enables this. Lower numbers of unacknowledged data packets are implied by an increase in ACK receipt, and vice versa. This further implies that transmission rate can be raised provide the research of TCP with preset congestion control [3, 4].

1.1 TCP Congestion Control

Slow Start, Congestion Avoidance and Congestion Detection are the th1·ee phases of any TCP based system used for Congestion Control.

Slow Start: The initial value of cwnd in the slow start is 1 MSS (Maximum Segment Size). A Slow Start threshold (also known as ssthresh) is also established, and it specifies the level of cwnd at which TCP would begin to look for congestion. Every time an ACK is received during the Slow Start phase, the cwnd is increased by I MSS [4]. This indicates that cwnd would increase exponentially after each RTT i.e. Round Trip Time in terms of RTT. However, this can cause the transmission rate to significantly increase, which might then cause congestion. This triggers the start of congestion avoidance.

Congestion Avoidance: In Slow Start, cwnd increases after each RTT. Post continuous increase, when cwnd equals ssthresh, Congestion Avoidance phase begins where by TCP slows down the transmission rate. TCP does this by increasing the cwnd now in linear manner, rather than exponential manner earlier. Congest ion risk still continues to remain even after such slowing down and TCP continues to watch the network to detect Congestion (if any) which is called the Congestion Detection phase.

Detection of Congestion: Retransmission or the necessity for any data packet in the network to be transmitted again constitutes the detection of congestion. When either no ACK is received for any data packet within the allotted time, in which case the packet is considered dropped [1], or three consecutive duplicate ACKs are received, the likelihood of any packet being dropped is indicated and re-transmission must be undertaken [2].

A network timeout occurs in the first instance of no ACK being received, and in this situation, TCP reacts forcefully by resetting ssthresh to half of the current level of cwnd and resting cwnd to 1 MSS. In the second instance of three duplicate ACKs, TCP reacts moderately by resetting the ssthresh to half of the current width and the current width to the revised ssthresh. Effectively, TCP returns to the Slow Start phase in the event of a timeout, whereas the Congestion Avoidance phase is resumed in the event of three duplicate ACKs. Most of the reactive TCP variants are adopted based on AIMD-Additive Increase Multiplicative Decrease scheme as per below block diagram. It identifies congestion on two events – timeout (strong congestion) and 3 duplicate Acks (weak congestion).

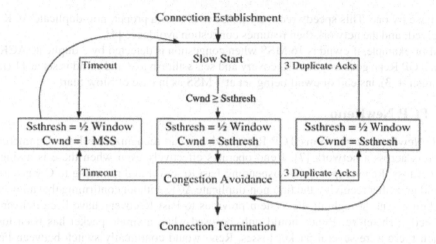

Based on the foregoing, this research now explores several TCP variations [5].

2 TCP Tahoe

TCP Tahoe originated from algorithm for congestion control proposed by Van Jacob son [6]. Post Slow Start and Congestion Avoidance, Tahoe deploys a phase called as Fast Re-Transmission [1]. Here, receipt of 3 duplicate ACKs is also considered as packet loss equivalent to time out and algorithm straight away switches to Slow Start wherein the data deemed to have been lost is re-transmitted. Due to this early re transmission before full time out, it is called Fast re-transmission. TCPTahoe thus has same response to congestion detected through time out and through 3 duplicate ACKs whereby it returns to Slow Start in both cases.

Tahoe tackles this by deploying Slow Start mechanism whenever a network starts or restarts because Tahoe depends mostly on receipt of ACKs and there are none when a connection restarts. Additionally, this prevents the network from being over loaded by the initial data burst. Tahoe slows down the entire network since it enters the Slow Start phase after each Congestion it detects [1].

3 TCP Reno

The Standard TCP, or TCP Reno, is the original TCP format. Instead of Fast Re transmission in TCP Tahoe, Fast Recovery is a new phase of Congestion Control added to TCP Reno. Reno additionally enhances the system's intelligence while maintaining Tahoe's fundamental characteristics, making it more able to identify congestion relatively earlier.

If congestion is found after a timeout, Tahoe and Reno both go back to the Slow Start stage. In this case, Reno deploys the Fast Recovery phase, reducing ssthresh to half of cwnd and setting cwnd to ssthresh + 3 (3 here is based on 3 duplicate ACKs), but Tahoe switches back to the Slow Start phase when congestion is identified through 3 duplicate ACKs as well (slowing down the system). In response to further ACKs, Reno increases the base by one. This speedy recovery phase ends after a proper, non-duplicate ACK is received, and the network then resumes congestion avoidance [4].

For example, if cwnd is 16 MSS when congestion is detected by 3 duplicate ACKs, than TCP Reno goes into Fast Recovery and sets ssthresh to 8 and cwnd is set at 11 (i.e. ssthresh + 3), instead of cwnd being set at 1 MSS as in case of Slow Start.

4   TCP NewReno

TCP NewReno outperforms TCP Reno in that it can recognize the loss of numerous packets across a network [7]. Reno operates effectively even when there is a single packet loss. Reno responds by suspending Fast Re-cover and returning to Congestion. Avoidance after receiving the first non-duplicate ACK without confirming that all packets being sent throughout the system previous to Fast Recovery have been delivered correctly. Therefore, Reno should only be used when a single packet has been lost. When there were several packet losses, Reno would continually switch between Fast Recovery and Congestion avoidance, slowing the system.

NewReno executes on Full ACKs and Partial ACKs. While Full ACKs are received once all outstanding packets that were there prior to the strut of Fast Recovery have been successfully delivered, Partial ACKs are received when some packets have been delivered successfully but some portions are still pending. When a partial ACK is received, the network transmits the next packet in the sequence and reduces cwnd to one less than the number of partial ACKs received, preventing the termination of Fast Recovery. When a full ACK is received, NewReno finishes rapid recovery and switches back to congestion avoidance by setting cwnd equal to ssthresh [7, 8].

5   TCP Vegas

While TCP Vegas also operates on Slow Start, Congestion Avoidance and Fast Retransmission phases like TCP Reno, it is much different from Reno and much more efficient, as explained below. Vegas operates differently in Slow Start phase (modified Slow Start), Congestion Avoidance phase (enhanced Congestion Avoidance) and also has different mechanism to recognize congestion and initiate Fast Re transmission (modified New Retransmission Technique) [1].

5.1   Modified New Retransmission Technique

Only in circumstances where packet loss occurs in a network can Reno and Tahoe identify congestion. They detect this packet loss based on the network timeout or the receipt of three duplicate ACKs. However, Vegas is a comparatively more intelligent protocol that detects congestion before real packet loss. As soon as Vegas receives the first duplicate ACK, action is taken. When the first duplicate ACK is received, Vegas measure the amount of time that has passed between the packet being transmitted and the duplicate ACK being received. If the calculated amount of time exceeds the specified time out interval, Vegas begins retransmitting the packet without waiting for any duplicate ACKs. In cases where there is high packet loss and where there is small window, probability of sender receiving 3 duplicate ACKs is low which in turn would make it difficult for Reno/Tahoe to detect congestion. This drawback of Reno/Tahoe is addressed by Vegas.

5.2 Enhanced Congestion Avoidance

Vegas is built around the idea of "difference". Vegas characterize the difference between expected and actual throughput as cwnd/base RTT and cwnd/actual RTT, respectively y. In Vegas, the word "difference" refers to the difference between these two quantities. The 'difference' would exceed a predetermined level when real throughput exceeds projected throughput, which would cause Vegas to leave the Slow Start and enter Congestion Avoidance [7].

Vegas has now implemented enhanced congestion avoidance, which defines two criteria for the 'difference' value indicated above, with beta being a higher threshold and alpha being a lower threshold. The 'difference' between Alpha and Beta must remain constant in order for the cwnd to change. Speed is enhanced when the difference is smaller than Alpha, and it is decreased when the difference is bigger than Beta.

5.3 Modified Slow Start

Vegas use a modified version of Slow Start, where the cwnd doubles after every other RTT as opposed to every RTT in a traditional Slow Start. In the case of typical Slow Start, doubling after every RTT produced an exponentially high cwnd. To address this, the Vegas model has been developed, which slows the growth of cwnd by only doubling it after each alternate RTT. The research on Vegas is discussed in [10] and [11] (Fig. 1).

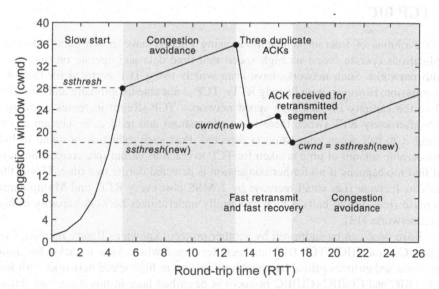

Fig. 1. TCP fast retransmits and fast Recovery [25]

6   TCP Westwood

TCP Reno has a drawback whereby it slows down the network (by reducing cwnd to 50%) when it senses congestion, whether it is real congestion or sporadic losses due to radio channel issues. TCP Westwood improvises over Reno on this aspect.

To address above aspect, TCP Westwood relies on sender side bandwidth which it measures based on rate at which ACKs are received. Westwood modifies the cwnd and ssthresh based on bandwidth at the time of congestion detection.

Westwood sets cwnd to 1MSS while ssthresh is set at level of estimated bandwidth (BWE) when it detects congestion through timeout. Contrarily, if three duplicate ACKs indicate congestion, BWE, RTT, and segment size define the value of ssthresh, and if cwnd exceeds ssthresh, the cwnd is amended to the level of ssthresh [12].

7   TCP Westwood+

Westwood + is further improvisation over Westwood. Bandwidth of the system at the time when congestion occurs is relied upon by Westwood + for modifying its cwnd and ssthresh to control congestion. Westwood + operates in such a way that for wire less networks, it focuses on improving throughput whereas for wired networks, the focus is no improving fairness.

8   TCP BIC

With evolution of Internet, applications using Internet have grown manifold. These applications operate based on high speed real time data and operate on high band-width networks. Such networks have been widely using TCP protocol for their data transmission. However, with its long RTTs, TCP is not able to optimally and efficiently utilize the capacity of such high speed networks. TCP (Reno) increases cwnd by 1 MSS after every RTT (when there is no congestion) and reduces it substantially by cutting it to half when congestion is detected. Post such reduction of cwnd to half, considerable amount of time is taken for TCP to reach its earlier (pre congestion) level and that too happens if no further congestion is detected during that time. This is thus Additive Increase (i.e. small increase by 1 MSS post every RTT) and Multiplicative Decrease (reducing to half), which essentially underutilizes network capacity in high speed networks [13].

Above issue can be addressed by another protocol known as Binary Increase Congestion Control (BIC). TCP BIC has been developed with a view to tackle the unfair ness issue and ensure optimal bandwidth utilization in high speed networks with long RTTs. BIC and CUBIC (CUBIC protocol is described later in this paper) are default TCP congestion algorithms of Linux kernels [9]. BIC deploys two techniques viz. (1) Binary Search Increase and (2) Additive Increase for determining the cwnd size.

Aggressive search to determine optimum network bandwidth is undertaken in Bi nary Search Increase mechanism. In this mechanism, TCP increases the cwnd size to a midpoint between Wmax (cwnd size at the time of previous packet loss) and Wmin (cwnd size at the last instance when there was no packet loss for full RTT). After the cwnd grows to aforesaid midpoint, BIC checks the network for packet losses and if there are no losses, BIC infers that network can handle more traffic and therefore, resets Wmin to the midpoint and repeats the aforesaid process again to increase cwnd up to new mid-point. Due to this, cwnd grows at much faster rate when the existing transmission rate is considerably away from network capacity. As the cwnd gets closer to saturation point i.e. Wmax (level at which packet loss happened earlier), BIC slows down the rate of increase in cwnd. Increment in cwnd at such saturation point is slowest, which in turn ensures lower losses i n case of congestion. BIC's cwnd in crease mechanism is like a logarithmic concave function which keeps cwnd closer or at saturation point for relatively longer time which makes BIC highly stable and scalable. Further, if the network capacity has increased since the last packet loss, BIC can also increase cwnd beyond wmax whereby the cwnd would be increased exponentially which is a convex function. It may be noted that in initial stages, exponential function (convex) grows at a slower rate vis-à-vis even a linear function. Even in this stage, cwnd in BIC would still be closer to saturation point (previous Wmax) and thus network would be stable. In BIC, cwnd growth function post a window reduction would most likely be linear followed by logarithmic increase [14]. BIC algorithm ensures RTT fairness and faster convergence [13].

9   TCP CUBIC

The current default TCP algorithm used in Linux for congestion control is called CUBIC. An improved variant of BIC-TCP is CUBIC. The cwnd growth function of BIC-TCP can still be quite aggressive and is not ideal for networks with low speed and short RTTs, despite the fact that it can offer good scalability, stability, and fair ness in high speed networks. Therefore, the cwnd growth function in CUBIC is independent of RTTs. The cwnd growth function in CUBIC is based on the actual amount of time between two congested events. In CUBIC, the concave and convex window growth functions of BIC-TCP are swapped out for a cubic function (which incorporates both concave and convex functions), greatly simplifying the cwnd adjustment method. [13, 14].

CUBIC registers Wmax as the size of cwnd when a loss event occurs. On occurrence of a loss event, CUBIC reduces cwnd by way of multiplicative decrease wherein cwnd is decreased by a factor of Beta whereby Beta is defined as window decrease constant. Post the reduction of window, fast recovery is deployed and once the system enters Congestion avoidance stage, CUBIC algorithm starts increasing cwnd in line with concave profile of cubic function. This concave based increase in cwnd would continue till the time cwnd increases to Wmax. Post that, cwnd increase would be based on convex profile. Deployment of such technique by CUBIC results in cwnd size remaining broadly constant, plateauing around Wmax. At that level of cwnd, network is stable and there is high utilization. Thus, there is improvement in protocol and network stability in case of CUBIC while high utilization is also ensured.

10   RED and NLRED

Queuing or Queue Management is used in any network to schedule network traffic and to decide on when to drop packets in the event of traffic jam i.e. in the event of congestion. Taildrop is simplest amongst the various queue management algorithms whereby the network system (operated through router or other equipment) buffers as many data packets as possible, and when the buffer gets full, it drops all incoming packets till the time some space is created in the buffer for incoming data. Full buffers indicate congestion in the network. There is unfair distribution of buffer space in this tail drop mechanism and all TCP connections are held back simultaneously making the network flooded and under-utilized.

To address above issues, another queue discipline viz. Random Early Detection (RED) has been developed. RED operates by dropping packets preemptively, rather than waiting for the buffer to be full. RED relies on predictive models to decide which packets to drop. RED provides early alelt to TCP to reduce its transmission rate rather than waiting for tail drop losses in the event transmission rate is not reduced.

RED model supports an ECN (Early Congestion Notification) approach whereby endpoints which may be developing in a bottleneck queue are notified, without any packet drops. Mini mum and Maximum queue thresholds are defined and when aver age queue length is between these two thresholds, the incoming packet is not dropped but is marked as ECN.

NLRED is a variant of RED which uses a nonlinear quadratic function for packet dropping rather than linear function used in RED [15]. Due to this, there is aggressive packet dropping in heavy traffic while in light traffic, packet dropping is relatively moderate.

The most recent and ongoing changes to TCP are described in [16, 17] depict a wireless and wired network model. TCP over Wi-Fi's potential applications are discussed in [18]. Six modern congestion control methods for TCP have been examined. The fairness-aware TCP-BBR technique is discussed in [19]. Congestion control in high-speed lossless data center networks is covered in [20]. High precision congestion control and congestion control management in high speed networks discussed in [21] and [22] respectively. A simple and efficient traffic flow control approach and an adaptive congestion control algorithm, respectively, are discussed in [23] and [24].

11   Simulation

Network Congestion mainly occurs due to overflow at intermediate nodes. These nodes could be made more congestion friendly with sufficient amount of memories and processing capabilities. But it is very expensive. Alternatively different early detection techniques can be used. We have performed analysis with RED and NLRED using NS3. NS3 is open source tool. It is used to be used to simulate a wide range of network types, including wired m1d wireless networks. NLRED is a variant of RED in which the linear packet dropping function of RED is replaced by a nonlinear quadratic function. Results of the analysis are provided in Table 1 (Figs. 2 and 3).

Table 1. Performance analysis of NewReno with RED and NLRED

TCP	Number of Nodes	Technique	Max Packets allowed in the queue	Throughput in Kbps
TCP NewReno	5	RED	150	742.45
TCP NewReno	5	RED	100	676.32
TCP NewReno	5	RED	50	611.34
TCP NewReno	10	RED	150	645.33
TCP NewReno	10	RED	100	602.37
TCP NewReno	10	RED	50	553.45
TCP NewReno	15	RED	150	589.33
TCP NewReno	15	RED	100	522.49
TCP NewReno	15	RED	50	467.83
TCP NewReno	5	NLRED	150	779.45
TCP NewReno	5	NLRED	100	708.32
TCP NewReno	5	NLRED	50	632.34
TCP NewReno	10	NLRED	150	671.33
TCP NewReno	10	NLRED	100	635.37
TCP NewReno	10	NLRED	50	575.45
TCP NewReno	15	NLRED	150	615.33
TCP NewReno	15	NLRED	100	533.49
TCP NewReno	15	NLRED	50	478.83
Average		RED		601.21
Average		NLRED		625.55

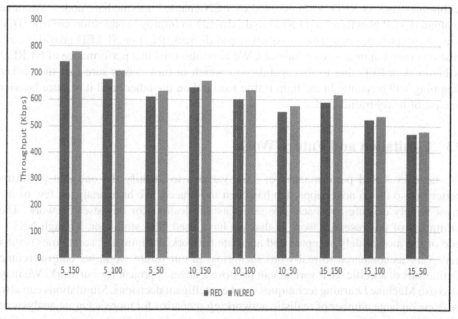

Fig. 2. Performance analysis of NewReno with RED and NLRED. Here, X axis represents a scenario. For example, 5_150 is a network of 5 nodes with 150 Max Packets allowed in the queue.

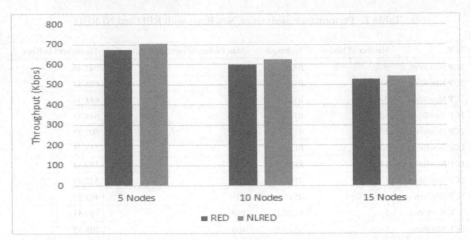

Fig. 3. Performance analysis of NewReno with RED and NLRED. Here, X axis represents all scenarios of 5 Nodes with different values for Max Packets allowed in the queue.

12 Conclusion

We have evaluated performances of TCP variants to identify the one that performs better in different scenarios. As TCP is end-to-end protocol, it does not directly take care of intermediate nodes but indirectly take care by analyzing various parameters like delay, loss, throughput etc. End-to-end TCP variants do not get explicit feedback from intermediate nodes but some latest TCP variants get explicit feedback based on various techniques such as RED being adopted by ECN enabled intermediate nodes. We have evaluated TCP NewReno with RED and NLRED to improve congestion control. TCP New Reno provides congestion control at end devices. RED or NLRED provides congestion control at intermediate devices. We have observed that performance of NLRED is better than RED due to its capability to which in turn makes sure that the packet dropping will be gentle in the light traffic load md on the other hand it is more heavier in case of heavy traffic load.

13 Limitation and Future Work

We have evaluated performances of TCP variants to identify the one that performs better but so far no novel approach has been introduced. We have analyzed few of the most widely existing approaches to select as a milestone for our research work. The limitation of this research work is that we have used NS3 simulator. Though NS3 is one of the most widely accepted and accurate networking simulator, sometimes results may vary as compared to real-word scenarios. In our future work, we can overcome limitations of specific TCP variant can propose a novel approach for our work. We may also use Machine Learning techniques to take intelligent decisions. Simulations can also be done on large number of realistic networking scenarios for more accurate analysis of performances.

References

1. Chaudhary, P., Kumar, S.: Comparative study of TCP variants for congestion control in wireless network. In: 2017 International Conference on Computing, Communication and Automation (ICCCA). IEEE (2017)
2. Callegari, C., Giordano, S., Pagano, M., Pepe, T.: A survey of congestion control mechanisms in Linux TCP. In: Vishnevsky, V., Kozyrev, D., Larionov, A. (eds.) Distributed Computer and Communication Networks, pp. 28–42. Springer International Publishing, Cham (2014). https://doi.org/10.1007/978-3-319-14228-9_3
3. Richard Stevens, W.: TCP/IP Illustrated, Vol. 1: The Protocols (Addison-Wesley Professional Computing Series) (1994)
4. Abed, G.A., Ismail, M., Jumari, K.: Exploration and evaluation of traditional TCP congestion control techniques. J. King Saud Univ. Comput. Inf. Sci. 24(2), 145–155 (2012)
5. Qureshi, B., Othman, M., Hamid, N.A.W.: Progress in various TCP variants. In: International Conference on Computer, Control and Communication, 2009. IC4 (2009)
6. Taruk, M., Budiman, E., Setyadi, H.J.: Comparison of TCP variants in long term evolution (LTE). In: 2017 5th International Conference on Electrical, Electronics and Information Engineering (ICEEIE). IEEE (2017)
7. Kaur, H., Singh, G.: TCP congestion control and its variants. Adv. Comput. Sci. Technol. 10(6), 1715–1723 (2017)
8. Parvez, N., Mahanti, A., Williamson, C.: An analytic throughput model for TCP NewReno. IEEE/ACM Trans. Network. 18(2), 448–461 (2009)
9. Sangolli, S.V., Thyagarajan, J.: An efficient congestion control scheme using cross-layered approach and comparison of TCP variants for mobile ad-hoc networks (MANETs). In: 2014 First International Conference on Networks & Soft Computing (ICNSC2014). IEEE (2014)
10. Lawrence, S.B., O'Malley, S.W., Peterson, L.L.: TCP Vegas: new techniques for congestion detection and avoidance. In: SIGCOMM 1994 Proceedings of the Conference on Communications Architectures, Protocols and Applications (1994)
11. Mathis, M., Mahdav, J.: Forward acknowledgment refining TCP congestion control. In: Pittsburgh Supercomputing Center- -ACM SIGCOMM, vol. 26, number 4 (1996
12. Forouzan, B.: TCP/IP Protocol Suite, 4/e, McGraw-Hill (2012)
13. Xu, L., Harfoush, K., Rhee, I.: Binary increase congestion control (BIC) for fast long-distance networks. In: IEEE INFOCOM 2004, vol. 4, pp. 2514–2524. IEEE (2004)
14. Ha, S., Rhee, I., Xu, L.: CUBIC: a new TCP-friendly high-speed TCP variant. ACM SIGOPS operating syst. Rev. 42(5), 64–74 (2008)
15. Kumhar, D., Kewat, A.: QRED: an enhancement approach for congestion control in network communications. Int. J. Inf. Technol. 13(1), 221–227 (2021)
16. Abdeljaouad, I., Rachidi, H., Fernandes, S., Karmouch, A.: Performance analysis of modern TCP variants: a comparison of Cubic, Compound and New Reno. In: Communications (QBSC), 2010 25th Biennial Symposium on 2010, pp. 80–83 (2010)
17. Pentikousis, K.: TCP in wired-cum-wireless environments. IEEE Commun. Surv. Tutorials 3(4), 2–14 (2000)
18. Grazia, C.A.: Future of TCP on Wi-Fi 6. IEEE Access 9, 107929–107940 (2021)
19. Jia, M., et al.: MFBBR: an optimized fairness-aware TCP-BBR algorithm in wired-cum-wireless network. In: IEEE INFOCOM 2020-IEEE Conference on Computer Communications Workshops (INFOCOM WKSHPS). IEEE (2020)
20. Huang, S., Dong, D., Bai, W.: Congestion control in high-speed lossless data center networks: a survey. Futur. Gener. Comput. Syst. 89, 360–374 (2018)
21. Li, Y., et al.: HPCC: high precision congestion control. In: Proceedings of the ACM Special Interest Group on Data Communication, pp. 44–58 (2019)

22. Bazi, K., Nassereddine, B.: Congestion Control Management in High Speed Networks. In: Bennani, S., Lakhrissi, Y., Khaissidi, G., Mansouri, A., Khamlichi, Y. (eds.) WITS 2020. LNEE, vol. 745, pp. 527–537. Springer, Singapore (2022). https://doi.org/10.1007/978-981-33-6893-4_49

23. Millán, G., et al.: A simple and fast algorithm for traffic flow control in high-speed computer networks. In: 2018 IEEE International Conference on Automation/XXIII Congress of the Chilean Association of Automatic Control (ICA-ACCA). IEEE (2018)

24. Verma, L.P., Verma, I., Kumar, M.: An adaptive congestion control algorithm. J. Homepage **92**(1), 30–36 (2019). http://iieta.org/journals/mmc_a

25. Lorincz, J., Klarin, Z., Ožegović, J.: A comprehensive overview of TCP congestion control in 5G networks: research challenges and future perspectives. Sensors **21**(13), 4510 (2021)

Impact of Scalability on BSM PDR Messages in VANETs

Satveer Kour[1], Butta Singh[2($\boxtimes$)], Manjit Singh[2], and Himali Sarangal[2]

[1] Department of Computer Engineering and Technology, Guru Nanak Dev University, Amritsar, India
[2] Department of Engineering and Technology, Guru Nanak Dev University Regional Campus, Jalandhar, India
bsl.khanna@gmail.com

Abstract. Vehicular Ad-hoc Networks (VANET) has been considered as the prospective techniques for improving safety and providing other services to drivers and passengers. It has evolved as a critical component of the smart transport system. Several efforts have been made in this direction, but security in VANET has received little attention. Security is a crucial concern for VANET routing since various applications influence life-or-death decisions and unauthorized interference can impose critical disasters. When compared to other communication networks, the characteristics of VANETs exacerbate the difficulty faced in the secure routing problem. Another issue related to routing is effective data dissemination and data sharing in VANETs. More areas for advancement include the incorporation of privacy and security measures into routing protocols, as well as the establishment of priority routes for emergency and safety communications. Scalability refers to a VANET's ability to accept a rising number of communicating vehicles without experiencing disruption or loss in data transfer or traffic loading, which increases administrative complexity and reduces network performance. The designed VANET model is analyzed in this technical work across low and high scalable networks (based on number of nodes) and its impact on Basic Safety Messages (BSM) Packet Delivery Ratio (PDR) on a designed VANET scenario. The experiment is performed over four VANET routing protocols. The results are shown in graphical and tabular form, one of the best routing protocol is selected after the result analysis. Destination Sequenced Distance Vector (DSDV) is chosen as the best routing protocol in low and high scalable scenarios.

Keywords: VANET · Routing Protocols · Basic Safety Messages · Packet Delivery Ratio

1 Introduction

Over the last decades, the wireless communication technology has brought tremendous advantages. It enhances the conventional computer networks with efficient workflow and high node mobility/movement in an economical way. In general, wireless technologies have categorized into two types. The first classification deals wide area technologies

S. Rajagopal et al. (Eds.): ASCIS 2023, CCIS 2039, pp. 415–425, 2024.
https://doi.org/10.1007/978-3-031-59100-6_29

(GSM, GPRS or UMTS) which need moderate bandwidth. The later one handles only local area technologies (WLAN, MANET) which require much higher bandwidth. The WLAN standard has further classified as two types namely High-Performance LAN (HIPERLAN) and IEEE 802.11. European Telecommunications Standards Institute (ETSI) has released HIPERLAN and 802.11 from the technical organization called IEEE [1]. Nowadays the entire market was predominated by the standard IEEE 802.11. The wireless LAN has also classified as Infrastructure based WLAN Infrastructure less/Adhoc networks. In this paper, the focus has given for VANET which is the subclass of Mobile Adhoc Network (MANET). MANET has distinguished from cellular networks in terms of partial dependence of traditional infrastructure. This type of network has used in vehicular communication [2]. The architecture of the VANET has illustrated in Fig. 1. The static nodes are called roadside units (RSU) which have connected through dedicated wires. The vehicles with onboard sensor mote (OBU) has named as mobile nodes. The mobile nodes have communicated with each other through a wireless medium [3]. The vehicular communications are categorized as follows-

1. Vehicle to wired roadside infrastructure (V2IC) communication
2. Vehicle to vehicle (V2VC) communication
3. Infrastructure to infrastructure (I2IC) Communication

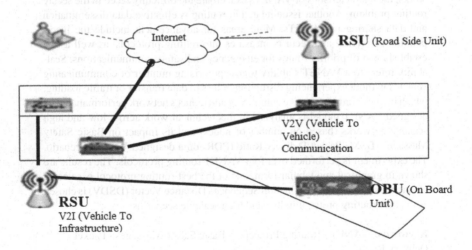

Fig. 1. VANET architecture

This technology's major goal has been to improve the overall safety of automobile travel. VANETs are generated by moving vehicles or nodes that are spread and decentralized. These networks feature very high node mobility and constrained mobility patterns. A network is a collection of objects that are linked to one another. Based on well-defined rules, a network allows information to be circulated among all of these entities [4]. Vehicles connect with each other through VANET without the use of any pre-existing components. It is also linked to a roadside unit. Roadside devices serve as gateways, allowing mobile nodes to connect to infrastructure. The On-Board Unit (OBU) functions as a radio system on the vehicle network, while the Road Side Unit (RSU) functions as a stationary unit [5, 6].

The V2IC communication connects vehicles with wired roadside infrastructure through Internet access. The V2V communication organizes the vehicles as nodes of the self-organized network and shares information without the intervention of central administration. I2I communication has performed among WRSUs. Based on the type of data and service given, VANET applications have divided as safety and information service providence applications. Safety applications provide information about accident occurrence, traffic conditions and pre-accident warnings. These are used to inform drivers of any change and perform suitable actions. Figure 2 depicts the essential key functions of each communication type [7, 8].

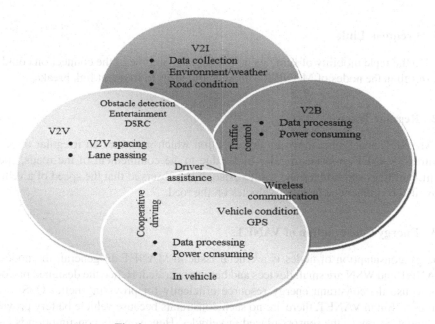

Fig. 2. Communication types of VANET

A wide range of wireless technologies are used in VANET for effective data transfer. Wireless communication is based on IEEE 802.11 standards. These standards are utilized in the implementation of VANET, however they are not directly used in VANET. IEEE 802.11p is an Intelligent Transportation System (ITS) standard that allows Wireless Access in Vehicular Environments (WAVE) and data transfer between vehicles and Road Side Units (RSU) [9]. Vehicles are employed in Intelligent Transportation Systems (ITS) to send and receive routing information from one node to another. The IEEE 802.16 standard is utilized in WiMAX technology to provide high-speed data across a broad region. With the use of scalable OFDMA, channel bandwidths for these approaches range between 1.25 MHz and 20 MHz. Dedicated Short-Range Communications (DSRC) frequency channels are utilized for communication in vehicular networks, and these bands are also used for Intelligent Transportation System (ITS). The first device to use this technology is expected to be police and fire vehicles that conversate with one another for secure reasons. Ad hoc network trends enable a choice of deployment architectures for local cars and between vehicles and local fixed roadside equipment. VANETs intend to deploy a number of wireless technologies including DSRC. Rest cellular systems include cellular, radio, and WiMAX [10].

2 VANETs Features

The VANET is differing from MANET by the node type (vehicles) which subjected to current traffic conditions and rules. In specific VANET exhibit the following features and unique properties [11–13].

2.1 Frequent Link

Due to the rapid mobility of vehicles in VANET, the lifetime of the connection could be shorter than the nodes of MANET. This scenario leads to frequent link breakage.

2.2 Regular Trace

In MANET, nodes may move in any direction which generates an irregular trace. In contrast, VANET produces regular traces due to the confinement of the roads, speed limit, buildings and bridges and traffic. Also, it has observed that the speed of a vehicle may also be influenced by other vehicles on the road.

2.3 Energy Consumption of VANETs

Energy consumption of nodes is a crucial issue in MANET. In general, the nodes in MANET and WSN are small devices and battery operated. Hence the designed protocol has to use the constraint energy resource efficiently for providing better QoS to the end user. But in VANET, there are no such constraints because vehicle battery provides sufficient energy to the sensors placed in vehicles. Hence energy consumption is not a significant issue in VANET.

2.4 Varying Environment for Communication

The different types of road, lane, traffic signal and its related environments are the crucial factors which influenced the performance of the vehicular network. Typically two different types of environment (urban and NH) are used by the application of VANET. Due to traffic signal and congestion, the vehicles/nodes travel slower with more complicated traffic patterns in the urban scenario. The presence of buildings and traffic signals also affects radio propagation. In NH scenario, high-speed vehicles are moving in straight lanes and have less interference from RSU.

3 Path Finding in VANET

Routing on VANETs has been extensively studied during the last few years. The key distinction between MANETs and VANETs is the movement pattern and abruptly changing topologies since VANET is a specific sort of ad-hoc network. The commonly used ad-hoc routing protocols are first constructed in MANETs, tested in various circumstances, and then evaluated for application in a VANET environment. As a result, the various existing addressing techniques employed in MANETs are rarely applicable in an excessively VANET environment [14]. Routing protocols for VANETs are classified into three classes based on their role claim and route updating processes. As illustrated in Fig. 3, they are Positioned, Topology, and Cluster [15].

Topology-based uses the network's available connection information to transfer packets from the origin device to the target device. It can be divided into three major categories. 1) Proactive 2) Reactive 3) Hybrid.

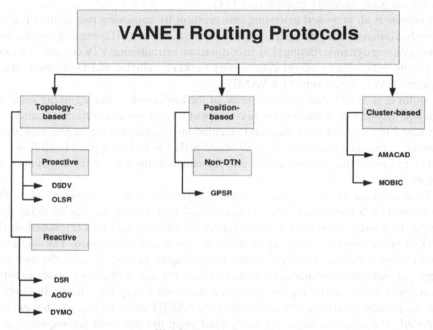

Fig. 3. Routing protocols

The protocol selects the route path in Proactive Routing Protocol, which generally relies on shortest path techniques. These routing protocols are Destination-Sequenced Distance-Vector (DSDV), Topology Broadcast based on Reverse-Path Forwarding (TBRPF) & Optimized Link State Routing (OLSR) [16].

Reactive routing protocols define the suitable routing path and preserve only the presently in use routing ways until only a few possible routing paths are in use at any given moment, minimizing network overhead. Reactive routing is especially beneficial in situations when data sharing between vehicles can only take use of a very limited range of links. Examples are- Dynamic Source Routing (DSR), Temporally Ordered Routing Protocol (TORA), and Ad hoc On Demand Distance Vector (AODV) [17].

The third category partitions the network into two areas in Hybrid Ad-hoc Routing Protocols: local and global. The Zone Routing Protocol (ZRP) improves reliability and scalability by combining local constructive and global reactive routing protocols to decrease overhead and interrupt routing caused by route discovery.

4   Review of VANET Routing Techniques and Methodology

A graph theory model and a new efficient car Internet routing system based on graph theory for the MANET connection diagram on the highway was developed in [18]. The extended graph theory can assist in capturing the evolutionary properties of the network's topology and determining the most efficient path in the routing process to boost Quality of Service (QoS). The software will determine the best reliable path from source to destination using MANET graph theory [18].

Oubbati et al. proposed extending this protocol by approving two distinct routing methods: (i) transmitting data packets solely to the earth; and (ii) spreading data packets to the sky using dynamic routing [19]. In comparison to traditional V2V communications, the results indicate that hybrid connectivity between vehicles and Unmanned Aerial Vehicles (UAVs) is best suited for VANETs.

Shilin et al. established the assessment of the likelihood of making flying vehicles. Here you may find the contact network concept of several isolated portions of cars using UAVs and to carry out modelling and calculations to compute the largest number of segments which can represent the UAV-based node for various types of call flows, as well as to explain the planning circuit and the output in the form of the actual network segment [20].

Bhuvaneswari et al., created a routing algorithm that is cognizant of multi-constrained QOS constraints. The suggested model comprises two phases: delay time computation and communication phase for secure message transfer [21]. Based on the AODV routing protocol, the delay aware routing protocol is discussed. The suggested system, which employs an elliptic curve cryptography method, ensures the trustworthiness of vehicular communications and vehicle privacy, and allows nodes to reply to vehicular reports including cryptographic data with a very short delay. In order to offer secure and efficient communication in the VANET environment, a technique was proposed. Malicious messages are recognized using the described techniques. It also identifies accidents and other issues in the cars' path.

For research methodology framework, a literature study is done about the wireless network, VANET, and its routing protocols. A network scenario is designed on the basis of low and high scalable scenario. Then the experiment is performed on the network simulator and movements are generated by SUMO tool. Then the performance metrics are analyzed on performance metrics.

5 Performance Metrics and Result Analysis

The Basic Safety Messages (BSM) Packet Delivery Ratio (PDR) performance indicator is compared across two network sizes in this paper. In the experiment, a node spreads 10 BSMs every second. The complete packet delivery ratio for each BSM is computed for the whole time of simulation. A high PDR is found to provide more dependable network connection. It is calculated using the following Eq. 1 as:

$$BSMPDR = ReceivedBSMPackets/TransmittedBSMPackets \qquad (1)$$

The simulation environment is installed on the Ubuntu 20 platform. The network simulator NS-3.29 simulator was utilised for execution. Over a performance metric, the reactive protocols AODV and DSR, as well as the proactive routing methods DSDV and OLSR, are studied. The simulation setup is detailed in Table 1. The experiment is run in two categories: low density (40 nodes) and high density (166 nodes). The experiment is then repeated for four different routing protocols by picking the category for node scalability. The movements are generated by the Mobility Generator Tool for Simulation of Urban Mobility (SUMO) [22–25]. The example of the movements generated by SUMO tool is graphically represented in Fig. 4.

Table 1. Parameters

Parameter	Value
Experiment time	30 s
Dimensions	X = 1500 m, Y = 1500 m
Communication range	50 m–500 m
Vehicle speed	20 mps
Number of vehicles	40, 166 nodes
Routing protocols	AODV, DSR, DSDV, OLSR
MAC Layer	IEEE 802.11p
Size of Safety message	200 byte
Transfer rate of Safety message	10 messages per second at 6 Mbps

Figure 5 depicts the BSM PDR values for 10 sent packets per second, divided into two sections: low node density and high node density. Table 2 shows the average of the BSM PDR metric. As a result, DSDV is the best routing protocol for low and high node scalability, with values of 0.79 and 0.92, respectively. The reason for this is that DSDV was one of the first algorithms, and it is ideal for constructing networks with a small density of nodes. DSDV also avoids unnecessary bandwidth by employing incremental updates. It also keeps the best or shortest path to each location. Following that, OLSR performs as a secondary number in both node densities, with values of 0.78 and 0.92. Because it does not require a central administration system to handle its routing process,

OLSR functioned successfully. Furthermore, the link is reliable for BSM messages and messages transmitted on a regular basis, thus there is no need for sequencing.

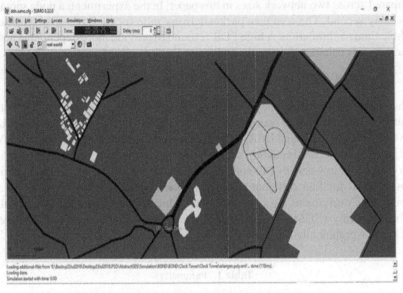

Fig. 4. Movements generated by SUMO

Table 2. Average values of BSM PDR metric

Routing Protocols	Low Node Density	High Node Density
AODV	0.772505	0.915695
DSDV	0.795699	0.920911
DSR	0	0
OLSR	0.788059	0.925098

Another feature of the OLSR routing protocol is that it is well-suited for high-density networks and does not permit large delays in packet transmission. With values of 0.77 and 0.91, AODV ranks third among routing protocols in the defined scenario. Because routing information that is not used expires after a pre-specified time, it requires less storage space than other reactive routing systems. It is capable of handling highly dynamic VANETs. AODV allows multitasking and is capable of swiftly recovering broken links. DSR is the worst routing protocol in the overall comparison, with BSM PDR values for both networks. It is comparable to AODV but has long route discovery latency. DSR does not perform well in dense networks because the amount of overhead conveyed in the packet rises as the network diameter increases. DSR's performance is also subpar because to its high reaction time and greater packet header size. DSDV is 1.02% better in low node density and OLSR is 1.01% better in high node density scenarios.

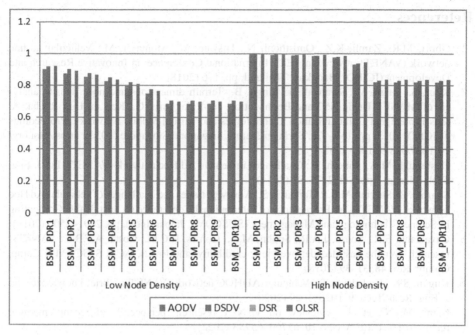

Fig. 5. BSM PDR ratios

6 Conclusion and Future Scope

The VANET is being developed to address traffic issues. The primary reason for the development of VANET was driving safety. The routing protocols were developed and tested using the NS-3 (Network Simulator-3 V. 3.29), SUMO, and OpenStreetMap. The NS-3 package was used to simulate node generation, SUMO, a real-time traffic and mobility simulation software, was used to construct the mobility model, and Open-StreetMap was used to import a local map. Simulations in Vehicular Ad hoc Networks are used to do performance evaluation, information prediction utilizing available data, and decision-making based on current updated information. SUMO was used to construct a real-time traffic situation using a local map acquired from OSM. The SUMO created the movement pattern and the NS-2 used to test and analyze the performance of VANETs. The designed VANET environment is analyzed in this technical work across low and high scalable networks (based on number of nodes) and its impact on Basic Safety Messages (BSM) Packet Delivery Ratio (PDR) on a designed VANET scenario. The experiment is performed over four two reactive (AODV, DSR) and two proactive (DSDV, OLSR) VANET routing protocols. On the basis of scalability parameter, DSDV routing protocol is recommended as a best routing protocol in the designed scenario.

The VANET study is still active and ongoing in order to determine the best technique for vehicular communication. Cooperation, handover, vehicular cloud computing, big data, cross layer design, and other open research challenges are among them. We will focus on multimedia data transfer between VANET nodes in real-time data communication in both static and dynamic situations in future studies.

References

1. Ghori, M.R., Zamli, K.Z., Quosthoni, N., Hisyam, M., Montaser, M.: Vehicular ad-hoc network (VANET): review. In: IEEE International Conference on Innovative Research and Development (ICIRD), Bangkok, Thailand, pp. 1–6 (2018)
2. Kour, S., Singh, M., Sarangal, H., Singh, B.: Terrain dimensions and node density analysis of MANET Using NS2 and BonnMotion. In: Rajakumar, G., Ke-Lin, Du., Rocha, Á. (eds.) Intelligent Communication Technologies and Virtual Mobile Networks: Proceedings of ICICV 2023, pp. 163–175. Springer Nature Singapore, Singapore (2023). https://doi.org/10.1007/978-981-99-1767-9_13
3. Deshmukh, M.A., Dinesh, D.: Challenges in vehicle Ad Hoc network (VANET). Int. J. Eng. Tech. Manag. App. Sci. 2, 76–88 (2014)
4. Sharma, B., Sharma, M.S.P., Tomar, R.S.: A survey: issues and challenges of vehicular Ad Hoc networks (VANETs). In: Proceedings of International Conference on Sustainable Computing in Science, Technology and Management (SUSCOM), Jaipur, India, pp. 2491–2503 (2019)
5. Cavalcanti, E.R., Souza, J.A.R., Spohn, M.A., Gomes, R.C.M., Costa, A.F.B.F.: VANETs' research over the past decade: overview, credibility, and trends. ACM SIGCOMM Comp. Comm. Rev. 48, 31–39 (2018)
6. Kugali, S.N., Kadadevar, S.: Vehicular ADHOC network (VANET):-a brief knowledge. Int. J. Eng. Resh. Tech. 9, 1026–1029 (2020)
7. Mahi, M.J.N., et al.: A review on VANET research: perspective of recent emerging technologies. IEEE Access 10, 65760–65783 (2022)
8. Kour, S., Singh, J.: Performance evaluation of enhanced Manhattan mobility model over GM, RWP, manhattangrid, SLAW, and TLW mobility models in MANETs. Rec. Adv. Comp. Sci. Comm. 15, 992–1000 (2022)
9. Abdeen, M.A.R., Beg, A., Mostafa, S.M., Ghaffar, A.A., Sheltami, T.R., Yasar, A.: Performance evaluation of VANET routing protocols in Madinah city. Electronics 11, 777 (2022)
10. Singh, K., Mishra, G., Raheem, A., Sharma, M.K.: Survey paper on routing protocols in VANET. In: 2nd International Conference on Advances in Computing, Communication Control and Networking, Greater Noida, India, pp. 426–429 (2020)
11. Phull, N., Singh, P., Shabaz, M., Sammy, F.: Enhancing vehicular Ad Hoc networks' dynamic behavior by integrating game theory and machine learning techniques for reliable and stable routing. Secur. Commun. Netw. 2022, 1–11 (2022). https://doi.org/10.1155/2022/4108231
12. Asra, S.A.: Security issues of vehicular Ad Hoc networks (VANET): a systematic review. TIERS Info. Tech. J. 3, 17–27 (2022)
13. Kaur, R., Singh, G., Kumar, A., Kour, S.: A review study of VANET, mobility models and traffic generator tools. In: Proceedings of 5th International Conference on Contemporary Computing and Informatics, Uttar Pradesh, India, pp. 1055–1060 (2022)
14. Pande, S., Sadakale, R., Ramesh, N.V.K.: Performance analysis of AODV routing protocol in VANET using NS-2 and SUMO. In: WCNC-2021: Workshop on Computer Networks & Communications, Chennai, India (2021)
15. Kour, S., Singh, J.S.: Performance analysis of mobile nodes in mobile ad-hoc networks using enhanced manhattan mobility model. J. Sci. Ind. Res. 78, 69–72 (2019)
16. Kour, S., Singh, J.S.: A novel approach to predict mobility pattern of mobile nodes in mobile Ad-hoc networks. J. Sci. Ind. Res. 77, 629–632 (2018)
17. Kour, S., Singh, J.S., Singh, M.: QoS improvement using enhanced manhattan mobility model on proposed Ant Colony optimization technique in MANETs. J. Sci. Ind. Res. 82, 616–628 (2023)

18. Li, J., et al.: EPA-CPPA: an efficient, provably-secure and anonymous conditional privacy-preserving authentication scheme for vehicular ad hoc networks. Veh. Commun. **13**, 104–113 (2018)
19. Oubbati, O.S., Lakas, A., Zhou, F., Güneş, M., Lagraa, N., Yagoubi, M.B.: Intelligent UAV-assisted routing protocol for urban VANETs. Comput. Commun. **107**, 93–111 (2017)
20. Shilin, P., Kirichek, R., Paramonov, A., Koucheryavy, A.: Connectivity of VANET segments using UAVs. In: Galinina, O., Balandin, S., Koucheryavy, Y. (eds.) NEW2AN/ruSMART -2016. LNCS, vol. 9870, pp. 492–500. Springer, Cham (2016). https://doi.org/10.1007/978-3-319-46301-8_41
21. Bhuvaneswari, M.M.: An efficient secure and delay aware routing protocol for VANETs. Int. J. Adv. Res. Comput. Eng. Technol. **5**(11), 2599–2604 (2016)
22. Lim, K.G., Lee, C.H., Chin, R.K.Y., Beng, K., Teo, K.T.K.: SUMO enhancement for vehicular ad hoc network (VANET) simulation. In: IEEE 2nd International Conference on Automatic Control and Intelligent Systems (I2CACIS), Kota Kinabalu, Malaysia, pp. 86–91 (2017). https://doi.org/10.1109/I2CACIS.2017.8239038
23. Lan, K.-C.: MOVE: a practical simulator for mobility model in VANET. In: Huang, C.-M., Chen, Y.-S. (eds.) Telematics Communication Technologies and Vehicular Networks: Wireless Architectures and Applications, pp. 355–368. IGI Global (2010). https://doi.org/10.4018/978-1-60566-840-6.ch021
24. Weber, J., Neves, M., Ferreto, T.: VANET simulators: an updated review. J Braz ComputSoc **27**, 8 (2021). https://doi.org/10.1186/s13173-021-00113-x
25. Härri, J., Fiore, M., Filali, F., Bonnet, C.: Vehicular mobility simulation with VanetMobiSim. SIMULATION **87**, 275–300 (2011). https://doi.org/10.1177/0037549709345997

Contrastive Analysis of Healthcare Management System Using Different Use Cases Based on Blockchain Technology

G. Mahesh(✉) and Renu Mishra

Department of Computer Science and Engineering, SET, Sharda University, Greater Noida, India
mahesh.guru08@gmail.com, renu.mishra@sharda.ac.in

Abstract. The distributed, decentralized and secure network based Blockchain technology is used to store information about the patients in the medical field with patient centric control option. This information is spread out among many nodes and can't be easily altered. There are different levels of how complicated patient information can be, like in the case of Covid19. Only authorized doctors or staff can safely access this information for treatment reasons with the patient's permission. People outside of the patient's care team can decrypt the information for treatment or advise, but only they can see it. Along with the use of blockchain technology in medicine, new technologies like IPFS and IoT have been introduced to make things safer, more efficient, and easier to remember. Security, authentication, data collection, and the sharing of encrypted medical information all need to be improved, though. As part of a suggested review, papers would be compared based on platform, programming language, system application, consensus algorithm, key findings and tools used, which would included from different studies based on the use cases and challenges in blockchain based Electronic health record(EHR) management system along with the issues raised.

Keywords: Blockchain · IPFS · IoT · Encryption · Decryption

1 Overview of Blockchain Technology

Blockchain technology is introduced with the concept of cryptocurrency named as Bitcoin [1, 2], invented by Satoshi Nakamoto. In this technology the details of transactions as well as transmission can be stored. It contains the collection of blocks to store the information, each individual block can be linked with the nodes created previously, this combination of blocks form a blockchain. The transmission of data can be confirmed using peer to peer network, so it also called as type of ledger in the form of distribution spread over the network, Blockchain is attracted by many fields of applications such as insurance, industry, energy, financial, banking, healthcare to store the information in immutable form with IPFS technology, that cannot be altered, if it tried to alter then lot of efficiency required, due to decentralized, distributed as well as secured nature. Here central authority does not exist to administer the network. Data can be gained using the agreement of consensus algorithm nature among the nodes (Fig. 1).

© The Author(s), under exclusive license to Springer Nature Switzerland AG 2024
S. Rajagopal et al. (Eds.): ASCIS 2023, CCIS 2039, pp. 426–439, 2024.
https://doi.org/10.1007/978-3-031-59100-6_30

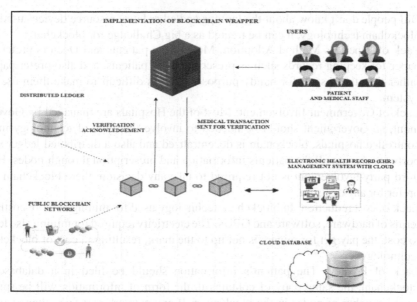

Fig. 1. Electronic Health Record management using Blockchain Technology

Blockchain technology is divided into 3 forms they are i) Public, ii) Private and iii) Consortium. These three forms can vary as per their data transparency and the consensus process will perform. In a Public type each and every participant involved in the ledger accessing, adding data as well as consensus processing. In a Private nature of Blockchain method, accessing of ledger as well as participation to consensus activities only if they get the permission from the Organization owner. Whereas in third category i.e., Consortium process can be controlled not by a single one but instead of that several organizations [20], here accessing of the ledger can be any of types public or private. Blockchain can use cryptography of asymmetric nature, that is public key used for encryption but the private key intended for the person can receive the sent message, others cannot view the message. Here public key is obtained by deriving process by private key, COVID-19 is type of spreadable diseases by SARS-CoV2 virus, diseases varied in the range of mild cold such as cough to complex serious illnesses as pneumonia, as per the World Bank information [3], the global economy of the year 2020 reduced to 5.2% that result in recession in almost all fields. To overcome this type of crisis and to improve the economic growth nation wise to achieve normal economic range, it was required to monitor people's health recording information to check if people got infected by COVID-19 for a given period, if so there required a vaccination for people to reduce the crisis. For the same reason the COVID-19 certificates proposed [4].

1.1 The Various Challenges in Healthcare Using Blockchain Technology

The various challenges in healthcare using blockchain may be as follows:

1. Lack of Technical Knowledge: The required hardware and software cannot be acquired by all the people who want to use the blockchain technology based system.

Old people don't know about the laptops and other latest resource devices used for blockchain technology, it can be treated as a big Challenge for blockchain.

2. Lack of Paperless Method Adoption: Most of the patients and Doctors prefer the paper for keeping records such as prescriptions of patients, and also prefer papers rather than the system for handy purposes, so it is difficult to make them use the system.

3. Lack of Government Involvement: Most of the Hospitals are managed by Government, so Government should be needed to involve this type of technology in all controlled hospitals, blockchain is decentralized and also a distributed ledger supports for sharing all the patients information and prescription through nodes. Here third party involvement is not required to take any decision, there blockchain can prefer for any decision.

4. Lack of cost reduction: In blockchain technology used for mining is more costly in terms of hardware, software and GPUs. The electricity required for mining also leads to cost, the pay get for miners is not up to the mark, resulting in cost of blockchain technology.

5. Lack of Privacy: The patient's information should be filed in a database of blockchain, the same copy of contains in the form of information will be spread over a number of nodes in the blockchain. If any network part fails, then also the data will not be altered and can be updated later at any time. Patients also prefer to maintain their healthcare information with no need to disclose for unauthorized persons.

6. Lack of Incentive: In a blockchain technology miners are required to verify the block. Blockchain technology offers independence in finance then also it can pay very less incentive for the miners, so miners try to mine more and more blocks to get a good incentive. Example for this for mining of 1 bitcoin 10 min time will be spent even though the machine is so powerful. Incentives paying for

7. Lack of Cryptocurrency Acceptance: Doctors will not prefer to get a cryptocurrency payment till now, they prefer only online payment methods and also cash payments. To make blockchain technology successful it is required to make arrangements of payment in terms of cryptocurrencies.

8. Lack of Cyber security: In a blockchain technology security provided for patient information without third party involvement, even though many hackers will hack to steal money most of 51% of attacks will take place, and also hackers try to get more incentives with mining not required blocks and also network traffic will increase.

9. Lack of Central Healthcare: If the healthcare data is distributed in most of hospitals in more numbers of times, then usage of blockchain becomes a hectic task. The streamlined system is required, without that it is not possible to keep the medical information in a blockchain. Consider an example if a person Amar visits a hospital in one location, for the second time he can visit the same hospital branch in another location, then getting the previous record of patient Amar is a challenging task.

10. Lack of speed: The blockchain technology prefers the highest speed, because processing speed is more than data sharing time becomes slow.

2   The Use Cases of the Blockchain Technology

The use cases of the Blockchain oriented technology can be defined as follows.

i) Medical Record Management

a) In "Secure Electronic Medical Records Storage and Sharing Using Blockchain Technology", Muhammad Usman et al. [5], concluded that Electronic medical records (EMRs) are type of electronically more sensitivity based information of private nature, which contains the details such as how to give treatment for the patients as well as diagnosis of the diseases.

b) In the paper "A blockchain-based secure storage scheme for medical information", by the Zhijie Sun et al. [6], proposed that the information in the medical record contains a patient's private sensitive information about the disease in the big data eta. The huge amount of information is important as well as accurate such information is also cause risk due to privacy information leakage and risk in sharing.

c) In a paper "Patient-centric soulbound NFT framework for electronic health record (EHR)", authors Namrta Tanwar et al. [7], proposed that "Patient-centric approach" used patient as a centre of heal care by giving the full controlling of patient records in terms of confidence timeliness. The proposed paper contains framework for solving of problems associated with the safety medical recording to address, secrecy, scalability, cost, interoperability and also timeliness.

ii) Clinical trials

a) In paper "A Permissioned Blockchain-Based Clinical Trial Service Platform to Improve Trial Data Transparency" the authors Lei Hang et al. [8], proposed that the research in the field clinical have several challenges starting from the patient data privacy along with the enrolment till requirement of controlling various costs. Blockchain technology can assist for resolving challenges with the transparent and immutable characters.

b) In paper "Blockchain for drug traceability: Architectures and open challenges", Mueen Uddin et al. [9], proposed that Hyperledger Fabric and Besu two architectures of blockchain base used for drug have the qualities of transparency, trust, privacy, security, authentication, authorization and also scalable.

c) In the paper "From clinical trials highly trustable clinical trials: Blockchain in clinical trials, A game changer for improving transparency?", the authors Mehdi Benchoufi et al. [10], proposed that clinical research quality is minimized with misconduct, fraud and error, which reduce the trustiness in proposed paper the authors specified that how blockchain technology used to check and control the clinical trials process in order the reduce the issues raised.

iii) Traceability for prescription drug

a) In a paper "BBTCD: blockchain based traceability of counterfeited drugs", the author Bipin Kumar Rai et al. [5], proposed blockchain based traceability of counterfeited drugs (BBTCDD) that supports to tracking the erroneous drugs with technology of smart contracts on the blockchain, that is Ethereum based.

b) In a paper "Drug Traceability in healthcare supply chain: A Blockchain solution", the author Osemwingie Osadolor et al. [6], proposed that this article gives a solution of blockchain based to improve traceability of supply chain, it is remarkable and also virtual type of drug recording transactions system by Ethereum.

c) In paper "Blockchain for drug traceability: Architectures and open challenges", Mueen Uddin et al. [7], proposed that Hyperledger Fabric and Besu two architectures of blockchain base used for drug have the qualities of transparency, trust, privacy, security, authentication, authorization and also scalable.

iv) Management of Medical devices

a) In paper "A blockchain-based secure storage scheme for medical information", authors Zhijie Sun et al. [11], proposed that the hyperledger fabric and attribute based access control combination of these techniques used for security of healthcare, here the system uses first attribute based access control technique for getting the medical data in fine grained form that data can be saved in blockchain in the form of nodes which results in tamper proof as well as secured one.

b) In paper "eHealthChain—a blockchain-based personal health information management system", authors Pravin Pawar et al. [12]., proposed that eHealthchain is blockchain based PHIMS for organizing the health data with medical of IoT devices based applications, it has four layers for gathering the data of personal healthcare.

c) In paper "MedRec: Using Blockchain for Medical Data Access and Permission Management" the authors Asaph Azaria et al. [10], proposed that the MedRec a decentralized record management system using for control the EMRs, with the help of blockchain technology, this system patient details in terms of immutable log details.

v) Telemedicine

a) In a paper "Decentralized Telemedicine Framework for a Smart Healthcare Ecosystem", authors Ahed abugabah et al. [13], proposed that framework of blockchain base can be used to release healthcare future with improved services, the author also proposed that Ethereum smart contract also used to improve a parameters such as transparency, protected framework and also confirm that central controlling of patient data management will be removed.

b) In paper "Multi-Access Edge Computing and Blockchain-based Secure Telehealth System Connected with 5G and IoT" authors Tharaka Hewa et al. [14], proposed that Multi access Edge Computing (MEC) with blockchain technology using the certificates with weightless ECQV (Elliptic Curve Qu Vanstone) to get the real-time features such as integration, privacy and also authentication among the IoT, MEC and cloud.

c) In paper "International Journal of Medical Informatics" authors Raja Wasim Ahmad et al. [15], proposed that blockchain technology is a technique used for qualities such as privacy, transparent, immutable, traceable of data and also to find the error with the record of patients. Blockchain can also improve the telemedicine tasks with the healthcare based on remote mode, and support the find the error accurately.

vi) Drug Development

a) In a paper "Blockchain Technology in the Pharmaceutical Industry" the authors Manuela M. Schoner et al. [16], proposed that a blockchain based method can be used to increase security for Pharmaceutical industry with the supply chain. Drug Supply Chain Security Act (DSCSA) developed by the country U.S. for the purpose of avoiding drug duplication problem.

b) In a paper "An IoT-Based Traceable Drug Anti-Counterfeiting Management System" the authors CHEN Chin-ling chen chen et al. [9], proposed that nowadays the mostly used removal of false systems using the QR codes for market is available. The currently available false system could be detected using QR that could not be trustworthy.

c) In paper "Integration of Machine Learning and Blockchain Technology in the Healthcare Field: A Literature Review and Implications for Cancer Care" the authors Andy S. K. Cheng et al. [17], proposed that the machine learning (ML) uses and blockchain technology (BCT) combination for data management of clinical field and investigate healthcare.

vii) Personalized medicine

a) In a paper "Blockchain Technology in Pharmaceutical Industry to Prevent Counterfeit Drugs Health Insurance" the authors Ijazul Haq et al. [18], Olivier Muselemu Esuka proposed that each and every year the tracking of counterfeiting reached in billions numbers, here ownership of drugs will change from manufacturer to distributor in a pharmacy industry supply chain. The authors also explained blockchain usage in the supply chain of the pharmacy industry.

b) In paper "An Adaptive Decision-Making Approach for Better Selection of a Blockchain Platform for Health Insurance Frauds Detection with Smart Contracts: Development and Performance Evaluation", authors Rima Kaafarania et al. [6], propose that defines the divisions among the different blockchain platforms. The authors designed a decision map approach where blockchain with smart contracts can be used in uncovering the errors within healthcare insurance system

c) In paper "Implementation of Electronic health record and health insurance management system using blockchain technology", the authors Lincy Golda Careline S et al. [19], proposed that people having insurance or health policies can be used to get a claim for the treatment. In earlier days the claiming process was taking long duration to complete, so people could not able to discharge or settle the money for treatment within a given time (Tables 1 and 2).

Table 1. Different recent inventions on healthcare management system along with Key findings and features

Sl. No	Title	Year	Author	Key findings	Features	Technology used
1	BlockMedCare: A healthcare system based on IoT, Blockchain and IPFS for data management security	2022	Kebira Azbeg, Ouail Ouchetto, Said Jai Andaloussi	Three main points such secured, scalable, and time of process. The author implemented results oriented system interface for the management of diabetes	In proposed method two types of security features are provided i) Blockchain security features benefit ii) The proxy re-encryption feature	IoT

(*continued*)

Table 1. (*continued*)

Sl. No	Title	Year	Author	Key findings	Features	Technology used
2	Decentralized Children's Immunization Record Management System for Private Healthcare in Malaysia Using IPFS and Blockchain	2022	Faiqah Hafidzah Halim, Nor Aimuni Md Rashid a, Nur Farahin Mohd Johari a, Muhammad Amirul Hazim Abdul Rahman	Symmetric and Asymmetric keys used for encryption for patient record security with help of Wireshark i) To find out the system performance at patient's record sharing, ii) it uses also automated agents for system keeping	i) The main goal of framework is to to offer immunization privacy record with centralized form along the recipient's information in vaccine form, ii) It assist for user's uploading of Hash key	IoT
3	A blockchain-based secure storage scheme for medical information	2022	Zhijie Sun, Dezhi Han, Dun Li, Xiangsheng Wang, Chin-Chen Chang and Zhongdai Wu	i) The distributed knowledge of consensus and authenticate system used for managements of information and decentralization mechanisms ii) It supports for data access control with permission dynamically management iii) Using policies of accessing, workflow of system, capable of data saving and query	i)This system can be implemented performance optimization in distributed system ii) It is built by the consensus mechanism called Kafka, iii) It supports a combination of IPFS as well as blockchain to minimize the storage of the blockchain	HyperLedger Fabric
4	An Application of blockchain to securely acquire, diagnose and share clinical data through smartphone	2022	Hasib Mahmud, Tanzilur Rahman	i) Health care services and complies with General Data Protection Regulation (GDPR) ii) Blockchain system for healthcare sector management in terms of privacy, data security and immutability, cost feasibility, patients' reports availability and usability	i) Patient side: Here the patient can record heartbeat, load, see report and payment done ii) Doctors side: Load the Feedback from patient, See the report of patient, and Give the feedback and further action for report	IoT

(*continued*)

Table 1. (*continued*)

Sl. No	Title	Year	Author	Key findings	Features	Technology used
5	A Blockchain Technology and Internet of Things to secure in Health care system	2023	Shaikh Abdul Hannan	It is decentralized and offers more improvement in safety by using IPFS, the blockchain supports mature agreement, innovation in blockchain takes care of patient information, protects patient data information and gives assurance of patient data securing	i) there will be a security issue for patient information, ii) it also causes problem for the programmers to get the patient information from framework, iii) there will be an issue without involving third party in information exchange between systems	HyperLedger Fabric
6	Securing Medical Records of COVID-19 Patients Using Elliptic Curve Digital Signature Algorithm (ECDSA) in Blockchain	2022	Andi, Carles Juliandy, Robet, and Octara Pribadi	This is more developed compared with previous version of workframe with two parts (front and backend tool), the simulations are implemented by providing the security with required level in patient's data	Elliptic Curve Digital Signature Algorithm (ECDSA) Algorithm is used to achieve security in the information of medical field such as Covid-19 patients details	Not specified
7	Integrating IoT with Health Record Management System using IPFS and Blockchain	2022	Waseem Khan, Gargi Kumbhare, Pradnya Pugaonkar	i) It problems acquired by conventional method of storing medical records can be overcome, it avail the mechanism of off-chain storage, along with the patient full control over system with trust among all users in all time ii) It is nature network of local blockchain reveals disputes related to secure, distinguishing, and flexibility of data sharing	i) Patient's physiological parameters can be measured E.g. BP, Body temperature, BPMminute, oxygen level in blood (SpO2), ECG etc., ii) IOT devices used for monitor patient's condition in all time iii) The true owner can get the patient's information when patient give permission	IoT

(*continued*)

Table 1. (*continued*)

Sl. No	Title	Year	Author	Key findings	Features	Technology used
8	Highly private blockchain-based management system for digital COVID-19 certificates	2022	Rosa Pericas-Gornals, Macia Mut-Puigserver, M. Magdalena Payeras-Capell	i) It supports for getting the data controlling with more private nature, avoiding vulnerable, entity regulation. Security and verification easily ii) proxy re-encryption service offers more privacy oriented, authentication and self controlling of data	The proposed system is used for resolve issue and fulfils in terms of confidentiality, integrity, availability, non-avoidance, immutable, self-sovereignty, authorization, auditable and traceable in patient's information system	Not specified
9	BFG: privacy protection framework for internet of medical things based on blockchain and federated learning	2023	Wenkang Liu, Yuxuan He, Xiaoliang Wang, Ziming Duan, Wei Liang & Yuzhen Liu	i) Gives good expected performance of the form accurating data, robustness in information, and privacy protection of patient data ii) The system reduces the storage pressure in blockchain to get a balancing between the privacy and global budgets and neglects the negative impacting value	In this paper the author propose IoMT framework works for i) Preserving privacy of patient's information ii) It upgrades using Federated Learning tasks storage for both dual on-chain and off-chain iii) It minimizes the blockchain storage pressure and assist in decentralization	IoMT
10	Patient-centric soulbound NFT framework for electronic health record (EHR)	2023	Namrta Tanwar and Jawahar Thaku	i) Secret of information, interoperability option, scalable as per requirement, price-effective, and timeing issues overcome ii) The framework constructed for assessing performance and service as a benchmark in the framework design	i) Owner: As admin can build NFT Non Fungible Tokens, and add minters in a network but cannot transact ii) Minter: The Doctors can include patients in the network, he can mint and burn the token. iii) Patients: view and validate the records after Doctron mint	Ether-eum
11	An Immutable Framework for Smart Healthcare Using Blockchain Technology	2023	Faneela, Muazzam A. Khan, Suliman A. Alsuhibany, Walid El-Shafai, Mujeeb Ur Rehman and Jawad Ahmad	It can be used in multiple areas for different tasks in the medical field, used in intrusion detection in a critical problem with an implementation of major societal activities	i) This system is prefer for blockchain based smart healthcare uses, ii) It works with fast, lightweight, adjustable and private nature of blockchain with IoMT iii) It used in less weighted Elliptic Curve Digital Signature Algorithm (ECDSA)	MHyperLedger Fabric

(*continued*)

Table 1. (*continued*)

Sl. No	Title	Year	Author	Key findings	Features	Technology used
12	Implementation of blockchain as covid-19 test and vaccine certificate storage system	2022	Dendi Arya Raditya Prawira Putra, Yudha Purwanto, Marisa W. Paryasto	i) The authenticity of Covid19 Certificate can be find out using hash values stored in smart contracts ii) The smart contract transactions can be affected by nodes on the Rinkeby network, here more transactions implemented randomly	The proposed system has three features 1. Register issuer: New user can register as an issuer, only Regulators controls this process 2. Verify certificate: The Certificates can be verified and used by all the users 3. Register certificate: Here new covid-19 certificate can be registered, issuer control this certificate	Ether-eum
13	Evolution of Health Information Sharing Between Health Care Organizations: Potential of Nonfungible Tokens	2023	Pouyan Esmaeilzadeh,	This paper gives practical knowledge like the for information sharing what are technological foundations required in the field of healthcare, developed and varied from earlier stages	NFT technology can be a bes used for HIE networks because having properties of i) Noninterchang-eable ii) Immutable iii) Owner required for every NFT	Nonfungible Tokens
14	Privacy Preservation in Patient Information Exchange Systems Based on Blockchain: System Design Study	2022	Sejong Lee, BS; Jaehyeon Kim, BS; Yongseok Kwon, BS; Teasung Kim, BS; Sunghyun Cho	Patient Information Exchange (PIE) allows to combine, control, patient information data with the blockchain nodes It provides security for patient data at the time of exchange result in increased efficiency, safety, data encryption can utilized for effective data exchange process	i) Blockchain based Patient Information Exchange (PIE) medical system manages and shares the medical data ii) PIE system encrypts the patient's information which avoids personal information of patients iii) Reencrypt-ion key allows for grant decryption rights for data in other system also	Hyperledger Fabric

Table 2. Comparison between the Literature papers

Sl. No	Title	Technology used	Consensus Algorithm used	Implemented? (Y/N)
1	BlockMedCare: A healthcare system based on IoT, Blockchain and IPFS for data management security	IoT	Proof of Authority	Yes
2	Decentralized Children's Immunization Record Management System for Private	IoT	Not mentioned	No
3	A blockchain-based secure storage scheme for medical information	HyperLedger Fabric	Mechanism of Kafka	Yes
4	An Application of blockchain to securely acquire, diagnose and share clinical data through smartphone	IoT	Not mentioned	No
5	A Blockchain Technology and Internet of Things to secure in Health care system	HyperLedger Fabric	Not mentioned	No
6	Securing Medical Records of COVID-19 Patients Using Elliptic Curve Digital Signature Algorithm (ECDSA) in Blockchain	Not specified	Proof of Work	Yes
7	Integrating IoT with Health Record Management System using IPFS and Blockchain	IoT	Proof of Stake	Yes

(*continued*)

Table 2. (*continued*)

Sl. No	Title	Technology used	Consensus Algorithm used	Implemented? (Y/N)
8	Highly private blockchain-based management system for digital COVID-19 certificates	Not specified	Not mentioned	No
9	BFG: privacy protection framework for internet of medical things based on blockchain and federated learning	IoMT	Consensus Mechanisms	No
10	Patient-centric soulbound NFT framework for electronic health record (EHR)	Ether-eum	Not mentioned	No
11	An Immutable Framework for Smart Healthcare Using Blockchain Technology	MHyperLedger Fabric	Not mentioned	No
12	Implementation of blockchain as covid-19 test and vaccine certificate storage system	Ether-eum	Not Mentioned	No
13	Evolution of Health Information Sharing Between Health Care Organizations: Potential of Nonfungible Tokens	Nonfungible Tokens	Not mentioned	No
14	Privacy Preservation in Patient Information Exchange Systems Based on Blockchain: System Design Study	Hyperledger Fabric	Not mentioned	No

3 Conclusion

In conclusion briefly define that blockchain technology capable of radically transform the healthcare field by developing in area of data privacy, data security, transparency as well efficiency. In the telemedicine, drug development, medical device management, drug traceability, clinical trials, personalized medicine and healthcare record keeping issues are resolved. With the blockchain based systems such as Hyperledger proves that it is possible to empower patients, boost data integrity and transparency in data, risk reducing, ensuring protection of patient data to improve the healthcare by providing solutions for various critical challenges and promoting a future that is safer and patient controlled system, the number of implemented papers for these field are very less as shown in above table, so in future more research should be expose with latest technologies combination such as Blockchain technology based Medicalchain platform for further improvement of secure and sharable healthcare data sharing system with (EHR) electronic health record management for achieving secured, risk reduced, patient controlled and efficient data sharing with healthcare systems.

References

1. Kumar, G., Singh, A., Patel, U., Yadav, A., Kumar, A.: Tourist and hospitality management using blockchain technology 11(08), 28670–28672 (2021)
2. Chaudhry, N., Yousaf, M.M.: Consensus algorithms in blockchain: comparative analysis, challenges and opportunities. In: Proceedings of the 2018 12th International Conference on Open Source Systems and Technologies (ICOSST), Lahore, Pakistan, 19–21 December 2018, pp. 54–63 (2018). [CrossRef]
3. COVID-19 to Plunge Global Economy into Worst Recession since World War II, 08 June 2020. https://www.worldbank.org/en/news/press-release/2020/06/08/covid-19-to-plunge-glo baleconomy-into-worst-recession-since-world-war-ii
4. EU Digital COVID Certificate. https://ec.europa.eu/info/live-work-travel-eu/coronavirus-res ponse/safe-covid-19-vaccines-europeans/eu-digital-covid-certificate
5. Usmana, M., Qamar, U.: Secure electronic medical records storage and sharing using blockchain technology. Procedia Comput. Sci. **174**, 321–327 (2020)
6. Sun, Z., Han, D., Li, D., Wang, X., Chang, C.-C., Zhongdai, W.: A blockchain-based secure storage scheme for medical information. J. Wirel. Com. Netw. **2022**, 40 (2022)
7. Tanwar, N., Thakur, J.: Patient-centric soulbound NFT framework for electronic health record (EHR). J. Eng. Appl. Sci. **70**, 33 (2023)
8. Hang, L., Kim, B., Kim, K., Kim, D.: A permissioned blockchain-based clinical trial service platform to improve trial data transparency. BioMed Res. Int. **2021**, 22 (2021). Article ID 5554487
9. Uddin, M., Salah, K., Jayaraman, R., Pesic, S., Ellahham, S.: Blockchain for drug traceability: architectures and open challenges. Health Inf. J. (2021)
10. Benchoufi, M., Altman, D., Ravaud, P.: From clinical trials highly trustable clinical trials blockchain in clinical trials, a game changer for improving transparency? **2** (2019)
11. Pawar, P., Parolia, N., Shinde, S., Edoh, T.O., Singh, M.: EHealthChain—a blockchain-based personal health information management system. Ann. Telecommun. **77**, 33–45 (2022)
12. Mahajan, H.B., et al.: Integration of healthcare 4.0 and blockchain into secure cloud-based electronic health records systems. Appl. Nanosci. **13**, 2329–2342 (2023)

13. Zhuang, Y.: Development of a blockchain framework for virtual clinical trials **2020**, 1412–1420 (2021)
14. Zhuang, Y., et al.: Re-engineering a clinical trial management system using blockchain technology: system design, development, and case studies **24**(6) (2022)
15. Rai, B.K.: BBTCD: blockchain based traceability of counterfeited drugs. Nature **23**, 337–353 (2023)
16. Osadolor, O.: Drug traceability in healthcare supply chain: a blockchain solution, January 2023
17. Salah, K., Jayaraman, R., Arshad, J., Al-Hammadi, M.D.Y., Ellaham, S.: A blockchain-based approach for drug traceability in healthcare supply chain **4** (2016)
18. Aslam, M., Jabbar, S., Abbas, Q., Albathan, M., Hussain, A., Raza, U.: Leveraging ethereum platform for development of efficient tractability system in pharmaceutical supply chain. Systems **11**, 202 (2023)
19. Azaria, A., Ekblaw, A., Vieira, T., Lippman, A.: MedRec: using blockchain for medical data access and permission management. IEEE Computer Society (2016)
20. Kumar, R., Marchang, N., Tripathi, R.: Distributed off-chain storage of patient diagnostic reports in healthcare system using IPFS and blockchain. In: International Conference on COMmunication Systems & NETworkS (COMSNETS), Bengaluru, India, pp. 1–5 (2020). https://doi.org/10.1109/COMSNETS48256.2020.9027313

A Survey on SCADA's Security, Concerns and Attacks

T. John Sunder Singh[1]([✉]), J. I. Sheeba[1], and S. Pradeep Devaneyan[2]

[1] Puducherry Technological University, Puducherry, India
johnsundersingh@ptuniv.edu.in
[2] Sri Venkateshwara College of Engineering and Technology, Puducherry, India

Abstract. The SCADA (Supervisory Control and Data Acquisition) system is an essential component for maintaining the smooth operation of critical infrastructure systems, including water supply, transportation, oil pipelines, and electricity. Its primary function is to monitor data from vital components such as pumps, valves, and transmitters. Over time, SCADA has evolved from a stand-alone system to a highly interconnected network, resulting in several advantages, including improved efficiency and reduced costs. But that has also made the SCADA system more vulnerable to cyberattacks. Currently, SCADA security relies primarily on IT systems, which may not be enough to counter the danger and hazard from field operations. Therefore, it is crucial to evaluate the potential cyber threats associated with SCADA. This survey aims to explore the security vulnerabilities of the SCADA system, categorize the relevant threats, attacks. Finally, the survey concludes by proposing a brief outlined hybrid IDPS (Intrusion Detection and Prevention System) to detect, prevent and mitigate cyberattacks on SCADA systems.

Keywords: SCADA · ICS · IDPS · IoT

1 Introduction

SCADA systems obtain real-time data from sensors, control systems, and devices to manage processes and make informed decisions. They process data to human operators and management systems for analysis and decision-making. Typically, SCADA systems rely on a centralized control system that communicates with remote sensors and devices via different communication networks, including wireless and wired networks. SCADA systems also offer remote access, control, and monitoring features that enable operators to manage processes from remote locations. Due to the critical role of SCADA systems in crucial infrastructures and their increasing connection to the internet, they have become a prime target for cyber-attacks. Consequently, the necessity for strong security measures to safeguard against cyber-attacks and other potential threats.

Throughout its four stages of development, from being monolithic to becoming integrated with IoT, SCADA systems have undergone significant evolution. Along with this evolution, the security measures for each stage have also evolved. Technology offers several benefits to Industrial Control Systems (ICSs), including cost savings, increased flexibility, and improved performance efficiency [1]

The flow of this paper contains Sect. 2, which discusses the related works of SCADA with IoT, Machine Learning with SCADA and Deep Learning with SCADA, Sect. 3, describes Cyber-physical attacks and their effects. Sect. 4, illustrates about the brief Outlined Novel Intrusion Detection and Prevention System (IDPS) model for SCADA networks.

2 Related Works

Including an IoT-based solution can enhance security by providing remote monitoring, anomaly detection, and secure data transfer, which are frequently lacking in traditional SCADA systems. This all-encompassing strategy offers server and application protection for each step of the data center operation. When it comes to data-driven production, security is essential, and running such a system demands a knowledgeable infrastructure. By ensuring that assets are closely monitored, networks are secure, and risks can be analyzed for improved decision- making, implementing an IoT SCADA system may provide value to the whole organization.

INTEGRATION OF SCADA WITH IoT

Global SCADA systems might be dramatically impacted by the Internet of Things (IoT). The Internet of Things (IoT) is a network of physical "things" that communicate data over the internet using sensors, software, and other technologies. When used in industrial settings, IoT can bring considerable advantages to SCADA systems. The biggest benefits of IoT for SCADA systems are that it can help to improve efficiency. By connecting sensors and devices to the internet, SCADA systems can collect real-time data on the performance of industrial assets. This data can then be used to identify inefficiencies and make improvements to operations. IoT can also help to improve safety. By connecting sensors and devices to the internet, SCADA systems can monitor for potential hazards and take corrective action before an incident occurs. For example, sensors can be used to monitor the temperature of a boiler and send an alert if it gets too high. This can help to prevent a boiler explosion. IoT can also help to improve security. By connecting sensors and devices to the internet, SCADA systems can be monitored for unauthorized access. This can help to prevent cyberattacks that could disrupt operations or damage critical infrastructure. [2]

MACHINE LEARNING IN SCADA

Osama Bassam [3], a study on the performance of the Deep Random Kernel Forest Classification (DRKFC) in SCADA systems, finding that it outperformed benchmarking with high accuracy. Tomas [4], from the Industry IoT Consortium published a comprehensive review of architectures in the field but did not provide detailed comparisons. Md Ohirul Qays [5], collected data from battery energy storage systems, evaluating their cost-effectiveness and reliability, but the findings were not applicable to all renewable energy sources, particularly in the electrical datasets. Mohammed H. Alquwatli [6], automated shell code analysis to identify weaknesses that cyber/physical attacks exploit, though their scope was limited.

C. Rohmingtluang [7], MOVEREAL for energy management schemes in the Greater Aizawl Water Supply, highlighting potential data loss issues due to internet connectivity in the GAWSS DATASETS. Upma Singh [8], assessed the performance of Random Forest and Long Short-Term Memory (LSTM) models using various statistical criteria but found that these models were only capable of short-term predictions in forecast datasets. Manar Alanazi [9], conducted a comparison of ICS and IT requirements in reviewing SCADA solutions from different perspectives, although they did not provide datasets related to SCADA vulnerabilities. Sagarika Ghosh [10], proposed a quantum-based signcryption approach, which was vulnerable to some attacks, including those using Shor's algorithm. Mustafa Alta [7], developed the FC-AE-IDS (Function Code Autoencoder IDS) for DNP3 networks but did not address other aspects of SCADA in their datasets. Allo O. Khadidos [8], MDCAM (Multifacet Data Clustering Model), which minimized computational operations but required more training, particularly in SCADA datasets.

DEEP LEARNING IN SCADA

Asaad Balla [11], Convolutional Neural Networks (CNN) and Recurrent Neural Networks (RNN) for developing robust Intrusion Detection Systems (IDSs) using Deep Learning (DL) algorithms. They noted a lack of a standard procedure for evaluating DL classification algorithms, with a focus on the (BATADAL) dataset.

Pampapathi [12], a Filtered Deep Learning Model for Intrusion Detection. This model, based on Neural Network and Artificial Neural Network algorithms, ensured that no local private data was exchanged. However, they pointed out the challenge of lacking available datasets, with reference to the TON IoT dataset. Sharjeel [13], Genetic Algorithm (GA) and Particle Swarm Optimization (PSO) to improve existing methods in intrusion detection. They achieved relatively lower accuracy compared to other methods and based their evaluation on the KDDCUP99 dataset. Ons Aouedi [14], novel Federated Semi-supervised learning scheme, emphasizing data privacy by avoiding local private data exchange. They highlighted the difficulty in obtaining labeled data and conducted their research using a SCADA system dataset. Jun Gao [15], utilized Feedforward neural network (FNN) and Long-Short Term Memory (LSTM) models for detecting temporally uncorrelated and correlated attacks. They acknowledged the need for further improvement of their model, with reference to the CICIDS 2017 dataset. Mayra Macas [16], a generic framework and suitable datasets for deep learning architectures in cybersecurity. However, their study did not discuss the potential security risks associated with using deep learning methods. Park [17], Auto-Encoder (AE) in sensory data and network traffic data to develop an Intrusion Detection System (IDS). They based their work on sensory datasets. Wang [18], employed Deep Neural Networks (DNN) for an IDS designed to withstand adversaries. They noted that their study used older datasets, particularly the NSL KDD dataset. Ali [19], DNN and Machine Learning (ML) methods to develop a Network Intrusion Detection System (NIDS). Their research also relied on older datasets, specifically the KDD dataset. Karatas [20], explored the Synthetic Minority Over-Sampling Technique (SMOTE) for ML-based Network Intrusion Detection Systems (NIDSs).

They highlighted the trade-off involving a higher execution time and referenced datasets, particularly the CSECIC-IDS2018 dataset.

3 Threats and Attacks on SCADA

3.1 Hardware Attacks

SCADA systems are vulnerable to a variety of hardware attacks, including:

- **Backdoor attacks:** Backdoor attacks are vulnerabilities that allow attackers to gain unauthorized access to SCADA systems. These vulnerabilities can be introduced by malicious software or by hardware components that have been tampered with.
- **Wireless attacks:** Wireless devices used in SCADA systems are often not adequately protected from attack. This is because wireless devices are designed to be low-power, which makes them difficult to secure. Attackers can exploit this vulnerability by using wireless devices to gain unauthorized access to SCADA systems.
- **JTAG port attacks:** JTAG ports are used by engineers to test and debug SCADA hardware. However, these ports can also be used by intruders to gain unauthorized access to SCADA systems. Attackers can exploit this vulnerability by connecting a malicious device to the JTAG port and then using that device to gain access to the system.
- **Malicious USB drives:** Malicious USB drives can be used to infect SCADA systems with malware. When a user inserts a malicious USB drive into a SCADA system, the malware will be automatically executed. The malware can then be utilized for unauthorized access and to damage the system.

3.2 Software Attacks

There are a variety of ways that software attacks can be executed on SCADA systems. Some common methods include:

- **Malware injection:** Attackers can inject malicious code into SCADA systems, such as viruses, worms, and Trojan horses. This malicious code can then can be utilized to illicitly obtain unauthorized entry into the system, steal data, or cause damage.
- **Command/response injections:** Attackers can inject malicious commands into SCADA systems. These commands can then be used to control the system, such as turning off power or opening valves.
- **Phishing and spear-phishing:** Attackers can send phishing emails to SCADA system users. These Emails might include harmful links or attachments that have the potential to infect the user's computer with malware. DoS attacks: Attackers can launch DoS attacks against SCADA systems. These attacks can overwhelm the system with traffic, making it unavailable to authorized users.
- **SQL injection attacks:** These vulnerabilities can be used to steal data from the system or to gain unauthorized access.
- **Man-in-the-middle attacks:** Attackers can use man-in-the-middle attacks to intercept communications between SCADA systems. This can allow them to steal data or to modify data in transit.
- **Advanced Persistent Threats (APTs):** APTs can use a variety of methods to attack SCADA systems, and they can be very difficult to detect and defend against.

- *Vulnerabilities of communication protocols:* Communication protocols can be vulnerable to attack. These vulnerabilities can be exploited by attackers can be utilized to illicitly obtain unauthorized entry into the system to the system or to cause damage.

The following were the limitations that are derived from the above survey.

1. Most papers focused on specific research works and does not covers the different types of attacks.
2. The survey on different topics have certain limitations, specific to certain scenarios or not considering the wider aspects of IIoT systems.
3. Most Intrusion Detection System (IDS) not properly handling the imbalanced nature of ICS datasets, which can affect their effectiveness in detecting and preventing attacks.
4. Some Existing systems only focuses on the DNP3 Protocol and don't address the other aspects of SCADA systems. Machine Learning faces problem related to the complexity in classification, requiring more time for training and testing, as well as mis-prediction results and error outputs
5. There could be issues with the low-cost IoT gateway and sensor module used to collect data, which may affect the accuracy and reliability of the Intrusion Detection System (IDS).
6. The testbed architecture may not be able to capture and analyze all possible scenarios in the SCADA environments.

4 Proposed Intrusion Detection and Prevention Systems (IDPS) for SCADA Networks

Figure 1, shows Creating an Intrusion Detection and Prevention System (IDPS) using deep learning involves several steps. The following were the steps in developing the IDPS.

1. *Goals of proposed IDPS:* Start by defining the objectives of IDPS, such as what kind of attacks want to detect and prevent, what kind of data want to monitor, and what kind of responses want to trigger in case of an attack.
2. *Data Collections:* Identify the data sources want to monitor, such as networktraffic, system logs, and user behavior. Consider using a variety of data sources to increase the accuracy and completeness of the IDPS.
3. *Data Preprocessing:* Collect and preprocess data from the identified data sources. Preprocessing may include cleaning the data, normalizing the data, and feature engineering to extract meaningful features from the data.
4. *Implementation Detection DL platform:* There are many ML platforms available, both open-source and commercial. Evaluate different platforms based on requirements, including the ability to handle large volumes of data, scalability, ease of use, and cost.
5. *Classification using DL Techniques:* Choose the algorithms want to use for anomaly detection and threat identification. Some popular algorithms used in IDPS include decision -trees, support vector machines, neural networks, and clustering algorithms.

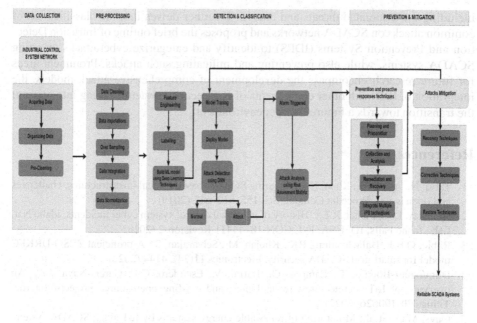

Fig. 1. Intrusion Detection and Prevention Systems (IDPS)

6. *Train DL algorithms:* Train algorithms using labeled data to identify patterns of normal behavior and potential attacks. Use both historical and real-time data to improve the accuracy and effectiveness of the IDPS.

7. *Set up alerts and notifications:* Set up alerts and notifications to trigger when the IDPS detects an attack. Consider using multiple channels, such as email, SMS, and push notifications, to ensure that the right people are notified promptly.

8. *Implement Prevention and Mitigation mechanisms:* Implement response mechanisms to prevent or mitigate attacks, such as blocking traffic, isolating compromised systems, and quarantining infected files. Consider automating response mechanisms to reduce response time and minimize human error.

9. *Test and Refine:* Test the IDPS in a variety of scenarios to ensure that it is effective and accurate. Refine algorithms and response mechanisms based on feedback and performance data.

10. *IDPS 24*7 Monitoring:* Monitor IDPS regularly to ensure that it is working properly and that it is detecting and preventing attacks. Maintain IDPS by updating algorithms, adding new data sources, and keeping up to date with the latest threats and vulnerabilities.

5 Conclusion

SCADA systems constitute intricate cyber and physical infrastructures that serve as the backbone of modern society, making secure operations crucial to national security. This work presents an examination of the communication architecture of SCADA systems, including the associated threats and attacks. It further delves into the classification of common attacks on SCADA networks and proposes the brief outline of Intrusion Detection and Prevention Systems (IDPS) to identify and categorize cyberattacks targeting SCADA systems, while also preventing and mitigating such attacks. Prominent areas for future research encompass the development of comprehensive attack models, the integration of IDS with other components of ICS security systems, taking into account the transition towards a Future Internet environment.

References

1. Tariq, N., Asim, M., Khan, F.A.: Securing SCADA-based critical infrastructures: challenges and open issues. Procedia Comput. Sci. **155**, 612–617 (2019)
2. Hemsley, K.E., Fisher, R.E.: 'History of industrial control system cyber incidents, Idaho Nat. Lab., Idaho Falls, ID, USA, INL/CON-18–44411-Revision-2 (2018)
3. Rabie, O.B.J., Balachandran, P.K., Khojah, M., Selvarajan, S.: A proficient ZESO-DRKFC model for smart grid SCADA security. Electronics **11**(24), 4144 (2022)
4. Domínguez-Bolaño, T., Campos, O., Barral, V., Escudero, C.J., García-Naya, J.A.: An overview of IoT architectures, technologies, and existing open-source projects. Internet Things **20**, 100626 (2022)
5. Qays, M.O., et al.: Monitoring of renewable energy systems by IoT-aided SCADA system. Energy Sci. Eng. **10**(6), 1874–1885 (2022). wileyonlinelibray.com/journal/ese3
6. Singh, U., Rizwan, M.: SCADA system dataset exploration and machine learning based forecast for wind turbines. Results Eng. **16**, 100640 (2022)
7. Alanazi, M., Mahmood, A., Chowdhury, M.J.M.: SCADA vulnerabilities and attacks: a review of the state-of-the-art and open issues. Comput. Secur. **125**, 103028 (2023)
8. Ghosh, S., Zaman, M., Plourde, B., Sampalli, S.: A quantum-based signcryption for supervisory control and data acquisition (SCADA) networks. Symmetry **14**(8), 1625 (2022)
9. Altaha, M., Hong, S.: Anomaly detection for SCADA system security based on unsupervised learning and function codes analysis in the DNP3 protocol. Electronics **11**(14), 2184 (2022)
10. Khadidos, A.O., Manoharan, H., Selvarajan, S., Khadidos, A.O., Alyoubi, K.H., Yafoz, A.: A classy multifacet clustering and fused optimization based classification methodologies for SCADA security. Energies **15**(10), 3624 (2022)
11. Balla, A., Habaebi, M.H., Islam, M.R., Mubarak, S.: Applications of deep learning algorithms for Supervisory control and data acquisition intrusion detection system. Cleaner Eng. Technol. **9**, 100532 (2022)
12. Pampapathi, B.M., Nageswara Guptha, M., Hema, M.S.: Towards an effective deep learning-based intrusion detection system in the internet of things. Soc. Sci. Res. Netw. (2022)
13. Riaz, S., et al.: Malware detection in internet of things (IoT) devices using deep learning. Sensors **22**(23), 9305 (2022)
14. Aouedi, O., Piamrat, K., Muller, G., Singh, K.: Federated semisupervised learning for attack detection in industrial internet of things. IEEE Trans. Ind. Inform. **19**(1), 286–295 (2022)
15. Gao, J., et al.: Omni SCADA intrusion detection using deep learning algorithms. IEEE Internet Things J. **8**(2), 951–961 (2020)
16. Macas, M., Wu, C., Fuertes, W.: A survey on deep learning for cybersecurity: progress, challenges, and opportunities. Comput. Netw. **212**, 109032 (2022)
17. Park, S.T., Li, G., Hong, J.C.: A Study on smart factory-based ambient intelligence context-aware intrusion detection system using machine learning. J. Ambient Intell. Hum. Comput. **11**(4), 1405–1412 (2020)

18. Wang, Z.: Deep learning-based intrusion detection with adversaries. IEEE Access **6**, 38367–38384 (2018)
19. Ali, M.H., Al Mohammed, B.A.D., Ismail, A., Zolkipli, M.F.: A new intrusion detection system based on fast learning network and particle swarm optimization. IEEE Access **6**, 20255–20261 (2018)
20. Karatas, G., Demir, O., Sahingoz, O.K.: Increasing the performance of machine learning-based IDSs on an imbalanced and up-to-date dataset. IEEE Access **8**, 32150–32162 (2020)

Comparative Analysis of Routing Algorithms in Opportunistic Network

Riddhi A. Joshi(✉) and Kalpesh A. Popat

Marwadi University, Rajkot, Gujarat, India
{riddhi.joshi,Kalpesh.popat}@marwadieducation.edu.in

Abstract. Opportunistic networks are developed by connecting interfaces for short-range communication. Routing is difficult in this type of Network. The existing routing algorithms are discussed in this paper and comparison is shown for the five algorithms which are used wisely in this Network. The comparison is made in Epidemic routing, Spray and Wait, First Contact routing, Prophet routing and Maxprop routing. In the comparison, we can see that in all routing algorithms overhead ratio is decreasing when buffer size is increased. And due to increase in buffer size, the delivery probability is also increased. Each algorithm has its own advantages and disadvantages.

Keywords: Overhead Ratio · Delivery Probability · MANET · Opportunistic Mobile Social Network

1 Introduction

Interconnection of computing devices that can share data and resources is known as Computer Network. There are mainly 2 types of Networks: Physical cables are used in wired networks to link computing devices to the internet or other networks. Ethernet cables, fiber-optic cables, and other wired connections are examples of these cables.

On the other side, wireless networks do not require physical wires since they employ electromagnetic (radiofrequency) or infrared waves to transport data between devices. Wireless devices can communicate over the airways because they have sensors or antennas that can send and receive signals.

There are decentralized wireless network types like Mobile Adhoc Networks (MANET) and Wireless Adhoc Networks (WANET). Adhoc networks function without an established infrastructure, like routers or access points. In these networks, nodes interact directly with one another, and the decision of which nodes to send data is determined dynamically based on the connectedness of the network and the chosen routing algorithm. This dynamic routing technique enables flexible and versatile device communication in a variety of contexts, including those where infrastructure-based networks are not practicable or possible [1].

In Opportunistic Mobile Social Network, self-organizing mobile nodes exchange and forward data as needed. For information exchange, these mobile nodes also take into account one another's social characteristics. In opportunistic networking, data is sent

S. Rajagopal et al. (Eds.): ASCIS 2023, CCIS 2039, pp. 448–461, 2024.
https://doi.org/10.1007/978-3-031-59100-6_32

from the source node to the destination node using nodes that are within the transferring node's transmission range [7].

1.1 Wireless Network Types [2]

- Wireless networks can function in either an infrastructure mode or an ad hoc manner.

Fig. 1. Ad-hoc mode

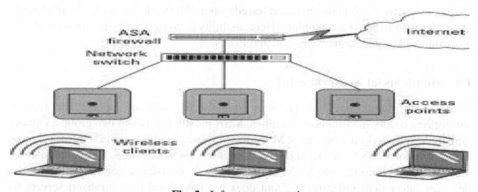

Fig. 2. Infrastructure mode

- In infrastructure mode (Fig. 2), a wireless network's access point (wireless router) serves as the central hub for communication between all connected devices.
- In ad hoc mode (Fig. 1) communication can be done using wireless network adapter.

1.2 Ad Hoc Network [3]

- These networks do not require a central access point or pre-existing infrastructure for communication between individual devices or nodes.
- This decentralized strategy has a number of benefits, including adaptability and rapid deployment, which makes it suited for a variety of contexts, including peer-to-peer mobile communication, military applications, and emergency response situations.

- Ad hoc networks are susceptible to security risks like eavesdropping, data tampering, and denial of service attacks because they lack centralized supervision. In order to protect data transmission between nodes, various encryption and authentication procedures are being developed. As a result, maintaining the security of communications in ad hoc networks is a key area of research.

1.3 Types of Wireless Adhoc Network [4]

Classes of wireless ad hoc networks have been established. Few illustrations:

- A mobile device ad hoc network. (MANET)
- Ad hoc Network for Vehicle (VANET),
- Smartphone ad hoc network (SPAN),
- Wireless mesh network,
- Army tactical MENT,
- Wireless sensor network

1.4 Social Network [5]

Social networks serve as networking tools that enable user interaction. There are two categories of this Network: social networks on the internet and on mobile devices. Social networks on the internet are the ones that rely on desktops as the primary communication tool. Social networking platforms are referred to as mobile social networks (MSNs) when the nodes within them have mobility. Here, mobility is brought on by the use of portable electronics like tablets, smart phones, and PDAs.

1.5 Mobile Social Networking [6]

Users use their tablet or mobile phone to communicate with one another. This type of networking occurs in virtual communities. MSN mostly belongs to two groups: Opportunistic MSN (also known as Future MSN or OMSN) and traditional MSN Infrastructure-based traditional MSN uses local or centralized servers and operates across the internet or an intranet. Opportunistic MSN, in contrast, uses short-range communication technologies rather than infrastructure and does not have local or centralized servers to function.

1.6 Opportunistic Mobile Social Networks [7]

OMSN (Fig. 3) is a type of Mobile Ad-hoc Network (MANET) in which self-organizing mobile nodes exchange and forward data as needed. For information exchange, these mobile nodes also take into account one another's social characteristics. The only thing between OMSN from MANET is how data is routed. Vehicular Social Networking is one of the most prevalent applications and significant types of opportunistic networking. Therefore, this form of networking will be dependable and efficient for these networks. In opportunistic networking, data is sent from the source node to the destination node using nodes that are within the transferring node's transmission range. If the range of transmission is devoid of nodes. If there are no other nodes within its transmission range, the transferring node holds the data and delays delivering it to another node. The nodes have a store-carry-forward method of operation. Therefore, opportunistic networks are regarded as a specific class of delay tolerant networks (DTNs).

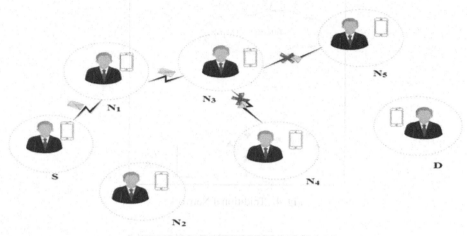

Fig. 3. Opportunistic Mobile Ad hoc Network

1.7 Architecture of Opportunistic Mobile Social Network [7]

Different short-range communication methods, including direct WiFi, Bluetooth, NFC, etc. can be used by mobile nodes to directly communicate with one another within the OMSN (Fig. 5) without the need for the Internet. When one moves into the other's transmission range, the data and information from the two mobile nodes are shared.

1.8 Overview of OMSN [7]

A new class of applications has evolved as a result of the widespread use of smartphones in daily life and their expanding capabilities. To accomplish message routing and data sharing, OMSN take advantage of human social features like similarity, daily routines, movement patterns, and hobbies. These networks allow users of mobile devices to quickly establish social networks where they may communicate and exchange information. There are a number of limitations because users often need the Internet to share content on social networks (Fig. 4). OMSN (Fig. 5) leverages opportunistic links between users' mobile devices that share social commonalities to distribute news and updates rather than requiring an Internet connection.

1.9 Opportunism in Social Networks (Fig. 6) [8]

According to the GSMA, more than 5 billion people use mobile phones globally as of January 2019. More than half of humanity is represented by that. The majority of

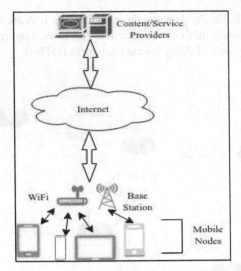

Fig. 4. Traditional Network

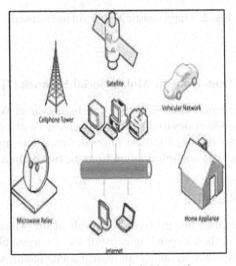

Fig. 5. Opportunistic Network

modern mobile phones come with Wi-Fi, Bluetooth, cameras, sensors, and many other features. Additionally, the majority of contemporary automobiles come equipped with both communication interfaces and sensory technology. A significant number of chances for human interaction are created by the widespread usage and accessibility of mobile communication devices, which is essential for the development of opportunistic mobile social networks. Since human movement is a major component of opportunistic communications, message transmissions may be delayed as long as people using mobile devices stay out of each other's line of sight. In order to construct effective message

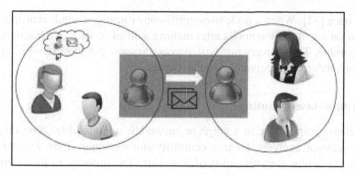

Fig. 6. OMSN

routing models with minimal message delays, many research projects are carried out over the world to examine human mobility and social interaction patterns.

Advantages [8]
No infrastructure is as economical, Low power consumption, use in disaster assistance, best technology for use in poor and rural areas, and avoids pointless communications are all benefits of this technology. Applications for OMSNs include sending messages and files, sending audio and video, disseminating and sending social content, and searching neighbours, which enables users for meeting people nearby at events, malls, big businesses, etc.

Challenges [8]
Due to the constant interruptions, delays, and patchy connectivity environment, opportunistic mobile social networks suffer various difficulties. One of the main issues is the unsecured communication that occurs in these networks since it is unable to use mature security techniques, like encryption, which depends on centralized trusted authorities, because of their distributed structure. Furthermore, because of the unconnected and decentralized ecosystems, it is particularly challenging to maintain trust across peer nodes. The participating entities can exchange information about one other's reputations in order to create reliable trust scores.

Routing Algorithms [9]
A routing algorithm decides whether data packets should travel along a particular path or in a particular direction. They aid in effective Internet traffic control. A data packet can take a variety of pathways from its source to its destination after leaving it.

2 Opportunistic Mobile Social Networks Routing Algorithms [10]

The three key social characteristics of OMSN are tie, similarity, and centrality. Single-copy routing refers to the practice of a node sending messages directly to the next hop node rather than copying them after receiving them from other nodes. Local copies of forwarded messages are then deleted. As a result, each communication in the network only exists once [33]. When a node uses multi-copy routing, it sends multiple copies of messages to various next-hop nodes after making multiple copies of them in accordance with the algorithm. The delivery rate will increase to some extent in a multi-copy routing because more nodes are receiving message copies.

2.1 Centrality-Based Routing

A node's relative importance in a graph or network is quantified by centrality in graph theory and network analysis. Degree centrality (for example, node degree) is one of the three most popular measurements of centrality. The quantity of direct connections involving the present node, as well as proximity Indicators of how quickly information spreads from one node to another in a network include centrality, which calculates the inverse of the average shortest distance between the present node and other nodes, and Betweenness centrality measures how closely a node is located to other nodes along a path that connects them. Sending messages to nodes with high centrality would undoubtedly increase the rate at which data is delivered and, to a certain extent, reduce latency. Centrality measures the relative importance of nodes in a network. The social connections between nodes are not taken into account when determining a node's centrality.

2.2 Similarity-Based Routing

It has been found that the majority of similarity-based routing algorithms use the assumption that nodes with high similarity are more likely to be in communication and have opportunities for data forwarding. Similarity takes into account the social connections between nodes and can help to increase routing efficiency to some level. However, in some situations, when the network is somewhat sparse, a lack of efficient data transmission mechanisms may result in a reduction in packet delivery ratio, and it is clear that more research is required in this area.

2.3 Tie Strength-Based Routing

The centrality and similarity stated above do not account for the social interactions and link strength between nodes, which surely have a significant impact on routing performance. In conclusion, routing algorithms based on tie strength efficiently increase the packet delivery ratio and decrease delivery delay by taking into account the social connections between nodes.

3 Related Work - Main Routing Algorithms

3.1 Epidemic Routing Algorithms

The epidemic routing algorithm follows the approach of multi copy routing which guarantees that each node in the network will obtain a copy of the data packet. Due to mobility nodes will come in contact with each other. This algorithm focuses on maximize throughput rate and minimize communication delay by making copies of the packets fast [11].

The authors of paper [12] have drawn attention to the problem with the epidemic routing method, which is that its replication process necessitates larger buffer sizes. The network will get crowded and messages will be lost if a node with a small buffer size tries to accept a new message. In this paper, the P-epidemic algorithm is also suggested. By allocating various transmission probabilities to various nodes, this approach is able to reduce the quantity of redundant messages and, as a result, the buffer overflows.

The authors of study [13] have emphasized the area of epidemic routing algorithm that consumes more resources and also suggest a limited epidemic routing scheme. This design calls for some nodes to be preplanned in order to build a small-size forwarding node group in order to manage conflicts in resources and overhead brought by message flooding.

In [14] examines the effectiveness of epidemic routing in mobile social networks while taking into account a number of groups that nodes commonly visit. Additionally, a monolithic Stochastic Reward Net (SRN) is suggested to assess the average number of transmissions under epidemic routing and the delivery latency by taking skewed location visiting preferences into account.

Paper [15] shows that epidemic is dangerous because of high infectious nature. In case of COVID-19, to break the chain primary methods were adopted like lockdowns, self isolation, social distancing. But than also it requires certain new strategy to control the spread of infection. This paper proposes to collect these types of data via cell phones and provide more comprehensive information to the authorities for better epidemic management, suggest an IoT-based infrastructure. If the software detects the existence of another user who may be affected nearby, the framework also sends alerts to other users via smartphones.

In paper [16], a simulation result is shown for different algorithms. The authors have taken different buffer sizes. And the simulation result shows that when buffer size is less at that time overhead ratio is more and when buffer size increases, the overhead ration decreases.

3.2 Spray and Wait

A technique known as "Spray and Wait" aims to reduce the cost of flooding-based schemes while attempting to maintain appropriate response times in relation to delivery rates and wait times. It doesn't require network updates like the past meeting's history like Epidemic requires [16].

The Spray and Wait method "sprays" several copies throughout the network and then "waits" until one of these nodes reaches the target. Direct transmission's simplicity and economy are combined with epidemic routing's speed in the Spray and Wait method. It "jump-starts" the distribution of message copies at first in a manner analogous to epidemic routing. The process ends and each node carrying a copy can start direct transmission after enough copies have been sent to ensure that at least one of them will reach the target shortly (with a high probability). To put it another way, Spray and Wait is a compromise between single-copy and multi-copy methods. Surprisingly, as we will demonstrate in a moment, its performance is better than all other feasible single and multi-copy systems in the majority of the scenarios taken into consideration in terms of both number of transmissions and delay [17].

Authors have developed a spray and wait algorithm that integrates social and non-social features in [18]. New spray-and-wait routing technique (NSSAW Router) has been proposed by the authors that selects relay nodes primarily using two different transmission values and dynamically distributes message copies between two nodes in the spray stage. This approach takes advantage of the social relationships between nodes in the DTN.

In paper [19], The authors' attention was drawn to the nodes' social network and their frequency of encounters. Based on a node social tree, they have suggested an enhanced spray and wait method. It will first decide the node's delivery capability value by combining the node's features and social ability. Following that, it will update the social node tree with each node's delivery capability. After which the encounter time between nodes will be determined. If it found message's destination node in the, the node will choose the encounter node as the relay node. If not, the relay node with the social tree with the highest propagation capacity will be chosen.

Paper [20] introduces QoN-ASW – Quality Of Node - Adaptive spray and wait algorithm with changes. The message handling capability and the enhanced delivery predictability are combined to create the quality of node (QoN) statistic, which the authors have presented. Finally, the QoN-based adaptive spray and wait routing method (QoN-ASW) has been put out. The QoN-ASW avoids replica distribution blindness.

According to simulation results of [16], spray and wait has highest packet drop ratio than epidemic, first contact routing, prophet.

3.3   First Contact Routing

In this routing, each node randomly selects a contact to transmit a message to. If none of the paths are open, the message waits for that particular path to open up before being assigned to the first contact that becomes open. Because of this, there is only one copy of each communication in the network. The receiving node only receives a message if it hasn't already been through it, to prevent two nodes who maintain a long-term connection from repeatedly exchanging the identical messages.

Authors in [21] has highlighted the overhead on network because of so many replicas of messages. The more recent opportunistic algorithms offer a solution to this problem, however with these algorithms as well, a message remains unnecessarily long in a node's buffer. In contrast to the current state-of-the-art routing protocols, they have developed first contact routing in the study that reduces the average message buffer time of a node while maintaining a desired message delivery ratio.

3.4   Prophet Routing Algorithm

The transitivity of mathematics and prior meetings are used by the probabilistic routing algorithm PROPHET [22] to assess each node's transfer probability ratio for each participating node. This method considers a node caching the data until a suitable next hop node is found to send the data to the destination, without checking the quality of the participating node's mobility pattern. The performance criteria cannot be met by PROPHET, the system with the least amount of communication.

In [23] PROPHET improved performance over pre-existing protocols by using transitivity and the history of node contacts. However, routing jitter issues arise as a result of changing probability values. In this study, we enhanced PROPHET and put forth an advanced PROPHET that forward massages using average delivery predictabilities. Advanced PROPHET eliminates routing jitter and takes into account the network's long-term performance. Simulations have demonstrated that improved PROPHET performs better than PROPHET.

3.5 Maxprop Routing Algorithm

MaxProp gives priority to both the schedule of packets to be forwarded and packets to be deleted by dividing the buffer into two halves.

In [24], the authors suggest a Time-To-Live (TTL)-based routing strategy that prioritizes packet delivery based on both TTL values and hop counts. High TTL message values are more accepted in our strategy to avoid early discarding. TTL-based routing system greatly increases the number of delivered messages while lowering the overhead ratio and delay, using the same amount of network resources as MaxProp, according to a series of simulations.

4 Other Related Work

- In one paper the existing problems in routing in OMSN are highlighted and also provided the overview of OMSN routing algorithms based on fuzzy logic. It also includes comparison based on fuzzy logic [25].
- One study gives the detailed description about selfishness of the node in routing. The authors have conducted simulation experience of 6 routing algorithms and conclude the challenges in designing of routing algorithms [10]. In one of the paper, the authors have highlighted the two problems of routing algorithms in OMSN, excessive calculation of key nodes and limited remaining cache of nodes. The authors have also introduced new routing algorithm EC-CW which improves the delivery rate [26].
- When forwarding a message in OMSN, authors of study [27] have called attention to issues such low message delivery rates and significant network resource consumption. This study also suggested a trust-based routing strategy for wireless mesh networks. Authors in [28] have highlighted the problem statement that how packet delivery can be improved. They have also proposed an algorithm which reduces communication cost and optimize the performance.
- The Bubble Rap algorithm in [29] has demonstrated that it is possible to extract significant social network characteristic characteristics from a wide range of actual human contact traces. In order to function best, BUBBLE prefers a hierarchical community structure. The EBR (Encounter Based Routing) algorithm, introduced by the authors in [30], maximizes delivery ratios while minimizing overhead and delay.

4.1 Comparison

Different authors have written different conclusion on comparison of routing algorithms. Few points are as under.

In [31] authors have made the comparison between epidemic, first contact and spray and wait. According to them, spray and wait algorithm is best among all the algorithms.

In [32] authors have provided the conclusion that flooding based algorithms are good but have network congestion problem. And they have proposed the prediction-based algorithm which works better.

In [16], a detailed survey and analysis of routing algorithms are produced and different results are also shown in the paper. According to the paper, main routing algorithms are Epidemic, Spray and Wait, First Contact based routing, and Prophet routing. Paper displays the detailed comparison by using different parameters like packet drop, delay, hop count average and buffer. Comparison is shown in the Table 1.

Table 1. Comparative Analysis of OMSN routing algorithms

Routing Algorithms	Deliver Probability	Ration dropped Vs. Relayed	Hop count Avg.	Overhead ratio
Epidemic Routing	The delivery probability is increased when buffer sizes are increased	Buffer size increases result in a decrease in the ratio of discarded packets to relayed packets	When buffer size is increased hop count average will be less	Overhead ratio is decreased when buffer size is increased Epidemic has lowest overhead ratio when buffer size is increased in comparison with other algorithms
Spray and Wait Routing	It is increased when buffer sizes are increased	Buffer size increases result in a decrease in the ratio of discarded packets to relayed packets. The highest packet drop ratio is with spray and wait	When buffer size is increased hop count average will be less	Overhead ratio is decreased when buffer size is increased
First Contact Routing	It is increased when buffer sizes are increased	Buffer size increases result in a decrease in the ratio of discarded packets to relayed packets	When buffer size is increased hop count average will be less. It is highest in First contact routing	Overhead ratio is decreased when buffer size is increased
Prophet Routing	The delivery probability is increased when buffer sizes are increased	When buffer capacity is raised, the ratio of packets discarded to relayed is reduced	When buffer size is increased hop count average will be less	Overhead ratio is decreased when buffer size is increased
MaxProp Routing	The delivery probability is increased when buffer sizes are increased. It has the highest delivery probability	Increased buffer size results in a lower ratio of discarded packets to relayed packets	When buffer size is increased hop count average will be less	Overhead ratio is decreased when buffer size is increased

Parameters used for comparison (Table 1).
Delivery Probability - This is the proportion of total packet creation to total packet delivery to the destination.

Ratio Dropped Vs. Relayed
This is the proportion of packets that were dropped to those that were relayed.

Hop Count Average
The number of intermediate nodes that are located between a source and a target node.

Overhead Ratio - It reveals how many network resources are required to send a packet to its destination.

5 Future Scope

Many researchers have developed many algorithms for Opportunistic Mobile Social Network. Each algorithm mentioned in the paper has certain advantages and disadvantages. There is a future scope of developing better algorithm which can increase data transmission with less overhead ratio.

6 Conclusion

We have observed that routing is difficult in opportunistic Network. Total 6 algorithms are used mainly in opportunistic Network. Different authors have shown different parameters for comparison of these algorithms. Epidemic routing algorithm overhead ratio is decreased with increase in buffer size as compared to other algorithms. We have also observed that spray and wait has highest packet drop ratio compared to other algorithms. We have seen that different parameters may exhibit different consequences. We can conclude that when buffer size is increased, all the algorithms work properly and overhead ratio is also minimised. We will focus on developing an algorithm which can increase packet delivery ratio with less overhead.

References

1. Amazon. What is Computer Networking? - Beginner's Guide to IT Networking - AWS. Amazon Web Services, Inc. https://aws.amazon.com/what-is/computer-networking/
2. How are infrastructure and ad hoc networks different? https://manuals.konicaminolta.eu/ineo-4020/EN/ntwk_guide/types-wireless-networks-topic.html#:~:text=Wireless%20netw orks%20can%20operate%20in. Accessed 09 Oct 2023
3. Wireless ad hoc network. Wikipedia (2023). https://en.wikipedia.org/wiki/Wireless_ad_hoc_network#:~:text=A%20wireless%20ad%20hoc%20network. Accessed 09 Oct 2023
4. M. P. W. F. L. writer M. P. has 5+ years' experience writing about consumer-oriented technology and is an expert telecommuter our editorial process M. Pinola. Features and Uses of an Ad Hoc Wireless Network. Lifewire. https://www.lifewire.com/what-is-an-ad-hoc-wireless-network-2377409

5. Social network. Wikipedia (2021). https://en.wikipedia.org/wiki/Social_network#:~:text= A%20social%20network%20is%20a

6. Wikipedia Contributors. Mobile social network. Wikipedia (2019). https://en.wikipedia.org/ wiki/Mobile_social_network

7. Vidhya Lakshmi, V.R., Gireesh, K.T.: Opportunistic mobile social networks: architecture, privacy, security issues and future directions. Int. J. Electr. Comput. Eng. (IJECE) **9**(2), 1145 (2019). https://doi.org/10.11591/ijece.v9i2.pp1145-1152

8. Opportunistic mobile social network. Wikipedia (2022). https://en.wikipedia.org/wiki/Opp ortunistic_mobile_social_network#:~:text=Opportunistic%20mobile%20social%20netw orks%20are. Accessed 09 Oct 2023

9. Gumaste, S., Kharat, M., Thakare, V.M., Kharat, V.: Routing algorithm: an overview. Int. J. Innov. Eng. Manag. **2**(1), 61–73 (2013). ISSN 2319-3344

10. Cai, Y., Zhang, H., Fan, Y., Xia, H.: A survey on routing algorithms for opportunistic mobile social networks. China Commun. **18**(2), 86–109 (2021). https://doi.org/10.23919/jcc.2021. 02.007

11. Wang, R., Wang, Z., Ma, W., Deng, S., Huang, H.: Epidemic routing performance in DTN with selfish nodes. IEEE Access **7**, 65560–65568 (2019). https://doi.org/10.1109/access.2019.291 6685

12. Darmani, Y., Karimi, S.: Message overhead control using P-epidemic routing method in resource-constrained heterogeneous DTN (2021). https://doi.org/10.1109/icee52715.2021. 9544149

13. Hu, Y., Tian, T., Zhang, F., Chen, Q., Yu, G., Ma, D.: Restricted epidemic routing method in large-scale delay tolerant networks. In: 2021 IEEE 21st International Conference on Communication Technology (ICCT) (2021). https://doi.org/10.1109/icct52962.2021.965 7947

14. Rashidi, L., Dalili-Yazdi, A., Entezari-Maleki, R., Sousa, L., Movaghar, A.: Modeling epidemic routing: capturing frequently visited locations while preserving scalability. IEEE Trans. Veh. Technol. 1 (2021). https://doi.org/10.1109/tvt.2021.3057541

15. Datta, S., Roy, M., Kar, P.: Application of IoT in smart epidemic management in context of Covid-19 (2021). https://doi.org/10.1109/hpsr52026.2021.9481844

16. Singha, S., Jana, B., Jana, S.H., Mandal, N.K.: A survey to analyse routing algorithms for opportunistic network. Procedia Comput. Sci. **171**, 2501–2511 (2020). https://doi.org/10. 1016/j.procs.2020.04.271

17. Spyropoulos, T., Psounis, K., Raghavendra, C.S.: Spray and wait. In: Proceeding of the 2005 ACM SIGCOMM Workshop on Delay-Tolerant Networking, WDTN 2005 (2005). https:// doi.org/10.1145/1080139.1080143

18. Cui, J., Chen, H., Chang, Y., Chen, Z., Gong, S., Yang, Y.: An improved spray-and-wait routing algorithm based on social relationship between nodes in DTN. In: 2022 IEEE 19th International Conference on Mobile Ad Hoc and Smart Systems (MASS) (2022). https://doi. org/10.1109/mass56207.2022.00017

19. Cui, J., Gong, S., Chang, Y., Chen, Z., Chen, H., Yang, Y.: An improved spray and wait algorithm based on the node social tree (2023). https://doi.org/10.1109/icpads56603.2022. 00017

20. Cui, J., Cao, S., Chang, Y., Wu, L., Liu, D., Yang, Y.: An adaptive spray and wait routing algorithm based on quality of node in delay tolerant network. IEEE Access **7**, 35274–35286 (2019). https://doi.org/10.1109/access.2019.2904750

21. Misra, S., Pal, S., Saha, B.K.: Distributed information-based cooperative strategy adaptation in opportunistic mobile networks. IEEE Trans. Parallel Distrib. Syst. **26**(3), 724–737 (2015). https://doi.org/10.1109/tpds.2014.2314687

22. Sok, P., Kim, K.: PRoPHET routing based on distance mechanism in disruption-tolerant network (2014). https://doi.org/10.1145/2557977.2558024

23. Xue, J., Li, J., Cao, Y., Fang, J.: Advanced PROPHET routing in delay tolerant network. IEEE Xplore (2009). https://ieeexplore.ieee.org/abstract/document/5076883?casa_t oken=-HqdrhHLDRAAAAAA:HIrxTHPoJIHFo3u95HpjBMo85Y7EPc1xtGq5PQJg-DM0 FMefW_Syh0xevOtlE3OcSJYFGPb6wy-3. Accessed 15 Apr 2022

24. Venkat Das, M., Sarkar, S., Shahid: TTL based MaxProp routing protocol (2016). https://doi.org/10.1109/iccitechn.2016.7860159

25. Abbas, S., Ahmad, K.: Opportunistic routing protocols based on fuzzy logic: present and future directions (2021). https://doi.org/10.1109/icais50930.2021.9395955

26. Chen, J., Xu, G., Wu, X., Feng-qi, W., He, L.: Energy balance and cache optimization routing algorithm based on communication willingness (2021). https://doi.org/10.1109/wcnc49053.2021.9417387

27. Zhao, Y., Srivastava, G.: A wireless mesh opportunistic network routing algorithm based on trust relationships. IEEE Access 10, 4786–4793 (2022). https://doi.org/10.1109/access.2021.3138370

28. Li, N., Yan, J., Zhang, Z., Martínez-Ortega, J.-F., Yuan, X.: Geographical and topology control-based opportunistic routing for ad hoc networks. IEEE Sens. J. 21(6), 8691–8704 (2021). https://doi.org/10.1109/jsen.2021.3049519

29. Hui, P., Crowcroft, J., Yoneki, E.: BUBBLE rap: social-based forwarding in delay-tolerant networks. IEEE Trans. Mob. Comput. 10(11), 1576–1589 (2011). https://doi.org/10.1109/tmc.2010.246

30. Nelson, S., Bakht, M., Kravets, R.: Encounter-based routing DTNs. In: Proceedings of the IEEE INFOCOM, pp. 846–854 (2009). https://doi.org/10.1109/INFCOM.2009.5061994

31. Aneja, M., Garg, V.: Simulation of epidemic, spray and wait and first contact routing protocols in delay tolerant network. IOSR J. Electron. Commun. Eng. (IOSR-JECE). https://www.iosrjournals.org/iosr-jece/papers/AETM'15_ECE/06-ECE-173.pdf

32. Poonguzharselvi, B., Vetriselvi, V.: Survey on routing algorithms in opportunistic networks. In: International Conference on Computer Communication and Informatics (2013). https://doi.org/10.1109/iccci.2013.6466129

33. Popat, K.A., Sharma, P.: Opportunistic location update—a novel cost efficient reactive approach to remove pauses in cellular networks. In: Modi, N., Verma, P., Trivedi, B. (eds.) ComNet 2016. AISC, vol. 508, pp. 459–467. Springer, Singapore (2017). https://doi.org/10.1007/978-981-10-2750-5_48

Author Index

S. Rajagopal et al. (Eds.): ASCIS 2023, CCIS 2039, pp. 463–464, 2024.
https://doi.org/10.1007/978-3-031-59100-6

Printed in the United States
by Baker & Taylor Publisher Services

Printed in the United States
by Baker & Taylor Publisher Services